Consumer Economics in Action

Consumer Economics in Action

Roger LeRoy Miller
Clemson University
Clemson, South Carolina

Alan D. Stafford
Niagara County Community College
Sanborn, New York

West Publishing Company
St. Paul   New York   Los Angeles   San Francisco

Copyeditor: Janet Greenblatt
Art: Miyake Illustration
Index: Terry Casey
Composition: American Composition and Graphics, Inc.
Production, Prepress, Printing and Binding: WEST PUBLISHING COMPANY
Photo credits follow index

WEST'S COMMITMENT TO THE ENVIRONMENT:
In 1906, West Publishing Company began recycling materials left over from the production of books. This began a tradition of efficient and responsible use of resources. Today, up to 95 percent of our legal books and 70 percent of our texts are printed on recycled, acid-free stock. West also recycles nearly 22 million pounds of scrap paper annually—the equivalent of 181, 717 trees. Since the 1960s, West has devised ways to capture and recycle waste inks, solvents, oils, and vapors created in the printing process. We also recycle plastics of all kinds, wood, glass, corrugated cardboard, and batteries, and have eliminated the use of styrofoam book packaging. We at West are proud of the longevity of the scope of our commitment to our environment.

ISBN 0-314-00330-4 (Student Edition)
ISBN 0-314-00329-0 (Teacher's Annotated Edition)

Library of Congress Cataloging-in-Publication Data
   Miller, Roger LeRoy.
      Consumer economics in action/Roger LeRoy Miller, Alan D. Stafford
          p. cm.
      Includes index.
      1. Consumption (Economics)   2. Finance, Personal.   I. Stafford, Alan D.   II. Title.
   HB801.M494   1992
   381.3—dt20   91-42677
                                                     ∞CI

Contents in Brief

Contents

TO THE STUDENT

Making Responsible Consumer Decisions

This book is about people like you. You are a **consumer**. A consumer is any person who buys or uses products to satisfy his or her needs or wants. You buy and use products every day of your life. In doing this, you make choices. In many ways, the quality of your life depends on the choices that you make. If you make good choices, you will have a better life. To make good choices, you need to have many types of knowledge and a wide range of consumer skills. It is difficult to make good choices if you don't really know about the different possibilities from which you can choose. As your knowledge increases, so does your ability to make good choices.

THE RESPONSIBLE CONSUMER

Part of the knowledge you need to be a responsible consumer is a basic understanding of our economic system. Although it may surprise you, you already know many facts about our economy and how it works. For example, you probably know that most people buy less of something when it costs more. You also know that companies that sell poorly made products will soon lose their customers. These are only two of the many facts you already know about our economic system. The course you are taking will help you learn more about how our economy works and how you can use this knowledge to make better consumer decisions.

To make good choices, you need certain skills. You need to be able to read with understanding, write clearly, solve basic mathematical problems, and reason logically. These skills will allow you to find and evaluate (judge) the information you need to make future choices. They will also enable you to communicate with others so that your choices can be carried out quickly and effectively. This course in consumer economics will help you develop the skills that will allow you to make decisions that can improve the quality of your life.

Most of the decisions that you and other Americans make are free choices. Making a free choice means that you are able to take the alternative you like best and reject other possibilities. When you make a free choice, you are responsible for the consequences of your decision. Almost all decisions involve both benefits and costs. When you make a choice, you should compare the benefits you expect to get from your decision with the costs you believe will be paid. This type of comparison will help you make better choices.

When we make consumer decisions, we take one alternative and give up the opportunity to do something else instead. If you spend your income going to a restaurant, you cannot use the same money to buy a new pair of shoes. Building materials and labor used to construct a new shopping mall cannot be used for public housing. Oil used to produce the gasoline that runs our automobiles today will not be available to heat our homes in the future. All Americans need to weigh the benefits and costs of their decisions.

As Americans, we need to realize that we do not live alone in the world. The choices that we make have a *global* impact on the people who live in our own country as well as on those who live in other nations. Citizens of the United States consume more than any other group of people in the world. What we consume cannot be used by citizens of other nations. If we make careless choices that waste the raw materials available to us, there may not be enough products to meet the needs of all the people in the United States or in other nations of the world. We need to be responsible to the global interests of other people.

Americans need to be **responsible consumers**. People who are responsible consumers are aware of how their individual decisions affect other members of society. They consider other people's interests when they make choices.

BEING RESPONSIBLE TO YOUR FAMILY

Most Americans live together in family groups. When people make choices, they often bring about benefits and costs for other members of their families. For example, if you choose to go to college after you graduate from high school, your decision will clearly affect you, but it will also affect your family. Spending current family income to pay the cost of your college tuition may force other members of your family to give up things they would like to have now. However, a college education may increase your future income and eventually allow you and your family to have a better standard of living.

In other cases, choices made by individuals can hurt members of their families. A parent who buys an expensive car may not have enough money left over to buy adequate food or clothing for his or her children. To be a responsible consumer, you must consider how your choices will affect other members of your family.

BEING RESPONSIBLE TO YOUR COMMUNITY

You, your family, and most of your friends live in a community. Members of a community depend on each other in many ways. If you build a house or buy a car, your decisions affect other people. Your new home could block your neighbors' view or require greater spending for government services. Every new car adds to traffic congestion. If you have the engine in your car properly tuned, then other members of your community will benefit from reduced air pollution. Playing a radio at full volume in your back yard will affect people who live near your home.

You may think of your free choices as individual decisions, but they almost always affect other people who live in your community. Being a responsible consumer means considering the interests of other members of your community when you make choices.

BEING RESPONSIBLE TO YOUR COUNTRY

Most Americans are proud of their country. They are aware of their good standard of living and of the opportunities they enjoy.

Although we receive many benefits as U.S. citizens, we also have certain obligations. One obligation is to use our raw materials wisely. Another obligation is to pay our fair share of the cost of supporting our government. The taxes we pay when we earn income, own property, or spend money allows the government to provide products that benefit society.

Good citizens should be careful not to waste these products. In addition, each American has a duty to pay his or her fair share of the cost of government. If some individuals avoid paying taxes, other Americans must pay more than their fair share.

You will learn about other consumer obligations as you read this text. Being a responsible consumer means considering the interests of our country and its people when you make choices.

BEING RESPONSIBLE TO THE ENVIRONMENT AND TO FUTURE GENERATIONS

There is a limited amount of raw materials in the world. Many raw materials cannot be replaced after they are used. As responsible consumers, Americans need to limit their use of these materials through conservation and recycling. If we are careful not to waste our raw materials, they will last longer and satisfy more of society's needs and wants.

We should also think about how the products we buy and use affect our environment. There are steps we can take as consumers that will ensure an adequate supply of materials and a clean environment for future generations. Being a responsible consumer means considering our environment and the interests of people who have not yet been born when you make choices.

BEING RESPONSIBLE TO YOURSELF

Although our families, communities, and government try to protect our interests, we, as individuals, are most responsible for the choices that affect our lives. To have a free society, we must rely on people to make most of their own decisions. Individuals benefit from making good choices and suffer from making bad ones. One important choice you can make now is to gain knowledge and develop your consumer skills so that you will be able to make better decisions in the future. Being a responsible consumer means considering your own interests when you make choices.

This text and the course you are taking can help you to become a responsible consumer. However, only you can make the choice to take advantage of this opportunity.

Getting Started

As you begin your study of consumer economics, there are a number of questions that you will probably have. You might wonder what economics is, what consumer economics is, and how they are different from each other. You will want to know what these subjects have to do with your life and your interests. What are their practical applications? In this first unit you will begin to get answers to these questions. You will learn about a decision-making process that can help consumers make better choices in their lives, and you will learn about the basic economic decisions that all people need to make.

Chapter 1

You, the Consumer

Chapter Objectives

After completing this chapter, you will be able to do the following:

- Describe situations in which consumers must pay opportunity costs.
- Explain why consumers need to set priorities.
- Describe situations that show why it is easier to make responsible consumer decisions when you know the facts.
- Describe situations that show why it is easier to make responsible decisions when you have good consumer skills.
- Use a decision-making process that can help consumers organize and evaluate information to make complex choices rationally.

Key Consumer Terms

In this chapter you will learn the meaning of the following important consumer terms:

- Consumer
- Opportunity Cost
- Consumer Decision
- Rational Choice
- Priority
- Goal
- Objective

Everyone makes decisions. The kinds of choices people need to make depend on many factors, such as their age, where they live, the amount of money they have to spend, and the kind of job they hold. When you were a child, you weren't able to make many important decisions for yourself. Your parents or other adults put food on the table, bought your clothes, and decided where you would live. As you grew older, you were probably expected to make more of your own decisions. Now the choices you make are likely to include what clothes to buy, what classes to sign up for, and when to study your schoolwork. You may also be asked for your opinion on important family decisions, such as where your family should live or how your family's income should be spent.

Soon you will be responsible for yourself. As an adult you will be able to help make political decisions by voting. You may contribute your time or money to community organizations. You will need to decide what career to pursue, whether or not to get married, or if you want to move to a different part of the country. You will need to find a way to earn enough money to support yourself. To a large extent, the decisions you make in the next few years will determine what kind of life you will lead. Your decisions will also affect your family, community and country, as well as people in other nations and future generations.

When you use your income to buy products, you are a **consumer**. You are also a consumer when you use things that have been purchased by others, including the government. When you attend school for example, you are consuming goods and services even though you may not have paid for them yourself. A consumer is any person who buys or uses goods or services to satisfy his or her needs or wants.

SECTION 1

MAKING RATIONAL CHOICES

While you read, *ask yourself . . .*
- ◆ *Why must people pay opportunity costs when they make choices?*
- ◆ *What choice have you made recently? What opportunity cost did you pay?*

You have learned that when people use goods and services to satisfy their needs and wants, they are consumers. Our ability to consume is usually limited by our income. We cannot use more goods and services than we can afford to buy. Because we have limited income, we must spend our money wisely to get the greatest possible satisfaction from the things we purchase.

Note to students: Throughout this text at the bottom right corner of most right-hand pages you will find *Vocabulary Builder* features such as this. These will include glossary entries for all of the key consumer terms found on the preceding two pages.

Vocabulary Builder

Consumer Any person or group that buys or uses goods or services to satisfy personal needs and wants.

Paying Opportunity Costs

Every time you spend part of your limited income to purchase a product, you give up the ability to use that money to buy something else instead. Economists call this idea **opportunity cost**. Opportunity cost is the value of your second choice, which you give up when you take your first choice.

Imagine that you have $20 to spend. You need a new shirt, and you would also like to buy a compact disk for your portable CD player. If you buy either of these items, you will spend almost all of your money. You can't afford both products, so you must choose the one you want most. If you buy the CD, the value you would have received from owning the shirt is your opportunity cost. To make this choice, you must believe that the CD has more value than the shirt.

When you decide how to spend your income, you make a **consumer decision**. In doing this, you also try to make a **rational choice**. Economists define rational choice as the alternative that has the greatest value and that results in the least possible cost.

Consumers make rational choices when they purchase the goods and services that they believe can best satisfy their needs and wants. Responsible consumers make rational choices.

Consumers sometimes make decisions that are irrational. They make choices that do not have the greatest values and the least costs. For example, suppose Jean decided to spend her money going out with her friends instead of buying gasoline for her car. Although she would enjoy her evening out, she might have to take a bus or chance running out of gas on her way to work. Consumers who make irrational choices usually do so because they don't take time to consider the benefits and costs of their decisions.

All decisions result in opportunity costs—even decisions that do not involve money. For example, if you join your school's swimming team, you might not have time to take a job

◆ When consumers buy one product they pay an opportunity cost that is the value of another use they could have made of their money. What opportunity costs may these consumers make when they purchase their CDs?

Consumer News

When Fewer Bases Require More Land

Would you like to live next to a military testing range? Thousands of Americans do, and more may in the future.

After a decline in tensions between the United States and the Soviet Union in the late 1980s, the Bush administration began to reduce the number of military bases the United States maintained in other countries. The reaction of the military to this choice was somewhat surprising.

In May of 1990, Pentagon officials announced their intention to add roughly 4.5 million acres of land to the current 25 million acres held by the U.S. military. The stated reason for this decision was to provide space to house military units returning from other nations. Some of the new land was to be used for war games and artillery practice that could no longer take place in Europe. Although more than half of the land chosen was not developed in 1990, at least one-third was used for farming or other purposes.

What types of opportunity costs will some American citizens pay if this plan is carried out?

Setting Priorities

Consumers who make rational choices when they buy goods and services get the most value for their money. However, there is no one choice that is rational for all people. This happens because different people value different things. The things you like best are probably not the same things your friends or relatives prefer. This is why different choices may still be rational choices when they are made by different people.

To be a responsible consumer, you need to consider your values when you make choices. Set **priorities** by ranking objectives you would like to achieve according to how much you value them. Making rational choices, budgeting your time and money, and planning for the future will help you reach more of the objectives you set for yourself. Other people with different values will set different priorities. They will make different choices. Their different choices may still be rational decisions for them because of their different values. Being rational consumers does not mean we must all make the same decisions.

Summing Up   *When people make consumer decisions, they pay opportunity costs by giving up the value of their second choice. If they make rational choices, they will take the alternative with the greatest value and least cost. People with different values make different rational choices.* ◆

after school. The value of the income you could earn would be your opportunity cost. If you do your homework instead of watching your favorite television program, what opportunity cost are you paying? All decisions that you make, including consumer decisions, result in opportunity costs that are measured in terms of the value of the second best use for your time or money.

Vocabulary Builder

Consumer decision   A choice made by a person concerning how to use resources or products.
Opportunity Cost   The value of a second choice that is given up when a first choice is taken.
Priority   A ranking of goals or objectives in the order of their value or importance.
Rational choice   The decision that maximizes the benefits at the lowest possible cost.

USING KNOWLEDGE AND CONSUMER SKILLS TO MAKE DECISIONS

While you read, *ask yourself . . .*
- *Why do consumers need knowledge to make rational choices?*
- *What consumer skills do you have today that you did not have a year ago?*

People sometimes are forced to make decisions when they don't know which alternative is best. Even if consumers have knowledge, they need to know how to use it to help them make the best choice possible.

Building Consumer Knowledge

Suppose that your uncle sends you to the hardware store to buy a valve for your bathroom sink. When you reach the store, you discover that there are about ten different types of valves you can buy, and you have no idea which is the correct one. You can ask a clerk which valve to buy, but there is a good chance you'll be making a mistake.

Think how much easier it would be if your uncle gave you more specific instructions or if you had a part number to look for. If you had purchased this type of valve before, you might know which one to buy. Consumer decisions like this are much easier to make when you have enough knowledge.

Imagine that Sue needs to buy a calculator for a business class she is taking. She goes to a store and finds twenty different products to choose from. They all have different features and different prices. If her teacher had told her that she needed a calculator that could find square roots and percentages, she would have knowledge that could help her buy the best type of calcula-

tor for her needs. Without this knowledge, she might choose a calculator that won't allow her to complete the problems in her class. She might be forced to spend more money to buy a different calculator later on. These simple examples demonstrate how important knowledge is to making good choices.

Using Consumer Skills

People who use consumer skills, are better able to make rational choices. Products that appear to be the same at first glance may prove to be quite different on closer examination. If you want to buy a new microwave oven, how do you choose which one to buy? There are many models you can choose, and most of them look pretty much the same. However, if you read the owner's manuals, you discover that there are important differences between them. The power levels of most microwave ovens range between 500 and 800 watts. Some have only two or three power settings, while others have ten or more. Some have built-in sensors that turn the power off when the food reaches a desired temperature. Others have built-in turntables. Many microwave ovens may be used as timers. Some can be programmed to turn on at a preset time. Microwave ovens can be very different from each other.

If you are unable to read the owner's manuals with understanding, you may have a hard time making a rational choice because you may not understand the different features of each product you can buy. Suppose you want a way to heat food for your supper before you get home from school. Think how you would feel if you spent $300 for a microwave oven only to find you had misunderstood its instructions and that it could not be preset to turn on at a desired time.

Consumers often need to communicate through writing. Imagine that you have or-

◆   Consumers need skills like being able to read and solve basic mathematical problems to make the best choices possible. What do you think this woman is doing as she reads the labels?

dered an adjustable drafting table from a mail-order catalog. When the table arrives, "some assembly" is required. Although you carefully follow the directions, you find an extra bracket #2-B has been included and an adjustable clamp #4-C is missing. To get the correct part, you need to write a letter to the manufacturer explaining the problem and requesting the missing part. No matter how much the company may want to provide good service and quality products, it won't be able to help you if it doesn't know what you want. Responsible consumers need to be able to write clearly and include relevant information in their written messages.

In other cases, making a rational choice requires the ability to solve basic mathematical problems. Imagine that you go to the grocery store to buy laundry detergent. You discover that the brand you want comes in bottles of various sizes. You wonder if it is a better choice to buy a 2-quart bottle for $3.99 or a 48-ounce bottle for $2.49. You remember that 2 quarts is equal to 64 ounces. You use this fact to figure out how much the detergent in each bottle will cost per ounce. By dividing 64 ounces into $3.99, you find that the detergent in the larger bottle costs 6.23 cents per ounce. The cost of the detergent in the smaller bottle is equal to $2.49 divided by 48 ounces, or 5.19 cents per ounce. As a result, you decide to buy the detergent in the smaller bottle. Using a basic mathematical process has allowed you to make the better, rational choice.

Often you need to use logic and reason to make rational choices. Suppose that you are a few years older and want to buy new furniture for your apartment. You visit a store where a

◆ Consumers must often use reason and logic to make good choices. Would it make sense to buy an expensive oven like the one in the photograph if you only used it once a month?

salesperson suggests that you would be better off renting furniture rather than buying the items you want. To buy furniture, you would need to borrow money and make payments of $50 a month over 48 months. The salesperson offers to rent you the same furniture for only $35 a month and tells you that this choice will be much better for you. You will have $15 extra each month to spend for other things.

If you use logic and reason, you will realize that if you buy the furniture, you will own it after four years and will no longer need to make any payments. If you rent, the payments will go on as long as you use the furniture, and you will never own anything as a result of your payments. If you can afford the $50 payments, you might decide that buying the furniture is the better, rational choice.

Responsible consumers need knowledge and skills to make rational choices. They should be able to read with understanding, write clearly, solve basic mathematical problems, and use logic and reason in making deci-

sions. This book and the course you are taking will help you develop these skills.

Summing Up *Consumers are better able to make rational choices when they have the necessary knowledge and are able to use consumer skills.* ◆

SECTION 3

MAKING MORE COMPLICATED DECISIONS

While you read, ask yourself . . .
  ◆ *What are several complicated decisions that you have recently had to make?*
  ◆ *How can the process described in this sentence help you make better choices?*

The choices that people make are often much more complicated than determining which size of detergent to buy or whether to buy or rent furniture. Simple decisions may involve one clear, best choice. More complicated decisions often involve many different objectives and values. When this type of choice must be made, it is more difficult to determine the rational choice.

Suppose that you are trying to decide what to do after you graduate from high school. You have considered going to a university, attending a vocational school, joining the military, or looking for a job. This is a type of consumer choice because your decision is likely to affect your income and ability to purchase goods and services for the rest of your life.

Deciding whether to start a career or go on with your education involves many different objectives. You should only make such an important decision after you have considered your personality, aptitudes, and values. This kind of choice should be made through a process that helps you to evaluate the different choices you could make.

The Decision-Making Process

When you need to make a complicated decision, a series of decision-making steps can help you make a rational choice.

These steps are:

1. Identify the problem.
2. Determine the broad goals.
3. Establish the specific objectives.
4. Identify alternative choices.
5. Evaluate each alternative choice.
6. Make the choice.
7. Evaluate the results.

The first things you should do are (1) identify the problem and (2) determine the broad **goals** you want to achieve. You might, for example, identify your problem as, "What should I do after I graduate from high school?" Your broad goal might be to gain financial security by holding a job that gives you a sense of satisfaction.

Consumer News

Less Water Usage The Law

In 1991, a drought had been going on in southern California for six years. Reservoirs were low, and some areas were in danger of running out of water. Natural habitats for birds and other animals were being destroyed. As a result, a law was passed in Los Angeles that required each household to reduce water consumption to an amount 10 percent below 1985 levels in March of 1991 and by another 5 percent in May. Many people complained. They said that the law would result in an unfair distribution of what water there was.

Use logic and reason to identify several reasons why this law may not have been fair.

How would you write a law that would reduce water consumption in a more equitable way?

How does this situation demonstrate our need to be responsible consumers?

The next step you should take is to (3) establish the specific **objectives** you would like to achieve. These are important because they will give you a way to measure your success and tell you if you should change your plans. Your

Vocabulary Builder

Goal Something to be accomplished in a certain period of time.

Objective A specific condition that an individual or organization wishes to achieve.

Consumers in Action

Bikes, Helmets, and Safety

Would you wear a bicycle helmet if your parents said you had to, or would you take it off as soon as you were out of their sight? How important would your friend's opinions be to your decision? Like it or not, bicycle helmets are becoming more common. Some communities have even considered making it illegal to ride a bicycle without a helmet.

Many high school students use bicycles for transportation. Bicycles have many advantages. They don't have to be expensive. You don't need to buy insurance to ride them. They give you lots of exercise. They are easy to park. And if you ever get caught in a traffic jam, you can just pick them up and carry them away.

Unfortunately, there are a few drawbacks to bicycles. They aren't much fun when it rains, and there may be times or places that you don't want to use one. But the most important problem with bicycles is they can be dangerous. If you are involved in a bicycle accident, you may be seriously injured or killed. In 1990 over 1,000 bicyclists died in accidents. About 85 percent of the victims suffered fatal head injuries. It was estimated that more than half of these deaths could have been prevented if the bicyclists had been wearing safety helmets.

New helmets used for mountain climbing, horseback riding, bicycling, and other sports are made of lightweight expanded polystyrene (EPS) foam like that used in picnic coolers. The EPS may be coated with a thin layer of plastic that can be colored or white. These helmets weigh as little as half a pound and have openings to allow ventilation. In a fall the EPS absorbs the shock and tends to slide along the ground, reducing the chance of neck injuries. If you buy a bicycle helmet, you should look for an American National Standards Institute (ANSI) sticker that shows that the helmet has passed tests for impact resistance and chin strap strength.

The price of bicycle helmets in 1991 ranged form a low of roughly $30 to as much as $85. The higher-priced models generally offered special decorations rather than greater safety.

If you wouldn't use a bicycle helmet because your parents told you to, would you decide for yourself to use one to reduce your chance of being killed in an accident?

---

objectives might include moving into your own apartment within two years, having a job managing a restaurant, learning how to program a computer, completing a two-year degree in electronic technology, or earning an income that will allow you to buy a house by the time you are twenty-five years old.

Once you have established your objectives, you should (4) identify alternative choices you could make. In our examples, your options include attending college, going to a two-year vocational school, joining the military, and looking for a job. When you think about these choices, you will probably recognize that there are other possible alternatives to consider. You could take a job and go to school part-time in the evening. You might work for a year and then go on to school.

When you are satisfied that you have identified all your possible choices, you should (5) evaluate each alternative choice in relation to how it will help you achieve your objectives. Remember, choices involve both benefits and costs. When you need to make decisions, you should weigh the value of the benefits you expect to receive against the costs you believe you will pay. You should then (6) make the choice that offers the greatest expected benefits with the least expected costs.

After you make a choice, you should carefully keep track of and (7) evaluate the results of your decision. There is no guarantee that every decision you make will have the results you expect. You may not have understood the situation you faced. Conditions may have changed. You may discover that your values and priorities change over time. By monitoring the results of your decisions, you may find reasons to change your mind. There is nothing wrong with changing a decision when doing so is possible and useful.

Summing Up *Consumers are better able to make complicated decisions when they organize their objectives, knowledge, and values in a decision-making process that allows them to evaluate their alternatives to make the best possible choice.* ◆

◆   The decision to attend college involves many costs and benefits. To benefit the most from their choice, students need to use their opportunities wisely. Do you think the students in the photograph are making good use of their time?

Review and Enrichment Activities

VOCABULARY REVIEW

1. Column A contains the key consumer terms from this chapter. Column B contains a scrambled list of definitions for these terms. Match the correct meaning with each term. Write your answers on a separate sheet of paper.

Column A	Column B
1. Consumer	a. a general condition to be accomplished in a period of time
2. Opportunity Cost	b. a choice made by a person to use money or a product in a particular way
3. Consumer Decision	
4. Rational Choice	c. a ranking of conditions a person wants to achieve in order of their value or importance
5. Priority	
6. Goal	d. a specific condition to be accomplished in a period of time
7. Objective	e. a person who uses products
	f. the value of a second best choice that is given up when a first choice is taken
	g. making a decision that results in the greatest benefits and the least costs

2. Explain the difference between simply making a *choice* and making a *rational choice*.

CHECKING WHAT YOU'VE LEARNED

Write your answers for the following exercises on a separate sheet of paper.

1. Describe an important decision you have recently made. Identify the opportunity cost that resulted from your choice.
2. Explain why consumers should set their priorities before making decisions.

3. How can one consumer's decision to buy a new car be a rational choice, while a different consumer's decision *not* to buy the same car is also a rational choice?
4. Why is it easier to make rational choices when you have knowledge about the choices?
5. What are the four consumer skills identified in this chapter that can help people make responsible decisions?
6. Identify and describe the seven steps in the decision-making process discussed in this chapter.

PRACTICING YOUR CONSUMER SKILLS

Write your answers for the following exercises on a separate sheet of paper.

1. For each of the following situations, decide what should be done. Explain the reasons for your answer.

    a. John purchases a new printer for his computer. The salesperson helping John says that it is easy to operate. However, when John gets it home, he discovers that it has an operator's manual that is 120 pages long. John doesn't read the manual, but just plugs the printer into his computer and tries to print a report he has completed for his English class. All he gets is a page full of meaningless letters. John tries to read the manual but can't understand it. John begins to think he has wasted the $399 he spent on the printer.

       What should John do? How does this situation show that being able to read with understanding can help you make good consumer decisions?

    b. Suppose that you are in the habit of taking one vitamin tablet a day. Your supply of tablets is running low, so you need to buy a new bottle. At the drugstore you discover that the brand you want comes in two sizes. One bottle contains 200 tablets and costs $4.99. The other bottle contains 500 tablets and costs $9.99. You immediately recognize that the tablets in the larger bottle are less expensive, but you see that there is another problem. Both bottles have an expiration date that is 413 days from today. You don't want to take any of the tablets after they expire.

       Which bottle should you buy? How does this situation show that being able to solve basic mathematical problems can help you make good consumer decisions?

    c. Your family is looking for a new refrigerator for your home. The one you have now is not working well, and your family agrees that buying a new one makes more sense than having the old one fixed. You all go to an appliance store looking for the same 14-cubic-foot model that just fits in the space in your kitchen. The salesperson who waits on you says that the refrigerator you are looking for is no

Review and Enrichment Activities Continued

longer made. He recommends that you buy a new 24-cubic-foot model that is on sale this week for just $699.99. He also tells you that it is much more energy efficient than the old model.

Should you buy this refrigerator because it is on sale? How does this situation show that being able to use reason and logic can help you make good consumer decisions?

2. Suppose that your friend Terry has come to ask your advice. Terry has a hard time in school. He tries to do his work and study, but his grades are not very good. He is afraid he may fail English and not graduate next spring. Terry's family doesn't have much money, and he sometimes feels embarrassed because he can't afford to buy nice clothes and other products he would like to own.

Terry has been offered a part-time job clearing tables at a local restaurant. If he accepts the job, he must agree to work from 5 P.M. to 8 P.M. every weekday and from 11 A.M. to 7 P.M. each Saturday. He would earn $138 a week. That's more money than Terry has ever had, but he is afraid that he will fail English and possibly other classes if he accepts the job.

Use the seven steps of the decision-making process to help Terry make the best choice possible. Write a description of each step you take.

USING NUMBERS

Solve the following problem to help make the best possible choice. Write your solution on a separate sheet of paper. Be sure to show all your work.

A local theater sells a book of ten theater passes for $35. The passes are only good on weekday evenings. They will expire in three months if they are not used. The normal price of a ticket is $6. How many passes would you need to use to come out ahead on this offer? How much would you save if you used all of the passes? Identify and explain other factors you should consider when you decide whether or not to buy the book of passes.

PUTTING IDEAS IN YOUR OWN WORDS

The following quotations are from this chapter. Explain these quotations in your own words to make sure you understand what they mean. Write your answers on a separate sheet of paper.

1. "All decisions result in opportunity costs—even decisions that do not involve money."

2. "There is no one choice that is rational for all people."
3. "Responsible consumers need knowledge and skills to make rational choices."

CONSUMER ECONOMICS IN YOUR LIFE

Write your answers for the following exercises on a separate sheet of paper.

1. Identify an item you would like to own. Describe an opportunity cost that might result if you bought this product.
2. Describe a specific piece of knowledge you have recently gained that will help you make better consumer decisions.
3. Describe a decision you have recently made that was easier to make because you have the ability to carry out mathematical computations.

◆   Would you consider riding across the mountains on a bicycle to be a rational choice? How would you use choose to spend your vacation?

Chapter 2

What is Economics?

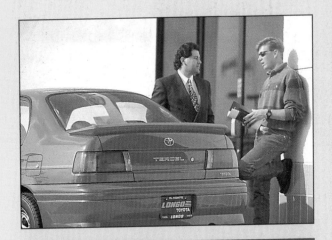

Chapter Objectives

After completing this chapter, you will be able to do the following:
- Identify ways that consumers may benefit from learning about economics.
- Explain why scarcity is the basic economic problem, and why it is the result of our limited productive resources.
- Describe examples of trade-offs that scarcity forces us to make.
- Explain why basic economic decisions are made in different ways in different economic systems.

Key Consumer Terms

In this chapter you will learn the meanings of the following important consumer terms:
- Economics
- Resource
- Consumer economics
- Goods
- Services
- Tangible
- Scarcity
- Trade-off
- Productive resource
- Land
- Labor
- Capital
- Entrepreneurship
- Factors of production
- Entrepreneurs
- Production
- Productivity
- Economic system

Economics is the study of how individuals and nations make choices about how to use scarce resources to fill their needs and wants. A **resource** is anything people use to make or obtain products that satisfy their needs and wants. There are different parts of economics that may be studied. One part concerns how people and businesses use resources to create the products they want. Another part of economics examines how people consume those products. The second kind of study is called **consumer economics**. It is the main topic of this book.

SECTION 1

WHY STUDY ECONOMICS

While you read ask yourself . . .
◆ *What goods and services do you consume each day?*
◆ *How does scarcity force you to make choices and pay opportunity costs?*

Most Americans enjoy a good standard of living compared to many other people in the world. This is because so many products are produced in our nation. Still, most Americans know of products that they would like to have but don't.

Goods and Services: Satisfying Our Needs and Wants

Goods and **services** are products that satisfy our needs and wants. Goods are **tangible** products that can be touched or felt, such as houses, cars, and swimming pools. We need certain goods in order to survive. We want other goods so we can enjoy a comfortable life.

Services are actions that satisfy our needs and wants. Unlike goods, services are products that are not tangible and cannot be touched or felt. When a doctor gives you a medical examination or when your teacher explains how a computer works, you are receiving a service. If you mow your neighbor's lawn or deliver newspapers, you are providing a service. People want to receive services that will improve the quality of their lives. In general, the more goods and services people receive, the happier and more satisfied they feel.

Studying economics will help you understand how resources are used to produce goods and services. It will also help you make decisions that will enable you to acquire more goods and services to satisfy your needs and wants.

Scarcity, the Basic Economic Problem

The basic problem of economics is **scarcity**. Economists say that scarcity exists when peo-

Vocabulary Builder

Consumer economics The study of how people consume goods and services that are produced.
Economics Study of how individual and nations make choices about ways to use their scarce resources to fill their needs and wants.
Goods Items of value that can be physically touched or measured.
Resource Anything people can use to make or obtain the goods or services they need or want.
Services Tasks completed by people or machines to satisfy human wants and needs and which cannot be touched or measured.
Tangible Something that can be touched.

◆ Every time a consumer makes a purchase he or she makes a trade-off that involves paying an opportunity cost. What trade-off may the person buying the car be making?

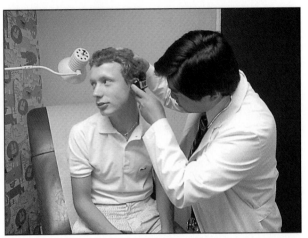

◆ Regular physical examinations are important to our health. What trade-off might a person make who does not have a check-up each year?

ple are unable to acquire everything they would like. Anything you have to pay for is scarce. Even something as common as a notebook is scarce because you must give up something of value (your money) to get it.

Scarcity exists because we don't have enough resources to produce all the goods and services necessary to satisfy every need and want we have. No matter how many goods you own or services you receive, there are likely to be other products you would like to have. The same is true of other members of society. Almost everyone wants more than they have.

Did you ever wonder why people don't own all the goods or receive all the services they need or want? Is it because people don't have enough money, or is there another reason? Think about this for a moment. If you had more money to spend, you would certainly be able to satisfy more of your needs and wants. Although this would make you happier, would it solve the problem of scarcity for other members of society? You would receive more of the available goods and services, but other people would receive less.

Scarcity is the result of our *limitless* desire for goods and services and our *limited* ability to produce goods and services. Giving everyone more money would not increase the quantity of resources we have or the quantity of goods and services we are able to produce. This is why scarcity forces us to choose the things we want most and give up alternatives that have less value.

Making Trade-Offs

In Chapter 1 you learned that whenever you make a decision, you pay an opportunity cost. When you take your first choice, you are giving up the value of your second best choice. Opportunity costs are the result of scarcity. If we could have everything we wanted, we wouldn't need to give up the value of any other choice. However, scarcity does exist. Therefore, it is important that we examine our values and our alternatives when we make choices. In this way we can receive the greatest possible benefit while paying the least possible cost. This is how people make rational choices and become responsible consumers.

Consumer News

Scarcity and Medical Care

On May 2, 1990, the Oregon Public Health Commission announced a plan to rank 1,600 medical ailments for the purpose of state funding. The ranking would be done by a computer according to each ailment's cost of treatment, the expectation of cure and recurrence, and the quality of life a patient could expect during and after treatment. Under this plan, people with diseases that are expensive to treat and who have a lesser chance for recovery, like lung cancer patients, would not receive state assistance. People with less serious ailments or with diseases with a high cure rate would find it easier to receive aid. By rationing aid, state officials believed that the number of individuals who could be helped would grow from 130,000 to roughly 250,000 a year.

Do you agree or disagree with the state officials who suggested this policy? Explain the reasoning behind your position.

How does this situation demonstrate the problem of scarcity?

When consumers make choices, they trade off the value of their first choice against the value of other possible alternatives. The term **trade-off** refers to the act of making a decision. The opportunity cost is the value of the second best choice that is given up.

Summing Up *Economics is the study of how we choose to use our resources to produce goods and services that satisfy our needs and wants. Scarcity prevents us from having all the products that we want.* ◆

SECTION 2

TYPES OF RESOURCES

While you read, ask yourself . . .
- ◆ *What productive resources are used to create some of the products you use each day?*
- ◆ *What do the words* land *and* capital *mean to the average person, and what do they mean to an economist?*

Four types of **productive resources** are necessary to produce the goods and services that satisfy our needs and wants. These are **land**, **labor**, **capital**, and **entrepreneurship**. Economists call these productive resources **factors of production**. Although you may think that you know what these words mean, economists have special meanings for them. You need to learn these special definitions to understand economic concepts in this book and in real-life situations.

Vocabulary Builder

Capital All property—machines, buildings, and tools—used to produce goods and services; in some situations, the money necessary to undertake a business venture. Value of a person's or business's assets; one of the "four Cs of credit."

Entrepreneurship The ability and willingness to be resourceful and innovative and to take the risks associated with operating a business.

Factors of production Economic resources such as land, labor, capital, and entrepreneurship used to produce goods and services.

Labor Work or effort performed by people to produce goods and services.

Land In economic terms, natural resources; all things found in nature.

Productive resources Any of the factors of production; land, labor, capital, or entrepreneurship.

Trade-off A term that implies an opportunity cost in which one alternative is accepted at the cost of a second alternative that is given up.

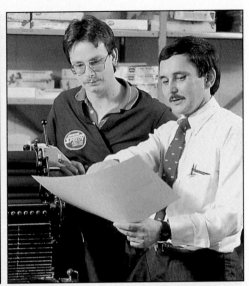
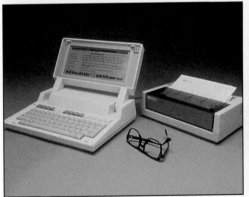

◆ These photographs show examples of the factors of production. Any one of them alone could not satisfy consumers' needs for goods and services. However, when combined natural resources found in land, labor provided by workers, capital made up of the tools of production, and organization provided through entrepreneurship, allow most Americans to have a good standard of living. What factors of production could you provide?

The term *land* refers to resources found in nature. It is more than the surface area of a piece of land. It also includes things found in, on, and under the ground. Oil, iron ore, animals, trees, and nutrients in the soil are all examples of land.

Location is an important aspect of land. An acre of land in the middle of a large city has a different usefulness and amount of productive value than an acre of land in the middle of a desert or swamp. Without natural resources and a location to construct a productive enterprise, it would be impossible to create goods and services.

Labor is the effort people make to produce goods and services. Labor includes people's skills, education, training, and other personal abilities. It is not enough to *want* to produce a product. It is also necessary to have the skills needed to complete the task.

Consumer Close-Up

What Are Wetlands?

To economists, land means natural resources, but to environmentalists, wetlands are homes to thousands of endangered species. In the mid-1970s, scientists convinced Congress that a steady loss of wetlands was endangering public safety as well as many animals and plants. They said that marshes filtered water, prevented floods, and provided habitats for many animals. As a result, a series of laws were passed to protect at least 100 million acres of wetlands.

The laws passed in the 1970s did not clearly define what the term *wetland* meant. Therefore, a team of scientists from four government agencies created a definition in 1989. It was decided that any land with standing water on it for seven consecutive days at

any time of the year was an official wetland and could not be altered without government permission. In one interpretation of this law, land that had moisture 18 inches below the surface could be considered wetland.

As a result of the law, many people were fined, and some went to jail. In 1990 a man named John Pozsgai cleaned some junk off his land to build a shop. For his effort he was sent to jail for filling in 5 acres of federally protected wetland that he happened to own. The land he filled in was part of a junkyard where no plants or animals lived. Across the nation hundreds of developments were held up or blocked. Farmers were told that they couldn't fill in ruts in their fields. Homeowners had to leave low parts of their yards alone where mosquitoes could breed.

Needless to say, many people were angry.

In August of 1991, President Bush took steps to solve the problem by redefining the term *wetland*. The new definition required the land to have standing water for at least 15 days each year and to remain saturated for 21 days. To try to prevent environmentalists from reacting too strongly, the president also classified land according to its ecological importance.

Land used for development cannot be used for natural habitats. Protecting natural habitats may prevent people from producing goods and services that consumers need to satisfy their wants.

What opportunity costs have been paid in this situation?

Capital includes the tools, factories, buildings, and other human-made objects that are used to produce goods and services. A machine that helps produce a camera is capital. The camera is not normally thought of as capital unless it is used to produce some other good or service, such as when a photographer takes pictures for a newspaper.

Many people believe that money is capital. Most economists do not agree. They point out that money does not actually produce any-

thing. If you were marooned on an island with $100,000 in cash, the money would do you no good—unless you used it to start a fire. The natural resources, workers, and tools, that money pays for are the resources that may be used to produce goods and services. Money is important. It allows people to pay for the production of goods and services. But it does not produce goods or services itself. Some people call money *liquid capital*.

The first three types of productive resources must be organized to bring about the production of goods and services. This organization is called entrepreneurship. **Entrepreneurs** are people who organize resources to bring about the production of goods and services. They must be resourceful, perseverant, innovative, and willing to take risks. These are some of the traits needed to own and operate a successful business.

Production is the result of combining different amounts of the factors of production in various ways to bring about the creation of new goods and services. **Productivity** is a measure of the relationship between the value of resources used to make goods and services and the value of the products that are produced. The more value that can be produced from a certain quantity of resources, the greater the productivity. Different combinations of productive resources result in different levels of productivity. For example, a modern farmer who plows a field with a tractor is much more productive than the farmer's great grandfather was when he used a horse-drawn plow. The more productive we are, the greater the quantity of goods and services we will create to satisfy our needs and wants.

Factors of production occur in limited quantities. As a result, there is a limit to the amounts of goods and services we can produce to satisfy our unlimited wants. This is why we are all faced with the problem of scarcity. By using our resources more efficiently, we can increase our productivity and satisfy more of our needs and wants. However, this will not eliminate the problem of scarcity. No matter how many goods and services we produce and receive, we will always want more. We will continue to make choices and pay opportunity costs.

Summing Up *The four factors of production are land, labor, capital, and entrepreneurship. These factors exist in limited quantities, making us choose the products we want most.* ◆

SECTION 3

THE FOUR BASIC ECONOMIC DECISIONS

While you read, *ask yourself . . .*
- ◆ *What are several ways that our economic system provides order in our lives?*
- ◆ *How do American businesses decide which products to produce?*

All consumers and producers in this country are part of our **economic system**. An economic system is a set of principles that governs how resources are used to produce goods and services. There have been many different types of economic systems in the world. Economic systems fulfill several necessary functions. They provide order and make it easier for people and businesses to work together.

Although different economic systems make decisions in different ways, there are four basic **economic decisions** that must be made in all nations. These are:

1. What goods and services should be produced?
2. Who should produce which goods and services?
3. How should these goods and services be produced?
4. For whom should these goods and services be produced?

What Goods and Services Should Be Produced?

All countries have a limited supply of resources with which to produce goods and services. The citizens, their leaders, or some other institution must decide which products should be produced, and in what quantity, from these

◆ Clothing may be produced in many ways. The workers in the photographs are completing most of their work by hand. In other factories similar garments could be made automatically by machines. Do you believe you have skills that would qualify you for any of these jobs?

limited resources. If a nation has 5 million acres of farmland, someone must decide how the land will be used. Should wheat, corn, potatoes or other crops be grown? Exactly how many acres of each crop should be planted? Each nation must decide which uses for its scarce resources will result in the greatest total satisfaction for its people.

Over time the types of goods and services people want will change. In the 1800s Americans wanted wooden wagon wheels. By the early 1900s, they wanted rubber tires for their automobiles. There must be a way to adjust production to accommodate changes in the types of products that consumers want. All economic systems need a way to communicate this type of information to decision makers so that they can adjust production.

Who Should Produce Which Goods and Services?

Many types of tasks must be completed to produce goods and services in each economic system. All nations need a method of determining which individuals should do each job that needs to be done. People are not equal in their ability to do different types of work. Some individuals are skilled at electrical work, while others may know how to prepare meals or construct houses. Each individual worker has his or her own unique set of skills and abilities.

People also have different values and personalities. Workers who enjoy working with their hands or being outside should not have a job in an office taking orders over a telephone. The total production of goods and services will be

Vocabulary Builder

Economic system A set of understandings that governs how resources are used to satisfy people's needs and wants.

Entrepreneur A person who takes the risks necessary to operate a business.

Production Combining factors of production to create goods and services that satisfy human needs and wants.

Productivity The measure of the relationship between the value of resources used to make goods and services and the value of the products produced.

Consumer News

Solution May Cause Problem

In 1990, the McDonald's Corporation stopped using Styrofoam packages for its hamburgers and other sandwiches and replaced them with cardboard containers. This decision was at least partially the result of pressure from environmental groups that argued that the Styrofoam packages contributed to the depletion of the earth's ozone layer and created waste that is not biodegradable.

Although McDonald's choice may have resulted in a partial solution to one problem, the cardboard containers have caused a different problem. The cardboard boxes are made from paper that requires more wood pulp. As a result, some people are saying that the paper containers are more harmful to the environment because they are causing the destruction of our forests.

What solutions can you think of to solve this problem?

How should our production be adjusted?

What should a responsible consumer do?

greater when people are responsible for tasks that they enjoy doing. Decision makers in each economic system need a method of placing people in jobs where they will be able to contribute the greatest possible value to production.

How Should These Goods and Services Be Produced?

There are many different ways for resources to be combined to produce a desired product.

Suppose that a society decides to manufacture 100,000 hubcaps. The hubcaps can be made by hand or by automated machines. The types of tools needed and the skills and abilities that the workers will need are different for each method.

The most efficient method of production in a country with highly skilled and well-paid workers will be different than in a country that has less-skilled and lower-paid workers. Countries with different natural resources or climates also may choose to produce products in different ways. Decision makers need a way to determine the best way to use their nation's productive resources.

For Whom Should These Goods and Services Be Produced?

In all economic systems there must be a way to decide how goods and services should be distributed. Should each person receive an equal share? Should some individuals receive more than others? What should be the basis for this decision: fairness, need, or equity? Another important consideration is the effect that the distribution of goods and services might have on people's willingness to work to the best of their ability. A totally equal distribution of goods and services might discourage people from making their best effort.

Suppose that you worked in a large factory where all the workers earned exactly the same wage no matter what they did. Some workers were skilled, others were not. Some worked very hard, while others accomplished very little. If you knew that your income would be the same no matter what you did, how hard would you work? You might think, "Why should I work hard when I won't earn any more money than those other people who are doing a poor job?"

The *Global* Consumer

Free Trade and Jobs

In the spring of 1991 President George Bush spoke in favor of creating a free trade agreement between the United States, Canada, and Mexico. He suggested gradually eliminating tariffs on goods and services traded between these nations. Under his plan, businesses in each country would be allowed to offer their products for sale in either of the other nations without paying a tax when the products crossed international boundaries. President Bush said that this would create new jobs in the United States because Mexicans would earn more income from selling products like clothing and shoes to the United States and Canada. He believed that this income would allow Mexicans to buy more products in this country.

Products like clothing can be produced by workers who have relatively little training and with a limited investment in tools and machinery. This type of production is well-suited to Mexico, which has many less-skilled workers who are willing to accept low wages. Many Mexican firms have been willing to break child labor laws, employing children at low wages to produce clothing and shoes. Most Mexican firms use many workers because they lack the money to invest in machines that could reduce their need for labor.

Leaders of the American labor movement (unions) argued against this plan, stating that it would cause many U.S. employees to lose their jobs and encourage the exploitation of lower-paid workers in Mexico. President Bush's position was that most of these jobs would be lost in any case owing to lower-priced imported goods. He said that if his plan was implemented, many U.S. workers would be able to find new jobs that would pay higher wages.

Union leaders replied that most of the people who would gain employment from exported U.S. goods would be different individuals than those who lost jobs. These leaders believed that industrial workers would be harmed, while the better-skilled, upper-income workers would benefit.

Which point of view do you believe is probably correct?

Would you be willing to buy U.S.-made garments at prices that are higher than the price of Mexican-made products to save U.S. jobs?

Do you believe that Americans should be concerned about the exploitation of workers and children in other countries?

What do you think a responsible consumer should do?

Would you work harder if your income depended on the number of goods you completed and on their quality? Decision makers need a way of determining the best method to distribute goods and services both in terms of fairness and equity and in terms of the impact on production within the economic system.

Different nations have different social values, economic systems, and political processes. As a result, they make the four basic economic decisions in different ways. Still, these choices must be made in all nations. This text will concentrate on explaining the way these choices are made in the United States.

Summing Up   *The four basic economic decisions that every nation must make are (1) what should be made, (2) who should make which products, (3) how should the products be made, and (4) for whom should the products be made?* ◆

Review and Enrichment Activities

VOCABULARY REVIEW

1. Column A contains key consumer terms from this chapter. Column B contains a scrambled list of phrases that describe what these terms mean. Match the correct meaning with each term. Write your answers on a separate sheet of paper.

Column A	Column B
1. goods	a. The measure of the value of resources used in production in relation to the value of the goods and services that are produced
2. land	b. The basic economic problem that results from our limited resources and unlimited needs and wants
3. trade-off	c. Tangible items that satisfy our needs and wants
4. labor	d. A set of principles that governs how resources are used to produce things that satisfy needs and wants
5. scarcity	e. Resources that are used to create the goods and services that satisfy our needs and wants
6. services	f. Actions that satisfy our needs and wants
7. productivity	g. Machines, buildings, and tools used to produce other products
8. capital	h. People's effort used to produce goods of services
9. economic system	i. Natural resources
10. factors of production	j. When one choice is given up so another may be taken

2. How is an economist's definition of land different from the way this word is more commonly used?

CHECKING WHAT YOU'VE LEARNED

Write your answers for the following exercises on a separate sheet of paper.

1. How can consumers benefit from studying economics?
2. What is the difference between a good and a service?
3. Explain why the problem of scarcity exists.
4. Describe at least one choice that scarcity has forced you to make.
5. What is an opportunity cost that resulted from the choice described in exercise 4?
6. What is the difference between making a trade-off and paying an opportunity cost?
7. Describe an example of each of the four factors of production.
8. What are the four basic economic decisions that must be made in all economic systems?
9. Why do people in different economic systems have different ways of making the four basic economic decisions?

PRACTICING YOUR CONSUMER SKILLS

Write your answers for the following exercises on a separate sheet of paper.

1. The term *handmade* is often used to try to convince consumers that a particular product has superior quality. Although this may be true in some cases, in others it is clearly not the case. For which of the following products would this term show superior quality, and for which ones would it not? Explain your answers.
   a. wooden furniture
   b. computer microchips
   c. camera lenses
   d. clothing

   What do these examples show about trade-offs between labor and capital that are made by producers?
2. Suppose that you have often played basketball with your friends after school at a community gym. The cost of keeping the gym open is paid by your city and by contributions from local organizations. The building is owned by the city. A clothing manufacturer offers the city $2 million for the building so that it can build a factory on the land that will employ 40 workers.
   a. What do you think the city should do?
   b. What opportunity cost might result from your recommended choice?
   c. How does this situation demonstrate the concept of scarcity?
   d. How does this situation demonstrate the concept of trade-offs?

Review and Enrichment Activities Continued

3. In the 1970s, organizations representing farm workers asked Americans to boycott (refuse to buy) grapes. These groups said that the grape growers were exploiting their employees by not paying them fair wages or providing benefits, such as health insurance. Many people chose to support this boycott, while others ignored it. Eventually, most grape growers improved wages and benefits for their workers, and the boycott ended.
   a. Do you believe that you would have supported this boycott by not buying grapes? Explain why or why not.
   b. Why might the improved wages and benefits for workers have caused grape farmers to give a different answer to the basic economic question, how should grapes be produced?
   c. How could a person's decision to either support or not support a boycott of a product like grapes demonstrate the idea of being a responsible consumer?

USING NUMBERS

Solve the following problem to help make the best possible choice. Write your solution on a separate sheet of paper. Be sure to show all your work.

Suppose that you are in charge of producing brooms in a factory. There are two methods you can use to manufacture the product. There is a machine that you can buy that will form, sew, and trim the brooms automatically at a rate of one broom a minute. The machine costs $280,000 and should last ten years before it needs to be replaced if you use it 8 hours a day, five days a week. If you buy the machine, you will need to hire a skilled mechanic to keep it in good working order for $30,000 a year. You will also need to hire two other workers to feed raw materials into the machine for $15,000 a year each.

Instead of buying the machine, you can hire six workers to make the same number of brooms by hand. You would need to pay each of them $15,000 a year. Whichever method of production you choose, you will have to pay $1 for straw, string, and other supplies to make each broom.

How much would it cost you to run the factory *per year* with each method? Which method would you choose? Explain your reasons for your choice. Remember, money may not be the only important consideration.

PUTTING IDEAS IN YOUR OWN WORDS

The following quotations are from this chapter. Explain these quotations in your own words to make sure you understand what they mean. Write your answers on a separate sheet of paper.

1. "Anything you have to pay for is scarce."
2. "The more value that can be produced from a certain quantity of resources, the greater the productivity."
3. "A totally equal distribution of goods and services might discourage people from making their best effort."

BUILDING CONSUMER KNOWLEDGE

Write your answers for the following exercises on a separate sheet of paper.

1. Describe a situation you know about where someone (possibly yourself) chose to pay more for something than was necessary because the person thought it was the responsible thing to do.
2. Many states require consumers to pay a bottle deposit when they buy soft drinks. This law is supposed to reduce pollution and also reduce the use of our limited resources. Some people argue against this law because they feel that it puts a financial burden on producers of soft drinks and the stores that offer this type of product for sale because they need space to store returned bottles or pay workers to keep track of them. Explain your point of view concerning this issue. Relate your feelings to the idea of being a responsible consumer.
3. Local governments have zoning laws that limit the way land can be used in different areas of a community. Suppose that a local businessperson wanted to open a meat-packing business in a residential area.
    a. How might the people who live in the community benefit?
    b. What costs might they pay?
    c. Why might the local government refuse to allow the business to open in such a location.
    d. What does this show about the production of goods and services in our economic system?

Basic Economic Principles

This unit builds on the knowledge that you gained in Unit 1. It provides a foundation of information that will help you understand the role of consumers and producers in making choices that determine how our economy works. In Unit 2 you will learn how prices are set and how we decide which products to man- ufacture and how they will be made. You will learn about the different ways we determine who receives the products that are produced. Finally, Unit 2 will help you understand how consumers benefit from competition between businesses.

Chapter 3

Free Market Economies

Chapter Objectives

After completing this chapter, you will be able to do the following:

- Explain why both buyers and sellers benefit from free exchange.
- Identify the basic characteristics of a command economy.
- Explain the central concepts of a free market economy.
- Describe situations that show how the four basic economic decisions are made in a free market economy.
- Explain how resources are allocated in a free market economy.
- Identify the characteristics of our economic system that make it a mixed market economy.

Key Consumer Terms

In this chapter you will learn the meanings of the following important consumer terms:

- Market
- Free market
- Voluntary exchange
- Command economy
- Free market economy
- Capitalism
- Profit motive
- Private property
- Decentralized decision making
- Incentive
- Profit
- Consumer sovereignty
- Allocation of resources
- Mixed market economy

Any transaction in which a good or service is bought and sold is part of a **market**. Markets are made up of exchanges of goods, services, money, or other things that have value. Markets often involve the use of stores, cash registers, money and other locations or objects, but these things are not the market. It is important to understand how markets work because most consumer decisions you make take place in markets.

Almost everyone has shopped at a farmer's market at one time or another. Consider the story of Shelly and Mark. Shelly buys fresh vegetables and fruit at a local farmer's market every week. Mark is a farmer who offers his produce for sale at the same location where Shelly shops. Mark and Shelly have made many transactions over the years.

Most people think of the stands, the produce, or the location where people meet to buy and sell produce as being the market. However, to an economist, transactions, such as those between Shelly and Mark, make up the market. The same can be said of other markets you know about. The stock market in New York City is not the building, the computers in the building, or the brokers who take orders to buy and sell. The market is made up of the exchanges between people when they buy and sell shares of stock.

To understand how our economic system works, you need to learn how the transactions we make in markets help make the four basic economic decisions you learned about in Chapter 2.

FREE MARKETS AND VOLUNTARY EXCHANGE

While you read, *ask yourself . . .*
- ◆ *What are several free exchanges you have made recently?*
- ◆ *How did you gain from these exchanges?*
- ◆ *How did other people who took part in these exchanges gain?*

In the United States, people like Shelly and Mark usually carry out transactions in a **free market**. This means that our government puts few restrictions on the types of transactions Shelly and Mark are able to make. Mark can choose where he wishes to sell his produce. Shelly is free to choose where she buys it.

Consumers Benefit from Voluntary Exchange

All transactions made in a free market are **voluntary exchanges**. Voluntary exchanges take place when buyers and sellers complete exchanges because they want to, not because anyone forces them. When a voluntary exchange occurs, both the buyer and the seller benefit. For example, when Shelly buys a sack of tomatoes from Mark for $1.50, she must feel that the tomatoes have greater value than the money she is spending. Mark, on the other hand, must feel that the $1.50 he receives in exchange for his tomatoes has the greater value. Both parties feel happier after the exchange is completed because they have different values. Voluntary exchanges lead to an increase in the satisfaction people enjoy.

Markets do not have to be free. Although many changes took place in the economic systems of Eastern Europe by the end of the 1980s, before that time these countries had various forms of **command economies**. In this type of economic system, a central authority (usually an agency of the government) makes most economic decisions. Individuals are not allowed to own productive resources or decide what products should be created from the resources. They can only buy products that the government chooses to have produced. The prices, locations of stores, types and quality of products offered for sale, and most other economic choices are made by the government.

Although command economies do not allow free markets, markets do exist when transactions take place. In general, people do not gain as much value when transactions are made in command economies because they are not free to produce and sell products of their choice or buy the goods or services they would most like to have. Today it is difficult to find a good example of a country that has a command economy, although many nations still have some characteristics of this type of economic system. Cuba, under the dictatorship of Fidel Castro, was probably the best example of a command economy in 1991.

Free Market Economic Systems

A **free market economy** is an economic system characterized by consumers and producers who are free to make transactions without the involvement of the government or any other authority. A free market economy exists when two conditions are met. First, people must own the productive resources and be free to use these resources to produce goods and services of their choice. Second, consumers must be free to buy any goods or services they can afford. Free market economies are often referred to as **capitalism**.

Consumer News

What Products Would You Buy?

When consumers are free to buy whatever they want, they often end up with some strange goods. In the 1990 Christmas season the following products sold well:

- A $16 plastic pig that could be mounted on a refrigerator and oink loudly whenever the door was opened
- A 6-inch basketball hoop that could be placed over wastebaskets for people to aim at
- A mirror that laughs at you when you stand in front of it

Would you consider buying any of these products?

How many of them do you believe would have been produced if our government decided how our resources should be used?

Vocabulary Builder

Command economy An economic system in which the government owns the factors of production and makes decisions about their use.

Free market A market in which individuals own the factors of production and decide the answers to the basic economic questions; also referred to as capitalism.

Free market economy An economic system characterized by individuals who own the factors of production and decide the answers to the basic economic questions.

Market The actions through which an exchange of goods, services, money, and other things of value takes place.

Voluntary exchange Transactions in which buyers and sellers work out their own terms of exchange without outside interference.

◆   Consumers in Russia often had to wait many hours to buy poor quality goods in the early 1990s. How would American consumers react to this type of situation?

Our example of Shelly and Mark demonstrates many characteristics of a free market economy. Mark owns a business and uses resources to produce products to offer for sale. Mark is free to use his resources to produce beans instead of tomatoes if he wants to. When he offers his products for sale, he may set his own price and conclude transactions as he and his customers see fit.

As a consumer in a free market, Shelly is able to use her money to buy Mark's products if she chooses to. She may also choose to buy products from another farmer instead. Her decision will be based on factors such as the price Mark charges, the quality of his products, the price and quality of other farmers' products, and the amount of money she is willing and able to spend on tomatoes. When Shelly decides to buy a bag of Mark's tomatoes for $1.50, they both gain, and their transaction becomes part of a free market.

Summing Up   *Free markets are made up of voluntary exchanges between buyers and sellers. A free market economy is one that allows people to own resources and determine how they will be used to produce goods and services to satisfy consumer needs and wants.* ◆

SECTION 2

THE MAIN CONCEPTS OF A FREE MARKET ECONOMY

While you read, *ask yourself . . .*
- ◆ *What might cause you to open a business of your own in the future?*
- ◆ *How hard would you be willing to work if you could not use your income to purchase private property?*
- ◆ *Who is best qualified to determine the goods and services you want?*

Free market economies are based on a set of economic ideas, or concepts. Among these concepts are the **profit motive**, **private property**, and **decentralized decision making**. The basic reason, or **incentive,** people have for running a business in a free market economy is their desire to earn a **profit**. Other objectives, such as personal satisfaction or pride of ownership, may be important, but a business that does not earn a profit will not stay in business for very long in a free market economy.

Mark will earn a profit from his business if he is able to generate income that is greater than the costs he pays to produce the goods or services he offers for sale. To accomplish this, Mark must produce goods and services that consumers want to buy and offer them at prices they are willing to pay. Mark's desire to earn a profit forces him to serve the interests of his customers. Businesses that offer products that consumers don't want or that charge more than consumers are willing to pay will not earn a profit and will soon go out of business.

In a free market economy the profit motive serves the interests of both the producers and the consumers. It also "weeds out" businesses that are inefficient, that produce products that consumers do not want to buy, or that charge prices consumers are not willing to pay.

The reason business owners work hard to earn a profit in a free market economy is their desire to use that profit to buy goods and services they want for themselves. Mark might want to buy more land to expand his business, or he might want to purchase a boat for family vacations. Both of these are examples of private property. Private property is any asset, or object that has value, and is owned by an individual or business. People's clothing, homes, cars, and other material goods are private property. The same may be said of any money, bank accounts, or stocks and bonds that people own. Factories, tools, and other items owned by private businesses are also private property. Earning money would have little purpose if you were not able to buy the goods and services you wanted with your income. The profit motive is the basic incentive to produce in free market economies because business owners want to use the money that they earn to buy private property.

In a free market economy, many firms produce and offer products for sale to many consumers who buy goods and services. Economic decisions are made by different people in different locations. This decentralized decision making is unlike the situation in command

---

Vocabulary Builder

Capitalism   Another name for a free market economy.
Decentralized decision making   copy to come.
Incentive   A reason for doing something.
Private property   Goods or assets owned by individuals or groups of individuals rather than by the government.
Profit   The amount of money left over after all expenses of a business are paid.
Profit motive   A desire to earn money from running a business that provides the basic incentive for producing goods and services in a free market economy.

Consumers in Action

What Brand of Sunglasses Do You Wear?

Most Americans own one or more pairs of sunglasses. In the 1970s and early 1980s, the most popular nonprescription brand in the United States was Foster Grants. In 1985 Foster Grants's annual sales were over $60 million, and the Massachusetts-based company employed 1,000 workers. The average price of a pair of Foster Grants was about $10.

Five years later, on August 16, 1990, Foster Grants filed for bankruptcy. What happened to this firm? The answer seems to be that it produced a product that most American consumers no longer wanted.

In the late 1980s American markets were flooded with low-price, low-quality, plastic sunglasses from Asian countries. These products sold for as little as $3. A number of restaurant chains gave millions of these products away as sales promotions. Consumers who wanted inexpensive sunglasses were not willing to pay $10 for Foster Grants when they could get other products for much less.

At the same time, manufacturers of high-quality sunglasses promoted their products in the $100

or more range. For example, Bausch & Lomb's sales grew by 25 percent between 1985 and 1990. People who wanted high-quality sunglasses were not interested in Foster Grants. As a result, the firm's sales dropped roughly 20 percent, and employment fell to 500 workers. In 1990 the firm was unable to pay its debts and was forced to file for bankruptcy. The free market economy had "weeded out" Foster Grants.

Do you believe that what happened to this firm was a good thing for American consumers?

economies, where one authority is in charge of making most economic choices. There are probably thousands of farmer's markets in the United States. Although there are certainly many similarities between them, the products offered for sale and the prices charged and paid will vary from one market to another. Different people are free to make their own decisions in different locations. In a free market economy there is no central authority that regulates the transactions. In general, people gain more value when their transactions are made

in a free market economy rather than in a command economy because people are free to produce and sell products of their choice and buy the goods or services that they would most like to have.

Summing Up   *Three concepts of a free market economy are profit, private property, and decentralized decision making. A company is most likely to be profitable if it offers consumers what they want at prices they are willing to pay.* ◆

SECTION 3

HOW BASIC ECONOMIC DECISIONS ARE MADE IN A FREE MARKET ECONOMY

While you read, ask yourself . . .
- ◆ *What products have you purchased in the last week? What information did you give to the company by buying their product?*
- ◆ *What qualities do you have that could make a company want to hire you to produce goods or services?*
- ◆ *What are several factors that will help determine the amount of income you will earn in the future?*

In Chapter 2 you learned that four basic economic decisions must be made in all economic systems. These decisions are (1) what goods and services should be produced, (2) who should produce which goods and services, (3) how should these goods and services be produced, and (4) for whom should these goods and services be produced? There is a particular way that each of these questions is supposed to be answered in a free market economic system.

What Goods and Services Should Be Produced?

People run businesses in free market economies to earn a profit. The only way to earn a profit is to offer for sale those goods or services that people are willing to buy. When a firm's sales generate an income that is greater than its costs, the business will earn a profit. It is impossible to earn a profit from products that are not sold. Every time a consumer buys a good from a producer, he or she is telling the producer to make more of the product. When consumers do not buy goods or services, they are also sending a message to the producer. They are telling the firm not to make more of the product.

In a free market economy consumers determine which products will be produced when they decide how to spend their money. Economists call this idea **consumer sovereignty**. The word *sovereignty* means being in control of something. For example, in the 1700s the king of England was in control of the British government. He did not have to follow the advice of Parliament if he chose not to. Therefore, the king was sovereign.

Consumer sovereignty means that consumers are in control of deciding which businesses will succeed and which will fail. They use their control when they decide where to shop and what to buy. They also determine the quantity of each product that will be manufactured. When Shelly buys tomatoes from Mark, she is telling him to grow more of them in the future. If she and other consumers chose not to buy his tomatoes, they would be telling him to grow better tomatoes or to use his resources to produce some other product.

Who Should Produce Which Goods and Services?

The type of work that each individual does in a free market economy is the result of decentralized decision making. These decisions are related to each business owner's desire to earn profits. The production of goods and services

---

Vocabulary Builder

Consumer sovereignty A situation in which consumers decide which products and styles will survive in the marketplace through their buying decisions.

Consumer News

Would You Buy a Turtle?

Would you believe that someone could successfully market a product based on young, genetically altered reptiles who are skilled in the martial arts? You might not think so, but this has been accomplished. The "Teenage Mutant Ninja Turtles" (TMNTs) were invented in 1983 by Peter Laird and Kevin Eastman. Six years later, sales of TMNT products totaled nearly $250 million. The TMNTs had their own television show and a movie that grossed $30 million in ticket sales in its first week. Comic books told of their adventures, and a TMNT breakfast cereal was produced along with many other products.

What factors do you believe caused American children to demand TMNT products?

How does this demonstrate the way America answers the basic economic question, What products should be produced?

requires the use of labor. Business owners hire workers who they believe will produce goods and services with the greatest value at the lowest possible cost.

Different workers have different skills and abilities. Business owners hire people who can complete necessary tasks and who do not have unneeded skills that might cause them to demand higher wages. If Mark decided to employ workers on his farm, he would look for people who know how to grow crops and operate the tools and machines he owns. He wouldn't hire workers who could pilot air-

planes or teach astrophysics but know little about farming. Not only would these workers possess unneeded skills, but they would probably demand higher wages than Mark could afford to pay.

Firms that employ the appropriate number and types of workers will be more efficient and will have a better chance to earn profits. Firms that employ too many or too few workers or that hire workers with too many or too few skills will be less efficient and will probably earn smaller profits.

How Should These Goods and Services Be Produced?

The methods used to produce goods and services in a free market economy are also the result of business owners' desire to earn profits. There are many different combinations of resources that could be used to make most products. Tomatoes, for example, may be grown in a field or in a greenhouse. Farmers may rely on rain, sprinklers, or irrigation ditches to keep plants moist. The plants may be grown with organic or chemical fertilizer or with no fertilizer at all. Tomatoes may be picked and packed by hand or by machine. Whatever methods of production are chosen, the end product is still a tomato.

Business owners in a free market economy produce products in whatever way they believe will result in the lowest possible cost. By having low costs, they are better able to charge customers lower prices and earn greater profits.

For Whom Should These Goods and Services Be Produced?

In a free market economy the amount of goods and services that people are able to buy depends on their income. People's income depends on the value of the contribution they

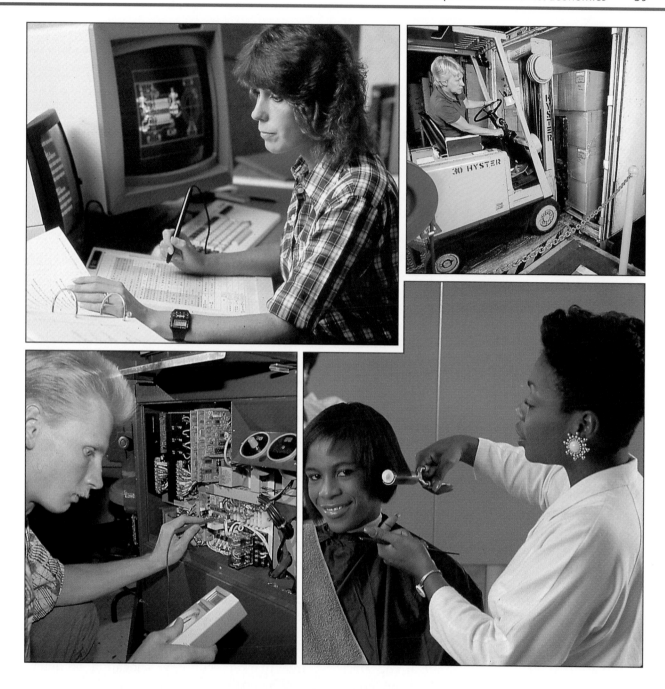

In a free market economy people are paid according to the value of their contribution to production. How much would you expect each person on this page to earn in his or her job? How may these people have prepared for their careers? What steps could you take now to increase the value of your labor in the future?

Some Advantages and Disadvantages of a Free Market Economy	
Advantages	**Disadvantages**
1. People are able to produce and buy the things they want most.	1. There will be an unequal and possibly unfair distribution of goods and services.
2. People are rewarded for hard work with greater wages or profits.	2. Many resources may be used to make luxury goods for the rich.
3. Resources will be distributed to the firms that are most efficient.	3. Resources may be wasted or the environment polluted when firms only consider profit.
4. People are able to choose the type of work they like most.	4. Some people may not be able to find a job.

◆   **Table 3-1**   Free Market Advantages and Disadvantages

make to production. People earn income in many ways in a free market economy. Some people receive income from selling their labor for a wage or salary. The amount that they earn depends on the value of their contribution to the production of the goods or services created by their employer. Other people earn income by selling or renting resources such as land or buildings to other people or to businesses. Interest is earned when people deposit their money in banks or lend money to others. Entrepreneurs like Mark earn income when the businesses they run are profitable. All of these ways of earning income are related to production in one way or another. In a free market economy the basic economic question, For Whom? is answered according to the value of each person's contribution to production.

You should realize that the words *skill* and *value* do not have the same meaning. It is possible for a person to be very skilled at doing something that no one cares about. If you are able to paint a picture on the head of a pin, you may be very skilled, but it is not clear that you would earn much money doing it. The value of your labor depends on the amount that someone else is willing to pay you to do it. If no one wants to buy your painted pin, your skill has little value. On the other hand, if you are a plumber and can repair leaks, your skill has value to many people, and you will be well paid.

The Allocation of Resources in a Free Market Economy

Profits are more than just an incentive to run businesses and produce goods and services in a free market economy. They are also the basic method for the **allocation of resources**. The word *allocation* means the way that something is distributed or shared out. For example, when a mother tells her children, "Take only one cookie apiece," she is allocating the cookies. The allocation of resources is the way that resources are distributed to some firms and denied to others. All economic systems have some method for allocating resources. In a command economy, the government does it. In a free market economy, allocation is determined by profit.

In a free market economy, businesses that are run efficiently and that offer goods and services that consumers want to buy at prices they are willing to pay are likely to earn a profit. These firms will be able to use their profits to buy additional resources, such as land, labor, and capital. This greater supply of resources will allow them to produce more goods and services and potentially earn even greater profits in the future.

Other firms may be less efficient or may offer goods and services that consumers do not want. Or perhaps they charge prices that are higher than consumers are willing to pay. These firms will not earn profits, which means that they will not be able to buy resources to produce additional goods and services. In free market economic systems, resources are automatically allocated to the most efficient and productive businesses because these businesses earn the greatest profits.

Summing Up *The way that each of the four basic economic questions is answered in a free market economy is related to businesses owners' desire to earn a profit. Firms that are profitable are able to buy more resources to produce more goods and services.* ◆

SECTION 4

OUR MIXED MARKET ECONOMIC SYSTEM

While you read, *ask yourself . . .*
- ◆ *How do laws or government regulations limit the types of work you can do or how you may spend your income?*
- ◆ *Why do you think the government has created these laws or regulations?*

Just as there are no good examples of command economies in the world, there are also no pure free market economies either. Every nation's economic system has characteristics of more than one theoretical system. However, there are many nations, including the United States, that have economic systems that are

◆ Raw materials that are taken from the land must be allocated in all economic systems. In market economies they flow to firms that are the most profitable. Do you believe this always results in the best possible allocation?

nearly free market economies. The American economic system is a **mixed market economy**. It is similar to a free market economy, but with limited government regulation.

Vocabulary Builder

Allocation of resources   The way that resources are distributed and used.
Mixed market economy   An economic system that has elements of both free market and command economies.

One hazard of a market economy may be the freedom people have to pollute the environment. In our mixed market economy the government takes steps to try to control this type of problem.

Although most economic decisions in the United States are free choices, some are not. Our government takes actions to limit our choices in situations where decisions made by individuals could harm other people. For example, businesses are not free to pollute the environment. The least expensive way to produce paper might involve spilling chemical wastes into our rivers. This might result in the greatest possible profits for the firms that produce paper, but it would cause great harm to our health and to future generations. As a result, our government attempts to protect the environment by limiting our choices. Businesses are not given the freedom to discharge pollutants into the environment. They are required to treat, reduce, or eliminate waste materials that result from their manufacturing process. The costs that businesses pay for controlling their pollution are passed on to consumers in higher prices. Therefore, consumers are not free to buy less expensive products that have been produced in an irresponsible way.

Some American firms would be powerful enough to set their own prices if the government did not regulate them. For example, consumers of natural gas and electricity would probably be willing to pay high prices to use these products if they had to. Government agencies in the United States tell the firms that produce these products what prices to charge. These companies are not allowed to make free choices because they could abuse the public if they were given the opportunity.

Government involvement in our economy is necessary because of problems that would result from a totally free market economy. At the same time, most of our productive resources are owned and controlled by individuals, and in most cases the four basic economic decisions are made by people. Thus, the United States and most other countries have mixed market economies.

Summing Up   *Although the United States economy is most like a free market economy, limited government involvement makes it a mixed market economy.* ◆

Review and Enrichment Activities

VOCABULARY REVIEW

1. Column A contains key consumer terms from this chapter. Column B contains a scrambled list of phrases that describe what these terms mean. Match the correct meaning with each term. Write your answers on a separate sheet of paper.

<table>
<tr><td align="center">**Column A**</td><td align="center">**Column B**</td></tr>
<tr><td>1. market</td><td>a. An asset or object that has value and is owned by an individual or a business</td></tr>
<tr><td>2. free market economy</td><td>b. An economic system in which people own businesses and are free to use resources to produce goods and services</td></tr>
<tr><td>3. profit motive</td><td>c. A reason for doing something</td></tr>
<tr><td>4. private property</td><td></td></tr>
<tr><td>5. allocation of resources</td><td>d. The freedom to make transactions as people want to</td></tr>
<tr><td>6. command economy</td><td>e. An economic system in which resources are owned and production is controlled by an agency of the government</td></tr>
<tr><td>7. voluntary exchange</td><td></td></tr>
<tr><td>8. consumer sovereignty</td><td>f. An economic system in which people own and control most resources but that also has limited government control of some resources</td></tr>
<tr><td>9. incentive</td><td></td></tr>
<tr><td>10. mixed market economy</td><td>g. The basic reason for producing goods and services in a free market economy</td></tr>
<tr><td></td><td>h. Determining how factors of production will be distributed and used</td></tr>
<tr><td></td><td>i. When business success is determined by purchases made by consumers in the market</td></tr>
<tr><td></td><td>j. Transactions in which products and other things that have value are exchanged</td></tr>
</table>

Review and Enrichment Activities Continued

2. Explain why profits would not be an important incentive if there were no private property in our economic system.

CHECKING WHAT YOU'VE LEARNED

Write your answers for the following exercises on a separate sheet of paper.

1. Why do both buyers and sellers gain from a voluntary exchange?
2. What is the difference between the way most economic decisions are made in a command economy and the way they are made in a free market economy?
3. What are two roles that profits play in a free market economy?
4. Describe how each of the four basic economic decisions are made in a free market economy.
5. Explain the difference between how resources are allocated in a free market economy and how they are allocated in a command economy.
6. Why has the U.S. government become involved in our economic system, making it a mixed economy?

PRACTICING YOUR CONSUMER SKILLS

Write your answers for the following exercises on a separate sheet of paper.

1. The cafeteria in your school probably is not a free market. Identify and describe at least three problems you see in how your cafeteria produces and serves the food it offers for sale. Explain how these problems might be reduced or eliminated if students and the cafeteria cooks had more freedom to make their own choices.
2. Most American workers are employed by firms that belong to other people. Employees work to earn a wage rather than to earn a profit for themselves. Explain why employees who do not share in the profits should care whether or not their employer earns a profit. Why might these workers feel that they have a profit motive as an incentive to work hard?
3. Suppose that you want to earn money next summer by cutting grass for people who live in your community. You decide to buy a lawn mower, but you're not sure what type to purchase. You could buy a nonpower mower that you must push for $189. You could also choose a power mower for $329. Your final alternative is a riding lawn mower for $899

that you would sit on and steer. Make a list of the factors you need to consider before you make your final decision. What does this have to do with the basic economic question, How should these goods and services be produced? and the way this question is answered in our economic system?

4. For many years Americans who wanted to smoke could light a cigarette almost anywhere. Public buildings, restaurants, buses, airplanes, even some college classrooms were filled with smoke. Smoking was regarded as a free choice by many people, regardless of its effect on nonsmokers. In recent years a number of states have passed laws that restrict smoking in public places. Employers are required to provide smoke-free workplaces. Smoking is no longer allowed on commercial flights within this country. The government has stepped into our free market economy to limit what consumers are able to do. Why do you believe that people have been restricted in where they are allowed to smoke? Do you believe that this is a proper thing for our government to have done? Explain your answer.

USING NUMBERS

Solve the following problem to help make the best possible choice. Write your solution on a separate sheet of paper. Be sure to show all your work.

Darryl owns a store that sells health foods. He employs two clerks who each work 40 hours a week. Darryl does most of the other work himself. He has $52,000 invested in goods he stocks in his store. His rent and other costs (but not employee wages) of doing business are $900 a week. His average weekly sales are $5,000. He takes a 50 percent markup on all products that he sells. He wants to earn a 10 percent yearly return on his investment and $500 a week in salary. How much income will he have left over each week with which to pay his two workers? How much would you recommend he pay them? What does this situation have to do with the way the fourth basic economic decision is made in a free market economy?

PUTTING IDEAS IN YOUR OWN WORDS

The following quotations are from this chapter. Explain these quotations in your own words to make sure you understand what they mean. Write your answers on a separate sheet of paper.

1. "When a voluntary exchange occurs, both the buyer and the seller benefit."
2. "Every time a consumer buys a good from a producer, he or she is telling the producer to make more of the product."
3. "You should realize that the words *skill* and *value* do not have the same meaning."

Review and Enrichment Activities Continued

BUILDING CONSUMER KNOWLEDGE

Write your answers for the following exercises on a separate sheet of paper.

1. Describe a situation in which you or a member of your family has recently sold or purchased a product. Was this a free choice? In what ways did both the buyer and the seller gain from this transaction?

2. You are probably aware that different adults hold different jobs for which they earn different incomes. Without identifying specific individuals, describe three of these jobs and explain why these people earn different incomes. How does this demonstrate the way the basic economic question, For whom should these goods and services be produced? is answered in a free market economy?

3. Identify a specific business in your community that has recently expanded its store or factory. Explain the characteristics of this firm that made it able to afford this expansion. Explain how this situation demonstrates how resources are allocated in a free market economy.

Chapter 4

Demand and Supply

Chapter Objectives

After completing this chapter, you will be able to do the following:

- Describe a situation that demonstrates the law of demand.
- Identify and explain events that will increase or decrease demand.
- Describe a situation that demonstrates the law of supply.
- Identify and explain events that will increase or decrease supply.
- Explain how the laws of demand and supply interact to establish an equilibrium price for a product.
- Explain how a change in demand or supply results in a change in a product's equilibrium price.

Key Consumer Terms

In this chapter you will learn the meanings of the following important consumer terms:

- Demand
- Law of demand
- Substitute goods
- Supply
- Law of supply
- Cost of production
- Equilibrium price
- Surplus
- Shortage

H ave you ever noticed how the price of some goods and services seems to go up or down rapidly? When electronic calculators were first produced and marketed in the early 1970s, they cost $100 or more and could only add, subtract, multiply, and divide. Now, for only a few dollars, you can buy a calculator that performs all these functions and more. Why did the price of calculators go down so much?

Have you ever been surprised by a rapid change in the price of fresh fruits or vegetables? The head of lettuce you could buy one week for 50 cents may cost $1.29 the following week. Tomatoes that cost $1.90 a pound in February may sell for 49 cents a pound in August. Have you wondered how these prices are determined and why they change so rapidly?

Consumers want to pay the lowest possible price for the quality and type of products they want to buy. Sellers want to receive the highest possible price for the goods or services they offer for sale. In our free market economy, prices are determined by agreements voluntarily reached between buyers and sellers in the market.

Buyers and sellers don't actually all come together and meet in one place to make exchanges. The market is made up of transactions that take place in all the various department stores, supermarkets, shopping malls, travel agencies, beauty salons, automobile showrooms, and so on. Transactions are also made through the mail and over the telephone. There are more than 250 million Americans and roughly 17 million businesses making transactions in the marketplace. Each one has a different set of needs and wants. Together their decisions determine prices in our economic system.

SECTION 1

CONSUMERS AND THE LAW OF DEMAND

While you read, ask yourself . . .
- ◆ *Do you only buy certain products when they're on sale?*
- ◆ *What are several products that you wanted a few years ago that you no longer desire? What has happened to your demand for these products?*

The Law of Demand

When you go to the store to buy a bottle of soda pop or a new pair of shoes, your purchase represents part of the demand for that product. **Demand** is the amount of goods or services that consumers are willing and able to buy at various prices. The **law of demand** states that the lower the price, the more of a good or service consumers will buy; the higher the price, the less consumers will buy.

For example, suppose that you went to a store expecting to pay $12 for a T-shirt that you wanted. You are pleased to find that the shirts are on sale in many colors for $8 each. Would you be tempted to buy more than one shirt at this lower price? Many consumers would. The owners of the store will sell more T-shirts at $8 than they could sell at the normal $12 price. This example demonstrates the law of demand.

On the other hand, suppose that you had saved $15 to buy a particular compact disk recording. But when you went to the store, you discovered that its price had been increased to $18. What would you do? You wouldn't have enough money to pay for the CD you wanted to buy. You could either save more money or buy a different, less expensive CD now. In either case, the owners of the store will sell fewer copies of the CD you wanted at the new higher price than could have been sold at the lower price. Again, this demonstrates the law of demand.

Changes in Demand

A change in demand happens when consumers are willing to buy either more or less of a product at each possible price. There are several possible reasons for a change in demand. Consumers are likely to buy more ice cream and cold lemonade on hot summer days than in the middle of winter, even if the prices of these products are the same in both seasons. The demand for these products changes with the seasons.

And what do you think would happen if the government suddenly announced that a scientific study had determined that whole wheat bread reduced the risk of cancer by 50 percent? Consumers would probably buy more whole wheat bread and less white bread, even if the prices remained the same. When consumer preferences change, consumer demand also changes.

Changes in demand also occur when consumers earn more income or less income. Sup-

Consumer News

The Demand for Gossip

On April 9, 1991, Simon & Schuster released Kitty Kelley's book *Nancy Reagan: The Unauthorized Biography*. Kelley portrayed former first lady Nancy Reagan in an uncomplimentary manner. She suggested that Nancy Reagan was often the real power in the Reagan administration. Former president Ronald Reagan referred to the contents of the book as "flagrant and absurd falsehoods . . . [which] . . . clearly exceed the bounds of decency." Although there is doubt about the information and conclusion drawn by Kelley, 150,000 of the first 600,000 copies were ordered on the first day the book was available for sale.

What do you believe causes consumers to demand an expensive ($24.95) book that is said to be largely the result of gossip and unfounded accusation?

Do you believe that people who buy such products are responsible consumers?

pose that a new industry paying higher wages moved into your community. As the average income of consumers went up, they would be

Vocabulary Builder

Demand   The amount of goods and services that consumers are willing to pay for at various prices.

Law of demand   An economic rule stating that as the price of a good or service falls, a larger quantity of it will be bought; as the price of a good or service rises, a smaller quantity will be bought.

◆ According to the law of demand consumers are willing to buy more products at lower prices than at higher prices. Why do stores advertise sales like the one in this photograph?

able to buy more products. Their demand would increase because of the increase in their incomes. On the other hand, if an important business in your community closed down and many workers were laid off, the demand for many products would fall. A change in consumer income results in a change in demand.

Another possible reason for a change in demand is a change in the price of a **substitute good**. There are many alternative products for most goods or services you buy. Suppose that you prefer a particular brand of potato chips. However, this week a different brand is on sale at 50 percent off. The lower price of the alternative brand may cause you to substitute this less expensive product for the brand you like best. Therefore, your demand for your preferred brand will fall. Most advertising and marketing efforts carried out by businesses are intended to change consumer demand for their products.

Summing Up *Consumers' willingness to demand products depends on many factors, including the price of goods and services offered for sale, consumer income, consumer preferences, and the price of substitute goods.* ◆

SECTION 2

PRODUCERS AND THE LAW OF SUPPLY

While you read, *ask yourself . . .*
- ◆ *If you found a job that paid you $20 an hour, would you be willing to work more hours (supply more labor)?*
- ◆ *If there was an invention that made it possible to produce televisions at half the cost, what do you think would happen to the number of television sets offered for sale?*

The Law of Supply

When a store sells you a bottle of soda pop or a new pair of shoes, the goods it offers for sale are part of the supply of those products. The **supply** is the amount of goods or services that producers are willing to provide for sale at various prices. The **law of supply** states that the higher the price, the more of a good or service producers will supply; the lower the price, the less they will supply.

You might think of price as a type of measuring device that helps sellers decide how much of a product they are willing to supply. For example, if peanut butter cost $5 a pound, you might think that was a high price. Many other people and businesses would probably have the same opinion, but they might see the high price as an opportunity to earn a profit. The high price would cause more people to produce and offer peanut butter for sale, so the quantity supplied would increase. Firms already making peanut butter would probably be earning a large profit at this price. They would be encouraged to produce even more of the product. Soon the quantity of peanut butter supplied would be much greater because of the high price.

Suppose that the price of peanut butter fell to only $1 a pound. At this price many producers would earn little or no profit. They would be encouraged to use their resources to produce some other product that had a higher price and that would earn a greater profit. A lower price causes the quantity of products supplied to fall.

Think of the law of supply from a personal point of view. Suppose that you washed cars in your neighborhood to earn money. If you could only charge $2 each, how many cars would you wash? At such a low price, you probably wouldn't bother to wash any cars unless you were desperate for money or had nothing else to do. On the other hand, if many people in your neighborhood were willing to pay you $10 a car, you would probably be willing to wash many cars. If you are like most people, the higher the price people were willing to pay you, the more cars you would be willing to wash. This example demonstrates the law of supply.

◆ According to the law of supply more resources or products will be supplied at a higher price than at a lower price. How many young men would be willing to paint this house if the owner paid $20 an hour instead of $5?

Vocabulary Builder

Law of supply   An economic rule stating that as the price of a good or service falls, a smaller quantity of it will be offered for sale; as the price of a good or service rises, a larger quantity will be offered for sale.

Substitute goods   Two or more goods that may be used to fill the same purpose.

Supply   The amount of products businesses are willing to offer for sale at a particular price.

◆   When workers go on strike they earn no income and they produce no products. How do strikes affect the demand and supply of goods and services that are produced and sold?

Changes in Supply

A change in supply is in many ways similar to a change in demand. Supply changes when businesses are willing to supply more products or fewer products to the market at each possible price. There are many events that may cause a change in supply—some due to forces beyond the control of business owners. If there is a freeze in California that destroys large parts of the orange crop, the supply of oranges will be smaller. If there is particularly good weather in Iowa and Kansas, the supply of corn will be larger. Similar changes in supply can result from good catches of fish or from the

discovery of a new oil field. No one can control or even predict these kinds of events that change supply.

Remember, people run businesses to earn a profit. A profit is the result of a firm receiving more income from sales than is spent running the business. Any event that changes a firm's income or its costs will affect its profits and its willingness to offer goods for sale.

A possible reason for a change in supply is a change in the **cost of production**. When the cost of making a product or providing a service goes up; a business will earn less profit at the price it had been charging. If it cannot increase price, it may be discouraged from producing as much of the product. Lower profits may also cause some firms to use their resources to produce an alternative product. Either of these events would reduce the supply offered for sale.

On the other hand, lower costs of production should increase the profit that a business earns and encourage greater production, even if there is no change in price. If a firm discovers a new way to manufacture paper that has 10 percent less waste, it should earn a greater profit. This will encourage the firm to produce and offer greater quantities of paper for sale. Technological developments often have dramatic effects on the cost of production and therefore on the willingness of firms to supply products to the market.

Summing Up   *The ability and willingness of businesses to supply products for sale depends on the price they are able to charge, their costs of production, and other events that are often beyond their control.* ◆

SECTION 3

CONSUMER, PRODUCERS, AND THE EQUILIBRIUM PRICE

While you read, *ask yourself . . .*
- ◆ *Why do so many stores charge almost the same prices for similar products?*
- ◆ *If a store charges a price that most consumers feel is too high, what is likely to happen to this business?*

At any point in time there is a price at which the quantity of a particular product consumers are willing to buy is exactly equal to the quantity producers are willing to supply. This is the **equilibrium price**. There are forces in a market economy that tend to force the market price to

Consumer News

The Cost of Crude

In August of 1990 Iraq invaded Kuwait. Within a few hours the cost of crude oil on world markets skyrocketed. Over the following months the prices of products manufactured from crude oil changed frequently. This may be seen in the price of gasoline.

How would changes like those shown in the following table affect your life?

Monthly Percentage Change In Price of 1 Gallon of Gasoline

Month	Percent Change
8/90	+ 7.6%
9/90	+20.6%
10/90	+ 8.0%
11/90	+ 0.3%
12/90	- 4.8%
1/91	-10.0%

(From: *Facts On File*, 1990 & 91)

the equilibrium price in a reasonably short period of time.

Suppose that you enjoy eating fresh tomatoes during the summer. A nearby store is selling tomatoes for $1.98 a pound. Although you

Vocabulary Builder

Cost of production   Money spent producing or marketing a product.

Equilibrium price   The price for a product at which the amount producers are willing to supply is equal to the amount consumers are willing to buy.

like tomatoes, you and many other customers are unwilling to pay such a high price. Mark, the store's owner, had ordered 100 pounds of tomatoes at 99 cents a pound from a vegetable wholesale firm. By the end of the first day, he has only sold 25 pounds of tomatoes. There is a **surplus** of 75 pounds. Mark soon realizes that if he doesn't lower his price, many of his tomatoes will rot and he will lose part of his investment. Mark lowers the price of his tomatoes to $1.49 a pound and sells out in two days. In the future he continues to order 100 pounds of tomatoes every three days and sell them all for $1.49 before he receives his next order. You are willing to buy some of his tomatoes at that price. Mark's surplus of tomatoes forced him to lower his price to the equilibrium price of $1.49.

In other cases a business may charge a price below the equilibrium price. Suppose that Joan starts a clothing alteration service. Her work has good quality and she completes her jobs on time. At first she only charges her customers $6 an hour for her labor. She soon has far more customers than she can possibly serve. There is a **shortage** of Joan's service at $6 an hour. This situation encourages her to raise her price to $10 an hour. Although many of her customers are willing to pay the higher price, some are not. Joan discovers that at the higher price of $10, she has enough work to fill a 40-hour week. The $400 a week she earns is enough for her to pay her bills, so she is satisfied. The shortage at the original price enabled Joan to raise the price of her labor to the equilibrium price of $10 an hour.

If Mark and Joan had taken the time to investigate other businesses that offered tomatoes or alteration services, they would have found that many of these firms were charging roughly $1.49 for tomatoes and $10 an hour for alterations. In market economies most firms

◆   Falling prices are often the sign of a surplus of products. Why would the owner of a business reduce prices by almost 70 percent?

Consumers in Action

The Price of a Low-Fat Diet

If the price of a product increased 40 percent, would you buy more or less of that product? If nothing else changed, you would probably buy less. But what if something else did change? Maybe the price went up because you and many other people wanted to buy more of the product. This is what happened to the demand and price for fish in the United States between 1980 and 1988.

In 1980 the average American consumed 15 pounds of fish a year. That amount grew to about 18.5 pounds by 1988. This increase occurred even though there was also a 40 percent increase in the average price of fish products. What happened to cause consumers to buy more fish at higher prices? What happened was a desire on the part of many Americans to reduce the amount of fat in their diets. In these years a series of scientific studies associated high-fat diets with heart disease. Many Americans seem to have decided to eat a lower-fat diet regardless of the price. Therefore, fish became a more common food for many Americans because most fish is very low in fat.

According to the U.S. Food and Drug Administration, a 3-ounce serving of steak contains 27 grams of fat, a 3-ounce serving of pork has 21 grams of fat, and a 3-ounce serving of haddock has only 5 grams of fat. In general, consumers are able to reduce their consumption of fat by 50 to 80 percent when they replace other sources of animal protein with fish products.

Although there are many consumers who continue to eat large quantities of red meat, there is a clear trend toward less demand for this type of product and a greater demand for fish and other low-fat foods.

How is this trend likely to affect the price of beef, pork, and fish in the future?

---

charge about the same price for similar goods and services. That price is the equilibrium price.

Summing Up   *There is an equilibrium price for all products at which the quantity demanded is equal to the quantity supplied. Prices above the equilibrium price will result in a surplus that will force the price down. Prices below the equilibrium price will result in a shortage that will encourage the producer to raise the price.* ◆

Vocabulary Builder

Shortage   A situation in which there is a larger quantity of a product demanded than supplied at a particular price.

Surplus   A situation in which there is a greater quantity of a product supplied than is demanded at a particular price.

CHANGES IN THE EQUILIBRIUM PRICE

While you read, ask yourself . . .
- ◆ *What is one example of a price change that has affected you recently?*
- ◆ *What caused this price change, and how did the price change affect the amount you were willing to buy?*

We opened this chapter wondering about the changes in the price of calculators and other products. You now know that most products are sold at their equilibrium prices most of the time. If this is true, why should the price of a good or service change quickly? The answer is that prices most often change when the supply or demand for a product changes. Let's take a second look at some of the examples presented earlier.

Suppose that the government really did discover that eating whole wheat bread helped prevent people from getting cancer. As a result, the demand for whole wheat bread would grow. The sales of this product would be greater than the quantity supplied at the current price. A shortage would result. This shortage would encourage producers to charge a higher price. The higher price would cause new bakeries to open and existing ones to make more whole wheat bread. A new and higher equilibrium price would be reached that would result in a greater quantity of whole wheat bread being supplied.

Now suppose that many workers in a community were laid off when a major company closed down. Many consumers in the area who used to buy take-out pizza at local restaurants would no longer be able to afford this product. The restaurants would find that their workers had little to do and their ovens were being used only part of the time. Therefore, some of the pizza restaurants would lower their prices to encourage customers to buy their products again. Others might go out of business, reducing the supply. Eventually, a new equilibrium price would be reached at which the number of pizzas that customers were willing to buy was equal to the number of pizzas that businesses were willing to supply.

Mass Production and Lower Prices

We now come to the price of calculators. When electronic calculators were first invented, manufacturers spent vast amounts of money to develop them. They did not have the ability to produce many of them, but there were many people who wanted them. People who worked with numbers for a living would save valuable time and effort if they owned an electronic calculator. The supply was small while the demand was large. Therefore, the original equilibrium price was very high.

Prices for these calculators fell rapidly because of new technological developments that reduced the cost of making these products. Soon calculators could be produced by the million at a cost of only a few dollars each. This increased the supply and resulted in a surplus of calculators that forced the equilibrium price down so that more customers could afford to buy them. The same type of event resulted in lower prices for VCRs, microwave ovens, and many other products.

Forces Beyond Our Control

The price of fresh fruits and vegetables changes quickly because of changes in grow-

◆ When crops are damaged by droughts or by disease the supply of these products will fall even if prices are high. Why have bad years for crops turned out to be good years for some farmers' incomes?

ing seasons and the weather. Consumers would like to eat about the same amount of fresh lettuce and apples throughout the year. However, these products are only plentiful when they are in season. If consumers want fresh strawberries in February, the strawberries must be shipped in from Mexico or grown in a greenhouse. This is expensive and can only be done on a limited scale. As a result, the supply of many fruits and vegetables is limited for most of the year. This in turn causes the equilibrium price to be high. On the other hand, when these products are in season, there are large quantities available, and producers will set a much lower price to avoid a surplus.

Rapid changes in the price of fresh fruits and vegetables are often the result of unexpected changes in the weather. If there is a storm or drought that destroys large parts of the lettuce crop, the price of lettuce may double in only a few days. It may take weeks or months for the

price to fall back to the original equilibrium price as new crops are planted and mature to increase the supply to normal levels.

Businesses sometimes charge prices that are higher or lower than the equilibrium price as part of a marketing promotion. However, most businesses try to charge the equilibrium price for their products most of the time. To do anything else invites a surplus or shortage of their products. Consumers who think that a business is charging prices substantially higher or lower than competing firms should be suspicious and consider the situation carefully before making a purchase.

Summing Up   *A product's equilibrium price can change rapidly as the result of a change in demand or supply. Consumers and businesses often have little control over these changes and need to keep track of them to be able to make responsible choices.* ◆

Consumer Close-Up

What Will You Give Me for My Mickey Mantle?

How much would you be willing to pay for an old piece of cardboard about 2 inches by 3 inches in size? If it was a 1909 Pittsburgh Pirates shortstop Honus Wagner baseball card, you would have had to pay $115,000 to get it in 1990.

Honus Wagner was a non-smoker who sued when his picture was placed on an American Tobacco Company baseball card. He won, and most of the cards were destroyed. It is estimated that the world supply of this card may be as few as fifty.

There are millions of baseball card collectors in the United States. In recent years the demand for older baseball cards has been greater than the supply. As a result, the prices of these cards have been forced up to unbelievable levels.

Baseball cards don't need to be more than a few years old to be valuable. Often the most demanded cards are rookie cards printed in a player's first year in the major leagues. For example, a 1952 Mickey Mantle rookie card was worth about $6,000 in 1990, while a card printed only a few years later could be purchased for about $400. Many collectors buy thousands of rookie cards each year. Although most of these cards will end up being worthless because the players won't become superstars, there are a few that will be worth thousands of dollars in only a few years.

Word of the profits that can be made from baseball cards has increased the number of people who collect cards. This increased demand has forced the price of cards up. Although the number of new cards produced each year has grown with the demand, this has no effect on the supply of cards printed in the past. Every increase in demand only serves to push the price of these cards higher.

What would happen to card prices if most collectors decided to sell their cards all at the same time?

◆ Many people think of collecting baseball cards as a child's hobby. Why do you believe most of the collectors in this photograph are adult men? Is there any reason women shouldn't collect baseball cards too?

Review and Enrichment Activities

VOCABULARY REVIEW

1. Column A contains key consumer terms from this chapter. Column B contains a scrambled list of phrases that describe what these terms mean. Match the correct meaning with each term. Write your answers on a separate sheet of paper.

Column A

1. demand

2. law of supply

3. equilibrium price

4. substitute goods

5. shortage

6. surplus

7. cost of production

8. law of demand

9. supply

Column B

a. two products that may be used to fill the same purpose

b. the amount of goods or services that producers are willing to provide for sale at various prices

c. money spent by a firm to offer products for sale

d. the amount of a product consumers are willing to buy at various prices

e. the price at which the quantity of a product demanded is equal to the quantity supplied

f. consumers will buy a larger amount of a product at a lower price than at a higher price

g. when a greater amount of a product is offered for sale than consumers are willing to buy

h. businesses will offer a larger amount of a product for sale at a higher price than at a lower price

i. when a smaller amount of a product is offered for sale than consumers want to buy

2. Explain the difference between the effect that a surplus and a shortage of a product would have on the price of the product.

Review and Enrichment Activities Continued

CHECKING WHAT YOU'VE LEARNED

Write your answers for the following exercises on a separate sheet of paper.

1. Describe a situation you have experienced that demonstrates the law of demand.
2. Explain why an increase in the price of apples is likely to result in an increase in the demand for oranges.
3. Explain why people run businesses in a market economy.
4. Describe a natural event that would result in a change in the supply of a product you use.
5. Why would the supply of many goods decrease if the cost of labor increased?
6. Define equilibrium price.
7. Explain why a price above a product's equilibrium price tends to be forced down over time.
8. Describe why a price below a product's equilibrium price tends to increase over time.
9. Identify a product that you use that has changed in price recently. Why do you think the price changed, and how did that change affect the amount you were willing to buy?

PRACTICING YOUR CONSUMER SKILLS

Write your answers for the following exercises on a separate sheet of paper.

1. Explain what would happen to the demand for each product described.
   a. What would happen to the demand for suntan oil if there was a cold, wet summer?
   b. What would happen to the demand for tea if the price of coffee went up 50 percent?
   c. What would happen to the demand for expensive sports cars in a community where many workers had lost their jobs?
   d. What happens to the demand for pencils and notebook paper in most communities at the end of August each year?
2. Explain what would happen to the supply of each product described.
   a. What would happen to the supply of grapes if a machine was invented that could pick them automatically and workers were no longer needed?
   b. What would happen to the supply of plastic boats if the price of oil fell 25 percent? (Plastic is made from oil.)

c. What would happen to the supply of lumber if the government stopped letting businesses cut trees in national forests?

d. What would happen to the supply of apples if there was a drought in the states of Washington and Oregon?

3. Explain what would happen to the equilibrium price of each product described.

a. What would happen to the equilibrium price of garlic if scientists discovered that eating garlic every day made people live longer?

b. What would happen to the equilibrium price of grapefruits if workers who harvest grapefruit in Texas received a 10 percent wage increase?

c. What would happen to the equilibrium price of houses if a new factory employing 1,500 workers opened in a community that had low housing prices?

d. What would happen to the equilibrium price of strawberries if a freeze destroyed about half the strawberry crop?

USING NUMBERS

Solve the following problem to help make the best possible choice. Write your solution on a separate sheet of paper. Be sure to show all your work.

Ben used to sell imported silk ties for $20 each in his store. His sales averaged 30 ties a week. He pays $12 to buy the ties he sells. Ben wondered if he could increase his profit by raising his price to $25. He tried this for a month, but his sales fell to 20 ties a week. How much money did Ben take in at the old price, and what was his profit at the old price? How much income did he receive at the new price, and what was his profit at his new price? Should he keep the new price? Explain how this example demonstrates the law of demand.

PUTTING IDEAS IN YOUR OWN WORDS

The following quotations are from this chapter. Explain these quotations in your own words to make sure you understand what they mean. Write your answers on a separate sheet of paper.

1. "In our free market economy, prices are determined by agreements voluntarily reached between buyers and sellers in the market."

2. "Any event that changes a firm's income or its costs will affect its profits and its willingness to offer goods for sale."

3. "There are forces in a market economy that tend to force the market price to the equilibrium price in a reasonably short period of time."

Review and Enrichment Activities Continued

BUILDING CONSUMER KNOWLEDGE

Write your answers for the following exercises on a separate sheet of paper.

1. Describe a situation you know about where a consumer decided not to buy a product because of an increase in price. Then describe a different situation where a consumer decided to buy a product even though it had increased in price. Explain why different choices were made in these two situations.

2. The price of a first-class stamp increased from 25 cents to 29 cents in February 1991. All other postage rates increased at the same time. Explain how this would have affected a business that sends advertising through the mail. How might it have affected the firm's willingness to offer its services at the same price it had charged before the increase in postage rates?

3. When microwave ovens were first introduced in the late 1950s, their price was between $700 and $800 at a time when people earned much less than they do now. You can now purchase a microwave oven for several hundred dollars. Describe what has happened to the demand for and supply of these products over the last thirty years.

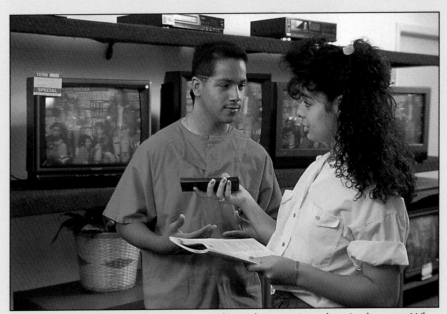

◆   Consumers buy more televisions today at lower prices than in the past. What has happened to the demand for, and supply of these products?

Chapter 5

Forms of Competition

Chapter Objectives

After completing this chapter, you will be able to do the following:
- Identify characteristics of firms that do business in a competitive market.
- Describe conditions necessary to achieve a competitive market.
- Identify firms that operate in various types of imperfect competition.
- Compare the benefits and costs of competitive markets with the benefits and costs of markets have imperfect competition.
- Explain how people can be responsible consumers when they buy from businesses that operate in imperfect competition.

Key Consumer Terms

In this chapter you will learn the meanings of the following important consumer terms:
- Competition
- Imperfect competition
- Competitive market
- Price taker
- "Invisible hand"
- Laissez-faire
- Monopoly
- Differentiation
- Monopolistic competition

C onsumers can usually find the products they want in many different locations. When many businesses offer the same product for
sale at the same price to many customers, there is **competition**.
Economists believe that competition between firms benefits customers
by ensuring the lowest possible prices and the best possible quality.
Competition also encourages innovation and technological
improvement.

Although many American businesses operate in competition, some
do not. These other firms do business in various forms of **imperfect
competition**. Imperfect competition exists when businesses have
some, but not all, of the characteristics of firms in competition. Firms
in imperfect competition have some control over their prices. There
are benefits and costs for consumers and producers that result from
competition and imperfect competition.

SECTION 1

FIRMS IN PERFECT COMPETITION

While you read, ask yourself . . .
- ◆ *What are several goods or services that you often buy that are available from many different businesses?*
- ◆ *If the stores where you often buy these products raised their prices, what would you do?*
- ◆ *If the stores where you often buy these products offered inferior quality, what would you do?*
- ◆ *How much choice do these businesses have in setting their prices and quality standards for the products that they offer?*

When consumers choose between products that they feel have equal value, they often consider the price first when they decide where to make their purchase. Suppose that you had a job in a factory and wanted to buy a pair of inexpensive jeans to wear to work. There might be ten or more stores near your home where you could buy them. If the products offered by each firm were the same, you would probably choose to buy your jeans at the store that had the lowest price. In this situation, a business that charged a higher price than other firms would have few, if any, customers. Firms that sell the same or similar products in the same area are in competition with each other. They do businesses in a **competitive market**.

Competitive Markets Where You Shop

Many products that you use, such as milk, eggs, gasoline, pencils, candy bars, and notebook paper, may be purchased from businesses that operate in what are basically competitive markets. These products would be much the same regardless of where you bought them. Can you think of other products that you buy in competitive markets?

When you purchase products in a competitive market, you probably consider three factors: (1) the price of the product offered for sale, (2) the convenience of the store that sells the product, and (3) the quality of any service offered with the product. When competitive firms are equally convenient and offer similar

◆ The owner of this farm runs a business in competition. Most people would not care where the celery they buy was grown. What would happen if this celery was offered for sale at $2 apiece when other celery was selling for $1?

service, price remains the chief consideration. This is why businesses in perfect competition are sometimes called **"price takers."** They must take the same price for their products that competing firms charge. If they try to charge more, they will not be able to sell their products.

Firms in competition must offer products that have equal or better quality then those offered by competing firms. If a business sold low-quality jeans with seams that came undone the first time they were worn, its owners would soon find their customers shopping elsewhere. Even if their prices were equal to, or lower than prices charged by other firms, the inferior quality of their product would drive customers away.

To be successful, firms in competition must offer products that have similar quality and similar prices to those offered by competing firms. When the owners of competitive firms do this, they are looking out for their own self-interest. An owner who charges higher prices or who offers products of inferior quality will lose customers and fail. This idea was called

the **"invisible hand"** by Adam Smith, a famous economist of the late 1700s. He said that owners of competitive businesses serve the best interests of consumers when they work for their own success. He believed that the only way that competitive firms could succeed was to provide the best quality products at the lowest possible prices. It is as if an "invisible

Vocabulary Builder

Competition The rivalry among producers or sellers of similar goods to win more business by offering the lowest prices and best quality.

Competitive market A market characterized by firms that are in competition.

Imperfect competition A market situation in which firm's sell or customers buy products and are able to affect prices on their own.

Invisible hand Symbol of Adam Smith's theory of economic competition that states that individuals will serve the interest of society in general when they are allowed to work for their own self-interest.

Price taker A firm in perfect competition.

hand" forces the owners to do things that benefit consumers.

Relatively few American firms do business in perfect competition. In most cases there are differences in quality, service, or convenience that causes consumers to be willing to pay more for one firm's products than for those of a competing firm. However, there are many businesses that come close to working in perfect competition. These firms are not able to charge prices or offer products that are significantly different from those of competing firms without losing many customers.

Summing Up *Firms in competition offer similar products for sale. As a result they must charge similar prices and provide similar quality to sell their products.* ◆

ACHIEVING COMPETITION

While you read, ask yourself . . .
- ◆ *What are some examples of products you buy but that work in ways you don't understand?*
- ◆ *How far would you be willing to travel to save $5 on the next pair of shoes you buy?*

Competition does not just happen. There are a number of conditions that need to exist for competition to function successfully.

◆ For competition to work efficiently businesses must be able to ship products at a low cost. One way the government helps create competition is to build roads. What would happen to competition if businesses had to pay the full cost of the highway system?

Conditions Needed for Competition

Of all the conditions needed to achieve competition, probably the most important is that there be many producers and many consumers of a product. Consumers must be free to buy a product from many firms so that they can be assured of receiving the lowest possible price and the best quality. The firms must be free to offer goods or services to many different consumers. This situation will prevent any one consumer or producer from having enough power to influence prices.

To have competition, consumers need knowledge so that they can make the best possible choice. They need to understand how to compare the quality and prices of the products they are considering buying. When consumers do not have enough knowledge, firms can sell inferior goods or charge higher prices than their competition without losing many customers. How would you go about finding the store with the best prices and quality if you wanted to buy a pair of jeans?

Perfect competition requires free entry to and exit from production. If good profits are being earned by producers in a competitive market, other entrepreneurs should be free to enter this market and offer the same products for sale. This will increase the supply of the product, lower the equilibrium price, and reduce profits to a more reasonable level. On the other hand, if little or no profits are being earned by firms in a competitive market, some businesses will close, or exit from production, reducing the supply of the product being offered for sale. This will cause the equilibrium price and profits to increase to a more reasonable level. To have competition, nothing should keep people from starting a business or closing a business if they choose to do so.

Low-cost transportation of both people and products is necessary for competition. If a firm in another part of town offers a product you want at a better price, you should be able to go there to buy the product or have the product shipped to you without spending a great deal of money. If transportation costs too much, local firms will have an advantage over businesses in other locations. This will allow them to charge higher prices or offer inferior goods. It is impossible to reduce transportation costs to nothing, but the lower they are, the greater the competition between firms can be.

Finally, for competition to exist, no single firm or consumer can have enough power in the market to be able to influence prices. Businesses that have the power to set prices or offer low-quality products without losing sales and profits are not competitive. The owners of such businesses may benefit from their power, but they can also harm consumers' interests and the economy in general.

The Role of Government

When Adam Smith wrote about firms in competition, he used the French term **laissez-faire**—which means "to leave alone"—to describe the role he thought the government should play in the economy. Many people have misunderstood the meaning of what he said. They think that he meant that the government had no responsibility for helping the economy work well. This is not what Adam Smith meant. He did believe that the government should not try to regulate the economy. However, he said

Vocabulary Builder

Laissez-faire French term meaning "do not touch"; applies to Adam Smith's theory of economic competition.

Consumer News

Competition Among the Airlines

In recent years there have been many "fare wars" between different airlines. This has contributed to low profits in the airline industry and a number of business failures, including Eastern Airlines, Braniff, and Midway. Consider the following example of a "fare war."

On March 13, 1991, American Airlines announced "special low fares" on all its flights for travelers who would book their flights seven days in advance by April 8, 1991, and stay over a Saturday night at their destination. A week earlier Northwest Airlines had started a "fare war" by reducing the price of round-trip tickets by as much as $100 between forty-nine cities. Delta Air Lines followed by offering 20 percent discounts to business travelers and requiring only a three-day advance purchase.

Why would airlines offer low-price tickets?

How does this situation demonstrate the benefits of competition?

that the government has a responsibility to encourage competition by helping to bring about the conditions needed for competition.

The government of the United States tries to create conditions that will lead to greater competition among businesses. More will be said of the government's role in Chapter 9.

Summing Up *Certain conditions are needed to achieve competition. The U.S. government makes an effort to create these conditions and encourage competition among firms in this country.* ◆

BENEFITS AND COSTS OF IMPERFECT COMPETITION

While you read, ask yourself . . .
- ◆ *What are several businesses you buy products from that have monopoly-like power?*
- ◆ *How have these firms been able to differentiate their products from those offered by other firms?*
- ◆ *Do you feel that you or other consumers are being harmed by these firms' monopoly-like power?*

Economists believe that consumers benefit when firms compete with each other. In many ways this is true. Firms in competition are likely to offer products of high quality at low prices. Competition encourages firms to find new and more efficient ways to produce and offer goods and services for sale. The most successful firms in competition are those that are most efficient and best able to offer products that consumers want at prices they are willing to pay. In Chapter 3 you learned that this ensures an efficient allocation of resources. Competition "weeds out" inefficient firms or businesses that do not offer products that consumers want at prices they are willing to pay. Although there are many benefits that come from competition, there are many situations in the U.S. economy where businesses do not or cannot operate in competition.

Businesses with Monopoly-Like Power

A **monopoly** is a business that is the only producer of a particular product. There are no substitutes for goods or services produced by monopolies. Most Americans believe that monopolies are bad for our economy, and in many cases they are correct. Monopolies have the power to charge high prices and offer products that have inferior quality. When consumers buy goods or services from a monopoly, they have no choice other than to buy the firm's product or do without. Monopolies do not need to find new methods of production or be responsive to the wishes of their customers. Monopolies are able to earn profits without being efficient.

It is difficult to find examples of perfect monopolies because there are substitutes for most goods and services. Still, many American firms have monopoly-like power. This means that they are large enough or powerful enough to have some control over the price and quality of the products that they sell.

Although firms with monopoly-like power can harm consumer interests, in special cases they may be unavoidable and even good for consumers and society in general. Some businesses need to be large to be efficient. For example, the cost of building a factory that can produce automobiles or steel is so great that consumers are better off when there are only a limited number of such facilities. It would be wasteful to have automobile or steel factories in every major city. The cost of building and running them would be very high. It is more efficient to have only a few of these factories to serve our entire nation. Businesses that are very expensive to build will have some monopoly-like power because there won't be many of them competing with each other.

There are a number of other reasons why firms with monopoly-like power may be good for our economic system. These businesses will probably earn greater profits than more competitive firms. Their profits can be used to pay for new investments, research and development, better wages for workers, and better service for customers. Because competitive firms tend to have smaller profits than firms with monopoly-like power, they are less able to do the things that could improve their efficiency over time.

◆   The cost of building large factories like steel mills is so great that it does not make sense to have very many of them. Why is it almost necessary for large firms to have monopoly-like powers?

Another potential problem of competitive firms with smaller profits is their possible failure in economic downturns. When businesses fail, many people are hurt. Owners lose their investments. Workers lose their jobs. Consumers lose a source of products they may want. People who sold resources to the business lose a customer. Even the government loses tax revenue as the firm and its workers stop paying taxes. Some businesses are inefficient and should be eliminated. Other businesses have failed simply because they lacked the money they needed to get through hard economic times. Firms with some monopoly-like power and greater profits are less likely to fail when the economy turns down.

Vocabulary Builder

Monopoly   A market situation in which only one firm offers a product for sale with no competition.

When Businesses Differentiate Their Products

Owners of businesses would prefer to have monopoly-like power to help them earn profits and improve their sense of security. To do this, most entrepreneurs try to convince customers that their products or services are superior to those offered by competing firms. This is called **differentiation**. A firm that succeeds in differentiating its products will be able to sell more goods and services and perhaps charge higher prices to earn larger profits. Firms that have some control over their prices have monopoly-like power and do business in a market characterized by imperfect competition.

Summing Up Some U.S. firms have monopoly-like power and operate in imperfect competition. Although such firms may use their power to take advantage of consumers, they can also afford investments, research and development, and specialized workers that can benefit consumers. ◆

SECTION 4

FIRMS IN IMPERFECT COMPETITION

While you read, ask yourself . . .
- ◆ What are several products that you have been convinced to buy as the result of advertising?
- ◆ At what store do you like to shop? What things about this store have caused you to differentiate it in your mind from other stores where you could shop?

Most firms in the United States do business in markets that have some degree of imperfect competition. This means that they have suc-

ceeded in differentiating their products. Economists call this situation **monopolistic competition**. Monopolistic competition is a special type of imperfect competition where many firms offer to sell products that are *almost* the same. These firms differentiate their products from those of competing firms in some way. Advertising, offering special services, or having superior quality are ways that firms in monopolistic competition differentiate their products. When this happens, the businesses have a monopoly on their name and reputation rather than on the product they offer for sale.

Using Advertising to Differentiate Products

Differentiation is often achieved through advertising. Differences between advertised products may be real or imagined. Consider the number of brands of soap you can choose to buy. They have different packages, colors, fragrances, and ingredients. However, they all do essentially the same thing: They help wash the dirt from your skin.

Most soap advertising provides few hard facts. People are seen having a good time after washing with particular brand of soap. Viewers are supposed to conclude that this is the result of using the advertised product. Think of other commercials you have seen that provided few facts but portrayed people being happy and satisfied while using a particular product. In each case the company was trying to differentiate its products from those of its competition. If it was successful, its sales and profits grew.

Some advertisements give specific facts and prices and describe qualities that may cause consumers to prefer the product over alternative goods or services. For example, most commercials for computer products provide

The *Global* Consumer

What Is an American Car?

Although many Americans would like to buy products made in the United States, this is often difficult to do. For example, when consumers buy cars from American manufacturers, they are also buying imported goods. All U.S. automobile companies buy parts for their "American" cars from foreign suppliers. Some cars with American names are assembled in other countries.

On the other hand, foreign-owned firms like Toyota, Honda, Nissan, and Mazda have now built automobile factories in this country. Even General Motors has undertaken a joint venture with Toyota in California, where automobiles are produced from parts made in Japan and the United States. International trade and the growth of international trade in the world economy has made it impossible to buy a car that is totally American-made.

It's not hard to see the changes that have taken place. In March 1986 there were almost 900,000 cars sold in the United States. Of these cars, 650,000 (72 percent) were made in the United States and 250,000 (28 percent) were produced in other countries. Of the 650,000 cars made in the United States, all but 30,000 were produced by American-owned firms.

Five years later the picture had changed dramatically. In March 1991, only 730,000 cars were sold because of a downturn in the economy. Of this number, 543,000 (74 percent) were made in the United States and 187,000 (26 percent) were imported. U.S. production accounted for a larger share of automobile sales in March 1991 than it had in March 1986. However, of the 543,000 cars produced in this country, 83,000 (15 percent) were manufactured in factories owned by foreign firms. Cars produced by foreign-owned firms accounted for more than one-third (37 percent) of all automobiles sold in the United States in March 1991.

Do you believe that a car assembled in the United States by a foreign-owned firm is more American than a Ford or Chevrolet that is partially made of imported parts or assembled in Canada and shipped to the United States?

What is an imported car? These days it is hard to say.

How have foreign producers differentiated their products to compete successfully with American manufacturers?

---

extensive and specific information about what the products are able to do. Firms that convince consumers that their products are superior by providing factual information also differentiate themselves from competing firms.

Offering Superior Service to Differentiate Products

Offering superior service or warranties is another way a firm may differentiate its products from those of competing firms. In the early 1980s most American automobile manu-

Vocabulary Builder

Differentiation   The process used by manufacturers to convince customers that their products are in some way superior to similar products offered by other firms.

Monopolistic competition   A market situation in which there are numerous sellers, each with some control over price as the result of having successfully differentiated their products.

◆   Sales of cars produced by Honda Motors in the United States grew rapidly in the early 1990s. What may this have had to do with the quality many consumers felt Honda cars had?

facturers offered warranties on their cars for one year or 12,000 miles or for two years or 24,000 miles. The Chrysler Corporation differentiated its products by offering warranties that lasted seven years or 70,000 miles. People who might have doubted the quality of Chrysler's products or who compared the warranties of the three major automobile producers could see a difference between what they were being offered. As a result, they were more likely to purchase a Chrysler product.

A similar type of differentiation can be seen in firms that service the products they sell. If you wanted to buy a bicycle, you might find one with the lowest price at a discount store. However, if the bicycle was defective, the discount store probably couldn't repair it. On the other hand, if you purchased the bicycle at a bicycle shop, its price might have been a little higher, but the shop would be able to repair the product if it was defective. When you decide where to purchase a product, consider the service that is offered as well as the price.

Offering goods and services of superior quality is a common method of differentiation.

Many consumers are willing to pay more to receive products they believe are the best available or most up-to-date. Although providing such products may result in higher costs to a business, these costs may be justified by higher prices some consumers are willing to pay. There are usually fewer businesses offering high-quality goods. Therefore, firms in this part of a market are likely to be less competitive and have monopoly-like power. Examples of such businesses include stores that offer the latest styles of clothing. Fashion-conscious customers are often willing to pay higher prices for new styles.

The Responsible Consumer

Consumers who buy from firms in monopolistic competition should be sure that they are paying for a product's quality and not just its name. Many well-known brands are much the same as other products that are not so well known. This does not mean that consumers should avoid buying goods or services from firms that have differentiated their products to gain some monopoly-like power. It does mean that consumers should use the problem-solving skills you learned about in Chapter 1 to reach the best decision possible.

Remember that some businesses need to be large to be efficient. There is no advantage in buying a product at a higher price from a competitive firm if a better product could be purchased for less money from a firm with some monopoly-like power.

To be responsible consumers, people should carefully consider claims made by businesses regarding the price and quality of goods or services. Paying too much or buying inferior goods not only hurts individual consumers and their families, but may also harm society and the economy in general. When a firm succeeds in charging prices that are too high or selling inferior goods, other firms are encouraged to do the same. Profits earned in such ways may result in an inefficient allocation of resources. Consumers who waste their money making unwise purchases cannot use the same money to buy the things they really need. The better our consumer choices are, the more efficiently our economic system works. We all have a responsibility to make the best choices possible.

Summing Up *Firms in monopolistic competition try to differentiate their products from those of competing firms. They do this by advertising or by offering superior service or quality. Consumers who buy from firms in monopolistic competition should be sure that they are paying for a product's quality, not just its name.* ◆

Consumer News

What's in a Trademark?

Businesses have used trademarks to differentiate their products for many years. It can be a shape like the Chevrolet emblem, a picture like the RCA dog sitting in front of a gramophone, or even a color. Try asking someone who was alive before 1940 where the "green in Lucky Strikes" went.

Recently, many firms have returned to their old trademarks to try to sell new products. In 1990, for example, Buick was planning to bring out a new line of full-size cars and was looking for a name that would be recognized and remembered by consumers. After considering hundreds of possibilities, the firm chose the name Roadmaster—the same name it used in the 1940s and 1950s. When Chase & Sanborn Coffee was bought by Hills Brothers in 1984, they discovered that there was a small but loyal group of consumers who wanted to buy Chase & Sanborn Coffee. The firm kept the name and sold about $120 million worth of coffee under it in 1990.

The U.S. Patent and Trademark Office has 680,000 active trademarks registered. More and more firms are using their registered names over again. This may be the result of having used up many of the best names, or it may be the result of consumer loyalty. Whatever the reason, it is clear that many trademarks are here to stay.

Review and Enrichment Activities

VOCABULARY REVIEW

1. Column A contains key consumer terms from this chapter. Column B contains a scrambled list of phrases that describe what these terms mean. Match the correct meaning with each term. Write your answers on a separate sheet of paper.

Column A	Column B
1. differentiation	a. When many firms offer the same product for sale to many customers
2. the "invisible hand"	b. The only producer of a product that has no substitutes
3. imperfect competition	c. Presenting a product as being superior to other similar products
4. Laissez-faire	d. The idea that business owners in competition serve the interests of consumers when they work to earn a profit for themselves
5. competitive market	e. When there are many firms that produce similar products that are differentiated from each other so that the firms have a monopoly on their names and reputations more than on the product they sell
6. monopoly	
7. competition	f. A term that is used to describe businesses in perfect competition
8. price taker	g. Where exchanges take place in perfect competition
9. monopolistic competition	h. A market that has some but not all of the characteristics of perfect competition
	i. A term used by Adam Smith that suggested the government should not interfere with the free market

2. Explain how a firm that is in competition can change its market to one of imperfect competition by differentiating its product.

CHECKING WHAT YOU'VE LEARNED

Write your answers for the following exercises on a separate sheet of paper.

1. Describe a firm in your community that is in competition.
2. Describe a firm in your community that is in imperfect competition.
3. Why are firms in competition often called "price takers"?
4. Describe three different ways consumers are supposed to benefit from firms that are in competition.
5. Describe three different ways consumers may benefit from firms that are in imperfect competition.
6. Why do some businesses need to be large to be efficient?
7. Describe three different ways that a firm could create differentiation for the products it sells.
8. If a firm in monopolistic competition has established differentiation for the product it sells, what does it have a monopoly on?
9. What should consumers do when they buy goods or services from firms in imperfect competition?

PRACTICING YOUR CONSUMER SKILLS

Write your answers for the following exercises on a separate sheet of paper.

1. For each of the following situations, say whether the firm is in competition or imperfect competition. Explain your answer in each case.
    a. Mel is an artist who makes metal sculptures. He heats iron over a coal fire before he shapes it with his hammer. Mel can buy coal from at least twelve different businesses within 20 miles of his home. The firm he has bought coal from for the past ten years increased the price of its product, so it now charges 10 percent more than other firms that offer coal for sale.
    b. Arnold is not a secure person. He lacks self-confidence. He is particularly nervous when he talks to girls. He saw a commercial on television where a strong, handsome, confident young man used a brand of cologne produced by Platinum Products for Men Inc. In the advertisement, the man was pursued by many beautiful women. Arnold is thinking of buying some of this product, even though its price is $27 for a 2-ounce bottle.
    c. Paula has a job selling expensive modern furniture. Most of her customers are young urban professionals who have lots of money to spend. Paula earns a good salary but feels that she must dress to

Review and Enrichment Activities Continued

impress her customers. She often pays between $300 and $500 for each outfit she buys at Mimi's Fashion Boutique. She could buy similar dresses and suits for much less if she waited a few months and bought them at other less fashionable stores.

2. For each of the following situations, explain why the market being described is not an example of competition. Explain how consumers may be harmed by the current situation.

   a. John owns a bookstore on a college campus. Although there are other bookstores in a nearby community, the college administration will not allow anyone else to open a bookstore on the campus. John pays the college a fee equal to 10 percent of his sales.

   b. Lewanda owns the only dry cleaning business in a rural community in Nebraska. Her customers would have to travel over 40 miles to take their business to another dry cleaners. Lewanda's prices are about 15 percent higher than the prices in larger communities, like Omaha.

   c. Sheldon repairs broken television sets. He is not exactly dishonest, but he often replaces parts that are not yet broken. He justifies this by telling himself, "I'm really saving my customers time and money because the parts I replace might have broken soon, and this is saving them from having to bring their TV back in the future." Sheldon's customers are not aware of what he does. Although they often complain of his high prices, they pay and often bring their television sets back the next time they break.

3. Explain how each of the following firms is trying to differentiate its product. Then describe how consumers will be affected by each firm's actions.

   a. The Acme Golf Ball Company hires beautiful women to stand next to golfers using their products on television commercials.

   b. The Super Clean Vacuum Company guarantees its products for ten years, while most other vacuum producers only offer five-year guarantees.

   c. A traveler's check company hires a former U.S. representative to advertise its products on television.

   d. Bob's Convenient Foods stays open 24 hours a day, while most grocery stores close at midnight.

USING NUMBERS

Solve the following problem to help make the best possible choice. Write your solution on a separate sheet of paper. Be sure to show all your work.

Brenda always buys a particular brand of cosmetics. It is not uncommon for her to go to her local drugstore and spend $25 or more on this type of product. She recently was told about a discount store on the other side of town that sells the brand she likes for 20 percent off if a customer spends $100 or more. Brenda figured out that driving to this store would take about an hour of her time and cost her $5 in gas and tolls on a bridge. If she goes to the discount store and spends $112, how much money will she save? What other factors should she consider when making her choice? Do you believe that her trip will be worthwhile? Explain your answer.

PUTTING IDEAS IN YOUR OWN WORDS

The quotations are from this chapter. Explain these quotations in your own words to make sure you understand what they mean. Write your answers on a separate sheet of paper.

1. "He [Adam Smith] said that owners of competitive businesses serve the best interests of consumers when they work for their own success."
2. "Competition does not just happen. There are a number of conditions that need to exist for competition to function successfully."
3. "A firm that succeeds in differentiating its products will be able to sell more goods and services."

BUILDING CONSUMER KNOWLEDGE

Write your answers for the following exercises on a separate sheet of paper.

1. Identify a product that you buy regularly in a market that you believe is close to being in perfect competition. Describe this market, and explain how you benefit from its being in perfect competition.
2. Identify a product that you buy regularly in a market that you believe is in imperfect competition. Describe this market, and explain how you may benefit or may be harmed by its being in imperfect competition.
3. Identify two different local businesses that you feel have successfully differentiated themselves from competing firms.
   a. Describe how the differentiation was accomplished in each case.
   b. Describe how the owners of each firm have benefited from this differentiation.
   c. Describe how each firm's customers have benefited or been harmed by the differentiation.

Economics in Action

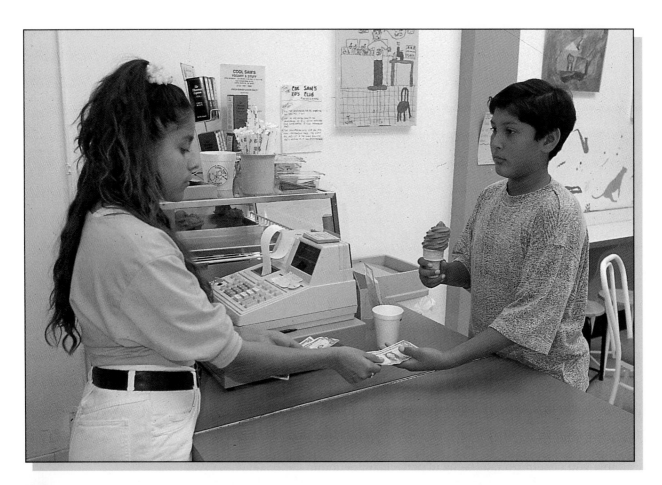

Unit 3 completes the foundation of knowledge that will help you understand consumer economics. In this unit you will discover that the economy of the United States is constantly changing and that consumers need to be aware of these changes to make responsible decisions. You will learn how the government measures, predicts, and controls these economic changes—and also how it helps provide a reliable system of money and banking. You will also learn to identify our government's sources of income and types of spending. Finally, you will come to understand how our trade with other nations affects both our ability to earn income and the prices we pay for products.

Chapter 6

Understanding Money

Chapter Objectives

After completing this chapter, you will be able to do the following:
- Identify and explain the functions of money in our economic system.
- Explain the various ways that money is spent in our economic system.
- Explain how banks earn income when they operate under the fractional reserve system.
- Explain the expansion of money and its role in our economic system.
- Describe the relationship between the amount of money in circulation, prices, and interest rates.

Key Consumer Terms

In this chapter you will learn the meanings of the following important consumer terms:
- Money
- Barter
- Debt
- Double coincidence of wants
- Commodity money
- Representative money
- Full-bodied money
- Fiat money
- Currency
- Demand deposit
- Fractional reserve system
- Reserve requirement
- Federal Reserve System
- Expansion of money
- Monetary policy
- Tight money
- Easy money
- Inflation
- Unemployment

Y ou can't eat money or wear it, and a roof made out of money wouldn't keep much rain off your head. Money doesn't keep you warm, and it can't guarantee happiness. If money can't do any of these things, why do most people feel that they need it? Although you use money almost every day, you might have trouble explaining what it is—or, for that matter, why it is so important to our economic system. These and other questions about money will be answered in this chapter.

SECTION 1

THE FUNCTIONS OF MONEY

While you read, ask yourself . . .
- *What are several ways that you have used money in the past few days?*
- *How have the functions of money been demonstrated by these events?*

Money is anything that is generally accepted as a *medium of exchange*, a *unit of account*, and a *store of value*. These terms used to define money really describe the functions of money in our economic system.

Money as a Medium of Exchange

When used as a medium of exchange, money helps people carry out transactions quickly and efficiently. This means that people are willing to accept money as payment for a **debt**. The alternative to money is **barter**, where actual goods or services are traded.

Barter is almost always inefficient. It requires a condition called a **double coincidence of wants**. This means that each person in a transaction must want what the other person has to trade and must be willing to accept the other person's property as equal in value to his or her own.

For example, you might be willing to trade one of your books for a friend's tennis racket. If your friend agrees to this trade, the exchange can easily be made. But what if your friend doesn't want your book? Many transactions may need to be completed involving other people and products. You might trade your book for someone else's CD recording, then trade the CD for a calculator, then trade the calculator for the tennis racket you want. Such exchanges can be more trouble than they are worth and are often not completed.

Think how much easier it would be to complete the exchange using money. You could sell your book and use the money to buy your friend's racket. Your friend could then use the money from the sale of the racket to buy a good or service he or she really wants.

The usefulness of money increases with the complexity of the transactions being made. Picture a chicken farmer trying to buy an automobile by bartering hens and eggs. Without the use of money, this transaction would probably be impossible. Barter can only be used effectively in small groups with few goods or services that need to be exchanged. The use of money allows our complex economic system to function successfully.

Money as a Unit of Account

Money helps consumers and business owners compare different values of goods and services. Suppose that you are interested in owning a new bicycle, a new jacket, and your brother's old softball glove. To buy these products, you are willing to trade the value of your labor used to cut your neighbor's lawn. Could you carry out the necessary transactions without money? Think about this for a moment. How would you exchange the value of your labor for any or all of the three items you want if you have to rely on barter? Could you determine which products you can afford? The necessary exchanges would be difficult or impossible.

If you are able to use money, the exchanges will be easy to complete. Suppose that you earn $15 a week working for your neighbor. Over the summer you save $120. You could use your money to buy the bicycle at a price of $120, or you could pay $95 for the jacket and $20 for the glove, leaving you with $5 to buy something else. Money in this example is used as a medium of exchange and as a unit of account. When money is used as a unit of account, it is used to compare the values and prices of different resources, goods, or services. Your choice of what to buy will be easier because you can compare the value of each of the goods you want.

◆   In the past beads and other items have served as money in many societies. What problems would prevent beads from being an efficient type of money in the United States?

Money as a Store of Value

There are many times when consumers want to save to buy a product in the future because they can't afford it at the present or they won't need the product until later. Suppose that a family owns a dairy farm and sells milk for a living. This family has decided to send the oldest child to college after high school. The cost of tuition will be equal to the value of one-half of the milk the family sells each year. To afford this, they have been setting aside 10 percent of their milk production for each of the past five years. Try to imagine paying the col-

Vocabulary Builder

Barter   Exchanges that take place without the benefit of money.
Debt   Something of value that is owed to someone else.
Double coincidence of wants   A situation in which two individuals each want exactly what the other has, allowing a direct exchange of goods or services without the use of money.
Money   Anything used as a medium of exchange, a unit of account, and a store of value.

Consumer News

Paying for a Quick Return

The annual National Football League draft for new players was held on April 21, 1991. On the day before the draft, many people assumed that the Dallas Cowboys would use their first choice to pick Notre Dame's Raghib (Rocket) Ismail. Ismail, a wide receiver, was best known for his great speed (40 yards in 4.3 seconds) and kick returns. Ismail ran back two kickoffs for touchdowns against Michigan in one game. Ismail, however, signed a four-year contract with the Toronto Argonauts for a minimum of $18 Million.

Consider how difficult it would have been to complete this transaction without the use of money.

Could the Toronto football fans, television networks, and advertisers have paid for Ismail's services without the use of money?

How was money used as both a medium of exchange and a unit of account in this transaction?

What characteristics of money were demonstrated in this situation?

lege tuition in milk that has been saved over the last five years.

Saving becomes easy when the milk is sold for money that can be accumulated. Without this function of money, it would be difficult or impossible to produce or acquire expensive goods or services like homes, factories, or a college education.

Summing Up   *Money serves important functions in our economy. It is a medium of exchange, a unit of account, and a store of value.* ◆

SECTION 2

TYPES OF MONEY IN THE U.S. ECONOMY

While you read, *ask yourself . . .*
- ◆ *How much money does your family spend in currency, how much through checks, and how much through credit cards?*
- ◆ *Why do you trust that the money you have in your pocket or purse has value?*

You know that the coins and dollar bills in your pocket are money. But do you know what type of money they are? Why are people and businesses willing to accept your money as payment?

Different Types of Money

Anything that people are willing to accept in exchange for goods or services can serve as money. At different times in history many things have been used as money, including cattle, salt, pieces of stone, gems, and tobacco. Each of these things possessed some of the characteristics of money shown in figure 6-1 and fulfilled the functions of money in a particular economic system. Items that serve as money and are useful in and of themselves are called **commodity money**. Often commodity money is not easily transported or divided, nor is it stable in value, durable, or generally accepted.

Commodity money may be better than no money at all, but it is not very efficient as a medium of exchange.

Representative money offers a much more efficient way of carrying out transactions. Rep-

CHARACTERISTICS OF MONEY

Characteristic	Description
Durable	The material that is used as money must be able to withstand the wear and tear of being passed from person to person. Paper money lasts on the average of only one year, but old bills can be easily replaced. Coins, on the other hand, last for years.
Portable	People need a medium of exchange that they can carry around easily so they can buy things whenever and wherever they want. Though paper money is not very durable, it is very portable. People can easily carry large sums of paper money.
Divisible	It must be possible to divide money into small parts so that purchases of any price can be made. Carrying large amounts of coins and small bills is not handy, but these make it possible to make purchases of any amount.
Stable in Value	Money must be stable in value. Its value cannot change rapidly or its in value usefulness as a store of value will decrease.
Scarce	Whatever is used as money must be scarce. That is what gives it value.
Accepted	Whatever is used as money must be accepted as a medium of exchange by those who use it. They must be willing to accept it in payment for debts and to pass it on to others. In the United States, that acceptance is based on the knowledge that others will continue to accept paper money, coins, and checks in exchange for desired goods and services.

◆ **Table 6-1**   Characteristics of money.

resentative money has no usefulness of its own, but is accepted as having value. When money can be exchanged for some commodity that people believe has value, like gold, it is called **full-bodied money**. For example, before 1933, paper dollars could be exchanged for gold from the U.S. Treasury. People believed that the gold had value, so they were willing to accept paper money.

Since 1933, the U. S. dollar has been **fiat money**. This means that it is money because our government says it is money, not because it can be converted into a commodity that has value. The U.S. dollar cannot be cashed in at

Vocabulary Builder

Commodity money   Money that has value as a commodity or a good, aside from its value as money.

Fiat money   Money that has value because a government has established it as an acceptable means for the payment of debts.

Full-bodied money   Money backed by a commodity that people believe has value, like gold.

Representative money   Money that is not valuable in itself for nonmoney uses, but which can be exchanged for valuable items.

◆   These photographs show consumers spending money through cash, writing a check, or by using a credit card. Why isn't it practical to use cash for all types of spending?

the U.S. Treasury for gold, silver, or anything else of value. The next time you see a U.S. dollar, read the small print that says "This note is legal tender for all debts, public and private." This means that the U.S. dollar must be accepted as payment for debt. Anyone who refuses the U.S. dollar as payment for a debt in this country gives up the legal right to receive payment. This is what makes the U.S. dollar "legal tender."

How Money Is Spent

There are three basic ways to spend money in the United States. You can spend money using currency, checks, or credit cards (also called charge cards or "plastic money"). **Currency** is the cash, or paper money and coins that people sometimes use to buy products. A check is a paper that transfers ownership of money deposited in a bank account from one party to another. Deposits in checking accounts are called **demand deposits** because consumers or businesses can spend money by writing a check against their deposits at any time and any place. They can "demand" the use of their money when they want it. Checks are based on currency, but they are not legal tender. Although most people and businesses accept checks as payment for debts, the law does not require them to do so.

Currency and demand deposits are regarded as money by economists, but credit cards are not considered money. Using a credit card creates a debt that eventually results in a transfer of money from one party to another. Credit cards are important to our economy because they let us use our money quickly and efficiently. People who have credit cards don't have to carry large amounts of cash with them or keep large balances in their checking accounts. However, a credit card itself is not money.

Most transactions in the United States are carried out through the use of currency. But these transactions tend to be small. When you buy a carton of milk or a ticket to a movie, you pay in cash. Large transactions, however, are usually carried out through checks.

Roughly 80 percent of the spending that takes place in the United States is carried out through the use of checks. Think of large transactions that your family has made. Workers usually receive their wages in a paycheck. When people buy cars, homes, or boats, they use checks. This tendency to use checks is even more apparent when the government or businesses are involved. The government almost never makes a payment in cash. Businesses may receive cash from customers, but usually pay their bills through checks. It is impossible to understand the role of money in the United States economy without having a basic understanding of how our checking system works.

Summing Up *The U.S. dollar is fiat money. It is legal tender and must be accepted for payment of debts in the United States. People spend money by using currency, checks, or credit cards.* ◆

SECTION 3

HOW THE CHECKING SYSTEM WORKS

While you read, *ask yourself . . .*

- ◆ *When you were a child, what did you think banks did with the money people deposited? Were you surprised when you found out what really happened to deposited money?*
- ◆ *Does it bother you to know that banks lend your deposits to other people?*

Like any other business in a free market economy, banks are run to earn a profit for their owners. Banks earn most of their income by lending money they receive in deposits to borrowers. They pay lower interest rates to depositors than the interest rates they charge borrowers. The difference between these interest rates allows banks to pay their costs and earn a profit.

Suppose that you deposited $1,000 in a checking account in 1991. At that time, you could have expected to earn a little less than 5 percent interest on your deposit. The bank could have used your money in a number of ways. It could have made a mortgage loan, a car loan, or a loan to a business. The bank might have chosen to use your deposit to buy a government bond, build a new office building, or make other investments that would have earned income for the bank. There probably would have been a difference of from 4 to 9

Vocabulary Builder

Currency   Cash, or paper money and coins, that may be used to buy goods and services.

Demand deposit   Money deposited in a bank that can be withdrawn at any time; checking accounts are demand deposits.

Consumer Close-Up

The Thrift Industry Disaster: What's Your Share of the Bill?

Most Americans are aware of the many failures of savings and loan associations (S&Ls) in the late 1980s and early 1990s. You may have heard that American taxpayers will eventually pay over half a trillion dollars to "bail out" the S&L industry. Have you thought about how much money that really is? What else could have been done with this money and the resources it could buy? How could our government allow such events to take place? Who is at fault? Who will pay for the mistakes that were made?

One-half of $1 trillion is roughly $2,000 for every man, woman, and child who lived in the United States in 1991. That amount of money distributed to our nation's poor could have brought all Americans above the official poverty level for over five years. It could have paid for 1 million low-income housing units or sent 800,000 students to college for a full four years. However, the money and the resources it could have bought will be used to pay off the debt of failed S&Ls.

The roots of the S&L disaster can be found in the banking regulations of the 1950s and 1960s. Savings and loan associations were limited in the kind of deposits they could accept and the loans they could make. They could not take commercial deposits or have checking accounts. They were only allowed to make loans for mort-

gages and some home improvements. They were intended to serve the needs of small savers and borrowers, who larger commercial banks were less interested in serving.

The S&Ls were assured a low-cost source of deposits because of a rule made by the government called Regulation Q. Regulation Q set a maximum rate of interest that could be paid on saving deposits of less than $100,000. Small savers earned the same interest rate no matter where they deposited their money. S&Ls seemed friendly and interested in their business, so small savers often deposited their money in S&Ls. The S&Ls took the money and made long-term fixed interest rate mortgages. This seemed to be a safe way to

percent between the interest rate you received for your deposit and the return earned by the bank.

The Fractional Reserve System

American banks operate under a **fractional reserve system**. This means that out of each dollar a bank receives as a deposit, it must hold a minimum percentage in reserve. The remainder of each dollar may be lent out or in-

vested in other ways by the bank. The percentage of each deposit that must be held on reserve is called the **reserve requirement**.

The reserve requirement is different for different types of deposits. In 1992 the reserve requirement for most money deposited in checking accounts was 10 percent. Therefore, when you deposited $1,000 in your checking account, the bank was required to keep a minimum of 10 percent or $100, on hand in cash or deposited in the **Federal Reserve System**. The Federal Reserve System is the agency of the

Consumer Close-Up, continued

do business. Depositors earned 5 percent, borrowers paid 7 percent and the S&Ls kept 2 percent to pay their costs.

In the 1970s the government changed the rules. New types of deposits were created that allowed small savers to earn much higher rates of interest on their deposits. To keep small savers from withdrawing their money, the S&Ls had to pay interest rates that were as high as those offered by other institutions. By the early 1980s these interest rates were as much as 12 to 14 percent. However, the S&Ls still earned their income from long-term fixed interest rate mortgages that paid the S&Ls 7 to 8 percent a year. Many S&Ls lost large amounts of money as a result of this situation.

Congress and the president tried to help the S&Ls in 1982 when the Garn-Fernand St Germain Act was passed. With this law, savings and loans associations could make some commercial loans to businesses, finance shopping centers, and oil exploration, and make many other types of investments. Nevertheless, the S&Ls still had billions of dollars tied up in fixed interest rate mortgages. They continued to lose money every year on these loans. If the S&Ls were to stay in business, they had to earn large profits from the new types of loans to make up for the money they were losing on mortgages. This encouraged the S&Ls to make investments that promised large returns but also had large risks. Many of these

investments failed, and the S&Ls lost even more money.

Many of the people involved in the S&L crisis were dishonest. Others showed poor judgment. However, the problem had its roots in the regulations established by our government. It would be difficult to find any one person who is most responsible for what has happened. But it is clear that the cost will now be paid by American taxpayers.

How does the S&L disaster demonstrate how important it is for consumers to be aware of the actions of their elected government officials?

---

federal government that regulates banking. The other 90 percent or $900, could have been lent out or invested in other ways to earn income for the bank.

Most people who deposit money in checking accounts intend to write checks against their deposits. When they do, they spend their money. However, when a bank lends part of someone's deposit to another person, more spending takes place. Money deposited in checking accounts can actually allow two people to spend the same money at the same time.

Vocabulary Builder

Federal Reserve System   An agency created by the federal government to regulate banking in the United States and implement monetary policy.

Fractional reserve system   A method of banking in which banks must keep a fraction of money deposited on reserve; the remainder may be lent out or otherwise invested.

Reserve requirement   The percentage of deposits that a bank must keep as cash or deposited with a Federal Reserve bank.

When people deposit money in checking accounts they are able to spend that money by writing checks. Banks then lend part of this money to allow even more spending.

Expansion of Money

In recent years currency has made up about one-third of the money in circulation in our economy. For example, on April 3, 1991, the Federal Reserve System estimated that the currency in circulation in the United States was $322 billion, while the total amount of money in circulation was around $852 billion. The $530 billion that was not currency was made up of checking deposits that had been "created" by the American banking system. Knowing how this process works will help you understand the role of checking accounts in the American economy.

Although banks must keep part of the deposits they receive on reserve, money held on reserve earns no income for the bank. Therefore, banks try to lend or invest as much of their deposits as they legally can as quickly as possible. When you deposited your $1,000, the bank lent or invested most of the $900 it was not required to keep on reserve. If the money was lent, you can be sure it was spent. Few people would pay interest to borrow money that they don't intend to quickly spend. If the bank used the $900 to buy a bond or build a new office, the result would be the same. The money would quickly be put into circulation or deposited in a bank by the party who sold the bond or by the firm that built the office.

All money that is spent becomes income to someone else. If you buy a new car for $20,000, the money you spend is income to the owners of the car dealership. This income allows the dealers to pay their bills and employees. People or businesses who receive income spend it again or deposit it in a bank. People and businesses tend to hold as little currency as possible to avoid losing the interest that they could earn if they deposited their money in a bank.

The $900 that the bank was able to lend as a result of your deposit would have been spent, becoming someone else's income. The person who received this $900 as income would have spent it again or deposited it in a bank. Eventually, a bank would receive the money as a deposit. It would keep 10 percent on reserve and lend or invest the remaining 90 percent. This new loan would again be spent, become someone's income, and be deposited once more. When this cycle goes on many times, it is called the **expansion of money**. Although you only deposited $1,000 in currency, banks and checking accounts allowed many thousands of dollars to be lent and spent as the result of your deposit. Most of the money in circulation in the United States is created through the expansion of money.

◆   Money that is borrowed from banks is almost always quickly spent. This creates income for other people and more spending in the economy. When consumers deposit money in checking accounts they are helping banks expand the supply of money.

Why Banks Keep Excess Reserves

You might wonder if the bank would have a problem if you wrote a check against the $1,000 you originally deposited or withdrew the $1,000 in cash. The answer is no.

If you or anyone else writes a check or demands cash, your intention probably is to spend the money. Remember, when you spend money, it is someone else's income. Most of the income that results from your spending $1,000 will be quickly redeposited into the banking system. If banks keep a small amount of excess reserves, they should have no problem when depositors write checks or withdraw cash. Most of the money will be returned to the banking system within a few days. Even if a bank finds itself short of cash, it can easily borrow extra money from another bank or from

the Federal Reserve System. The expansion of money is not stopped by people demanding currency.

Summing Up   *American banks operate under the fractional reserve system. This allows money that is deposited in checking accounts to be spent by two people, the depositor and a person who borrows from the bank. Most of the money being spent in our economic system is a result of the expansion of money.* ◆

Vocabulary Builder

Expansion of money   Repeated cycles of deposits, loans, spending, and new deposits that provide a large part of the money used to buy goods and services in our economic system.

SECTION 4

THE AMOUNT OF MONEY IN CIRCULATION

While you read, ask yourself . . .
- ◆ *If you had more money, what would happen to the price you would be willing to pay for the products you wanted?*
- ◆ *If you had less money, what would happen to the price you would be able to pay for the products you wanted?*

Economists believe that there is a relationship between the amount of money in circulation and the prices that people pay for the

◆ If there was more money in circulation there would be no quick increase in the amount of gasoline or other products offered for sale. The first result would be higher prices.

resources or goods and services they buy. Each year there is some quantity of goods and services produced and offered for sale. The amount of products available doesn't change very much from one year to the next. It doesn't matter if businesses and consumers have more money to spend or less money to spend. There will be no large or quick change in the amount of products offered for sale. There will, however, be a change in the prices charged for the goods and services that are sold.

How Money and Prices are Related

Suppose that 100,000 bicycles are produced each year by the Acme Bicycle Corporation. The firm could not produce more products without investing in new machines and hiring additional workers. If it sold fewer products, it would be forced to lay off some of its workers and would find it difficult to pay its mortgage and other costs. The owners of this firm need to produce and sell about the same number of bicycles every year.

Last year the price of the bicycles was $100 each. There were 100,000 customers who wanted to purchase an Acme bicycle, and each had $100 they could afford to spend. As a result, the business sold all of its products at the price it wanted to receive, and all the people who wanted to buy a bicycle at that price were satisfied. Everyone was happy.

Suppose that the amount of money in circulation increased this year, and people had 50 percent more money to spend. As a result, there were many more consumers who could afford to buy the bicycles at $100. The owners of the Acme Bicycle Corporation quickly realized that they had more customers than they had bicycles to sell. This shortage encouraged them to increase the price of their product until the number of customers was just equal to the number of bicycles they were willing to produce and offer for sale. This shows that an increase in the amount of money in circulation tends to force prices up.

On the other hand, if the amount of money in circulation fell, consumers would have less money to spend. As a result, there would be fewer consumers who could afford to buy bicycles at $100. The Acme Bicycle Corporation would produce more products than it could sell. This surplus would force the firm to lower its price until the number of customers who were willing and able to buy its product was equal to the number of bicycles the company needed to sell. A decrease in the amount of money in circulation tends to force prices down.

Who Controls the Amount of Money in Circulation?

The Federal Reserve System is the agency of the federal government that regulates banking. It can take actions that will either increase or decrease the amount of money in circulation. By regulating the supply of money in our economy, the Federal Reserve System tries to keep prices stable, fight unemployment, and encourage other economic conditions that will benefit businesses and consumers alike.

The Federal Reserve System (often referred to as the "Fed") was created in 1913. The Fed is responsible for maintaining a secure banking system and for carrying out **monetary policy**. Monetary policy is made up of actions that are intended to help the economy work efficiently. These actions adjust the supply of money in circulation and affect the interest rates that people and businesses must pay when they borrow money.

The Federal Reserve System is a sort of "bank" for banks. Banks may deposit their reserves in the Federal Reserve System. They may also borrow money from the Federal Reserve System if they run short of cash. The Fed-

eral Reserve System has the power to set the reserve requirement that banks must hold within a range set by Congress. In 1992 the Fed set this requirement at 10 percent for most checking deposits.

At times the Federal Reserve System has reduced the supply of money in circulation, or made money "**tight**." When money is tight, it is more difficult to borrow money, and interest rates tend to increase.

At other times the Federal Reserve System has increased the supply of money in circulation, or made money "**easy**." When money is easy, it is easier to borrow money, and interest rates tend to fall.

By making money tight or easy, the Federal Reserve System influences interest rates and how much money people and businesses choose to borrow and spend. This power allows the Federal Reserve System to influence the entire economic system of the United States.

Summing Up   *When there is more money in circulation, prices tend to go up. When there is less money in circulation, prices tend to fall. The Federal Reserve System tries to help the economy work better by carrying out monetary policy that makes money either tight or easy.* ◆

Vocabulary Builder

Easy money   A policy designed to stimulate the economy by making credit inexpensive and easy to get.

Monetary policy   The decisions of the Federal Reserve System concerning the money supply, intended to influence interest rates and help our economic system meet objectives.

Tight money   Policy designed to slow the economy by making credit expensive and in short supply.

SECTION 5

HOW FEDERAL RESERVE DECISIONS AFFECT CONSUMERS

While you read, *ask yourself . . .*
- ◆ *Did you ever hear your parents complain about high interest rates?*
- ◆ *Do you know of a recent time when interest rates have either increased or decreased rapidly? How did consumers react?*

In recent years, the decisions of the Federal Reserve System have had important results for American consumers. In the early 1980s the Federal Reserve System did not allow the sup-

ply of money to grow as rapidly as prices. The result was tight money and high interest rates. People who borrowed money for home mortgages paid as much as 16 percent in 1981. If you borrowed $100,000 to buy a home in 1981, your interest payment alone would have been almost $16,000 the first year. High interest rates made it impossible for many people to buy a house in 1981. At the same time, rates for automobiles, home improvements, and other types of loans were as high as 20 percent. These interest rates discouraged consumers from borrowing and spending for other products.

The Federal Reserve System forced interest rates up to try to reduce the 13.5 percent rate of **inflation** that had existed in 1980. Reduced spending discourages businesses from increasing prices because they are likely to have sur-

◆   The men and women who control the Federal Reserve System have power that allows them to affect the interest rates you receive when you deposit your savings or pay when you borrow money. Why would borrowers and savers have a different point of view of higher interest rates?

pluses of their products. This effort by the Federal Reserve System was successful. The rate of inflation dropped to 3.2 percent by 1983.

At other times the Federal Reserve System has increased the supply of money in circulation to force interest rates down. In 1985 the amount of money in circulation grew over 15 percent. This easy money brought interest rates for home mortgages down from an average of 16 percent in 1982 to 10.1 percent in 1986. Lower interest rates encouraged businesses and people to borrow and spend more money. Increased spending helped reduce unemployment from 10.4 percent in 1982 to 6.8 percent in 1986.

When the Federal Reserve System increases or decreases the supply of money in circulation, it is trying to achieve economic goals. From 1980 through 1982, it was trying to fight inflation with tight money and high interest rates. In the mid-1980s the Federal Reserve System fought unemployment with easy money and lower interest rates. These are examples of monetary policy.

Unfortunately, it is impossible for the Federal Reserve System to achieve all of its economic goals. For example, when there is unemployment and inflation at the same time, the Federal Reserve System cannot create both easy money to fight unemployment and tight money to fight inflation. Like consumers, the Federal Reserve System must set priorities for the objectives it wants to achieve. If it works to solve one problem, it may not be able to solve another.

Consumers often borrow money to buy the goods and services they want. The interest rate that they must pay to borrow money is influenced by the Federal Reserve System. It is important for responsible consumers to be aware of the Federal Reserve System's powers and policies and to use this knowledge when they make decisions. You will learn more about interest rates, banks, and your consumer choices in Unit Eight.

Consumer News

Interest Rates and Affording a Home

How important do you think interest rates are to someone who's thinking of buying a new home? Would your family be more likely to consider moving into a new house if interest rates were low?

In 1978 the American economy was doing well, interest rates for home mortgages averaged 9.7 percent and 817,000 new homes were sold. Four years later, in 1982, sales, profits, and employment in our economy were down. Interest rates for home mortgages averaged 16 percent, and new home sales dropped by almost one-half to 412,000. By 1986 the economy had recovered, interest rates had fallen to 10.1 percent and new home sales grew to 750,000.

It is hard to say how much of the difference in sales was the result of factors other than interest rates. However, it is clear that there is a relationship between interest rates and new home sales.

Summing Up *The Federal Reserve System can take steps to fight inflation with tight money or reduce unemployment with easy money. Unfortunately, it is not able to do both of these at the same time.* ◆

Vocabulary Builder

Inflation A sustained increase in the prices of goods and services.

Unemployment The situation in which people are unable to find a job.

Review and Enrichment Activities

VOCABULARY REVIEW

1. Column A contains key consumer terms from this chapter. Column B contains a scrambled list of phrases that describe what these terms mean. Match the correct meaning with each term. Write your answers on a separate sheet of paper.

Column A

1. easy money

2. debt

3. commodity money

4. tight money

5. full bodied money

6. barter

7. inflation

8. monetary policy

9. fiat money

10. reserve requirements

Column B

a. when exchanges take place without the use of money

b. something that is money because a government says it is money

c. money that is not difficult to borrow when interest rates are low

d. something that serves as money and is also useful in and of itself

e. money that is difficult to borrow when interest rates are high

f. the percentage of a deposit banks must keep on hand in cash or deposited in the Federal Reserve System

g. decisions of the Federal Reserve System that are intended to influence the money supply and interest rates

h. a financial obligation that is owed to another party

i. money that is backed by a commodity that people believe has value but that is not useful in and of itself, like gold or silver

j. a sustained increase in the average level of prices

2. Explain why currency is legal tender but a demand deposit is not.

CHECKING WHAT YOU'VE LEARNED

Write your answers for the following exercises on a separate sheet of paper.

1. What is meant by a double coincidence of wants?
2. Describe a situation where you have used money as a medium of exchange.
3. Describe a situation where you have used money as a unit of account.
4. Describe a situation where you have used money as a store of value.
5. Explain the difference between commodity money and representative money.
6. What is a fractional reserve system?
7. Why is a deposit in a checking account also called a demand deposit?
8. What is the Federal Reserve System responsible for?
9. What is monetary policy?
10. What is the difference between tight money and easy money?
11. Under what economic conditions would you expect the Fed to have tight money?
12. Under what economic conditions would you expect the Fed to have easy money?

PRACTICING YOUR CONSUMER SKILLS

Write your answers for the following exercises on a separate sheet of paper.

1. Sara has a job selling automobiles. She wants to buy a new dress, rent the most reasonable apartment possible, and eventually go to college. Write a story about Sara that demonstrates how she benefits from money as a medium of exchange, as a unit of account, and as a store of value.
2. Suppose that the following transactions took place one week last month. Write a paragraph placing these events in order and demonstrating your understanding of how the expansion of money works.
   a. Frank borrowed $1,800 from the City National Bank to pay for having his car fixed after he ran it into a tree.
   b. Mary, a vice president of the City National Bank, placed $200 in the Federal Reserve to meet her bank's reserve requirement.
   c. Sam fixed Frank's car and was paid $1,800 for his work. He deposited the check he received from Frank in his own checking account at the First Trust Bank.
   d. Terry deposited the $2,000 she received when she cashed in a government savings bond in her checking account at the City National Bank.
   e. The officers of the First Trust Bank held 10 percent of Sam's deposit on reserve and used the remaining 90 percent to help pay for a new office building.

Review and Enrichment Activities Continued

3. Explain how each of the following people may be affected if monetary policy is changed from one of easy money to one of tight money.
   a. Mario works as a carpenter, building new homes.
   b. Gene wants to borrow money to buy a new car next year.
   c. Ellen often leaves an unpaid balance on her credit card at the end of the month.
   d. Karen wants to borrow $5,000 to pay for next year's college tuition.

USING NUMBERS

Solve the following problem to help make the best possible choice. Write your solution on a separate sheet of paper. Be sure to show all your work.

Norman has been saving to buy a home. He has $20,000 set aside for his down payment, but he is worried.. He needs to borrow another $80,000 to buy the home he wants. Interest rates for mortgages have gone up from 10 percent to 12 percent. On the other hand, his bank has increased the interest rate it pays him for his deposit from 6 percent to 8 percent. He is not sure that interest rates will remain this high. He is willing to put off his purchase for one ye if it makes good financial sense. To help Norman solve his problem, answer the following questions.
   a. How much more will Norman have to pay over the next 30 years if he takes out this mortgage at 12 percent rather than at 10 percent?
   b. How much will he earn on his savings at the bank over the next year?
   c. What other factors should Norman consider when he makes his decision?
   d. What do you think Norman should do? Explain your opinion.

PUTTING IDEAS IN YOUR OWN WORDS

The following quotations are from this chapter. Explain these quotations in your own words to make sure you understand what they mean. Write your answers on a separate sheet of paper.

1. "Barter can only be used effectively in small groups with few goods or services that need to be exchanged."
2. "All money that is spent becomes income to someone else."
3. "The Federal Reserve System is a sort of bank for banks."

BUILDING CONSUMER KNOWLEDGE

Write your answers for the following exercises on a separate sheet of paper.

1. Figure 6-1 identifies and describes six characteristics of money. Write several sentences that describe a transaction you have recently made. Explain how your transaction demonstrated at least three of the characteristics of money.

2. Discuss the importance of interest rates with a parent or other adult. Ask how this person's saving, borrowing, and spending decisions might change if interest rates were 2 percent higher or lower. Do not ask about specific amounts of money. Write a paragraph that explains the adult's answers and what they show about the importance of interest rates to consumer decisions.

3. Look in the financial pages of a newspaper or magazine to find an article about interest rates going up or down. Write a short paper summarizing the information in the article. State whether the information in the article indicates that the Federal Reserve System is increasing or decreasing the supply of money in circulation. Be sure to identify the title of the article, the name of the newspaper or magazine, the date of publication, and the page number the article appeared on.

◆ Although making purchases with checks is often convenient consumers should expect to be asked for identification. What do you suppose the clerk is asking this customer?

Chapter 7

Measuring the Economy

Chapter Objectives

After completing this chapter, you will be able to do the following:

- Identify the five measurements of production and income that are most often used in the United States.
- Describe how our government measures the value of production in the U.S. economic system.
- Describe several problems in accurately measuring the value of production in the U.S. economy.
- Describe how inflation can be taken into account in evaluating the measurements of production and income.
- Describe several difficulties in evaluating national income data accurately.

Key Consumer Terms

In this chapter you will learn the meanings of the following important consumer terms:

- National income accounting
- Gross domestic product (GDP)
- Net national product
- National income
- Personal income
- Disposable personal income
- Double counting
- Depreciation
- Transfer payment
- Underground economy
- Nominal value
- Current dollars
- Real value
- Constant dollars

Suppose that you produced yo-yos for a living. Each day for a year you went to your basement and used lumber, paint, string, and tools to make yo-yos as quickly as you could. At the end of the year there was a tremendous pile of yo-yos sitting on the floor of your basement. There were other yo-yos you had made and sold. At this point you might want to know how many yo-yos you had produced and how much money you had earned. This information could help you decide if you should make more or fewer products next year. You could find out if you had been using your resources efficiently and how you had spent the income you earned from making yo-yos. This information could help to find better ways to produce yo-yos in the future, or you might decide to use your resources to make some other product instead.

Just as you would like to have information about your business, government officials, business owners, and economists want to have information about the production of goods and services in the entire economy. This type of information can help them make better choices. The same information can help you make better consumer decisions.

SECTION 1

NATIONAL INCOME ACCOUNTING

While you read, ask yourself . . .
◆ *What are some things that you or other members of your family do that contribute to our nation's GDP?*
◆ *Which types of personal income does your family receive? Which types of income don't they receive?*

Measuring the nation's economic performance is called **national income accounting**. Through this process the overall value of production and income is determined. There are five important measurements of the nation's income and production. These are **gross domestic product (GDP)**, **net national product**, **national income**, **personal income**, and **disposable personal income**. Although these measurements are related, each one provides a different type of information and is used in a different way.

Vocabulary Builder

Disposable personal income   The income that people have left to spend or save after all taxes have been paid.

Gross domestic product (GDP)   The total dollar value of all final goods and services produced by a nation regardless of ownership during a given period, usually one year.

National income   Total income earned by everyone in the country.

National income accounting   Measuring the economy's income and output and the interaction of its major parts—consumers, businesses, and government.

Net national product   The value of GDP less wear-out or depreciation.

Personal income   Total income received by individuals before personal taxes are paid.

Gross Domestic Product: The Basic Measure of Production

The broadest measure of our economic production and income is the gross domestic product (GDP). This is the total dollar value of all new final goods and services produced in the nation in a single year regardless of ownership. The GDP is the most frequently used measure of the amount of production and income earned in a year. It also gives an indication of the supply of new products we can buy. The GDP is often used to compare production in one year with production in another year, indicating changes in our economic condition. If you cook hamburgers in a fast-food restaurant, the value of your labor and the hamburgers that you cook are part of the GDP.

There are three words in the definition of gross domestic product that you need to understand. One of these words is *value*. Simply adding up all the goods and services produced in a year wouldn't really tell us how produc-

◆ Suppose we know this worker made 50 brooms a day. They were worth $5 each and the supplies used to make each broom cost $2. How much value did he add to GDP?

tive our economy was. What good would it do to know that we made 5 billion safety pins and 782 million pairs of shoes last year? There would be so many numbers and types of goods and services that the result would be difficult or impossible to understand. Therefore, the GDP is measured in dollar values regardless of the specific products or quantities. This is one way that money is used as a unit of account. It allows us to understand and compare the value of our production regardless of what is produced.

The word *final* is also important. To measure our production accurately, economists must avoid **double counting**. For example, suppose that Joe produces 1,000 bricks and sells them to Sam for $200. Sam then uses them to make a sidewalk worth $500 for Mrs. Webster. How much value was produced: $200, $500, or $700? The final product is worth $500. It would be easy to make the mistake of counting the value of the bricks twice—once when Joe sold them to Sam and again when they were part of the income Sam earned building the sidewalk. To avoid double counting, economists only include the value of final or finished goods and services when they determine our GDP.

The word *new* is also important to the measurement of GDP. When we measure production, we must be careful not to include the value of goods or services produced in an earlier year. If Maxine buys Gerry's three-year-old car, the value of that car was not produced in this year and should not be counted as part of the GDP. If your family buys a house that was built in 1958, the $100,000 price should not be included in this year's GDP. However, the real estate agent's $5,000 commission on the sale should be included in the GDP because it was earned this year.

The GDP gives us a very broad picture of how the economy is doing. We can also get more specific information about the economy by looking at the four kinds of production that together make up the GDP:

◆   In many years Americans have bought more goods from foreign countries than we have sold to them. This encouraged greater production in other countries and less in the United States. Do you try to buy American made products?

1. *Consumer Products.* Goods and services bought by consumers to directly satisfy their needs and wants.

2. *Business, or Producer Products.* Resources, goods, or services bought by businesses to produce other goods or services. This includes products purchased to be held in inventory.

3. *Government Products.* Goods and services purchased by federal, state, and local governments to carry out their responsibilities.

4. *Net Exports.* The difference between the value of goods and services sent to other countries and the value of goods and services purchased from other countries. This value will be negative if we purchase a

greater value of goods and services than we sell to other nations.

Although the GDP is the most widely used measure of production and income in the United States it does not provide enough specific information for all purposes. Other measures provide more specialized information.

Vocabulary Builder

Double counting   Including the value of a product in national income accounting more than once.

Net National Product

When goods and services are produced, tools and machines eventually wear out. The same may be said of some of the consumer products people own. Each year that you keep a car, it loses some of its value. This loss of value is called *depreciation*. The GDP does not take this factor into account. Some of our output must be used to replace goods that wear out. Net national product (NNP) accounts for this loss of value. It measures the GDP minus the loss in value in goods resulting from depreciation.

In recent years the amount of depreciation has been about 10 percent of the GDP. Therefore, if the GDP were $6 trillion, depreciation would be about 10 percent of that value, or $600 million. This results in a net national product of roughly $5.4 trillion. The net national product is a measure of the value of *additional* goods and services that we have to use as the result of our GDP.

National Income

National income (NI) is a measure of the total income earned by everyone in our nation. National income includes all income earned by people as a result of their labor, ownership of resources, or operation of a business. National income is equal to the net national product minus indirect business taxes, such as sales and property taxes, and license fees. National income is divided into five types of income:

1. Wages and salaries paid to employees as the result of their labor
2. Income earned by people who are self-employed, including farmers
3. Rentals and royalties paid to property owners
4. Corporate profits paid to stockholders

5. Interest earned on savings and other investments

Although each of these types of income contribute to NI, wages and salaries account for about three-fourths of the total.

Personal Income

Personal income (PI) is the total income received by individuals before personal taxes are paid. To find the PI, we first subtract corporate income taxes, profits invested by business owners into their firms, and Social Security contributions made by employers from the national income. We then add the value of **transfer payments** to this amount to arrive at the PI. Transfer payments include any cash payment made to an individual from the federal, state, or local government that is not in exchange for a good, service, or resource received from that person. Examples of transfer payments include welfare, unemployment compensation, and Social Security payments.

Disposable Personal Income

Everyone pays taxes. Even poor people pay taxes when they buy clothing or pay their heating bills. Disposable personal income (DPI) is what is left from personal income after personal taxes are subtracted. DPI is an important indication of the economy's health because it tells us how much money people have that they can spend or save.

Look at Table 7-1. Think of the kinds of income that your family receives and the spending that your family carries out.

Where would these values be included in Table 7-1?

Summing Up ⎢ *Although gross domestic product is the most often used measure of production, other measures used in national income accounting provide more specific information about different parts of the economy.* ◆

National Income Accounting - 1991
(Figures in billions of dollars)

ADD TOGETHER:

PERSONAL CONSUMPTION EXPENDITURES	+ $3,943.7
GROSS PRIVATE DOMESTIC INVESTMENT	+ $ 747.9
GOVERNMENT PURCHASES OF GOODS & SERVICES	+ $1,079.5
NET EXPORTS	- ($ 31.4)
EQUALS GDP	= $5,739.7
MINUS DEPRECIATION	- $ 596.7
EQUALS NET NATIONAL PRODUCT	= $5,143.0
MINUS INDIRECT BUSINESS TAXES	- $ 553.7
EQUALS NATIONAL INCOME	= $4,589.3
MINUS UNDISTRIBUTED CORPORATE PROFITS	- $ 41.8
MINUS SOCIAL SECURITY TAXES PAID BY BUSINESSES	- $ 386.6
MINUS CORPORATE INCOME TAXES	- $ 84.8
PLUS GOVERNMENT AND BUSINESS TRANSFER PAYMENTS	+ $ 819.2
EQUALS PERSONAL INCOME	= $4,895.3
MINUS PERSONAL TAXES AND OTHER PAYMENTS TO THE GOVERNMENT	- $ 618.4
EQUALS DISPOSABLE PERSONAL INCOME	= $4,276.8

(Source: Economic Indicators 3/92)

* Estimated values

◆ **Table 7-1** National Income Accounting

SECTION 2

DIFFERENT WAYS TO MEASURE PRODUCTION AND INCOME

While you read, *ask yourself . . .*
- ◆ *How is income created for other people when you spend your money?*
- ◆ *What do you do that creates something of value so you receive income?*

The government has different ways of measuring our nation's gross domestic product. None of these methods are perfect, but they are the best we can do with the tools we now have.

Even if they are not perfect, they still provide us with a good idea of changes that are taking place in our economy.

Vocabulary Builder

Depreciation A loss in value that occurs as a result of wear and age. A fall in the value of a nation's currency due to the forces of demand and supply.

Disposable personal income The income that people have left to spend or save after all taxes have been paid.

Transfer payment Financial assistance by the state or federal government that is not in exchange for any current productive activity by an individual.

The Expenditures Approach

One way to find the GDP and the other measures of production and income is called the expenditures approach. This method counts the value of all money spent buying the final goods and services produced in the country in a year. It includes money spent by individuals on consumer goods, business investments in new capital or inventory, government spending on goods or services, and the difference between the value of our exports and the value of our imports. Notice that these are the same categories of GDP listed earlier.

In using the expenditures approach, we must be careful not to double count or to count products that were produced in previous years. Americans spend large amounts of money each year on products that are not part of the GDP.

The Income Approach

The value of GDP may also be found by adding the value of all income earned producing final goods and services in a year. In this process we add up the five components of national income listed earlier (wages, profits of those who are self-employed, rents, corporate profits paid to stockholders, and interest). Then we add in the value of depreciation, indirect business taxes, and reinvested business profits to get the GDP. Again, we must be careful not to double count or to include the value of sales of products made in previous years. If a firm sells a car it produced last year, the value of that car is not part of this year's GDP.

The two methods of measuring GDP are similar in many ways. One method measures spending to buy products that are part of the GDP. The other method measures income earned from selling products that are part of the GDP. Spending and income are different ways of looking at a transaction. Any money that you spend is income to the person who sells you a good or service. The value of your spending and his or her income is the same.

Problems in Making Accurate Measurements

Measurements of production and income cannot be totally accurate. One reason for this problem is the **underground economy**. When people produce goods and services that they receive income for, they are legally required to report this income to the government. The value that they are creating should be included in the GDP. However, many people choose not to report parts of their income to avoid paying taxes. Their unreported labor, income, and production are part of the underground economy.

For example, if your neighbor pays you $500 to paint his garage, you are supposed to report that income to the government. But if you don't report the payment, there is a good chance that the government will never find out. Although failing to report income is against the law, it does happen. Production and income of this nature cannot be included in the GDP.

◆   If these workers are paid for their labor and do not report this income on their tax returns it is part of the underground economy. Have you ever earned money you did not report?

Consumer Close-Up

How Important Is the Underground Economy?

At one time or another, most people receive some income in the underground economy. Perhaps you have earned a few dollars cutting a neighbor's lawn or baby-sitting. If you did not report this income to the government, your labor and income were part of the underground economy. This sort of labor is also called working "off the books" because it goes unreported.

If the few dollars you earned was your total income, the government lost little tax income. Because your income was small, you probably wouldn't have paid income tax in any case. However, when people earn large incomes that go unreported and untaxed, the government loses substantial revenue. For example, people who earn more than $400 in income from self-employment are required to pay 15.3 percent of it in Social

Security tax in addition to income tax. Those who fail to pay taxes on all their income force a larger tax burden on other citizens.

Suppose that Jane is an electrician who works for a contractor during the week. If she takes a job wiring a house on weekends and earns $2,000, the government can lose as much as $948.60 in taxes if she fails to report her extra income. Electricians are often paid high wages. Assume that Jane pays income taxes at the maximum rate of 31 percent. She also should pay 15.3 percent of the $2,000 in Social Security taxes. Therefore, according to the law, the government is entitled to 46.3 percent of the $2,000 she has earned. Jane may also owe taxes to her state or local government, in which case she may end up paying more than half her extra income in taxes. You may argue that the tax rate is too high, but Jane is breaking the law if she doesn't report this income and pay taxes on it.

How large is the underground economy? No one is sure. But estimates place it between 3 and 20 percent of the GDP. In 1989 the GDP was $5.23 trillion. The underground economy for that year was therefore between $156 billion and $1.05 trillion. If this income had been taxed at 28 percent + 15.3 percent for Social Security, the government would have received anywhere from $68 billion to $455 billion in additional tax revenue. State and local governments would also have received new tax revenue. This would have helped the government balance the budget or reduce taxes paid by other citizens.

The underground economy is a serious problem to our country.

When you receive income, do you feel a responsibility to report it to the government and pay your share of taxes?

A similar problem involves the barter of services. If one person knows how to repair plumbing and another understands how to repair television sets, they may exchange services without any exchange of money. When this happens, there is production of services without income. This type of transaction is also missed when the GDP is measured.

Vocabulary Builder

Underground economy The production of goods and services resulting in income that is not reported to the government.

The value of production and labor is only included in the GDP when it is paid for. If you paint your own house, the value of your labor is not included in the GDP. If your neighbor pays you to paint her house, it should be included. When economic times are hard, people tend to do more things for themselves. This change in production is not included in the GDP.

Although the GDP and the other measurements of production and income are not perfect, they are better than having no measurements at all. The inaccuracies in measurement are the same each year. These measurements are used most often to study changes in our economy from one year to another. For this purpose they provide valuable and reliable information.

Summing Up *The government uses two basic methods to measure our GDP: the expenditures approach and the income approach. Although neither method is perfect, they do provide a good indication of changes in our economy.* ◆

SECTION 3

NOMINAL AND REAL VALUES

While you read, ask yourself . . .
- ◆ *In 1963 the minimum wage was 90 cents an hour. Why doesn't this fact tell you much about the importance of the minimum wage in that year?*
- ◆ *How would your family be affected by a very cold winter? How might a different family living in a different part of the country be affected?*

If you read about the GDP in a newspaper, you may come across the words *nominal* and *real*. It is important to know what these words mean. If you don't understand them, you might not understand what you are reading.

◆ Suppose a "car-hop" at a drive-in restaurant earned $1.50 an hour 20 years ago. Would a clerk who earns $5 an hour today be better off financially? What other information do you need to be able to answer this question?

Nominal Values

A **nominal value** is any amount of money that has not been adjusted for inflation. Nominal values are expressed in what are called **current dollars**. Even if you knew you would earn $100,000 a year by the year 2010, you wouldn't be able to predict your standard of living for that year. If prices remain the same from now until 2010, you could have a good income and a comfortable life. If prices go up 20 percent a year until 2010, you might live in poverty, even with an income of $100,000.

Nominal values provide little useful information if you want to compare values over time. The longer the period of time over which nominal values are compared, the less meaningful they are likely to be.

Real Values

A **real value** is one that has been adjusted for inflation. When we want to evaluate change, real values are much more useful than nominal values. Real values are often expressed in what are called **constant dollars**. A constant dollar is based on the amount of purchasing value a dollar had in some specific year or period of time. For example, if you earned a nominal income of $11,830 in 1988, it would have been equal to a real income of $10,000 in constant dollars from 1982. This means that your income in 1988 would buy the same quantity of goods and services as $10,000 would have bought in 1982 because of the 18.3 percent inflation between 1982 and 1988.

When prices go up, the value of nominal GDP grows even if there is no change in the quantity of final products produced. Real GDP values give us a more reliable way to evaluate changes in production and income from one year to another because they do not change when prices change. Study Table 7-2 to see how real values gives you a much clearer understanding of changes in our economic system.

Summing Up *Consumers need to understand the difference between nominal and real values when they compare values over time. Real values have been adjusted for inflation and are therefore more useful than nominal values.* ◆

Consumer News

A Drop in Real Disposable Income

How do you think members of your family would feel if they worked just as hard as they used to but were able to buy less with what they earned? According to the federal government, a typical American family with two workers lost $614 in real disposable income in 1990. This is the result of several changes in our economy. The average income for a two-income family increased from $49,990 to $51,421, or by $1,431, between 1989 and 1990. However, the taxes they paid went up $582. Therefore, their after-tax income increased by $849, from $39,381 to $41,130.

However, there is also inflation to think about. The 6.1 percent rate of inflation in 1990 reduced the purchasing power of this $41,130 in disposable income to $38,767. Although the nominal income of a two-income family increased from an average of $29, 627 to $51,421 between 1980 and 1990, their real disposable income only grew by $3,228. The rest of the increase was eaten up by taxes and inflation.

Vocabulary Builder

Constant dollars Dollar amounts that have not been adjusted for inflation.
Current dollars Dollar amounts that have not been adjusted for inflation.
Nominal value A value that has not been adjusted for inflation.
Real value A value corrected for inflation.

Gross Domestic Product in Current and Constant Dollars, 1981–1991 (Dollar Values in Billions)				
Year	GDP in Current Dollars	Percent Change in Nominal GDP from Previous Year	GDP in Constant 1982 Dollars	Percent Change in Real GDP from Previous Year
1981	3,031	+ 8.1%	3,843	-1.6%
1982	3,150	+ 3.9%	3,760	-2.2%
1983	3,405	+ 8.1%	3,907	+3.9%
1984	3,777	+10.9%	4,149	+6.2%
1985	4,039	+ 6.9%	4,280	+3.2%
1986	4,269	+ 5.7%	4,405	+2.9%
1987	4,540	+ 6.3%	4,540	+3.1%
1988	4,900	+ 7.9%	4,719	+3.9%
1989	5,244	+ 7.0%	4,837	+2.5%
1990	5,514	+ 5.1%	4,885	+1.0%
*1991	5,673	+ 2.9%	4,849	-.1%

◆ **Table 7-2**   Gross Domestic Product, 1981–1991

SECTION 4

EVALUATING NATIONAL INCOME INFORMATION

While you read, ask yourself . . .
- ◆ *If someone in your family received a wage increase, would your family be able to buy more goods and services than they could a year ago?*
- ◆ *How would your life be affected if a relative who had no income came to live with your family?*

Information gathered through national income accounting is used by economists, business owners, and government leaders. It provides an indication of our economic system's efficiency and productivity. The GDP

◆   When we mine resources from the land we often destroy its value for any other purpose. Do you believe some amount should be subtracted from GDP to take the cost of this damage into account?

and other measures of production and income are often used to measure changes in our standard of living and economic health. Unfortunately, people who do not understand national income accounting methods may draw the wrong conclusions from the information.

A common mistake that people make is assuming that a change in the GDP always causes a change in people's standard of living. There is no guarantee that increases in GDP will result in additional products being distributed equally to all people. Increases in the GDP may be the result of increased production of consumer goods and services, or increased production of products purchased by businesses, the government, or people in foreign nations.

If the production of consumer goods does increase, these additional goods may be distributed to only some people, leaving other individuals no better off. The GDP may increase as the result of additional military spending by the government. Such spending may be important and necessary, but it will do little to improve individual consumers' standard of living. Investments in casinos or video games add to the GDP, but it is not clear how they contribute to an improved standard of living for most people. Increased GDP does not provide information about how the increased production is allocated or used.

Another factor that should be considered is growth in our population. We produced a real GDP in 1988 that was about twice as large as that in 1965. However, the population of the United States grew by roughly 33 percent in these years. As a result, the real GDP per person increased by about 65 percent. This still shows growth in production per person, but it is not as large as people might have first believed.

Changes in the GDP do not provide information about the natural resources used to produce the GDP. This sort of consideration goes beyond the depreciation that is taken into

Consumer News

Increasing Nature's Production

In 1980 Mt. St. Helens erupted, destroying 150,000 acres of forests in Washington State. Many people assumed that it would take centuries for nature to replace the trees that were destroyed. However, Weyerhaeuser, a forest and lumber products company, stepped in to start replanting the devastated lands in 1981. By 1990 over 18 million seedlings had been planted, and some had already reached a height of 25 feet. The firm estimates that some of its trees will be ready for harvest as early as the year 2010.

Do you believe that the growth of these trees should be included in the measure of our nation's production?

account when the NNP is determined. When trees are cut down to make lumber for houses, when we turn farmland into shopping malls, or when rivers or lakes are polluted by factories, society is paying a cost. Our method of measuring GDP does not take these costs into account. Rapid growth in the GDP may be the result of irresponsible use of our resources and damage to our environment. These costs may affect our standard of living in the future.

To understand the meaning of information gathered through national income accounting, business owners, government leaders, and consumers must evaluate the information carefully. They should consider other factors that are not included in these measures of production and income. Only then can we make decisions as responsible producers and consumers.

Review and Enrichment Activities

VOCABULARY REVIEW

1. Column A contains key consumer terms from this chapter. Column B contains a scrambled list of phrases that describe what these terms mean. Match the correct meaning with each term. Write your answers on a separate sheet of paper.

Column A	Column B
1. Gross domestic product	a. including the value of a product in a measure of production more than once
2. Personal income	b. the value of all money earned in the economy less wear out and indirect business taxes
3. Disposable personal income	c. the dollar value of all final goods and services produced in a year
4. Depreciation	d. production of goods or services that is not reported to the government
5. Underground economy	e. individual income after personal taxes have been paid
6. Transfer payment	f. money paid by the government to people, but not in exchange for a good or service
7. Net national product	g. the process of measuring the value of a nation's output and income
8. National income	h. individual income before personal taxes have been paid
9. National income accounting	i. a loss of value that results from wear and age
10. Double counting	j. the value of new final production less wear out

2. Explain the difference between nominal and real values.

CHECKING WHAT YOU'VE LEARNED

Write your answers for the following exercises on a separate sheet of paper.

1. Describe each of the five measures of production and income that are used in national income accounting in the United States.
2. Three key words in the definition of the gross national product are *value, final,* and *new*. Explain why we need to include each of these words in the definition of GDP.
3. Describe how the GDP is measured through the expenditures approach.
4. Describe how the GDP is measured through the income approach.
5. Give an example of double counting. Do not use the same example that was used in this text.
6. Give an example of the underground economy. Do not use the same example that was used in this text.
7. Why doesn't it mean much when an adult says, "When I was your age, I only earned ninety cents an hour"? Include the terms *nominal value* and *real value* in your answer, making it clear that you understand what these terms mean.
8. Explain two reasons why GDP figures alone cannot provide complete information about our standard of living.

PRACTICING YOUR CONSUMER SKILLS

Write your answers for the following exercises on a separate sheet of paper.

1. Choose the situation in column B that best demonstrates each measure of production and income in column A.

Column A	Column B
1. Gross domestic product	a. Jeff's wages are $500 a week, but he only takes home $347.53 after taxes.
2. Net national product	b. The Apex Golf Ball Co. wore out a machine that cost $38,00 last year.
3. National income	c. The Ibex Pogo Stick Co. took in $500,000 from sales last year before.
4. Personal income	d. The Amalgamated Export Co. paid a $5,000 license fee to the government to operate its business.
5. Disposable personal income	e. Erwin earned $40,000 in profit last year from his insurance business.

Review and Enrichment Activities Continued

2. Identify each of the following as being a part of the GDP as measured by the *expenditures* (E) approach or the *income* (I) approach.
   a. The board of education paid the Gross Construction Co. $13,000,000 to have a new middle school built.
   b. Terry earned $350 a week working on the new school building.
   c. A school purchased $1,238 worth of typing paper last year.
   d. The Gross Construction Co. bought a new truck for $18,000.
   e. Terry's husband spent $84.32 on groceries last week.
   f. The Gross Construction Co. earned a profit of $292,043 last year.
3. Explain why each of the following statements is wrong.
   a. All people are better off now than they were five years ago because the GDP is 20 percent larger.
   b. Francine adds $5 to the GDP for each of the cakes she bakes and sells for $5 each.
   c. The GDP includes the value of all goods and services produced in this country.
   d. Tom increases the GDP when he cuts his own lawn.
   e. Inflation has no impact on the value of the GDP.

USING NUMBERS

Solve the following problem to help make the best possible choice. Write your solution on a separate sheet of paper. Be sure to show all your work.

Franklin is a labor negotiator for a union. He wants to gather information that he can use in negotiations. He wants to know what has happened to the real value of wages his union members have earned over the last ten years. In 1980 their hourly wage rate was $7.48. It is now $10.20 in 1990. Complete the following table to determine what the hourly wage would have had to be in each of the last ten years to have as much purchasing power at the 1980 wage. How much of a raise do you think Franklin should demand? What other factors should he consider? Explain your answers.

Year	1980 Wage	×	Price Change Factor	=	Wage with Equal Purchasing Power
1981	$7.48		1.10		_____
1982	$7.48		1.17		_____
1983	$7.48		1.21		_____
1984	$7.48		1.26		_____
1985	$7.48		1.31		_____
1986	$7.48		1.33		_____
1987	$7.48		1.38		_____
1988	$7.48		1.44		_____
1989	$7.48		1.51		_____
1990	$7.48		1.60		_____

PUTTING IDEAS IN YOUR OWN WORDS

The following quotations are from this chapter. Explain these quotations in your own words to make sure you understand what they mean. Write your answers on a separate sheet of paper.

a. "To measure our production accurately, economists must avoid double counting."
b. "Unreported labor, income, and production are part of the underground economy."
c. "Real values are often expressed in what are called constant dollars."

BUILDING CONSUMER KNOWLEDGE

Write your answer for the following exercises on a separate sheet of paper.

1. Ask an adult to tell you how much income he or she earned at your age and how much could be purchased with that income. Use this information to describe the impact of inflation on the value of income since this person was a student.
2. Describe production you are aware of that is not included in the measure of the GDP. Do not include names if you discuss an example of the underground economy.
3. Describe a cost of producing GDP that is paid in your community but that is not included in our national income accounting measures. Refer to the next to the last paragraph in section 4 of this chapter for ideas to help you answer this question.

Chapter 8

Economic Cycles and Changes

Chapter Objectives

After completing this chapter, you will be able to do the following:

- Describe each of the four phases of the business cycle.
- Explain the economic meaning of the unemployment and employment rates.
- Describe different types of unemployment.
- Explain the difference between demand-pull inflation and cost-push inflation.
- Describe how the consumer price index is determined and explain its significance.
- Give examples of leading indicators and explain how they may be used to predict future economic conditions.

Key Consumer Terms

In this chapter you will learn the meanings of the following important consumer terms:

- Business cycle
- Peak
- Boom
- Contraction
- Recession
- Depression
- Trough
- Recovery
- Expansion
- Labor force
- Frictional unemployment
- Seasonal unemployment
- Cyclical unemployment
- Structural unemployment
- Demand-pull inflation
- Cost-push inflation
- Consumer price index (CPI)
- Weighted average
- Leading indicator

Most American families have experienced good economic times and other times that were not so good. The events that made times seem good or hard may have included changes in family income, promotions for a wage earner, a family member losing a job, or changes in prices. For people who own businesses, these good and hard economic times may have been related to changes in sales, profits, the number of workers they could afford to employ, and their ability to invest in new capital.

When changes in economic conditions are viewed over time, they tend to move up and down to form what is called the **business cycle**. The kinds of decisions that consumers make influenced by the business cycle. It is important for you to understand the causes and effects of the business cycle to be able to make rational decisions and be a responsible consumer.

SECTION 1

PHASES OF THE BUSINESS CYCLE

While you read, ask yourself . . .
- *What phase of the business cycle does the economy seem to be in at the present time?*
- *What are the economic indicators that allow you to answer the question above?*

When you studied Table 7-2, you may have realized that the change in our GDP does not happen at a constant rate. In some years our real GDP has increased rapidly. At other times it has stayed almost the same or has even decreased. These changes in the quantity of final goods and services produced in a year are the most obvious signs of the business cycle. Other indicators of the business cycle include changes in employment, earnings, sales, inventories, and profits.

Figure 8-1 shows an idealized business cycle. This graph demonstrates how the business cycle is divided into four phases. It begins with an economic **peak**, or **boom**. This is a period of prosperity. New businesses open, factories are producing at full capacity, real growth in GDP is high, there is full employment, and

profits are likely to be good. Most people enjoy good economic times during a boom.

Eventually, the rate of growth in real GDP begins to decline. During this part of the business cycle, a **contraction** of the economy occurs. Businesses experience lower sales, inventories grow, workers are laid off, and profits decline. Economic contractions often become **recessions**. A recession is defined by the government as a period of two quarter years, or six months, when real GDP does not grow. In recessions, consumers and businesses are less likely to make expensive purchases, investment in new equipment declines, fewer

Vocabulary Builder

Boom That portion of the business cycle in which economic activity is at its highest point.

Business cycle The periodic ups and downs in the nation's economic activity.

Contraction A portion of the business cycle in which economic activity is slowing down.

Peak A portion of the business cycle in which economic activity is at its highest point.

Recession A portion of the business cycle in which a nation's output does not grow for at least six months.

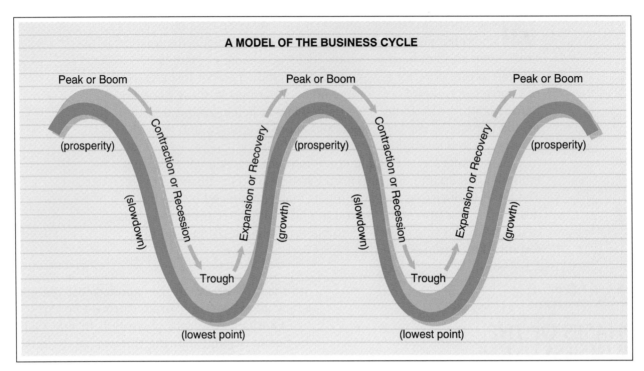

Figure 8-1   A Model of the Business Cycle

new businesses open, and more businesses fail. Tax revenues collected by the government fall, while government programs to provide assistance to individuals grow. A very deep recession may become a **depression** when the economy operates far below its capacity. Many people suffer hard economic times during recessions.

At some point economic conditions stop becoming worse. Production may be far below capacity, sales may be poor, and there may be high rates of unemployment, but at least the economy has stopped its contraction. This leveling off of economic activity is called a **trough** and is a sign that the economy may soon begin to recover.

Recovery, or an economic **expansion**, is a period of time when real GDP grows at an increasing rate. In an expansion, sales increase, businesses earn larger profits, new businesses

are formed, employment grows, and government tax revenues increase. Economic recovery leads to a boom economy. When economic booms, contractions, troughs, and expansions follow each other they form the business cycle.

Remember that Figure 8-1 is an *idealized* view of the business cycle. In the real world the business cycle is not this neat. The ups and downs of economic activity do not occur smoothly or last for equal periods of time. Examine Figure 8-2. You can see how the level of business activity changed at uneven rates over the past 130 years. Although the changes were not smooth or even, you can still see evidence of the business cycle in this graph. It clearly shows that there were good economic times and hard economic times.

Consumers and business owners need to be aware of changes in economic conditions to be able to make better choices. They cannot rely on each phase of the business cycle to last an equal length of time or for all changes in economic activity to be the same size.

Summing Up ▶   *There have always been periods of time when economic conditions were good and other times when they were bad. Changes in economic activity form the phases of the business cycle. These phases do not always last the same length of time or involve the same amount of change in economic activity.* ◆

SECTION 2

EMPLOYMENT AND UNEMPLOYMENT IN THE BUSINESS CYCLE

While you read, ask yourself . . .
   ◆ *Do you know an adult who would like a job but does not look for work? Do you know why this person doesn't seek employment?*
   ◆ *What might cause this person to look for a job?*

One of the first things the owners of a business are likely to do if their sales fall is to reduce production and lay off workers. When sales grow, business owners often choose to produce more products and hire additional workers. Two important signs of economic activity are the employment and unemployment rates. Many people believe that these two figures are the same idea looked at from different points of view. If you feel this way, you aren't exactly right. They are related to each other, but they do not provide the same information.

The Unemployment Rate

To understand the meaning of the unemployment rate, you first need to understand the term **labor force**. The labor force is made up of all individuals sixteen or older who are

◆   To receive unemployment compensation people must be willing to look for work. What reasons can you give that would explain the difference in dress between people who are waiting to pick up their unemployment checks and those who are applying for a job?

Vocabulary Builder

Depression   A major slowdown of economic activity, during which millions are out of work, many businesses fail, and the economy operates far below its capacity.
Expansion   A portion of the business cycle in which economic activity is increasing; also called recovery.
Labor force   All people who are sixteen or older who are able to work and who either hold a job or are looking for a job.
Recovery   A portion of the business cycle in which economic activity is increasing.
Trough   A portion of the business cycle in which economic activity is at its lowest point.

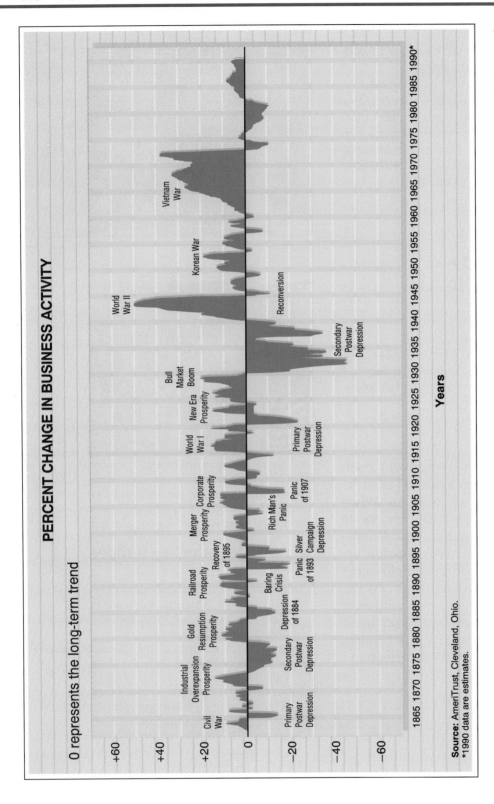

PERCENT CHANGE IN BUSINESS ACTIVITY

0 represents the long-term trend

Source: AmeriTrust, Cleveland, Ohio.
*1990 data are estimates.

◆ **Figure 8-2** Business Activity in the United States, 1863–1990. Although this graph does not follow the idealized business cycle seen in Figure 8-1, it does show that there have been many ups and downs in the economy. Notice that many large changes in business activity took place at the same time as other important events. Some economists believe that the business cycle is most often caused by political, social, or natural events. Even if this is true, it does not change the fact that the business cycle has an important effect on consumers.

Labor Statistics, 1980–1990 (in thousands)					
Year	Working-Age Population	People With Jobs	People With Jobs As Percent Of Working-Age Population	People Unemployed	Unemployment Rate
1980	169,349	100,907	59.6%	7,637	7.0%
1982	173,939	101,194	58.2%	10,678	9.5%
1984	178,080	106,702	59.9%	8,539	7.4%
1986	182,293	111,303	61.1%	8,237	6.9%
1988	186,322	116,677	62.6%	6,701	5.4%
1990	189,686	119,550	63.0%	6,874	5.8%
(Statistical Abstract of the United States, 1991, p. 384)					

◆ **Table 8-1** Labor Statistics

able to work and who either have a job or are looking for a job. The unemployment rate is the percentage of people in the labor force who cannot find work. People who have no job and who are not looking for work are not counted in the labor force and are not counted as being unemployed.

The unemployment rate may change as a result of two different types of events. When workers lose their jobs and try to find new employment, the unemployment rate will grow. It will also increase when people who have not been part of the labor force choose to look for work but are not successful in finding a job. Both of these events will cause an increase in the unemployment rate, but they do not show the same things about economic conditions.

Imagine that a friend of yours has become discouraged and has given up looking for work because the economy is in a recession. As a result, this person is not counted in the labor force or as unemployed by the government.

Then suppose that there is an economic recovery and your friend decides to look for a job. Until he or she finds work, there will be an increase in the unemployment rate. However, this increase would be the result of improving economic conditions. This situation is very different from one where the unemployment rate grows because workers are laid off as the economy falls into a recession.

The Employment Rate

Many people who study labor statistics believe that the employment rate is a better measure of economic conditions. This figure simply states how many people have jobs. When production grows and economic conditions are good, more people have jobs. When production declines, there are fewer jobs. Study Table 8-1 to see the difference in the unemployment and employment information for the 1980s. Think how these different types of information could cause people to reach different conclusions about economic conditions.

Types of Unemployment

People may be out of work for many reasons. In some cases they have a serious, long-term problem, but in other situations their unemployment may only be temporary. Some types of unemployment may even be good for the person who is out of work and for the economy in general. Economists have identified four types of unemployment: **frictional**, **seasonal**, **cyclical**, and **structural**.

Frictional Unemployment. People who are frictionally unemployed are temporarily out of work. They may be new to the labor force, or recently fired or laid off, or they may have quit a job to look for a new one. The common factor among people who are frictionally unemployed is that they have all been out of work for only a short time.

Some workers will always be frictionally unemployed. There are even some benefits to this type of unemployment. It is good for the economy when people who have not been looking for work decide to try to find a job. Other workers who are dissatisfied with their jobs are not likely to contribute as much value to production as they could. They would probably be more productive if they found

◆   Many agricultural workers suffer seasonal unemployment. Why don't children of farm workers often have the same opportunity for a good education as other children? How may this reduce their chance of having a steady job when they become adults?

other work they liked better. Frictional unemployment is not regarded as a problem by most economists. The unemployment rate will never fall much below 5 percent because there are always some workers who are frictionally unemployed.

Seasonal Unemployment. Some types of jobs only exist during specific times of the year. People who are employed in construction often do not expect to work in January or February if they live in the North. There are normally few agricultural jobs when there are no crops to plant or harvest. People who produce swimming suits or winter coats may not be employed at all times of the year. Workers who are temporarily without jobs at certain times of each year are seasonally unemployed. Although unemployment for these individuals may cause them economic difficulties, they are aware of the situation and can plan for their unemployment. They also may look forward to being called back to work in a relatively short time.

Cyclical Unemployment. During a contraction of the economy, some workers lose their jobs. This is called cyclical unemployment because it is the result of the business cycle. People may be cyclically unemployed for many months or even for years. Cyclical unemployment is an important problem for both the people without work and for the economy in general. People who are unemployed for extended periods of time cut back on their spending. Their reduced spending causes reduced sales for businesses and may cause other workers to be laid off. People who are cyclically unemployed at least can expect to find the same type of job once the economy recovers.

Structural Unemployment. The type of unemployment that causes the greatest problems for people and for the economy is structural unemployment. People who are structurally unemployed do not have skills that allow them to earn an adequate income. Structural unemployment is often the result of technological

Consumer News

Cyclical Unemployment Among Urban Youth

Unemployment is a serious problem for anyone who loses a job. However, unemployment does not happen to all groups in our society at the same rate. In 1990 the U.S. economy was in a recession. The unemployment rate grew from a low of 5.1 percent in 1989 to almost 7 percent at the end of 1990. However, for specific groups the unemployment rate was much higher. The jobless rate for all sixteen-to twenty-four-year-olds reached 11.8 percent and would have been even higher if many young people had not given up looking for work. (Remember, if you don't look, you're not counted.)

To find the highest unemployment rate in the nation, you needed to look at young, minority males who lived in urban areas. The unemployment rate among this group reached, and in some places exceeded, 50 percent in 1990. When the economy turns down, these people are often the first to lose their jobs. And when the economy improves, they are among the last to be rehired.

Vocabulary Builder

Cyclical unemployment Unemployment that is the result of a downturn of the business cycle.

Frictional unemployment A situation in which people are unemployed for a short time; people between jobs.

Seasonal unemployment A situation in which people are unemployed during a specific time of the year.

Structural unemployment A situation in which people are unemployed because they lack the skills that employers demand.

improvements. For example, the production of steel used to require large numbers of workers who possessed specialized skills. In recent years many steel mills in the United States have either closed or become more automated. There are fewer jobs in the steel industry today. The people who do work in the steel industry have different skills than those who worked there thirty years ago. Many people who used to produce steel are structurally unemployed because their skills are no longer demanded and have little value in our economy.

People who are structurally unemployed need to be trained to develop new skills before they can earn an adequate income. This process takes time and is expensive for both the individual worker and for the economy in general. This is why structural unemployment is the type that causes the most serious problems for our economic system.

Summing Up   *Looking at the unemployment and employment rates can help us determine the phase of the business cycle the economy is in. The most serious type of unemployment is structural unemployment because these workers need training.* ◆

◆   When factories close many workers become structurally unemployed. Why can't some skilled workers find work that will provide a reasonable standard of living? Should inefficient factories be kept open just to provide jobs?

INFLATION AND THE BUSINESS CYCLE

While you read, ask yourself . . .
◆ *What are several products you buy that have recently gone up in price? Why do you believe their prices have increased?*
◆ *How would students react to an increase of 50 cents for the price of lunch in your school cafeteria? What would this do to the number of jobs for cafeteria workers at your school?*

In Chapter 6 you learned that inflation is a sustained increase in the average price level. Inflation often occurs during the expansion and boom phases of the business cycle. In special cases it has also happened during contractions. There are two basic situations that result in inflation. Both situations are related to the laws of demand and supply that you learned about in Chapter 4.

Demand-Pull Inflation

Prices go up when there are fewer products for sale than consumers want to buy. Such a shortage of goods and services may be the result of demand increasing at the current price when there is no increase in the quantity of products offered for sale. The shortage of products will tend to force prices up. These higher prices will encourage producers to make and offer more products for sale and will cause a decrease in consumers' willingness to buy goods and services. This type of price increase is called **demand-pull inflation** because it is caused by an increase in demand.

An example of demand-pull inflation occurred in the mid-1960s. During that time the U.S. government was buying materials that were used to fight the war in Vietnam. There

Consumer News

Inflation and the Cost of Energy

The year 1986 seemed to be a good one for the economy. The government reported that inflation was only 1.1 percent (the lowest rate in twenty-five years). Unfortunately, the low rate of inflation was almost entirely the result of one event, the drop in the cost of crude oil. The record in other parts of the economy was nowhere near as good.

In 1985 the Organization of Petroleum Exporting Countries (OPEC) did away with their restrictions on how much oil could be produced. As a result, world oil production grew by almost 20 percent between 1985 and 1986. This caused the price of crude oil to fall by more than 50 percent. The price of gasoline in the United States declined 30 percent. Other energy prices also fell, although not as much or as rapidly.

However, prices in other parts of the economy continued to grow. Food prices increased by more than 5 percent, housing went up almost as much, and the price of appliances increased by more than 6 percent. Although the *average* rate of inflation in 1986 was low, this rate could not last. The cost of oil and other sources of energy could not fall another 50 percent to keep the rate low in 1987.

Vocabulary Builder

Demand-pull inflation   An increase in prices that is the result of a total demand for goods and services that exceeds their supply.

was also a large increase in government spending to fight poverty in the 1960s. Almost everyone who wanted a job had one. Because of high wages, consumers tried to buy products that they would not have otherwise been able to afford. More products were demanded than businesses were able to supply. This shortage resulted in higher prices. Demand-pull inflation most often happens during the expansion phase of the business cycle. It is associated with growing production, investment, and employment.

Cost-Push Inflation

Shortages may also be the result of a decrease in the supply of products offered for sale. When businesses must pay more to produce goods and services, their profits go down unless they are also able to increase their prices. When the costs of raw materials, labor, or tools increase, businesses often react by reducing production. The result is a shortage of products that tends to force prices up. This type of price increase is called **cost-push inflation** because it is the result of an increase in the costs of making goods and services. When there is cost-push inflation, sales often go down, resulting in less investment and fewer jobs.

Cost-push inflation usually occurs when the economy is in a contraction phase of the business cycle. It is associated with falling production, investment, and employment. A recent example of cost-push inflation occurred in the mid-1970s. In 1973 there was a war between Israel and several Arab nations in the Middle East. One result of this war was a rapid increase in the cost of fuel. Crude oil cost almost four times as much in 1975 as in 1972. Many firms found that their costs of producing goods and services were much higher. They reacted

by reducing production, causing shortages of many products. Prices grew, and there was a recession that lasted through much of 1974 and 1975. The inflation during this time was largely cost-push inflation.

Measuring the Rate of Inflation

You are aware of inflation when it causes the price of products you buy to increase. However, if you were asked to measure the rate of inflation, how would you do it? The federal government is faced with this problem. It has established a method of gathering, organizing, and evaluating price information to measure inflation for the types of products consumers tend to buy. This measure is called the **consumer price index (CPI)**.

To determine the consumer price index, the government has identified several hundred goods and services that consumers often buy. Each month employees of the Department of Labor Statistics record the prices of this "market basket" of goods and services at approximately 21,000 stores. These prices are averaged and then weighted, forming a **weighted average**. Weighting means counting the price of some products more often than others to reflect the frequency with which consumers buy those goods and services. For example, consumers buy many more cartons of milk each year than television sets. Therefore, the price of milk is counted more times in the index than the price of television sets. The weighted prices are totaled and compared with prices in an earlier period of time, called the base year.

In 1991 the base year was the average of prices in 1982 through 1984. The average prices in these years were given a value of 100. Percentage increases in prices in following years have been recorded as an increase in this value. This value is the consumer price index.

In 1987 the CPI was 118.3. This means that according to the CPI, the average price of products that consumers buy increased 18.3 percent between the base year (1982–1984) and 1987.

Weaknesses in the CPI

The CPI is not a perfect measure of inflation. It does not take into account the fact that different people spend their money in different ways. The products and weights chosen for use by the government cannot reflect the buying patterns of all consumers. If you never buy an automobile but always use a bus, including automobile prices in the CPI makes little sense for you. The CPI only tells us what happened to prices *on an average*. It tells us little about individual people.

Another problem occurs when new products are introduced into the market. It is difficult to work them into the CPI. Today many people own VCRs and home computers. Twenty years ago these products were rare. It is difficult to compare prices now with those of the past because the types and qualities of products that consumers buy have changed.

The CPI may also be misleading because of changes in the types of products people buy as they age. A young family is more affected by changes in the price of food, housing, and clothing. Older people are more affected by changes in the price of medical care or retirement homes. The consumer price index does not take these differences into account.

Although the CPI does have some weakness, it is the best measure of inflation we have. Changes in the CPI are one indication of economic trends and of the business cycle.

Summing Up *Inflation may happen in any phase of the business cycle, but it is most common in an expansion. It may be caused by increased demand or decreased supply. The government measures the rate of inflation through the consumer price index.* ◆

PREDICTING THE BUSINESS CYCLE

While you read, ask yourself . . .
- ◆ *How would your decisions be different if you knew that there would be a boom next year and that good jobs would be easy to find?*
- ◆ *How would your decisions be different if you knew that there would be a recession next year and that it would be difficult to find a job?*

Business owners and consumers could benefit if they knew when the economy was about to turn up or turn down. This type of knowledge would allow them to make better choices. Business owners would hire more workers, produce more products, and make more investments if they knew that the economy would expand in the next year. If they believed that the economy was entering a recession, they would cut back on spending.

The same type of information would help consumers make better decisions. When consumers believe that the economy is about to enter a recession, they do not buy expensive cars or build as many new houses. When the

Vocabulary Builder

Consumer price index (CPI) A measure of changes in average prices over a period of time for specific group of goods and services used by the average household.

Cost-push inflation An increase in prices that is the result of wage demands of labor, an increase in the costs of raw materials or tools, or the excessive desire for profits by owners.

Weighted average An average that counts some components (parts) more often than others.

economy is expanding, consumers are willing to take on greater financial responsibilities.

Leading Economic Indicators

Each month the Department of Commerce publishes statistics for 300 economic indicators covering all aspects of the economy. By studying this information, people and businesses can better predict future economic conditions. Statistics that point to what will happen to the economy in the near future are called **leading indicators**. Their activity often changes a few months before similar changes occur in overall economic conditions.

When employees work fewer hours, for example, it is a sign that production will soon fall. When more permits are issued to build new houses, it is a sign that construction is about to increase. An increase in the number of new machines ordered indicates a future increase in production and jobs. Economists use leading indicators to predict which phase of the business cycle the economy is moving into.

Weaknesses of Leading Indicators

Although leading economic indicators are important in making economic predictions, they are far from perfect. Different indicators

◆   Americans are living longer lives. Therefore, there will be a need for more nursing homes in the future. Why would this information cause people to invest in building nursing homes?

Consumers in Action

What's in the Newspaper?

Are you aware of what is going on in the world? Do you read a newspaper regularly? Do you listen to the news on radio or television? Do you believe that there is any value in trying to keep up with world events? The following is a list of statements that appeared in news magazines in the first six months of 1990. What do you believe each might have shown about the near future of our economic system?

"Fed Expects Inflation to Fall to 4%"
"Unemployment Holds Steady at 5.4%"
"Auto Sales Remain Weak, Down 9% from Last Year"
"GNP Grows at Annual Rate of 2.1%"
"Interest Rates on Treasury Bonds Hits 9%"
"Corporate Profits Down 10.8% from 1989"
All of these statements were printed before

August 1990, when Iraq invaded Kuwait. Think about how this single unpredicted event changed the situation referred to in each statement. Clearly, the economic predictions made in early 1990 were not correct.

Does this mean that we shouldn't pay any attention to the economy?

often give conflicting information. Sometimes predicted changes in economic activity happen quickly, and at other times months or years may pass before they take place.

The greatest problem with using leading indicators to make predictions is that they cannot foresee events outside the economy. Political, social, or natural events may take place that can result in significant changes in economic conditions. For example, there was no way to predict the impact of the Middle East war of 1973 before it happened. The drought of 1986 could not be predicted and included in the leading indicators. There was no way to know that Iraq would invade Kuwait in 1990. These events had important effects on our economy that could not be predicted or included in the leading indicators.

Leading indicators may not be a totally reliable way to predict future economic conditions, but they are better than nothing at all. Consumers should try to be aware of changes in these indicators so that they know about economic trends and the business cycle.

Summing Up *Consumers and business owners use leading economic indicators to predict future economic activity. Although these indicators are not always reliable, they are better than nothing at all.* ◆

Vocabulary Builder

Leading indicator A statistic that points to what will happen in the economy in the near future.

Review and Enrichment Activities

VOCABULARY REVIEW

1. Column A contains key consumer terms from this chapter. Column B contains a scrambled list of phrases that describe what these terms mean. Match the correct meaning with each term. Write your answers on a separate sheet of paper.

Column A	Column B
1. Contraction	a. Workers who have been without a job for only a few weeks
2. Cyclical unemployment	b. The share of people who could work and who have a job or are looking for a job
3. Peak	c. A period of time when economic activity is falling
4. Frictional unemployment	d. Workers who are without a job because of a downturn in economic activity
5. Business cycle	e. A period of time when economic activity is increasing
6. Leading indicator	f. A period of time when economic activity is at its highest point
7. Recession	g. When a nation's output does not grow at least six months
8. Labor force	h. A period of time when economic activity is at its lowest point
9. Trough	i. A statistic that points to what will happen in the economy
10. Expansion	j. Periodic ups and downs in the nation's economic activity

2. Explain the difference between the causes of demand-pull inflation and cost-push inflation.

CHECKING WHAT YOU'VE LEARNED

Write your answers for the following exercises on a separate sheet of paper.

1. Describe each of the four phases of the business cycle.
2. Explain what an unemployment rate of 6.5 percent means.
3. Explain why some economists believe that the employment rate is a better measure of economic activity than the unemployment rate.
4. Describe each of the four types of unemployment.
5. Why is it unlikely that the unemployment rate will ever go much below 5 percent?
6. Why is structural unemployment regarded as the most serious type by many economists?
7. What is inflation?
8. What phase of the business cycle is most likely to have demand-pull inflation?
9. What phase of the business cycle is most likely to have cost-push inflation?
10. Explain why the consumer price index isn't a perfect measure of the rate of inflation.
11. What is a leading indicator supposed to do? Give an example of a leading indicator.
12. Why aren't leading indicators always reliable?

PRACTICING YOUR CONSUMER SKILLS

Write your answers for the following exercises on a separate sheet of paper.

1. For each of the following economic situations, identify the phase of the business cycle that the economy is in. Give reasons for your answer.
    a. For eight months the unemployment increased until it reached 9.7 percent five weeks ago. Since then, it has stayed almost the same. Factories are only working at 69 percent of capacity, but at least they are able to sell what they now produce. Some economists have predicted that economic conditions will soon start to improve.
    b. The rate of inflation began to fall six months ago and is still going down. There is an increasing rate of business failure. Unemployment rates are going up, and sales are dropping rapidly.
    c. The economy isn't doing very well, but things are getting better. The unemployment rate has come down from 9.7 percent to 8.1 percent and is still falling. Business profits are gradually improving, and government tax collections are going up.
    d. Most businesses are working at full capacity. Unemployment is at 4.9 percent. Most businesses have been earning the same high profits for several months. Inflation is running at 11.5 percent. Some

Review and Enrichment Activities Continued

economists have predicted that economic conditions will soon turn down.

2. Identify the type of unemployment described in each of the following stories. Give reasons for your answer.

    a. Barbara works as a hostess at a ski lodge in Vermont. In the winter she works long hours. In the fall she works because tourists come to see the fall colors. In March it rains, and very few people come to the lodge. Most days in March Barbara doesn't work at all. It is now March, and Barbara hasn't worked in three weeks.

    b. Doug used to work in a shoe store until two weeks ago. His job was putting away shoes that people had tried on but not bought. Doug hated his job. He never got to talk to anyone. He got so bored that he fell asleep in the storeroom. When the owner found him asleep on the job, Doug was fired. Doug isn't worried. He is sure that he will soon find a job he likes better.

    c. Paula used to help manufacture television sets. Her job was screwing printed circuit boards into television tuners. About two years ago Paula's employer started using electronic tuners in the television sets. These tuners were automatically installed by a computer-controlled robot. Paula lost her job and has not been able to find a job that pays as well as her old job. She keeps looking, but would live in poverty if her husband didn't have a job.

    d. Leroy used to have a job at a factory that produced power boats. The boats had big engines, used lots of gasoline, and were quite expensive. As a result of a war in the Middle East, the price of gasoline went up and the economy went into a recession. Although Leroy has been out of work for eight months, he expects to be called back to the same job as soon as the war is settled and the economy picks up.

USING NUMBERS

Solve the following problem to help make the best possible choice. Write your solution on a separate sheet of paper. Be sure to show all your work.

Wayne builds homes that he sells through a real estate agent he knows. In recent years he has asked a price for his homes that is 25 percent higher than his cost of building them. The agent receives 5 percent of this profit, and Wayne keeps 20 percent. Wayne has found a piece of property that he would like to buy for $100,000. He could build roads and install sewers for another $200,000. The land could be cut up into ten lots. He would like to build homes he would sell for $140,000 on each lot. He believes that the cost for materials and labor on each home would be $80,000. To accomplish all this, Wayne would need to borrow $500,000 from a bank. He believes that he could put up the rest of the money himself.

Figure out how much money Wayne needs to complete his project. If interest rates are 12 percent, how much interest would he pay the bank over one year? If he finishes the project and sells all of his houses in one year, how much profit will Wayne earn? What could go wrong with Wayne's plan? Explain why Wayne should be interested in studying leading economic indicators.

PUTTING IDEAS IN YOUR OWN WORDS

The following quotations are from this chapter. Explain these quotations in your own words to make sure you understand what they mean. Write your answers on a separate sheet of paper.

1. "The ups and downs of economic activity do not occur smoothly or last for equal periods of time."
2. "People who are structurally unemployed need to be trained to develop new skills before they can earn an adequate income."
3. "The products and weights chosen for use by the government cannot reflect the buying patterns of all consumers."

BUILDING CONSUMER KNOWLEDGE

Write your answers for the following exercises on a separate sheet of paper.

1. Read three or more articles from the financial section of your local newspaper that concern economic conditions in your community. Decide what phase of the business cycle your community is currently in. Write a paragraph explaining your conclusion. Make specific references to the articles you read.
2. Interview an adult you know who has changed jobs in recent years. Ask the person why he or she changed jobs, if he or she was unemployed, and if so, for how long. Find out how this person's family was affected. Write a paragraph summarizing what you learned. Identify the type of unemployment that this person represented.
3. Go to the library and ask to see a copy of a newspaper from two years ago. Look for advertisements for five different goods or services, and check each product's price. Only use "regular" prices, not "sale" prices. Compare the old prices with current prices for the same or similar products. Divide each product's old price into the difference between the product's old price and its current price. For example, if the old price was $1.50 and the new price is $1.80, you would divide $.30 by $1.50 to find a 20 percent increase. This will give you the percent of change in the product's price in the past two years. Write a paragraph describing the information that you found. Explain how consumers may have reacted to the changes in prices.

Chapter 9

The Government's Role

Chapter Objectives

After completing this chapter, you will be able to do the following:

- Evaluate government spending as it relates to other types of spending in our economic system.
- Describe the functions of government in our economic system.
- Evaluate sources of tax revenue for federal, state, and local governments.
- Evaluate responsibilities of federal, state, and local governments.
- Discuss reasons for government borrowing and describe its impact on the economy and consumers.

Key Consumer Terms

In this chapter you will learn the meanings of the following important consumer terms:

- Public goods
- Income redistribution
- Social insurance
- Public assistance
- Social Security
- Workers compensation
- Unemployment compensation
- Aid to Families with Dependent Children (AFDC)
- Medicaid
- Fiscal policy
- Tariff
- Benefits-received principle
- Ability-to-pay principle
- Progressive tax
- Regressive tax
- Proportional tax
- National debt
- Deficit

You might say that the government is our nation's biggest business and consumer. Roughly one-third of the income earned in the United States passes through some level of government each year. All levels of government—federal, state, and local—use resources, employ workers, and consume products so that they may provide goods and services for our citizens.

SECTION 1

GOVERNMENT'S PLACE IN THE ECONOMY

While you read, ask yourself . . .
- ◆ *What are several ways in which your local government acts like a consumer?*
- ◆ *What are several activities that your local government is involved in that are similar to those of a private business?*

In Chapter 3 you learned that our nation's economy is similar to a free market economy, but government involvement makes it a mixed market economy. Individual Americans make most of the decisions that answer the four basic economic questions you studied in Chapter 2:

- What and how much should be produced?
- Who should produce what?
- How should goods and services be produced?
- For whom should goods and services be produced?

In some situations the government influences these decisions or makes these decisions for us. To do this, the government passes laws that limit our freedom to make economic choices. The government collects taxes or borrows money to obtain the funds it uses. It also provides money, goods, or services to people who need help to maintain a minimum standard of living.

Differences Between the Government and Business

Although our government often seems to operate like a business, there are many important differences between the government and business. One of the most important differences is that the government is not run to earn a profit. It is run to provide leadership, to achieve social order, to establish relations with foreign countries, and to help Americans maintain and improve their standard of living. We do not expect the government to earn a profit while carrying out these responsibilities.

When the government makes choices, its decision-making process is not the same as that found in business or used by individual consumers. Businesses make choices that are intended to increase their profits. Consumers make choices that are intended to satisfy their needs and wants. Government choices are made to achieve social, political, and economic objectives. They are based on laws created by elected representatives.

Decisions that make good economic sense may not be socially or politically acceptable. For example, in April 1991, Secretary of Defense Richard Chaney suggested closing many military bases to save money for the government. Although this plan made good economic sense, many representatives and senators in Congress demanded that the cuts not be made. They may have taken this position to protect jobs and political support in their home districts. This illustrates how political and economic objectives are not always the same.

Growing Role of the Government in Our Economy

The role of the government in our economy has grown rapidly over the past thirty years. In 1960 the federal government's budget was 18.2 percent of our GDP. By 1970 this figure had grown to 19.3 percent. In 1980 it was 21.1 percent, and by 1988 it was 22.3 percent. Similar rates of growth occurred in spending by state and local governments.

The government's role in the economy is not just a matter of the additional money it gathers and spends. It may also be seen in increased regulation of the economy. Many government agencies have been created in recent years that limit what businesses and consumers may do. One example is the Occupational Safety and Health Administration (OSHA), which regulates workplace safety and health conditions. Others include the Environmental Protection Agency (EPA) and the Equal Employment Opportunity Commission (EEOC). Each of these, as well as many other government agencies, has specific objectives that are intended to benefit American citizens. However, in carrying out their responsibilities, they also limit the individual choices we can make.

Summing Up   *The government's role in our economy has been growing in recent years. This may be seen in the government's growing share of the GDP and in its greater regulation of our economic activity.* ◆

THE FUNCTIONS OF GOVERNMENT

While you read, ask yourself . . .
- ◆ What are several examples of public goods that you benefit from?
- ◆ How are people you know affected by social insurance programs or public assistance programs?

Government in the United States fulfills four important economic functions:

1. It provides public goods.
2. It protects public well-being.
3. It regulates economic activity.
4. It promotes economic and social objectives.

Federal, state, and local governments share responsibility for the first three functions. The fourth function is almost entirely the responsibility of the federal government.

Providing Public Goods

Public goods are goods or services provided by the government to the people. These goods can be used by many individuals at the same time without reducing the benefit that each person receives. Public goods include education, national defense, and some types of health care.

National defense is one of the few public goods provided only by the federal government. Usually, different levels of government share the responsibility of providing public goods. For example, the legal system, which is a type of public good, involves all three levels of government. Federal, state, and local governments maintain separate systems of courts, correctional institutions, and law enforcement agencies.

There is no practical way to provide many necessary services other than through the government. Would it make sense to have each person provide his or her own fire protection?

Society has decided that all Americans deserve at least some minimum standard of living. To help accomplish this the government provides food stamps to people with low incomes.

Protecting Public Well-Being

Another function of government is to provide for the public well-being by giving assistance to specific groups, such as the aged, the ill, the poor, or other people who are economically disadvantaged. Through our political process, Americans have decided that there is a minimum level of income that every citizen is entitled to. This is accomplished through **income redistribution**—taking income from some people and giving it to others. Government programs that redistribute income fall into two categories: **social insurance** and **public assistance.**

Social Insurance.   Social insurance programs pay benefits to retired and disabled workers and their families and to the unemployed. Benefits are financed by other workers and employers who pay into the programs. **Social Security** is a program of the federal government that provides monthly payments to people who are retired or unable to work. **Workers compensation** is a state program that provides care and payment to workers injured

on the job. Workers who are unemployed may receive payments through state-run and federally supported **unemployment compensation** programs. A feature of all social insurance

Vocabulary Builder

Income redistribution Taking income from some groups of people or businesses and paying it to members of other groups.

Public assistance Government programs that make payments to people based on their need.

Public goods Goods or services supplied to everyone by the government; can be used by many individuals at the same time without reducing the benefit that each person receives.

Social insurance   Programs designed to provide insurance against the problems of old age, illness, and unemployment.

Social security   A federal program that provides monthly payments to millions of people who are retired or unable to work.

Unemployment compensation   Money paid by the government to people who have recently become unemployed.

Workers compensation   A state-run program to extend payment for medical care to workers injured on the job.

Consumer Close-Up

Is There a Good Place to Be Poor?

No one would choose to live in poverty. Welfare programs run by each state are intended to provide an economic "safety net" to prevent Americans from falling into poverty. However, the size of this net and who it catches vary widely from state to state.

For example, Aid for Families with Dependent Children is funded by the federal, state, and local governments. In general, federal support for AFDC matches spending by state and local governments up to some maximum amount. If state and local governments spend $300 per month on AFDC, the federal government will also contribute $300. If the state and local governments spend $100, the federal government contributes $100. Because of this method of funding, AFDC payments are different in each state.

Some state and local governments make substantial payments into the AFDC program. Others pay much less. For example, in 1988 California paid an average of $1,194 per year for each person on AFDC. The federal government paid the same amount, bringing the total to $2,388. In California a family of four on AFDC received an average of $9,552 in benefits per year. The same family in New York would have received $9,024, or $7,704 in Michigan. No one suggests that it would be easy to support a family of four on any of these incomes, but it would have been harder still in many other states.

In 1988 a family of four on AFDC in Alabama would have received $1,908 in aid for an entire year. In Mississippi the amount would have been $1,920, and in Louisiana the amount paid would have been $2,644. The benefits in these states were much lower because the state governments spent smaller amounts for the federal government to match.

Some of the differences in benefits may be explained in terms of the lower cost of living in some locations. In rural areas it usually costs less to support a family. A large part of the difference is the result of lower housing costs. However, the fact remains that the standard of living that can be supported through AFDC payments varies widely from state to state.

What are some social and economic results of this inequality in the welfare system?

---

programs is that the benefits are provided to specific groups of people from funds paid by members of the same group or by their employers.

Public Assistance.   Public assistance programs are often called welfare. These programs provide payments and other benefits to people based on need. Public assistance payments are made from general government funds rather than from payments made by members of specific groups. Programs of this type include food stamps and payments to the aged, blind, and disabled. The largest number of people who are helped through public assistance receive aid through the **Aid to Families with Dependent Children (AFDC)** program. AFDC provides money to needy parents who are raising small children. **Medicaid** is another public assistance program. It provides free health care for people with low incomes and the disabled.

Many Americans depend on benefits from social insurance or public assistance programs as the basic means of their support. There have been many debates over the amount of aid that should be provided to people who are economically in need in the United States. However, there are few people who would dispute that there is a need for these types of programs.

Regulating Economic Activity

All levels of government make and enforce laws and take actions intended to protect the public from being taken advantage of by businesses. The federal government encourages competition and regulates some businesses. It enforces laws that protect our environment and conserve our resources.

State and local governments also protect consumers. They establish laws that determine when young people may work and what types of jobs they may take. Businesses and homes must follow zoning laws and building codes. These and other government regulations are discussed in Chapter 12 and in other sections of this text.

Promoting Economic and Social Objectives

The government taxes income, property, and activities to collect revenue. It uses money from taxes to buy the goods and services that it needs to carry out its functions. The manner in which government collects and spends money can also influence how people and businesses behave. People and businesses are less likely to choose to have or do anything that is taxed. For example, tobacco products are taxed to collect money for the government and to discourage people from smoking. Taxes on expensive cars discourage people from buying such products.

In other cases our government provides tax relief or financial support to people or businesses to encourage certain types of behavior.

For example, if you contribute to a church or charity, you may reduce your income tax payment by claiming the gift as a deduction. If a business invests in an economically depressed area or hires disabled workers, it often receives tax reductions or cash payments from state or local governments. On a federal level, taxes and government spending are carried out in a way that attempts to influence economic conditions in our nation.

Carrying Out Fiscal Policy

The federal government carries out its **fiscal policy**, which is made up of the government's taxing and spending decisions. Fiscal policy is intended to help the economy achieve full employment, steady growth in production, and limited rates of inflation. An example of fiscal policy was the removal of a 7 percent federal tax on new cars in 1971 to encourage the sale of automobiles. And in 1981 businesses that purchased new machines were allowed to reduce their federal income tax by 10 percent of the cost of their investment. This was designed to increase business investment and improve their efficiency of production. Another example of fiscal policy took place between 1977 and 1981, when President Carter led Congress to expand the Comprehensive Employment

---

Vocabulary Builder

Aid to Families with Dependent Children (AFDC) Public assistance program that provides money to needy families with children.

Fiscal policy The federal government's policies concerning spending and taxing that are intended to stabilize economic conditions.

Medicaid A government program that provides health care for people with low income and the disabled.

and Training Act (CETA), providing government-funded jobs to hundreds of thousands of Americans. This program reduced the unemployment rate significantly in the late 1970s.

Summing Up *The government carries out many important functions in our economy. As a citizen and consumer, you will have opportunities to contribute to the process that determines how our government uses its economic powers.* ◆

SECTION 3

GOVERNMENT BUDGETS

While you read, *ask yourself . . .*
- ◆ *What similarities are there in the way the government makes decisions in its budgetary process and the way you decide how to spend your money?*
- ◆ *What differences are there between the way the government makes decisions in its budgetary process and the way you decide how to spend your money?*

The Federal Budget

Every year our federal government receives hundreds of billions of dollars from taxes and borrows even more to spend and transfer to American citizens. How the federal government decides to use its powers to tax, borrow, and spend may be the most important choices made in our economic system.

Every year a complex process occurs in Washington, D.C., that results in the federal government's budget. Eighteen months before the fiscal (financial) year begins on October 1, The executive branch of the federal government begins to prepare a budget. Employees of the Office of Management and Budget (OMB) start the process, with the advice of the Council of Economic Advisers (CEA) and the Treasury Department. The OMB makes an outline for a tentative budget. Various federal departments and agencies receive this outline and negotiate for larger allocations.

The president submits the budget that results from this process to Congress in January of each year. The president's budget is then examined by various committees and subcommittees of the Congress that are advised by the Congressional Budget Office (CBO). Congress is supposed to pass a second budget resolution setting limits on spending and taxes for the upcoming fiscal year. In practice, however, the budget resolutions often are not passed on time. Moreover, when they are passed, the government does not always follow its own limits.

As a result of delays in this process, the fiscal year sometimes starts without a budget. Federal agencies are then allowed to operate under a special type of legislation that is called a continuing resolution. In the budget debate of 1990, President Bush briefly refused to sign a continuing resolution in an effort to put pressure on Congress to reach an agreement on the budget. This forced large sections of the federal government to close for a short period of time.

Under the federal government's budget, tax revenues have often been less than government expenditures. This has forced the government to borrow hundreds of billions of dollars in recent years. At the start of 1991 the total amount that the federal government owed was over $3.2 trillion. More will be said about this debt later in the chapter.

State and Local Budgets

Figure 9-1 shows the sources of federal, state, and local tax revenue and the types of spending carried out in a recent year. The largest source of tax revenue for local governments was the property tax. Local governments were very dependent on transfers of

Federal, State, and Local Government Revenues and Spending, 1988
(Given as Percent of Total*)

Tax Revenue Source	Federal	State	Local
Individual income taxes	39.6%	14.8%	—
Social insurance taxes	31.6%	—	—
Corporate income taxes	9.3%	4.0%	—
Property taxes	—	—	25.7%
Sales taxes	—	24.0%	5.3%
Intergovernment transfers	—	19.8%	32.9%
Insurance trust revenue	—	16.7%	20.4%
Fees and utility revenue	—	21.6%	—
Other	19.5%	20.7%	14.5%
Spending and Transfers			
National defense	27.3%		
Payments to individuals	46.9%	22.8%	5.6%
Interest	14.3%	—	5.0%
Intergovernment transfers	10.8%	31.3%	—
Education	—	13.2%	36.0%
Highways	—	6.9%	4.4%
Correction, police, and fire	—	3.3%	8.3%
Other	.7%	22.5%	40.7%

*Values smaller than 3% combined in "Other."
Statistical Abstract 1991, p. 280

◆ **Table 9-1**   Government Revenues and Spending

funds from state and federal governments. Sales taxes were important for both state and local governments. State governments also received significant aid from the federal government in transfers. Income taxes were the second greatest source of tax revenue for most states.

The greatest share of local government spending was used to support education. The two largest expenditures for most states was for education and social services. Although most states and some local governments have sometimes spent more money than they have received from taxes, they generally do not have the same types of problems with debt that the federal government has.

Summing Up   *Federal, state, and local governments have budgets to help them plan where they will obtain money and how they will spend the money they receive. In many years the federal and many state budgetary processes have been slow and inefficient.* ◆

◆   When drivers pay to use roads they benefit from the money they pay. How do other people who don't use these roads benefit from the fact that they exist?

TAXATION

While you read, *ask yourself . . .*
◆ *What benefits-received tax do you pay?*
◆ *What ability-to-pay tax do you or someone you know pay?*
◆ *Are most of the taxes you pay progressive or regressive?*

There are many different types of taxes you will pay in your lifetime. Some of the more obvious taxes are income taxes, Social Security taxes, sales taxes, and property taxes. You will pay other taxes that you may not be aware of. When Americans buy alcoholic beverages, cigarettes, or gasoline, part of the price they pay is an excise tax that is paid by the producer and

passed on to the consumer in the price of the product. **Tariffs** are taxes on imported goods. If you ever buy a Japanese or German automobile, part of the price you will pay is a tariff. If you buy expensive jewelry, boats, or cars, you will pay a luxury tax. You may find that your life seems to be full of taxes.

Principles of Taxation

People are usually taxed according to one of two major principles. Under the **benefits-received principle of taxation**, those people who use a particular government service support it by paying taxes in proportion to the benefit they receive. The $1 you pay to cross a toll bridge helps to pay for the bridge and its maintenance. If you are charged a $15 fee to camp in a national park, the fee helps pay the cost of operating the park. The more you use the bridge or park, the more you pay to support these government services.

Although there are many situations where benefits-received taxes make sense, there are other cases where they clearly cannot work. Large families could not possibly pay the cost of education for their children. People who receive welfare or disability payments from the government could not pay to support these services. In such cases other people must pay the cost of the government programs.

An alternative principle of taxation is the **ability-to-pay principle**. Under this type of taxation, people with higher incomes pay a larger share of their income in taxes than people who have smaller incomes. These taxes are collected regardless of whether the individual taxpayers directly benefit from the government programs their taxes support. For example, school taxes are paid by all property owners, even when they have no children attending the schools. Our government leaders often choose to impose taxes on individuals with greater incomes to support programs that benefit members of society who have smaller incomes or that benefit society as a whole.

Forms of Taxation

All taxes fall into one of three possible categories: **progressive**, **regressive**, or **proportional**. These forms of taxation are determined by the percentage of income people pay in taxes.

Progressive Taxes. A progressive tax is one that falls most heavily on people with higher incomes. Any tax that requires people with greater incomes to pay a larger percentage of their income in taxes than people with smaller incomes is a progressive tax. Ability-to-pay taxes are usually progressive taxes. The federal and most state income taxes are progressive,

Consumer News

Changes in Military Spending

How much are the armed forces worth to you? In 1990 the U.S. government spent just over $1,300 per American to support our military. That worked out to be about 6 percent of our GDP. Do you think that was too much, too little, or just about right?

The amount of military spending thirty years earlier, in 1960, was just $250 per person. Although this may appear to be much less than we spent in 1990, in reality it was much more. The military budget in 1960 was 9 percent of our GDP. Our economy grew and prices went up between 1960 and 1990. Therefore, we spent many more dollars, but the military burden was smaller because we produced more goods and earned more income.

Vocabulary Builder

Ability to pay principle   A system of taxation in which people with larger incomes pay a higher rate of tax than those with lower incomes.
Benefits-received principle   A system of taxation in which those who use a particular government service support it with taxes in proportion to the benefit they receive.
Progressive tax   Tax that takes a larger percentage of higher incomes than of lower incomes.
Proportional tax   A tax that takes the same percentage of all incomes.
Regressive tax   A tax that takes a larger percentage of lower incomes than of higher incomes.
Tariff   Tax levied on imported products.

based on the amount of a person's taxable income. In 1991 the federal income tax brackets were 15, 28, and 31 percent. As people's taxable income increased, they were required to pay a larger percentage of any additional income they earned in taxes.

Suppose that you were single and earned $10,000 in taxable income in 1991. You would have paid 15 cents in federal income tax on the next dollar in taxable income you earned. If you earned $25,000 in taxable income, you would have paid 28 cents of your next taxable dollar of income. And if your taxable income was $50,000, you would have paid 31 cents of your next taxable dollar of income.

It is important to realize that this tax rate applies to *taxable* income that is left after total income has been adjusted according to the number of people a taxpayer supports and other expenses he or she must pay. Because of these adjustments it is possible for a person with a large income to pay taxes at a low rate. You will learn more about these taxes in Chapters 23 and 24.

Regressive Taxes.   A regressive tax falls most heavily on people with lower incomes. Any tax that requires people with lower incomes to pay a greater percentage of their income than people with larger incomes is a regressive tax. This does not mean that people with smaller incomes pay more dollars. If you earned $50,000 a year and paid $10,000 in taxes, you would be paying at a 20 percent rate. If your best friend earned only $12,000 a year and paid $3,000 in taxes, he or she would be paying at a 25 percent rate. Although you would have paid more than three times as much tax as your friend, this tax structure would be regressive because you would have paid a lower percentage of your income in taxes.

Many taxes in the United States are regressive. This is particularly true of state and local taxes. Gasoline taxes, property taxes, and sales taxes are usually regressive. They take a larger share of income from people with lower earnings. Although it is easy to condemn such taxes as being unfair, you should remember that people with lower incomes also receive the bulk of benefits from government assistance programs.

Proportional Taxes.   A third form of taxation is the proportional tax. A proportional tax is one that takes the same percentage of everyone's income. There are no true proportional taxes in this country. Social Security taxes are proportional up to some maximum amount of earned income but become regressive on earnings above that level. Some economists and government officials have suggested that the tax system could be simplified and made more fair by charging all citizens a tax equal to 18 percent of their income with no adjustments allowed. It is not likely that such a law will be passed at any time in the near future.

Summing Up   *Taxes may be classified in a number of ways. They may be based on the benefits-received principle or ability-to-pay principle. They are also classified as progressive, regressive, or proportional. Although people with lower income may pay a greater percentage of their income in taxes, they also receive the bulk of government transfers.* ◆

SECTION 5

THE NATIONAL DEBT

While you read, *ask yourself . . .*
- ◆ *How is your future likely to be affected by the growth in our national debt?*
- ◆ *What steps, if any, do you believe should be taken to control the growth of our national debt?*

To spend more money than you earn, you must use some of your savings or go into debt. The federal government has no savings. Therefore, when its spending exceeds its income, it must borrow. The total amount of debt that the federal government has accumulated over the years is called the **national debt**. From 1940

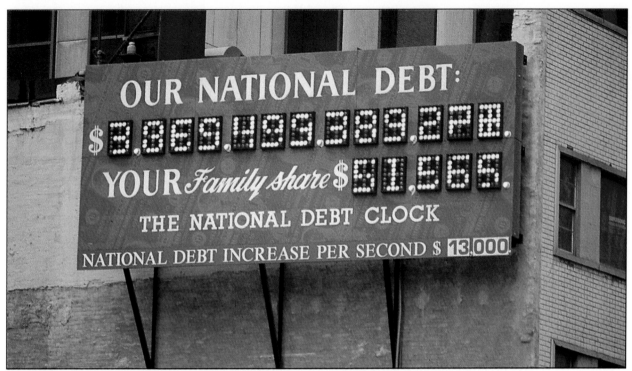

◆   This photograph was taken on April 4, 1992. What objective do you suppose the people who put up this sign were trying to achieve?

through 1990, the federal government had a **deficit** (shortage) in forty three out of fifty one years. In the 1980s, federal, state, and local government spending together averaged about 9 percent more than total tax revenues. The difference was made up by borrowing.

How the Government Borrows

Our government borrows by selling securities to individuals, businesses, banks, and government trust funds. If you have ever bought a government savings bond, you have made a loan to the federal government. People who own savings bonds may cash them in at a bank at any time. There are other types of government securities that may not be cashed in until they come due. However, they may be sold to other people in a bond market that works much like a stock market. You will learn more about these securities when you study investing in Chapter 28. Most of the national debt has been financed by selling these other securities.

When the federal government needs to borrow money, it creates new debt by issuing and selling new securities. It raises money to pay off old securities that come due in the same

Vocabulary Builder

Deficit   The difference between income and spending in an accounting period (or in a specific period of time).
National debt   Total amount of debt owed by the federal government.

The Growth of Our National Debt				
1 Year	2 National Debt in Current Dollars	3 National Debt in Constant 1982 Dollars	4 National Debt as a Percent of GDP	5 Interest Payment on the National Debt as a Percent of the Federal Budget
1960	$284.1	$957.4	56.0%	7.5%
1970	380.9	999.7	37.5%	7.4%
1980	908.5	1,108.4	33.3%	9.1%
1982	1,136.8	1,136.8	35.9%	11.6%
1984	1,564.1	1,501.5	41.5%	12.7%
1986	2,120.1	1,929.3	50.0%	13.7%
1988	2,600.8	2,210.7	54.4%	14.2%
*1990	3,200	2,467.2	58.9%	15.5%
*estimated (Note: Both current and constant dollars in billions of dollars.)				

◆   **Table 9-2**   The Growth of Our National Debt

way. In recent years the size of the national debt has been growing at a rapid rate. There is a wide debate over the importance of the national debt to our nation's future.

Evaluating the National Debt

In 1991 the total national debt was about $3.2 trillion. This amount was equal to roughly $12,800 for every person in the United States. Many people are concerned about the size of the national debt. Others believe that its growth and importance can be controlled. There are many ways to measure and evaluate growth in the GDP, as shown in Figure 9-2.

Looking at column 2 in Table 9-2, you can see the growth in our national debt in current dollars (not adjusted for inflation). You can see that the debt is large, but there is little informa-

tion to help you judge the debt's importance. You need something to measure it against. The third column in Table 9-2 shows the national debt in constant 1982 dollars. This allows you to see the growth of the debt after it has been adjusted for inflation. This is an improvement over using current dollars, but it still provides limited information.

A better way to evaluate the importance of debt is to measure the ability of the borrowing person or group to carry that debt. If you owed $100,000 as a high school student, you would probably have trouble carrying your debt. But if you were a corporate vice president earning $90,000 a year, you might have no trouble making payments on this debt. The same principle applies to the debt of the United States. Its importance can be evaluated in terms of our ability to carry the debt.

The basic measure of our nation's yearly income is the GDP. According to column 4 in Figure 9-2, the national debt declined as a percent of GDP between 1960 and 1980. After 1980 it grew as a percent of the GDP. Many economists use these statistics to evaluate the importance of changes in our national debt. Between 1960 and 1980 our nation's ability to carry the debt was increasing. Therefore, the debt was becoming less important. After 1980 its importance increased.

Another way to measure the significance of the national debt is to consider the interest payment that the federal government makes on the debt as a percent of its budget. When this value grows, the importance of the debt also increases. By studying column 5 in Figure 9-2, you can see that the payment on the national debt has become a larger part of the federal government's budget in recent years. In fact, the payment on the debt has grown more rapidly than the debt itself. This more rapid rate of growth is the result of higher interest rates the federal government must pay to borrow money. In 1960 the federal government had to pay roughly 4 percent to borrow money. In 1990 it paid over 8 percent. The amount of interest that must be paid on any debt depends on the rate of interest and the amount borrowed. The size of the payment on our national debt has grown because the debt itself is larger and because interest rates have increased.

Although the federal debt has grown in recent years, some people say it is manageable. They believe that before steps are taken to reduce the debt, we should consider the cost of such steps. To reduce its deficit, the federal government would have to either cut its spending, increase taxes, or take both of these actions. Many Americans would be hurt by higher taxes or cuts in government spending. As always, we need to weigh the benefits and costs of any decision.

As an American you have the right to participate in our political process. If you're not yet

Consumer News

New Causes For Growth in the National Debt

According to federal laws, the government's annual budget deficit was supposed to fall in each year in the 1990s until the budget was balanced after 1993. Events of 1990 and 1991 resulted in new costs that prevented this. The greatest new cost was the more than $100 billion that the Treasury provided to help bail out many failed savings and loan associations. The war in the Persian Gulf added many billions in spending that had not been anticipated. The recession of 1991 increased the need for government spending for social programs and at the same time reduced tax receipts. As a result, in August 1991, the Congressional Budget Office predicted that the debt for the 1990–1991 budget would be between $350 billion and $370 billion. That was another $1,400 to $1,500 per American.

How will this growth in the national debt affect you?

old enough to vote, you soon will be. You can also help people campaign for public office. You will have the opportunity to help decide how our nation deals with its debt. How you use your political rights will help determine whether you are a responsible citizen and consumer.

Summing Up   *The national debt has grown rapidly in recent years. Since 1980 it has increased both in terms of its percent of the GDP and in terms of its percent of the federal budget.* ◆

Review and Enrichment Activities

VOCABULARY REVIEW

1. Column A contains key consumer terms from this chapter. Column B contains a scrambled list of phrases that describe what these terms mean. Match the correct meaning with each term. Write your answers on a separate sheet of paper.

Column A	Column B
1. Social Security	a. Goods or services supplied to all citizens by the government
2. Benefits received principle	b. People paying taxes in direct relation to their income
3. Ability to pay principle	
4. Fiscal policy	c. As income increases, percentage paid in taxes increases
5. Regressive tax	d. As income increases, percentage paid in taxes decreases
6. National debt	e. People paying taxes in direct relation to the value they receive from the program supported by the tax
7. Tariff	
8. Progressive tax	f. Spending and taxing decisions made by the federal government to help the economy work more efficiently
9. Medicaid	
10. Public goods	g. The total amount of money owed by the federal government
	h. A federal program that is intended to provide financial assistance to people when they retire
	i. A program that is administered by state governments that provides health care for people who need public assistance
	j. A tax on an imported good

2. Explain the difference between the way social insurance programs and public assistance programs are paid for.

CHECKING WHAT YOU'VE LEARNED

Write your answers for the following exercises on a separate sheet of paper.

1. What has happened to the share of the GDP that governments take through taxation and borrowing in recent years?
2. How are the objectives of the decision-making process for the government different from those of businesses and consumers?
3. Describe each of the four functions of government.
4. Describe how the federal budget is prepared.
5. What is the most important source of federal tax revenue?
6. What type of spending takes the largest share of the federal budget?
7. What is the most important source of tax revenue in most states?
8. What is the most important source of tax revenue for most local governments?
9. Explain the benefits-received principle of taxation, and give one example of this type of tax.
10. Explain the ability-to-pay principle of taxation, and give one example of this type of tax.
11. Explain what a progressive tax is, and give one example of this type of tax.
12. Explain what a regressive tax is, and give one example of this type of tax.
13. What happened to the national debt as a percent of GDP between 1960 and 1980? What happened after 1980? Why do many economists believe that this information is important?
14. What happened to the interest payment on the national debt as a percent of the federal government's budget after 1970? What are two reasons for this trend?

PRACTICING YOUR CONSUMER SKILLS

Write your answers for the following exercises on a separate sheet of paper.

1. The four functions of government are to (a) provide public goods, (b) protect the public well-being, (c) regulate economic activity, (d) ensure economic stability. Identify the function demonstrated in each of the following situations. Give reasons for your answer.
   a. Ted was injured while he was at work last month, and he now receives workers compensation payments.
   b. The federal government increased its spending for highway construction to try to provide jobs and reduce unemployment.
   c. The town council voted to buy 5 acres of land for a public playground.
   d. When Jeff wanted to open a restaurant, he had to receive a license from the county health department.

2. Identify each of the following taxes as an example of (a) a benefits-received tax or (b) an ability-to-pay tax. Give reasons for your answer.
    a. Jerry paid $3,562 in federal income taxes last year. The tax revenue is used to help support all government programs.
    b. Sally pays 15 cents in tax for each gallon of gasoline she buys. The tax revenue is used to repair the roads.
    c. Joan paid $3 to visit the city art museum last week. The money was used to pay for renovations to the museum.
    d. Felix paid $589 in school taxes last year. He is eighty-one years old and hasn't had any children of school age for forty years.

3. Identify each of the following taxes as an example of (a) progressive, (b) regressive, or (c) proportional taxes. Give reasons for your answer.
    a. When Tim was an assistant store manager, he earned $20,000 a year and paid a property tax of $500 on his home. The following year he was promoted to district supervisor. In his new job he earned $60,000 a year and moved to a larger house, where he paid $1,200 in property taxes.
    b. When settlers came to the New World, they agreed that each person would pay a tax of $5 to support the government, regardless of how much income they made.
    c. A state placed a 2 percent tax on any income earned from rent in excess of $5,000 a year. The state also placed a 5 percent tax on this type of income over $10,000 a year.
    d. Suppose that the federal government placed a tax on automobiles according to the size of the engine. Any person whose automobile had an engine greater than 150 horsepower would be required to pay an annual tax of $1 for each additional horsepower.

USING NUMBERS

Solve the following problem to help make the best possible choice. Write your solution on a separate sheet of paper. Be sure to show all your work.

Paul wants a new building for his industrial cleaning business. His firm uses solvents to remove grease and other materials from work clothes used by employees of a nearby chemical factory. His business is rapidly becoming too large for his old location.

Paul has found a piece of property about 10 miles from town that he could buy and build on. He estimates that the entire cost would be $1.5 million. If he build there, he would pay $40,000 in property taxes and would have to spend $50,000 a year to have his waste products removed to a toxic waste disposal facility.

He could also buy an old factory in a depressed urban area for $750,000. To use this factory, he would need to spend another $800,000 for remodeling so that it would meet his needs. However, the local government would provide him with the following benefits if he chooses this location:

• Reduced property taxes of $20,000 a year for ten years
• $15,000 to hire and train local people to work in his plant

- Permission to dispose of some of his waste products in city sewers, cutting his disposal costs to $30,000 a year

How much would Paul save over ten years if he chose to locate his business in the old factory? What other factors should he consider? Where would you recommend he place his business? Explain your reasons for your recommendation.

PUTTING IDEAS IN YOUR OWN WORDS

The following quotations are from this chapter. Explain these quotations in your own words to make sure you understand what they mean. Write your answers on a separate sheet of paper.

1. "When the government makes choices, its decision-making process is not the same as that found in business or used by individual consumers."
2. "Many taxes in the United States are regressive. This is particularly true of state and local taxes."
3. "A better way to evaluate the importance of debt is to measure the ability of the borrowing person or group to carry that debt."

BUILDING CONSUMER KNOWLEDGE

Write your answers for the following excercises on a separate sheet of paper.

1. Make a list of at least four types of taxes that you now pay. Identify each of these taxes as a benefits-received tax, an ability-to-pay tax, or a tax that isn't clearly either of these.
2. The budgets of local governments are documents of public record. This means that citizens have the right to see them. Obtain a copy of the budget for your school district, county, town, or city. List the major sources of revenue and types of spending for the budget you study. Do you believe that the money is being collected fairly? Do you believe that the money is being spent on programs that are needed? Explain your answers.
3. Take a survey of five adults. Don't choose more than one from your own family. Ask them how large they think the federal debt is at the present time. Don't provide them with the answer if they don't know. Ask them if they feel that the size of the debt is an important problem to our nation. Ask them what they would do about the debt if they had the power to make the decision. Record their answers and be prepared to explain them to other members of your class.
4. Local projects that require government spending are often discussed in the community. Your teacher will identify such a project for you. Write an essay explaining whether you believe that the project is a good or bad idea. How can responsible citizens let their elected officials know how they feel about this project?

Chapter 10

The Consumer and International Trade

Chapter Objectives

After completing this chapter, you will be able to do the following:

- Describe benefits and costs associated with international trade.
- Explain the impact of tariffs, quotas, and exchange rates on the price of imported goods.
- Explain the arguments for and against buying imported goods.
- Discuss the impact of international trade agreements on American businesses, national income, and consumers' ability to buy domestic and imported goods and services.

Key Consumer Terms

In this chapter you will learn the meanings of the following important consumer terms:

- Import
- Export
- Specialization
- Barrier to trade
- Quota
- Domestic
- Exchange rate
- Fixed exchange rate
- Negative balance of trade
- Positive balance of trade
- Devaluation
- Flexible exchange rate
- Appreciation
- Depreciation

Do you like chocolate? Do you drink coffee or eat bananas? Do you buy gasoline for a car or watch television? If you answered yes to any of these questions, you depend on foreign trade. Many of the products we take for granted in our lives are available in sufficient quantities only because we trade with other countries.

S E C T I O N   1

THE IMPORTANCE OF FOREIGN TRADE

While you read, *ask yourself . . .*
◆ *What are some products that you use that were produced in other countries?*
◆ *Who do you know whose job depends on our ability to sell American goods to foreign countries?*

What would happen if the United States could no longer buy products from other countries or sell goods in return? Many Americans do not realize the many ways in which trade changes their lives. For example, if you are wearing athletic shoes, they were probably made in a different country. Over 25 percent of the automobiles that Americans bought in 1990 were not manufactured in the United States. More than half of the petroleum we use was taken from the ground in other countries. Without trade, there would be no coffee, chocolate, or pepper for Americans to use. The list of **imports** we buy from other countries goes on and on.

THE VALUE OF TRADE

In 1990 the value of U.S. imports was about 12 percent of our GDP. If Americans could not have bought these goods, they would have been inconvenienced, at the very least. Shortages of these products could have occurred that would have pushed prices up. Many

American firms that depended on imported resources and manufactured goods would have been forced out of business. Their workers would have lost their jobs and might have needed assistance from our government. In one way or another, most Americans would lose if we couldn't buy imported goods.

Imports are only half of the trade story. Many American workers depend on our ability to sell goods and services to other countries. In recent years our most important **exports** were machinery and equipment, food products, chemicals, and raw materials. If we could not export these products, millions of American workers could be unemployed, and some businesses would fail. Government assistance programs would need to grow, and taxes could increase. Clearly, the U.S. economy and every American citizen depend on our ability to export and import goods and services. We take part in international trade because we benefit from it.

Why Nations Trade

If the seat on your bicycle came loose, you could probably fix it. However, trying to man-

Vocabulary Builder

Export   A good or service sold to individuals or groups in another country.
Import   A good or service bought from another country.

Consumer News

Which U.S. Firms Depend on Trade the Most?

Most American businesses don't depend on foreign trade very much, right? WRONG! Many American businesses would be in deep trouble without trade. For example, in 1989 the Boeing Corporation exported more than $11 billion worth of aircraft and parts to customers in other nations. These exports were 54 percent of the firm's total sales. General Electric's exports totaled $7.2 billion, IBM's foreign sales were $5.4 billion, and Eastman Kodak sold $2.8 billion in other nations. Each of these firms, as well as the thousands of workers they employ, would have been seriously hurt by a reduction in foreign trade. Many economists feel that reducing imports to the United States would also reduce the willingness and ability of foreign nations to buy American products.

What do you think?

ufacture a bicycle from raw materials would be a waste of your time. You lack the skills and tools necessary to complete the task. We are able to accomplish many tasks, like tightening a bicycle seat, because we have the skills and tools needed to do the work. Other tasks are beyond our ability. These are the tasks we pay someone else to do. This demonstrates the idea of **specialization**. When people or businesses specialize at certain tasks and trade with others for goods and services that they cannot pro-

duce as efficiently, resources are better used and production increases.

The principle of specialization applies to countries as well as to individual people and businesses. Nations trade with each other because they do not produce all products equally well. For example, some nations are better suited for growing coffee beans, while others produce sewing machines more efficiently. To produce the greatest quantity of goods possible, each country should specialize in making the products it can produce most efficiently. If these countries trade coffee beans for sewing machines, both nations will gain. International trade exists because the nations of the world benefit when they trade.

The benefits of trade are the result of each country having different types and amounts of the factors of production. Some nations have large amounts of a natural resource like copper, bauxite, or cobalt. Others have good farmland or abundant water power. Many countries have a skilled labor force or advanced technology that allows them to produce complex products. Nations may have warm, cold, wet, or dry climates. Because different nations have different resources, they cannot produce all products equally well. When each country specializes in making the goods and services it is best suited to produce, it can use its resources most efficiently. It should trade for other products it is not able to produce as efficiently.

Trade allows countries to make the best use of their resources and to increase the total production of goods and services in the world. International trade helps all countries benefit from specialization.

Summing Up *The U.S. economy depends on foreign trade. We buy many products from other countries and sell them many of the goods that we produce. Trade allows specialization, which leads to greater efficiency and production.* ◆

◆   Countries that have few machines and many workers who are willing to accept low wages often are best suited to produce agricultural products.

◆   Other countries that have more capital and skilled workers are better suited to produce technologically advanced goods and services.

SECTION 2

BARRIERS TO TRADE

While you read, ask yourself . . .
- ◆ *Why do you choose to buy imported goods?*
- ◆ *How would you be affected if a 50 percent tariff was placed on the imported goods you buy?*

If the governments of the world completely believed in the benefits of trade, there would be no **barriers to trade**. However, for a number of reasons, countries have established **tariffs** and **quotas** that restrict the flow of trade between countries.

Tariffs

A tariff is a tax on an imported good. Its effect is to increase the price of the good and to discourage people from buying it. Throughout history, tariffs have been established for several reasons. In the late 1700s and early 1800s revenue tariffs were used by the United States primarily to raise money for the federal government.

Protective tariffs have been established to protect businesses from foreign competition. In 1930 the Hawley-Smoot Tariff was passed to establish a "high degree of self-sufficiency," for the United States. Essentially, the law pushed tariffs so high that few people could afford to buy imported goods.

In a few cases, punitive tariffs have been established to punish specific countries for actions our government did not approve of. In 1987 the United States put a special tariff on Japanese computer chips because we believed that the Japanese firms had been selling them below cost in the United States, hurting American producers. Tariffs today are lower than at many times in history, but they still represent a barrier to trade.

Vocabulary Builder

Barrier to trade   Obstacle to free trade, such as a tariff or quota.

Quota   A fixed limit on the importing or exporting of a product.

Specialization   Producing a good or service for which a person, business, or nation is particularly well suited.

The Global Consumer

Free Trade in North America

In the spring of 1991 President Bush spoke in favor of creating a free trade agreement between the United States, Canada, and Mexico. He suggested gradually eliminating tariffs on goods and services traded between these nations. Under his plan, businesses in each country would have been allowed to offer their products for sale in either of the other nations without paying a tax when the products crossed international boundaries. President Bush said that this would create new jobs in the United States because Mexicans would earn more income from selling products like clothing and shoes to the United States and Canada. He believed that this income would allow Mexicans to buy more products made in this country.

Producing products like clothing requires workers to use relatively limited skills and training and a limited investment in tools and machinery. This type of production is well suited to Mexico, which has many poorly skilled workers who are willing to accept low wages by U.S. standards. Some Mexican firms have been willing to break child labor laws and employ children at low wages to produce clothing and shoes. Most Mexican firms use many workers because they lack the money to invest in machines that could reduce their need for labor.

Leaders of the American labor movement (unions) argued against the plan, stating that it would cause many U.S. employees to lose their jobs and would encourage taking advantage of lower-paid workers in Mexico. President Bush's position was that most of these jobs would be lost in any case because of lower-priced imported goods. He said that if his plan was implemented, many U.S. workers would be able to find new jobs that would pay higher wages. Union leaders replied that most of the people who would gain employment from exported U.S. goods would be different individuals than those who lost jobs because of lower Mexican wages. These leaders believed that industrial workers would be harmed while the more skilled upper-income workers would benefit.

Which point of view do you believe is probably correct?

Would you be willing to buy American-made garments at prices that were higher than the prices of Mexican-made goods?

Do you believe that Americans should be concerned about the exploitation of workers and children in other countries?

What do you think a responsible consumer should do?

Quotas

Quotas are maximum limits on the quantity of a particular type of product that may be imported into a nation. Quotas are intended to fill a **domestic** shortage of a product while maintaining a desired price level. Suppose that a country's farmers produce sugar, but not as much as its people want to buy at the present price. If there were no imports, shortages of sugar would occur and force the price of sugar to go up. But if the government allowed an un-limited quantity of sugar to be imported, there would be a surplus that would cause the price to fall, hurting the farmers. To solve this problem, the government sets a quota to allow just enough sugar to be imported to fill the domestic shortage at the current price and prevent both price increases and decreases.

The use of quotas requires the government to estimate both domestic demand and domestic supply of the product. This is not easy to do. For example, when farm products are involved, production depends on rainfall and

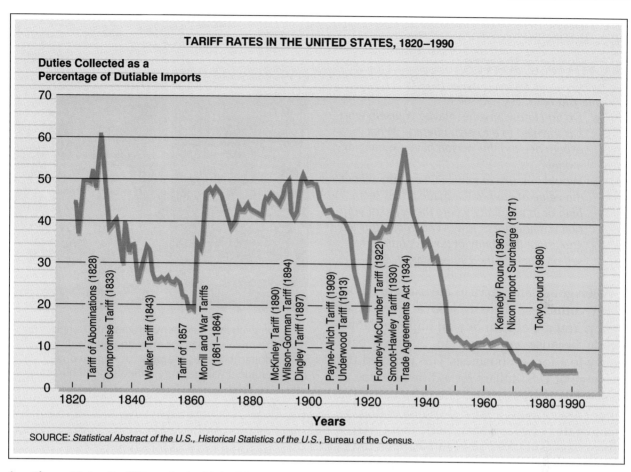

TARIFF RATES IN THE UNITED STATES, 1820–1990

SOURCE: *Statistical Abstract of the U.S., Historical Statistics of the U.S.,* Bureau of the Census.

Figure 10-1   Tariff Rates in the United States, 1820–1990

other weather conditions. There is no way for a government to know in April if there will be a good harvest in September. Therefore, the government can't know how much of any crop will be supplied.

Changes in demand happen when there are changes in economic conditions. Consumer demand for almost all products, including imported goods, will fall in a recession. There is no way for a government to be sure what the economic conditions will be like in the future. For these reasons, it is difficult for a government to accurately predict the size of a domestic shortage. Although quotas are used by many countries as barriers to trade, they are not always used successfully.

Summing Up   *Countries have established tariffs and quotas as barriers to trade. Tariffs may be used to raise revenue, protect industries, or punish other nations. Quotas are generally intended to help maintain a desired price level.* ◆

Vocabulary Builder

Domestic   A good or service that is made within the country in which it is sold.

SECTION 3

EXCHANGE RATES

While you read, ask yourself . . .

◆ *Do you know anyone (maybe yourself) who has traveled to a foreign country? What experience did this person have exchanging money?*

◆ *Would you like to travel in a country where the value of your dollar made prices seem high or in a country where the value of your dollar made prices low? What might this tell you about the ability of these countries to sell products to the United States?*

When goods and services are exchanged between countries, there is also a transfer of money. You are able to buy an imported automobile because an American business paid money to a foreign business. This required the exchange of U.S. dollars for a different type of money, like marks or yen. The price you must pay for any imported good depends on the **exchange rate** between dollars and other types of money. The same type of events happen when Americans sell products to other nations. If American oranges are exported to Japan, the Japanese importer must convert yen into dollars to pay the American exporter. The price of the fruit to the Japanese firm depends on the exchange rate between the dollar and the yen. It is impossible to study trade in a meaningful way without considering exchanges rates.

Fixed Exchange Rates

From 1944 to the early 1970s, the relative values of different types of money were set through a **fixed exchange rate** system. Under this system there was a specific value for each nation's currency in terms of other types of money. This value did not change for extended periods of time. For nearly thirty years, most of the noncommunist developed nations used

◆ The exchange rate between currencies helps determine the price we pay for imported goods. If the value of the dollar increases the price of imported goods will be lower and it will be more difficult to sell our goods in other countries.

the fixed exchange rate system. Unfortunately, there was a problem with the system. There were unequal rates of inflation.

Countries that had high rates of inflation found it difficult to sell their products to other nations. However, citizens of these countries bought many imported goods that were less expensive than their own. As a result, countries with high rates of inflation often had a **negative balance of trade**. This means that the value of the country's imports was greater than the value of its exports.

Countries with a negative balance of trade tend to have higher rates of unemployment, less profitable businesses, lower rates of investment, less income for the government to tax, and a greater need for government social programs. Therefore, countries do not want to have a negative balance of trade. They prefer to have a **positive balance of trade**. This happens when the value of a country's exports is greater than the value of its imports. Countries

U.S. Exports and Imports of Goods and Services, 1970–1990 (Values in Millions of Dollars)			
Year	Exports	Imports	Balance of Trade
1970	$ 65,674	$ 59,901	+ $ 5,773
1975	$155,729	$132,745	+ $ 22,984
1980	$342,485	$333,360	+ $ 9,125
1982	$352,127	$349,936	+ $ 2,191
1984	$371,101	$462,818	− $ 91,717
1986	$391,958	$575,626	− $183,668
1988	$529,806	$641,698	− $111,892
1990	$648,738	$726,961	− $ 78,223

◆   **Table 10-1**   Exports and Imports 1970–1990

with a positive balance of trade tend to have less unemployment, profitable businesses, higher rates of investment, more income for the government to tax, and less need for government social programs. The only economic problem that is frequently associated with a positive balance of trade is an increase in inflation. When people from other countries buy a nation's products the extra demand may force prices up. Table 10-1 shows you the value of U.S. trade and our balance of trade in recent years.

Under the fixed exchange rate system, countries with a negative balance of trade often tried to reduce their economic problems by devaluing their currency. **Devaluation** occurred when a country lowered the value of its money in terms of other types of currencies. When a country devalued its money, foreign products seemed more expensive to its own citizens, while its own products appeared less expensive to foreigners. This usually made its balance of trade less negative, at least for a while.

Unfortunately, devaluation did not offer a long-term solution to the economic problems of countries with high rates of inflation. This was because devaluation did nothing to solve the real problem: the inflation. If the country devalued its money but its rate of inflation continued to rise, it was only a matter of time before it had a negative balance of trade again. Eventually, the fixed exchange rate system was replaced with a different system that solved some of these problems.

Vocabulary Builder

Devaluation   Lowering the value of a nation's currency in relation to other currencies by government order.

Exchange rate   The value of a nation's currency in relation to that of any other nation or to a fixed standard, such as gold.

Fixed exchange rate   A system in which a government sets the value of its currency in relation to other types of currency so there is an official exchange rate between currencies that does not change for extended periods of time.

Negative balance of trade   When the value of a country's imports is greater than the value of its exports.

Positive balance of trade   When the value of a country's imports is less than the value of its exports.

Flexible or Floating Exchange Rates

In the spring of 1973 the **flexible exchange rate** system was introduced into world money markets. Under this system, the forces of demand and supply were allowed to determine the value of different types of currencies in terms of each other. When many people wanted to trade their money for a particular type of currency, the value of that type of money would **appreciate**, or go up. Other types of money that few people wanted would **depreciate**, or go down in value. Adjustments in exchange rates were made continually by banks and other international financial institutions. This is why they were called **flexible** exchange rates.

Under a flexible exchange rate, anything that causes people to exchange different types of money will cause exchange rates to change. There are many reasons to trade one type of money for another that have little to do with foreign trade. For example, countries with higher interest rates will attract investors. In the early 1980s interest rates in the United States were higher than in many other countries. As a result, foreigners demanded dollars so that they could invest in American securities or make deposits in American banks. This forced the value of the dollar up. At the same time, the United States was seen as a safe place to invest by many people who felt that political and social problems in other countries made them too risky. When foreigners invested in the American stock market or bought American property, they traded their currency for U.S. dollars. Again, the value of the dollar appreciated.

Between 1980 and 1985, the value of the American dollar roughly doubled in terms of many other types of currencies. This made it more difficult for U.S. firms to sell products to foreign countries and encouraged Americans to buy many foreign products. As a result, by 1984 the United States had a very negative balance of trade and the economic problems that are associated with this condition.

Following 1985 the value of the U.S. dollar depreciated. Again, this happened for reasons that were not entirely caused by our prices or trade. In these years we had lower interest rates and rapid growth in our national debt. Other economic systems were being more successful, and we were having problems with our banking and savings and loans industries. All of these events made people want to hold fewer U.S. dollars. As a result, many people exchanged dollars for other types of currencies and the value of the U.S. dollar went down. The flexible exchange rate system is a better system than the fixed exchange rate system, but it is not perfect. By studying Table 10-2 you can see how the value of the dollar compared to other types of money changed in recent years.

Summing Up   *Foreign trade requires people and businesses to exchange different types of currency. In recent years exchange rates for most currencies have been set by demand and supply. Any factor that causes people to demand more or less of a type of currency will affect its exchange rate.* ◆

SECTION 4

FOREIGN TRADE AND THE RESPONSIBLE CONSUMER

While you read, *ask yourself . . .*
- ◆ *Do believe it is important to buy American-made products whenever you can?*
- ◆ *How much more would you be willing to pay for an American-made pair of shoes than for an imported pair of similar quality?*

Percentage Changes in the Value of Currencies From Their Values in Terms of the U.S. Dollar in 1980				
Year	Franc (France)	Yen (Japan)	Lira (Italy)	Mark (Germany)	Pound (Great Britain)
1980	$0.226	$0.004	$0.0012	$ 0.55	$ 2.32
1981	–18.5%	+2.6%	–25.0%	–20.0%	–12.9%
1982	–32.7%	–9.9%	–41.7%	–24.6%	–25.0%
1983	–42.0%	–4.8%	–41.7%	–29.1%	–34.5%
1984	–49.1%	–4.8%	–50.0%	–36.4%	–42.2%
1985	–50.9%	–4.9%	–58.2%	–38.1%	–44.4%
1986	–36.3%	+36.2%	–41.7%	–16.4%	–36.6%
1987	–26.5%	+56.7%	–33.3%	+ 1.8%	–29.3%
1988	–25.7%	+76.8%	–33.3%	+ 3.6%	–23.3%
1989	–33.8%	+64.1%	–37.6%	– 3.4%	–29.5%
1990	–22.4%	+56.6%	–28.5%	+12.4%	–23.2%

◆ **Table 10-2** Percentage Changes in Value of Currencies

Some Americans try to limit their purchases of products made in other countries. They feel that buying American products shows a sense of loyalty or patriotism toward American firms and American workers. Do you believe that this is a reasonable and responsible feeling for American consumers to have? There are arguments on both sides of this issue.

Should You "Buy American"?

When consumers buy products made in this country, they are sending a message to American manufacturers to produce more of these goods and services. Production in the United States creates jobs for American workers. The owners of American businesses will be more likely to earn profits. Increased sales of U.S. products will encourage American firms to invest in new equipment. The government finds it easier to collect taxes when people earn wages and businesses are profitable. There will also be a smaller need for government assistance when more people are employed. For these and other reasons, many Americans choose to buy products manufactured in this country.

Vocabulary Builder

Appreciation   An increase in the value of a currency under a flexible exchange rate.

Depreciation   A loss in value that occurs as a result of wear and age. A fall in the value of a nation's currency due to the forces of demand and supply.

Flexible exchange rate   System of setting the values of currencies in terms of each other according to the demand and supply for each type of money.

◆   Many people believe Americans have a duty to buy American products. Others think they should be free to buy any product they want no matter where it was made. What do you believe?

Are there reasons to buy goods and services made in other countries? Individual consumers often pay lower prices for imported goods and may receive higher-quality products for their money. For example, statistics prepared by *Consumers' Report* consistently rank automobiles manufactured in Japan as amount the most reliable that consumers could buy. Most American-made automobiles are ranked significantly lower.

Should Americans buy products that may be less reliable simply because they were made in this country? Some people would say yes, but sales figures show that many Americans do not feel this way. Over 2 million foreign automobiles were sold in the United States in 1990.

The consumers who bought these automobiles may have felt that the price of the foreign-made product was lower or that the quality was better than similar American-made cars. It is clear from their choices that they believed that they would be better off owning an imported product.

Consumers who buy foreign-made products are sending messages too. They tell foreign manufacturers to produce more products. Part of the money they spend stays in the United States to pay the dealers and American workers who prepare and deliver the foreign-made goods, but a larger part of their money is paid to the foreign firms that produce the products.

Can Our Economy Benefit When We Buy Imports?

Some people believe that our economic system will work better when American consumers buy foreign-made products. They say that Americans have more money left over to spend on other goods when they buy foreign products that have lower prices or that last longer. Others believe that competition from foreign manufacturers has forced American firms to invest in new technology and to be more efficient.

Some Americans say that it is inefficient for skilled workers in this country to do jobs that could be done cheaper by people in foreign nations. If foreign workers do jobs that require less skill, American workers may be able to do jobs that require higher skills and are better paid.

Other people believe that trying to keep jobs in this country when they can be done at lower costs in other countries is useless. They believe that sooner or later these jobs will leave the United States. They suggest that we should use our time and resources to find new types of work that we are able to do better.

In some cases it is impossible for consumers to buy American-made products. There are many goods that Americans want to buy that are not made in this country. For example, it is difficult or impossible to buy a VCR or video camera that was manufactured in the United States. When Americans want these products, they must buy imported goods.

All of these arguments probably sound weak to an American worker who is unemployed. But it is worth considering all points of view.

Individual consumers need to examine their values and the benefits and costs of alternatives before making a decision to buy domestic or imported goods. In this way we can be responsible citizens and consumers.

Consumer News

What's Dumping?

How would you feel if you could buy a product for less than other people had to pay to buy the same good? You'd probably think you had a good deal. However, there are laws against selling products in foreign countries for less than a firm charges consumers in its own country. This practice is called "dumping."

You might wonder why a firm would want to "dump" its products at low prices in other countries. There are several possible reasons. Dumping may be an attempt to destroy competing firms in other countries with the intention of raising prices later. It may also be done because local laws require firms to pay workers whether they produce products or not. It can be cheaper to sell products at low prices than have workers do nothing.

In 1990 Lorenzo Zambrano, owner of the Mexican cement company Cemex, was accused of dumping cement in the American market to destroy American cement producers. In August of 1990, a 58 percent tax was placed on Zambrano's cement. The result was higher prices for cement for American consumers.

Do you believe that this was a correct decision for the U.S. government to make?

Summing Up *There is little agreement about the benefits and costs of buying American-made products instead of those produced in other countries. Regardless of your personal feelings, it appears that trade will continue to grow and the U.S. economy will become more dependent on foreign nations.* ◆

Review and Enrichment Activities

VOCABULARY REVIEW

1. Column A contains key consumer terms from this chapter. Column B contains a scrambled list of phrases that describe what these terms mean. Match the correct meaning with each term. Write your answers on a separate sheet of paper.

Column A	Column B
1. Specialization	a. When the value of a currency is reduced in terms of gold and other types of money
2. Devaluation	b. When the value of a country's exports is greater than the value of its imports
3. Appreciation	c. When a country only allows some maximum amount of a product to be imported
4. Exchange rate	d. Something made within a country
5. Positive balance of trade	e. When the value of a type of money increases under a flexible exchange rate
6. Import	f. A good or service sold to an individual or group in another country
7. Negative balance of trade	g. Producing a product that a person or a nation is particularly well suited to
8. Quota	h. The value of a nation's currency in relation to other nations' currencies
9. Export	i. When the value of a country's imports is greater than the value of its exports
10. Domestic	j. A good or service purchased from an individual or group in another country

2. Explain how the value of a type of currency would be set under a fixed exchange rate and how it would be set under a flexible exchange rate.

CHECKING WHAT YOU'VE LEARNED

Write your answers for the following exercises on a separate sheet of paper.

1. Explain why nations benefit when they trade with each other.
2. What are three reasons why a country might establish tariffs?
3. Explain what a quota is and why countries establish quotas.
4. What are three advantages that a country could expect to have as the result of a positive balance of trade?
5. Explain why unequal rates of inflation resulted in problems under the fixed exchange rate system.
6. Why did countries devalue their currencies under the fixed exchange rate system? Why didn't devaluing money solve a country's negative balance of trade problems for very long?
7. What factors can cause the value of a country's money to increase under a flexible exchange rate?
8. Give two reasons why some Americans are opposed to buying foreign-made goods.
9. Give two reasons why some Americans believe that buying foreign-made goods may help the American economy.

PRACTICING YOUR CONSUMER SKILLS

Write your answers for the following exercises on a separate sheet of paper.

1. There is a mistake in each of the following statements. Identify and explain each mistake.
   a. Every person in the United States is better off because of foreign trade.
   b. The only reason we have tariffs is to collect more money for the government to spend.
   c. The value of the U.S. dollar always keeps going down.
   d. The United States has had a negative balance of trade in every year since World War II.
   e. There is no advantage for the American economy when U.S. consumers buy imported goods.
2. Between 1980 and 1985, the value of the U.S. dollar increased compared to most other types of currency in the world. Explain how this would have affected each of the following people.
   a. Steve, who owns a farm where he grows wheat that is sold in foreign nations
   b. Tammy, who wants to buy a small, fuel-efficient car
   c. Rita, who works in a factory that produces women's shoes
   d. Larry, who owns a store that sells radios, TVs, and other electronic devices
   e. Jim, who sells American-made cars for a living

3. Describe the effect that each of the following events would probably have on the value of the U.S. dollar.
   a. The rate of inflation in many other countries grows much higher than the inflation rate in the United States.
   b. The interest rates paid by banks in other nations become much higher than the rate paid by American banks.
   c. There is a drought that destroys crops in many nations, but not in the United States.
   d. There is a war in another part of the world that causes many nations to want to buy American-made weapons.
   e. There is a new tax placed on American-made goods that makes them 10 percent more expensive.

USING NUMBERS

Solve the following problem to help make the best possible choice. Write your solution on a separate sheet of paper. Be sure to show all your work.

Paula is a buyer for a small business that manufactures women's blouses. In an average year, she purchases 100,000 yards of different types of fabric that is used to produce 50,000 garments. She can buy material that was produced in foreign countries or in the United States. This year she has discovered that the domestic fabric would cost about one-third more than imported goods. The average price of domestic fabric is $4 a yard. Her employer charges a price for the blouses that is equal to $15 more than the cost of the fabric used.

a. How much less money would the firm spend by purchasing imported fabric instead of domestic fabric?
b. What average price would the firm charge for its blouses if it used domestic fabric?
c. What average price would the firm charge for its blouses if it used imported fabric?
d. Which type of fabric do you believe the firm should purchase? Explain your answer.

PUTTING IDEAS IN YOUR OWN WORDS

The following quotations are from this chapter. Explain these quotations in your own words to make sure you understand what they mean. Write your answers on a separate sheet of paper.

1. "Nations trade with each other because they do not produce all products equally well."
2. "It is impossible to study trade in a meaningful way without considering exchange rates."

3. "When consumers buy products made in this country, they are sending a message to American manufacturers to produce more of these goods and services."

BUILDING CONSUMER KNOWLEDGE

Write your answers for the following exercises on a separate sheet of paper.

1. Survey five adults about their willingness to buy imported goods. Do they feel it is a good or bad thing to do? Ask them to explain specific reasons for their opinions. Ask them to identify the brand of car they own. Is it American-made? Do they seem to follow their own beliefs when they buy goods? Be prepared to explain their comments to other members of your class.

2. Go through the clothes in your closet. Look for tags that tell where the garments were manufactured. How many of the clothes you own were made in the United States? How many were imported? Are you surprised about what you found? Explain your answer.

3. Go to a public library and ask for a recent copy of the *Wall Street Journal*. In the third section, there is a boxed feature titled "Key Currency Cross Rates." It will look like the one from July 29, 1991, shown below. The value of other currencies in terms of U.S. dollars is found in the bottom row. Compare the current values with those from 1990. Has the dollar appreciated or depreciated since 1990? How should this have affected the ability of the United States to sell its products in other countries?

Key Currency Cross Rates
Late New York Trading July 29, 1991.

	Dollar	Pound	SFranc	Guilder	Yen	Lira	D-Mark	FFranc	CdnD/r
Canada	1.1493	1.9325	.75295	.58376	.00834	.00088	.65768	.19342	.....
France	5.9420	9.991	3.8928	3.0181	.04311	.00456	3.4003	.....	5.1701
Germany	1.7475	2.9384	1.1449	.88760	.01268	.00134	.....	.29409	1.5205
Italy	1304.0	2192.7	854.32	662.35	9.46	.....	746.23	219.46	1134.6
Japan	137.84	231.78	90.304	70.012	.....	.10570	78.878	23.198	119.93
Netherlands	1.9688	3.3105	1.2898	.....	.01428	.00151	1.1266	.33134	1.7130
Switzerland	1.5264	2.5666	.....	.77529	.01107	.00117	.87348	.25688	1.3281
U.K.	.59471	.....	.38961	.30207	.00431	.00046	.34032	.10009	.51745
U.S.	.....	1.6815	.65514	.50792	.00725	.00077	.57225	.16829	.87009

Source: Telerate

UNIT 4

Consumer Issues

U nit 4 explains various issues in our economic system that directly concern consumers. This unit provides a transition from the economic topics of the first three units to consumer economics by showing how many of the earlier topics are related to problems faced by consumers. In Unit 4 you will become familiar with consumer rights and responsibilities in our economic system. You will also have an opportunity to use the decision-making process from Unit 1 to make choices that involve consumer issues.

166

Chapter 11

Consumer Rights—Consumer Responsibilities

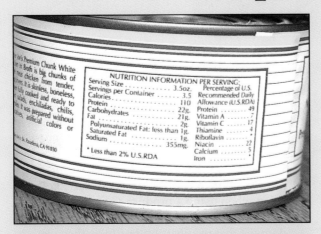

Chapter Objectives

After completing this chapter, you will be able to do the following:

- Explain the consumer rights recognized by the federal government.
- Explain the responsibilities that consumers have in our economic system.
- Explain the meaning of ethical behavior and give examples of decisions that consumers make that demonstrate ethical behavior.

Key Consumer Terms

In this chapter you will learn the meanings of the following important consumer terms:

- Redress
- Bankruptcy
- Food and Drug Administration (FDA)
- Department of Justice
- Antitrust law
- Lobby
- Acid rain
- Chlorofluorocarbon
- Consumer Product Safety Commission (CPSC)
- Claimant
- Fraud
- Ethical behavior
- Nuisance suit

A s a consumer in the U.S. economic system, you have many rights. You expect to receive fair value for your money and to be treated with honesty and respect. The rights of American consumers are protected by the government. All branches of the government help to carry out this responsibility. The legislative branch passes laws to protect consumers. The administrative branch enforces laws passed by Congress and suggests new legislation. The judicial branch interprets the law, determines responsibility, and sets punishments for those who break the law.

SECTION 1

CONSUMER RIGHTS

While you read, ask yourself . . .
- ◆ *Why do most Americans feel safe and confident when they go into a grocery store to buy foods?*
- ◆ *If you buy a product that doesn't work, what rights do you have? What organizations guarantee these rights?*

To protect your consumer rights, you need to understand what these rights are. In 1962 President John F. Kennedy sent a consumer protection program to Congress in which he called for the recognition of four fundamental consumer rights:

1. *The Right to Safety.* Goods cannot be dangerous to life or health.
2. *The Right to Be Informed.* Businesses must provide consumers with the information they need to make rational choices.
3. *The Right to Choose.* Many firms must exist in a competitive market, and the government must intervene when such competition no longer exists.
4. *The Right to Be Heard.* Consumers have a right to have their interests heard when governmental policy decisions are being made.

To these four rights, following presidents have added the following rights:

5. *The Right to a Decent Environment.* Consumers have a right to live in an environment that is not dangerous to their health.
6. *The Right to Consumer Education.* Consumers have a right to be taught skills they need to make rational choices.
7. *The Right to Reasonable **Redress**.* Consumers have a right to sue for physical damages suffered when using a product. Consumers have a right to seek fair compensation for injuries or damage that results from products they use.

Now let's consider each of these consumer rights in greater detail. Keep in mind, however, that the following sections include just a sampling of the many laws and measures that protect us.

The Right to Safety

How would you feel if there was a product in your home, your school, or your workplace that was slowing killing you? If you discovered this danger, what would you want done about it? Should the firm that manufactured and installed the product take responsibility for any harm that the product was causing? Should the manufacturer be held responsible even if it didn't know that the product was dangerous? What should the government do in this situation? This type of event is not imaginary. It happened to the Mansville Corporation and to people who lived or worked with asbestos products before the 1970s.

Asbestos is a lightweight mineral that does not burn or transmit heat easily. For many years asbestos products were used extensively as insulation and to reduce the risk of fire in buildings, ships, and other structures. Heating pipes were wrapped in asbestos. It was sprayed on metal beams in buildings to keep them from melting in case of fire. The navy used asbestos to reduce the chance of fires spreading on warships. The list goes on and on. It was impossible to live in the United States without coming in contact with asbestos products in some way.

In the 1970s asbestos was found to be carcinogenic (a cause of cancer) and the cause of a lung disease called asbestosis, similar to emphysema. The further use of asbestos in most cases was banned, but what of the thousands of structures already containing asbestos? And what of the thousands of people who were already ill or who might become ill because of their contact with asbestos?

Before the 1970s, the Mansville Corporation was the largest manufacturer of asbestos in the Western world. In 1982 it was ranked number 181 in size in *Fortune's* list of the 500 largest industrial firms in the United States. The firm was worth $1.1 billion and had annual sales of just under $1 billion. With the ban on asbestos products, Mansville changed its business to the production of fiberglass and other building products. However, it still had a responsibility for the asbestos it had produced and sold in previous years. Thousands of suits were filed against Mansville for both property damage and health problems. Mansville determined that these cases could eventually result in costs of over $2 billion. Although Mansville earned $60 million in profits in 1982, the firm filed for **bankruptcy** on August 27, 1982, to halt the legal proceedings against it until a plan to reorganize could be approved by a court.

A plan to resolve the asbestos claims was approved in 1986. Between 1982 and 1986 almost no claims were paid by Mansville, leaving indi-

When asbestos was found to be carcinogenic it was often removed from buildings. Later it was found that this could release the material into the air. Why is finding the safest decision often difficult?

viduals, businesses, and the government to deal with the problems of asbestos as best they could. In the 1986 plan, Mansville agreed to set up a fund that would eventually total $2.5 billion to pay claims against the firm. The initial fund would start with $615 million from insurance companies, $200 million from Mansville and half of Mansville's corporate stock. Starting in 1990, Mansville was required to pay an additional $75 million plus 20 percent of its profits into the fund each year. In exchange, Mansville

Vocabulary Builder

Bankruptcy   An inability to pay debts based on an individual's or firm's wealth and income.
Redress   The right to seek and obtain satisfaction for damages through legal action.

was given the right to emerge from bankruptcy and continue to operate as a business.

Four years later the fund was almost out of money, and only 22,000 of 150,000 claims had been paid. Although the average amount asked for in each case was almost $800,000, the average settlement had been $43,000. The costs to the victims far exceeded the amount of the settlements in most cases. In fact, many of the victims were dead.

There is no end in sight to the asbestos problem. The diseases caused by asbestos take twenty to forty years to appear in the victims. There will continue to be new cases of cancer and asbestosis appearing well into the twenty-first century.

The Right to Be Informed

In past years you might have gone into a grocery store and bought "light" food products only to discover that they had 65 calories per tablespoon. No one knew what terms like *low fat*, *low sodium*, or *reduced calories* meant. Until 1990 these words had no standard meaning. Manufacturers could use them as they saw fit. Many consumers were misled into buying foods that they believed were healthy but that really weren't good for them.

People's health often depends on their knowing what is in the food they eat. People who are diabetic must avoid sugar and excessive amounts of fat. People with circulatory diseases need to avoid sodium. People with heart problems should avoid eating foods with high cholesterol or saturated fats. When food products didn't have labels listing ingredients and nutritional values, it was hard for people with medical conditions to know which products they could safely consume and which they couldn't.

In 1990 the federal government passed legislation that went a long way toward solving problems related to inadequate product labels.

On July 12, 1990, the secretary of Health and Human Services, Louis W. Sullivan, announced a proposal from the **Food and Drug Administration (FDA)** to require labeling that would clarify and standardize nutritional information on packaged foods. As a direct result of this FDA proposal, the House of Representatives and Senate passed legislation that required food packages to provide the calories, fat, saturated fat, cholesterol, fiber, sodium, sugar, protein, and total carbohydrates per serving. Serving sizes were also established for 159 types of food. The secretary of Health and Human Services was given the power to devise standards for the meaning of the words *light* and *low fat*. On November 9, 1990, this bill was signed into law by President Bush. Now when you pick up a box of food from a shelf in a grocery store, you can tell what is in it and whether it is something you should choose to buy and eat.

The Right to Choose

Suppose that you are completing your senior year in high school. Your grades have been exceptionally good, you are president of the student council and the French club. You were the leading scorer on the school basketball team and won the all-city debating contest.

You have been accepted at several well-known universities. The only problem is that you need financial aid to attend any private school. Your parents can afford to pay only $5,000 a year. They don't have a large income, and you have five brothers and sisters at home. The colleges that you applied to charge tuition that is between $13,150 and $19,310 a year plus room and board. You may see the average yearly costs for public and private colleges in the 1980s in Table 11-1. When you received your acceptance letters, you discovered that each school offered you financial aid. To your surprise, the final cost for each school was

Average Yearly Cost For Tuition, Fees, and Books Public and Private Colleges 1980–1990		
Year	**Public Four Year College**	**Private Four Year College**
1980	$ 840	$3,811
1981	$ 915	$4,275
1982	$1,042	$4,887
1983	$1,164	$5,583
1984	$1,284	$6,217
1985	$1,386	$6,843
1986	$1,536	$7,344
1987	$1,651	$8,118
1988	$1,750	$8,770
1989	$1,846	$9,451
1990	$2,006	$10,400
Statistical Abstract of the United States, 1990, p. 160		

◆ **Table 11-1**   Average Yearly College Costs

within $50 one way or the other of $5,000. Something seems a little "fishy" to you, but you are getting ready to attend the college that offers the academic program you like best.

Events like this really did take place for almost thirty years in the United States. Since the 1950s, twenty three top-name colleges and universities sent representatives to a special meeting twice each year. The purpose of the meeting was to screen top college candidates and compare financial aid information. To apply for financial aid, students were required to provide information about their family's financial condition. Some people suggested that the meetings were held to decide what each student's family could afford to pay. The schools would then offer enough aid to bring the cost of tuition down to that amount, regardless of what school the student chose to attend. As a result, thousands of the nation's best students ended up with no real choice in the cost of their education.

This practice of the colleges became public knowledge in August 1989, when the **Department of Justice** announced that it was investigating the schools for possible violation of **antitrust laws** (laws intended to limit the monopoly powers of businesses). Representatives of the colleges said that their meetings were intended to avoid damaging "bidding wars" for the best students. It is possible that a result of this practice was reduced financial aid and

Vocabulary Builder

Antitrust law   Legislation that prohibits attempts to monopolize or dominate a particular market.
Department of Justice   To Come
Food and Drug Administration (FDA)   Federal agency responsible for administering federal laws that regulate the quality of foods and drugs offered for sale.

Consumer News

FDA Sets New Label Standards

The labeling bill signed into law by President Bush in 1990 gave the Food and Drug Administration the power to establish standard definitions for terms used on food labels. On November 6, 1991, the FDA announced the following definitions that food manufacturers must follow.

- **Free:** Less than five calories; less than 0.5 grams of sugar; less than 5 milligrams of sodium; less than 0.5 grams of fat; less than 2 milligrams of cholesterol and 2 grams of saturated fat—each per serving.
- **Low:** Less than 140 milligrams of sodium; less than 40 calories; 3 grams or less of fat; 1 gram or less of saturated fat and not more than 15 percent of calories from saturated fat; 20 milligrams or less of cholesterol and 2 grams or less of saturated fat—each per 100 grams of food.

- **High**: Benefits the consumer by providing more than 20 percent of the amount recommended for daily eating, as in high-fiber.
- **Source of**: Beneficial because it provides 10 percent to 19 percent of the amount of the nutrient recommended to be eaten each day.
- **Reduced**: One third the calories; half or less the sodium, fat, saturated fat or cholesterol.
- **Less:** 25 percent or less the sodium, calories, fat, saturated fat or cholesterol.
- **Light:** One third fewer calories. Any other use of the term must specify that it is a reference to look, taste or smell, as in "light in color."
- **More:** At least 10 percent more of the nutrient, as in "more fiber," "more potassium."
- **Fresh**: Raw food. Never frozen, processed or preserved.

   How may these standard definitions make it easier for consumers to make responsible choices?

greater college costs for our nation's best students. Despite protests that they had done nothing wrong, Yale University and Barnard College stopped participating in the meetings in 1990. The meetings were not held at all in 1991 to show a "spirit of cooperation" with the government investigation.

The Right to Be Heard

Do you believe that Americans have the right to own and bear arms? The Second Amendment to the U.S. Constitution reads, "A well-regulated militia being necessary to the security of a free state, the right of the people to keep and bear arms shall not be infringed." Do you suppose that those who added the Bill of Rights to the Constitution in 1791 ever imaged that the Second Amendment would cover the right to own assault rifles or to buy "Saturday night specials"? Times and weapons have changed in the past 200 years. The meaning of the Second Amendment is now the topic of wide debate.

Legislation known as the Brady Bill was introduced into Congress in 1991. This bill would have required a seven-day waiting period for people who wanted to buy a handgun. Lines were drawn between those who support-

◆   Many Americans have trouble understanding their rights. They may believe they have a right to own and drive a car and the right to a clean environment. Why is it difficult to protect all our rights?

ed the legislation and those who opposed it. **Lobbies** pressured members of Congress on both sides of the issue. Supporters of the legislation said that the waiting period would make it more difficult for criminals to acquire weapons that could be used against innocent victims. Honest citizens would be willing to wait a week while their identity was checked.

Those who opposed the bill argued that it was a step down the "slippery slope" leading to identification of gun owners and to possible confiscation of their arms. Others felt that the law would have little or no effect on the ability of criminals to buy guns on the streets. They argued that a computer system to instantly check the identity of gun customers was a better choice (although they admitted that such a system would take many years and millions of dollars to install).

The decision to buy a gun is a type of consumer decision. Americans have demonstrated their right to be heard as they tried to influence the Brady Bill and other gun control legislation. Regardless of which side you take on this issue, you have the right to be heard.

Vocabulary Builder

Lobby Special-interest group that pressures members of Congress to vote for or against legislation that would support the group's point of view or benefit the group.

The Right to a Decent Environment

How much is clean air worth to you? In 1991 citizens of Mexico City, one of the most polluted cities in the world, could stop at sidewalk booths and pay $1.50 to breathe pure oxygen for 1 minute. Sales were brisk. The air in most areas of the United States is much less polluted than that in Mexico City, but our government has found it necessary to pass and enforce clean-air legislation.

President Bush signed a new Clean Air Act on November 15, 1990, declaring it "an important milestone in preserving and protecting America's natural resources." The bill sets standards for air pollution that will result in an estimated $30 billion annual cost to American businesses. Some people believe that the cost of the bill will exceed the value of any benefits resulting from it. Others say that the eventual costs of not improving air standards would be much greater in terms of health care and environmental damage. The legislation concentrated on setting standards that would improve the quality of air in cities where the problem was the greatest. A number of objectives were set, including the following:

1. By 1994 automobile tailpipe exhaust must contain 60 percent less nitrogen oxide and 40 percent fewer hydrocarbons, and the emission control equipment must last ten years or 100,000 miles.
2. By 1995 only cleaner-burning gasoline can be sold in the smoggiest metropolitan areas.
3. An effort will be made in California to produce and sell vehicles that use cleaner-burning methanol.
4. Electric utilities will be required to reduce smokestack emissions of sulfur dioxide and nitrogen oxide by 50 percent to reduce the **acid rain** in the Northeast.
5. Factories that emit cancer-causing substances into the air must install the best available equipment to reduce the emission of toxic chemicals by 90 percent by the year 2003.
6. Production of **chlorofluorocarbons**, which are linked to the destruction of the earth's ozone layer, must end by the year 2000.

These standards will increase the costs of production to the nation's businesses and will be passed on to consumers in higher prices. It is estimated that one effect of the new law will be to increase the cost of owning and operating an automobile by an average of about $1,200, or 20 percent, a year. Also, the costs will not be evenly distributed. People who live in rural areas will pay less than those who live in cities with a smog problem.

The Right to Consumer Education

The government's performance in providing adequate consumer education has met with mixed reviews. During the 1960s and 1970s Congress passed many laws and established federal agencies intended to help protect consumers' rights and provide information to consumers that allow them to make better decisions. Among the agencies was the Office of Consumer Education (OCE). This office provided printed materials to consumers to help them make better choices.

Under the Reagan administration in the 1980s, the OCE was phased out through budget cuts. Some of its responsibilities were taken over by other government agencies, such as the **Consumer Product Safety Commission (CPSC)**. These other agencies also received reduced financial support from the government in the 1980s.

The federal government took a less active role in consumer education and protection in the 1980s than it had in the 1960s and 1970s. State and local governments, our schools, and private organizations took on more of this responsibility.

Consumer News

The CPSC and Safe Toys

The CPSC sets and enforces standards for toys with small parts and sharp points and edges and checks for levels of lead in paints. It also carries out public information campaigns to inform consumers of which toys are safe for different-age children. It investigates consumer complaints and reports of toy-related injuries and deaths. When a dangerous toy is found on the market, the CPSC issues a press release to alert retailers and consumers. Such press releases often lead to product recalls by manufacturers and stores to avoid possible law suits. For example, in 1990, the F. J. Strauss Company voluntarily recalled roughly 3,600 "Music Maker" toys because of excessive levels of lead and too many small parts that could be swallowed.

With the enormous number of new toys brought to market each year, the CPSC may not be able to stop all dangerous toys from reaching toy stores. To reduce this problem, the CPSC and U.S. Customs Service jointly undertook "Operation Toyland" in 1987. Through this program, shipments of toys are inspected as they enter the United States. In 1990 roughly 1.1 million toys with a value of $4.7 million were prevented from entering this country. This program also discourages firms from trying to import and sell dangerous toys.

Federal involvement in consumer education began to grow again after President Bush took office in 1989. Funding for the CPSC and other federal agencies has increased. Leadership of the agencies has been more aggressive in its pursuit of businesses that mislead or harm consumers. Although the federal government appears to be taking a more active role in consumer education, individual consumers are still responsible for their own decisions and for their own education. You will learn more about government consumer protection agencies in Chapters 12 and 13.

The Right to Reasonable Redress

When you buy a product from a well-known and respected manufacturer, you probably expect it to be safe and reliable. How would you feel if you bought an automobile and later found that similar automobiles had been known to catch fire when they were involved in an accident? This happened to many American consumers when they bought not one, but many different models of vehicles.

Probably the best-known case involved the Pinto, a small economy car manufactured by the Ford Motor Company in the late 1960s and

Vocabulary Builder

Chlorofluorocarbon Any of a group of chemicals used in many products that contribute to the depletion of the earth's ozone layer.
Consumer Product Safety Commission A federal agency that regulates all potentially hazardous consumer products.

Consumer News

The Supreme Court and Punitive Damages

Punitive damages are awarded by courts to people who have been harmed by a product as a way of punishing a firm that is sued and found guilty of negligence. Juries in the 1970s and 1980s awarded larger and larger punitive damage settlements, reaching amounts in the hundreds of millions of dollars.

In 1990 a case involving punitive damages reached the U.S. Supreme Court. Pat Haslip, an employee of Roosevelt City, Alabama, had paid for health insurance, but her agent had kept her payments and held back her cancellation notices from the company. When she became ill, the company refused to pay her bills, saying that they were not responsible for the actions of their agent. Haslip sued for her $4,000 in medical bills and for $1 million in punitive damages for destroying her credit record. On March 4, 1991, the Supreme Court ruled in her favor, upholding the $1 million judgment of a lower court. In so doing, the Court also upheld the concept of punitive damages as a means of encouraging firms to be more careful in how they treat consumers.

early 1970s. The Pinto's gas tank was in a location that increased the possibility of rupture when the car was struck from behind in a collision. Many people were killed in such accidents, and even more were seriously injured as a result of fires. Ford was sued by hundreds of people and by the families of people who were killed in accidents involving Pintos. Although the company denied responsibility, courts awarded **claimants** judgments that were as large as $10 million.

Summing Up *The government has identified many consumer rights and has passed laws intended to protect those rights. However, each consumer needs to take responsibility to protect his or her own rights by making responsible consumer decisions.* ◆

SECTION 2

CONSUMER RESPONSIBILITIES

While you read, ask yourself . . .
- ◆ *What are several ways that you take responsibility in making consumer choices?*
- ◆ *What would happen to our economic system and the freedoms we enjoy if most people chose not to be responsible consumers?*

As consumers we enjoy certain rights in our economic system. But we must also act responsibly for our economic and legal systems to work efficiently. Here are several important consumer responsibilities:

1. *The Responsibility to Use Products Safely.* Consumers should use products as they were meant to be used and follow instructions carefully.
2. *The Responsibility to Learn.* Consumers should look for information about products that they plan to buy and should use that information to compare and evaluate different brands and models.
3. *The Responsibility to Give Correct Information.* Consumers should give accurate information.
4. *The Responsibility to Seek Redress.* Consumers should report defective goods and let businesses know when goods and services do not measure up to their expectations. They should report wrong doing in consumer dealings to the appropriate government agencies.

◆   Many tools can be dangerous if they are not used properly. Why should you always read and follow the instructions for products you buy?

The Responsibility to Use Products Safely

How many times have you purchased a product and not bothered to read the instruction manual? If the instructions concern the proper way to make instant mashed potatoes, your decision not to read them probably makes little difference. However, if you buy a table saw, pressure cooker, electric generator, or new brake shoes for your car, you could be in serious trouble if you fail to follow the manufacturer's directions.

We live in a free society. It would be impossible for the government or manufacturers to keep track of how we use all of the products we buy and use. For example, in the early 1980s leaded gasoline was less expensive than

Vocabulary Builder

Claimant   The person who sues someone else in a court of law.

unleaded. Many consumers put leaded gasoline in their cars to save money. In so doing, they destroyed the pollution control devices in their exhaust systems, causing the cars to release dangerous chemicals into the air whenever they were driven. Manufacturers fulfilled their responsibility to build cars that created less pollution, but some consumers prevented the pollution control devices from working to save a few pennies. Consumers must fulfill their responsibilities—including the responsibility to use products in the manner they were intended to be used.

The Responsibility to Learn

One of the skills that responsible consumers need is the ability to read with understanding. Consumers need this skill so they can understand how to use products safely. Over your lifetime the kinds of products you use will change. The day may come when you toast your bread in a laser oven or heat your home with a fusion furnace. These ideas seem farfetched now, but fifty years ago microwave ovens and VCRs would have seemed out of the question.

As new products become available, consumers will need to learn how to use them properly. They are less likely to be harmed if they read the instructions provided with new products before trying them. Do you know anyone who has tried to cook an egg in a microwave oven? It tends to make a mess. If consumers read the instructions provided with microwave ovens, they will know not to do this.

Exploding an egg in a microwave probably won't hurt anyone, but not venting a new furnace properly can cause people to die from carbon monoxide poisoning. Manufacturers must provide adequate instructions with the products they produce and sell, but they can't make consumers read them. Consumers have a responsibility to learn many things—including how to use products properly and safely.

The Responsibility to Give Correct Information

When you go to an amusement park, you see signs that say that people with heart disease should not go on certain rides. If a consumer with heart disease chooses to go on such a ride and suffers a heart attack, it is not reasonable to hold the amusement park responsible.

As you grow older, you will need to make different types of consumer decisions. To buy a car or house, to obtain credit, and to complete many other transactions, you will be required to provide certain kinds of information. At some point, you will probably file a claim with an insurance company. You will be asked to provide information about the claim. As a responsible consumer, you should give complete and correct information so that you and other consumers may be treated fairly.

Some people have the attitude that they aren't hurting anyone when they cheat businesses by making false claims. However, false claims cost businesses money, and that money comes from sales made to other consumers. Suppose that Joe says that a $500 set of golf clubs was in his car when it was stolen. However, Joe never owned any golf clubs. He just wanted a larger settlement from the insurance company. This sort of behavior is called **fraud** and is against the law. Fraud increases the cost of doing business for insurance companies. The higher a firm's costs, the more it must charge its customers. When one customer cheats a business, other customers pay. Consumers have a responsibility to provide correct information to the businesses they deal with.

The Responsibility to Seek Redress

When a firm provides inferior products, its customers have a responsibility to tell the firm that they are not satisfied. The owners of such a business should be given the chance to correct a problem that they may not have been aware of. Providing this sort of information to a manufacturer is particularly important if there is a chance of personal injury resulting from the product. If you receive a shock from a defective iron, you should inform the firm so that it can warn other customers who have purchased the product.

If the firm refuses to correct a problem, the consumer also has a responsibility to report the problem to an appropriate authority. This may be a private organization like the Better Business Bureau or a government agency. Then again, the situation may require legal action. Letting a problem "slide" means that someone else will probably experience the same problem. Responsible consumers should realize that their actions will affect the relationship that all consumers have with businesses. They have a responsibility to seek legal **redress** when necessary.

Summing Up *Consumers should be responsible for their decisions. They should read product instructions, use products properly, provide accurate information, and seek redress when they have not received the quality of good or service they were promised.* ◆

SECTION 3

ETHICAL BEHAVIOR

While you read, ask yourself . . .
◆ *What are several ethical decisions you have made recently?*
◆ *What are several unethical decisions that have been made by others? What was the impact of these decisions on other people?*

Ethical behavior means acting in accordance with one's moral convictions as to what is right and what is wrong. Many commonly held ethical convictions are written into our laws. But ethical behavior requires more than just obeying laws merely because we don't want to get caught breaking them.

All consumers make decisions that involve ethical behavior. Sometimes people have an opportunity to break the law and not be discovered. Suppose that you use the automated teller machine (ATM) at your local bank. You punch in your code, put your card in the slot, and request $100 from your account. To your amazement, instead of giving you $100, the machine gives you $1,000. You also receive a receipt charging your account with a $100 withdrawal. There are hundreds of other people who will use the machine. There is no way for the bank to trace the extra $900 to you. You have the opportunity to gain 900 "free" dollars. If you don't tell the bank about the mistake, you are breaking the law, but you almost certainly will not be caught. What would you do in such a situation?

A more common ethical dilemma occurs when you are not billed correctly by a clerk in a store. At one time or another, almost everyone has been charged the wrong price for a product. If you are charged too much, you probably complain loudly. But if you are charged too little, what do you do? Suppose that you are in a grocery store and you are buy-

Vocabulary Builder

Ethical behavior Acting in accordance with one's moral convictions as to what is right and what is wrong.

Fraud Providing incorrect information for the purpose of obtaining payments one does not deserve.

Redress The right to seek and obtain satisfaction for damages through legal action.

Consumers in Action

Shopping at Smokin Joe's

If you could find a store that offered very low prices for the products you buy, would you shop there? Most people probably would. But you might ask yourself: "Why are the prices so low? Is there something going on here that's against the law?" For many people living in upstate New York in 1991, this was a real situation.

Federal law recognizes native American tribes as being independent nations. Native Americans do not have to pay federal, state, or local taxes on money earned on their reservations. In the 1980s native Americans opened stores on their reservations, where they paid and collected no tax. But many of these stores appeared to be intended less for native American consumers than for people who weren't native Americans but were able to enter the reservations and purchase goods at lower prices.

One such store was Smokin Joe's, on the Tuscarora Reservation in Niagara County, New York. Joe sold regular unleaded gasoline for 99.9 cents a gallon when gas stations only 2 miles away charged $1.219. The difference in the price was the federal and state gas tax that Joe didn't collect. Joe also sold cigarettes, gold, and many other items at much lower prices than stores off the reservation. Joe's business was booming. Lines 30 or 40 cars long were often found at his pumps. His store overflowed with people looking for a bargain. You could hardly blame these consumers. Or could you?

A consumer buying gasoline from Joe was benefiting from paying a low price. On the other hand, Joe was making a profit by taking advantage of a loophole in the law. The treaties signed by the federal government and the native American leaders were never intended to give the general public a way to avoid paying their fair share of the taxes that support our government. When the federal, state, and local governments lost tax revenue from people who shopped at Joe's, other taxpayers had to pay more than their share of the tax burden. Merchants in surrounding areas experienced lower sales and profits because of a situation that was beyond their control. When Joe earned more profit, other entrepreneurs earned less. Was this fair?

Consumers who shopped at Joe's probably were not breaking any laws.

Do you believe that they were being ethical? Should consumers take advantage of loopholes to avoid taxes?

What would you do if you were in this situation?

ing two bottles of soda pop. As you check out, the clerk only rings up one. You have been given one bottle for "free." Do you say something to the clerk or do you keep quiet? Would your decision be different if you didn't discover the mistake until you got home? Then you would have to go back to the store and explain what happened. This would cost you time and effort, and you had no intention of taking anything without paying for it. Do you think, "The store can afford it"? What is the right thing to do?

When faced with an ethical consumer decision, try to remember that someone always has to pay. If you receive something of value for "free," others are receiving less value than they should. It may be the owners of a store, the workers, an insurance company, or the government. All businesses and the government receive their money in one way or another from people. If you get something for "free," the store will have to charge other customers more or its owners will earn less profit. There is no such thing as getting something for nothing. Somebody always pays.

There are many ways for consumers to demonstrate ethical or unethical behavior.

Making false claims under warranties is a common event. Suppose that Jayson buys a large air conditioner and plans to install it in a rear window of his home. The air conditioner weighs about 200 pounds, so Jayson uses a wheelbarrow to bring it around to the back of his house. Suddenly Jayson hits a rock, and the wheelbarrow tips over. The air conditioner is still in its box, but Jayson is worried. He carefully opens the box. Just as he suspected, the case is now bent and a fan has been pushed into a cooling coil. Jayson closes the box and takes the air conditioner back to the dealer. He says that it was defective when he received it. Jayson is given a new air conditioner and is

more careful this time. His behavior is clearly unethical. However, he tells himself: "The $599 that the air conditioner cost means very little to the firm that made it. But I would have to work for almost two weeks to earn that much money. They should pay because they can afford to, and I can't."

What Jayson is overlooking is the long-term consequences of his behavior. In the short run, the manufacturer of the air conditioner will pay for Jayson's carelessness. But in the long run, other consumers will pay as the firm is forced to raise its prices to cover the cost of Jayson's dishonesty and that of other consumers. It take little imagination to picture the dozens of ways that consumers can behave dishonestly or unethically to gain personal benefit at the expense of others.

Unethical behavior can be seen in other situations. Airlines and hotels often have reduced charges for children. Suppose that a friend of yours is traveling with his parents. They stop at a hotel that allows children sixteen or under to stay for free. Your friend is seventeen years old. The hotel would charge an extra $5 a night for your friend, but his father says that he is fifteen years old and "big for his age." Is your friend's father doing anything wrong? What would you do in a similar situation?

Suppose that Wilma is walking down an aisle in a discount store, talking to her friend Clair. Wilma is so busy talking that she doesn't look where she's going. She walks right into a stack of paint cans, knocking them down. One of the cans lands on her foot. She sues the store for $5,000, although she was clearly at fault. She figures that the store has insurance, and after all, she did break her toe. Wilma thinks that someone ought to pay for her pain and suffering. In such situations, stores often settle out of court because it is less expensive than defending themselves. The store may be insured, but its premiums are likely to increase if it has many claims. **Nuisance suits** are a form of unethical behavior.

Ethical and unethical behavior can also involve perfectly legal activities. There is no law against using many types of products that can damage our environment. Spraying too much weed killer on your driveway may kill all the weeds and keep them from coming back, but all that poison goes into the environment. There may be no law against dumping old appliances, automobile tires, and discarded furniture in your backyard, but you will probably offend your neighbors. Even keeping a dog that barks at night or frightens children involves an ethical decision. At what point do your rights interfere with those of others? What is the responsible, or ethical, choice you should make?

Clearly, there is no exact formula for ethical behavior. Everyone has his or her own set of values and moral principles, and every situation is different. But it is important to remember that our behavior always affects those around us. This is true in all of our activities as family members, citizens, employers, employees and consumers. Ethical decision making involves becoming aware of how our behavior affects others and evaluating whether these consequences are desirable. This is something that all individuals must decide for themselves.

Summing Up *The meaning of ethical behavior for each consumer depends on his or her individual values. However, all consumers should realize that their choices affect other people and future generations. Consumers need to learn not to be self-centered and shortsighted when they make their consumer decisions.* ◆

Vocabulary Builder

Nuisance suit A suit filed for the purpose of bothering a person or organization rather than for redress of a grievance.

Review and Enrichment Activities

VOCABULARY REVIEW

1. Column A contains key consumer terms from this chapter. Column B contains a scrambled list of phrases that describe what these terms mean. Match the correct meaning with each term. Write your answers on a separate sheet of paper.

Column A	Column B
1. lobby	a. an agency of the government charged with evaluating goods and protecting consumers from hazardous products
2. redress	b. laws intended to limit the powers of large businesses to take advantage of consumers or to harm other businesses
3. claimant	
4. Food and Drug administration	c. an agency of the government that administers laws that regulate the quality of foods and drugs offered for sale
5. Consumer Product Safety Commission	d. compensation for a wrong act or injury
6. fraud	e. an attempt to influence the votes of legislators
7. chlorofluorocarbon	f. a person who sues someone else in a court of law
8. acid rain	g. the division of the government that is responsible for enforcing all federal laws
9. Department of Justice	h. providing incorrect information for the purpose of obtaining payments one does not deserve
10. antitrust law	i. when reactions in the air cause rain to be acidic, thought to be the result of burning fossil fuels

Review and Enrichment Activities Continued

      j. chemicals used in many products that contribute to the destruction of the earth's ozone layer

2. Explain how it is possible for a person to not break any laws at the same time he or she fails to follow ethical behavior.

CHECKING WHAT YOU'VE LEARNED

Write your answers for the following exercises on a separate sheet of paper.

1. The following list contains the seven consumer rights identified by the government. Describe a situation that demonstrates each right. Do not use the same examples described in this chapter.
   The right to safety
   The right to be informed
   The right to choose
   The right to be heard
   The right to a decent environment
   The right to consumer education
   The right to reasonable redress
2. The following list contains the four consumer responsibilities identified in this chapter. Explain and give an example of each. Do not use the same examples described in this chapter.
   The responsibility to use products safely
   The responsibility to learn
   The responsibility to give correct information
   The responsibility to seek redress
3. Describe a decision you have recently made that involved ethical behavior.
4. Explain why ethical behavior may not be exactly the same for all people.

PRACTICING YOUR CONSUMER SKILLS

Explain the consumer right and consumer responsibility demonstrated in each of the following situations. Write your answers for the following exercises on a separate sheet of paper.

1. Lucy buys a new type of convection oven for her kitchen. The oven comes with a book of instructions that is 128 pages long. Lucy doesn't bother to read them and just puts a roast in the oven and turns it on. An hour later the roast is burned to a crisp.

2. Raymond buys a band saw to use in his shop. The saw comes with many different types of guards and other types of safety equipment. Ray thinks that these things get in his way and slow down his work. He takes them off. Then Ray almost cuts off his thumb and needs 28 stitches after catching his hand in the saw.

3. A local businessman applies for a permit to open a theater in a residential neighborhood. He says that he intends to show "adult" films to people who are at least twenty-one years old. Many citizens from the community complain to the town council. One woman says that she has data proving that movies like that warp people's minds and increase violent attacks in communities where such films are shown. Later she admits that she just made up the data because she thought it "sounded good."

4. Maxine buys a new lawn mower. She pays an extra $20 to have it assembled at the store so that she won't have to do this herself. When she gets it home, she goes out and starts to cut her grass. Soon the mower begins to vibrate. Before she can turn it off, the mower's blade comes loose, digs into her lawn, and then crashes through a window in her house. Maxine is so happy that she hasn't been injured that she almost forgets to be angry about the mower having been improperly assembled. Eventually, she complains to the store where she bought it. The store's owners refuse to pay for her window, so she takes them to court, where she wins $1,500.

USING NUMBERS

Solve the following problem to help make the best possible choice. Write your solution on a separate sheet of paper. Be sure to show all your work.

You decide to attend a concert with your best friend and his four younger brothers. When you buy the tickets, you ask for two "adult" tickets for $21.50 and four "child" tickets for $11 each. The tickets look exactly the same except for the price stamped in small print in one corner.

On the night of the concert, two of the children are sick and can't go. However, two of your other friends, who are old enough to be considered "adults," decide that they want to go. You think that you can probably sneak them in if you hand in all the tickets at once with the adult tickets on top. You can also choose to pay extra to trade for adult tickets.

How much more will you need to spend to exchange the tickets? What do you believe is the ethical decision? Explain.

Review and Enrichment Activities Continued

PUTTING IDEAS IN YOUR OWN WORDS

The following quotations are from this chapter. Explain these quotations in your own words to make sure you understand what they mean. Write your answers on a separate sheet of paper.

1. "Although the federal government appears to be taking a more active role in consumer education, individual consumers are still responsible for their own decisions."

2. "False claims cost businesses money, and that money comes from sales made to other consumers."

3. "There is no such thing as getting something for nothing. Somebody always pays."

BUILDING CONSUMER KNOWLEDGE

Write your answers for the following exercises on a separate sheet of paper.

1. Describe two events that you or a member of your family has recently been involved in that demonstrates consumer rights.

2. Describe two situations in which you or a member of your family has demonstrated consumer responsibility.

3. Describe two situations in which you or a member of your family has demonstrated ethical behavior.

4. Describe two events that you believe demonstrate unethical behavior. Do not name specific people.

Chapter 12

Consumer Protection

Chapter Objectives

After completing this chapter, you will be able to do the following:

- Explain changes in our economic system and in the products we buy that have increased our need for consumer protection.
- Describe the functions of government agencies that are charged with providing consumer protection.
- Describe limitations on the ability of the government to protect consumers from harm.
- Explain why consumers must rely on their own skills and abilities to protect themselves.
- Identify actions that consumers can take if they feel they have been taken advantage of.

Key Consumer Terms

In this chapter you will learn the meanings of the following important consumer terms:

- Caveat emptor
- Caveat venditor
- Consumer Affairs Council (CAC)
- Federal Trade Commission (FTC)
- Cease-and-desist order
- Price discrimination
- Consumer Credit Protection Act
- Consumers Union
- Consumers' Research, Inc.
- *Consumer Reports*
- *Consumers' Research Magazine*
- Better Business Bureau
- Investigative reporting
- Warranty
- Magnuson-Moss Warranty Act
- Full warranty
- Limited warranty
- Implied warranty of merchantability
- Implied warranty of fitness

Two hundred years ago, most products that consumers bought were relatively simple and easy to understand. Determining the quality of a bushel of corn, a hand ax, an animal, or woolen fabric was a task most people had learned to do through experience. There was little need for our government to provide consumer education or protection. This situation has changed.

Today we all own products that are useful but that work in ways we don't understand. For example, you may have a general idea of how a refrigerator, television, or home computer works, but you certainly wouldn't be able to build or repair one of these products. You probably wouldn't even be able to determine how dependable such products were on your own.

As the products we buy have become more complex and technologically advanced, our ability to evaluate them has declined. We often need expert advice to determine which products will meet our needs, offer the best value for our money, and are safe to use. In many cases federal, state, and local governments require manufacturers to provide the information we need to make responsible consumer decisions. In other situations they force products that may be dangerous from the market. In so doing, the government provides a public service.

Private organizations also provide expert information and help consumers solve problems relating to product sales and services. Many industries have established consumer divisions to deal with concerns or complaints about their products. Today consumers are often able to receive information or help in solving a problem by making a toll-free telephone call.

There was a time when the watchword for consumers was **caveat emptor**, or "Let the buyer beware." This meant that consumers had to rely on their own knowledge and skills to evaluate products they wanted to buy. Now it is the seller who must be careful not to violate consumer protection laws. Caveat emptor has been replaced by **caveat venditor**, "Let the seller beware." Major federal consumer legislation is summarized in Figure 12-1.

SECTION 1

FEDERAL CONSUMER PROTECTION AGENCIES

While you read, ask yourself . . .
- *What are several products that you don't understand but that you or other members of your family use regularly?*
- *How were you or members of your family able to choose these products when you don't understand them?*
- *How much do you depend on government protection when you buy goods and services?*

The federal government has tried to provide some level of consumer protection for over 100 years. In 1887, for example, the Interstate Commerce Act was passed to prevent railroads from setting "unreasonable" rates that would harm producers and consumers. This federal law was followed by many others that had different degrees of success. For many years consumer protection laws were not well enforced, and many were not clear enough to be used successfully in court. This shows that passing consumer protection laws is only part of the government's responsibility. Legislation must be written clearly, administered consistently, enforced, and kept up-to-date.

In 1979 President Carter established the **Consumer Affairs Council (CAC)**, which is composed of representatives of the cabinet-level departments and is led by the president's special assistant for consumer affairs. The CAC's responsibility is to establish a broad federal policy to guide agencies in responding to consumer issues. Two important consumer protection agencies are the Federal Trade Commission and the Consumer Product Safety Commission.

The Federal Trade Commission

The **Federal Trade Commission (FTC)** is the most important federal consumer protection agency. It was created in 1914 in response to a growing realization that consumers needed protection from dishonest or careless manufacturers. The FTC's activities are divided among three bureaus—the Bureau of Consumer Protection, the Bureau of Competition, and the Bureau of Economics. Through the Bureau of Consumer Protection, the FTC can stop any "unfair or deceptive act or practices" that treat consumers unfairly in their purchasing decisions.

Suppose that you send away for a "portable piano" you have read about in a magazine advertisement. The advertisement says that the piano plays "quality music with concert hall sound." You pay $19.99 plus $3.50 for shipping. When your "piano" arrives, it is about 6 inches long and ¼ inch thick, and it makes music that sounds like a smoke alarm going off. If this really happened, you could file a complaint with the FTC. If the FTC receives many complaints about a product, it can hold a hearing and then issue a **cease-and-desist order** to keep the firm from using misleading advertising in the future. If the advertisement is run again, the firm can be fined as much as $10,000 for each time the commercial is used.

The Bureau of Competition works with the Justice Department to enforce antitrust laws. They could take action, for example, if a firm was selling the same product for different prices in different locations. This kind of activity may be **price discrimination**. Federal law states that firms must offer their products for sale to all customers at the same price unless differences can be justified by differences in cost. For example, if one store is right next to the factory that makes the product, while another is 2,000 miles away, the firm could justify a difference in price because of greater shipping costs. A firm that is found guilty of price discrimination can be forced to charge all its customers the same price and pay damages to consumers who have been discriminated against.

The FTC's Bureau of Economics provides economic advice to the other two bureaus and

Vocabulary Builder

Caveat emptor Latin for "Let the buyer beware."
Caveat venditor Latin for "Let the seller beware."
Cease-and-desist order An administrative or judicial order commanding a business to stop conducting "unfair or deceptive acts or practices."
Consumer Affairs Council (CAC) A group of representatives from cabinet-level department that guides federal agencies in responding to consumer issues.
Federal Trade Commission (FTC) Most important federal consumer protection agency, created in 1914.
Price discrimination Selling the same product at different prices to different customers.

MAJOR FEDERAL CONSUMER LEGISLATION

Statute or Agency Rule	Purpose
Advertising	
Federal Trade Commission Act (1914/1938)	Prohibits deceptive and unfair trade practices
Public Health Cigarette Smoking Act (1970)	Prohibits radio and TV cigarette advertising
FTC Rules of Negative Options (1973)	Federal Trade Commission rules regulating advertising of book and record clubs
Smokeless Tobacco Act (1986)	Prohibits radio and TV advertising of smokeless tobacco products; requires special labeling to warn consumers of potential health hazards associated with smokeless tobacco
Credit	
Consumer Credit Protection Act (Truth-in-Lending Act (1988)	Offers comprehensive protection covering all phases of credit transactions
Fair Credit Reporting Act (1970)	Protects consumers' credit reputations
Equal Credit Opportunity Act (1974)	Prohibits discrimination in the extending of credit
Fair Credit Billing Act (1974)	Protects consumers in credit-card billing errors and other disputes
Fair Debt Collection Practices Act (1977)	Prohibits debt collectors' abuses
Counterfeit Access Device and Computer Fraud and Abuse Act (1984)	Prohibits the production, use, and sale of counterfeit credit cards or other access devices used to obtain money, goods, services, or other things of value.
Home Equity Loan Consumer Protection Act (1988)	Prohibits lenders from changing the terms of a loan after the contract has been signed; requires fuller disclosure in home equity loans of interest-rate formulas and repayment terms
Health and Safety	
Pure Food and Drug Act (1906)	Prohibits adulteration and mislabeling of food and drugs sold in interstate commerce
Meat Inspection Act (1906)	Provides for inspection of meat
Federal Food, Drug, and Cosmetic Act (1938)	Protects consumers from unsafe food products and from unsafe and/or ineffective drugs (superceded Pure Food and Drug Act of 1906)
Flammable Fabrics Act (1953)	Prohibits the sale of highly flammable clothing
Poultry Products Inspection Act (1957)	Provides for inspection of poultry
Child Protection and Toy Safety Act (1966)	Requires child-proof devices and special labeling
National Traffic and Motor Vehicle Safety Act (1966)	Requires manufacturers to inform new car dealers of any safety defects found after manufacture and sale of auto
Wholesome Meat Act (1967)	Updated Meat Inspection Act of 1906 to provide for stricter standards for slaughtering plants of red-meat animals
Consumer Product Safety Act (1972)	Established the Consumer Product Safety Commission to regulate all potentially hazardous consumer products

◆ **Figure 12-1**   Major Federal Consumer Legislation

conducts economic studies concerning the impact of government regulations on businesses and consumers and on the economy in general. Regional offices of the FTC are located in major cities across the country to assist consumers.

The Consumer Product Safety Commission

The **Consumer Product Safety Commission (CPSC)** was created by an act of Congress that

MAJOR FEDERAL CONSUMER LEGISLATION

Statute or Agency Rule	Purpose
Health and Safety (continued)	
Department of Transportation Rule on Passive Restraints in Automobiles (1984)	Requires automatic restraint systems in all new cars sold after September 1, 1990
Toy Safety Act (1984)	Allows the Consumer Product Safety Commission to quickly recall toys and other articles intended for use by children that present a substantial risk of injury
Drug-Price Competition and Patent-Term Restoration Act (Generic Drug Act) (1984)	Speeds up and simplifies Food and Drug Administration approval of generic versions of drugs on which patents have expired
Labeling and Packaging	
Wool Products Labeling Act (1939)	Requires accurate labeling of wool products
Fur Products Labeling Act (1951)	Prohibits misbranding of fur products
Textile Fiber Products Identification Act (1958)	Prohibits false labeling and advertising of all textile products not covered under Wool and Fur Products Labeling Acts
Hazardous Substances Labeling Act (1960)	Requires warning labels on all items containing dangerous chemicals
Cigarette Labeling and Advertising Act (1965)	Requires labels warning of possible health hazards
Child Protection and Toy Safety Act (1966)	Requires child-proof devices and special labeling
Fair Packaging and Labeling Act (1966)	Requires that accurate names, quantities, and weights be given on product labels
Smokeless Tobacco Act (1986)	Requires labels disclosing possible health hazards of smokeless tobacco; prohibits radio and TV advertising of smokeless tobacco products
Sales and Warranties	
Interstate Land Sales Full Disclosure Act (1968)	Requires disclosure in interstate land sales
Odometer Act (1972)	Protects consumers against odometer fraud in used-car sales
FTC Door-to-Door Sales Rule (1973)	Federal Trade Commission rule regulating door-to-door sales contracts
Real Estate Settlement Procedures Act (1974)	Requires disclosure of home-buying costs
Magnuson-Moss Warranty Act (1975)	Provides rules governing content of warranties
FTC Vocational and Correspondence School Rule	Federal Trade Commission rule regulating contracts with these types of schools
FTC Used-Car Rule (1981)	Federal Trade Commission rule requiring dealers in used-car sales to disclose specified types of information in "Buyer's Guide" affixed to auto
FTC Funeral Home Rule (1984)	Federal Trade Commission rule requiring disclosure by funeral homes regarding prices and services

◆ **Figure 12-1**   Continued

was signed into law by President Richard Nixon in 1972. The purpose of the CPSC is to regulate all potentially hazardous consumer products. Although many laws had been passed before 1972 to deal with specific consumer safety is-

Vocabulary Builder

Consumer Product Safety Commission   A federal agency that regulates all potentially hazardous consumer products.

Consumer News

FTC Takes Stronger Actions

Janet Steiger, former chairwoman of the U.S. Postal Commission, was appointed head of the FTC by President Bush in 1989. Since taking over, she has helped make the commission an aggressive investigator and protector of consumer interests. In 1990 the FTC took actions that blocked twenty planned mergers, compared to only seven cases in 1987. In 1990, Steiger announced the investigation of plastics manufacturers who have made claims that their products are biodegradable and therefore less harmful to the environment. Steiger is considering a major effort by the FTC to look into environmental claims made by manufacturers in general. In 1990 the FTC also initiated investigations of health care and cosmetic surgery advertisements. Concerns over advertising directed at children are also on the FTC's list of matters to investigate.

sues, the CPSC is concerned with the overall safety of all consumer products.

The 1972 act states that "any article, or component part thereof produced or distributed for sale to a consumer for use in or around a permanent or temporary household or residence, a school, in recreation or otherwise, or for the personal use, consumption or enjoyment of a consumer" shall be subject to regulation by the CPSC. The CPSC can set safety standards for consumer products as well as ban the manufacture and sale of any product it believes to be hazardous to consumers. The CPSC obtains data from hospital emergency rooms concerning those products that cause frequent con-

sumer injuries. The CPSC uses this information to determine which products are hazardous.

Summing Up The two government agencies that play the greatest roles in consumer protection are the Federal Trade Commission and the Consumer Product Safety Commission. Consumers who feel that they have been cheated or sold unsafe products may report their problems to these agencies. ◆

SECTION 2

OTHER CONSUMER PROTECTION ORGANIZATIONS

While you read, ask yourself . . .
- ◆ *Have you or a member of your family ever bought a product that you later found had been marketed in a fraudulent way?*
- ◆ *How could you use either* Consumer Reports *or* Consumer's Research Magazine *to help you make better consumer decisions?*

Although the federal agencies tend to be better known, there are many state and local government organizations and laws that help consumers defend their rights. Private organizations also make important contributions to this effort.

State and Local Consumer Protection

While federal consumer protection agencies take actions that concern national consumer issues, state and local governments go much further in protecting consumers in specific situations. For example, each state determines what sort of actions constitute consumer fraud within that state. Consumer fraud is a deliberate deception intended to cause a consumer to give up property or some lawful right.

◆   How would you feel if you discovered there was a plan to build a chemical plant like this one a few hundred yards from your home? What would you expect your government to do about it?

Suppose that your family decides to buy a particular dishwasher because the salesman says that it has a five-year full warranty. Moreover, you are encouraged to sign the sales agreement without reading the document. Later you discover that the full warranty only lasts for six months. After that there is a $50 deductible charge that you must pay out of each service bill. The salesman in this situation has committed consumer fraud because he did not tell you the truth. Consumers may report events that they believe involve fraud to their state attorney general's office. The attorney general has the responsibility to see that state laws are enforced and can prosecute firms that violate consumer protection laws. Many states also have consumer protection agencies that are listed in the telephone book.

States set standards for firms that offer credit, insurance, health, and sanitation. Many problems that became national issues for federal agencies were first addressed at a state level. For example, both California and New York passed legislation to protect the rights of consumers in credit transactions in the 1950s.

Massachusetts passed the first truth-in-lending law, which led to the passage of the federal **Consumer Credit Protection Act** in 1968. In effect, Massachusetts was a pilot case for the national legislation.

Local governments are also involved in protecting consumer rights. Local laws usually involve special issues that are important in a particular community. For example, most local governments enforce health and building standards. They may license firms that offer plumbing or electrical services. Zoning ordinances prevent some types of businesses from moving into residential communities. Where wider issues are involved, local governments sometimes assist individuals when they appeal

Vocabulary Builder

Consumer Credit Protection Act   A truth-in-lending law that requires lenders to inform borrowers of the annual rate of interest and the finance charge they will pay for their loan.

to either state or federal consumer protection agencies. One factor that limits what local governments can do is the cost of investigating complex issues. For example, most local governments could not afford to do the necessary tests to determine what sorts of fertilizer should be used on lawns and which should not. Consumer protection of this nature must be provided at the federal or state level.

Private-Sector Consumer Protection

Private organizations have provided different types of consumer protection for many years. However, most private consumer protection organizations have suffered from limited and unreliable funding. Private consumer groups tend to be organized to confront consumer issues as they arise. When a problem is resolved, many of these groups fade away. This is not a bad thing. It shows that people are able to respond to situations as they develop. However, there are several private organizations that stand out in the fight for consumer protection. Two are the **Consumers Union** and **Consumers' Research, Inc.**

Consumers Union is a not-for-profit organization chartered in the state of New York in 1936. It publishes *Consumer Reports*, a magazine that provides useful information to consumers to help them make rational consumer decisions. Consumers Union buys goods in the open market and brings them to the Consumers Union laboratory for testing.

Approximately 3.5 million people now read *Consumer Reports* every month. Consumers Union, which accepts no advertising in its magazine, gives advice about purchasing on credit, insurance, and drugs. Consumers Union gives special attention to testing auto-

mobiles. In addition, Consumers Union has published articles on ecological topics, such as pesticides, phosphates in detergents, and lead in gasoline. It often criticizes government agencies when they are slow to act on consumer interests.

Consumers' Research, Inc., was founded in 1929 and publishes *Consumers' Research Magazine* with a monthly circulation of several hundred thousand. This magazine contains ratings for products, such as motion pictures, and video tapes and gives other types of advice to consumers. Consumers' Research carries out extensive product testing and reports results in its magazine. It also announces product recalls.

Both of these organizations pride themselves on stressing safety and efficiency in the products that they recommend. They have also provided information to government agencies that have led to legal actions against specific firms and products.

There are **Better Business Bureaus** in most towns and cities. These private agencies are supported by local businesses. The National Better Business Bureau has existing since 1916. It has three main goals:

1. To provide information to consumers on the products and selling practices of businesses
2. To provide businesspeople with a source of localized standards for acceptable business practices
3. To provide a method of mediating grievances between consumers and sellers

The Better Business Bureau has no enforcement powers. Any action that it recommends is voluntary. The Better Business Bureau depends on the business community for its membership and support. Therefore, some people believe that it will not want to risk making businesses angry and will therefore tend to take their side in disputes with consumers. Almost all disputes involving substantial amounts of money or significant claims are settled through the courts rather than the Better

The *Global* Consumer

Was Nintendo Zapped?

Do you like to pay video games? If you owned a video game system in 1990, the chances are that it was a Nintendo system. Nintendo is a Japanese firm based in Kyoto that dominated the video game market in 1990. In that year it accounted for two-thirds of the video game industry's sales, or $2.5 billion. It was estimated that Nintendo earned $350 million in profits on its U.S. sales in 1990.

Nintendo was different from many firms that produced video games. Instead of only producing software (the computer program), it also manufactured and marketed the hardware needed to change an ordinary family television set into a video arcade. The Nintendo Entertainment System console that plugged into the back of the TV cost $99. Nintendo relied on selling games that retailed for $50 and up to earn most of its profits. After establishing itself as the dominant force in the video game market, could Nintendo maintain its sales and profits, or would it shrink as consumers became bored with the games?

Nintendo apparently tried to solve this problem by forcing dealers not to discount its products. In 1990 the FTC accused Nintendo of price fixing and demanded that the firm allow retailers to set their own prices for Nintendo products, as well as allow other firms to manufacture products that would run on Nintendo systems. By keeping prices high, Nintendo had protected the profit it earned on each game sold, and avoided satisfying all its consumer demand. As a result, consumers paid more for Nintendo games than they might otherwise have paid and were able to buy fewer products.

Although Nintendo never admitted to doing anything wrong, in April of 1991, the firm agreed to pay up to $30 million to settle its dispute with the FTC. It promised to mail up to $25 million worth of $5 discount coupons to registered owners and to pay nearly $5 million to the states that had done most of the legal work to bring the case to the FTC.

Do you believe that the Nintendo settlement was fair?

What would you do if you had the power to make the decision in this case?

Business Bureau. The Better Business Bureau is not really effective as a consumer protection agency. In many communities it only keeps files on businesses regarding consumer complaints.

Newspapers, radio and television stations, and magazines often publicize stories that deal with consumer protection. The main goal of such organizations is to increase the number of people who use their service. Their efforts are not well organized or coordinated on a national level. Still, **investigative reporting** has often focused public attention on specific problems and brought about important results that have benefited consumers.

Vocabulary Builder

Better Business Bureau   A private agency supported by businesses and intended to improve customer relations and resolve disputes.

Consumer Reports   A magazine published by Consumers Union that provides information to help consumers make rational decisions about products they buy.

Consumers' Research, Inc.   An organization that publishes *Consumers' Research Magazine*.

Consumers Union   A not-for-profit organization that publishes *Consumer Reports*.

Investigative reporting   Actions taken by news media to investigate and report on various situations, including consumer issues.

Industry Self-Regulation

Firms benefit from having satisfied customers who will give them repeat business and who will make positive recommendations about the business to friends and relatives. Businesses will be harmed if they abuse their customers. They lose sales and public respect. For these reasons, many industries have developed forms of self-regulation. Self-regulation generally consists of (1) setting standards for the industry's products and services, (2) publishing these standards, and (3) enforcing the standards. The willingness of many industries to regulate themselves may in part be the result of a desire to avoid government regulation.

Many industry associations help to resolve disputes between their members and consumers. For example, the Automotive Consumer Action Program (AUTOCAP) is a consumer action group created by the National Automotive Dealer Association to resolve disputes between consumers and automobile dealers. In a similar way, the Major Appliance Consumer Action Panel (MACAP) helps to resolve problems between consumers and business firms in the appliance industry. Over forty other similar associations have been organized in the past twenty years. Although these organizations provide an important service to consumers, they are funded by industry. As a result, some people believe that they favor industry's point of view in many disputes. Anyone who is dissatisfied with an action taken by such a consumer action group has the right to take legal action through the courts.

Summing Up *Consumers are protected by state and local governments and by private organizations. Consumers need to recognize that some private organizations are supported by businesses and may not be totally unbiased. They may be more interested in protecting businesses than in protecting consumers.* ◆

WARRANTIES

While you read, ask yourself . . .
- ◆ *Do you read the warranty card when you buy a product? Do you send in registration cards for warranties? Why do you believe some consumers choose not to do these things?*
- ◆ *What experiences have you or members of your family had in having a warranty honored when a product was defective?*

Consumers often buy products that turn out to be defective and need repairs or replacement. We are used to buying products with "money-back guarantees" or "full satisfaction guarantees." But such guarantees have often been worth little more than the paper they were printed on. In the past, consumers often did not know what was being guaranteed and what was not. In the 1970s a survey by the Major Appliance Consumer Action Panel showed that many **warranties** did not state the name and address of the warrantor, did not mention the product or part covered, did not indicate the length of the warranty, and did not state what the warrantor would actually do and who would pay for it. What's more, most warranties were written in language that was difficult for many consumers to understand.

The Magnuson-Moss Warranty Act

The **Magnuson-Moss Warranty Act** of 1975 closed many of the loopholes contained in some warranties. The act does not force a manufacturer to provide a written warranty. But if a warranty is offered, the firm must comply with the following provisions of the law:

◆   When consumers buy appliances and many other goods they expect to receive warranties with these products. Why is it important for consumers to read these warranties carefully?

1. Any warranty on a product that costs $15 or more must include a simple, complete, and easily seen statement of the following: the name and address of the warrantor, a description of what is covered and for how much, a step-by-step procedure for placing warranty claims, and explanation of how disputes between the parties will be settled, and the warranty's duration. This information must be available to the consumer before the purchase is made.

2. Manufacturers cannot require as a condition of the warranty that the buyer of the product use it only in connection with other products or services that are identified by brand or corporate name. For example, the maker of a flashlight cannot require the purchaser to use only one brand of batteries in that flashlight for the warranty to be effective.

Full versus Limited Warranties

If a firm offers a warranty that meets minimum federal standards, it can be designated as a **full warranty**. If it doesn't meet these standards, it must be designated as a **limited warranty**. When a full warranty is offered, a consumer simply needs to present the product to the firm and inform the warrantor how the product is defective. The warrantor must then fix the product without charge to the consumer. If the product cannot be successfully repaired in a reasonable period of time, the customer has the right to choose between a new product or a refund of the purchase price. Full warranties apply to both the original purchaser of a prod-

Vocabulary Builder

Full warranty   A promise by a supplier to provide for the repair or replacement of faulty merchandise within a reasonable period of time; meets minimum federal standards.

Limited warranty   A warranty that does not meet minimum federal standards and must state how it fails to meet these standards.

Magnuson-Moss Warranty Act   A law passed in 1975 that sets federal standards for warranties.

Warranty   A guarantee made by the seller of a product that it will meet specific standards over a period of time, or it will be repaired, replaced, or its price will be refunded.

Consumer News

Guaranteed Service

If you bought a new tape recorder, you would expect it to have a warranty that would protect you if it broke shortly after you bought it. But what would you expect if you ordered bottled gas or oil for your home and it was delivered late? Would you expect anything more than an apology?

In recent years a number of firms have begun guaranteeing their service as well as their products. JWS Technologies, in New Jersey, guarantees on-time deliveries to its customers of bottled gas or there is no charge for the product when it is delivered. And many restaurants promise that your food order will be brought to your table within a certain period of time or it's free.

Consumers are often willing to pay much more to receive service guarantees. Prism Inc. is a pest control service that guarantees a full refund of its fee if a single bug is found in any building that it treats on a regular basis. The firm's sales continue to grow, although it charges two to three times as much as competing firms.

How much more would you be willing to pay to be sure that a job was done right?

uct and to those who buy the product second-hand during the warranty period.

Limited warranties must specifically state in what ways they offer less warranty than a full warranty. For example, if the warranty only covers parts and not labor, this must be stated in writing when the consumer buys the product. When you buy any product, be sure to find out what sort of warranty you are being offered.

Implied Warranties

In some cases the law states that an implied warranty is made when a product is sold, even if there is no written warranty offered to the consumer. When a dealer who specializes in camping equipment sells a tent, the customer receives what is called an **implied warranty of merchantability**. This means that the customer can expect that the tent doesn't leak and that it isn't defective in any other way. A tent sold in a garage sale would not have an implied warranty because the customer should realize that the product is not new and that the seller is not in the business of selling tents for a living.

Another type of warranty in an **implied warranty of fitness**. This means that the customer can rely on the merchant to sell a product that is appropriate for the use the product will be put to. For example, if you tell a salesperson that you want to buy paint for the outside of your house, that salesperson should not sell you indoor paint that would wash off in the first rainstorm. However, to qualify for an implied warranty of fitness, the customer must be sure that the seller "has reason to know" the purpose for which the product is being bought. If a customer points to a can of indoor paint and says, "I want four of those," the salesperson will naturally assume that the paint will be used for a room and not the outside of a house.

Whenever there is a problem with a product, customers must make sure that their warranty is honored. A company cannot carry out the terms of a warranty unless it is made aware of the problem. This means that consumers must have the skills and abilities necessary to recognize those problems that a warranty covers and the willingness to ask for it to be honored.

Summing Up   *Products are often protected by full or limited warranties. When you purchase a product, you should be sure to find out what sort of warranty is included with your purchase. In some situations consumers are also entitled to an implied warranty.* ◆

SECTION 4

CONSUMER PROTECTION TODAY

While you read, *ask yourself . . .*
◆ *What is your opinion of the general trend in government consumer protection during the 1980s?*

Over the past thirty years the government's commitment to consumer protection has changed many times. Starting with the Kennedy administration in 1961 through the Carter presidency of the late 1970s, consumer protection occupied an important and often growing role in government priorities. However, under the Reagan administration (from 1981 to 1989), federal consumer protection agencies suffered repeated cuts in budgets and employees. In 1981, for example, David A. Stockman, director of the Office of Management and Budget, justified a 30 percent cut in the Consumer Product Safety Commission's budget, saying that it had "largely accomplished" its goal to "ferret out hazardous products" and therefore needed fewer resources. Funding for the CPSC remained between $31 million and $37 million a year under the Reagan administration, although price increases totaled roughly 35 percent in these years. This forced a cutback in the commission's employees from over 1,000 workers in 1980 to just over 525 in 1989.

The Reagan administration was often said to be probusiness and anticonsumer. In 1983 Congressman John D. Dingell accused the Federal Trade Commission of "deliberately narrowing the commission's authority to prosecute dishonest and deceptive conduct." In the same year, Michael Perschuck, chairman of the Federal Trade Commission under Carter, responded to an FTC decision to redefine and limit the meaning of deceptive advertising by saying,

"Of all the destructive anticonsumer efforts this administration has pursued, none of them has been potentially more disastrous."

The level of federal government involvement in consumer protection began to grow again under the Bush administration. In October 1990 the Consumer Product Safety Commission was reauthorized, and its funding was increased to $42 million. The powers of the CPSC to keep track of businesses that were found guilty of producing or selling hazardous products were expanded. At the same time, the CPSC's power to suspend its own rules to benefit manufacturers was severely limited. The CPSC was directed to develop safety standards for several potentially hazardous products, including cigarette lighters and garage door openers. It is not clear how far the trend toward greater government involvement in consumer protection will go. But in the early 1990s the federal government was taking on a larger role. Whether or not this increased effort continues, it is clear that consumers need to do their best to make responsible decisions to protect their own interest.

Summing Up *Funding and support for consumer protection has not been consistent. Although support grew in the early years of the Bush administration, there is no guarantee that it will remain at that same level. Consumers cannot rely on the government to protect them. They need to make responsible choices and protect themselves.* ◆

Vocabulary Builder

Implied warranty of fitness An implied promise that a product is appropriate for the buyer's stated purpose.
Implied warranty of merchantability An implied promise by the seller that an item is in good condition and can be used for the purpose for which it was sold.

Review and Enrichment Activities

VOCABULARY REVIEW

1. Column A contains key consumer terms from this chapter. Column B contains a scrambled list of phrases that describe what these terms mean. Match the correct meaning with each term. Write your answers on a separate sheet of paper.

	Column A		**Column B**
1.	Consumer Affairs Council	a.	the federal agency that is most responsible for consumer protection
2.	warranty	b.	a private organization that helps resolve problems between producers and consumers
3.	Consumer Credit Protection Act	c.	a private organization that publishes *Consumers Reports*
4.	cease-and-desist order	d.	the federal law that protects the rights of consumers who borrow money
5.	Better Business Bureau	e.	a group of representatives from government departments that exists to coordinate federal consumer protection policies
6.	caveat emptor		
7.	Consumers Union		
8.	caveat venditor	f.	a guarantee made by a seller that a product will meet specific standards
9.	price discrimination	g.	selling the same type of product to different customers at different prices
10.	Federal Trade Commission	h.	let the buyer beware
		i.	an official command to stop doing something
		j.	let the seller beware

2. Explain the difference between full and limited warranties.

CHECKING WHAT YOU'VE LEARNED

Write your answers for the following exercises on a separate sheet of paper.

1. Explain why there is a greater need for consumer protection now than there was 200 years ago.
2. Explain the difference between the terms *caveat emptor* and *caveat venditor*.
3. Describe the membership and responsibility of the Consumer Affairs Council.
4. Under what circumstances would the FTC issue a cease-and-desist order?
5. What is price discrimination?
6. What is the responsibility of the Consumer Products Safety Commission?
7. Why may the definition of consumer fraud be different in different states?
8. What is the most important functions of both Consumers Union and Consumers' Research, Inc.?
9. Why isn't the Better Business Bureau a true agency for consumer protection?
10. What was the basic function of the Magnuson-Moss Warranty Act?
11. Describe the two types of implied warranties.

PRACTICING YOUR CONSUMER SKILLS

Write your answers for the following exercises on a separate sheet of paper.

1. Suppose that you have just moved from Chicago to a small town in rural Iowa. When you lived in Chicago, there was a particular brand of potato chip you really liked and bought for $1.19 per 7-ounce bag. The local store in Iowa charges $1.39 for the same bag. You write a letter to the FTC complaining of price discrimination. Explain why this may not be a case of price discrimination.
2. Amanda paid over $20,000 for a new car last year. In the first nine months she owned the car, its engine died on an interstate highway, the gas gage broke, the speedometer stopped working, the air bag was recalled, she had to have new rotors put on her front disk brakes, and several of the doors came loose and ran into each other, so she had to have them painted. All of these defects were repaired free of charge by the automobile dealer, but Amanda has had her car in the shop eight times in nine months. Amanda is afraid to take the car on a trip or into heavy traffic for fear something else will go wrong. What alternatives does Amanda have?

Review and Enrichment Activities Continued

3. Make up a full warranty for a Fax machine manufactured by the Amalgamated Copy Corporation of 435 South Oak Street, Newton, NJ 09875. Check the Magnuson-Moss Warranty Act to find the other types of information you need to include. Make up the rest of the information you need. Be reasonable.

USING NUMBERS

Solve the following problem to help make the best possible choice. Write your solution on a separate sheet of paper. Be sure to show all your work.

Martha wants to buy an air conditioner for her bedroom. She has read *Consumer Reports* and has chosen the make and model she wants to buy. She has already visited several local stores to find the one with the best price. Martha has decided where to buy her air conditioner, but she has another choice to make. If she pays $349, she will receive a full warranty for one year and a limited warranty that covers the cost of replacing the compressor for five years. She could choose to pay $419 instead to receive a ten-year service warranty in addition to the manufacturer's warranty. The service warranty will pay the full cost of parts and labor if the air conditioner breaks.

Martha asked how much a typical repair on an air conditioner costs. She was told that air conditioners don't break very often, but when they do, there are three parts that tend to fail: the motor, the thermostat, and the compressor. Currently, a new motor costs $129, a new thermostat costs $89, and a new compressor costs $149. Using current costs, determine how much Martha would save if she purchased the service warranty and any of these parts failed after she owned the air conditioner for six years. Would you recommend that she pay for the service warranty? Explain.

PUTTING IDEAS IN YOUR OWN WORDS

The following quotations are from this chapter. Explain these quotations in your own words to make sure you understand what they mean. Write your answers on a separate sheet of paper.

1. "Consumer fraud is a deliberate deception intended to cause a consumer to give up property or some lawful right."
2. "Most private consumer protection organizations have suffered from limited and unreliable funding."
3. "The willingness of many industries to regulate themselves may in part be the result of a desire to avoid government regulation."

BUILDING CONSUMER KNOWLEDGE

Write your answers for the following exercises on a separate sheet of paper.

1. Look through local newspapers to find an example of a controversy that involves consumer protection in your community. Write an essay that explains both sides of the issue.

2. Ask an adult to describe a situation that he or she experienced that involved consumer protection issues. Write a paragraph describing what happened and what, if anything, the adult believes should have been done by the government to protect his or her consumer rights.

3. Interview the owners of a local store. Ask them to explain how their business is affected by consumer protection laws. Do they feel that these laws are necessary? How would they run their business differently if there were no consumer protection laws? Be prepared to explain your findings to the class.

Chapter 13

Understanding Advertising

Chapter Objectives

After completing this chapter, you will be able to do the following:

- Explain the purpose of advertising from the point of view of the advertiser.
- Identify various types of advertising and explain how consumers may be helped or harmed by these types of advertising.
- Identify several types of deceptive advertising that consumers should be aware of.
- Explain the objectives of laws that govern advertising in the American economy.

Key Consumer Terms

In this chapter you will learn the meanings of the following important consumer terms:

- Informative advertising
- Brand-name advertising
- Consumer recognition
- Comparative Advertising
- Verifiable claims
- Defensive advertising
- Persuasive advertising
- Deceptive advertising
- Bait and switch
- Counteradvertising
- Mediation
- Small claims court
- Litigation

Pick up any newspaper and make a list of the words used to describe the products that are advertised. Phrases like "best quality," "long lasting," "lowest prices," "new and improved," and "easy payments" abound. If you read carefully, you will discover that for all the words that advertising uses, many of them provide little specific or useful information. Remember, businesses must pay for advertising (a total of almost $150 billion in 1992). Business owners are willing to spend this money because they believe that they will earn more profit as a result. Businesses advertise to encourage consumers to buy greater quantities of their products, possibly at higher prices, than they otherwise would. Advertising is intended to serve the interests of people who own businesses. Advertising may help consumers, but you should realize that this is not its primary purpose.

S E C T I O N 1

TYPES OF ADVERTISING

While you read, ask yourself . . .
- ◆ *What types of advertising do you most frequently see or hear?*
- ◆ *Do you find the advertising you see or hear helpful or confusing?*
- ◆ *How important is advertising in your consumer choices?*

Most firms advertise to achieve product differentiation for their business. Their objective is to convince consumers that they offer superior-quality goods or services, are more reliable or stylish, or have consistently lower prices than other competing firms. If consumers believe that a particular firm offers better value for their money, they are likely to buy more products from that firm. As a result, the owners will be more successful and earn a greater profit. Advertising is the most common method businesses use to differentiate their products.

Informative Advertising

It's not hard to figure out what **informative advertising** means. It's advertising that pro-vides information to consumers. Grocery and discount stores pay to have advertising supplements placed in newspapers, providing consumers with page after page of product names and prices. By studying informative advertising, consumers may find the best price and quality for a product they wish to buy.

Most of the advertising you see or hear provides some information. However, this does not mean that the information provided by advertising is complete or balanced. The firm that places the advertisement wants you to buy its products. It will therefore provide you with information intended to convince you that it offers the best value for your money. If a different business offers the same lawnmower for $20 less than Al's Hardware Store, you should not expect Al to point this out in his advertisement. Consumers may be helped by advertising that provides information and allows them to make better choices. But consumers must read the advertising carefully and evaluate what they read.

Vocabulary Builder

Informative advertising Advertising that provides information about a product.

This process requires consumer skills and a knowledge of what to look for.

Consumers need to study the real meaning, or lack of meaning, in advertisements. It is against the law for advertisers to make false claims or to lie about the products they sell. However, consumers should realize that it is possible to tell the truth in a way that may encourage people to draw incorrect conclusions. If your friend tells you, "I just got the best test score I ever earned," you might be impressed. But if your friend's previous best score had been only 52, then this latest score might only be a 54—which really isn't so good. You would have drawn the wrong conclusion because your friend did not provide you with enough information. Advertisers often use similar methods.

Businesses may use incomplete information in their advertising. If a store advertises chairs at 25 percent off, you need to know "off of" what? The price may be 25 percent less than their price last week. The problem is that their price last week may have been 50 percent higher than the price of chairs offered by other stores. As a result, the store's price may still be higher than prices at other stores. Any time you see words like "better," "lower priced," or "longer lasting," you need to ask yourself, "Than what?" When an advertisement says that the price of a product has been lowered by $20, it has provided information, but not particularly useful information.

A similar problem is that of "hidden charges." Your family probably receives "junk mail" advertising almost every day. Although many mail-order businesses offer high-quality products at fair prices, this is not always the case. When a firm offers a product at a price that seems too good to be true, it probably is. Some mail-order businesses offer products that appear to have very low prices. When you receive such an advertisement, it pays to be suspicious. Always look for shipping or handling charges. A $15 shirt does not look so inexpen-

sive if there is a $7.95 charge for sending it to your home. Be sure to find out if the product can be returned without having to pay a fee, and find out who pays the return postage—you or the firm?

Consumers can benefit from informative advertising if they are careful. Remember, the main purpose of all advertisements is to increase the profits of the firms placing the ads.

Brand-Name Advertising

Much of the advertising you see or hear is intended to create consumer loyalty to a particular brand or product. This is called **brand-name advertising**. Buying a brand-name product offers both benefits and costs for consumers. Nationally known brand-name products are likely to have consistent quality. But one problem of buying brand-name products is the possibility of overlooking a better product that is not widely known. You could buy a McDonald's hamburger in almost any town in the United States, and the hamburger would always be about the same. But while McDonald's may be convenient and reliable, you might be missing out on a truly wonderful hamburger at Jeff's Diner.

Another factor you should consider is price. Because most firms that produce brand-name products are large, they may be able to offer products at lower prices than small firms. However, this is not always the case. Manufacturers of brand-name products often achieve **consumer recognition** by advertising. This adds to their cost of doing business. These extra costs may be passed on to consumers in higher prices. Off-brand products that do little advertising may provide better value to consumers who are willing to shop carefully.

As with any decision, there are benefits and costs to buying brand-name products. By buying such products, you don't have to worry about making a big mistake. However, you may spend more than you need to, and you may miss the opportunity to buy a less-known but higher-quality product.

Comparative Advertising

Many advertisements compare the quality and prices of different products. Until recent years, **comparative advertising** rarely mentioned competing products by name. Consumers almost always saw "brand X," which was inferior in some way to the advertised product. In the last few years, however, many advertisers have been using the specific names of competing products. Whenever a firm comments on a competing product, it must make sure that it is making a **verifiable claim** or one that can be proven.

For example, automobile advertisements sometimes make statements about other automobiles. These claims are usually the result of tests run by independent organizations. But just because some specific information is being given about the products, that doesn't mean that all relevant information is being given. A car that has rapid acceleration is probably less efficient than a different car with less power. As a result, the manufacturer is likely to include information about its product's power and ignore its fuel efficiency in its advertisements. Comparative advertising is selective and will show only what the advertiser wants the consumer to know.

Firms that are the target of comparative advertising often respond with **defensive advertising** that is intended to rebut claims made by their competition. In the early 1990s, consumers in the United States experienced the "telephone wars." American Telephone and Telegraph (AT&T) and MCI, another long-distance telephone company, made conflicting claims about which firm had the lowest long-distance rates. Each business used advertising to defend itself against claims made by the other firm, trying to show its own superiority.

◆ Does this advertisement provide much useful information? Do you believe many consumers would bother to write for the $2 brochure that may provide more specific information?

Vocabulary Builder

Brand-name advertising Advertising that features a firm's name, picture, or logo to help consumers distinguish that firm's products from other similar products; intended to create consumer loyalty to the brand.

Comparative advertising A form of advertising that compares a firm's product to specific competing products.

Consumer recognition A feeling of knowing and trust amount consumers for a particular brand of product.

Defensive advertising Advertising intended to rebut claims made by competing firms about a firm's product or business practices.

Verifiable claim Claim made in comparative advertising that has been proved true.

Consumer News

Advertising in the Classroom?

In June 1989, Christopher Whittle, of Whittle Communication, announced plans to provide free cable news television to America's junior and senior high schools. Whittle offered schools that signed on for channel 1 free television receivers and hookups. He hired twelve educators to oversee his news programming. So what was the catch? To receive the channel 1 cable broadcasts, school districts had to allow students to see 2 minutes of paid advertising for each 10 minutes of news they viewed.

Many educators accused Whittle of trying to commercialize education. California banned channel 1 entirely. Many individual school districts did the same. Still, on the first day channel 1 went on the air, 2,900 schools had agreed to show Whittle's program, advertisements included. Whittle said that he didn't see what was wrong with commercials in the classroom. After all, most students see so many advertisements outside of school. He said that the free service and televisions made it a "reasonable tradeoff."

Do you believe that school districts that sign up for channel 1 programming are being responsible?

Persuasive Advertising

Some advertisements provide virtually no information about the products they recommend to consumers. They portray happy, successful, satisfied, and popular people using a product.

The advertisers hope that consumers will associate their products with success and satisfaction and will buy them for this reason. Many personal care products are advertised in this way. Commercials for perfumes or colognes almost never mention price. They show beautiful people in romantic settings being unreasonably happy. When is the last time you saw someone who was physically unattractive selling French perfume for $75 an ounce?

If a person is not popular, buying a particular brand of pickup truck is not likely to change that person's life very much, although many advertisements would have you believe otherwise. **Persuasive advertising** attempts to change consumers' tastes and preferences. It may be successful or useful from the point of view of the manufacturer. Whether it does any good for consumers is debatable.

Summing Up *Consumers are exposed to many types of advertising. Some advertising is helpful and provides valuable information. However, consumers should realize that all advertising is intended to encourage them to buy a particular product and is not likely to present complete or balanced information.* ◆

SECTION 2

DECEPTIVE ADVERTISING

While you read, ask yourself . . .
- ◆ *How often have you seen or read advertising that you believed to be deceptive?*
- ◆ *What made you believe that this advertising was intended to be deceptive?*

Unfortunately, some businesses deliberately try to mislead or cheat consumers through **deceptive advertising**. This type of practice may happen in many ways and in the long run is likely harm the business as much as the consumer. When a business treats its customers unfairly, the unhappy customers soon spread the word, and the business ends up losing even more customers. Nevertheless, deceptive advertising does occur, and consumers need to be on their guard.

The terms *unfair* and *deceptive* have very broad meanings. It is often difficult to determine when an event is the result of an honest misunderstanding and when it is the result of a deliberate attempt to deceive the customer. Suppose that you see an advertisement for "Teak coffee tables" for only $69.95. You immediately think that the store is offering an unbelievably good bargain, so you get in your car and drive 20 miles to the store. But when you get there, you discover that the table is made of particle board with a plastic coating. The store owner explains that the name of the company that produces the tables is Teak Manufacturing. He denies any attempt to mislead you or any other customer. Even if you don't believe him, this problem *could* be the result of a misunderstanding, and there is little you can do about it.

Bait and Switch

Suppose that Mike's refrigerator stops working one day. He needs a new one, and needs it fast. Mike looks through the local paper for refrigerator ads. He spots an ad from Marty's Appliance Emporium for an 18-cubic-foot refrigerator for only $399. Most of the other stores are advertising similar products for prices ranging between $500 and $600. When Mike arrives at Marty's store, he discovers that the advertised refrigerator is a demonstration model that has been in the store for the last year. It has a number of dents and makes a strange noise when it is turned on. It is also dirty, and the door doesn't fit quite right. When Mike complains to Marty, Marty points out some small print in his advertisement that says that the refrigerator isn't new. He suggests that no one would really want such an old ma-

chine and that a new and improved model with automatic defrosting and an ice maker, would be a better choice. He says that he can sell such a refrigerator for only $950. Mike refuses to buy the refrigerator for $950, but agrees to purchase a new one like the refrigerator in the ad for $599. Mike feels cheated, but he needs a new refrigerator before all his food spoils.

Mike was a victim of **bait and switch**. The bait was the unbelievably low price for the advertised refrigerator. The switch was to encourage Mike to buy a much higher priced product. Although this type of practice happens, it can only be successful if consumers take the bait and accept the switch. You have the right to walk out of the store if you don't like the deal you are offered.

Other Types of Deceptive Advertising

There are many other types of deceptive advertising you may encounter in your life. A business may call or write to tell you that you are a contest winner, but you have to buy something to collect your prize. Or the firm may require you to sit through a long sales pitch in order to receive your "free prize." These sales meetings may go on for hours, and the firm's

---

Vocabulary Builder

Bait and switch Advertising a product at a bargain price but then informing customers brought in by the offer that only a more expensive product is available; normally an illegal sales practice.

Deceptive advertising Advertising that is intended to mislead consumers.

Persuasive advertising Advertising intended to persuade consumers to buy a product by appealing to their need to be happy or socially accepted.

Consumer Close-Up

FDA Moves Against Misleading Claims

American consumers are concerned about the amount of fats and oils in the food they eat. Unfortunately, in the past many consumers may have been misled by the different terms used to describe oils. While phrases like "reduced saturated fats," "no tropical oils," and "no cholesterol" clearly had something to do with the fat content of foods, many consumers were confused about what these terms really mean! It appears that some manufacturers used this confusion to mislead consumers and sell more of their products.

In 1991 the Food and Drug Administration determined that statements made by Procter & Gamble Co., CPC International, Inc., and Great Foods of America, Inc., were deceptive. These companies all boasted that their products contained "no cholesterol." The FDA said that these claims left the impression that these products benefited the heart and overall health of consumers. The FDA threatened to take further action if the products weren't relabeled and the claims dropped from advertising. The companies denied that they had intended to mislead consumers, but agreed to cooperate and eliminate the claims.

FDA Commissioner David Kessler accused the firms of passing off "half truths" on health-minded consumers. He said that the labels on cooking oil "don't tell the whole story." The products are entirely fat, and eating too much fat is unhealthy. It increases the chance of cancer and other diseases as well as contributing to obesity.

Kessler said of FDA efforts, "We are systematically examining every food category to make sure no food company gets an unfair advantage by making misleading claims." They are looking particularly at advertisements that use the words "fresh" and "no cholesterol."

representative may refuse to give away the prize until you buy a different product.

Advertisements sometimes offer free or reduced-price goods with the purchase of a different, more expensive good. This type of advertisement may cause consumers to buy expensive products that they didn't want or need, just to receive "free goods." For example, if a store offers a two-for-one sale on furniture polish for $11.59, when the normal price for one jar is $5.99, the store isn't really cutting the price very much. But the advertisement may cause consumers to buy more polish than they need.

Sometimes the picture printed in a newspaper advertisement is not the product being offered for sale. Suppose that you see a chair advertised for $199. The picture in the ad shows a chair that would fit in with the early American furniture you already own. Later you find that the chair in the picture really has a price tag of $499. The $199 chair is made out of plastic and steel tubing. In this case the store is trying to deceive you through merchandise substitution. The firm appears to advertise one product, but offers a different product at a higher price when the customer comes to the store.

In recent years many manufacturers have offered cash back, or **rebates**, to consumers who buy their products. In many cases these are legitimate marketing methods. However, in some cases rebates have been used to cheat customers. Suppose that a customer responds to an advertisement for a portable computer. The ad promises a $150 rebate from the manufacturer. The customer is willing to pay full price for the computer because of the expected rebate. However, the rebate form states that to receive the money, the customer must also buy a $350 software package. If the dealership has not made this requirement clear to the customer, it has carried out deceptive advertising.

Deceptive advertising can only succeed when there are customers who can be taken advantage of. At one time or another, you will probably be deceived. But the more knowledge you gain, and the more skilled you become in evaluating goods and services, the more you will avoid being taken advantage of.

Summing Up *There are many types of deceptive advertising. Firms that try to deceive people can only succeed if consumers are not careful in making purchases.* ◆

SECTION 3

THE GOVERNMENT'S ROLE IN ADVERTISING

While you read, *ask yourself . . .*
- ◆ *Why do we no longer see television advertisements for hard liquor or cigarettes?*
- ◆ *Are there any advertisements that you believe should be banned by the government? What are they, and why do you believe that they should not be seen or heard?*

Numerous government agencies, both federal and state, have the power to protect consumers from deceptive advertising. At the federal level, the most important agency that regulates advertising is the Federal Trade Commission. (You read about other powers of the FTC in Chapter 12.) Under a 1938 amendment to the 1914 Federal Trade Commission Act, the FTC is authorized to prohibit "unfair or deceptive acts or practices" in the marketplace. Although the FTC tries to make sure that consumers are not misled by deceptive or

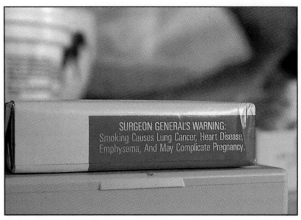

◆ How effective do you believe health warnings like this are in causing consumers to make rational choices about the products they use?

fraudulent advertising, it cannot be 100 percent successful in every situation. Individual consumers must rely on their own good judgment to avoid being taken advantage of by unscrupulous businesses.

What the FTC Can Do

The FTC received complaints of *alleged* violations. The fact that a complaint has been made does not prove that a firm is guilty of deceptive advertising or of any other violation of federal law. Also, the FTC receives so many complaints that it cannot possibly look into every one. When a significant number of complaints are made concerning a particular firm or a particular business practice, the FTC carries out an investigation to determine the facts. Whether or not the FTC takes action against a firm depends on its findings. In any case, results take time.

If the FTC finds sufficient evidence that a given advertisement is unfair or deceptive, it can conduct a hearing—similar to a trial—in which the company that has allegedly violated FTC rules can present its defense. If the FTC decides that the firm is guilty of the violation, it may issue a cease-and-desist order requiring

Consumer News

Should There Be Limits on Advertising?

Imagine a "dreamboat" actor holding a pack of a new brand of cigarettes on a billboard across the street from your classroom. Every day students see the sign as they come to school.

Public protests do not always succeed, but sometimes they do. In February 1990, the R.J. Reynolds Tobacco Co. withdrew the Uptown cigarette that many believed was directly targeted at young, poor African Americans. Public demonstrations, letter-writing campaigns, and threats of refusing to buy the firm's products may have contributed to the firm's decision. Regardless, RJR's decision was hailed as a victory for the right of consumers to limit the type of advertising that young people are exposed to.

What do you believe such an advertisement is intended to accomplish?

Do you think that there should be limitations on what and where businesses may advertise?

the challenged advertising be stopped. Businesses that disregard these orders may be fined as much as $10,000 for each time the offending advertisement is used after the order is issued.

A new type of punishment has recently been imposed by the FTC. In some cases firms have been required to place **counteradvertising** in their future advertisements to correct misinformation or deception in past advertisements. For example, Listerine advertised that its mouthwash could prevent or cure colds and sore throats. This claim was found to have no scientific proof. Therefore, the FTC required Listerine to state in future advertisements that its product did not prevent colds or sore throats.

The requirement to place health warnings on tobacco products is similar in that these warnings are intended to help consumers understand the true nature of the products they buy. There is also some controversy about whether alcoholic beverages should carry warnings, informing pregnant women that drinking alcohol can harm their unborn children.

What You Can Do

If you feel you have been victimized by unfair or deceptive advertising, there are many things you can do. You can report your problem to the Better Business Bureau. This organization will sometimes provide **mediation** of disputes between consumers and businesses. Unfortunately, many businesses do not abide by rulings of this organization. Also, some people suggest that the Better Business Bureau may not be completely unbiased in its decisions because it is funded by businesses.

Consumers always have the right to seek legal redress for their complaints. They should recognize that formal legal actions are expensive and do not guarantee success. One alternative is to go to **small claims court**. This is a court that does not usually require people involved in a suit to be represented by lawyers. It is therefore far less expensive than other types of legal action. There is maximum amount that may be sued for that varies between states. (The typical maximum amount ranges from $1,000 to $3,000.) Although settlements in small claims courts are less costly, there is no guarantee that they will be satisfactory to the litigants or that the party found to be at fault will pay any settlement without further **litigation**.

Consumers may also write to the FTC or to their state's attorney general's office. Many states have taken the lead in recent years in trying to protect the rights of consumers and limit

Consumer Close-Up

Ethical Advertising and Children

American businesses have decided to direct a large part of their advertising dollars toward children. One publisher recently stated that children make brand decisions very early in life and carry their preferences into adulthood. Spending on children's advertising reached $450 million in 1990, up 15 percent from 1989. Even firms like IBM and AT&T, which don't manufacture products intended for children, advertise on children's television programs. Many of these firms defend their decisions by stating that children often influence how parents spend money.

The list of new products for children is long, and growing longer every day. For example, few children have any real need for deodorant until they reach puberty. Yet BertSherm Products, Inc., has marketed a deodorant for children as young as seven years old. Other toiletries in the "kiddy market" include Gregory Boys's cologne for $15.50 an ounce and a skin moisturizer called Environmental Protection Cream that is supposed to protect children from the harmful effects of air pollution.

Convenience foods are particularly popular for the growing number of children who cook for themselves while their parents are at work. Products like Tyson's Daffy Duck Spaghetti and Meatballs and McCain's Turtles Pizza abound in grocery store freezer cases. What's more, children who are expected to do household chores can now vacuum with their own bright-colored Handy Cleaner for only $75.

With the flood of new children's products, it is becoming more and more important for parents to teach their children how to make responsible consumer decisions and how to exercise reasonable control. A good question to ask yourself before agreeing to any purchase by or for a child is, What's the point? If a product serves no useful purpose, there is probably no reason to buy it. Letting children have products simply because they have seen them advertised teaches children little about making rational decisions. If children are never too young to form brand loyalties based on advertising, then children are never too young to learn how to make good consumer decisions.

---

unfair or deceptive advertising. Depending on the nature of the complaint, a consumer may also want to contact the Food and Drug Administration (FDA), the U.S. Postal Service, the Federal Communications Commission (FCC), or the Securities and Exchange Commission (SEC).

Summing Up *There are government agencies and laws that protect consumers from deceptive advertising. Private organizations also help consumers resolve problems that concern misleading advertising. However, a consumer's best defense against deceptive advertising is his or her ability to evaluate advertising and to say no when necessary.* ◆

Vocabulary Builder

Counteradvertising   Advertising ordered by the Federal Trade Commission to correct earlier false claims made about a product.

Litigation   Law suit.

Mediation   Procedure by which a neutral person steps into a negotiation to try to get both sides to reach an agreement.

Small claims court   A state court that allows people to sue other parties for limited amounts of money without the services of a lawyer.

Review and Enrichment Activities

VOCABULARY REVIEW

1. Column A contains key consumer terms from this chapter. Column B contains a scrambled list of phrases that describes what these terms mean. Match the correct meaning with each term. Write your answers on a separate sheet of paper.

Column A

1. mediation
2. informative advertising
3. defensive advertising
4. counter advertising
5. deceptive advertising
6. brand-name advertising
7. litigation
8. small claims court
9. bait and switch
10. consumer recognition

Column B

a. when a firm responds with advertising to claims made by a competing firm in comparative advertising

b. when a firm advertises its name or a logo to help consumers distinguish its products from other similar products

c. when a firm provides information to consumers through advertising that helps them make decisions

d. when a firm is forced to correct unfair or misleading advertising in new advertising

e. when a firm misleads consumers by providing inaccurate or incomplete information in advertisement

f. a feeling of knowing and trust among consumers for a particular brand of product

g. when a neutral parts helps both sides reach an agreement in a negotiation

h. taking a dispute to court to be settled

i. advertising a product at a low price but trying to convince consumers to buy a more expensive product when they come to a store

        j. courts that allow people to sue for limited amounts of money without the need for a lawyer

2. Explain why comparative advertising requires firms to make verifiable claims so it is clear you know what these terms mean.

CHECKING WHAT YOU'VE LEARNED

Write your answers for the following exercises on a separate sheet of paper.

1. What is the purpose of any advertisement from the point of view of the firm that placed the ad?
2. Explain why businesses want to differentiate their products from similar goods or services offered for sale by competing firms.
3. Describe several examples of informative advertising.
4. Why should consumers be careful to evaluate the facts provided by firms in informative advertising?
5. How may consumers benefit from buying brand-name products?
6. What costs may consumers pay when they buy brand-name products?
7. How can comparative advertising be misleading when the facts listed in the advertising are correct?
8. Describe two examples of persuasive advertising. How do these advertisements try to appeal to consumers?
9. Why is it difficult to determine exactly which advertisements are deceptive and which are not?
10. Describe a real or fictional example of bait-and-switch advertising that is different from those mentioned in this chapter.
11. Why can't the FTC respond to every complaint that it receives by taking action against the accused firm?
12. What are some other government agencies that can protect consumers from deceptive advertising?
13. Why must consumers learn to rely on their own skills and knowledge to protect themselves from deceptive advertising?

PRACTICING YOUR CONSUMER SKILLS

Write your answers for the following exercises on a separate sheet of paper.

1. Identify each of the following advertisements as informative advertising, brand-name advertising, comparative advertising, defensive advertising, or persuasive advertising. One advertisement may demonstrate more than one type of advertising.

Review and Enrichment Activities Continued

a. The Apex golf ball lets you hit tee shots that average 10 yards longer than other golf balls tested. Recently, ten professional golfers hit ten balls each. Brands used included Acme, Gem, Longball, and #1 Driver. The drives using Apex balls averaged 287.4 yards. The average of all other brands was 276.9 yards. Apex golf balls are best.

b. Make an impression with McTavish sports clothes. Even if your golf scores won't win any tournaments, you can impress your friends and adversaries with McTavish pants or a McTavish golf jacket. The bold plaids of McTavish clothing leave no doubt about who you are. You make a statement without saying a word when you wear a McTavish product!

c. Lost Our Lease. EVERYTHING must go at or below cost. Our loss is your gain! Come to Ed's Discount Golf Pro Shop at 123 East South Street while there is still a wide selection of clubs and shoes to choose from. All merchandise has been reduced 50 percent or more from the original list price. We will be open from 10 A.M. to 9 P.M. every day this week.

d. Gem golf balls are the best value for your dollar. Recently, the Apex Golf Ball Co. ran a test to determine how far different golf balls could be driven. Their conclusion that their product goes farther is misleading. They compared the results of their balls with an average of nine other types of balls. Most of these other balls were unknown brands made of inferior materials. Although their balls went ten yards farther than the average of all the tested balls, it only went 6 inches farther than Gem golf balls. Gem balls are virtually the same as Apex balls, yet they cost about half as much. If you care about how you spend your money, buy only GEM GOLF BALLS!

e. Are you tired of being left out of social events? Do your dates want to go home at nine? When you enter a room, do other people remember somewhere else they were supposed to be? Maybe you need to use Marla's Mystery Mouthwash. Marla's secret is a patented blend of herbs and spices. No other mouthwash has her formula. Leave a lasting impression! Use Marla's Mystery Mouthwash. People will remember you.

The following situations involve deceptive advertising. Identify and explain each deceptive practice.

a. John advertises "free vacations" in Hawaii for any customer who buys a used car from him in February. Many people come to his car lot. Some buy cars from him expecting a free trip. It turns out that John is only offering a three-day stay in a small hotel about a mile from the beach. He will not pay for food or transportation to Hawaii. Many of his customers are angry when they find out what John is really offering.

b. Diedra owns a shoe store that specializes in women's shoes in large, wide, and small sizes. Most of her shoes are very expensive. Last week she advertised a "Special $29 Sale" on women's tennis shoes. Because of her reputation for stocking a wide selection of sizes, many women with large or small feet come to her store expecting to buy inexpensive shoes. It turns out that the $29 shoes only come in medium width in sizes between 6 and 11. When the women cannot fit into the inexpensive shoes, Diedra tries to convince them to buy other shoes that are more expensive.

    c. Ted sells garden supplies for a living. He advertises that anyone who buys a year's supply of fertilizer from him will receive $50 from the product's manufacturer. He fails to mention that to qualify for this refund, the customer must also purchase a fertilizer spreader that costs $129. Many of his customers are upset when they discover this fact.

3. Explain why you believe that the Consumer Products Safety Commission should or should not become involved in each of the following situations.

    a. Thelma buys a toy for her three-year-old son that he has seen advertised on a cartoon television program. The toy contains many small parts. The box that the toy comes in is clearly labeled "Recommended for children 8 through 12 year old." Her son swallows some of the parts and spends five days in the hospital. Thelma writes to the CPSC demanding that they force the manufacturer to take the toy off the market.

    b. Riccardo doesn't speak English very well. He sees an advertisement for a sewing machine that is guaranteed for life. What Riccardo doesn't understand is that the parts are guaranteed for life, but the customer will have to pay for labor when repairs are made. The contract that Riccardo receives with the sewing machine clearly states this fact, but he doesn't read the contract. Later, when the machine breaks, Riccardo is charge $58 for labor. He complains to the CPSC.

    c. Tina sends away for a silk blouse she sees advertised in a mail-order catalog. The advertisement says, "Satisfaction Guaranteed—Your money will be cheerfully refunded without question." Tina pays for the blouse with her charge card. The blouse arrives and the first time she wears it, she breaks out in a rash. She washes it and wears it again, but the same thing happens. Tina concludes that there is something in the fabric that she is allergic to, so she returns the blouse. However, the firm never credits her account. When she calls to complain, the firm's representative says that the blouse appears to have been worn and they will not refund her money. Tina writes a letter to the CPSC explaining what has happened.

USING NUMBERS

Solve the following problem to help make the best possible choice. Write your solution on a separate sheet of paper. Be sure to show all your work.

Review and Enrichment Activities Continued

Curtis has always purchased most of his clothing at a men's shop near his home. For the past year he has been paying $28 each for the cotton-blend shirts he wears to work. Curtis receives an advertisement in the mail that says in large letter, "BUY HIGHEST QUALITY MEN'S COTTON BLEND SHIRTS THROUGH THE MAIL FOR JUST $16.95 EACH!"

Curtis is interested, so he reads the advertisement more carefully. He finds that the $16.95 price is only good if a customer buys ten or more shirts. For smaller numbers, the price is $21.95. There is also a $4.50 shipping charge regardless of how many shirts are purchased. On the other hand, the mail-order business is located in a different state and will not charge Curtis the 5 percent sales tax he has to pay at the local men's store.

Curtis is thinking of ordering two shirts to see if their quality is good. If he does this, how much money will he save compared to the price at the men's store? Would you recommend that he place the order? Explain the reasons for your recommendation.

PUTTING IDEAS IN YOUR OWN WORDS

The following quotations are from this chapter. Explain these quotations in your own words to make sure you understand what they mean. Write your answers on a separate sheet of paper.

1. "Most of the advertising you see or hear provides some information. However, this does not mean that the information provided by advertising is complete or balanced."
2. "It is often difficult to determine when an event is the result of an honest misunderstanding and when it is the result of a deliberate attempt to deceive the customer."
3. "Deceptive advertising can only succeed when there are customers who can be taken advantage of."

BUILDING CONSUMER KNOWLEDGE

Write your answers for the following exercises on a separate sheet of paper.

1. Identify a specific advertisement that you believe helps consumers make better choices. Explain how it achieves this.
2. Identify a specific advertisement that you believe provides no help to consumers. Explain what the advertisement does and why it provides no help to consumers.
3. Identify a specific advertisement that you believe is harmful to consumers. Explain how the advertisement may harm consumers.

Chapter 14

The Responsible Consumer and The Environment

Chapter Objectives

After completing this chapter, you will be able to do the following:

- Investigate society's need for environmental protection.
- Identify benefits and costs associated with recycling and conserving resources.
- Explain why the least expensive or most convenient products may be harmful to the environment.
- Identify steps that consumers can take to protect the environment.

Key Consumer Terms

In this chapter you will learn the meanings of the following important consumer terms:

- Environment
- Pesticides
- Global warming
- Environmental Protection Agency (EPA)
- Formaldehyde
- Aquifer
- Ozone layer
- DDT
- Endangered Species Act
- Range
- Recycle
- Reuse
- Biodegradable

W hat factors do you consider when you decide which brand of cookies or soft drink to buy? You probably choose a product that has a flavor or texture you like. You may read the ingredients and avoid products with too much sugar or fat. The convenience of the product may be important to you. You certainly think about price. However, do you consider the product's impact on the **environment**? Do you believe that this is something that responsible consumers should think about when they make decisions?

SECTION 1

WHY WE NEED ENVIRONMENTAL PROTECTION

While you read, ask yourself . . .
 ◆ *What environmental problems exist in your community that you are aware of?*
 ◆ *What actions have you or people you know taken to try to protect the environment?*

If you are a typical American consumer, you will create 3½ pounds of trash today. Do you wonder where your trash goes? Do you care? If you don't, you should. If something isn't done to limit the amount of trash we produce, we will soon be living in it.

The Scope of the Problem

Some people wonder how great our need for environmental protection really is. We have a large nation with open spaces. We have many resources. Do we really have anything to worry about? If you doubt the importance of environmental issues, here are a few facts that you should consider:

• Americans produce 800 million pounds of garbage each day. This amounts to 3½ pounds per person. Only 10 percent of our garbage is reused. The rest is discarded into our environment.

• Only 3,500 of the more than 35,000 types of **pesticides** used between 1945 and 1989—that's less than 10 percent—have been tested for health hazards.

• America releases 6 tons of carbon dioxide per person per year into the air, contributing to **global warming**. Many people worry that a gradual increase in the earth's temperature will lead to drastic changes in our climate and in our ability to produce food to sustain life.

• Americans dump 16 tons of sewage into their water supplies every minute of every day. That totals 525 billion tons a year, or 2 tons for every person in the country.

• Each year enough rain forest is being burned or cut down to cover the entire state of California.

• The **Environmental Protection Agency (EPA)** estimates that the depletion of the earth's ozone layer will cause an additional million cases of skin cancer for Americans who were alive in 1989. It is not yet known how the depletion of the ozone layer will affect plants and our ability to grow food.

There are many other problems that could be added to this list. The United States and the world in general need to take steps to protect our environment for the benefit of all those who are alive today as well as future generations.

◆   Thousands of trailer park communities have been built across the United States. Many of these homes are made of materials that contain formaldehyde. Is there anything owners can do to protect their health?

The Impact on People

We all know someone who has been affected by the damage done to our environment. All we have to do is look in a mirror. We live in our environment. We are part of it. We cannot escape harm when it is damaged. The following examples demonstrate only some of the many ways people suffer.

Where We Live.   When you put on a new piece of clothing that is made of permanent-press fabric, the chances are very good that some of its "new smell" is **formaldehyde**. Manufacturers treat most permanent-press fabrics with formaldehyde to give them body. Some residues stay with the fabric and are released to be breathed when they are worn. Formaldehyde is also found in shampoo, many cosmetics, draperies, and tissues. It has been shown to cause nasal cancer in mice and rats and is suspected of doing the same in humans.

The amount of formaldehyde a person would be exposed to from a new shirt probably has little significance. This is not true of many mobile homes that are constructed from materials that contain large amounts of

Vocabulary Builder

Environment   The sum of our surroundings that we live in.

Environmental Protection Agency (EPA)   The federal agency charged with monitoring and enforcing laws that concern the protection of our environment.

Formaldehyde   A chemical found in many consumer products that has been associated with an increased incidence of cancer.

Global warming   A gradual increase in the average temperature of the earth's atmosphere.

Pesticide   A chemical intended to kill insects, and other pests.

Consumer News

New Emission Standards for Automobiles

On May 22, 1991, the Environmental Protection Agency announced tighter air emission standards for automobiles built in 1994. This is the first significant improvement since 1981. The new standards will reduce the limit of nitrogen oxides by 60 percent and the content of unburned fuel by 31 percent. New limits were also set for particulate matter that could be emitted from gasoline engines. The new standards will be phased in over three years. By 1994, 40 percent of new cars must meet the standards, 80 percent by 1995, and 100 percent by 1996. New cars will also have to be able to meet the standards for ten years or 100,000 miles—twice the current time. The EPA estimates that the cost of its new rules will be about $150 per vehicle, although experts in the automobile industry believe that the cost may be much more.

formaldehyde. Some Americans who live in mobile homes or in prefabricated housing breathe large amounts of formaldehyde every day.

Where We Go To School. Schools contain many substances that are potentially dangerous. Thirty years ago cleaning fluids made from alcohol, benzine, or tetracycline could be found in almost every school. Lead-based paints were common. Although most of these substances have been eliminated, risks remain. Asbestos, duplicating fluid, chemicals in laboratories, pesticides, and disinfectants used in gymnasiums still present potential dangers to students and teachers.

What We Eat. The list of additives in our food is far too long to be included here. Pick up any packaged food product and read the list of ingredients on the label. You will probably find that the ingredients contain many additives that you cannot identify. This may come as no surprise to you. However, one problem you may never have considered is the fact that many foods we use are wrapped in plastic film. DEHA is an additive used in manufacturing most types of plastic wrap. DEHA has the ability to cause cancer in laboratory animals. In 1990 some scientists suggested that DEHA might move from plastic wrap into food products. The use of plastic wrap may represent a health risk to consumers.

What We Breathe. Ice samples have been taken from glaciers in Greenland that were formed thousands of year ago. By studying tiny amounts of air trapped in the ice, scientists can determine what the composition of air was in the past. It has been found that the world's air today contains 2,000 percent more lead than the air 1,000 year ago. We all breathe air that contains lead that may damage our bodies. Lead poisoning mainly affects the central nervous system and our ability to think. There are many other pollutants released into our atmosphere. How much do you care about what they may be doing to your body?

What We Drink. A 1982 study showed that 45 percent of the **aquifers** in the United States are contaminated with organic chemicals. In some locations the problem is particularly acute. In New Jersey 100 percent of the state's major aquifers contain chemical contaminants of one type or another. It is becoming close to impossible to find drinking water that is "pure." Living in a rural area offers no guarantee of water purity. Because of all the chemicals used by our nation's farmers, well water contamination rates are as high as 97 percent in many rural communities. Even buying bottled water offers no assurance of purity. Many bottled water products have been filtered to re-

◆ Although modern sewage treatment plants are able to remove most organic pollutants from waste water they often cannot eliminate dangerous chemicals. How can you be sure the water you drink is safe?

move suspended particles. However, this does nothing to eliminate dissolved compounds in the water.

Where We Work.   On June 22, 1974, a firm in Louisville, Kentucky, announced that three of its workers had died of angiosarcoma, a rare cancer of the liver. The firm manufactured products from polyvinyl chloride (PVC). After further investigations, it was determined that an ingredient in the product, vinyl chloride, increased the chance of having this type of cancer several thousand percent. Of 3,000 workers surveyed, 64 had developed this type of cancer over a twenty-year period. Employees who worked with the material were at greatest risk. But consumers who used the vinyl products were also breathing in the vinyl chloride fumes released from the products.

Where We Play.   Most Americans enjoy a day in the country or at the beach. However, some people say that the destruction of the **ozone layer** has made spending a day in the sun life threatening. Brian Toon, of the National Oceanic and Atmospheric Administration, has said, "Without ozone, we'd all have to go back

Vocabulary Builder

Aquifer   A geological structure that is a source of water.

Ozone layer   A layer in the atmosphere that contains high levels of ozone that block most ultraviolet rays from reaching the earth's surface.

The *Global* Consumer

Ozone Depletion: It's Not Just an American Problem

A layer of ozone in the atmosphere is vital to the future of life on earth. A concentration of ozone occurs naturally in the stratosphere from 30 to 60 miles above the earth's surface. In 1991 the EPA announced that between 1978 and 1990, the level of ozone over the United States had fallen by 4 to 5 percent. It is possible that this loss may total 20 percent by the year 2010.

Ozone absorbs a large part of the ultraviolet radiation that reaches the earth's atmosphere from the sun. If the ozone balance in the atmosphere is disturbed, major climatic changes may result. Reduced ozone levels will also increase the probability of people and animals developing cancer. Moreover, there is reason to believe that a higher concentration of smog will result if greater amounts of ultraviolet radiation reach the lower levels of the atmosphere. The effect on animal and plant life is not entirely understood, but should be significant.

The destruction of the ozone layer is the result of several factors. Probably the most important cause is the use of chloroflurocarbons (CFCs) in aerosol sprays, plastic foam, refrigeration gas, and many other products, A number of steps have been taken to reduce the use of CFCs in the United States and other developed nations. In September 1986, DuPont, the largest producer of CFCs in this country, announced that it would produce a substitute for CFCs by 1991. New refrigerants are being used in cooling systems that reduce CFC emissions but increase cost. A tax was placed on CFC production in the United States in 1989 to collect $5 billion over five years and to discourage the use of CFCs in this country.

Internationally, a treaty between twenty-seven developed nations was signed in 1987 to limit the production and use of CFCs. It appeared that positive steps were being taken to protect the ozone layer by industrial nations. However, little was done to reduce the production and use of CFCs by less developed nations. In 1990, for example, India and China, the two most populous countries in the world, had taken no steps to reduce the use of CFCs. To try to remedy this situation, an agreement between developed nations was suggested in 1990 that would have paid less developed nations to reduce their use of CFCs. The total cost of the program was estimated to be roughly $40 billion. The U.S. share was to start at $20 million. In May 1990, the Bush administration refused to participate in the program and suggested that the reduction of CFCs be financed through loans from the World Bank. There is little reason to believe that this will happen.

The problem is that the CFCs released into the air in India, China, and other places will not stay there. They will destroy the ozone layer over your home as much as over the cities of New Delhi and Peking.

Do you believe that the United States should help less developed nations pay the cost of reducing their use of CFCs?

to living under the water." Researchers predict that if we continue to destroy the ozone layer over the next thirty years at the same rate as in the past thirty years, food shortages are likely, along with a significant increase in the number of cases of skin cancer.

Environmental damage is a reality we cannot avoid. We can, of course, take steps to reduce its effect on our lives. But it is even more important that we take steps to reduce such damage so that there is a world for future generations to use and enjoy.

ANIMALS AND PLANTS NEED ENVIRONMENTAL PROTECTION

While you read, ask yourself . . .
- ◆ *Are you concerned about the possible extinction of many types of animals and plants?*
- ◆ *Would you be willing to change the way you live to protect endangered plants or animals?*

If people are affected by environmental problems, you can be sure that plants and animals are too. Indeed, it is likely that because plants and animals are not able to think or defend themselves, they will suffer more than human beings. In the past few decades Americans have become aware that part of the environment we need to protect is made up of the plants and animals that share the earth with us.

This understanding became widespread after the publication of Rachel Carson's book *Silent Spring* in 1962. Carson depicted a world without birds—the result of the overuse of pesticides and other chemicals. The most widely used pesticide at that time was dichlorodiphenyltrichloroithane (**DDT**). This product had been found in the shells of bird eggs and is believed to cause them to be weak and prone to being crushed in the nest. In the 1960s it was discovered that bird populations were falling with alarming speed. For example, the peregrine falcon entirely vanished east of the Mississippi River. Public opinion helped force the government to ban the sale of DDT in 1972. This has contributed to the growth of bird populations in recent years.

In 1966 and again in 1973, the federal government passed the **Endangered Species Act**, which protects specified plants and animals.

Species may be nominated to the list of endangered species by any interested party. The U.S. Fish and Wildlife Service is charged with determining which candidates should be listed. A candidate may be listed as endangered if it is in danger of extinction in all or a significant portion of its **range**. If a candidate appears likely to become endangered, it is listed as threatened.

On the surface, the Endangered Species Act appears simple and clear. In reality, the law is neither. As it is written, the law would stop a natural process that has been happening since the beginning of time. It would have been impossible to legislate an end to the extinction of dinosaurs. It is impossible to stop the extinction of some species today. This means that the law will inevitably fail in some cases.

The steps to protect a species, as outlined in the law, pose no small problem. Before a species may be protected, it must be placed on the official list. This process can be time-consuming and subject to political pressure. When specific species are protected, there are usually groups of people who stand to be hurt economically or in other ways. There is a good chance that these groups will fight against listing the plant or animal in question. For example, consider the case of the snail darter.

In the 1970s the Tennessee Valley Authority had built a $50 million dam on the Tombigbee River to provide electricity and flood control. Just before the dam's reservoir was scheduled to be filled and the dam put into operation, it was

Vocabulary Builder

DDT   Dichlorodiphenyltrichloroithane, a powerful insecticide banned in the U.S. in 1972.
Endangered Species Act   A law that protects animals and plants designated as endangered species by the federal government.
Range   The geographical area in which a particular plant or animal may be found.

Consumer News

Businesses Change to Protect the Environment

Recent studies have shown that an increasing number of American corporations are paying closer attention to environmental issues. In 1990 AT&T received the Council on Economic Priorities's Corporate Conscience Award for its plan to stop using ozone-depleting chlorofluorocarbons. Procter & Gamble donated Dawn detergent to clean animals in the 1989 Alaskan oil spill. A British cosmetics firm, The Body Shop, has given up animal testing of its products. Another sign of changing corporate values is the success of the consulting firm Capital Missions Co., which advises businesses on how to be socially and environmentally responsible. It is increasingly apparent that businesses are concerned about their public image in relation to environmental issues. This may be the result of their desire to be environmentally responsible or their desire to remain profitable. The better a firm's environmental record, the less likely it is to be sued. In any case, it appears that consumer pressure is already making a difference to our environment.

and many people who had expected to have jobs or reduced flood damage to their property were harmed. After the Supreme Court's decision, Congress amended the Endangered Species Act in 1978 to force the Fish and Wildlife Service to be slower in placing new species on the list.

Another problem with the law is that a species must be nominated to be on the list. There are thousands of species of plants and animals that are not well known, attractive, or of interest to specific groups. They therefore have not been nominated, regardless of how endangered they may be. As a result, there is a potential for great loss to humankind. Many plants and animals may have important uses that are as of yet unknown. If they become extinct, we will never be able to use them.

Summing Up *Consumers suffer in many ways when the environment is harmed. We will have to find ways to protect our environment for our own sake and that of future generations. Part of our environment is also made up of the plants and animals that share the earth with us. Steps we have taken to protect their future have only been partially successful.* ◆

SECTION 3

CONSUMERS, BUSINESSES, AND THE ENVIRONMENT

While you read, ask yourself . . .
   ◆ *What products do you buy that you believe may be harmful to the environment? Why do you buy them?*
   ◆ *How much more would you be willing to pay for products that are environmentally sound?*
   ◆ *What products would you be willing to give up to protect the environment?*

discovered that the Tombigbee River was the only habitat of a small fish, the snail darter. Filling the reservoir would have destroyed the only habitat for the fish and caused its extinction.

The Fish and Wildlife Service added the fish to its endangered species list, and use of the dam was stopped. The case eventually reached the U.S. Supreme Court, which ruled in favor of protecting the snail darter. As a result, vast amounts of money and resources were wasted,

Americans have placed a high priority on environmental protection. In 1990 a *New York*

Times and CBS poll found that 81 percent of Americans felt that protecting the environment is so important that improvements must be made regardless of the cost. Some people believe that the protection of the environment is the responsibility of businesses and our government. They are partially correct. Businesses and our government must help, but citizens need to recognize that they share this responsibility. The environment needs to be protected by everyone.

Consumers and the Environment

One way for consumers to show their support for environmental protection is through the way they spend their money. Many consumers who say that they want to protect the environment buy products packaged in containers that can't be **recycled**, **reused**, or are not **biodegradable**. Their actions seem to contradict what they say. Using products that are environmentally sound may cost a little more than using other products, but in the long run it is a more responsible choice.

In recent years many books have been published that can help consumers make choices that are environmentally responsible. One of the best known is *50 Simple Things You Can Do to Save the Earth*, by John Javna. (You will read more about John Javna in Chapter 15.) Another useful book, *The Green Consumer*, was written by John Elkington, Julia Hiles, and Joel Makower and published by Penguin Books in 1990. This book contains over 300 pages of information and suggestions on how to be an environmentally sound consumer. *Changing Times* magazine published an "Environmental Shopper's Guide" in its February 1990 issue. All these publications emphasize the fact that individual consumers can make a difference to the environment. There is information and advice available for those who look for it. Consumers should make a personal commitment to help protect the environment.

Costs and the Environment

Everyone would prefer to pay less for a product rather than more. Unfortunately, some products are inexpensive because the manufacturer was not careful of the environment when the product was made. It is much less expensive to discharge pollutants into the environment than to properly treat them. It often costs more to use recycled materials than to use new resources. Generating electricity by burning high-sulfur coal, which contributes to acid rain, costs less than using low-sulfur coal or removing sulfur compounds from smoke before it is released into the air. If consumers buy products produced in ways that are bad for the environment, they may benefit from a low price in the short run. However, society will pay other costs in terms of environmental damage in the long run.

Many of the actions that producers take that are bad for the environment are more related to marketing than to production. Manufacturing a new electric blender may not be particularly

Vocabulary Builder

Biodegradable A quality of a product that allows it to break down into basic components over prolonged contact with the environment.
Recyclable A product which leaves remains that may be used as the raw material to make a new product.
Reusable A quality of a product that allows it to be used repeatedly.

Consumer News

How Far Is Too Far?

In recent years some individuals have been taking environmental protection into their own hands by practicing civil disobedience (breaking laws on purpose to achieve a goal). An organization called Earth First has been connected with actions that include putting sand in the fuel tanks of logging machinery, driving spikes into trees that would have been cut, sinking whaling ships, and destroying oil exploration equipment. Although such radical actions are not supported by most environmentalists, there are a growing number of people who are willing to break the law and risk punishment. As one environmentalist said, "The more you study ecology, the more radical you become."

What actions would you be willing to take part in to protect the environment?

aged and marketed this way. If consumers stop buying these products or write to the firms and ask them to use other, less damaging containers, the firms will change their packaging. They will change when they become convinced that other types of packaging will make their business more profitable. Consumers can force businesses to make environmentally responsible decisions if they work together. Consumers can stop firms from using wasteful packaging by refusing to buy it.

Summing Up *Consumers can make a difference in protecting the environment. By shopping carefully and buying environmentally sound products, they encourage firms to be environmentally responsible too.* ◆

SECTION 4

RECYCLING AND CONSERVATION

While you read, ask yourself . . .
  ◆ *Do you know what happens to the trash your family produces?*
  ◆ *How would you react to a decision by the government to build a landfill near your home or school?*

harmful to the environment. But wrapping it in plastic with Styrofoam "peanuts" and then placing it in a cardboard box made from trees has a significant impact. It uses resources and creates waste that will probably end up in a landfill.

In the 1960s most producers of laundry detergents turned to the use of plastic bottles because they were perceived as convenient by American consumers. These firms are in business to earn a profit. They used plastic containers because they believed that more consumers would buy their product when it was pack-

Americans produce more garbage than any other group of people in the world. In 1989 the average American produced 1,300 pounds of trash. American businesses produced another 250 million tons of often toxic waste.

Roughly 80 percent of all waste was dumped in landfills in the 1980s. We cannot burn most of this trash without creating air pollution. Most other countries are no longer willing to accept our garbage.

There is also the problem of disposing of our nation's radioactive and medical waste. In 1988 the hospitals of New York City alone gen-

◆   Containers that require a deposit have been shown to reduce the litter that is discarded into our environment. Why do some people oppose deposit laws?

erated an estimated 1.7 million pounds of infectious waste each week. The untreated liquid part of this waste could be dumped legally into the city's sewer system to flow into the ocean. When bacteria counts increased in the summer of 1988, beaches were closed on the Long Island and New Jersey shores. We are running out of places to put our garbage. One answer that has been suggested is recycling our trash.

Recycling: An Answer or Another Problem?

In individual states and local areas, recycling has been carried out for a number of years. On a national basis an average of 10 percent of our garbage was recycled in 1990. There are clear indications that Americans are willing to recycle more of their garbage. In the late 1980s, 60 percent of families in California participated in voluntary recycling. In Seattle 28 percent of household garbage was recycled. New York State passed a law requiring all communities to establish recycling programs by 1991. Estimates of the share of garbage that could be recycled range between 70 and 90 percent. Recycling costs money and requires more labor to sort garbage. However, it is clear that in the long run, it will cost more to continue using our limited landfill space.

Although many people believe that recycling is an answer to some of our environmental problems, not everyone supports this idea. Some people have suggested that the extra money and energy spent collecting and sorting garbage will be too great. They believe that conservation is a better alternative.

Reuse and Conservation

Resources that are never used don't turn into trash, don't need to be recycled, and don't take up space in landfills. Many people believe that conservation offers the best long-term hope for protecting our environment. An advantage of conservation is the ability that consumers have to take action individually and at the present. They do not need to join an organization or wait for government action.

Reuse of scarce resources is an alternative that is almost as good as not using them at all. It is possible to use glass containers in your refrigerator time after time. Taking your own fabric shopping bag to the store reduces your need to use resources. Using china plates instead of paper or plastic products may require washing them but reduces the amount of trash

◆   How are the people in this mini-bus helping to protect our environment? Could you or members of your family make similar choices?

we put into landfills. These are things that all consumers can choose to do. In many cases, the reuse or conservation of resources saves money as well as being environmentally sound.

There are other steps that you can take. Buy products in larger containers rather than smaller ones to reduce the amount of packaging. Plan your shopping and other trips to reduce the miles you drive. Remember, small cars get you where you want to go as easily as large ones that use more fuel. Better yet, take a bus.

Or use a bicycle or walk. Try to organize car pools. Avoid overheating or overcooling your home or workplace. The list is endless. If we all make an effort to conserve and reuse resources we can make a favorable impact on our environment.

Summing Up   *Although many communities are turning to recycling as a means of protecting the environment, some people believe that the reuse and conservation of our resources is a better alternative.* ◆

Review and Enrichment Activities

VOCABULARY REVIEW

1. Column A contains key consumer terms from this chapter. Column B contains a scrambled list of phrases that describe what these terms mean. Match the correct meaning with each term. Write your answers on a separate sheet of paper.

Column A	**Column B**
1. environment	**a.** a rock layer from which flowing water may be obtained
2. formaldehyde	**b.** the trend toward an increased average temperature of the earth's atmosphere
3. pesticide	
4. ozone layer	**c.** all conditions and influences the affect the existence of an organism
5. global warming	**d.** a part of the atmosphere that blocks most of the ultraviolet rays of the sun from reaching the earth
6. range	
7. aquifer	**e.** a chemical that is intended to kill insects
8. Endangered Species Act	**f.** the federal agency responsible for enforcing laws that concern protection of the environment
9. Environmental Protection Agency	**g.** a chemical found in many consumer products that has been found to cause cancer in laboratory mice
10. biodegradable	**h.** an area in which a particular plant or animal may be found
	i. able to break down into basic components over time
	j. a law that protects animals and plants designated by the government as being in danger of becoming extinct

Review and Enrichment Activities Continued

2. Explain the difference to the environment between products that can be recycled and those that can be reused.

CHECKING WHAT YOU'VE LEARNED

Write your answers for the following exercises on a separate sheet of paper.

1. Why should people consider the environment when they make consumer decisions?
2. What are several possible explanations for global warming?
3. What has happened to nearly half of our nation's aquifers?
4. What have scientists predicted the result will be if the earth's ozone layer is destroyed?
5. What did Rachel Carson write about in her book *Silent Spring*?
6. How may an animal or plant be placed on the endangered species list?
7. Why did many firms turn to packaging that cannot be recycled or is not biodegradable?
8. How can consumers encourage businesses to use packaging that is recyclable or biodegradable?
9. What share of our trash was recycled in 1990? What share could be recycled?
10. Why do some people believe that conservation is a better alternative to recycling?

PRACTICING YOUR CONSUMER SKILLS

Identify the environmental problem in each of the following situations, and explain a step that consumers can take to improve the situation. Write your answers on a separate sheet of paper.

1. Every weekday at 7 A.M. a traffic jam develops at the main entrance to an interstate highway in a suburb of a major city. Hundreds of drivers sit in their cars for 20 minutes or more while they wait their turn to get on the highway.
2. The mayor of a small town believes that communication between government and citizens is very important. Therefore, the town sends a newsletter to every registered voter each month. Some months there are important events to report. In other months there is little going on, and the letter is almost blank. However, it is sent out anyway.

3. A city in the Midwest used to take its drinking water from a river that flowed through town. The city's sewage treatment plant was built in the 1960s to serve 50,000 homes. There are now 80,000 homes that send waste water to the plant, and it has not been updated to use new technology. Bacteria levels in the city's water grew so high that the city council decided to drill wells to supply its water needs instead of using the river. Nothing has been done about the sewage treatment plant.

4. A local take-out restaurant switches from cardboard to Styrofoam containers. The owner says that the new containers don't leak and they keep the food warm longer. He uses an average of 500 containers a day.

5. A farmer used to own 1,000 acres of swampland in a remote area that he thought had little value. He enjoyed going to the swamp every fall and spring to watch migratory water birds on their way north or south. Some birds stayed and nested on his land. However, as a nearby city grew, homes were built in the area of his farm, and his property taxes began to go up. Soon the farmer felt he could no longer afford to own so much land. He sold the swamp to a firm that intends to drain most of it and turn it into a golf course.

USING NUMBERS

Solve the following problem to help make the best possible choice. Write your solution on a separate sheet of paper. Be sure to show all your work.

Lois buys fabric softener for her laundry. Until recently, she always bought a national brand that came in a 2-quart plastic jug that cost $2.99. Lois bought one of these jugs about every two weeks. This firm now offers concentrated fabric softener in 1-pint cardboard containers for $2.39. By mixing the concentrate with water, consumers can make 2 quarts of softener. This reduces the amount of plastic that will be discarded into landfills. When Lois tries this new product, she slips and spills water all over her foot and the floor. She also wonders what will happen to the plastic-coated cardboard container.

How much could Lois save in a year if she buys the concentrate? What would you recommend she do? Explain your reasons for your recommendation.

PUTTING IDEAS IN YOUR OWN WORDS

The following quotations are from this chapter. Explain these quotations in your own words to make sure you understand what they mean. Write your answers on a separate sheet of paper.

1. "We live in our environment. We are part of it. We cannot escape harm when it is damaged."

2. "On the surface, the Endangered Species Act appears simple and clear. In reality, the law is neither."

Review and Enrichment Activities Continued

3. "Many people believe that conservation offers the best long-term hope for protecting our environment."

BUILDING CONSUMER KNOWLEDGE

Write your answers for the following exercises on a separate sheet of paper.

1. Survey your school to identify any practices that may be harming the environment. For each practice, suggest an alternative that could reduce the harm to the environment. Do the same for your home.
2. Suppose there was no plastic. Make a list of the ways your life would be affected. How many of these ways are important, and how could you adjust to life without plastic? What groups of people would be affected more than you? How would they be affected?
3. List five ways your life will probably be different from that of your parents because of damage to our environment. How much value would you assign to these changes?

Chapter 15

Making Consumer Decisions

Chapter Objectives

After completing this chapter, you will be able to do the following:

- Use the knowledge you have learned and the skills you have developed to make consumer decisions.
- Explain how your knowledge and skills will help you make better consumer decisions in your own life.

Key Consumer Terms

In this chapter you will learn the meanings of the following important consumer terms:

- Boycott
- Clear-cut
- Bureau of Land Management (BLM)
- Old-growth forest
- Groundwater
- Radon gas
- Curie
- E-PERM test

T his chapter focuses on five situations that require a decision. Your task will be to use the decision-making process (a consumer skill) along with the knowledge you have gained so far to recommend a specific decision for each situation. In each case there is no *one* solution that is right. There are many possible answers. Don't waste your time looking for the "right" choice. Use your time to develop a choice that you believe will work.

In Chapter 1 you learned that most important consumer decisions involve benefits and costs that must be identified and evaluated so that the best possible choice can be made. You were provided with a process to help you make more complicated decisions. The steps in this process are listed here as a reminder. Take a few minutes to review them. If they are not clear to you, return to Chapter 1 and read about them again. The steps are:

1. Identify the problem.
2. Determine broad goals you would like to achieve.
3. Establish specific objectives you would like to achieve.
4. Identify the alternative choices you could make.
5. Evaluate each alternative choice in relation to how it will help you achieve your objectives.
6. Make the choice.
7. Evaluate the results of your decision.

Visit your library to get more up-to-date information on the topics discussed in this chapter. Important events may have taken place since this book was written. Be prepared to explain why you believe your decision is the best choice possible.

A brief list of terms follows each of the five discussions. After you complete the decision-making process, explain how these terms relate to the situation and your decision. Use this as an opportunity to show your understanding of the terms.

SECTION 1

DOLPHINS AND TUNA FISH SANDWICHES

Imagine that it is 1989 and Marcy has a problem. She thinks of herself as an environmentalist, but she also likes tuna sandwiches for lunch. Marcy feels that she should boycott canned tuna fish because of the danger some methods of tuna fishing pose to dolphins. She recently read about the problem in a newsletter from an environmental group she supports, the Earth Island Institute.

Marcy learned that in the 1970s, a new type of fishing net, called the drift net, became widely used by people who catch tuna because it was very effective in catching ocean fish. The net was as tall as the ocean is deep in areas where it was used. Weights were attached to its bottom to keep it on the ocean floor. Floats held the top at the surface. The drift nets could be thousands of feet wide. They swept along the ocean floor and caught everything that was alive: tuna fish, rays, turtles, sharks, and dolphins.

Dolphins are marine mammals. They must swim to the surface to breathe. When dolphins were caught in drift nets, they often drowned. An estimated 80,000 to 150,000 dolphins a year were being killed by these nets in the 1980s. It was feared that the use of drift nets could cause dolphins to become an endangered species.

It is possible to catch tuna with other types of nets that pose little threat to dolphins, but they are much less efficient. Fishermen from many nations, especially Japan, Taiwan, and other Southeast Asian countries argued that their nations needed the large quantities of tuna they catch with drift nets to sustain a nutritious diet for their people. Eliminating drift nets could also result in unemployment for fishermen from these countries. It was estimated that not buying from fishermen who used drift nets would add from 3 to 5 cents to the price of a can of tuna.

In 1988 consumers organized a movement in the United States and other countries to **boycott** canned tuna to put pressure on canneries not to buy tuna that had been caught in drift nets. Environmental groups demanded some form of international inspection to be established to prevent further killing of dolphins and other animals by drift nets.

Suppose it is 1989 and you, like Marcy, like tuna fish sandwiches for lunch. As a responsible consumer, what should you do? Use the decision-making process to make your choice. When you finish, explain how the following terms were related to the problem or to your solution.

- Scarcity
- Opportunity cost
- Demand

On April 12, 1990, Star-Kist, VanCamp Seafood, and Bumble Bee Sea Food announced that they would no longer buy tuna from boats that used drift nets. These firms accounted for 70 percent of the canned tuna sold in the United States in that year. An agreement was reached to put observers on 100 percent of U.S. fishing boats and on 30 percent of foreign vessels to assure the firms that drift nets were not used. The boycott on these brands of tuna was lifted. Soon after, most other firms that sell tuna in this country agreed to meet the same standards for their products.

◆ Fishermen need to earn a living. Can we protect animals like dolphins without harming people? Would you be willing to pay more for your food to accomplish these objectives?

Vocabulary Builder

Boycott   An activity in which the public is urged not to purchase a particular product to exert economic pressure on the producer of that product.

Consumer Close-Up

How Much Difference Can One Person Make?

John Javna is just one person. However, he is a person who saw a problem and decided to do something about it. Javna was convinced that many Americans truly wanted to do what they could to protect the environment but didn't know how to do it. He decided to produce a book that was understandable and easy to use, so that people could immediately take action. Javna said, "The message of the book is that we do have power, that it's not too late to do something." Javna's book, *50 Simple Things You Can Do to Save the Earth*, identifies things that ordinary people can do that will make a difference *now*.

Javna's book deals with many different environmental problems. It explains how to stop the junk mail that wastes paper and trees. The value of phosphate-free laundry detergents is discussed. How to save water, how to reduce evaporation of gasoline into the atmosphere, how to protect animals by cutting plastic rings on six-pack containers, and how to recycle motor oil are all included in his book. Most of the steps Javna recommends are simple. People just have to know enough to do them.

Rather than going to a professional publisher, Javna decided to produce and print the book himself. He worked with twelve other people to research and write the book. The process was largely one of searching the vast amount of available materials and selecting actions that were easy and simple for ordinary people to do. By doing most of the work independently, Javna was able to keep the final price low enough so that most people could afford to buy his book.

Javna's first printing of 25,000 copies of the 96-page book sold out in a few weeks. Soon it was at the top of the *New York Times* best-seller list and stayed there for months. About 1.2 million copies were sold in its first year of publication. Javna's final message in his book is to spread the word. He invites readers to send him suggestions for other things that people can do to save the earth so that he can include them in future editions. If you have any ideas you believe are worth sharing, his address is:

Earthworks Group
Box 25
1400 Shattuck Avenue
Berkeley, CA 94709

SECTION 2

WHICH IS ENDANGERED: THE SPOTTED OWL OR THE LUMBER INDUSTRY?

For many years privately owned lumber companies have been able to buy rights from the federal government to cut trees on public lands. These firms often "**clear-cut**" vast areas of forest because cutting down all trees is the most cost-efficient method to produce lumber. When only mature trees are cut, the cost of getting them out of the woods is much higher. Conservationists have condemned clear-cutting of forests as being destructive to the environment. Regardless of protests, the federal **Bureau of Land Management (BLM)**, which controls cutting rights in national forests, allowed firms to continue to clear-cut trees in the 1980s.

Suppose that you owned a restaurant and motel in Olympia, Washington. Olympia is located near many national forests and depends on money earned from lumber and tourism. Most tourists who stay in your motel have

◆   How does the photograph of a hillside that has been clear cut make you feel? How much more would you be willing to pay for forest products like lumber and paper to have more wilderness that looks like the picture on the right? Would you have a different opinion if you were employed in the forest products industry?

come to see the great national forests that surround Olympia. Many customers in your restaurant are workers on their way to cut trees in the forest. Your business depends on the forest being there to see and being there to be cut. You hope that when you retire, you will be able to spend more time hiking and camping in the woods. You have mixed emotions about the situation.

In the 1980s it was discovered that the northern spotted owl nested in parts of the northwestern forests that were scheduled to be cut for timber. The U.S. Fish and Wildlife Service placed the owl on our nation's endangered species list on April 26, 1989, stating that the owl was "imperiled over significant portions of its range because of continuous losses of it habitat." A ban on cutting was suggested on 2.5 million acres of **"old-growth" forest**. The decision was appealed through the federal

court system by businesses and people employed in the lumber industry. It was estimated that the ruling, if enforced, would cause the loss of 9,000 to 16,000 jobs in the economically depressed Northwest. Other effects of the decision would be an increase in the price of lumber for consumers and a greater dependency on imported wood products from Canada and other countries.

Vocabulary Builder

Bureau of Land Management (BLM)   The federal agency that oversees and controls the cutting of trees in national forests.
Clear-cut   To cut all trees in an area of forest, regardless of their size.
Old-growth forest   Forest made up of trees that are in the climax stage of the forest's growth.

People often gather in your restaurant to discuss and argue over what should be done. Both sides demand your support in the arguments. As a responsible consumer, which side should you support? Use the decision-making process to make your choice. When you finish, explain how the following terms relate to the problem or to your solution.

- Productive resources
- Voluntary exchange
- Supply

A federal court issued a ruling on May 23, 1991, stopping further sales of cutting rights on federal land near Olympia, Washington.

SECTION 3

HOW HIGH SHOULD YOU STACK IT?

There is a small community of about 6,000 people located in New York State about halfway between two larger cities with populations of several hundred thousand people each. We'll call this town Middleton for our *almost* true story.

For many years Middleton was the quiet home of farmers and a few small industries. A local entrepreneur, Joe Winner, ran a landfill that was used to dispose of garbage from Middleton and a few other communities no more than 10 miles away. Most people who lived in Middleton thought that their lives were good and their environment safe. However, in the late 1980s things began to change.

Garbage dumps that had served the larger cities were filled and new locations needed to be found. One morning, giant eighteen-wheel semi-trailers filled with garbage started driving through Middleton on their way to Winner's landfill. It was discovered that at a late-night town board meeting, a change had

been made in Joe's permit to allow him to accept trash from anywhere. Joe had also applied for and received state permission to expand his dump. People in Middleton were up in arms. They didn't want trucks carrying evil-smelling loads through their streets. They didn't want giant piles of garbage stacked near their community. They worried about the impact the trash could have on their **groundwater** and their property values. The leaders of the town council who had changed Joe's permit were defeated in the next election, but that didn't get rid of Joe or his landfill.

Joe tried to make peace with the citizens of the community. He agreed to pay large property taxes that allowed the new town council to reduce the taxes other people paid. He agreed to pay for repaving a country road for the trucks so that they wouldn't need to pass through the town. Joe could always be counted on to make contributions to every local charity and school fund raiser. People began to believe that maybe Joe wasn't such a bad person. Joe was also getting rich.

After a few years, Joe's landfill began to fill up. He applied to the town council for permission to make his mounds of garbage 100 feet high instead of stopping at the current 30-foot limit. This would have created a mountain of garbage that could have been seen from almost any point in Middleton. The town council refused. Joe said that his landfill would be full in four more years. He asked the town council where they intended to put their garbage after he closed down.

Meanwhile, the New York State legislature passed a law that required every community to start a recycling program by the end of 1991. This gave Joe an idea. He offered to run the recycling program in Middleton for free if the town council would allow him to stack his garbage higher and accept materials for recycling from other communities. Joe said that if the town refused, he would close his landfill, and the town would have to find another way to get rid of its garbage and **recycle** its trash. The members of the town council were reluctant to make this decision on their own. They put the question to a vote by the citizens.

How do you believe the people of Middleton should have voted? Use the decision-making process to make your choice. When you finish, explain how the following terms relate to the problem or to your solution.

- Rational choice
- Entrepreneurship
- Profit motive
- Public goods

The town agreed to Joe's terms, and the recycling program was provided for free. The landfill was expanded, and as this book is being written, Joe is continuing to earn a good profit. With the expansion, Joe's landfill will probably last ten to fifteen years before it is full. The ultimate effect on the environment of Middleton is still unknown.

SECTION 4

THERE'S RADIOACTIVE GAS IN THE BASEMENT

Thad and Wilma own a new single-story home in Pennsylvania. They have three children, all under the age of ten. Thad is employed as a production worker in a factory, while Wilma works as a waitress on weekends. At the end of most months, Thad and Wilma have only a few dollars left over after paying their bills. A few weeks ago Wilma read a magazine article about **radon gas** that made her worried. She learned many facts she wasn't sure she wanted to know.

Radon is a naturally occurring, colorless, odorless gas that is also radioactive. It tends to accumulate in the basements of homes built on radon-bearing rock. The amount of radon in air

Consumer News

It Isn't Just Trash We Need To Worry About

Some types of radioactive waste take 10,000 years to decay and become harmless to humans, plants, and animals. The United States has created thousands of tons of high-level nuclear waste, most of which was sitting in pools of water near nuclear power plants in 1991. The federal government plans to construct a burial facility near Yucca Mountain, Nevada, to house this material for at least 1,000 years.

The Yucca Mountain site was chosen because it is a geologically stable location with very little water that could transport radioactive materials to other areas. The water table in this location is about 2,000 feet deep. Yucca Mountain is also nearly 50 miles from any permanent human dwelling. However, some residents in Las Vegas and other communities oppose the facility. They argue that over the next 1,000 or more years, our climate could change, and the radioactive materials could be released into the environment.

What do you think should be done with our radioactive waste?

Vocabulary Builder

Ground water Water held in a geographical area's aquifer.
Radon gas A colorless, odorless, radioactive gas that occurs naturally in the soil.

is measured in many ways, but a common method is in **curies** per liter of air (pCi/L). The EPA has determined that 4 pCi/L is a safe level for indoor radon. Higher levels of radon have been associated with increased rates of lung cancer, particularly in the young and old. The EPA has recommended that action should be taken for homes with unsafe levels of radon gas:

- *Levels Higher Than 200 pCi/L.* Exposures in this range are among the highest observed in homes. Residents should undertake action to reduce levels as far below 200 pCi/L as possible. Temporary relocation is appropriate until the levels can be reduced.
- *Levels from 20 to 200 pCi/L.* Exposures in this range are considered above average for residential structures. Residents should take actions to reduce levels as far below 20 pCi/L as possible within several months.
- *Levels from 4 to 20 pCi/L.* Exposures in this range are considered above average for residential structures. Residents should take actions to reduce levels as far below 20 pCi/L as possible within a few years.

As homes have been better insulated, concentrations of radon gas have tended to increase. Some areas of the country (including large parts of Pennsylvania) have much greater problems with radon gas than others. The best way to find out if your home has a problem is to have it tested. Since the 1980s radon testing kits have been available in many stores for under $25. A common test is called the **E-PERM test**, which stands for "electret-passive environment radon monitor." This system uses electrostatically charged plastic disks to detect the electric charge associated with radon gas. Using this test allows consumers to know quickly if they have a radon problem.

After finishing the article, Wilma went to a hardware store and bought an E-PERM test kit for $14.99. When she received the results of the test, she was upset to find that her basement air had a radon level of 67 pCi/L. According to the EPA's recommendations, Thad and Wilma should take action to reduce the radon in their home within several months. Thad and Wilma called a contractor who specialized in radon problems to examine their home and make recommendations.

The contractor spent several hours with Thad and Wilma. He said that they should have ducts installed in their basement to collect air and blow it outside. He offered to do the job for $3,600. If Thad and Wilma agree to this, it will use almost every penny they have saved.

What do you believe they should do? Use the decision-making process to make your choice. When you finish, explain how the following terms relate to the problem or to your solution.

- Private property
- Consumer protection
- Litigation

It might be possible for Thad and Wilma to bring legal action against the builder of their home. William Ethier of the U.S. National Association of Home Builders has stated that claims can arise against builders for the following reasons:

a. *Breach of express warranty: Written contract containing statements or representation about radon, or indirect "safety" statements that could be construed to include radon.*

b. *Breach of implied warranty: Those warranties placed on builders by statutes or courts, which, since the wording is often vague, may or may not include statements that can be applied to radon.*

c. *Negligence: Could include poor siting, poor construction, and not warning buyers of potential high radon levels.*

d. *Fraud and misrepresentation: Failure to warn about radon.*

e. *Strict liability: The house is considered a product, and like all other faulty products, the maker may be held liable.*

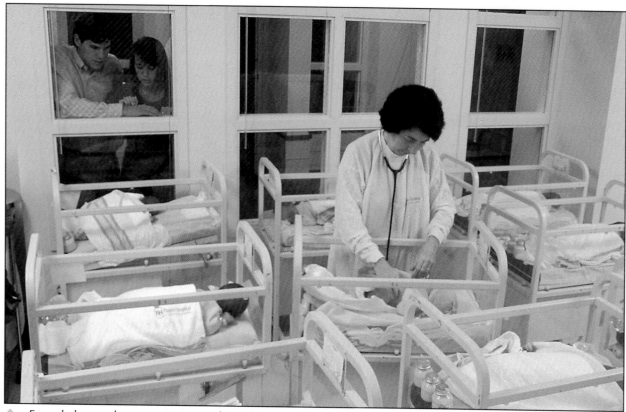

◆ Every baby needs resources to use through his or her life. Would you be willing to use fewer resources today to assure an adequate supply in the future?

SECTION 5

DIAPERS: SHOULD YOU WASH THEM OR TOSS THEM?

Paula and Fred are new parents. Little June brightens their days and teaches them the meaning of responsibility. June may be the joy of their lives, but she is also the cause of a long and heated debate. Paula wants to use disposable paper diapers because she believes that they are more convenient and are less likely to leak and make a mess. Fred argues in favor of cloth diapers because they cost less and because he believes that they are less damaging to the environment. Paula doesn't think cotton diapers are any better for the environment than paper ones. Both Paula and Fred have done research and found information to support their points of view.

Fred discovered that Americans bought about 18 billion paper diapers a year in the late 1980s. This required the use of 67,500 tons of plastic film that will take hundreds of years to

Vocabulary Builder

Curie A measure of an amount of radioactivity.
E-PERM Test A test used to determine the amount of radon gas in the air.

break down in landfills. When diapers are buried, they contain viruses that could eventually reach the groundwater that people drink. Thousands of acres of trees are cut down each year to make paper diapers. Fred believes that using paper diapers is not environmentally sound. He also found that cloth diapers cost about one-third less to use than paper disposables and can be reused as many as 200 times before they are recycled.

Paula feels that cloth diapers are not good for the environment either. She argues that the land used to grow cotton for the diapers is often overfertilized, causing water pollution. Also, soil nutrients are depleted, and the soil tends to erode. When a diaper service is used, the firm's trucks burn fuel and emit carbon dioxide into the air. Cotton diapers must be washed, a process that requires more energy than producing paper diapers. The water used for washing diapers puts a strain on limited supplies of fresh water in many locations and often is not hot enough to kill germs. Discarded wash water may be dumped into sewer systems and may find its way into our lakes and rivers. Besides, it is possible to buy paper diapers that are biodegradable, even if they do cost a few pennies more.

Do you believe that Paula and Fred should buy paper diapers or cloth diapers for June? Use the decision-making process to make your choice. When you finish, explain how the following terms relate to the problem or to your solution.

- Consumer sovereignty
- Substitute goods
- Monopolistic competition

In 1989 Proctor & Gamble Co. produced 8 billion disposable diapers a year that accounted for 17 percent of its sales. As a result of the disposal problem, the firm has been investigating uses for recycled paper diapers. Several possible answers are composting them for use in agriculture or making them into backing for drywall construction. Although these ideas may offer hope for the future, the firm believes that the cost of landfills will have to go up first. When dumping paper diapers becomes too expensive, other ways of using them probably will be found.

Review and Enrichment Activities

VOCABULARY REVIEW

1. Column A contains key consumer terms from this chapter. Column B contains a scrambled list of phrases that describe what these terms mean. Match the correct meaning with each term. Write your answers on a separate sheet of paper.

Column A	**Column B**
1. E-Perm test	a. water below the water table that is tapped by wells
2. old growth forest	b. a measure of radioactivity
3. ground water	c. area of trees that have never been logged
4. boycott	d. removing all trees from an area of forest
5. curie	e. an odorless radioactive gas naturally released from rock and soil formations
6. radon gas	f. a method used to determine the amount of radioactive gas in the air
7. clear cut	g. an agency of the federal government that controls cutting of trees in national forests
8. Bureau of Land Management	h. when consumers are urged not to buy a product to put economic pressure on the producer of that product

2. Why should people be concerned if they find there is radon gas in their homes?

CHECKING WHAT YOU'VE LEARNED

Write your answers for the following exercises on a separate sheet of paper.

1. Why were consumers asked to boycott canned tuna fish in 1988?
2. Why do logging firms prefer to clear-cut forests instead of cutting only mature trees?

Review and Enrichment Activities Continued

3. How did placing an animal's name on the endangered species list prevent tree cutting in national forests?
4. Why are landfills in many rural communities being used up very rapidly?
5. How have state requirements for recycling been used to almost force some communities to accept waste disposal sites?
6. Why do new homes often have more problems with radon gas than older homes?
7. How can consumers find out if their homes have a radon gas problem?
8. Why do some people feel that cloth diapers are as much of a threat to the environment as disposable paper diapers?
9. How has the decision-making process helped you to recommend choices in the situations described in this chapter?

PRACTICING YOUR CONSUMER SKILLS

Each of the following stories includes several events. Each event represents a step in the decision-making process. On a separate sheet of paper, identify the step and explain why it is important to the decision-making process. The decision-making steps are repeated here:

1. Identify the problem.
2. Determine broad goals you would like to achieve.
3. Establish specific objectives you would like to achieve.
4. Identify the alternative choices you could make.
5. Evaluate each alternative choice in relation to how it will help you achieve your objectives.
6. Make the choice.
7. Evaluate the results of your decision.

1. Jerry is a college student who has been offered a part-time job working in a research laboratory 8 miles from his home. He has been offered $8 an hour to work 20 hours a week. He needs the money, and the work is directly related to the organic chemistry he is studying in college. If he takes the job, he will need to find a way to get to work.
   a. Jerry thinks that he can take a bus, buy a car, or ride his bicycle to work.
   b. Jerry needs to get to work on time. He needs to limit his cost. He also needs to have a way to get to work when it is late at night or stormy.
   c. Jerry finds that buying and insuring a car would cost at least $5,000 a year. The bus costs $1 each way, but the nearest stop is half a mile from his job. Jerry already owns the bicycle, but he doesn't like riding it in the rain.
   d. On nice days Jerry rides his bicycle. If it rains he takes the bus.

2. Lori has decided to do as much as she can to protect the environment. She no longer buys products that use Styrafoam, aerosol propellants, plastic containers, or other products that result in what she thinks is "unnecessary waste."
   a. Lori decides to buy milk in plastic jugs instead of cardboard containers.
   b. Lori wants to buy milk for her children in containers that do the least damage to the environment.
   c. Lori discovers that the cardboard containers she bought were coated with a plastic film that would not biodegrade. She also finds a firm that recycles plastic milk jugs into insulation for houses.
   d. Lori takes about twenty jugs a month to the insulation firm and sometimes watches as the jugs are ground into insulation.
3. The City Memorial Hospital maintains a garden for its patients. The doctors are convinced that people who are ill are happier and recover more quickly when they can enjoy a place that is green and full of life. Their problem is that they can't afford to spend much on the garden.
   a. They can hire a professional gardener who would take care of the garden for $120 a day. They can hire a garden service that would come once a week for $75 to cut the grass and spray the plants with fertilizer and insecticide. They can try to find local volunteers to take care of the garden.
   b. They decide that they do not want any chemicals or artificial fertilizers used because some patients could have bad reactions. They decide that they can't afford to spend more than $100 a week. They also want to encourage community involvement in the hospital.
   c. After a year the program is doing well. Over twenty volunteers put in time each month, totaling roughly 30 hours a week.

USING NUMBERS

Solve the following problem to help make the best possible choice. Write your solution on a separate sheet of paper. Be sure to show all your work.

Sam has just had an energy use survey completed for his house by the firm that sells him natural gas. According to the survey, he could reduce his energy consumption by roughly 22 percent if he increased his insulation and replaced several old and leaky windows. Installing the insulation would cost $1,250. The windows would add another $700. Last year Sam spent $893 on gas. If gas prices and his use do not change, how long would it take Sam to save the cost of insulation and windows? What factors, other than cost, should he consider? What choice would you recommend for Sam? Explain the reasons for your recommendation.

Review and Enrichment Activities Continued

PUTTING IDEAS IN YOUR OWN WORDS

The following quotations are from this chapter. Explain these quotations in your own words to make sure you understand what they mean. Write your answers on a separate sheet of paper.

1. "Firms often "clear-cut" vast areas of forest because cutting down all trees is the most cost-efficient method to produce lumber."
2. "As homes have been better insulated, concentrations of radon gas have tended to increase."
3. "When diapers are buried, they contain viruses that could eventually reach the groundwater that people drink."

BUILDING CONSUMER KNOWLEDGE

Write your answers for the following exercises on a separate sheet of paper.

1. Select a product that you believe is produced or marketed in a way that is not environmentally responsible. Write a letter to the producer of this product, stating your opinion and what you believe the firm should do about the situation. Be polite, but make your point of view clear. If you get a response to your letter, report this to your class.
2. Identify a specific consumer issue in your home, school, or community. Use the decision-making process to recommend the choice that you believe would result in the greatest possible benefit to society at the least possible cost. Be prepared to explain how you reached your decision.
3. Choose a specific consumer issue that you feel should be addressed by the government. Write a letter to one of your representatives, clearly and politely stating your opinion and the action you would like to see the government take. If you get a response to your letter, report this to your class.

UNIT 5

The Business World

We are consumers so long as goods and services are being produced that we may buy and use. Unit 5 explains how businesses function in the U.S. economy. In this unit you will learn about the different types of businesses found in our economic system and the different ways they may be organized. You will also come to understand the relationship between your ability to earn income as a producer and your ability to pay for products as a consumer.

Chapter 16

The Variety of American Business

Chapter Objectives

After completing this chapter, you will be able to do the following:

- Explain the difference between goods-producing businesses and service-producing businesses.
- Identify business groupings that have been designated by the federal government and explain how the goods or services they produce are important to consumers.
- Discuss how different industrial groups work with each other in the American economy to provide goods and services that satisfy consumer needs.

Key Consumer Terms

In this chapter you will learn the meanings of the following important consumer terms:

- Standard industrial classification (SIC)
- Sector
- Division
- Group Retail

- Industry
- Wholesaler
- Retail
- Intermediaries

ave you ever picked up a newspaper and read an article that went something like this?

"The Department of Commerce announced today that the nation's service sector grew by 3.5% last year. This growth was led by an expansion of 5.2% in retail trade. The division with the lowest growth rate was government services, which expanded by only 1%..."

Did you understand everything you just read? What is a "sector" or "division" of the economy? By learning what these terms mean, you will be better able to understand what is happening in our country's economy and will be able to make better consumer choices.

SECTION 1

HOW THE GOVERNMENT CLASSIFIES BUSINESSES

While you read, ask yourself . . .
- *What kinds of goods and services does your family use?*
- *How will knowing the different types of businesses that exist in the U.S. economy help you make better consumer choices?*

The federal government classifies businesses into divisions, groups, and industries through the **standard industrial classification (SIC)**. There are other methods of classification, but SIC is the most commonly used. In this system all American businesses are divided into two **sectors**, those that produce goods, and those that provide services. These two general classifications are then broken down into ten **divisions** that are again subdivided into **groups**. Finally the groups are divided one more time into specific **industries**. See Figure 16-1.

For example, all businesses in the retail division are concerned with selling products to the final customer, regardless of whether their sales are $10,000 or $10 million a year. Toy stores, stationery shops, and newsstands are all members of the retail division. What retail firms have in common is selling goods to consumers.

Businesses in the manufacturing division have a different common characteristic. Some may manufacture computer parts, while others produce soap. Some may have one factory, while others may have many factories in different states and in other countries. Their main purpose, however, is to earn a profit by manufacturing a product in the most efficient way possible.

Vocabulary Builder

Division   One of ten types of businesses that all firms are divided into in the government's Standard Industrial Classification; a subheading under the two sectors, goods and services producing firms.

Group   A sub-heading for one of the ten divisions in the government's Standard Industrial Classification.

Industry   A group of businesses that operate in a similar fashion to provide the same type of goods or services.

Sector   One of the two basic classifications in the government's Standard Industrial Classification; either goods or services producing.

Standard industrial classification (SIC)   A government listing of businesses and industries divided into ten basic classifications that are further divided into groups and industries.

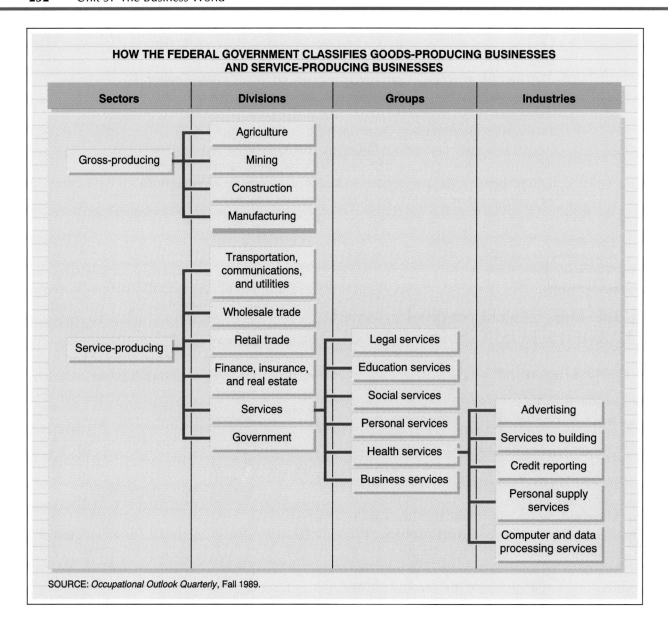

HOW THE FEDERAL GOVERNMENT CLASSIFIES GOODS-PRODUCING BUSINESSES AND SERVICE-PRODUCING BUSINESSES

SOURCE: *Occupational Outlook Quarterly*, Fall 1989.

◆ **Figure 16-1** How the Federal Government Classifies Goods-producing Businesses and Service-producing Businesses.

Some firms provide services rather than products. The insurance industry, for example, provides many different types of insurance, including homeowner's, automobile, medical, and life insurance. Some businesses in the insurance industry may specialize in only one type of insurance, while others may offer a wide range of policies. However, they all provide protection for people and businesses from unexpected loss.

Summing Up *It is often easier to think about businesses when they are classified into industries like those in the government's standard industrial classification.* ◆

INDUSTRIES YOU DEAL WITH

While you read, ask yourself . . .
◆ *What industries do you deal with on a regular basis?*
◆ *How do firms in these industries benefit from the consumer purchases you make?*

Many consumers find it useful to have an idea of the types of businesses that exist in the American economy. Organizing similar businesses into groups can help you understand what they do. A common way to classify businesses is by industry. An industry is a group of businesses that operate in a similar fashion to provide the same type of goods or services. Businesses that make up an industry have a common characteristic that causes them to have similar goals and objectives and to behave in similar ways.

Let's look at some of the major industries in the United States that consumers depend on. Remember, there are many businesses throughout the country that together make up each industry. These firms share one or more common characteristics, but they are each individual firms. They do not all need to be exactly the same to be in the same industry.

◆ Many cities now have massive industrial parks that contain many different types of industries. Why do these firms choose to be located so close to each other?

Automotive Industry

If you are like most Americans, you will eventually own an automobile. You could buy an American car made by General Motors, Chrysler, or Ford. Or you could purchase a Japanese vehicle produced by Toyota or Nissan. There is about one automobile on the road for each adult in the United States. The American love of automobiles, trucks, and recreational vehicles keeps hundreds of thousands of

workers employed in the United States and in other countries.

In recent years the U.S. automobile industry has fallen on hard times. In the first three months of 1991, 33 percent of the automobiles sold in this country were produced by foreign firms (although some of those automobiles were produced in factories in this country). Because of cost cutting, better engineering, and improved quality in American-owned companies, there is hope that the U.S. automotive industry will turn around and grow in the future.

Chemical Industry

You use chemicals every day. When you wash your dishes, the detergent you use is a chemical. The antifreeze in your car's radiator is a chemical. When paints and solvents are sold in stores, chemicals are being purchased. The plastic chairs that consumers buy for their patios and the vinyl flooring in their homes are made from chemicals. Firms like DuPont, Dow Chemical, and Monsanto are among the largest producers in the American chemical industry. Americans also import chemical products from firms like BASF in other countries. Although some chemical companies have received bad publicity in recent environmental debates, we need many of the products they produce to maintain our standard of living.

Defense Industry

Companies in the defense industry design and produce weapons, such as tanks, airplanes, and missiles. The importance of these products was demonstrated by the 1991 war in the Persian Gulf. American soldiers using "smart" bombs and other sophisticated weapons devastated the fourth largest army in the world in little more than a month. Although most citizens will never have any personal need for such products, their production protects the interests of Americans and other people in the world who desire freedom.

The defense industry has been substantially scaled back to reduce the size of the federal deficit and because of a reduction in international tensions in recent years. Many military bases have been closed and weapons systems canceled or reduced in size. This has caused a significant loss of jobs and income in many communities. It is hoped that a reduction in the use of our resources for the defense industry will enable a greater allocation of resources to other uses.

Entertainment Industry

When you go to a movie or turn on your television, you are receiving a service provided by the entertainment industry. Consumers often do not pay directly for entertainment. When you listen to the radio or watch broadcast television, the cost is paid for by advertisers. Consumers support this type of service indirectly as part of the price they pay when they buy the advertisers' products.

In recent years the entertainment industry has provided more services that consumers pay for directly and indirectly through the government. Cable television and rental videotapes are two examples of direct payments made by consumers. Educational programming is supported by consumers through donations and tax dollars provided by the government.

Financial Services Industry

Most people and businesses rely on various types of financial services. When consumers open checking accounts, they receive a financial service. Most home buyers need a mortgage. People who deposit money in a saving account are earning interest. Many consumers buy corporate stocks or bonds through a broker. Some people hire a financial advisor to help them plan for their retirement or save for their children's education. These are all examples of services provided by the financial services industry.

In recent years businesses in the financial services industry have experienced difficulty. In the 1980s many savings and loan associations failed. A number of banks also had problems as a result of having made risky loans. The Congress and president have taken action to resolve many of these problems.

◆   Reduced government spending on national defense has allowed more resources to be used for other purposes. What industries may have grown from government's decision to build fewer airplanes for the military?

Health Care Industry

There are times when every consumer needs the services of a doctor or a dentist, even if it is only for a regular check-up. Many consumers are healthy and don't use the services of a doctor or hospital very often. However, their insurance payments still support these services for people who do need them.

One of the most rapidly growing industries in the United States is the health care industry. This is the result of two trends. Americans are living longer, so a larger part of our population is older and in greater need of health care services. Also, many new medical advances allow us to help more people but require a greater allocation of resources. In the 1990s the number of workers in the health care industry will

Consumer News

A New Financial Service: The Reverse Mortgage

In May 1991 the Federal Housing Administration (FHA) announced that it was expanding a program that allowed homeowners who were sixty-two or older to borrow against the value of their homes to receive monthly income. This new financial service helped older homeowners on limited incomes to continue living in their homes. A survey carried out by the American Association of Retired People in 1990 showed that 86 percent of older Americans want to remain in their homes until they die. Without special help, many will not be able to afford this.

Under the "reverse mortgage" plan, homeowners can receive payments as long as they live in their home. Once they can no longer live at home, the house is sold to pay off their debt. When the homeowner moves or dies, the heirs may pay back the loan and keep the home if they choose. The maximum amount of the loans is between $67,500 and $124,875, depending on the value of the home. There are about 15 million homes owned by people who could qualify for this financial service.

Do you believe that this "reverse mortgage" is a good idea?

What advantages and disadvantages of the program can you think of?

◆ As our economy has changed more businesses have opened in the food service industry. Why are more Americans buying prepared foods today?

Food Service Industry

There are many kinds of businesses that prepare and serve food. They include everything from the local Pizza Hut to the most expensive French restaurant in New York City. Many school districts have even agreed to have restaurants like McDonald's provide meals in their school cafeterias. As more people work longer hours, our need for restaurants and the food service industry will grow.

There is almost a 50 percent chance that you will hold a job in the food service industry yourself. Statistics collected by the government show that about half of young workers today have been employed at some time either preparing or serving food, often in fast-food restaurants.

Differences Within Industries

What is true of one firm in an industry may not be true of all firms in that industry. You've probably heard at some time or other that a

grow to 12 million. Health care will be provided by individual doctors and nurses in offices and small clinics, as well as by giant interstate firms like Humana, National Medical Enterprises, and National Health Laboratories.

particular industry is not doing well. For example, you may have read that the computer industry is in a slump or that the aluminum industry has turned down. Your teacher may tell you that the banking industry is doing better this year than last. This does not mean that every bank is successful. It means that banks, on an average, are doing better. Some banks could be doing very well, while others could be losing money. Statements about an industry provide little information about specific businesses in that industry.

Summing Up   *Students and consumers may use the government's SIC to learn about the industries they deal with.* ◆

SECTION 3

ACTIVITIES THAT BUSINESSES PERFORM

While you read, ask yourself . . .
   ◆ *What are several activities that businesses perform that benefit you or other members of your family directly?*
   ◆ *How do you benefit indirectly from other activities that businesses perform?*
   ◆ *How do businesses interact with one another?*

You have seen how businesses have been grouped by the government according to the types of products they produce. Another way the government groups businesses is according to the main types of *activities* they perform. Some companies perform only one function, while others perform several. A few companies perform all five of the activities identified by the government. Consumers do not have direct dealings with businesses that carry out some of these activities. However, all five activities are necessary to produce the goods and services consumers buy to satisfy their needs

Consumer News

Selling the Legend of the "Old West"

In a sun-baked deserted street, two men in cowboy boots march slowly toward each other. They stop. One draws his gun. There is a deafening roar. The man in the black hat falls dead. The hero rides off into the sunset, leaving behind a grateful town that is now safe for law-abiding citizens.

Does this sound a bit "corny" to you? Corny or not, the legends of the "Old West" sell and earn good money. In 1991 the tourism industry as a whole was not doing well. Increased airfares, a recession, fears of terrorism, and other factors had caused sales to be essentially flat. But this was not true of Dodge City, Kansas, which exploited its history as the home of many famous lawmen and gunfighters. A nineteenth-century, Old West town was built near Dodge City, featuring saloons, dance halls, and regularly scheduled gunfights. Sales from tourism in the area increased by over 25 percent from 1990 levels. Many of the visitors were tourists from Europe, Asia, and South America, who were looking for a little piece of the "real" America.

and wants. You will find this method of classification useful in understanding how businesses are related to each other.

Producing or Extracting Raw Materials from Nature

Raw materials (land, to economists) are materials that occur naturally in our environment.

◆ Workers who extract resources provide the raw materials that allow other firms to carry out different business activities. Why is extracting resources often a very competitive business?

Businesses that use or extract (take) raw materials from the ground, water, or air are grouped accordingly.

Farmers who grow oranges use the nutrients in the soil and the rain that falls on the land to produce the fruit you eat. The oil workers in Texas or California who drill for petroleum and the foresters who harvest trees are also examples of people who perform this extracting activity. Consumers do not often carry out transactions directly with these businesses, but the materials that these businesses produce are used to make goods and services that satisfy human needs and wants.

Processing Raw Goods

Some raw goods are ready to use as they are taken from the environment. An apple, fish, or Christmas tree does not need to be changed before it is consumed. Most raw materials, however, need to be processed before consumers or other businesses can use them. When a raw material is processed, a series of actions is performed that changes the raw material into something useful.

Crude oil as it is taken from the ground has little value to consumers. The same may be said of wheat, or of wool as it is sheared from sheep. These raw materials need to be processed into gasoline, flour, and fabric before they are useful to consumers. All businesses that change natural materials from their original forms into more finished forms are involved in activities related to the processing of raw goods. The output of these businesses is called processed goods. Processed goods such as lumber may be purchased by consumers, or they may be purchased by other firms that will use them to make goods like furniture or houses.

Manufacturing

Businesses that use processed goods to produce finished goods are called manufacturers. Finished goods are often used by consumers to satisfy their needs and wants. If you buy a bicycle, the firm that produced the bicycle is a manufacturer. However, other firms that contributed to the production of the bicycle are also manufacturers. The different businesses that produced the tires, bicycle chain, and reflectors also manufactured final products. These products were not changed by the firm that assembled the bicycle. They were simply attached to the bicycle.

A bakery that produces bread from flour made by a firm that processed wheat into flour is a manufacturer. A factory that takes sheet steel made by a processing firm and makes it into doors for automobiles is also a manufacturer. When the door is finally used to make a car, it will not be changed. The door itself is a final product.

◆ Businesses that manufacture goods rely on marketers and distributors to sell their products. If you were in charge of marketing plastic turtles how would you encourage consumers to buy your products?

Some firms perform both processing and manufacturing. H. J. Heinz, for example, processes the ingredients needed to make ketchup and manufactures the bottle of ketchup you buy in the grocery store.

Marketing and Distributing

American firms employ skilled workers and use advanced technology to manufacture thousands of different products that are able to satisfy consumers' needs and wants. However, consumers must know how and where to buy these products for the firms to earn a profit. The activities of marketing and distribution involve many steps that bring the countless products and services from their producers to the consumer.

You would find it very difficult and expensive to make a direct transaction with the producer of every good or service you wanted to buy. Imagine having to go to Hawaii to buy a pineapple every time you wanted to make a fruit salad. Businesses that move goods from producers to consumers are called **intermediaries**.

One type of intermediary is a **wholesaler**. Wholesalers may distribute goods to businesses or sell to **retailers**. Retailers buy from producers or wholesalers and sell directly to consumers. Any business where consumers buy final products is a retailer.

Other types of businesses are also in this grouping. Firms that distribute advertising, deliver packages, or perform market research are involved in marketing. Firms involved in marketing and distribution add value to products because they make it easier for consumers to obtain the goods and services they want.

Providing Services

A service is an action done for you that satisfies a need or want that you have. Services are needed by consumers and businesses alike. Large firms like Coca-Cola or General Motors hire advertising firms to plan and create advertising campaigns. Employment agencies often find workers with specific skills for businesses. Many firms hire accounting firms to do their tax returns. These are all examples of services that businesses buy.

Vocabulary Builder

Intermediary A go-between between the producer of a product and its consumer.
Wholesale When a firm buys products from a manufacturer for resale to another business.

Consumer Close-Up

The Need for Child Care

Child Care for working parents is a growth industry. Although more men are staying home with children, most parental child care is still provided by mothers. However, most mothers work outside their homes at least part-time. In 1988 there were 16,617,000 working mothers with 28,309,000 children under the age of fifteen. More than one-third of these children had no one to watch them while their parents were at work.

A survey of working parents conducted by the Bureau of the Census in 1986–1987 provided the following information:

The share of preschool children (up to six years old) cared for in licensed day-care centers reached 23 percent in 1985. More states are regulating in-home day care provided by an unrelated person. Some states require such people to receive training and be screened for health or mental problems. One result of this increased regulation has been a decrease in the availability of in-home day care. As more mothers are employed, and with changes in government regulations and support, a growing number of children will probably need to be placed in licensed day-care centers.

In 1990, federal programs were supposed to provide day care for socially, educationally, or nutritionally disadvantaged children. Although 450,000 children were in federal programs, almost 2 million more qualified but could not be placed because of inadequate funding or lack of approved day-care facilities. In an attempt to address the shortage of day care, in 1990 President Bush signed a bill into law providing grants to help pay for new day-care centers, improve the quality of existing centers, and reduce the cost of child care for low-income workers.

State and local governments also provide assistance for day-care services. Many states provide funds for after-school day-care centers for students, and some provide day care for preschool children whose mothers are attending school. In 1990, 29 states helped to pay for child care through special tax deductions or by funding day-care centers to reduce the cost to low-income parents.

Employment in the day-care industry has grown with the increased need for licensed day-care centers. In 1976 there were 215,000 paid workers. By 1988 that number had grown to 406,000. There is every indication that this number will continue to grow at an even greater rate.

How would you go about finding and choosing a quality day-care center for your children (if you had any)?

Percent of Children Under 15 Years Old	
Cared for in a private home	47.0%
by a relative	31.7%
by an unrelated person	15.3%
Attended a day-care center	11.5%
Parent cared for child while working	6.1%
Child cares for self	35.4%

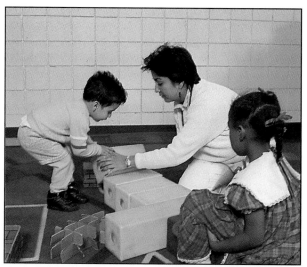

Once baby sitters were hired to "watch" children. What extra services do we expect of our child care workers today? What special skills do they need?

Consumers purchase services when they don't know how, or don't want to take the time to do something. Some consumers hire tax consultants to help them prepare their tax returns because they don't understand how to complete the forms themselves. Other consumers pay a lawn service to cut their grass because they have other things they would rather do with their time. In both these situations, consumers are buying services.

As more people have taken jobs and spend less time at home, our need for services has grown. The service industry has been the most rapidly growing part of the American economy in recent years. One of the most rapid growth areas has been in child care. With a larger number of mothers in the labor force, our need for child care services will continue to grow.

Businesses Work Together

Businesses that perform different activities depend on each other in many ways. A firm that extracts iron ore from the soil needs the services of a railroad to transport the ore to the processing firm where it is made into steel. The steel processor needs a manufacturer to buy its product to make it into a car or file cabinet. The manufacturer needs the services of marketing and distribution firms.

All businesses depend on consumers. Even firms that never make transactions with consumers depend on consumers. The businesses they sell products to could not afford to pay their bills if consumers did not buy finished goods and services. The success of all businesses depends on the willingness and ability of consumers to purchase goods and services that generates income for businesses.

Our Changing Needs for Goods and Services

As time goes by the kinds of products consumers want to buy will change. Technological advancements will alter the way we produce goods and services. In the future our needs for resources will be different than they are at the present. As a result, the relationship that exists between businesses now will also change. Businesses will still carry out the same five types of activities, but they may be different businesses and they will be completing different tasks.

To be a responsible consumer you should recognize that businesses and the products they offer for sale will change. You should expect to continue to learn about new or different goods and services for the remainder of your life. Consumers who fail to learn about new products will probably not gain the greatest possible satisfaction from the money they have to spend.

Summing Up   *Businesses may be classified according to the activities they perform. Businesses depend on each other and on consumers for their success.* ◆

Review and Enrichment Activities

VOCABULARY REVIEW

1. Column A contains key consumer terms from this chapter. Column B contains a scrambled list of phrases that describe what these terms mean. Match the correct meaning with each term. Write your answers on a separate sheet of paper.

Column A	Column B
1. intermediary	a. One of two business classifications whereby goods or services are produced
2. industry	b. A method of classifying all businesses according to the types of goods or services they produce
3. standard industrial classification	
4. wholesaler	c. A business or a person who acts as a go-between between a buyer and a seller
5. division	d. one of ten basic types all businesses are classified into by the government
6. retail	e. businesses that operate in a similar way to produce the same type of product
7. sector	f. the ten basic types of businesses are sub-divided into this more specific type of classification
8. group	g. a business that sells products directly to consumers
	h. a business that buys products from a manufacturer and resells them to other businesses

2. How do the activities of marketers and distributors differ from those of manufacturers?

CHECKING WHAT YOU'VE LEARNED

Write your answers for the following exercises on a separate sheet of paper.

1. Name two examples of each of the four classifications in SIC: sectors, divisions, groups, and industries.
2. Explain the difference between a goods-producing industry and a service-producing industry.
3. Explain why something that is true of an industry is not always true of each firm in that industry.
4. Identify the business *division* that each of the following businesses probably belongs to:
    Al's Independent Insurance Agency
    Morton's Sporting Goods
    WXXX TV
    Sasha's Home Building Co.
    The 2nd National Bank
5. Identify the *activity* that each of the following businesses is likely to perform:
    The Amalgamated Broom Company
    Ted's Bait Shop
    The Acme Rolled Steel Company
    The Deep Load Mine
    Martha's Home Decorating
6. Explain why firms that never sell products directly to consumers still depend on consumers for their success.

PRACTICING YOUR CONSUMER SKILLS

Write your answers for the following exercises on a separate sheet of paper.

1. Consider the following products:
    a. Advice on how to save for retirement
    b. A solvent to clean bugs from the front of a car
    c. A new television comedy about a family that adopts an aardvark
    d. A homeowner's insurance policy
    e. A van that seats ten passengers

    Identify each product as an example of a good or service. Then state whether a high school student would be likely to use the product. Finally, identify the industry that would produce the product, choosing from the following list of industries:

Insurance industry	Automotive industry
Chemical industry	Defense industry
Entertainment industry	Financial services industry
Health Care industry	Food service industry

Review and Enrichment Activities Continued

2. For each of the following activities, identify a firm that demonstrates the activity:

Producing or extracting raw materials

Processing raw goods

Manufacturing

Marketing or distributing

Providing services

3. Just about every American has eaten at a restaurant that serves pizza. Identify the activities that different businesses carry out that contribute to the production and distribution of pizza. Explain how this exercise demonstrates the way businesses work together and depend on each other.

USING NUMBERS

Solve the following problem to help make the best possible choice. Write your solution on a separate sheet of paper. Be sure to show all your work.

The following data show the value of production added by each of the ten business divisions in 1987 in billions of dollars. Find the percentage of the total that was generated by each division by dividing the value of the total production into the amount for each division and then moving the decimal in your answer two places to the right to change the number to a percent. Of these divisions, agriculture added the least to total production, while services contributed the most—almost seven times more than agriculture. Does this mean that services were about seven times more important to our country than agriculture? Explain.

	Value in 1987 (in billions)	Percent of Total
Total production	$3,847	100%
Agriculture	$ 96.1	_____
Mining	$117.5	_____
Construction	$175.8	_____
Manufacturing	$839.5	_____
Transportation, communications, and utilities	$349.5	_____
Wholesale trade	$291.7	_____
Retail trade	$368.3	_____
Finance insurance, and real estate	$559.4	_____
Services	$610.8	_____
Government	$415.7	_____

PUTTING IDEAS IN YOUR OWN WORDS

The following quotations are from this chapter. Explain these quotations in your own words to make sure you understand what they mean. Write your answers on a separate sheet of paper.

1. "Businesses that make up an industry have a common characteristic that causes them to have similar goals and objectives and to behave in similar ways."
2. "Statements about an industry provide little information about specific businesses in that industry."
3. "You would find it very difficult and expensive to make a direct transaction with the producer of every good or service you wanted to buy."

BUILDING CONSUMER KNOWLEDGE

Write your answers for the following exercises on a separate sheet of paper.

1. Identify three specific firms in your community that operate in different industries. For each firm, identify the industry it is part of, and explain the characteristics of the firm that enable you to make this judgment.
2. Identify three different firms that consumers are not likely to have direct transactions with. Explain why the activities of these firms are still important to consumers.
3. Identify three goods and three services that you don't need today, but that you are likely to need in ten years. What additional knowledge or skills will you need in order to use these goods and services ten years from now?

Chapter 17

Business Organizations and Consumers

Chapter Objectives

After completing this chapter, you will be able to do the following:

- Identify goals and objectives that are common to all businesses.
- Explain the basic characteristics of the sole proprietorships, partnerships, and corporations.
- Explain why different types of business are likely to have different forms of organization.
- Explain what a franchise is and describe the benefits consumers may receive and the costs they may pay when they deal with a franchise.

Key Consumer Terms

In this chapter you will learn the meanings of the following important consumer terms:

- Sole proprietorship
- Partnership
- Corporation
- Unlimited liability
- Asset
- Dissolved
- Legal entity
- Stock
- Stock Exchange
- Closely held corporation
- Limited liability
- Unlimited life
- Charter
- Franchise

People run businesses in the United States because they expect to earn a profit. To accomplish this goal, firms produce and distribute goods and services that satisfy consumer needs and wants. Some businesses sell products directly to consumers. Others provide goods and services to other businesses. All businesses depend on consumers to buy final goods and services.

Businesses must be organized to produce goods and services. In Chapter 2 you learned that entrepreneurship is one of the factors of production. Entrepreneurship involves taking the risks and making the decisions necessary to organize the production of goods and services from productive resources. In the United States there are three basic forms of business organization: **sole proprietorships**, **partnerships**, and **corporations.** Although these forms of business organization have similarities, there are also important differences between them and between the types of goods and services they are likely to offer for sale.

SOLE PROPRIETORSHIPS

While you read, ask yourself . . .
- ◆ *What are several businesses you deal with that are sole proprietorships?*
- ◆ *In what ways may you benefit from these firms being sole proprietorships?*
- ◆ *In what ways may you pay a cost because these firms are sole proprietorships?*

Many of the businesses where you shop are sole proprietorships. A proprietor is the owner of a business or firm. The word *proprietor* comes from the Latin word *proprietas*, meaning "property." A business is a type of property that people own. *Sole* means "the only one." Therefore, a sole proprietorship is a business owned by only one person.

Sole proprietorships are the most common form of business ownership in the United States. The owner may have help in operating the business, but he or she is the owner and is the only person responsible for the business.

There are certainly many sole proprietorships in your community—perhaps including the hair salon that perms your hair, the corner drugstore, and your local hobby shop. About 75 percent of all businesses in the United States are sole proprietorships. They are almost always small. Although sole proprietorships are the most common type of business organization, they carry out only about 10 percent of the dollar value of business sales in the United States owing to their small size.

Vocabulary Builder

Corporation   An organization owned by many people but treated by the law as though it were a person. It can own property, pay taxes, make contracts, sue or be sued, and so on.

Partnership   A form of business organization owned and operated by two or more people under a contractual agreement.

Sole proprietorship   A form of business organization owned by only one person, who is totally responsible for the business.

Advantages of Being a Sole Proprietor

Suppose that you want to open a Mexican restaurant in your community. Assume that you have had experience working in restaurants and your grandmother has agreed to teach you how to cook authentic Mexican food. You don't know much about the business end of running a restaurant but believe that you can learn "on the job."

Being a sole proprietor offers many advantages. A sole proprietorship is the easiest type of business to start because you don't have to reach an agreement with other owners. Depending on local laws, the only requirement may be to obtain a license from your local government. Other forms of business organization are usually more difficult to get started.

Sole proprietors have much greater control over their firms than owners of other types of business. A proprietor is free to make most of his or her own decisions about running the business. This allows sole proprietors to act quickly to take advantage of new opportunities. As the sole proprietor of a restaurant, you could decide at any time to change the items on your menu or the hours you stay open if

◆   The greatest advantage of being a sole proprietor may be the satisfaction it gives you to be your own boss. On the other hand, how much time do you imagine this owner spends in his store?

you believed that these changes would be good for business. You would not have to convince other owners to accept your ideas.

Sole proprietors control the use of their firm's profits. However, they are also responsible for any losses that their business suffers. Sole proprietors are taxed as individuals and therefore may pay fewer taxes or be taxed at lower rates than other forms of business organization. Sole proprietors, for example, do not pay corporate income taxes.

Sole proprietors are not totally free to run their business in any way they see fit because they must meet various government regulations. For example, your restaurant would need to be inspected by health officials. You could not hire workers who were too young or who were sick. However, there are often fewer regulations for sole proprietors than for other forms of business organization.

Many sole proprietors will tell you that one of the most important benefits they receive from their business is a sense of pride of ownership. Building a successful restaurant or other type of business could give you a sense of accomplishment you would not achieve working for someone else. On the other hand, if your business does not do well, you could decide to go out of business, and you would not need to consult other owners.

Disadvantages of Being a Sole Proprietor

Just as there are advantages of being a sole proprietor, there are important disadvantages you should know about. Sole proprietors have **unlimited liability**. This means that the owner of a sole proprietorship is personally responsible for all debts incurred (entered into and owed) while doing business. For example, if a customer at your restaurant falls on poorly lighted steps, you could be completely respon-

Consumer News

Retirement Success

In 1981 Walter Lappert settled in Hawaii to enjoy his retirement. Lappert had been a waiter in a large hotel and had run his own French crepe business for fourteen years. He decided that the ice cream in his new home was inferior and decided to go into the ice cream business himself. Walter invested $110,000, which was most of his savings, and started producing ice cream in the small town of Hanapepe. In his first three weeks he sold as much ice cream as he had expected to sell in six months. His product was "superrich" (14 percent butter fat) and made mostly from local ingredients. Ten years later Lappert's products were known throughout the islands. Sales from his "retirement job" totaled more than $15 million in 1990.

What special qualities must Walter Lappert have had to make his sole proprietorship such a success?
What costs might he have paid?

sible for the cost of the accident. Courts could take your personal belongings as well as your business property to satisfy claims that resulted from the injury.

Sole proprietors are limited in the amount of money, land, tools, and machinery that they

Vocabulary Builder

Unlimited liability   The risk that sole proprietors and partners take that all their assets may be taken to satisfy the debts of their firm.

can use in their business by the amount of money and **assets** that they have. If the total value of everything you own is $20,000, it would be difficult for you to organize a restaurant or other business that has a value greater than this amount. People, businesses, and banks are not likely to make business loans that are greater than the value of assets belonging to the owner of the firm. Because most individuals have limited assets, they are only able to own small businesses. This explains why most sole proprietorships are small.

Sole proprietors need to carry out many different responsibilities. The pride of ownership that many sole proprietors feel may make them unwilling to share the responsibility for making decisions with employees or others. As a result, many sole proprietors work long hours. They also may try to make decisions that require a variety of knowledge and skills. When sole proprietors lack the skills and knowledge needed to make decisions, they may make mistakes that could cause their business to fail. It is difficult for anyone to be an expert in everything.

Consumers and Sole Proprietors

All consumers carry out transactions with sole proprietors. It would be impossible to lead a normal life and not do so. However, you should recognize that the advantages and disadvantages of being a sole proprietor have an impact on consumers.

If you are looking for a low price on a new central home air-conditioning system, you might find a sole proprietor who is willing to install one for less than a larger firm would charge. However, if the firm is new or small, there is a chance that it will not be in business in several years when you might need service. The owner may be trying to do too many different tasks and may not be able to do them all well. If there is a problem with the system and

your home is damaged by water leakage, the sole proprietor's assets may not cover the cost of repairing your home. Consumers should be careful whenever they buy products. They should be especially careful when they buy expensive products from small businesses.

Summing Up   *The most common form of business organization in the United States is the sole proprietorship. These businesses tend to be small. Although consumers may benefit from lower prices and personal service when they deal with sole proprietors, such firms are likely to have fewer assets to put behind their products.* ◆

SECTION 2

PARTNERSHIPS

***While you read**, ask yourself . . .*
- *Are there any businesses that you deal with that are partnerships?*
- *Why are there fewer partnerships in your community than sole proprietorships?*

Suppose that after a year, your Mexican restaurant is doing well, particularly when you consider the fact that you really didn't know much about the business of running a restaurant. Although you have hired an accounting service to keep your books, you occasionally experience difficulties in keeping enough money on hand to pay for food and other supplies that you need to order. You would also like to buy some new equipment for your kitchen that you can't afford.

Now suppose that a friend of yours named Andrew graduated from college a few years ago with a degree in business. He has been working in the accounting department of a large business for the past three years. He has saved $10,000 and wants to buy into your business by becoming a partner. A partnership is a type of organization that has two or more people who share ownership and control of a business under a legal agreement. Only about 8 percent of all businesses in the United States are partnerships. If you agree to Andrew's suggestions, you will receive certain benefits and pay certain costs.

Advantages of Partnerships

In general, partnerships are able to raise larger amounts of money than sole proprietorships because they can call on the assets of two or more people. Partnerships can also borrow more money because creditors are often willing to lend larger amounts when two or more people are responsible for repaying the loan. If Andrew becomes your partner, the two of you will be able to raise more money together than either of you could raise alone.

Partners are able to share responsibilities and skills. You have learned to prepare authentic Mexican food. Andrew understands accounting and many other functions necessary to run a business. By sharing responsibilities, the two of you can run the restaurant more efficiently together than either of you could alone.

Partners often develop a special type of shared satisfaction. They feel a sense of pride in what they have accomplished and may enjoy a personal friendship in addition to a business relationship. People who are not totally confident of their own abilities may benefit from having a partner with whom to share business responsibilities.

Like sole proprietorships, partnerships are taxed in the same way as individuals. Therefore, partnerships pay fewer taxes and lower rates than some other types of business organization.

Partnerships are a very old form of business organization. Their legal status has been defined by many court cases over the years. These cases can be used as examples if issues arise between partners like you and Andrew.

Lawyers are able to provide extensive legal advice about partnerships.

Disadvantages of Partnerships

Probably the most important disadvantage of forming a partnership is unlimited liability. Each partner is liable (responsible) for the partnership's debts. This means that each partner is responsible for the debts of the other partners as well as for his or her own. If Andrew was not careful with the firm's money and ran up large debts that you were not aware of, you would still be responsible for paying these debts. This is one reason to choose partners very carefully.

Partnerships are more likely to be **dissolved**, or closed, than any other form of business organization. When partners do not agree, they may not be able to work out their differences. The result may be a decision to dissolve the partnership. Disagreements are often the result of different opinions on how profits should be divided. If you work 60 hours a week at your restaurant and Andrew only puts in 40 hours, do you deserve more of the profit? You might believe so, but Andrew might believe that his time has a greater value because of his education and training.

A related problem can occur when one of several partners wants to withdraw from the agreement and take his or her investment out of the business. If money is invested in a building or tools, it may be difficult or even impossi-

Vocabulary Builder

Asset   Anything of monetary value that is owned by a consumer, business, or government.
Dissolved   Describing a business that is closed, its assets distributed to the owners.

ble to turn these assets into cash to be paid to the partner who wishes to withdraw. Again, the final result may be the dissolution of the entire partnership.

Consumers and Partnerships

Consumers are most likely to deal with partnerships when they seek professional services. Doctors often form partnerships, as do lawyers, to share the costs and responsibilities of their profession. When doctors are partners, they can rely on each other to take care of patients when they are away on business or vacation. Doctors can also share the cost of running a laboratory or of hiring a nurse or office staff. They may also share the cost of expensive equipment.

From the point of view of a consumer, dealing with a partnership requires careful evaluation of the business and communication with the partners. Suppose that you develop a sense of trust and understanding with one doctor. If this doctor is out of town when you need help, you might not be pleased to find yourself discussing a personal medical problem with another doctor you do not know. Consumers should also keep in mind that partnerships are often dissolved. When a consumer is dealing with a partnership that is dissolved, he or she may be forced to choose which partner to do business with in the future.

Summing Up *The least common form of business organization is the partnership. Partners share the responsibilities of their business, but are also most likely to dissolve their business. Consumers should deal with those partnerships that they believe are reliable and that will serve them well over a period of time.* ◆

◆   Why could it be difficult for one doctor to provide all the services necessary to run an efficient and well supplied office? How may this explain why many doctors form partnerships?

SECTION 3

CORPORATIONS

While you read, ask yourself . . .
   ◆ *Are most of the corporations in your community large or small?*
   ◆ *Do you believe that these firms could have been successful if they were organized as sole proprietorships or partnerships?*

Suppose that your Mexican restaurant is very successful. With Andrew's knowledge of business and your skills as a cook, sales and profits grow rapidly. The two of you decide to look into opening similar restaurants in other locations across the state. However, your firm does not have the ability to raise the $1 million you estimate you need, and Andrew does not have enough experience to manage several businesses by himself. You think about adding more partners but decide against this. Neither of you wants to become personally responsible for the actions of more partners. You also don't want to have to consult more partners when decisions need to be made. What you need are financial backers who will let you use their money for the business and not expect to be consulted every time you need to make a decision for the firm. You decide to form a corporation.

A corporation is an "artificial being." It has a legal existence that is separate from the human beings who own or control it. A corporation has many legal powers, such as the right to buy and sell property and the right to enter into contracts. It can also sue or be sued. Corporations are **legal entities**. (An entity is an existing thing.) While your business may be owned by many people, it will be treated by the law as if it were a "person."

If your business becomes a corporation, other people will own part of your company. **Stock** is a share of ownership in a corporation.

Consumer News

Corporations as Family Businesses

Earl G. Graves, the owner of *Black Enterprise* magazine, a closely held corporation, is quoted as saying on its twentieth anniversary: "When I shut my eyes, I can still see the first magazine rolling off the presses and relive the emotion I felt. I was anxious about whether my 'paper child' was going to survive its birth and live a long and healthy life and, at the same time, so very proud to have my real children witness such an historic moment for our family and, yes, this country."

Graves's business venture was certainly a success. His family now owns one of the most widely read and respected minority publications in the United States.

What special talents do you suppose he had that enabled him to make his business a success?

Large corporations sell their stock through a **stock exchange**, a central market where stocks are bought and sold. The New York Stock Exchange (NYSE) is the largest and oldest stock

Vocabulary Builder

Legal entity   An organization, such as a corporation, that is recognized by the law and given many of the rights of a person under the law.
Stock   A share of ownership in a corporation that entitles the owner to a share of profits distributed to owners.
Stock Exchange   An organization that helps people who want to buy and sell stock in corporations complete transactions.

market in the United States. Having a central location to buy and sell stocks helps the economy by encouraging people to invest and save. It also helps corporations obtain the money that they need in order to grow.

A corporation may be owned by a single person, by several people, or by hundreds of thousands of shareholders. Large corporations like General Motors or International Business Machines have millions of stockholders.

Some corporations are owned by just a few people. In such cases, the company's stock is not sold to the general public through a stock exchange. These are sometimes called **closely held corporations**. The owners may be business associates or members of a single family. Closely held corporations often operate much like partnerships, with the few shareholders managing and directing the business. You might form a closely held corporation with Andrew and a limited number of your friends and relatives.

Advantages of Corporations

The legal status of corporations is important to owners because it means that they will not be held personally responsible for the debts of the business. In case of failure, an owner will only lose the value of assets he or she has invested in the firm. This advantage that owners of corporations enjoy is called **limited liability**. If your restaurant was organized as a corporation and you had invested $20,000, the most you could lose would be that $20,000. You would not be responsible for the debts of other shareholders, and your personal assets could not normally be taken from you if the business failed.

Another important advantage of corporations is their greater ability to raise money by selling shares of stock to many different people. The $1 million that your firm might need could be raised if 100 shareholders invested

$10,000 each. Most large businesses are corporations because the most effective way of raising large amounts of money is through the sale of stock. This is why corporations, while making up only 16 percent of all businesses in the United States, do about 85 percent of the business. There aren't as many of them, but they are often large.

Corporations also enjoy the advantage of **unlimited life**. When the owner of a sole proprietorship for one of the owners in a partnership dies or leaves the firm, the business ceases to exist and must be reorganized to continue to function. A corporation, however, can exist and function when individual stockholders die or sell their stock. The shares are transferred to new stockholders without interrupting the working of the business.

Because many corporations are large, they often can afford to hire professional managers to run the business, as well as paying for other specialized skills that may improve the firm's efficiency. Sole proprietorships and partnerships are often too small to be able to afford workers who have specialized skills. These types of business owners must often rely on their own abilities to carry out many, if not all, of the business functions.

Disadvantages of Corporations

A major disadvantage of corporations is that they must pay federal and often state and local income taxes on their profits. When remaining profits are paid to shareholders, the owners pay personal income taxes on the same income. In a sense, corporate profits are taxed twice. Profits earned by sole proprietorships and partnerships are only taxed once as personal income.

A corporation is more difficult to start than other forms of business organization because it involves applying for a **charter** from a state government. This may be an expensive and time-consuming procedure, depending on the laws of the state where the firm is organized.

A corporation is normally led by an elected board of directors. Most stockholders are given one vote for each share of stock they own. There may be disputes between stockholders when boards of directors are elected. This can slow down important decisions that need to be made. When any business becomes very large, it may be difficult to coordinate and control. At times, corporations suffer from this problem because they are the largest businesses in the United States.

Corporations experience greater levels of government control and regulation than other forms of business organization. This is partly because of their size and partly because they are chartered by the government. There are many laws and enforcement procedures that affect corporations but not sole proprietorships or partnerships.

Consumers and Corporations

When you buy a shirt, refrigerator, or automobile, the store where you shop may be a sole proprietorship or a partnership, but the product itself is likely to have been manufactured by a corporation. The money needed to build a factory to produce shirts, refrigerators, or automobiles is so great that only a corporation could operate such a business.

Buying products manufactured by large corporations offers important advantages to consumers. Large corporations are more likely to have full warranties and service contracts for their products. If you move to another part of the country, there may be branches of the same firm near your new home. Sears, for example, has stores in all fifty states. If you bought a lawn mower from a Sears store in Washington, you could have it serviced in Iowa. Because corporations have unlimited life, they are more

Sole Proprietorships, Partnerships, and Corporations in the United States, 1970–1987			
Year	Number, in Thousands	Sales, in Billions	Net Income, in Billions
Sole Proprietorships (nonfarm)			
1970	5,770	$ 198.6	$ 30.5
1975	7,221	$ 274.0	$ 39.6
1980	8,932	$ 411.2	$ 54.9
1987	13,091	$ 610.8	$105.5
Partnerships			
1970	936	$ 91.8	$ 9.8
1975	1,073	$ 146.0	$ 7.7
1980	1,380	$ 286.0	$ 8.2
1987	1,648	$ 411.4	$ −5.4
Corporations			
1970	1,665	$1,706.1	$ 65.9
1975	2,024	$3,120.4	$142.6
1980	2,711	$6,172.2	$239.0
1987	3,616	$9,185.5	$328.2

Source Note: *Statistical Abstract of the United States,* 1991, p. 525, & 1981, p. 534.

◆ **Table 17-1** Business Organizations Compared What does the data in the table above tell you about the relative importance of the three basic forms of business organizations in the American economy? How has this importance changed over time?

Vocabulary Builder

Charter A state's written agreement giving a corporation the right to operate a business.

Closely held corporation A corporation in which most of the stock and control is held by a single family or small group of people.

Limited liability The risk taken by a shareholder in a corporation that is limited to the value of money invested in the firm.

Unlimited life A characteristic of corporations that allows them to function through a majority of voted stock, even when an individual stockholder dies.

likely to continue in business over long periods of time. Corporations are closely regulated by the government and may therefore be more reliable than some firms organized in other ways.

Possibly the greatest problem in dealing with a large corporation is that the firm may be slow and impersonal in its service. When you deal with a sole proprietor or partner, your business is likely to be important to the firm. You may develop a personal relationship with the owner. This is not true of many large corporations. General Motors will not be seriously hurt if you buy a Ford rather than a Buick. When a firm employs thousands of workers, it may be difficult to have a personal relationship with any of them. Consumers may receive service, but it may take a long time to get it. Also, if it becomes necessary to take legal action against a large corporation, the firm will have well-paid lawyers that the consumer will have to face to receive just compensation for a problem.

Summing Up *Corporations dominate the American economy, accounting for more than 85 percent of the value of all sales. Owners of corporate stock enjoy many benefits, including limited liability and unlimited life, but the firm's profits are double taxed. Most large businesses are corporations.* ◆

SECTION 4

FRANCHISES

While you read, ask yourself . . .
- ◆ *What are several franchises in your community that you deal with?*
- ◆ *Do you believe that these firms are better run or more successful than the nonfranchise businesses they compete with?*

If you have ever eaten in a McDonald's or in a Kentucky Fried Chicken restaurant, you have purchased goods from a **franchise.** A franchise

◆ Which businesses in this photograph are probably franchises? Why have the number of franchised businesses grown so rapidly in recent years? Have consumers benefited from this growth?

Growth of Franchise Sales, 1989–1991 (in billions of dollars)			
	1989 Sales, in Billions	1991 Sales, in Billions*	% Growth 1989–1991
Total Sales by Franchises	$677.9	$758.5	11.9%
Restaurants	$ 70.1	$ 85.4	21.8%
Retailing, non-food	$ 26.7	$ 31.3	17.2%
Hotels and motels	$ 21.6	$ 25.9	23.3%
Business aids and services	$ 16.9	$ 20.7	22.5%
Convenience stores	$ 14.3	$ 14.9	4.2%

* Projected amounts

Source: *Nation's Business*, March 1991, p. 50.

◆ **Table 17-2**   Consider the data above. What does this table show about the importance of franchises in the economy?

is a way to start a business. It is not a form of business organization. A franchise may be organized as a sole proprietorship, partnership, or corporation. The owner of the business (franchisee) buys the right to sell some other company's (franchiser's) product in a fairly specific manner, in a specific area, and over a specified period of time and to use the firm's name or trademark.

Franchising is one of the fastest-growing segments of the U.S. economy. The 500,000 franchise operations in the United States accounted for an estimated $760 billion in sales in 1990. Table 17-2 summarizes franchise sales during the 2-years 1989-1991. This method of operating a business will continue to grow throughout our economy and in the world. There are now franchises of McDonald's and Pizza Hut in Russia.

does not work. Buying a franchise requires the payment of an initial investment and a percentage of sales over time. However, it relieves the owner from having to make many business decisions. The owner pays for a proven method of producing and marketing a product and is assured that no other franchisee from the same firm will open a competing business nearby. Franchise owners also benefit from the name and product recognition that has been established by the parent firm.

There are several potential problems in buying a franchise. One problem is the initial investment, which may be quite large. Another difficulty is that franchise owners may have little voice in how their business is run. The contract that they sign to buy the franchise may prevent them from carrying out some very good ideas.

Advantages and Disadvantages of Owning a Franchise

The greatest advantage of owning a franchise is the fact that someone else has already made the mistakes to find out what does and

Vocabulary Builder

Franchise   A business that buys the right to operate using an established name and method of production.

The Global Consumer

To Russia with Fries

On January 31, 1990, customers in Moscow stood under the golden arches and waited up to 4 hours to get into the 700-seat restaurant. Television crews were there to capture the scene for the world to see. The sign on the door read, "For Soviet rubles only." The Russian people, some spending as much as four days' pay, were amazed by the cleanliness, fast service, quality of food, and especially the polite and enthusiastic service—something almost unknown to consumers in Russia.

On the first day the golden arches of Pushkin Square attracted 30,000 Muscovites and served as much food as the average McDonald's serves in three months. How did McDonald's get the money, ingenuity, and permission to set up shop in the heartland of communism?

Ray Kroc didn't invent the "Bolshoi Mac" (Russian for Big Mac) that the soviet consumers were gobbling down, but he did change the eating habits of millions of Americans. In the early 1950s Kroc sold machines that could make six milk shakes at a time. When Maurice and Richard McDonald bought eight of them for their one restaurant, Kroc wanted to see the business that needed to be able to produce forty-eight milk shakes at a

time. He visited their operation and was so impressed that he convinced the McDonald brothers to franchise their business and let him take it to Illinois.

In 1955, at age fifty-two, Kroc opened his first McDonald's near Chicago. Five years later he had 250 outlets, and he bought out the McDonald brothers for $2.7 million.

Ray Kroc's standards of quality, service, cleanliness, and value are enforced in all McDonald's stores, including the one in Russia. The employees and managers of the Moscow McDonald's were Russian citizens who knew nothing of the standards that are part of the McDonald's trademark. Therefore, the top managers were sent for training in Toronto, Canada, and Oak Park, Illinois. The entire Moscow crew began training a month before the store opened.

McDonald's of Moscow set a new standard for quality and service for Russian consumers who had rarely received either. Perhaps the experience of eating there will inspire Russian consumers to become Russian entrepreneurs who will also supply quality products and service to other Russian citizens.

Another important problem is that each franchisee will be affected by the actions of other franchisees. For example, if you franchise a printing service, your business might be hurt by inferior work done by another franchisee with the same parent firm in a near-by community. If the parent company does not maintain tight control over each franchise's quality, other franchisees may be hurt.

Consumers and Franchises

Consumers often benefit from buying goods and services from a franchise. They can be reasonably certain of the quality they will receive and the price they will pay. When you check into a Holiday Inn, you know what kind of room you will get, even though you have never seen it before.

◆   Would you be willing to wait four or more hours to be able to buy a McDonald's hamburger and a bag of fries? Residents of Moscow were when the first store in Russia opened in 1990.

One problem of doing business with a franchise is that you can miss the opportunity to buy a superior product at a lower price from a competing business. If you are on a business trip, it is easy to stay at a Holiday Inn. However, you may miss staying at a very nice motel run by a sole proprietor who charges a lower price and gives better service. As in all other economic choices, there is a trade-off in choosing to deal with a franchise. Consumers receive the benefit of being able to easily receive assured quality and price. They pay the cost of missing the chance to receive a better product from a less-known firm.

Summing Up   *Franchises are growing as a part of the U. S. economy. They help people start businesses by providing a proven method of organization. Consumers may rely on franchisers to provide quality products. However they give up their opportunity to buy superior goods and services from the businesses that are not franchises.* ◆

Review and Enrichment Activities

VOCABULARY REVIEW

1. Column A contains key consumer terms from this chapter. Column B contains a scrambled list of phrases that describe what these terms mean. Match the correct meaning with each term. Write your answers on a separate sheet of paper.

Column A

1. dissolved
2. legal entity
3. charter
4. sole proprietor
5. stock exchange
6. unlimited life
7. asset
8. franchise
9. stock
10. closely held corporation

Column B

a. A legal document that must be obtained to operate a corporation
b. An organization that is treated by the law as if it was a person
c. A unit of ownership in a corporation
d. The only owner of a business
e. The purchased right to operate a business in a particular way with an established name or trademark
f. When a business is closed and its property distributed to the owners
g. When a small group of people own all the stock in a business
h. Anything that has value and is owned by a person, business, or the government
i. An organization through which units of ownership in corporations are bought and sold
j. The ability to continue to function that corporations have even when an owner dies

2. Explain the difference between the **limited liability** enjoyed by owners of corporations, and the **unlimited liability** of sole proprietors and partners.

CHECKING WHAT YOU'VE LEARNED

Write your answers for the following exercises on a separate sheet of paper.

1. Why are sole proprietorships the easiest form of business to organize?
2. Describe three advantages of operating a business as a sole proprietorship instead of as some other form of business organization.
3. Describe three disadvantages of operating a business as a sole proprietorship instead of as some other form of business organization.
4. Why might consumers receive better service from a sole proprietor than from a different type of business organization?
5. Why are partnerships the form of business organization most likely to be dissolved?
6. Describe two advantages of operating a business as a partnership instead of as a sole proprietorship.
7. Describe two disadvantages of operating a business as a partnership instead of as a sole proprietorship.
8. Why might consumers experience changes in the services offered by partnerships more often than with other kinds of businesses?
9. How are corporations treated differently under the law than either sole proprietorships or partnerships?
10. Describe three advantages that owners of corporations have that the owners of sole proprietorships and partnerships do not enjoy.
11. Describe two disadvantages that owners of corporations have that the owners of sole proprietorships and partnerships do not experience.
12. Why are most large businesses corporations?
13. What advantages may a person who buys a franchise have over a person who starts his or her own business?
14. What advantages may a consumer receive from shopping at a franchise instead of at an independent firm that offers similar products for sale?

PRACTICING YOUR CONSUMER SKILLS

Write your answers for the following exercises on a separate sheet of paper.

1. Identify each of the following businesses as being a sole proprietorship, a partnership, or a corporation. Then explain why the owner(s) of the firm probably chose this form of business organization.
   a. Jeff runs a dry-cleaning business with his brother John. The two brothers have invested nearly $250,000 in their store and equipment. They take turns running the store. They take turns working nights and weekends.
   b. Maria is the manager of a diaper service that is worth over $1.5 million. Her business has a fleet of fourteen trucks that pick up and deliver diapers. The firm has forty employees and does $2.5 million

Review and Enrichment Activities Continued

worth of business a year. Maria has invested $50,000 of her own money in the business.

c.   Juan runs a baseball card store. He started collecting cards when he was five years old. When he had over 50,000 cards, he decided he needed a place to store and trade them. He works in a factory during the day and opens his store at night and on weekends.

d.   Tony operates an indoor golf course. The business rents space in a mall. Golfers tee off on "fairways" that are really curtains painted to look like a golf course. The total investment in the business is about $150,000, of which Tony put up $10,000 of his own money. He was willing to risk this amount of money but no more. Other people bought into the firm to raise the other $140,000. He really isn't too sure the business will be a success.

2.   Identify the problem in each of the following situations. Explain how the problem could have been avoided if a different form of business organization had been used.

a.   Rod owns a store named "The Box Factory." He specializes in shipping items anywhere in the nation as quickly as possible. He stays open 24 hours a day, seven days a week. His motto is, "It can't be too big or too small to go in a hurry." Rod's business is a sole proprietorship. Rod can be found in his store seven days a week. Some days he even sleeps there.

b.   Carl used to run his restaurant by himself. However, three years ago he reorganized the business as a corporation and expanded it to seventeen locations. Carl now owns about 5 percent of the stock and finds himself taking orders from other people about how to run the restaurants. He is very frustrated.

c.   Betty and Bob own a cleaning service. They started the business three years ago when they thought they were going to be married. Their plans didn't work out. Bob married Teresa instead. Now, when Betty and Bob have to work together they often argue about what the best business decisions should be.

3.   Each of the following situations involves a consumer choice. What action would you recommend in each case? Explain the reason for your recommendation.

a.   Fred and Mary have been looking for a contractor to build their new home. They have received bids from two different contractors. Jim owns a sole proprietorship that employs three workers. He has been in business for two years and has built four homes. He offers to do the job for $97,000. Lou is a representative for Apex Construction. This firm is a corporation worth over $2 million. It has been in business for twenty-four years. Lou says his firm can build the house for $102,000. Which firm should Fred and Mary employ?

b. Ronda places a high value on personal service. She wants people to know her name and greet her when she walks in. She does not mind paying more for good service. Her dentist joined a partnership with six other dentists last year, but she liked him, so she continued to go to him. Last week she lost a filling and was forced to make an emergency appointment to have it fixed. When she arrived, she was told that her regular dentist was booked solid and she would have to see a new dentist who had just graduated from school. She was told she should feel special because she would be his very first patient. Should Ronda see him anyhow?

c. Roxanne has gone to the same jewelry store for years. She has always received prompt and friendly service. In recent years the owner has been getting quite old and somewhat forgetful. Last week she gave him a diamond ring to clean that was worth over $3,000. Because she trusted the owner, she didn't ask for a receipt. When she went to pick up her ring, the jeweler couldn't remember she had left it and could not find it. Roxanne does not believe that the man is trying to cheat her, but she wants her ring back. What should she do?

USING NUMBERS

Solve the following problem to help make the best possible choice. Write your solution on a separate sheet of paper. Be sure to show all your work.

Carla and JoAnn want to open a store to sell quality handbags, belts, and other items made from leather. They each have $20,000 to invest in the firm. They have found a location and have investigated the costs that they would need to pay to open and run their store. Here is a list of their projected costs.

Projected Costs for the C & J Leather Boutique

- They want to have money set aside to pay for six months of rent, at $800 a month.
- They plan to buy $12,000 worth of inventory.
- They want to buy display cabinets and other furnishings for the store that will cost $4,000.
- They need to pay for insurance in advance at a cost of $1,250.
- They want to spend $3,000 on advertising when they open their store.
- They must buy a cash register and other equipment that will cost $1,600.
- They must pay $500 to have their telephone and other utilities turned on.
- They want enough money set aside to pay for three months of their one employee's wages and benefits at a cost of $320 a week.
- They want at least $5,000 in reserve for unexpected expenses.

Determine how much money Carla and JoAnn will need and then recommend the form of business organization that they should choose. Explain your choice.

Review and Enrichment Activities Continued

PUTTING IDEAS IN YOUR OWN WORDS

The following quotations are from this chapter. Explain these quotations in your own words to make sure you understand what they mean. Write your answers on a separate sheet of paper.

1. "Many sole proprietors will tell you that one of the most important benefits they receive from their business is a sense of pride of ownership."
2. "Corporations are legal entities."16

3. "The greatest advantage of owning a franchise is the fact that someone else already made the mistakes to find out what does and does not work."

BUILDING CONSUMER KNOWLEDGE

Write your answers for the following exercises on a separate sheet of paper.

1. Look through the yellow pages of your local phone book. Identify businesses that are sole proprietorships, partnerships, and corporations. Explain why you believe one specific firm of each type was organized the way it was.
2. Identify a type of business you might consider operating someday. Choose the type of business organization you believe would be most appropriate to this type of business. Explain why you feel this way.
3. Identify a small, local business that you believe would be more efficient if it could grow larger. What form of business organization does the firm use now? Do you believe that the type of business organization now used is the best for this firm? Explain.
4. Identify a franchise that you shop at. Explain the advantages and disadvantages you receive because you shop at this business. Could you buy similar products from a business that was not a franchise? If you could, why don't you shop at the other business?

Chapter 18

How Businesses Work

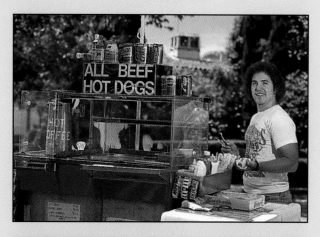

Chapter Objectives

After completing this chapter, you will be able to do the following:

- Review the relationship between a firm's ability to provide the goods and services that consumers want and its ability to earn a profit.
- Explain each of the four basic functions of business.
- Explain how consumers benefit when firms carry out the four basic functions of business efficiently and effectively.

Key Consumer Terms

In this chapter you will learn the meanings of the following important consumer terms:

- Marketing
- Accounting
- Management
- Capacity planning
- Facility location
- Inventory control
- Schedule
- Utility
- Marketing concept
- Target market
- Market research
- Cash flow
- Accounting process
- Liability
- Net worth
- Balance sheet
- Income statement
- Organizing
- Directing
- Controlling
- Feedback

Think of a business in your community that appears to be successful. It might be a restaurant, a clothing store, a dry-cleaning firm, or almost any other sort of business. What sorts of activities do the owners of this business carry out that cause them to be successful when other people might fail?

To be successful, firms need to carry out four basic business functions. These four functions are production, **marketing**, **accounting**, and **management**.

SECTION 1

PRODUCTION OF GOODS AND SERVICES

While you read, ask yourself . . .
- *How do you judge the quality of products you buy?*
- *If you buy a product from a store and find it is inferior, do you usually shop at that store again?*

Is there a particular type of soft drink or snack food that you like? If you stopped to buy something to eat on your way home from school, would you wonder how this product came to be offered for sale? Before you, or any other consumer, can buy a product, someone has to produce the good you want to buy. Production doesn't just happen. It must be planned and carried out. Consider the different steps a business must take to produce a good or service.

How Big Should a Business Be?

Business owners need to determine what products they will produce and in what quantity. This is called **capacity planning.** The owners or managers of every business need to decide whether they should produce and offer ten products, a million, or some quantity in between for sale each day. This decision will tell them how large a factory or store to build. They should have a facility (building) that is large enough to meet their needs, but not so large that they end up paying for unnecessary space.

Businesses that are large are often more efficient than those that are small. Large firms usually buy resources in larger quantities and at lower costs. Banks often charge lower interest rates to large firms. They are also better able to afford more efficient equipment. Although large firms may be able to produce products at lower costs per item, there is no advantage in producing more goods than can be sold. Capacity planning requires firms to consider both their costs of production and their ability to sell the products that they manufacture.

Where Should the Business be Located?

Once the size of a business has been decided, the managers must choose the best location for their business. **Facility location** can have an important effect on a firm's success. The managers need to consider the advantages and disadvantages of various locations. When selecting a location, they will need to investigate such factors as availability of qualified workers and resources, convenience for potential customers, and local tax rates.

There is always a trade-off between the benefits and costs of different locations. For example, the place with the lowest taxes may also be the least convenient for customers. Or a location with abundant supplies of raw materials may be many miles from where the nearest

◆   The decision to locate a business in a large city has many costs and benefits. Why might this be a good choice for a retail business but a bad idea for a manufacturing firm?

workers live. Location mistakes can be very expensive. Suppose that a firm that produces quality furniture opened for business in a rural area because it got a "really good deal" on a used factory. Although the cost of its building might be very low, it could soon discover that there are few qualified workers in the area. The extra cost of attracting these workers could far outweigh the savings from the building. Owners have to decide which location offers the greatest benefits and the least cost.

Starting Production

When a business is established, the managers must identify and purchase the resources they need to produce their product. They need to buy enough resources to fill their needs, but

Vocabulary Builder

Accounting   Measuring, interpreting, and communicating financial information for internal and external decision making.

Capacity planning   The decisions made concerning the right amount of products or services to manufacture or offer for sale.

Facility location   Choosing the location for a business that is most likely to contribute to its profitability.

Management   The achievement of organizational objectives through organizing, directing, and controlling employees and their use of resources.

Marketing   The actions associated with supplying products consumers want when, where and in the form that they want them, and making consumers aware of these products' availability.

Consumer News

Just-in-Time

Just-in-time (JIT) is a method of controlling inventory that results in having just enough supplies on hand to keep production going. The idea of JIT is to supply needed parts to the production line on a last-minute basis. Manufacturers that use JIT are able to keep fewer parts and resources in inventory than when other methods of control are used. This helps them keep production costs down. The just-in-time system enables a firm to respond rapidly to changes in markets, to maintain high-quality standards, and to keep employment in the production system as low as possible. JIT also forces a firm to keep its machinery in perfect running order.

JIT helped AT&T cut the production time of some of its products from 3½ weeks to 2½ weeks. JIT also helped Huffy Corporation become the most productive bicycle maker in the world.

In what ways might consumers benefit when firms use JIT?

not so much that they will have an unnecessary surplus that will waste the firm's money. This process of keeping just the right amount of resources and completed products on hand is called **inventory control**.

Finally, the managers of the firm must **schedule** the production of their product. Workers need to be told what to do and when to do it. Resources must be where they are needed, when they are needed, and in the amount that is needed. Someone has to package and ship products as they are completed.

All of this should be accomplished with as little effort and time as possible.

Firms that produce good quality products at the lowest cost are most likely to earn a profit. They also should be best able to charge consumers lower prices. Consumers benefit from dealing with businesses that produce products efficiently.

Summing Up *Producing goods and services involves more than making products. Owners must decide the best size and location for their business and then schedule and control their production.* ◆

SECTION 2

While you read, ask yourself . . .
- ◆ *How do you usually learn about new products?*
- ◆ *Do you shop at the same store over and over again without considering alternative places to shop?*

Brad's family eats fresh fish at least once a week. They have always bought this fish at a local grocery store where the quality is inconsistent and the prices tend to be high. They shop there because they don't know any other place to buy fish.

Suppose there is a fish market in a different part of town that offers high quality at reasonable prices. Brad's father could easily stop there on his way home from work, but he doesn't know it exists. As a result, the owner of the fish market loses business, and Brad's family pays too much for low-quality fish. Both the seller and the customer lose because of a lack of communication. The owner of the fish market offers a good product that customers would like to buy at a fair price, but he has not successfully marketed his product. Marketing involves supplying products that consumers want when, where, and in the form they want them. Marketing also involves making consumers aware that these products are available.

Creating Utility

The final objective of marketing is to sell products. However, marketing is related to other functions that involve many parts of the business and its dealing with customers. Marketing adds value, or **utility**, to a good or service that a firm offers for sale. Consider Brad's family and the fish market. If the owner of the store would advertise to make Brad's parents aware of his price and products, they would gladly buy fish at his store. He would have greater sales, and they would have a better product at a lower price. Advertising would clearly add utility to the product.

Marketing creates other types of utility. Form utility is created when a business converts a product into a form that is more useful to its customers. Selling pizza dough that has been rolled out flat and is ready to use instead of in a lump in a bag demonstrates form utility. Another example would be a store that sells pasta or candy by weight instead of in premeasured boxes. This allows people to purchase whatever amount they want.

Time utility is having a product available when a customer wants to buy it. Stores that stay open 24 hours a day provide time utility. They are able to attract customers who find it convenient to shop late at night.

Place utility is having a product available where a customer wants to buy it. Many consumers are attracted to businesses that are located in places that are convenient to their home or place of work. The decision to put a small grocery store in a residential neighborhood is at least partially a marketing decision.

All of these forms of utility are created through marketing. The basic products remain the same. They are simply offered to consumers in alternative ways that make them more valuable.

Developing a Marketing Concept

There was a time when most American firms put their efforts and resources into producing the best-quality product possible. Having completed this task, they would then move on to selling the product as if marketing was a separate function from production. As a result, companies sometimes produced products of high quality that almost no one wanted. In the 1950s many firms became sales oriented. They began to ask consumers what they wanted in the products they bought. As a result, goods and services were produced that were better able to satisfy consumer needs and wants. The businesses that were most successful in finding out what consumers wanted often earned the greatest profits.

Today most American business owners and managers realize that production and marketing are closely related. They often develop a

---

Vocabulary Builder

Inventory control   The process of keeping adequate supplies for production and sale while keeping down the cost of carrying inventory.

Scheduling   Making sure that workers, raw materials, and tools are where they are needed at the appropriate time so that production can be efficient.

Utility   An economic term that means value, or added value.

Consumer News

Targeting Minorities

Nielson Media Research is the leading provider of television information services in the United States. In March 1991 Nielson announced a new program designed to collect and report data on television viewing by minorities. Specifically, its monthly reports were expanded to include data on approximately twenty different groups of African Americans. This will allow advertisers to know which programs these groups are most likely to watch.

The purpose of the new effort was to allow businesses to target segments of the African American population and to offer goods and services for sale that are better able to serve the needs and wants of African Americans.

marketing concept that can be found in all parts of the business. The concept is to make each part of a business work to satisfy consumer needs and wants. All employees are trained to realize that their job is to help the business achieve this goal. The worker on the production line has the job of making reliable automobiles that consumers can trust—not just a job of making automobiles. An inferior product cannot be marketed successfully for a very long time. Workers who produce inferior products are likely to soon be out of work. Developing a sales orientation and a marketing concept is part of marketing a product and is beneficial to all the employees of a firm.

Choosing a Target Market

It is impossible for one firm to offer all products to all customers. Earlier in this chapter you learned that every business must decide what products to offer for sale. Businesses also need to identify the type of customers to try to sell products to. A **target market** is a group of consumers toward which a firm decides to direct its marketing efforts. The kind of products that a firm offers for sale must appeal to the customers in its target market. For example, a store that targets young women who want to look fashionable might make a mistake to offer full-length flannel skirts for sale.

Think of the advertisements you see for Wendy's and McDonald's restaurants. Wendy's advertisements almost always target adults, while many of McDonalds ads feature Ronald McDonald and are directed toward children. Although these two firms offer similar products for sale, they have chosen different target markets.

To successfully market a product to a group of consumers, it is helpful to have specific information about that group. Many businesses carry out **market research** to obtain such data. The owners of a business may collect data about customers on its own, or they may hire a firm that specializes in market research to do this for them.

There are two basic types of data that may be collected through market research. One type examines sales made by the firm to its current customers. The other looks at people who are potential customers.

Internal data are collected by a business from its current sales. For example, a firm might study the sales of a particular style of product it manufactures before it decides to make another one with a similar design. It could investigate which products are most often purchased by credit and which are bought with cash. Businesses often benefit from knowing what factors cause consumers

◆   By purchasing your own ice cream and cones you could make an ice cream cone for about thirty cents. Why can businesses sell ready-made ones for three to five times as much? Who would be willing to pay this price?

to become repeat customers. Firms that sell expensive products like automobiles are particularly interested in encouraging repeat sales.

External data are found outside the business. One way to obtain this type of data is by observation. Some companies count the number of potential customers who pass by a store, or they keep track of the sex and age of customers who buy products from their competitors. Direct surveys and questionnaires are also carried out. Frequently, information can be gathered from external sources like the government or trade organizations. For example, the U.S. Census Bureau provides extensive information about the types of people who live in various cities or even in specific neighborhoods.

Businesses that market their products successfully provide consumers with information through advertising, thereby helping consumers to make the best possible choices. Consumers must rely on their own judgment to determine what parts of the information provided by businesses are important. They should realize that the objective of the business is to sell more products. The objective of the

consumer is to receive the best possible value for each dollar spent. Although these objectives are different, businesses do provide consumers with information they may use in making responsible consumer decisions.

Summing Up   *Businesses have come to realize that marketing is more than selling. By providing products consumers want, when, where, and in the form they want, businesses add to the utility of their products. To market successfully businesses often develop a strategy, choose a target market, and complete market research.* ◆

Vocabulary Builder

Marketing concept   A business's decision to be sales oriented in its functions, to produce goods and services that consumers want, and to produce them when, where, and in the form they want them.

Market research   Gathering, recording, and analyzing information about the types of goods and services that people want.

Target market   A group of consumers toward which a firm directs its marketing efforts.

Consumer Close-Up

"Super Soaker" Super Sales Success

Probably every child in the United States would like to own a squirt gun that can soak their friends and enemies (mothers, fathers, brothers, and sisters?) from a range of almost 20 yards. In 1989 Lonnie Johnson, an employee of the Jet Propulsion Lab in California, invented a squirt gun that would hold up to half a gallon of water and could squirt a stream up to 55 feet. The difference between Johnson's gun and other products was a pressurized plastic tank to hold

water. A child (or adult) could simply fill the tank, pump it up, and shoot for 5 to 10 minutes without needing to reload.

Johnson took his invention to the toy industry's national fair in New York City, where he met A1 Davis of the Larami Corporation. Davis said that his firm invested in the gun because "I liked it and I thought the kids would like it." Larami was a small toy manufacturer that had never carried out any national advertising for its products. However, the firm invested $1 million for television advertising in twenty market areas in 1991. Within two

months the firm was rewarded with sales of nearly 4 million guns. First one kid on a block would have a gun and "get" all the other kids from such a distance that they couldn't fight back.

Soon every kid was demanding a "super soaker" too, so they could have a chance in the next water war. Parents reported driving to as many as ten stores to try to find a gun. Davis stated that his objective was to produce and market at least 24 million guns, one for every child in the country. After that there was the rest of the world to think about.

SECTION 3

ACCOUNTING

While you read, ask yourself . . .
◆ *How do you keep track of your own income and expenses?*
◆ *What happens when you run short of money?*

Businesses carry out accounting when they measure, interpret, and communicate financial information to help manage the firm and plan for the future. From the point of view of the business, it is important to have a systematic method of managing the firm's money. The owners must be sure that they can afford to buy resources and pay workers. They must make financial plans for investments and for

maintaining their equipment. They must be assured of an adequate **cash flow** through their business to allow them to pay their own bills on time. They must know who they owe money to and who owes money to them. If customers do not pay debts on time, there must be an established method of collection. All of these activities depend on an accurate record of a firm's financial transactions.

The Accounting Process

Accounting concerns the financial record keeping of all transactions that a firm has with customers, employees, suppliers, bankers, owners, and the government. Businesses con-

◆   All successful businesses need to keep accurate records of their financial transactions. Do you think computers could replace accountants or just make their jobs easier?

vert a record of individual transactions into a financial statement through the **accounting process.** The first step in the accounting process is to keep a record of each transaction in chronological order in a journal. (Chronological order is the order in which events occur.) This record is then posted into a book of accounts called a ledger. Many firms now maintain these records in computer data banks. Businesses keep separate accounts for items such as salaries, sales, inventory, accounts payable, and accounts receivable. At the end of an accounting period, the various accounts are totaled into two categories: assets, which are things of value that the firm owns, and liabilities, which are amounts of money that the firm owes others. The business's **net worth** is found by subtract-

ing its liabilities from its assets. This information is placed on a **balance sheet**, which lists the firm's assets, liabilities, and net worth (see

Vocabulary Builder

Accounting process   Steps that firms take to maintain records that are used to prepare financial statements for evaluating the firm's performance and for planning for the future.

Balance sheet   A financial statement that shows a firm's assets, liabilities, and net worth at a point in time.

Cash flow   The flow of money into and out of a person's, business's, or government's accounts.

Net worth   The difference between the value of a business's assets and its liabilities.

Balance Sheet for Karen's Kandy Shop			
Assets		**Liabilities**	
Current assets		Current liabilities	
Cash on hand	$ 4,531	Accounts payable	$ 6,439
Accounts receivable	$ 2,769	Accrued expenses	$ 560
Inventory	$ 7,982	Taxes owed	$ 1,295
Fixed Assets		Long-term liabilities	
Real estate	$54,250	Loan payable in more	
Fixtures & equipment	$13,400	than one year	$60,000
Other assets		**Total liabilities**	**$68,294**
Goodwill & reputation	$ 5,000	**Net worth** (assets minus	
Total assets	**$87,932**	liabilities)	**$19,638**

◆ **Figure 18-1**   Balance Sheet

Figure 18-1). Businesses also prepare **income statements**, which show the flow of cash through the firm and measure the firm's profit or loss (see Figure 18-2).

Financial statements like these are necessary for a business to be run efficiently. By studying this information, owners and managers can determine which parts of a business are working well and where there is need for improvement.

Accounting and the Consumer

Keeping complete and accurate financial records is also necessary for businesses to provide quality service to consumers. For example, by keeping accurate records, firms are able to send correct bills to their customers. You probably know people who have complained of being billed for something they did not buy. A good way for a business to lose customers is by causing them inconvenience and aggravation. Inaccurate billing is also likely to result in reduced cash flow for a firm while disputes are being settled.

Consumers benefit from businesses that offer goods and services they want to own. To stay in business and offer these goods and services, firms must be successful and earn a rea-

sonable profit. Keeping accurate financial records is necessary for firms to be successful. Therefore, consumers benefit from businesses that follow good accounting practices.

Summing Up   *Accounting is necessary for firms to provide quality products to consumers and an adequate flow of cash through the business.* ◆

SECTION 4

MANAGEMENT OF THE FIRM

While you read, ask yourself . . .
- ◆ *In what ways is your school managed like a business?*
- ◆ *How do the consumers of education (students) benefit when school administrators have good management practices?*

If you applied for a job as the assistant manager of a store, would you have a clear idea of the kind of work you would be asked to do? Try to think of all the possible tasks you might need to carry out. You might be responsible for making business plans, ordering inventory, di-

Income Statement for Karen's Kandy Shop		
Revenues		
Gross sales	$142,802	
Less returns and allowances	$ 1,143	
Net sales		$141,659
Cost of goods sold		
Beginning inventory	$ 8,321	
Purchases during year	$ 66,842	
Less ending inventory	($ 7,982)	
Cost of goods sold		$ 67,181
Gross profit		**$74,478**
Operating expenses		
Selling expenses		
Salaries and fringe benefits	$ 33,103	
Advertising	$ 2,500	
Depreciation of equipment	$ 2,500	
Miscellaneous selling expenses	$ 1,476	
Total selling expenses		$ 39,579
General and administrative expenses		
Salaries and fringe benefits	$ 21,500	
Office supplies	$ 1,439	
Depreciation of office equipment	$ 1,200	
Miscellaneous general expenses	$ 2,285	
Total general and administrative expenses		$ 26,429
Total operating expenses		$ 66,008
Net income before taxes		$ 8,470
Less: income taxes		$ 1,270
Net income		**$ 7,200**

◆   **Figure 18-2**   Income Statement

recting other employees, providing customer service, paying bills, placing advertisements, preparing displays, maintaining accurate records, and taking deposits to a bank. The list goes on and on. The point is that there are many jobs that managers have to do. Their general responsibility is to see that the firm runs efficiently.

Management may be divided into two general categories: managing the organization and managing people. In this chapter you will learn about managing the organization. Chapter 19 (the next chapter) is devoted to managing people and how this function affects consumers.

Vocabulary Builder

Income statement A financial statement that shows a firm's revenues, costs, and net income over a period of time.

Consumer News

Employees Need to Have Their Skills Updated

The growing use of computer-assisted manufacturing (CAM) has created a need for computer management. Just because computers exist in a business does not necessarily mean that the workers know how to use them or that the computers are even the right ones for the job. The development of new computer's and programs has progressed so rapidly that many employees have not been able to keep up with the changes. This has created a need for specialized workers whose job is to be sure that their employers computers and programs are the types needed and that they are used properly by other employees.

Consider how important this function is to the success of a firm.

Have you ever gone shopping at a store where the clerk did not understand how to use the computerized cash register?

How did the clerk's lack of knowledge affect the value of any return the firm received from its investment in the machine?

When this happens, how is customer service affected?

Making Plans

Probably the single most important function of management is making plans for the future. Change always takes place. Products that consumers want at the present may not be demanded in the future. New technology will cause the methods of producing goods and services to change. The costs of resources, taxes, transportation, and marketing are all likely to change. Businesses that are controlled by managers who do not plan for the future stand a good chance of not having a future.

Making plans is much like the decision-making process you studied earlier in the book. To make good plans, managers need to set goals for their firm. These goals should be general results or conditions that the managers would like to achieve. Examples might be having satisfied customers, expanding the firm's market into another city, and increasing the firm's profit.

Once a firm sets its general goals, it must determine specific objectives that need to be achieved. These objectives must include enough specific information to be useful. An objective might be to have no more than 5 percent of a firm's products returned for service in the year after they are sold. Increasing sales to $1 million in a new location would be another objective. Objectives are useful when they help managers coordinate the production or marketing of goods and services and evaluate their firm's success.

Organizing, Directing, and Controlling

Managers must coordinate the efforts of employees in such a way that objectives are met. This means getting everyone to work together and direct their efforts toward reaching some common objective. You know from your own experience what happens when people are disorganized. You probably have attended student meetings where many people were trying to talk at the same time and no one was listening to what others had to say. People may have become confused or angry. Think how much more could have been accomplished if people had been organized and had taken turns talking. They could have worked together to accomplish their goals.

Businesses also need organizing and coordinating. To accomplish this, managers must be capable of directing workers to carry out specific tasks in a particular way at the appropriate time. Managing a business often requires telling others what to do. This should be done in a polite, friendly, and understandable manner. However, managers must make decisions and see that their choices are carried out.

Controlling is making sure that the directions given by managers are completed in the proper way by employees. If workers are not carrying out directions, corrective measures must be taken. This does not mean firing or even disciplining workers. The directions that were given may not have been clear. Workers might have received different directions from different managers. When a business is not achieving its goals, the primary effort should be to correct problems, not to assign blame.

Management's controlling function can be looked at as a four-step process:

1. Setting standards for time, quality, quantity, and performance
2. Measuring and monitoring performance
3. Gathering data or **feedback** and evaluating results
4. Taking corrective action when necessary

Consumers Benefit from Successful Firms

Businesses that give a favorable first impression to consumers are often well run in other ways that are not as obvious. Suppose that you go to a store because you were attracted by a newspaper advertisement. You find that the store's products are displayed in a pleasing way that allows you to compare price and quality of different products you could buy. Signs throughout the store proclaim that the owners will not be "undersold." All of these clues indicate that the firm is performing the marketing function effectively.

If the firm is marketing its products well, the chances are good that it also offers quality product for sale, keeps accurate records, and manages its employees effectively. You may confirm your opinion by investigating the store further. Study the products to see if they are well made. When you are ready to pay for your purchase, ask if the store will take cash, checks, or charge cards. Perhaps they will allow you to lay away your purchase. These could be signs of good accounting practices.

Signs like these give you an indication of the store's ability to carry out business functions. They may give you a feeling of confidence about the effectiveness of the firm's management. The firm seems to have a plan for the future. You probably will choose to shop at this store again.

When businesses are well run, they are more likely to be successful. To be successful, they must serve the interests of their customers. Successful businesses and satisfied consumers are often found together.

Summing Up *Managing a business involves being sure that all parts of the firm operate properly by planning, organizing, directing, and controlling the business. Firms that are well managed are best able to satisfy the needs of consumers.* ◆

Vocabulary Builder

Controlling Evaluating and adjusting an organization's activities and performance to help it accomplish its objectives.
Directing Supervising and guiding workers to accomplish organizational goals.
Feedback A method of collecting and retaining information about an event or process. To help managers judge whether changes need to be made.
Organizing Coordinating the efforts of employees to help meet a business's goals.

Review and Enrichment Activities

VOCABULARY REVIEW

1. Column A contains key consumer terms from this chapter. Column B contains a scrambled list of phrases that describe what these terms mean. Match the correct meaning with each term. Write your answers on a separate sheet of paper.

Column A	Column B
1. directing	a. A measure of the value that consumers believe a product has
2. market research	b. The process of gathering data about the relationship between a business and customers who may buy the firm's products
3. target market	c. Offering products consumers want when and where they want them
4. utility	d. Working to achieve objectives by planning, directing, and controlling the use of resources and workers
5. accounting	e. A group of consumers toward which a firm directs its marketing efforts
6. controlling	f. Making sure workers, raw materials, and tools are available when they are needed to produce goods or services
7. liability	g. The claim on a firm's property by its creditors
8. management	h. Telling workers what to do to accomplish a firm's objectives
9. marketing	i. Keeping financial records to help a firm accomplish its objectives
10. schedule	j. Evaluating and adjusting business activities to help it achieve its objectives

2. Explain the difference between a firm's net income and its net worth.

CHECKING WHAT YOU'VE LEARNED

Write your answers for the following exercises on a separate sheet of paper.

1. Identify and give an example of each of the four basic business functions.
2. Describe two activities that are involved in production in addition to producing goods and services.
3. Explain the idea of a marketing concept.
4. Describe one way that marketing adds utility to products that are offered for sale.
5. What is the difference between internal and external data?
6. What are several items that would be found listed under *assets* and under *liabilities* on a firm's balance sheet?
7. Explain why planning may be the most important management activity.
8. What is the difference between directing and controlling the activities of a firm's workers?
9. Explain the four steps in the controlling process of management.
10. Explain how consumers benefit from businesses that are run efficiently and effectively.

PRACTICING YOUR CONSUMER SKILLS

Write your answers for the following exercises on a separate sheet of paper.

1. Identify the business function demonstrated in each of the following situations. Explain how consumers may benefit from the situation. The functions are production, marketing, accounting, and management.
    a. When the Idel Days Pool Co. invented a new self-cleaning pool filter, it placed advertisements in national magazines so that many consumers would become aware of the product.
    b. The Idel Days Pool Co. kept track of its sales and found that when it lowered the price of its new filter by 10 percent, its sales increased 32 percent, and its total profits went up by 8 percent.
    c. The Idel Days Pool Co. discovered that by keeping no more than three days' worth of parts in stock it could reduce its inventory and use the extra space to add another production line.
    d. In the past, the Idel Days Pool Co. has only sold its products on the West Coast. Plans have been made to expand the market of its highly successful filter into the midwest in the next two years and to the East Coast in five years.
2. Identify each of the following situations as examples of time, place, or form utility. Explain how each demonstrates the marketing function of business.
    a. The Best Ever Take-Out Pizza Factory has decided to open stores only at subway stops in residential areas (where people live) of large cities.

Review and Enrichment Activities Continued

  b. Jerry owns 40 push-carts from which his employees sell hot dogs, potato chips, and soft drinks in a large city. On days that it is supposed to rain, he also supplies his workers with umbrellas and rain hats to offer for sale.

  c. Betty runs a business that sells natural foods. She used to sell her products in prepackaged amounts. Many of her customers live alone and complained that her packages were too large for their needs. As a result, she now sells by weight. Customers tell her how much they want, and she packages just that amount to sell.

3. Explain how a management activity could have prevented each of the following problems.

  a. The Green Acres Natural Cheese Co. has been very successful, but its owners have a problem. They opened for business three years ago, when they made 1,000 pounds of goat milk cheese a day. They could now sell 2,000 pounds of cheese a day, but they have not increased the size of their factory. They cannot satisfy all of their customers.

  b. Mark owns an automobile repair shop. He has six employees. When a car is brought in to be fixed, he assigns it to the first worker he sees or thinks of. Some of his employees have too many cars to fix and fall behind. Others have little to do and waste time.

  c. Sally owns a flower shop. She has thousands of dollars worth of flowers in inventory at any time. It is important that cut flowers be kept watered and stored in a cooler to stay fresh. Sally has the proper equipment and has instructed her employees on how to take care of flowers. However, she keeps finding flowers left out and wilted. Sally throws away almost 15 percent of the flowers she buys before she can sell them.

USING NUMBERS

Solve the following problem to help make the best possible choice. Write your solution on a separate sheet of paper. Be sure to show all your work.

Molly wants to open a riding stable and rent stalls for horses. She has found two farms that she could rent that would fill her needs. Each has a barn and a large area where customers could ride. One is only 3 miles from town and would rent for $3,000 a month. The other is 15 miles from town and would cost $1,000 a month to rent. She intends to charge $10 for each half hour a customer rents a horse and $100 a month to stable a horse. In either case, she intends to hire no workers. Molly and her husband Bob will do all the work. Molly has completed market research and has projected the information on the following table. Copy these on a separate sheet and determine which location she should rent. What functions of business are demonstrated by this example?

	Possible Location	
	Closer to Town	**Farther from Town**
Estimated revenue per 30-day month		
Riders per day	40 — $_____	25 — $_____
Stalls rented	20 — $_____	10 — $_____
Total	$_____	$_____
Estimated costs per 30-day month		
Rent	$_____	$_____
Feed and other expenses for her own ten horses	$_____ 700	$_____ 700
Feed and other expenses for customer horses at $50 each	$_____	$_____
Insurance	$_____ 500	$_____ 500
Total	$_____	$_____
Estimated net income	$_____	$_____

PUTTING IDEAS IN YOUR OWN WORDS

The following quotations are from this chapter. Explain these quotations in your own words to make sure you understand what they mean. Write your answers on a separate sheet of paper.

1. "Marketing adds value, or utility, to a good or service that a firm offers for sale."
2. "The kind of products that a firm offers for sale must appeal to the customers in its target market."
3. "Goals are useful when they help managers coordinate the production or marketing of goods and services and evaluate their firm's success."

BUILDING CONSUMER KNOWLEDGE

Write your answers for the following exercises on a separate sheet of paper.

Review and Enrichment Activities Continued

1. Interview one or two people about the jobs that they hold. Ask them to discuss the ways in which their employers carry out each of the four basic business functions. Be prepared to report your findings to the class.

2. Examples of all the basic business functions (except marketing) can be found in most households. Identify an example of production, accounting, and management that takes place in your home. How does your family benefit when these functions are carried out efficiently and effectively?

3. Think of a business in your community that you believe is well run. Describe some of the things this business does that shows how it carries out each of the four business functions.

4. Imagine that you have recently moved into a new community. Describe factors that would help you decide where to shop for your groceries. Explain how these factors are related to the four business functions.

Chapter 19

Management, Labor, and the Consumer

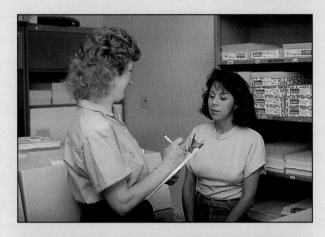

Chapter Objectives

After completing this chapter, you will be able to do the following:
- Explain the functions that make up human resources management.
- Investigate methods that businesses use to recruit and hire workers who have needed skills and knowledge.
- Identify various methods of training workers to complete necessary tasks.
- Discuss the relationship between worker compensation and job performance.
- Explain ways that consumers benefit from workers who are satisfied and motivated to perform their jobs well.

Key Consumer Terms

In this chapter you will learn the meanings of the following important consumer terms:
- Human resource management
- Recruitment
- Internal recruitment
- External recruitment
- Headhunter
- Hiring decision
- Training
- On-the-job training
- Apprenticeship
- Off-the-job training
- Wage
- Salary
- Compensation
- Fringe benefit
- Job evaluation
- Commission
- Profit sharing
- Gain sharing
- Bonus

P icture William in your mind. He is a twenty-one-year-old high school graduate who has worked for a landscaping firm for the past two years. William has managed to save $9,500 and wants to use the money to buy a used car. William has always like Ford Mustangs and sees a nice-looking red one in a used car lot as he walks to work. That afternoon, after work (and looking a little dusty), he stops to look at the car. The salespeople ignore him until he goes up to a man and politely asks for help. The salesman asks William what he wants. William explains that he would like to see the red Mustang and maybe take it for a drive. The salesman replies, "How're ya gonna pay fer it?" William explains that he isn't sure he wants to buy the car until he has driven it. The salesman says, "Welllll son, when you got the cash, and yer ready to buy, you come back an talk ta me. Right now I'm busy." William is tempted to say something rude, but thinks better of it and simply leaves.

How would you feel if something like this happened to you? Who paid a cost as a result of the salesman's behavior? He lost the commission he might have earned. The owner of the used car lot lost profit. William lost the chance to own a car that could have satisfied his need for transportation. How could this problem have been avoided? Who was more at fault, the employee or his manager? What management policies could have been used to encourage this employee to provide better service? The answers to these questions may be found in **human resource management**.

Human resource management is the process of recruiting, hiring, training, motivating and using workers properly to achieve a firm's goals and objectives. In doing this, managers and workers serve the interests of the firm's customers.

SECTION 1

RECRUITING AND HIRING EMPLOYEES

While you read, ask yourself . . .
◆ *If you owned a business, what characteristics would you look for in an employee?*
◆ *If you were looking for a job, what skills and talents would you be able to offer a potential employer?*

Managing people is very different from managing tools or inventory. If you use a machine seven days a week, it won't complain. When you install electric wires close together in a poorly lighted, cold room, they won't mind. If you say unkind things about a tool, it won't take it personally. However, if you try to do these things to an employee, that person is likely to react negatively and perform poorly on the job.

Employees are people. They need to be treated with respect and consideration. They are also individuals, with different values and personalities. Not every person is equally suited to all jobs. Employers need to choose and train employees who are able and willing to complete tasks that need to be done. Employees who lack necessary skills or who are unhappy in their work are not likely to produce quality products efficiently or provide superior service to customers.

Recruitment

Recruitment is the process of finding and attracting the best candidates for a job. In our vast economic system there were more than 115 million workers in 1990. These individuals possessed varying degrees of skills, experience, abilities, and motivation. It would be impossible for a business to interview every possible worker for each job opening. There must be some way of narrowing the field of applicants to those who are qualified for the job, likely to accept the job, likely to perform well on the job, and likely to remain with the business for a reasonable period of time.

Internal Recruitment. A common method of narrowing the field of applicants is to recruit from among current employees. If the Apex Glass Company needs a new production manager, it could invite applications from current production line workers. There are many advantages to this type of **internal recruitment**. The employer already knows about the worker's abilities, sense of responsibility, and motivation. Internal recruitment tends to increase the loyalty and morale of workers who hope to advance their careers with the firm.

There are, however, some possible problems with internal recruitment. If successful, it will result in the need to replace workers who advance to new jobs within the firm. Rivalries may develop between workers who apply for job openings. Some workers who do not advance may feel "passed over" and make less of an effort to do their jobs well.

External Recruitment. When a firm is unable or unwilling to recruit from its current employees, it must carry out **external recruitment**. Again, an important goal of external recruitment is to narrow the field of applicants to a number that can be evaluated in a reasonable period of time without using too many resources. This may be accomplished by asking for specific skills and experience from applicants.

Firms must be careful that the skills and abilities requested are job related. It is reasonable to ask for two years of selling experience for a sales job or a demonstrated knowledge of organic chemistry for a research opening at a pharmaceutical company. Such requirements are obviously related to the job. However, a firm that advertises for a truck driver who is also a "white Anglo-Saxon Protestant male" will soon hear from the government.

Methods used to contact potential applicants include advertisements in newspapers or journals, employment agencies, college placement offices, state departments of labor, unsolicited applications (applicants who did not respond to a specific job advertisement), and recommendations of current employees. Which method will be most effective depends on the types of skills and abilities needed to

Vocabulary Builder

External recruitment Recruiting applicants for a job opening from among people who are not current employees of a firm.

Human resource management The process of acquiring, training, developing, motivating and using people properly to achieve an organization's objectives.

Internal recruitment Recruiting for a job opening from a firm's current employees.

Recruitment The process of attracting the best-qualified candidates for a job opening.

Consumer News

There Aren't Enough Qualified Applicants

Many American businesses are experiencing a severe shortage of qualified applicants for job openings. For example, in 1991 the owner of a lumber mill in Virginia complained of not being able to find permanent employees for his factory. He had been forced to hire more than twenty migrant workers with no lumber mill experience to fill job openings.

Several national surveys completed in 1990 indicated that more than half of American businesses expected to have trouble attracting and hiring skilled workers in the 1990s. One-fifth of the firms that responded to one survey reported that they *always* experienced difficulties in finding workers with needed skills. Many firms said that they were forced to hire workers who had poor work habits. Higher rates of employee absenteeism, tardiness, and failure to perform quality work were frequently mentioned. A large number of responding firms reported that many new workers either could not or would not follow written or spoken instructions.

How do you believe the shortage of skilled workers will affect the quality of products that firms are able to offer consumers?

What steps can employers take to try to solve this problem?

meet the requirements of the job. For unskilled positions, qualified job applicants may be found by advertising in local newspapers. However, if a job requires specialized technical skills, such as a working knowledge of nuclear physics, advertisements should be placed in national journals that serve people with this type of training. When a very specialized skill is needed, a business may list the opening with an employment service or hire a **headhunter** (a firm that specializes in locating managers or other workers with particular, hard-to-find skills).

Hiring

Once suitable applicants are located, firms must determine which person is best qualified for the job. This process is subject to some legal requirements. Discrimination based on race, religion, or sex is prohibited by federal and state laws. The **hiring decision** must be based solely on the applicant's ability to meet the requirements of the job.

To determine the most qualified candidate, firms interview the applicants. This allows the firm to obtain additional information that was not provided in the original application and to gain insight into the personality of the applicant. Trained interviewers are able to determine the applicant's personal goals, attitudes toward work, and motivation for seeking the job in question.

Many firms ask applicants to complete tests that are intended to determine how skilled and knowledgeable they are about the job. At one time businesses often administered tests that were intended to measure intelligence or general aptitude. Most of these tests have been dropped because they tested for skills and abilities that were often not important to job performance. They also may have discriminated against people with specific racial, ethnic, or social backgrounds.

Businesses that hire the most qualified workers are better able to provide goods and services to consumers. They are able to place employees in jobs that allow them to use their skills and talents to best advantage and to contribute to their employer's success.

Summing Up   *Businesses need to recruit and hire the best-qualified worker for each job opening. The objective of recruitment is to narrow the field of applicants to a manageable number. Hiring decisions must be based solely on the qualifications of the applicants to complete the responsibilities of the job.* ◆

SECTION 2

TRAINING EMPLOYEES

While you read, *ask yourself . . .*
- ◆ *How much of what you know have you learned in a formal setting like a classroom, and how much have you learned from your life experiences?*
- ◆ *How will you keep up-to-date with changes as time goes by? Will you ever know everything you need to know?*

Almost every job requires some **training** for new and current employees. If a worker is only going to fry hamburgers, he or she may be able to learn the necessary skills in a few hours. However, the more complex the job, the longer the training period is likely to be. When The Boeing Aircraft Corporation hires new workers, they are not regarded as qualified until they have completed months of training, even if they are hired with a degree in engineering. It is one thing to learn about engineering principles in a classroom. It is something else to apply this knowledge in a real-life situation.

On-the-Job Training

When workers learn and acquire skills in their workplace, they are receiving **on-the-job training**. Some on-the-job training takes place when workers talk with each other and share knowledge. The value of this sharing can be increased by management through various organized methods. New workers may be assigned to a mentor (an experienced worker who helps the new worker gain necessary skills). There may be an **apprenticeship** program for specific trades. Classes or other forms of formalized training may be provide to employees at their place of work. Employers are often willing to pay for on-the-job training because they believe it will improve the productivity of their employees.

Unions often negotiate for training programs as a part of the bargaining process. They recognize that with changing technology, workers will have to acquire new skills to keep their jobs. On-the-job training assures union members of an opportunity to keep up with changes in their workplace. Training current employees also prevents managers from having to pay to find new workers with necessary skills.

Off-the-Job Training

Many jobs require skills that cannot be easily learned in the workplace. If a firm is going to buy a new computer system, it won't be able to train workers on a machine it does not yet

Vocabulary Builder

Apprenticeship   A form of on-the-job training in which new employees must complete a period of instruction to become certified as having a skill.

Headhunter   A firm that specializes in locating employees for firms to hire, particularly managers.

Hiring decision   Decision as to who is the best-qualified applicant for a job opening.

On-the-job training   Training that takes place in the workplace.

◆   Different workers have different abilities but all workers need income and a sense of personal fulfillment. We should learn to think of people in terms of what they can do rather than in terms of their limitations.

own. It will need to send workers to a different location where they can learn how to use the new type of machine.

It would make little sense to spend a lot of money to hire a specialist to train only one worker in a particular procedure. It would be more efficient to send that worker to a class where there are many students who need the same type of specialized training. When workers are sent to other locations to obtain knowledge or learn skills, they are involved in **off-the-job training**.

Consumers benefit from employee training programs. Workers who have the necessary skills are better able to produce products and provide services that satisfy consumer needs and wants. Employees who lack knowledge or skills cannot be expected to serve customers well. For example, workers who deal with the public need to understand and use social skills. It is probably acceptable to say something like "Hey, Whadoyawant?" to your friends in school. However, if you work as a clerk in a store, a question like "How may I help you?" is more likely to result in a sale. One reason some clerks are rude to customers is that no one has ever taught them to be polite. Employers need to take the time to help employees learn the social skills they need to be productive workers.

Consumer Close-Up

Protecting the Rights of the Disabled

Do you know a person who is disabled? What kind of life do you think this person leads? How do you believe people who are disabled should be treated? Should they have the same opportunities as other people? What would you be willing to give up to assure disabled people an equal chance to have a full and rewarding life?

According to the Library of Congress's Congressional Research Service, 43 million Americans, or about one out of every six in this country, have some sort of disability. Under legislation passed in 1989, disabled people must be given equal access and opportunity in employment, public and private transportation, public accommodations, and telecommunications. Most businesses will be required to offer disabled people equal opportunities by July 1994. These rights will be phased in starting in January 1992, when many businesses will have to offer equal access to disabled cus-

tomers. By January 1993 all new public buildings must be constructed to have complete access for people with disabilities. Between July 1992 and July 1994, small firms with twenty-five or fewer employees will be exempted from having to offer equal employment opportunities. After July 1994 only firms with fifteen or fewer employees will be exempted.

To be protected by the law, a disabled applicant or employee must be able to complete "essential functions" of a job. The employer must make "reasonable accommodations" to compensate for the employee's handicap unless it would cause "undue hardship" to the employer.

This means that employers must determine what the "essential functions" of each job classification are. Employers must be able to explain why these particular functions need to be completed if asked to do so in a court of law. Employers must also make the same training opportunities available to disabled workers that are offered to other workers, even if the cost is greater.

The penalties under the antidiscrimination law are the same as those under the Civil Rights Act of 1964. A judge may force an employer found guilty of discrimination to reinstate or employ a worker and award back pay. However, the worker may also sue the employer, and a jury may award much larger judgments against the firm. Businesses must be very careful to follow the new law to avoid expensive law suits. They will also benefit from the valuable contributions disabled workers are able to give to production.

How do you believe this law will affect the average consumer?

Do you think it will increase the cost of running a business?

How could the law reduce the burden on the government of providing benefits to disabled people?

Would it bother you to be waited on by a person who is disabled?

Do you feel that the law is justified and a good idea?

Summing Up *All workers benefit from regular training programs. This training may be provided on or off the job. Employers, employees, and customers benefit when workers are trained to complete tasks more efficiently.* ◆

Vocabulary Builder

Off-the-job training Training that takes place away from the workplace.

WORKER COMPENSATION

While you read, ask yourself . . .
- ◆ *When you take your first job, will your wage or the experience you gain be of greater value to you in the long run?*
- ◆ *What factors determine the value of your labor? How much do you feel your time is worth?*

It's nice to have a job that gives you a feeling of accomplishment and satisfaction. It is also nice to be paid an hourly **wage** or a **salary** that allows you to support yourself and your family in a manner that suits your needs. Wages are paid on an hourly basis, while salary is an amount contracted for over a period of time. Both wages and salary are forms of worker **compensation**.

Compensation is all of the direct and indirect payments that employees receive for their labor. While money is part of compensation, it is not the only thing of value that workers expect to receive for their labor. Most workers who have a full-time job receive **fringe benefits** like health insurance, paid vacation, and a retirement plan. They may also be provided with child care, a company car, or reduced prices for products that their employer produces. Another valuable benefit that all workers receive is job experience. Employees benefit from the knowledge and skills that they gain on the job, whether they stay with their current employer or eventually take a job with a different employer.

Compensation as a Reward

Workers expect to be paid. Employers expect to pay their workers. Beyond these simple expectations, the manner and amount of compensation can be used to reward workers who follow directions, who are responsible, or who suggest creative and innovative ideas that help the firm succeed. When managers use compensation to reward employees, it is important that all workers understand what is being rewarded. If Sue receives a raise because she made more sales than any other salesperson, she and other workers will be encouraged to work harder in the future *only* if they understand why Sue received more pay. Employee contests that result in bonuses or free vacations may be used to encourage greater efforts, but they must be perceived by workers as fair and reasonable or they may cause resentment among the workers who do not win.

Employers should provide a method of **job evaluation** to measure the worth of a worker's labor. This may be used as a basis for determining how much compensation each worker should receive. For this process to work, there must be standards to compare worker performance to. These standards may be established in a number of ways. The accomplishments of each worker may be compared with the average accomplishments of the others. Or managers and individual workers may establish mutual objectives that the worker agrees to try to achieve. Again, the important factor is fairness. Workers will not perform well if they feel they are not being treated justly.

Pay for Performance

Many businesses provide an incentive to workers by giving them a share of the income generated by their effort. This may take the form of a **commission** for sales they make. Another method that has been negotiated into many contracts in recent years is **profit sharing**. Examples may be found in the contracts agreed to by the United Auto Workers and General Motors, Ford, and Chrysler in the 1980s. **Gain sharing** rewards employees for increases in their productivity. **Bonuses** are given by many firms at a particular time of year to reward workers for their effort. The amount of the bonus may depend on the success of the firm or of the individual worker.

When workers are rewarded for their performance, they (and other employees) must understand why the extra compensation is being received. This reason must be associated with activities that contribute to the success of the firm. In this way the firm will encourage all workers to do their best.

Summing Up *Compensation is more than a way of paying workers for their labor. It is also a way to motivate employees to do their best work. To achieve this goal, methods of compensation must be perceived as fair and reasonable by employees.* ◆

wanted to buy cars manufactured in Japan. The demand for these products far exceeded the supply. Dealers who sold imported Japanese cars were able to sell every car they received almost immediately. Some of them even added a charge to their car's price that was labeled "EDP." EDP stood for *extra dealer profit*. Salespeople and service technicians were sometimes rude to customers. They were able to sell their cars because they were inexpensive and known for quality. However, customers were often angry about the service they received and over the way they were treated. Later, the price of Japanese cars increased. Customers did not forget the kind of service they had received at some dealerships. Many did not return to these businesses, and some of these businesses failed.

SECTION 4

HOW CONSUMERS BENEFIT FROM SATISFIED WORKERS

While you read, ask yourself . . .
- ◆ *If you were a salesperson, how would you treat your customers?*
- ◆ *If you worked on a production line, what would encourage you to produce the best-quality products possible?*
- ◆ *How much pride do you take in completing a job that is well done?*

When a consumer buys a product, that person is also buying the services offered by the business. These services include the help of the clerk who makes the sale, the work of the accountant who records the sale and sends a bill requesting payment, and the skills and effort of the workers who may service the product.

It is possible for a firm to offer superior products and yet fail because it provides inferior service. In the early 1980s many Americans

Vocabulary Builder

Bonus A form of compensation usually given in a lump sum at a particular time of the year to reward workers for their effort.

Commission A payment based on a percentage of the total amount or value of a good or service sold by a salesperson.

Compensation The direct and indirect payments that employees receive for their labor or job performance.

Fringe benefits Compensation other than salary or wages provided by employers to employees or their families.

Gain sharing A form of compensation where employees are paid a share of a firm's increase in profit or reductions in cost.

Job evaluation A method of determining job worth, often used to set levels of compensation.

Profit sharing A form of compensation in which employees are paid a part of a firm's profit, the amount often set by a contractual agreement.

Salary Employee compensation provided in exchange for labor over a specific period of time.

Wage Employee compensation calculated on an hourly basis.

Consumer News

Building a Winning Team

On June 12, 1991, the Chicago Bulls won the National Basketball Association championship by beating the Los Angeles Lakers by a score of 108 to 101 in the fifth game of a seven-game series. What functions of human resource management must the owners of the Bulls have carried out to develop this winning team? Consider their efforts to recruit and hire talented players and how these players must have been trained, directed, and compensated.

How did the efforts of the Bulls' managers pay off for themselves, the players, and the consumers (fans)?

◆   Success in most situations is the result of a team effort. Workers in a business need to work together no less than the members of an athletic team. Why can't everyone in a business be a star?

Businesses that use good human resource management to recruit, hire, and train workers will be better able to provide courteous, quality service to their customers. Workers who are well paid are more likely to value their jobs and work to keep them. They probably understand that the only way their employer can afford to pay them is to generate income from sales. Employees are able to protect their jobs and income by providing good service to customers.

The following ideas are related to each other. Owners generate income and earn profits when their businesses sell products. Employees are more likely to be paid good wages when they provide quality products and superior service to customers. Customers should receive quality products and superior service when workers are well compensated and business owners earn reasonable profits. Owners, workers, and customers all depend on each other for their success. If one group does poorly, the others will also suffer.

Summing Up   *Consumers often benefit when firms earn reasonable profits and workers are fairly compensated. These profits and compensation allow firms to supply quality products that consumers want to buy to satisfy their needs and wants.* ◆

Review and Enrichment Activities

VOCABULARY REVIEW

1. Column A contains key consumer terms from this chapter. Column B contains a scrambled list of phrases that describe what these terms mean. Match the correct meaning with each term. Write your answers on a separate sheet of paper.

Column A	Column B
1. human resource management	a. Choosing the individual who is best qualified for a job
2. job evaluation	b. The policies and decisions that cause employees to work to achieve the firm's objectives
3. headhunter	c. Direct and indirect payments that employees receive for their labor
4. hiring decision	d. A method of determining the value of an employee's labor
5. apprenticeship	e. The process of attracting applicants to a job opening
6. fringe benefit	f. Businesses that locate employees for other firms to hire
7. profit sharing	g. When employees are paid a share of a firm's increases in profit
8. compensation	h. A form of on-the-job training that requires new workers to complete a period of instruction before becoming certified as having a particular skill
9. gain sharing	i. When employees are paid a share of a firm's profits
10. recruitment	j. Benefits workers receive in addition to their salary or wage

2. Explain the difference between earning a **wage** and a **salary**.

Review and Enrichment Activities Continued

CHECKING WHAT YOU'VE LEARNED

Write your answers for the following exercises on a separate sheet of paper.

1. Identify each of the functions that together make up human resource management.
2. Explain why managing people is different from managing tools or inventory.
3. Why is recruitment often thought of as a process that narrows the field of applicants?
4. What advantages are there for a firm that uses internal recruitment?
5. Why are firms sometimes forced to use external recruitment?
6. Describe several factors that might determine the amount of training a new employee needs.
7. What advantages does a firm receive from providing training opportunities for its employees?
8. What factors may cause a firm to use off-the-job training rather than on-the-job training?
9. What are several ways that workers may be compensated for their labor in addition to the money they earn from wages or salaries?
10. Describe one specific way that compensation may be used to encourage desired worker behavior.
11. Explain the difference between profit sharing and gain sharing.
12. Explain how consumers benefit from firms that practice good human resource management.

PRACTICING YOUR CONSUMER SKILLS

Write your answers for the following exercises on a separate sheet of paper.

1. Evaluate each of the following business policies. Describe the reaction most workers would probably have to each policy, and state whether the policy is likely to help the firm achieve its objectives.
    a. The Acme Packaging Company offers its workers the choice of working five 8-hour days each week or coming in four times a week to work 10-hour days.
    b. The Sheldon Furniture Co. has a policy of promoting workers to higher positions in management except for the most highly skilled craftspeople. The owners have chosen not to promote these workers because they are very difficult to replace in their current jobs.

    c. The Martin Tool Co. assigns specific jobs to each employee and measures their performance. The owners have a policy of paying a bonus equal to 10 percent of additional income that results from increased worker productivity.

    d. Although the owners of the Amalgamated Carburetor Co. hires many women, they employ no female managers.

    e. The Central Printing Co. provides training opportunities for job advancement to workers who have been with the firm for five years or more.

2. The following questions were asked by the human resource manager of the Butler Bottling Co. during a job interview. The person being interviewed was applying for a job as a quality control specialist. State whether you believe each question was appropriate, and explain your reasoning.

    a. "Why are you seeking this position?"

    b. "Have you ever been arrested for anything more serious than a traffic violation?"

    c. "What training and experience do you have that qualifies you for this position?"

    d. "Do you have any medical or family problems that would prevent you from being able to get to work on time?"

    e. "Does working with people who have different ethnic, social, or racial backgrounds bother you?"

    f. What religious holidays would you expect to take off?

3. Evaluate each of the following compensation policies. Explain how each policy would probably affect the quality of products and service offered to customers.

    a. Tony's Fashion Shop pays a 5 percent bonus to clerks who complete $500 or more in sales in an 8-hour workday.

    b. Martha pays each of her twelve workers 1 percent of her store's profit at the end of each year.

    c. Ray likes to make raises a surprise. He awards them to workers at no particular time and for no apparent reason.

    d. Paula asks her regular customers to evaluate her employees. When workers receive many favorable comments, they are given a raise. If a worker receives many unfavorable comments, they are fired.

    e. Kerry pays his new workers $7 an hour. He gives them a 50-cent-an-hour raise every three months until they earn $10 an hour. All workers receive these raises unless they do so poorly that they are fired.

USING NUMBERS

Solve the following problem to help make the best possible choice. Write your solution on a separate sheet of paper. Be sure to show all your work.

George owns an appliance store. He is trying to decide what the best method of worker compensation is for his business. He has three plans he

Review and Enrichment Activities Continued

could use. One is to simply pay his salespeople $10 an hour regardless of what they sell. Another is to pay $5 an hour plus a 4 percent commission on their sales. His last idea is to pay workers an 8 percent commission and no wage at all. The following table shows how much each of George's four salespeople sell in an average 40-hour workweek. Copy the following worksheet to your paper. Determine how much each employee would be paid under each plan. Then recommend one of the plans to George, and explain the reasoning behind your choice.

Salesperson	Average Sales Per Week	Earnings Under Plan 1	Earnings Under Plan 2	Earnings Under Plan 3
Rosa	$5,789	—	—	—
Terry	$6,204	—	—	—
Bob	$3,937	—	—	—
Keren	$8,940	—	—	—

PUTTING IDEAS IN YOUR OWN WORDS

The following quotations are from this chapter. Explain these quotations in your own words to make sure you understand what they mean. Write your answers on a separate sheet of paper.

1. "Managing people is very different from managing tools or inventory."
2. "Businesses that hire the most qualified workers are better able to provide goods and services to consumers."
3. "It is possible for a firm to offer superior products and yet fail because it provides inferior service."

BUILDING CONSUMER KNOWLEDGE

Write your answers for the following exercises on a separate sheet of paper.

1. If you have a job, describe the process you went through to be hired. If you do not have a job, ask a friend who is employed to explain how he or she was hired.

2. Ask three different employed adults to describe training opportunities they are given by their employers. Try to interview people who work for different firms, so you can receive different information. Be prepared to explain your findings to the class.

3. The following list is made up of types of employees you are likely to have had contact with. Describe the type of service you received from each employee, and tell why you think you received that type of service.
   a. A cafeteria worker in your school
   b. A clerk at a discount store
   c. A worker in a government office (perhaps at a license bureau)
   d. A stock person in a grocery store
   e. A nurse in your doctor's office
   f. A salesperson at a clothing store

Your Career in the World of Work

Unit 6 outlines a method that you can use to evaluate your personal aptitudes, objectives, and values. You will discover that an understanding of yourself will help you make better choices for your future role in our economy. You will also learn how to investigate careers and how to prepare yourself for the career you choose. Finally, you will learn about various methods that can help you obtain and keep a job that fulfills your career goals.

Chapter 20

Getting to Know Yourself

Chapter Objectives

After completing this chapter, you will be able to do the following:

- Complete an inventory of your interests, aptitudes, skills, values, and personality.
- Use this inventory to define your self-concept and your attitude toward life.
- Explain how your inventory and self-concept can be used to identify career choices that would be appropriate for you.
- Explain how your inventory and self-concept can be used to make consumer choices that will best satisfy your needs.

Key Consumer Terms

In this chapter you will learn the meanings of the following important consumer terms:

- Personal inventory
- Attitude
- Self-concept
- Interests
- Aptitude
- Skill
- Values
- Life values
- Work values
- Personality

S uppose in a dream you find Aladdin's magic lamp. You rub the lamp, and a genie appears from a cloud of green smoke. He exclaims, "Oh possessor of the lamp, I will grant you three wishes."

You think to yourself, "Awesome! How about a mansion, yacht, and about a billion dollars?" But before you can open your mouth, the genie goes on: "You should know that the Intergalactic Genie's Union has made a new rule. They are tired of granting people useless wishes that they make without thinking. Before I grant you any wishes, you must complete a **personal inventory**. You must list your interests, aptitudes, skills, and values and describe your personality. When you have done this and know what you really want from life, we can talk about wishes." You start to protest, but the genie disappears in another cloud of smoke.

When you wake the next morning, you dismiss the dream as no more than the result of eating six slices of pizza before going to bed. However, the genie and your consumer economics teacher have given you the same assignment. They both want you to complete a personal inventory to help you learn about yourself.

SECTION 1

YOUR ATTITUDE AND SELF-CONCEPT

While you read, ask yourself . . .
◆ *Think of several people you know who you believe have a positive attitude toward life.*
◆ *What type of self-concept do you imagine they have of themselves?*

How do you see yourself? Are you self-confident or shy? Would you rather spend time by yourself or be with your friends? Would you be happier to be rich or to have an occupation you find interesting? If you had twenty-five words to describe what is important to you, what would you say? Have you ever really thought hard about what you believe in and why? If you expect to ever make plans for your future, you need to have a clear idea of what you want to achieve in life.

Your Attitude: How You Look at Life

Your **attitude** is your basic outlook on life. It is your personal way of looking at yourself and the world around you. If you believe that things usually go well and that you will succeed if you work hard, you have a positive attitude. A positive attitude is important to personal success because it encourages you to do your best.

Has an adult ever talked to you about your attitude? You might think that this is a favorite topic of parents and teachers. You may have been told that your generous attitude is a fine example for others to follow. Or someone might have said that your self-centered attitude is something you should change. The fact is, we all have an outlook on life. Some people expect to achieve their goals and objectives, while others are quite negative and expect the worst. Some people assume that the world is honest and good, while others are distrustful and suspicious. Some people angrily protect what they believe to be their rights, while others are easygoing and don't take life too seriously. All of these feelings and expectations contribute to people's attitudes.

Your Self-Concept: A Measure of Your Value

Your **self-concept** is the way you see yourself and your personal worth or value. A self-concept is formed over many years by many people. When parents love and care for their children, they are helping their children acquire a positive self-concept. Children who are popular and have close friendships learn to feel good about themselves. People who do well in school, succeed in sports, win community awards, or volunteer time and effort to charitable organizations are also building a healthy self-concept. Children who grow up without love, support, or success are likely to have a negative self-concept.

A person's attitude and self-concept often determine his or her behavior. When people have a positive attitude and value themselves, they are more likely to do their best to achieve their objectives in life. This will improve their chance of reaching their goals. People who have a negative attitude and self-concept might feel that they can't succeed and therefore will not make their best effort to achieve their objectives. In this chapter you will be asked to complete a personal inventory that will help you make plans for your future. The first step in this process is to honestly describe your attitude toward life and your self-concept.

Summing Up *All people have an attitude toward life and a self-concept that affect their behavior and success. The first step in preparing a personal inventory is to consider your own attitude and self-concept.* ◆

SECTION 2

IDENTIFYING YOUR INTERESTS

While you read, ask yourself . . .
- ◆ *What are several ways that your interests have changed in the past five years?*
- ◆ *How are your interests likely to change in the future?*
- ◆ *Why is it important to consider your future interests, as well as your current interests, when you make a career choice?*

If you take a job when you are eighteen years old and work 40 hours a week until you are sixty-five years old, you will work more than 95,000 hours. That is a long time to be doing something that doesn't interest you. It would be better to choose a career that you find challenging, rewarding, and interesting.

Interests go beyond enjoying paperback romance novels or watching football every weekend in the fall. You may enjoy these things, but you probably would not want to spend a large part of your life doing them. They are also not likely to give you a way to earn a living. To discover your real interests, you need to consider basic facts about yourself and what you like. To identify your interests, ask yourself the following questions.

Vocabulary Builder

Attitude One's basic outlook on life.
Interests The activities, objects, causes, or people that an individual finds personally rewarding or gratifying over extended periods of time.
Personal inventory An exploration of personal assets, needs, values, and personality.
Self-concept The way one sees oneself and one's feeling of self-worth.

◆   The way you spend your free time can be an indication of your interests. If you enjoy taking care of a car becoming an automobile technician might be a rewarding career choice for you.

- What sort of people do you like to be with? What do you do when you are with them? If you talk about automobile engines or computer programs with your friends, this could be an indication of something that interests you.

- What do you watch on television, listen to on radio, or read about in newspapers or magazines? If you read about the stock market or listen to news reports about medical advancements, this could be an indication of something that interests you.

- Which classes in school do you like best? Have you studied subjects outside of school just because you wanted to? Are there topics you would like to know more about? If you learned how to sew in school and as a result designed some of your own clothes, this could be an indication of something that interests you.

- How do you spend your spare time? Do you have hobbies, or are there social activities that you enjoy? If you volunteer to help at a local food bank or nursing home, this could be an indication of something that interests you.

- If you have a choice, do you prefer to work with people, facts, or things? Do you enjoy the personal relationships and exchange of ideas that result from working with people? Do you prefer to deal with facts, write reports, or create innovative ideas? Do you find working with tools or machines most rewarding? If you have a feeling of satisfaction when you take lumber and make it into a chair or table, this could be an indication of something that interests you.

When you understand the subjects and activities that you enjoy and find interesting, you will be better able to choose a career and life-style. This knowledge will help you complete your personal inventory.

Summing Up *People who are making plans for their future need to have a clear idea of the types of subjects and activities they find interesting. This will help them choose a rewarding career and life-style.* ◆

SECTION 3

DISCOVERING YOUR APTITUDES AND SKILLS

While you read, ask yourself . . .
- ◆ *Have you had broad life experiences, or have they been rather narrow? (Have you done many different things?)*
- ◆ *What skills do you have today that you did not have two years ago?*
- ◆ *Are you aware of all the aptitudes you have that could be developed into skills?*

It takes more than an interest to be successful in a career. Success requires **aptitudes** and **skills**. Aptitudes are the potentials or natural inclinations that help people develop the necessary skills to accomplish a type of task. Everyone finds some skills easier to learn than others. Some people have an aptitude for understanding mechanical devices. They read an instruction booklet once and can take a bicycle apart, fix the part that is broken, and reassemble the bicycle easily. Other people don't feel comfortable if they have to tighten a loose screw. You may be able to picture an object in your mind and draw it from memory, while someone else couldn't draw it if it was sitting right in front of them. Different people have different abilities to learn new tasks because they have different aptitudes.

The next step in completing your personal inventory is to identify the aptitudes that you could develop into skills. Here is a list of aptitudes you might have:

- *General aptitude.* Do you find learning and understanding new ideas, facts, or relationships to be easy or challenging? Can you use logic and reason to solve problems you have not dealt with before? Your success in school may be a good indication of your general aptitude.
- *Verbal aptitude.* Do you have the ability to explain ideas or directions to other people so that they understand your meaning? When you give a talk to your class or to a group of adults, do they understand and appreciate it? Are you able to convince people that your ideas are correct? If you are able to do these things, you might be successful in a career in sales or in managing other workers.
- *Numerical aptitude.* Are you able to work with numbers quickly and accurately? If you are presented with a problem that requires a numerical solution, are you able to choose the correct mathematical process to find the answer? An aptitude for numerical relationships can be seen in your success in math, science, or business classes.
- *Spatial aptitude.* Can you "see" what something will really look like from a flat drawing or photograph? Can you move or rotate pictures of objects in your mind? If someone describes something you have never seen, can you picture it in your mind? If you can do these things, you may have an aptitude that would help you design machines, be an architect, or do displays and layouts in a store.
- *Form perception.* Are you able to recognize small changes in objects? Do you know

---

Vocabulary Builder

Aptitude   A potential or natural ability that may be developed into a skill.
Skill   The ability to accomplish a specific task.

Consumer Close-Up

Home-Based Industry

Almost one out of every four Americans in the labor force works at home at least part of the time. In 1988 that was 26.6 million people. This number included those who were self-employed, salaried employees, contract workers, and free-lancers (people who do work under temporary contract to other businesses). The number of people involved in home-based work grew by 1.7 million in 1988 alone. What kind of people choose this type of work over a more traditional life on the job? Research indicates the following:

- About 60 percent are involved in some type of white-collar (administrative or professional) work.
- One-third are in sales or technical fields. Many are consultants.
- Many of them are between twenty-five and forty years old and have worked in a more traditional job setting before.
- More than half are women, and many female home-based workers are mothers with young children.
- Many are new entrepreneurs who work at home to save the cost of establishing a separate

place of business. About 70 percent of home-based entrepreneurs are women.
- Much of the growth in home-based work has been made possible by low-cost electronic connections with traditional business locations.

What does the growth in the number of people who do home-based work show about our changing values?

Why do you suppose most people who are involved in home-based work were first employed in a more traditional work setting?

when a friend has a new skirt or haircut? If one line is 2 inches longer than another, can you remember and recognize the difference when you don't see the lines together? If you have form perception, you have an aptitude for police work or for being a quality control manager.

- *Clerical perception.* When you read a newspaper, book, or a friend's homework assignment, do you find yourself recognizing errors and making corrections? Can you see mistakes in numbers, spelling, and punctuation? If you have clerical perception, you have an aptitude that would help you succeed in writing, publishing, or reporting the news.
- *Finger dexterity.* Can you work with small objects with ease and accuracy? When you were a child, did you ever take a watch

apart to see how it worked—and then put it back together so it worked? If you have good finger dexterity, you might be successful assembling small parts, adjusting precision machines, or being a surgeon.

- *Manual dexterity.* Are you able to use your hands easily and in a coordinated manner? Do you find it easy to use hand tools like wrenches and hammers? If you pound a nail, do you hit it on the head or do you miss and hit your thumb? If you have manual dexterity, you have an aptitude that could help you run machines or work with tools.
- *Motor coordination.* When you try to put a key into a lock, do you always hit the hole on the first try? Can you fit parts together easily? Motor coordination is the ability to use your eyes and hands together. This

◆ People who are able to communicate ideas and persuade others when they speak have a verbal aptitude. This ability could help them to become successful sales people or politicians.

would be a valuable aptitude for jobs like painting, adjusting machines, or working on a moving assembly line.

- *Eye-hand-foot coordination.* Do you have the ability to move both your hands and your feet at the same time in response to something you see? The obvious example of this is driving a car or truck or flying an airplane. There are many other jobs that require this type of ability. Even piano players need this aptitude.

- *Color discrimination.* Can you see small differences in color? Can you tell when colors go well together or when they clash with each other? If you have this ability, you

have an aptitude that will help you succeed in the fashion industry or in interior design.

This is not a complete list of every aptitude you might have. You may be able to distinguish between sounds. You may have an ability to taste or smell the difference between foods. You may even be able to put a ball through a basket from beyond the three-point line. All people—including you—have aptitudes. You just have to discover what they are.

An aptitude must be developed to become a skill that has real value to you and your career. Even if you have numerical aptitude, you cannot be a certified public accountant without

Consumer News

Does Leadership Equal Management?

Over the years many people have believed that the words *leadership* and *management* mean the same thing. Recently, it has become increasing clear that this is not the case. John P. Kotter has written a book on the subject: *A Force for Change: How Leadership Differs from Management*. According to Kotter, management is a process of "planning, budgeting, organizing, staffing, and controlling." Managers tend to accept the structure of a firm the way it is and fit workers into its organization. People who don't fit don't stay.

Leadership, Kotter believes, involves establishing a direction for a firm and then helping individual workers contribute to that direction according to their own abilities and personalities. Leaders think in terms of "renewal" or of adjusting an organization to suit the individual values and needs of people. Leaders are aware of the "larger realities" of the world beyond the firm they work for. As Kotter writes, "Leadership by itself never keeps an operation on time . . . and management by itself never creates significant useful change."

Would you rather be a manager or a leader?

What special talents would a leader need that a manager might not?

Would you rather work for a manager or a leader?

those that could be developed into skills. The final part of your personal inventory is to consider your values and personality.

Summing Up *Most people have aptitudes that can be developed into valuable skills. Finding and developing these aptitudes are important steps in choosing and succeeding in a career.* ◆

SECTION 4

WHAT DO YOU VALUE?

While you read, ask yourself . . .
- ◆ *Are your values most similar to those of your parents, friends, teachers or someone else you know?*
- ◆ *How do you feel when you are with people who clearly have different values than you?*
- ◆ *How important do you think your values are when you choose a career?*

What possessions or activities bring you the greatest personal pleasure? Is it more important for you to have many friends or only a few special relationships? Would you care more about the amount of money you earn on a job, the type of work you do, or the kind of people you work with? Do you learn new things because you like to know more about the world, or only when you are forced to? How important is your family, community, or religion to you? All of these questions could be answered according to your **values**. Values are the personal standards that you believe are important and worthwhile. Values are learned. The values you hold are probably similar to those of your family, friends, and other people you respect. Regardless of how you gained your personal values, they are now *your* values and should be considered when you choose a career.

Your **life values**—the values that determine how you live—are related to, but not always the same as, your **work values**. You may value

studying business practices, rules, and laws and gaining experience to pass a state test that earns you the right to your certification.

When you complete your personal inventory, you will list your aptitudes and identify

traveling to secluded places where you can commune with nature. A desire for peace and solitude is an example of a life value. You may find it necessary to work in a noisy, crowded factory to be able to afford your life value. Your work value may be earning enough money to be able to take vacations you desire. Consider your feelings toward the following values. Which do you believe are life values? Which are work values? Are there some that may be both?

- *Money.* How important is the amount of money you earn?
- *Security.* Do you need to know that you can count on having the same job for the rest of your working life?
- *Independence.* Do you need to be able to make most of your own decisions?
- *Health.* How important is leading a life or having a job with little health risk?
- *Personal recognition.* How important is it for other people to know and respect you?
- *Creativity.* Do you feel a need to develop new ideas or ways of doing things? Are you willing to take a risk to prove your own ideas?
- *Education.* Is it important to you to learn? Do you believe that knowing something is valuable, regardless of whether you ever use the knowledge?
- *Religion.* How important is your religion and its teachings?
- *Family.* Do you want to live close to your family? How important is the time you spend with your family?
- *Well-being of your community.* Do you feel a need to improve your community? Is helping other people important to you?
- *Living where you want to.* Is there a particular place or type of location where you would like to live? Do you like the excitement of big cities, the sense of family that can be found in small communities, or the solitude of living by yourself in the country?

Consumer News

Can You Satisfy Your Life Values in a Part-Time Job?

Many people hold full-time jobs that they find less than exciting to support themselves and their families. In general, jobs take less than 25 percent of our time. We spend the other 75 percent sleeping, playing, eating, and doing other things. Many people have used some of their free time to take second jobs or start businesses—not to earn money, but to enjoy doing something they find personally rewarding.

Arthur Whitaker is a statistician who works for the government. He bakes and sells fruitcakes in his free time. He says that the fruitcakes make him remember his childhood. Dr. Cleve Francis is a cardiologist in a hospital during the day and sings country and western songs in a club by night. Joyce Jones, a college personal counselor, operates an art studio in her free time. Many other people have found ways to satisfy their life values in jobs that are not their basic careers.

Can you think of a job or occupation you would like to try on a part-time basis?

Vocabulary Builder

Life values Values that determine how a person chooses to live.
Work values Values that help a person choose a job and career.
Values The personal standards that a person feels are important and worthwhile.

◆ The satisfaction people receive from life depends on their values and personalities. What do you imagine these people are feeling that apparently gives them such joy or sense of purpose. Do you have strong feelings about what you like to do?

• *Environment.* How important is protecting the environment? Would you live in a community where chemical waste has been stored? Would you work for a business that pollutes the environment? Are you willing to make sacrifices in your own life so that future generations will have a clean environment?

Again, this is not a complete list of all the values you might hold. When you consider the type of life you want to lead and the type of career you would like to choose, you should evaluate your choices by how they fit in with the things you value.

Summing Up *Although life values and work values are related, they are not the same for most people. When choosing a career, it is usually necessary to make a trade-off between these two types of values to achieve your personal objectives.* ◆

SECTION 5

YOUR PERSONALITY

While you read, ask yourself . . .
◆ *Do you find it easy or difficult to make friends?*
◆ *Do other people respect your opinions?*
◆ *Would you rather be with people who have personalities that are similar to your own or who are different?*

You are unique. There is no one else in the world quite like you. You have your own **personality** that is made up of the outward signs of your inner self. What you think, feel, and believe determines your personality and how you act. Other people judge your personality by the way you walk, talk, treat other people, give compliments or insults, respect property and the environment, and behave in hundreds of other ways.

When other people say that you are friendly, kind, or cheerful, they are telling you their opinion of your personality. If people say that you are mean, grouchy, or inconsiderate, they are also telling you about your personality. What other people think of you and your personality is important for a number of reasons.

Whether you like to or not, you will have to live and cooperate with other people for your entire life. If you do not have an outgoing or friendly personality, you may find this difficult, but you will still have to do it. However, you can choose a life and career that involves less contact with other people. You could become a forest ranger and spend your time sitting in a tower looking for forest fires. This might not be a very challenging job, but it would fit your personality. If you are naturally enthusiastic and friendly, you may find a job in sales or public relations to be fulfilling.

Read the following list of personality traits. Do you believe that you fit into any of these categories? What other personality traits can you think of that might describe you?

- *Realistic.* Realistic people like to work with machines, tools, and objects. They like answers that can be classified as right or wrong. They prefer to be able to quantify and measure things.
- *Investigative.* Investigative people like the challenge of solving a problem. They like to analyze physical, biological, or cultural problems and come up with solutions. They usually develop numerical and scientific skills.
- *Artistic.* Artistic people like to be involved in free, unregulated activities that give them the opportunity to express their creativity. They often develop skills in languages, art, theater, or music.

- *Social.* Social people like to help, teach, train, cure, and lead other people. They avoid working in areas where there is little human contact. They often develop skills in communications and interpersonal relations.
- *Enterprising.* Enterprising people like to lead and direct other people to achieve a goal. They may choose to run their own business. They often earn large incomes or seek political office.
- *Conventional.* Conventional people have also been called conformists. They like to fit in with other people. They desire the sense of security that can be found in groups. They are often most successful when they have jobs that require limited creativity, such as working on a production line or working as a file clerk.

When you complete your description of your personality, you have also completed your personal inventory. You will use this inventory in Chapter 21 to help you evaluate possible career choices. Remember, the purpose of this unit is to help you choose a satisfying career that will allow you to earn income to buy products to fill your needs and wants. People who don't make good career choices will be less satisfied in life and probably will have less income and be able to make fewer consumer choices.

Summing Up *Each person has his or her own unique personality that should be considered when making a career choice. People should choose careers that allow them to use their personality to its best advantage to contribute to their personal satisfaction and success.* ◆

Vocabulary Builder

Personality Sum of the outward signs and characteristics that show the inner values that a person holds.

Review and Enrichment Activities

VOCABULARY REVIEW

1. Column A contains key consumer terms from this chapter. Column B contains a scrambled list of phrases that describe what these terms mean. Match the correct meaning with each term. Write your answers on a separate sheet of paper.

Column A	Column B
1. Personality	a. Person's natural inclination to be able to do or understand something
2. Aptitude	b. The ability to accomplish a task
3. Skill	c. The way people see themselves and their worth
4. Values	d. A person's basic outlook on life
5. Self-concept	e. The things that a person is concerned with or curious about over a long period of time
6. Personal inventory	f. The outward signs and characteristics that show the inner values a person holds
7. Attitude	g. The personal standards one feels are important and worth while
8. Interests	h. An exploration of an individual's personal assets, needs, values, and personality

2. Explain the difference between **life values** and **work values**.

CHECKING WHAT YOU'VE LEARNED

Write your answers for the following exercises on a separate sheet of paper.

1. Describe the attitude toward life held by a person you like. Do the same for someone you don't care for. Don't include the names of these people in your response.
2. Explain what the term *self-concept* means.
3. Identify a specific sports figure or political leader. Describe what you imagine this person's self-concept is like.
4. Describe several interests that you or your friends have. Do the same for an adult in your family. How may your interests change as you grow older?
5. Explain why you should consider your interests when you choose a career.
6. Define aptitude, and describe two aptitudes that you have.
7. Explain the difference between having an aptitude for doing a particular task and being skilled in that type of work.
8. Explain why you should consider your aptitudes when you choose a career.
9. Are your life values or your work values more important? Explain the reasons for your answer.
10. Explain why you should consider your life values when you choose a career.
11. What is your personality the outward sign of?
12. Explain how a personal inventory may help you choose the type of life you want to lead and the career you should pursue?

PRACTICING YOUR CONSUMER SKILLS

Write your answers for the following exercises on a separate sheet of paper.

1. Several people are described below along with an interest they hold. Each person is considering a specific job offer. State whether you believe the job offer should be accepted, and explain your answer.
    a. Mary really enjoys learning about nature. She spends every free moment she has outside, finding specimens of plants and then looking them up in one of her many books. She has been offered a job as a receptionist in the office of a local chemical factory.
    b. Harry's hobby is fixing up old cars. He particularly likes working with engines. He is able to take them apart and put them back together easily. Harry has been offered a job that would require him to install air conditioners and ducts.
    c. Tanya enjoys being a volunteer at her church's food pantry. She packs sacks of groceries and gives them to people who are poor or out of work. Helping other people makes her feel good. Tanya is thinking of taking a job as a public relations representative in the billing department of an electric company.
    d. Peter really enjoys his business communications class. The type of assignment he likes best is writing answers to complaint letters from

Review and Enrichment Activities Continued

the point of view of a business. He earned an A in the class. Peter has been offered a job with a small community newspaper, where he would write about people who were dissatisfied with products they have purchased from businesses.

2. For each of the following people, identify a specific aptitude, choosing from the list provided on page 000. Explain the reasoning behind your answer.

    a. Kerry is the best video game player in school. When he goes to the game room at the local mall, he gets twice as many points as other people score. He is able to "zap" the space aliens at exactly the right moment.

    b. Molly has this "thing" she does when reading newspapers. Every evening she sits down with the front page of the local newspaper and draws red circles around every spelling and punctuation mistake she can find. She always find at least five or six. One day last month she found twenty-six and sent the page to the newspaper.

    c. Fred does very well in his accounting class at school because he always gets the answers right. Another student asked him if he ever made a mistake. Fred answered, "Sure, but I know when I do. If the answer looks wrong to me, I check my work and find my mistake. Somehow I just know when a number's wrong."

3. A list of values was provided in Section 4. Identify the value that is demonstrated in each of the following situations. Explain the reasoning behind your answer.

    a. Leroy is the senior class president. He is also president of the Spanish Club and treasurer of his church youth group. Leroy's most exciting memory is when he was interviewed by a local television reporter. He called all of his relatives to be sure they would watch him on the news.

    b. Gloria is very careful about what she eats. She buys only natural foods and never eats oils or fats if she can avoid it. She runs 5 miles every day and wears an electronic monitor so that she knows how fast her heart is beating.

    c. Roger was offered a chance to attend a summer camp in Oklahoma for free by a community organization. He thought about the idea but decided not to go because he didn't want to be away from his family for that long.

    d. Gina knows where almost every dollar she has ever earned is. Gina started delivering newspapers when she was twelve. Now she works 20 hours a week at a shoe store and baby-sits instead of going out on weekends. Gina knows which banks pay the highest interest rates. Although Gina is only seventeen years old, she has saved over

$7,500 from her own income. She says that she is going to use the money to go to college.

USING NUMBERS

Solve the following problem to help make the best possible choice. Write your solution on a separate sheet of paper. Be sure to show all your work.

Wayne wants to study chemistry and learn enough about toxic waste to work for the Environmental Protection Agency someday. He has done well in his science classes in school and has been accepted at the college he would like to attend. Unfortunately, the tuition is a problem. Wayne has been given a partial scholarship, but must pay $5,000 of his own money each year. His parents cannot afford to help. Any money Wayne can't earn he will have to borrow. He would rather not start out his career with a large debt to pay off.

Wayne has been offered three different summer jobs. He has mixed emotions about which one to take. Use the following information to determine how much he could earn working ten weeks at each job. Recommend a choice for Wayne, keeping his values and personality in mind. Explain your recommendation.

Job #1 Wayne could work for a local community action program that provides information about dangerous chemicals to small businesses and residents. His job would be to make telephone calls to people to ask for donations to the program. If he takes this job, he will earn $4.25 an hour and work 25 hours a week.

Job #2 Wayne could work as a summer replacement for a local sanitation service (garbage collector). Wayne would work from 6 A.M. until 4 P.M. five days a week, with an hour off for lunch. He would earn $8 an hour for his first 40 hours each week, and time and a half for each hour he works over 40.

Job #3 Wayne could work as a research assistant in a local plastics factory. He would work in an air-conditioned laboratory and would have an opportunity to learn about manufacturing plastics. He would be paid $10 an hour for a 40-hour week. The firm that has offered him this job has been accused by the government of illegally dumping toxic waste into a local landfill.

PUTTING IDEAS IN YOUR OWN WORDS

The following quotations are from this chapter. Explain these quotations in your own words to make sure you understand what they mean. Write your answers on a separate sheet of paper.

1. "A positive attitude is important to personal success because it encourages you to do your best."

Review and Enrichment Activities Continued

2. "A person's attitude and self-concept often determine his or her behavior."
3. "An aptitude must be developed to become a skill that has real value to you and your career."

BUILDING CONSUMER KNOWLEDGE

Write your answers for the following exercises on a separate sheet of paper.

1. Review the personal inventory you completed in this chapter. Identify any new facts that you discovered about yourself. Explain how your personal inventory may be helpful to you in making a career choice.
2. At the beginning of this chapter, your teacher asked you to write a paragraph to describe your self-concept. Having completed your personal inventory, write a new paragraph to describe your self-concept. Is the new one different from the old? How has your self-concept changed?
3. Describe the life-style you would like to lead ten years from now. Describe the trade-offs you may need to make between your life values and your work values to achieve this life-style.

Chapter 21

Exploring Careers

Chapter Objectives

After completing this chapter, you will be able to do the following:

- Explain how various sources of career information may be used to learn about different career choices.
- Explain how the information found in these sources may be used to investigate possible career choices and help you find careers that are suited to your individual interests, aptitudes, values, and personality.
- Discuss the importance of planning in achieving the career objectives and goals that people set for themselves.

Key Consumer Terms

In this chapter you will learn the meanings of the following important consumer terms:

- Job
- Career
- *Occupational Outlook Handbook*
- *Dictionary of Occupational Titles*
- *Guide for Occupational Exploration*
- Career consultation
- Cooperative education program
- Work-study program
- Work environment
- Logical progression

Do you remember when you were in grade school and your teacher asked you, "What do you want to be when you grow up?" You probably said that you wanted to be a fireman, astronaut, teacher, doctor, lawyer, or some other occupation you had heard or read about. You may have said, "I want to sell real estate like my mother," or "I think I'd like to be a chef in a restaurant like my father." It is common for children and young adults to consider choosing the same career as their relatives. These occupations are likely to be the ones they know the most about. Whatever your answer was, you probably did not put much thought into it. When you are older and are trying to choose a career that may determine the kind of life you lead for the next fifty years, you need to give your choice more careful consideration.

There is an important difference between holding a **job** and choosing a **career**. You may have a part-time job working for an ice cream store after school. This job may be important to you because it provides extra spending money and work experience. However, if you merely hold a job, you have no intention of keeping that type of occupation for the rest of your life. A career is a long-term commitment to a particular occupation. It requires planning, education, years of preparation, and a willingness to give up current income and consumption to achieve future success. A career choice should not be taken lightly.

Beware of simply "falling into" a career by just taking whatever work comes your way. The most important factor in your career choice should be what you want to do and be. You should choose a career that you believe will bring you personal happiness and satisfaction. Don't choose a career simply because someone offers you a job.

The decision-making process you learned about in Chapters 1 and 15 can be used to help you make a career choice. You may recall the seven steps in this process:

1. Identify the problem.
2. Determine broad goals that you would like to achieve.
3. Establish specific objectives that you would like to achieve.
4. Identify the alternative choices that you could make.
5. Evaluate each alternative choice in relation to how it will help you achieve your objectives.
6. Make the choice.
7. Evaluate the results of your decision.

Most people your age need more experience and knowledge to identify the career they want to commit themselves to. Many high school students have never carefully thought about their life values or investigated career opportunities that would help them make such an important choice. At this time, the most you should try to do is to select careers you find interesting and investigate them further. Therefore, step 1 of the decision-making process is to identify possible careers you might choose.

In Chapter 20 you completed a personal inventory that identified your interests, aptitudes, skills, values, and personality. This inventory should help you complete steps 2 and 3 in the decision-making process: to choose your broad goals and to set specific objectives that you want to achieve through your career choice.

One purpose of this chapter is to help you complete the remaining steps in the decision-making process. By finishing this process, you should gain a sense of personal direction that will help you make many different types of choices in your life.

SECTION 1

HOW TO RESEARCH CAREERS

While you read, ask yourself . . .
   ◆ *Do you know someone who has a career that you might enjoy and find personally rewarding?*
   ◆ *How could you find out about career opportunities in this or related fields?*

There is a wide range of sources for career information. You will need to sort through these various sources to find the ones most useful for your individual needs.

Printed Sources of Information

Books, magazines, directories, occupational guides, and government publications are excellent ways to find information about specific jobs. Some libraries devote entire sections to career information. These sections are often called Career Information Centers. It is worth your time to become familiar with three valuable references that are published by the federal government.

The *Occupational Outlook Handbook* (OOH) is the best source of general informa-

tion about occupations. It is reprinted every two years and describes about 250 occupations. These occupations account for about 80 percent of all jobs in the United States. The OOH provides information about job duties, working conditions, levels and places of employment, education and training requirements, advancement possibilities, job trends, and average earnings.

The *Dictionary of Occupational Titles* (DOT) describes the work activities of more than 20,000 jobs. It can help you learn about jobs you didn't even know existed and can help you focus your interests. Look up the name of the job you want to research in the alphabetical index of occupational titles in the

---

Vocabulary Builder

Career   A sequence of work-related experiences over a person's lifetime.

Dictionary of Occupational Titles   Publication that provides a brief description of over 20,000 jobs.

Job   A group of tasks to be accomplished while at work.

Occupational Outlook Handbook   A publication that provides general information about 250 occupations, covering about 80 percent of all jobs in the United States.

THE TWENTY FASTEST-GROWING OCCUPATIONS (1988–2000)

Occupation	Percentage Increase	Number-of-Jobs Increase
1. Paralegals	75%	62,000
2. Medical Assistants	70%	104,000
3. Home Health Aides	68%	160,000
4. Radiologic Technologists and Technicians	66%	87,000
5 Data Processing Equipment Repairers	61%	44,000
6. Medical Records Technicians	60%	28,000
7. Medical Secretaries	58%	120,000
8. Physical Therapists	57%	39,000
9. Surgical Technologists	56%	20,000
10. Operations Research Analysts	55%	30,000
11. Securities and Financial analysts	55%	109,000
12. Travel Agents	54%	77,000
13. Computer Systems Analysts	53%	214,000
14. Physical and Corrective Therapy Assistants	53%	21,000
15. Social Welfare Service Aides	52%	47,000
16. Occupational Therapists	49%	16,000
17. Computer Programmers	48%	250,000
18. Human Services Workers	45%	53,000
19. Respiratory Therapists	41%	23,000
20. Correction Officers and Jailers	41%	76,000

SOURCE: Adapted from *Outlook 2000*, Bureau of Labor Statistics, Fall, 1989.

Figure 21-1   Fastest Growing Occupations

back of the book. You will find a nine-digit code number for that job. You can then turn to the front section of the book to find the description of the job you want to investigate under that code number.

The *Guide for Occupational Exploration* (GOE) is organized into twelve interest groups. Each group is further divided into subgroups called worker trait groups. Each of the sixty-four worker trait groups has descriptive information, a listing of jobs within the group, and answers to questions about the following:

- The kind of work done
- Skills and abilities needed
- Interests and aptitudes needed
- How to prepare for this kind of work

There are many other printed sources of occupational information. The Bureau of Labor Statistics publishes the *Occupational Outlook Quarterly*, which contains recent articles about particular occupations. The Department of Labor publishes the *Monthly Labor Review*, which also provides current information about changes in the workplace. Figures 18-1 and 18-2 show the fastest- and largest-growing jobs.

Many federal and state agencies, professional societies, trade associations, labor unions, corporations, and colleges provide career information on request. These agencies and associations can sometimes furnish you with a list of schools that offer training in a particular field you are investigating. The addresses of these organizations can be found in your li-

THE TWENTY LARGEST-GROWING OCCUPATIONS (1988–2000)

Occupation	Number of Jobs to be Added	Percentage Increase
1. Retail Salespersons	730,000	19%
2. Registered Nurses (RNs)	613,000	39%
3. Janitors and Cleaners	556,000	19%
4. Waiters and Waitresses	551,000	31%
5 General Managers and Top Executives	479,000	16%
6. General Office Clerks	455,000	18%
7. Secretaries (except legal and medical)	385,000	13%
8. Nursing Aides and Orderlies	378,000	32%
9. Truckdrivers (light and heavy)	369,000	15%
10. Receptionists and Information Clerks	331,000	40%
11. Cashiers	304,000	13%
12. Guards	256,000	32%
13. Computer Programmers	250,000	48%
14. Food Counter, Fountain or Related Workers	240,000	15%
15. Food Preparation Workers	234,000	23%
16. Licensed Practical Nurses (LPNs)	229,000	37%
17. Secondary School Teachers	224,000	19%
18. Computer Systems Analysts	214,000	53%
19. Accountants and Auditors	211,000	22%
20. Kindergarten and Elementary School Teachers	208,000	15%

SOURCE: Adapted from *Outlook 2000*, Bureau of Labor Statistics, Fall, 1989.

◆ **Figure 21-2**   Larges-Growing Occupations

brary's reference section. Ask your librarian for help in finding the addresses you need.

Information about financial aid for higher education can be found in publications available in guidance offices, libraries, and college financial-aid offices. Information about financial assistance granted by the federal government is included in a pamphlet entitled *Student Consumers' Guide: Six Federal Financial Aid Programs*. Hispanics, African Americans, native Americans, and women may be interested in *Selected Lists of Postsecondary Education Opportunities for Minorities and Women*. This is an annual publication of the U.S. Department of Education that describes programs and other opportunities for these groups.

Your librarian will be able to help you find many other sources of information about occupations that interest you. Make sure the printed materials you use are up-to-date. Job opportunities can change quickly.

Vocabulary Builder

Guide for Occupational Exploration   A publication that organizes jobs into twelve interest groups that are further divided into sixty-four worker trait groups.

Guidance Services

Your school's guidance counselors are one of your best sources of information about the education and training that you need to qualify for various careers. They can give you a general idea of the costs and necessary time to prepare for these careers. Don't expect counselors to tell you what to do. They are not you, so they can't be sure what the best choice for you is. They can furnish information and help you discover facts about yourself and what you want from life. They may point out possible choices you had not thought of. But they cannot live your life for you. You should not ask them to make choices for you.

There are many private counseling firms that provide career guidance services to individuals. Remember, such services are in business to earn a profit for their owners. They may provide you with useful knowledge, but they will also charge a fee. Be sure to investigate the reputation and background of any private career-planning service that you consider using. A call to your local Better Business Bureau may save you time and money. The U.S. Employment Service can also help you select and plan a career.

In addition to reading about career choices or seeking information from counselors, you might consider using a computerized guidance program. Many state employment offices, libraries, and college guidance offices have computers that are programmed to ask users questions about their interests and abilities and to respond by providing information and suggestions. Again, a computer cannot make a career choice for you, but it can provide valuable information that will help you make a better choice.

◆ Many students learn about jobs by talking with people who have a career that interests them. What do you imagine this man is saying that holds the other people's interest?

Career Consultations

Another way to find out about a possible career choice is to talk with someone who actually is employed in a career you are considering. This type of **career consultation** provides you with firsthand information that is more up-to-date than any printed material can possibly be. Although this source of information is valuable, remember that the information you receive is only *one* person's opinion and may not be true of all people who have chosen the career you are investigating.

A good place to start asking about careers is with family and friends. Their experiences may provide you with important information or direct you to other people to talk with. Other people you may ask include teachers, counselors, business leaders, political officials, and religious leaders.

Be sure to prepare questions to ask before you talk with a person about his or her career. If you have not thought about what you would like to know, your interview may waste the person's time as well as your own. Here are just some of the questions you might want to ask:

- What do you like most about your job?
- What kind of education and training is needed to qualify for your job?
- What are the disadvantages of your job?
- What kind of work environment does your job involve?
- How did you choose this career?
- What hours do you work?
- What are your job responsibilities?
- What opportunities exist for new people who choose your career?

Work Experience

There is no better way to learn about a career than to actually work at a job in that career field. As a high school student, you probably won't be able to work at a job that you might like to hold when you are older and more experienced. However, you may be able to find employment in a related field that requires less skill and education. For example, if you want to be a research chemist, you might find a job cleaning up in a laboratory. You won't do any research, but you could see how it is done. The experience you gain will help you determine if the career you are interested in is one you might really like to choose, and it will help you when you apply for almost any future job.

You may gain work experience by taking part-time jobs after school or by accepting employment in the summer or during school vacations. You might consider volunteer work to gain experience. Many schools have **cooperative education programs** that give students a chance to work and earn school credits at the same time. There are various other programs in different states and localities. You may ask your guidance counselor about **work-study programs** in your area.

Summing Up   *Before making a career choice, people need to investigate the types of careers that interest them. You can find career information by reading printed materials, talking to guidance counselors, or gaining actual experience in a field you are considering.* ◆

Vocabulary Builder

Career consultation   A meeting with someone to obtain information about that person's career.

Cooperative education program   School program that allows students to earn school credits for learning that takes place while they work.

Work-study program   A school program that arranges jobs that allow students to work around their class schedule.

Consumer News

A Career is What You Make It

In 1990 Gail Pankey was a thirty-six-year-old African American who had been raised in a poverty-stricken area in New York. When she was four, her parents got divorced. Her family lived on welfare for four years and received surplus cheese, powdered milk, and dried eggs from the government to eat. When her mother re-married, her stepfather ran a TV repair shop in Queens but had a heart attack and became an alcoholic. When she was fourteen, Gail's best friend died of a heroin overdose. Gail was not the sort of person who you might have picked as most likely to succeed. Yet twenty-two years later, Gail Pankey was earning more than $100,000 a year as a floor broker at the New York Stock Exchange.

Gail's career began with a job as a messenger for the New York Stock Exchange in 1971. Over the next ten years she came to understand the workings of the market and was hired as a broker in 1981. In 1985 she become the head floor broker for Fahnestock & Co., Inc. Pankey attributes her success to never letting herself believe that her disadvantaged childhood would prevent her from being successful. It took years of hard work and planning, but Gail Pankey proved that it is who you are that's important, not where you come from.

If you could talk to Gail Pankey, what questions would you ask her?

WHAT TO RESEARCH

While you read, ask yourself . . .
- *Do you know an adult who was forced to change careers?*
- *How was this person and his or her family affected by the change?*
- *What does this show you about the possible danger of preparing for only one career?*

There is such a vast amount of information available on career choices that you need to spend some time deciding what information you want to look for and consider. The type of information you should look for depends on your values and interests. Consult your personal inventory from Chapter 20 as you read this section.

Changes in Job Opportunities

Before you choose a career, you should investigate the employment opportunities that exist in the general field that interests you. There is little point in training for a career that will not exist in the future. If you want to be a zookeeper, you should know that there are few schools you could attend to learn the skills you need for this career. There are also a limited number of jobs available in this career area. On the other hand, the rate of growth in nursing and other health care careers is very high. If you want to be a nurse, the opportunities for employment are good.

Nobody can be sure that their predictions of the future will be correct. However, the U.S. Department of Labor makes a projection called the *Labor Outlook*. It gives a general idea of the possible job opportunities for various occupations. You can find this publication in most public libraries.

◆   The skills people need for different careers often change over time. What abilities do we expect police officers to have today that might not have been as necessary thirty years ago?

Career Qualifications and Conditions

Most careers require employees to possess special skills and abilities. If you are interested in a career that you are not yet qualified for, you should investigate sources of education and training that will help you acquire the skills and abilities you need.

When you choose a career, you must also be sure that you understand the nature of the occupation you are considering. For example, many people are attracted to police work because they believe that being a police officer is exciting. However, many police officers will tell you that their occupations involve a great deal of routine paperwork and boredom. It would be frustrating to train for many years to qualify for a career only to find that you didn't like it. People should consider both their quali-

fications and the type of work they would be doing before they make a career choice.

The conditions that different employees work under vary widely. Some employees work in air-conditioned offices; others work outside in the heat or cold. Most employees commute to work each day; others work at home. Many workers punch a time clock; others are able to work when they choose to. Before you make a career choice, understand the **work environment** you may expect. Investigating a work environment requires finding

Vocabulary Builder

Work environment   The general conditions in which people work in a particular type of job.

answers to questions about where, when, how, and under what conditions employees in this career work. Many of the publications that provide career information also describe the work environment associated with different careers.

You should understand how you will be compensated in a career that you choose. Some careers offer greater current income, while others provide extensive fringe benefits, job security, or good retirement programs. If a sense of personal fulfillment from helping people is your primary career objective, you might consider being a worker for a nonprofit organization. If you want to earn money quickly, you could choose a career in sales. Financial reward isn't the only reason to choose a career, but it is one important reason.

The opportunity for personal advancement is another important consideration. A job may have a low entry-level wage, but it may provide an opportunity for rapid advancement in the future. Many sales jobs do not pay well at first. However, most people who stay with sales eventually are able to earn good incomes. When you consider a career, ask yourself, "If I take this job, what will I probably be doing ten years from now?" If you don't like the answer, you may want to consider a different choice.

Identifying, Evaluating, and Making Career Choices

By researching careers, you have completed step 4 in the decision-making process. This was to identify the alternative choices that you could make. You can now use the information you have gathered in your personal inventory to evaluate each career choice you have identified. In doing this, you will complete step 5 in the decision-making process: to evaluate each alternative choice in relation to how it will help you achieve your objectives.

You should not expect to identify the one career that is best for you at this time. However,

you should know enough about yourself and your possible career choices that you can take the next steps in preparing for your career. The knowledge that you have gained will help you choose the courses you should take in school, the type of part-time job you might look for, and how you should plan for your future.

Summing Up *People should investigate the qualifications they need for a career that interests them. They should learn how to acquire the needed skills and abilities. They should learn about working conditions and compensation. This information will allow them to identify and evaluate career choices. ◆*

SECTION 3

THE IMPORTANCE OF PLANNING

While you read, ask yourself . . .
- ◆ *What is likely to happen to people who fail to make long-range plans for their futures?*
- ◆ *What plans have you made for a time that is more than two years in the future?*

If something is important to you, then it is worth planning for. Have you ever let things slide to the point that you can't do everything you need to do? Suppose that your English teacher assigned a report on a novel you were supposed to have read two weeks ago. It's due tomorrow and you can't remember a single word you read. You also have five problems to finish for your accounting class. You promised to clean your room. The junk on your floor is about 6 inches deep. Your boss called and asked if you could come in and work from 5 to 8 P.M. this evening. You don't want to go, but you could use the money. As you look at your alternatives, you realize that you can't possibly do everything.

Problems like this can often be avoided by making and following a plan. Plans can save

Consumer Close-Up

Schools Where Students Work

Do you believe that you could qualify for an 80 percent scholarship at the Massachusetts Institute of Technology? Jeff Gonzalez, who was born in Cuba, never thought so, but he started attending classes as a freshman at MIT in the fall of 1991. How could an immigrant from a family that started with almost nothing be so successful? The answer is found in our nation's magnet schools. Jeff completed his high school program at the International Baccalaureate program in Coral Gables, Florida, in 1991. To graduate he took 23 hours of final exams that tested his knowledge of subjects from epistemology to a history of scientific thought in the world. Jeff's accomplish-ments are impressive, but they are not unique.

In recent years many public schools have been converted to magnet schools that specialize in different aspects of learning, including the arts, science, languages, business, and even theater. At first students were recruited in many cities to fill these schools. However, their success has led school districts to hold lotteries to choose which of many qualified applicants will be allowed to take one of the limited number of places in magnet schools.

In Long Beach, California, an urban high school became the Center for International Commerce. To attend CIC, students have to agree to take eight subjects a day, including either Japanese, Chinese, or Russian. They are required to complete classes in international marketing, accounting, computers, history, physics, calculus, international relations, and many other subjects. Out of an average of 300 yearly applicants, only 160 are accepted by CIC. Graduates of the school have been employed in Japan and by American firms involved in international trade.

What kinds of plans must students have that would make them attend a school that takes so much of their time and requires so much work?

Would you be willing to make this sort of commitment to your future?

---

time, effort, and sometimes money. They help you remember what needs to be done. The process of making a plan forces you to consider your alternatives and to organize your time and resources. Plans help you finish tasks on time. You need to make short-term plans for how to use your time for each week. You also need to make long-term plans to help you achieve your career goals.

Planning to Gain Skills and Education

You have identified one or more general types of occupations that you think could eventually provide you with a satisfying career. At this time you should not expect to have the skills and abilities you will eventually need. However, you should have a general idea of the aptitudes you need to begin to develop these skills.

Review the aptitudes you listed in your personal inventory that you believe could be developed into skills. For each aptitude, identify an activity that would provide you with some of the training you need. For example, if you want to be a plumber, you might investigate apprenticeship programs. If you think that you want a career in sales, you could consider taking a part-time job in a store. If a career deal-

◆   Most people follow a logical progression of steps to achieve their career goals. If you go to work for a grocery store you may start by collecting carts and work your way into a position that requires more responsibility and offers a better wage.

ing with biology interests you, you need to investigate colleges that offer biology programs. When you identify a college that you like, find out what the entry requirements are. You may need to plan your high school classes to fit the needs of the trade school or college you want to attend. If you make plans now to gain experience and skills, you will probably save yourself time and money in the future.

Be sure that your plans include a **logical progression** of objectives. You are not going to start off at the top in any career. If you want to be a reporter for a major city newspaper, you might start by writing sports stories for your school newspaper. The experience you gain could help you if you later apply for a job with a community newspaper. Each career step you take leads to the next. Plan how to work your way into the career you eventually want to have. Set reasonable objectives. As you achieve them, be ready to move on to new objectives.

Financing Your Career Plans

Many of the activities you undertake to prepare for your future career will cost money.

When people attend school or practice to gain skills, they give up money that they could have earned working at a different job that they were already qualified for. One reason people seek higher levels of education or training is to increase the total income they will earn during their lives. They give up current income to attend classes or training sessions so that they may earn more in the future. This does not change the fact that they must eat while they are attending class. Students need to plan a way to finance their education.

Personal saving is an obvious way to pay for education or training. Unfortunately, many people have limited income that they can save. Still, most people can save something if they make and follow plans. The first thing to do is to start now. People who plan to start saving tomorrow frequently never save at all. Set a realistic goal for each period of time. If you are paid every two weeks, you might set a goal of saving $10 or $20 from each paycheck.

Whatever goal you set, it should be realistic. Once you set your goal, keep it in mind. If you see a new recording that you want, your decision to set aside $10 a week may help you choose not to buy it. Be sure to place your savings in a bank or other type of investment that

Consumer News

What Are Your Academic Aptitudes?

Do you know what 1.3 million high school students do for 2½ hours every year? They take the College Board's Scholastic Aptitude Test (SAT). This test is intended to measure reasoning skills, math and verbal ability, and readiness for college.

What was begun in 1926 as a method of screening potential college students has become a hotly debated issue among the more than 1,600 colleges that review SAT scores when choosing which students to accept. Critics charge that SATs contain cultural and class biases that put women and minorities at a disadvantage. They believe that the test's multiple-choice format does not give students a reasonable opportunity to demonstrate reasoning ability.

In an attempt to satisfy some critics, the College Board has decided to change the SAT tests in 1994. There will be two SAT tests in the new plan: SAT I and SAT II. SAT I will test reasoning and math, with longer problems that require students to actually find solutions, not simply choose from multiple-choice alternatives. SAT II will devote 20 minutes to writing an essay that concerns an issue in world history.

These changes will not address the problem of sex or race bias. It is also not clear that the SATs predict college success accurately. Students who complete special courses before they take the SAT average as much as 100 points (out of a possible 800) better than those who don't. Cramming for the SAT to earn a better score probably has little to do with a person's true academic aptitude.

What has your experience been with the SATs or other forms of standardized testing?

Do you believe they have been a good measure of your aptitudes and can help you plan your future?

---

pays interest. For many people, an important help in saving is to never carry more cash than they intend to spend. If you have charge cards, you may want to leave them at home.

When you are considering what school or training program to attend, find out what sorts of financial aid are available. Schools often have scholarships for academically successful students or for people who are disadvantaged. Many have work-study programs that provide part-time jobs to help students pay their bills. You should also investigate various loan programs. The institution or program you are considering is best qualified to provide you with specific financial advice. However, no matter how much information you receive, you are the one who will be responsible for paying for your education or training. There is little point in choosing a school you can't afford. It is better to make an alternative choice than to run up a debt that you will have difficulty repaying.

Summing Up *Planning is a necessary step in achieving your long-term career goals. People need to plan how to turn aptitudes into skills by gaining education or training. They also need to make financial plans for achieving their goals. ◆*

Vocabulary Builder

Logical progression A series of steps that when taken in sequence will help a person or organization reach a goal.

Review and Enrichment Activities

VOCABULARY REVIEW

1. Column A contains key consumer terms from this chapter. Column B contains a scrambled list of phrases that describe what these terms mean. Match the correct meaning with each term. Write your answers on a separate sheet of paper.

Column A	Column B
1. Dictionary of Occupational Titles	a. The best general overview of career opportunities, reprinted by the government every two years
2. Occupational Outlook Handbook	b. Interviewing a person who has a particular occupation that interests you
3. Logical progression	c. A publication that organizes jobs into twelve occupations, and each occupation into trait groups
4. Guide for Occupational Exploration	d. A publication that lists a basic description of about 20,000 jobs
5. Work study program	e. An arrangement that allows students to hold a job and attend classes at the same time
6. Work environment	f. An arrangement that allows students to earn school credits for learning that takes place while they work
7. Career consultation	g. A series of steps that when taken together help a person reach a goal
8. Cooperative education programs	h. The general conditions in which people are employed

2. Explain the difference between a **job** and a **career**.

CHECKING WHAT YOU'VE LEARNED

Write your answers for the following exercises on a separate sheet of paper.

1. Explain why you should avoid "falling into" a career.
2. Why shouldn't most students attempt to choose a specific career before they graduate from high school?
3. Describe the three government publications that are often most useful in finding job and career information.
4. Describe the type of help a student should expect to receive from a guidance counselor.
5. Why shouldn't students expect a guidance counselor to make their career choices for them?
6. Why is it important to be sure that the job and career information that you get is up-to-date?
7. What is probably the best way to receive up-to-date and accurate information about a career?
8. Describe at least three different factors that are part of a work environment.
9. Explain why planning is important to your success in achieving a career choice.
10. Explain why financial planning is as important as planning where and how to acquire skills necessary for a career choice.

PRACTICING YOUR CONSUMER SKILLS

Write your answers for the following exercises on a separate sheet of paper.

1. Recommend a source of information that would be most appropriate in each of the following situations. Choose from the *Occupational Outlook Handbook*, the *Dictionary of Occupational Titles*, the *Guide for Occupational Exploration*, a school guidance counselor, and career consultation. Explain why you made each recommendation.
    a. Jeff has read about a career that interests him. He has found several jobs mentioned in his reading that he does not recognize. He would like to find information that would tell him what these jobs are. How can he find the career information he needs?
    b. Roxann believes that she might like to be an architect. She has read about this career, but doesn't feel she understands the actual day-to-day work and responsibilities that an architect carries out. How can she find the career information she needs?
    c. Patty has decided that she wants to work in the general field of health care, but is not sure what types of careers are available in this field or of the exact skills and training she would need to be qualified for this sort of career. How can she find the career information she needs?

Review and Enrichment Activities Continued

d. Although Todd knows that he would like a career that would allow him to use and develop his mechanical aptitude, he has very little idea of what occupations he should be investigating. He needs general advice about different types of career opportunities. How can he find the career information he needs?

e. Heather enjoys working with computers. She wants to choose a career that will allow her to develop this interest and keep up with new developments in computing technology. She feels that the best chance of doing this is to have a career that involves computers and is in a growing industry. How can she find the career information she needs?

2. Match the career information in column B with the person in column A who would find this information most useful. Explain why you made each choice. The numbers in column B are from the *Dictionary of Occupational Titles*.

Column A

1. Frank wants to work with his hands. He also wants to work outside most of the time.

2. Gretchen enjoys organizing people to accomplish tasks. She has an aptitude for making things work and a good memory.

3. Tammy wants to work in the fashion industry. She enjoys drawing clothes and choosing fabrics.

4. Anthony wants to work in a restaurant. He enjoys cooking, and he likes to be creative.

Column B

a. 142.061-018 *procurement services manager*: Directs and coordinates activities of personnel engaged in purchasing and distributing raw materials, equipment, machinery, and supplies.

b. 131.267-014 *chef de froid*: Designs and prepares decorated foods and artistic food arrangements for buffets in formal restaurants.

c. 405.684-012 *horticultural worker*: Plants, cultivates, and harvests horticultural specialties such as flowers and shrubs.

5. Leon likes to write about current events. He reads newspapers and magazines and prides himself on knowing what is happening.

d. 131.267-014 *newswriter*: Writes news stories for publication or broadcast from written or recorded notes.

e. 142.061-018 *clothes designer*: Designs . . . garments . . . , compares leather fabrics and other materials and integrates findings . . . with knowledge of design.

3. Describe the steps that the following people can take now to help them make meaningful preparations for their future. At the present, each is a high school junior with average grades. None of them has held a job or volunteered any time for community organizations. All of their families have incomes that would prevent them from paying cash for higher education.
   a. Glenn has decided to seek a career in law enforcement. He thinks that he might like to be a state trooper someday.
   b. Rose wants to work in advertising. She believes that she would enjoy developing television commercials.
   c. Domonic believes that he would like to be a radio announcer someday. He enjoys keeping up with the newest types of music.
   d. Nancy wants to work in education. She enjoys her science classes in school and thinks mathematics is interesting.

USING NUMBERS

Solve the following problem to help make the best possible choice. Write your solution on a separate sheet of paper. Be sure to show all your work.

John wants to be a reporter for a big city newspaper someday. He has been offered a full-time job working for a small community publication that would pay him $15,000 a year and give him practical experience in reporting news stories. He has also been offered a scholarship to study journalism at a well-known university. If he accepts the scholarship, he will still need to pay for his books and other expenses, which will cost him about $3,000 a year. When he graduates after four years, he should be able to earn at least $12,000 a year more than the job he has been offered, or $27,000 a year.

If John chooses to accept the scholarship, how long will it take him to

Review and Enrichment Activities Continued

make up the cost of his education and also the money lost by not taking the current job? To make this problem easier to solve, assume that John will not receive any raises at either job.

Use your answer to help make a recommendation to John about which choice he should take. Remember, money is not the only consideration. Explain your recommendation.

PUTTING IDEAS IN YOUR OWN WORDS

The following quotations are from this chapter. Explain these quotations in your own words to make sure you understand what they mean. Write your answers on a separate sheet of paper.

1. "1

Beware of simply "falling into" a career by just taking whatever work comes
    your way."
2. "Make sure the printed materials you use are up-to-date."
3. "Each career step you take leads to the next."

BUILDING CONSUMER KNOWLEDGE

Write your answers for the following exercises on a separate sheet of paper.

1. Visit your school or local public library and ask the librarian to help you find copies of the various printed materials identified in this chapter. Use these materials along with your personal inventory to identify three career choices you might be interested in investigating further. Take notes on the information you find. Be sure to copy down the sources that you used. Be prepared to discuss your findings with your class.
2. Choose the one career that seems most interesting to you. Go to your school's guidance office or your library and find information about where you could go for further training or education in this field. Identify specific schools and programs that you might attend, along with their costs.
3. Prepare a plan of steps that you could take to prepare yourself for this career. Your plan should include your academic training, work experience, and financial needs. Be sure that your plans have a logical progression of events. Remember, you are not likely to "walk into" most careers directly after you graduate from high school.

Chapter 22

Getting and Keeping a Job

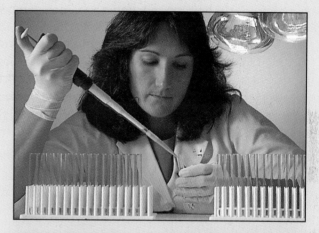

Chapter Objectives

After completing this chapter, you will be able to do the following:

- Identify different sources of information concerning job openings.
- Explain the steps that you should take when applying for a job.
- Discuss preparations that may be made and types of behavior that will improve your chance of being offered a job as the result of a job interview.
- Describe work attitudes and habits that will help you keep a job and advance to better positions.

Key Consumer Terms

In this chapter you will learn the meanings of the following important consumer terms:

- Job referral
- Chamber of Commerce
- Classified want ads
- Employment agency
- Temporary agency
- Reference
- Résumé
- Cover letter
- Punctuality
- Dependability
- Notice

Are you employed? If you are a senior in high school, there is about an even chance that you have at least a part-time job during the school year. How did most young people who are employed find their jobs? Some may have gone around to various businesses and filled out applications. Some may have had a friend or relative who helped them find their job. Some may have been offered employment through a work-study program at school. And some may have been recommended by teachers or other adults they know. Regardless of how people find a job, they always receive benefits and pay costs as a result of their employment.

Do most of your friends who work like their jobs? Some probably do. They may find their work rewarding and their compensation fair. Others probably hate going to work. Employees who do not like their jobs are at least partly to blame for their own dissatisfaction. It was their decision to take the job.

FINDING JOB OPENINGS

While you read, *ask yourself . . .*
- ◆ *Who do you know who might be able to help you identify job opportunities?*
- ◆ *If you were looking for employment, at what local business would you apply for a job?*

There isn't just one right way to look for a job. There are many different steps you can take. The more alternatives you find, the better your chances will be of being offered a job that provides you with the working conditions, experience, and compensation you want. You should avoid taking the first job that comes your way unless it offers you almost everything you could reasonably hope for.

Asking People You Know

You probably have a wide circle of relatives, friends, and acquaintances. You should let these people know when you are interested in finding a job. Some people believe that it is "unfair" for an employer to hire people with an "inside track." This does not change the fact that employers often hire people who have been recommended to them by someone they know and trust. If you know people who can help you find a job you would like, don't be bashful. Ask for their help.

Studies show that from 20 to 40 percent of all job applicants find employment through **job referrals**. In this situation, someone gives your name as a possible job candidate to an employer who is looking for someone to fill a position. Managers, owners, and personnel officials prefer hiring people who have been recommended by people they know. It's similar to buying a used car. Most people would prefer to buy a car from someone they know and trust, rather than from a stranger. Employers use job referrals because they expect to benefit from hiring more reliable, productive workers.

Workers also benefit from job referrals. Studies have shown that employees who accept a job offer resulting from a referral have better and higher-paying jobs. They also work for the same employer longer. This probably indicates that they are more satisfied with their work than many other employees.

◆   Many businesses keep files of job applicants they may call as job openings occur. It is often a good idea to apply at firms even if they have no current job openings.

If you want referrals, be sure to let as many people as possible know that you are looking for work. You should also explain the type of work you are looking for and your general qualifications. You can't expect to provide potential employers with complete information in this way, but you can avoid wasting their time and your effort when there is no chance you would be interested in or qualified for a particular opening.

Contacting Potential Employers

Many businesses keep files of applicants to contact when they have job openings. They may encourage potential workers to apply by putting up signs at their places of business. Studies show that between 25 and 33 percent of all people who accept employment contacted their employer and completed an application before they were aware of any specific job opening.

When you choose to contact employers directly, you should be selective in the types of

Vocabulary Builder

Job referral   Giving a person's name to an employer as a possible candidate for a job opening.

Consumer News

Working for a Temporary Agency

The temporary employment business has grown about 20 percent in both sales and earnings in the past five years. The National Association of Temporary Service estimates the payroll for 1 million temporary jobs in 1991 to $8.5 billion. Temporary assignments can last a day or a year, and companies often offer permanent jobs to efficient temporary workers. Some people become "temps" because they want the freedom to go to school or they want the time to spend with their children when they need to. Others look at temporary work as a chance to "try out" companies or careers before accepting a permanent job. Still others want a variety of different jobs or just can't find permanent employment.

Would you consider taking temporary employment?
What advantages could it offer you?
What abilities do you have to offer an employer?

businesses you apply to. If you want a job selling clothing, there is no point in applying to a firm that provides cleaning services. There are a number of ways to get information about the kinds of jobs that specific firms offer. You could ask about the business at the **Chamber of Commerce**. The Chamber of Commerce is an organization that has the purpose of improving business conditions in a community. It may provide information about the products that a firm manufactures or sells. This will give you an idea of the types of jobs different firms might offer.

Another possibility is to investigate businesses in your local library. You can look through local newspapers for information about specific local firms, or you can seek information about the types of jobs businesses offer from publications like those named in Chapter 21. Again, a good choice is to ask your librarian for help.

Formal Job Search Methods

Many firms advertise job openings in newspapers or magazines. They may also notify state or private employment agencies. Reading **classified want ads** is a good way to find information about the jobs that are open in your community, even if you don't reply to the advertisements.

Although there are "help wanted" advertisements in all issues of most newspapers, the largest number are printed on Wednesdays and Sundays. Although many people gain employment through want ads, you should realize that only about 25 percent of all job openings are advertised in this way. The ones that are advertised are often those that the employer has the greatest difficulty in filling. This may indicate that the jobs do not offer desirable working conditions or compensation. Some want ads are nothing more than "tricks" intended to convince you to buy something. Other want ads are placed by employment agencies that will require you to pay a fee if you take the job. This does not mean that you should not use want ads. It does mean that you should be careful when you respond to them.

Employment agencies may be run by private companies, by community organizations, or by the government. Private employment agencies earn money for their owners by charging a fee to applicants, employers, or both. Be sure that you understand what is being offered for what price if you deal with a private employment agency. Although government employment agencies can help you find a job, you should realize that the jobs listed with such agencies are not likely to be the most desirable. Better jobs are usually offered to applicants that firms have found through their own recruitment efforts.

A growing number of people are employed by **temporary agencies**. These are private firms that specialize in supplying short-term employees to businesses that have a temporary need for workers. This may be the result of a full-time worker being ill or on vacation, or it may be the result of a special job that needs to be done for a limited period of time. Working for a temporary agency often results in relatively low pay, but may provide an employee with valuable experience. Many temporary workers eventually become full-time workers for those firms.

Summing Up   *People who are looking for work can seek job openings by using job referrals, investigating local businesses, reading want ads, and using the services of employment agencies. The more job contacts you make, the better your chances will be of finding a job that will help you achieve your career goals.* ◆

SECTION 2

APPLYING FOR A JOB

While you read, *ask yourself . . .*
- ◆ *Who do you know who would be able to provide you with a favorable job recommendation?*
- ◆ *What advantage might you receive from going out of your way to be helpful and respectful to adults whom you know or work with?*

When you apply for a job, you are offering your labor for sale. Suppose that you have identified a job you would like to have. To be offered the position, you must convince the employer that you are the best person for the job. Everything you do or say in the application process will have an impact on the employer's opinion of you and on your chance of getting the job.

Completing an Application

When you apply for a job, you will almost certainly be asked to complete a written application form. It is important that you complete it fully, neatly, and accurately. The following suggestions will help you sell yourself to the employer.

- Read the entire application first, and follow all directions exactly. Work slowly and carefully.
- Be neat. The person reading the application will base part of his or her opinion of you on the appearance of your work. Bring your own black pen. If you make a mistake, ask for another form.
- Be prepared. Have all necessary information with you. Most applications will require you to provide:
  1. Your name, address, telephone number, and Social Security number

Vocabulary Builder

Chamber of Commerce   An organization whose purpose is to improve business conditions within a community.

Classified want ads   Advertisements in newspapers that seek qualified applicants for current job openings.

Employment agency   An organization that matches people with jobs.

Temporary agency   An agency that hires individuals for employers who need help for limited periods of time.

◆   People looking for work should fill out applications so they are complete, accurate, and neat. What else has this job applicant done to make a favorable impression with an employer?

2.   Information about your education and any other training you have completed
3.   A record of your work experience
4.   A description of the job you would like with the salary and benefits you expect to receive
5.   A list of **references**, or people who may be contacted to verify your training, experience, or personal character. (Be sure to ask these people for permission to use them as references *before* you provide their names to an employer.)

• Answer all questions that apply to you. If a question does not apply to you, write "NA" (not applicable).
• Spell words correctly and use proper English. Even if you are not applying for a job that will require you to write, correct spelling and proper English will improve the employer's opinion of you.
• Be specific about the type of work you want to do. If you only want to work in an office, there is no point in an employer offering you a job on a production line.
• Be positive about yourself and your abilities. Explain why you want the job in question. Always look for a way to describe your talents, training, and ability in the best possible light. Never put information on your application that is not true.
• Double-check your form when you are finished to be sure that you haven't made any mistakes.

Figure 22-1 shows a sample Application for Employment.

Preparing a Résumé

The word **résumé** means summary. It usually refers to a summary of a person's abilities, accomplishments, and personal objectives. Many job applicants provide résumés to their prospective employers. The kind of information included in a résumé is similar to that found in a job application. However, because the applicant prepares his or her own résumé, it may be organized to emphasize strengths and abilities and to include information that might not be brought out in an application form.

When you prepare a résumé, follow these simple guidelines:

- Make it simple. The person who will read your résumé wants information about you. Fancy print or paper is not likely to impress anyone.
- Make it brief. A résumé should not be more than two pages long. The person who reads your résumé has many others to read and will not be impressed by unnecessary length.
- Use action words and short sentences to describe your accomplishments. Words like *directed*, *improved*, *planned*, and *organized* provide a positive image of what you have done.
- Make it error-free. A single spelling error can ruin the impression left by an otherwise favorable résumé.
- Ask a parent, teacher, or counselor to review your first draft and make suggestions for improvement.
- Write it yourself. It's a good idea to get help, but your final résumé should sound like you. Professional interviewers will be able to tell if your résumé was written by someone else, and it may cause them to doubt your honesty.

Figure 22-2 illustrates a sample cover letter.

You should include a **cover letter** with your résumé. The purpose of a cover letter is to explain why you are applying for a particular job and what you will be able to accomplish for your potential employer. If you do not have an appointment for an interview, you may ask for one in your cover letter. This letter should be clear and factual. It should be polite and never "pushy." It should never appear that you are demanding anything of a potential employer. Instead you should emphasize what you have to offer.

Summing Up   *People who are looking for work will complete application forms that request basic information. Job applicants should also prepare a résumé that describes their work experience, training, skills, and abilities.* ◆

SECTION 3

SUCCESSFUL INTERVIEWING

While you read, *ask yourself . . .*
- ◆ *What opportunities have you had to speak with strangers whom you want to impress?*
- ◆ *Are you able to talk about yourself in a favorable way without sounding like you are bragging?*
- ◆ *Why is it important to have a positive self-image when you are being interviewed?*

Vocabulary Builder

Cover letter   A brief letter written to a potential employer intended to convince the employer to read the enclosed resume.

Reference   A written recommendation supporting a person who is being considered for a job opening.

Résumé   A one- or two-page summary of a person's job qualifications.

Application For Employment

All qualified applicants will receive consideration for employment and promotion without regard to race, creed, religion, color, age, sex, national origin, handicap, marital status or sexual orientation. This application is effective for 90 days. If you wish to be considered for employment thereafter, you must complete a new application.   Date _____

Name _____   Telephone (___) _____
            Last   First   Middle Initial   Area Code

Address _____
            Number & Street   Apt. #   City   State   Zip

Length of time at that address_____ Previous Address _____

Position you are applying for_____ Rate of pay expected $_____ per month

Were you previously employed by us?_____ If yes, when? _____

Typewriting words per minute_____ Shorthand or speedwriting words per minute_____

Other business Machines _____

State any other experiences, skills or qualifications which you feel would especially fit you for work with the company _____

Applying for: Full-time _____ Part-time Days_____ Evenings_____ Midnight_____ Alternating_____ Any _____

Location Preferred: Downtown St. Paul_____ Eagan_____ Westbury_____Other _____

Are you at least 18 years of age?_____ Will you take a physical examination?_____

List any friends or relatives working for us _____
                                              Name   Relationship

                                            _____
                                              Name   Relationship

Referred to our company by _____

_____

	School	Name and Location	Course of Major		Graduated
Elementary					❏ Yes ❏ No
High School					❏ Yes ❏ No
College					❏ Yes ❏ No
Business or Trade					❏ Yes ❏ No
Other (Specify)					❏ Yes ❏ No

Do you plan any additional education?_____ If yes, describe_____

_____

List in order all employers, beginning with your most recent employment:

	Name & Location of Company	From Mo Yr	To Mo Yr	Salary	Supervisor	Reason for Leaving
1)						
2)						
3)						

Describe the work you did with:

Company #1. _____

Company #2. _____

Company #3. _____

May we contact the employers listed above?_____ If not indicate by number which one(s) you do not wish us to contact

_____

CERTIFICATION OF APPLICANT

I hereby certify that the facts set forth in the above employment application are true and complete to the best of my knowledge. I understand that if I am employed, falsified statements on this application shall be considered sufficient cause for dismissal, and that no contractual rights or obligations are created by said employment application.

Signature of Applicant_____

◆ **Figure 22-1** When you apply for a job you will need to complete an application similar to the one above. Provide complete and accurate information, and be neat. If anything is not clear be sure to ask for an explanation. It is better to be slow and careful than to be quick and take the chance of making a mistake.

676 Costello Drive
Westlake, CA 93001
(818) 555-1294
May 21, 19XX

Ms. Jessica Louis
Human Resources Manager
Excalibur Advertising Company
5150 North Henry Avenue
Westlake, CA 93001

Dear Ms. Louis:°

Mr. George Smith, the work-study counselor at Westlake High School, has informed me of
your company s opening for an advertising trainee. As a design student, I am highly
interested in assuming this entry-level position once I graduate in June.

Since my junior year at Westlake High School, I have served as the advertising coordinator
for both the newspaper and the yearbook. As such, I have been responsible for soliciting
advertisements from local businesses. I often design the ads myself, using computerized art
programs.

I have fulfilled elective units with courses in the visual arts: Photography 1 and 2,
Commercial Design, and Drafting. A class in communications, furthermore, has introduced
me to the various methods of transmitting messages through the media. I believe these
studies have provided me with the ideal background for a job in advertising, which to a large
extent combines art with the media. Also, as my resum indicates, I have earned high marks
in the above-mentioned courses.

For over a year, I have spent afternoons answering phones and filing claims for a local
insurance company. I have become comfortable, therefore, working within a business
atmosphere.

I would greatly appreciate an interview, at your convenience. Thank you for considering my
application, and I hope to hear from you soon.

Cordially,

Sharon Chase

◆ **Figure 22-2**   When you send résumés to employers you should include a cover letter similar to the one above. A
cover letter explains why you are sending the résumé, what your abilities are, and why the employer should be interested in reading your résumé.

◆ When you are interviewed for a job remember you are trying to sell yourself. It is not enough to have job skills. Other applicants probably have similar skills. You need to convince the interviewer that you are the best person for a job opening.

A job interview is often the climax of your job search. This is your opportunity to convince the employer that you are the right person for the job. Most interviews last from 20 minutes to an hour. These can be some of the most important minutes in your life.

Typically, an interviewer will be considering several applicants for a job opening. Remember, you are here to sell yourself. As a consumer, you look for the best product for your money. Employers are no different. When they hire labor, they are looking for workers who will give them the best value for the wages they pay. It is your responsibility to convince the interviewer that you have the most to offer. Your chance of success will improve if you prepare for your interview.

The Importance of Preparation

Interviewers often ask job candidates to talk about themselves and why they want and are qualified for a particular job opening. You should anticipate this type of a question and be prepared with your answer. Here are some of the things you should expect to be asked about:

- *Information about your relationships with other people.* Most jobs require employees to work successfully with either workers or customers. Businesses want workers who are able to get along with other people. Most interviewers would like to know about your experiences and ability to take responsibility. If you have held leadership positions in school or on teams, you should mention this. Being a member of a religious group, the scouts, or a volunteer organization demonstrates your concern for others. Interviewers are not legally allowed to ask many types of personal questions, but you may volunteer information that shows your qualities.

- *Your work experience.* Be prepared to identify your work experience, not only in terms of where and when you have held a job, but in terms of what you accomplished. There is a big difference between saying, "I worked at McDonald's," and saying, "I directed three workers who prepared hamburgers at McDonald's and was able to produce 300 hamburgers an hour."

- *Your education and educational plans.* Be prepared to discuss the subjects you like and why you like them. Grades are important, but they often provide little specific information about what you are able to do. The fact that you participated in a history fair at your school and won third place for your essay on the settlement of Georgia by convicts provides more information about you than saying, "I got an A in American history." Be able to explain how you intend to further your education or training in the future.

- *Your hobbies, interests, and athletic abilities.* Activities that are not directly related to the job may not seem important enough to mention, but talking about them can provide an interviewer with insight into your character. If you were the captain of your little league baseball team, you may have leadership abilities that could be valuable to an employer.

- *Your plans for the future.* Be ready to talk about your goals, particularly those that relate to the job you are applying for. If an interviewer knows that you want to eventually sell insurance as a career, he or she may be more willing to offer you a job as a file clerk in an insurance office. Your goal might make you work harder and learn more.

One of the most important steps you can take to prepare for an interview is to learn everything you can about the firm you are applying to. This knowledge will help you appear informed and knowledgeable. It will also show your interviewer that you are seriously interested in the job you are being considered for. You should also gather as much information as you can about the position you are applying for. Try to be able to discuss the job responsibilities and how you can carry them out.

When you have gathered as much information as possible about yourself, the firm you are applying to, and the job you are applying for, it is time to practice. Make up a list of questions you might be asked, and have a parent, relative, or friend ask you these questions. The more often you answer these questions, the more confident you will become. The more confident you are, the less likely you will be to make a mistake when you are being interviewed.

It is particularly important to practice answering slowly and distinctly. If you answer an interviewer's question about your job experience by saying, "Iworkedatmybrother'sbowlingalleyfortwoyears," you will not make a good impression.

◆   Applicants who accept job offers must be careful to perform well. They should be punctual, dependable, responsible, and honest. Success in a first job is often your first step toward a successful career.

During the Interview

Think how you judge people that you meet for the first time. You look at the way they dress, you listen to how they talk. You watch their manners and how they act toward other people. In only a few minutes, you decide what sort of people they are. Professional interviewers are trained to look beyond their first impressions, but they are still human. If the interviewer is not impressed with you, he or she may wonder if other workers or customers would feel that way too. If an interviewer asks about your ability to make change and you answer, "Nah, I ain't too good in math," the interviewer might assume that you will talk the same way to customers. It is not likely that you will be offered a job.

An interview is a two-way method of communication. Try to avoid yes and no answers. Volunteer relevant information. Answer questions completely, but avoid going into unnecessary detail. If you are asked to describe the work you did for a prior employer, you can mention that you were responsible for closing the store at night. You don't need to explain

Consumer Close-Up

Acting at an Interview

The time when a job interview was a matter of simply answering questions about yourself is a thing of the past. Faced with a need to be sure that workers are able to deal with real on-the-job problems, many employers are asking job candidates to "put on an act." Potential employees may be shown a videotape of a job-related problem and be given 5 minutes to explain what they would do and why. These simulations present scenarios that vary with the type of job being considered.

A person who is applying to be a clerk in a store might see a customer become angry when an advertised product is not in stock. The applicant is asked to explain what he or she would do to calm the customer. A candidate being considered for a production job might be shown a videotape of a machine that stopped working. The applicant is asked to respond to the situation. The objective is to discover which applicants are best able to deal with stress and quickly solve problems in a creative way.

This interview practice appears to be working. At Colgate-Palmolive's Cambridge, Ohio plant, the use of simulations has reduced turnover of new employees from a range of 20 to 25 percent to a range of 5 to 10 percent. Furthermore, managers state that in four years, two-thirds of the employees hired using simulations were promoted. This is over three times the promotion rate for workers hired by the firm before it used the simulation method.

There is another advantage to using videotape scenarios. This method reduces the chance of being accused of hiring biases. When all applicants are asked to respond to the same tapes, there is a better chance that they are treated equally.

---

that your employer drove a Buick that you liked very much.

Don't be afraid to ask questions. You should find out what the potential employer expects of employees. If you would not want to work for a firm because of its personnel policies, it is better to find this out before you accept a job offer. A good interview involves a serious exchange between two people who are trying to find out what each has to offer.

You should always be neatly dressed for an interview. The type of clothing that is appropriate depends on the situation and type of job that you are seeking. If you are being interviewed for a managerial position, you should wear suitable business attire. If you are applying for a job as a production line worker, you may wear less formal clothes, but they must be neat and clean. You would not buy a box of breakfast cereal that was crushed and dirty. An employer is not likely to hire a worker who wears clothing that is mussed and needs to be laundered.

You should always be polite and respectful. Stand or sit with good posture. Keep your feet on the floor. Don't fidget or tap your feet, and don't chew gum or smoke. Try to sound friendly and confident of your own value.

You can usually tell when an interview is almost over. The interviewer is likely to ask you if you have any questions. Think of one or two relevant questions to ask before your interview. Be sure that they make sense, and show your interest in doing a good job for the firm.

Choose a question that will make a positive impression on the interviewer. It is better to ask about how you will be able to demonstrate your personal initiative or creativity on the job than to ask when you can expect your first raise.

When you get home, write a brief thank-you note and send it to the interviewer the same day if possible. Think about the interview and evaluate your performance. Identify what you did well and ways you could have improved your answers. This information can help you learn from your mistakes and do better in future interviews.

The final point to remember is not to give up. Don't be discouraged if you aren't offered the job. Finding a job that satisfies your needs is a challenge. Remember, employers are also looking for workers who satisfy their needs. Continue your job search until you receive an offer for a job that you believe will help you achieve your career goals. Then accept the offer and make your best effort to succeed.

Summing Up   *An interview is often the final step in seeking a job. People who are interviewed should be prepared, confident of their own value, and willing to ask questions about the job they are being interviewed for.* ◆

KEEPING YOUR JOB

While you read, ask yourself . . .
   ◆ *If you owned a business, how would you expect a new employee to behave?*
   ◆ *How well are you able to take and follow directions? Why are these important abilities for employees to have?*

You probably know people who have been "let go" or "fired" from a job. In some cases this happens because the employer no longer needs the employee's services. More often it is the result of an employer feeling that a worker

is not providing dependable labor. Being fired from a job is more important than a simple loss of income. The event is likely to become part of an employee's work record and may prevent a worker from being offered other jobs in the future.

Knowing What Is Expected of You

As you start a new job, there will be a period of time when you will need to learn the tasks you are expected to carry out. During this time you will probably receive oral or written instructions. It is important for you to listen or read carefully to avoid making mistakes. If an instruction is not clear to you, it is better to ask for a clarification than to do something wrong and find your mistake later. Remember, your employer hired you to do a job. He or she wants you to succeed and will provide you with a reasonable amount of help.

Workers should demonstrate good work habits, including the following:

• *Punctuality*. This means putting in a full day's work. You should get to work on time and take only as much time for breaks or lunch as you are scheduled for.

• *Dependability*. This means that your supervisor and co-workers can trust you to complete your work in an appropriate way and on time.

• *A willingness to learn*. This means that you have an open mind and are interested in learning new or better ways to accomplish tasks.

• *Enthusiasm*. This means that you work with energy and a positive attitude. You complete your tasks without having to be told to do your work repeatedly.

• *Honesty*. This means that your employer can trust you not to take money or items that do not belong to you. He or she can rely on you to do an honest day's work and can trust that you will not lie about mistakes you make or call in sick when you aren't.

Getting Along with People

Most businesses work like a team. The manager is the "coach," and the workers are the "players." When the players on a basketball team don't work together, they usually lose the game. The same is true of a business. As an employee, you will depend on other workers to do their jobs and on your superiors to provide coordination and directions. If you don't get along with your supervisor or co-workers, you won't be a good team member for your employer.

When you start a new job, have a positive attitude toward your supervisor and co-workers. They have more experience and can help you succeed. Recognize that you need to learn facts and skills that they already possess. Be polite, friendly, and helpful. Good personal relationships also contributes to job satisfaction. Everyone prefers to work with people they like. Getting along with others will improve your chance of receiving increased pay and promotions. Here are a few tips that can help you form better relationships on the job:

- *Accept differences.* People are not the same. They have different ethnic, social, and cultural backgrounds. Don't think that there is something wrong with someone who is different from you.
- *Treat others with consideration.* You will find that most people treat you the same way you treat them. On a new job you will need consideration from other people. This is one reason you should be considerate of others.
- *Be willing to compromise.* You can never have everything your own way. Most jobs have good and bad aspects. Don't demand only the good for yourself. As a new worker, you may be expected to do the less desirable tasks more often than other workers. You will need to earn the right to be assigned to better tasks.
- *Be polite and respectful.* When you take a new job, you will probably be younger than other workers and will certainly be less experienced than most. It is better not to call people by their first name until you sense that you are accepted as an equal. Watch how other workers act toward each other to guide your actions.
- *Keep a cheerful attitude.* In any new situation, you are likely to encounter problems and some failures. Don't let these events "get to you." If you act depressed and complain, other people may not want to talk to you or even be around you.

How to Complete Your Job

There are two basic ways you may be asked to complete a job. You may be given specific instructions, or you may be asked to use your own judgment to accomplish a task. When given instructions, always try to follow them to the best of your ability. There are almost always reasons for the instructions you receive as a new employee. In many cases they concern your safety and that of your co-workers. For example, if you are told to always turn off the gas on a stove before you clean it, this may be necessary to avoid an explosion.

Vocabulary Builder

Dependability Ability to complete a task on time and in the appropriate manner.
Punctuality Arriving at work and completing tasks on time.

Consumer News

Changing Jobs

Would you like a different job? If you are employed and between the ages of sixteen and twenty-four, there is a one-in-eight chance that you will change jobs this year. If you are forty-five to fifty-four years old, that chance is just one in fifty. The average employee between sixteen and twenty-four has held his or her current job for less than two years, while workers who are between thirty-five and forty-four have worked for the same employer for an average of ten years.

What are some possible reasons for younger workers changing jobs more frequently than older workers?

When you are asked to use your own judgment, remember that your objective is to help your employer achieve goals that include earning a profit. Actions that please you the most might not be best for your employer. For example, if you are a clerk in a store, you will probably wait on some customers who are demanding and unreasonable. If you are impolite to these people, you will damage your employer's business and reduce your opportunity for success with the firm. Keep your feelings under control, and make the best of the difficult situations you face.

When It's Time to Change Jobs

At some time in your career, you will probably need to quit a job. This may be the result of having a better opportunity elsewhere or of dissatisfaction with your current employment.

In either case, it is important to give your employer **notice** so that he or she may look for a replacement. Depending on the type of job you are leaving, two weeks to thirty days notice is appropriate. Remember to be polite when you give notice. You may need to ask your former employer for a recommendation in the future.

It is better to quit a job than to be fired. If you become convinced that a job you have taken is not providing you with the satisfaction, experience, or compensation that you need, you should discuss the situation with your supervisor. It is very likely that this person will have sensed your dissatisfaction and will not be surprised. Try to work out your problems if you can. If you are not able to reach a satisfactory agreement, respectfully give your employer notice that you are quitting. Quitting a job you don't like is almost as important to your career as taking a job you do like.

To be a consumer, you need income. A career can provide you with personal satisfaction and the income you need. Your first job is more than a means of earning income. It is the first step on the road to your career.

Summing Up   *Keeping a job requires workers to fulfill the expectations of their employers. Workers need to be responsible, productive, and able to get along with other workers and customers.* ◆

Vocabulary Builder

Notice   The advance warning that employees give their employer when they intend to leave their job.

Review and Enrichment Activities

VOCABULARY REVIEW

1. Column A contains key consumer terms from this chapter. Column B contains a scrambled list of phrases that describe what these terms mean. Match the correct meaning with each term. Write your answers on a separate sheet of paper.

Column A	Column B
1. Résumé	a. The quality of being trustworthy
2. Cover letter	b. A one to two page summary of job qualifications
3. Temporary agency	c. The quality of being consistently on time
4. Dependability	d. Informing an employer of your intention to quit a job
5. Notice	e. A brief message written to an employer intended to convince the employer to read one's summary of job qualifications
6. Employment agency	f. Advertisements in newspapers that seek qualified applicants for job openings
7. Punctuality	g. An organization that matches people who are looking for jobs with job openings
8. Chamber of Commerce	h. An organization that has the purpose of improving business conditions in a community
9. Classified want ads	i. An organization that hires workers for employers who need help for a limited period of time

2. Explain the difference between a job referral and a reference.

Review and Enrichment Activities Continued

CHECKING WHAT YOU'VE LEARNED

Write your answers for the following exercises on a separate sheet of paper.

1. How may friends, relatives, or acquaintances be used to help you find a job opening?
2. Explain why employers usually prefer to hire a candidate who has been referred by people they know.
3. Why should workers be careful when they use the services of a private employment agency?
4. Although most job openings are never advertised, want ads can provide applicants with important information. Explain why this is true.
5. Explain why working for a temporary agency may be a valuable type of employment, even when a worker's wages are not high.
6. Why is it important to fill out application forms completely and accurately without making any mistakes?
7. Explain what résumés are and how they are used.
8. Explain what cover letters are and how they are used.
9. Explain why applicants should practice their interview skills before they have a real interview.
10. Describe how job applicants should dress, talk, and answer questions when they are interviewed.
11. Explain why new employees depend on supervisors or co-workers.
12. Explain why it is important for all workers to get along well with other people.
13. Why is it important for a worker to be polite when he or she quits a job?

PRACTICING YOUR CONSUMER SKILLS

Write your answers for the following exercises on a separate sheet of paper.

1. Explain how Joe might obtain a job referral for each of the following job openings:
   a. Joe has heard that the town council wants to hire high school students who are athletic to work for its summer youth fitness program. Joe has been on his high school's football and baseball teams for each of the past two years.
   b. The largest factory in town always hires summer help when full-time workers go on vacation. One out of every ten adult workers in Joe's community is employed by this firm.

   c. A local department store hires many high school students each October to work during the Christmas shopping season. Joe's older brother has worked for this store for the last three years.

   d. A new shopping mall is about to open in Joe's community that will offer hundreds of jobs for clerks. Joe would like to work at a new branch of a local sporting goods store in the mall. Three of Joe's friends work for the store at its present location.

2. Use the following information to complete an application form for Felecia. When necessary, make up reasonable information.

   Felecia Ann Rodriguez was born on April 17, 1973, in St. Louis, MO. She now lives with her parents at 234 East Downing Street, in Livingston, NJ 07039. She has lived there since the summer of 1987. Felecia's telephone number is (201) 748-4312, and her Social Security number is 876-45-1234. She is applying for a full-time job opening as a data entry clerk she saw advertised in a newspaper. The position is offered by the New Jersey Trust Insurance Company, where her sister Maria works.

   Felecia graduated from Livingston Central High School in a secretarial/business curriculum in 1991. She has not had any other formal education, but did gain experience working with computers when she worked for the New Jersey State Department of Motor Vehicles from July 1991 until September 1992. Felecia can type 60 words per minute. When she was employed by the state, she entered information into a computer system to register new vehicles. She was laid off from that job because of state spending cuts. She would eventually like to attend business school, but has not been able to afford to yet. When Felecia was in high school, she volunteered to do typing for her church.

3. There are many mistakes in the résumé on the following page. Some involve spelling or grammar. Others involve content or style. Rewrite the résumé so that it is correct and will create a favorable impression of Sandra. She is sending her résumé to a furniture store that has advertised a position for an experienced sales representative.

Review and Enrichment Activities Continued

Sandy Kinderman
Address
413 West Lake Street
St. Paul, MN 55164
(612 347-2371

OBJECTIVE
To earn enough money to be able to attend college while I support my three children. I'm tired of depending on help from my parents to get buy. There income isn't very big and they really can't afford to give me much help. I want to become totally self supporting and think furniture is a good way too do this.

EDUCATION
Member of Future Business CLub in HighSchool
Graduated from East Rushford High School in 1989
Earned a 2.2 grade point average on a 4.0 skale
Voted most congeniel by my senior classmates

Work Experience
STOCK PERSON IN DOMESTICS DEPARTMENT AT K-MART
In this position I helped customers find towels, linnens and other things they wanted to buy. I worked thirty hours most weeks and earned $5.75 a hour when I quit because I was going to have my second child. My former husband works as a mechanic and runs his own repair shop. When I worked at K-Mart I sometimes sold patio furniture which I really liked to do. One day I was able to sell seven complete sets that cost a total of over $2,900.
CLEANING PERSON AT THROUGHWAY MALL
When I was in highschool I worked parttime as a cleaning person at the throughway Mall. I picked up discarded papers and swept the passage ways. I watched customers and how they were treated by sales people. I think this will help me be a good salesperson.

Hobbies
I enjoy sewing my own clothes and no a lot about fabrics.

REFRENCES
Refrences avalable on request.

USING NUMBERS

Solve the following problem to help make the best possible choice. Write your solution on a separate sheet of paper. Be sure to show all your work.

Andrew is going to be interviewed tomorrow for a job opening as an assistant manager of a fast food hamburger restaurant. He believes he is well qualified for the job because he has worked in another similar fast food restaurant for two years and has been responsible for closing three nights a week. Andrew's current wage is $7.84 an hour. He works at least 40 hours a week and often another five to ten hours of overtime. Last year his total gross income was $19,620. Andrew knows that the assistant manager of the restaurant where he now works receives an annual salary of $24,500. This assistant manager works an average of 50 hours a week but receives no overtime pay. If this person was paid an hourly wage and overtime for hours worked in excess of 40 per week, what would her hourly wage be? (HINT: she would receive time and one half for hours worked over 40 each week. If she is working 50 hours a week this would result in the same income as 55 hours of ordinary pay.)

If Andrew is offered the new job he has been told he will receive an hourly wage, not a salary. How much do you think he should ask for? Explain your reasoning. If he asks for too much he may not be given the job.

PUTTING IDEAS IN YOUR OWN WORDS

The following quotations are from this chapter. Explain these quotations in your own words to make sure you understand what they mean. Write your answers on a separate sheet of paper.

1. "When you apply for a job you are offering your labor for sale."
2. "Professional interviewers are trained to look beyond their first impressions, but they are still human."
3. "A good interview involves a serious exchange between two people who are trying to find out what each has to offer."
4. "It is better to quit a job than to be fired."

BUILDING CONSUMER KNOWLEDGE

Write your answers for the following exercises on a separate sheet of paper.

1. Identify three or more specific job openings in your community that you believe you are qualified to fill. Use the job search methods described in this chapter to find these openings. Do not use want ads as a source for more than one example.
2. Choose one of the job openings you have identified, and prepare a résumé about yourself that you could send to this employer.
3. Make a list of questions that you would like to ask if you were interviewed for the job opening you have identified.

UNIT 7

Managing Your Money

This unit describes the types of withholding that are taken from a worker's earnings, including payments for Social Security and federal and state income taxes. You will learn how to file your tax returns and how to choose the appropriate tax form. You will read about the different services offered by banks and other financial institutions in our economic system. Finally, Unit 7 explains why you should save and invest part of your income. It also describes several methods you can use to achieve your financial objectives.

Chapter 23

Analyzing Your Paycheck

Chapter Objectives

After completing this chapter, you will be able to do the following:

- Explain why money is withheld from employee income.
- Identify the types of information on a federal W-4 form.
- Describe methods of withholding for federal, state, and city income taxes.
- Explain other types of withholding that may be taken from an employee's income.

Key Consumer Terms

In this chapter you will learn the meanings of the following important consumer terms:

- Gross income
- FICA
- Net income
- Earned income
- Exemptions
- Deductions
- Unearned income
- W-4 form
- Internal Revenue Service (IRS)
- Allowance
- Overwithholding
- Refund
- Flat tax
- Payroll savings
- Credit union

everly started work as a part-time receptionist in a real estate office several weeks ago. Her job is to answer the phone, greet customers, and file papers. Her wage rate is $6.50 an hour. Beverly worked 34 hours in her first two weeks on the job. She expected her first paycheck to be well over $200 (34 hours × $6.50 = $221). To her dismay, she only received $185.79. When she read the stub to her check, she saw that her **gross income** was $221. However, $16.91 had been withheld for something called **FICA**. Withholding for federal income taxes took another $11.52, and the state income tax took $6.78. Beverly's **net income** was $35.21 less than her gross income. She asked her boss, Mr. Roberts, to explain why he held back so much of her pay.

Mr. Roberts told Beverly that he has no choice in how much he withholds from her pay. He explained that the government provides him with specific instructions and tables that tell him how much to withhold based on the amount of income Beverly earns and information that she supplied when she accepted his job offer. He said that there were ways Beverly might increase her current take-home pay, but she would end up paying the government the same amount of tax regardless of how much was withheld from her earnings at the present.

SECTION 1

WITHHOLDING FOR SOCIAL SECURITY

While you read, ask yourself . . .
- ◆ *Do you know people who receive Social Security payments? Do they believe that they receive a fair amount?*
- ◆ *How do you feel about paying 7.65 percent of your income into the Social Security program? Do you feel that it is money well spent?*

Ever since 1935, when the Social Security system was established, most Americans have had some income withheld from their earnings to cover the cost of Social Security benefits paid to others. This withholding is called FICA, which stands for Federal Insurance Contributions Act. In 1991, employers and employees each paid FICA taxes equal to 7.65 percent of the first $53,400 of income that an employee earned. Of this 7.65 percent, 6.20 percent paid for Social Security and 1.45 percent for **Medicare** (a federal health insurance plan for older Americans). Income over $53,400 was not taxed for Social Security; but it was taxed to support the cost of Medicare up to a maximum of $125,000. There was a maximum FICA of $5,123.30 in 1991 that could be paid by both employees and their employers:

First $53,400 taxed at 7.65% = $4,085.10
Next $71,600 taxed at 1.45% = $1,038.20
Maximum FICA paid on
    $125,000 or more = $5,123.30

Employers and employees have no control over the part of wages or salary that must be withheld and paid into the Social Security system. Unlike income taxes, there are no exemptions or deductions that may be used to reduce the amount of Social Security taxes. This tax is paid on all **earned income** up to the maximum amount. Above that amount there is no Social Security tax. There is also no tax taken from **un-**

◆   FICA withholding is taken from workers' earnings and used by the government to make Social Security payments to people who qualify for benefits under this program. Why do some Americans feel Social Security payments are too large while others feel they are too small?

earned income—income that people received but did not work to earn. Examples of unearned income include interest paid by your bank or dividends from stock that you own. People who are wealthy tend to have more of this type of income and pay a smaller percent of their total income in Social Security taxes. Therefore, Social Security taxes as a whole are regressive.

The Social Security program is not a retirement program. It is intended to provide "supplemental" income to people who are retired or disabled. Each citizen is expected to plan for his

or her own retirement and should only expect a certain amount of help from the government.

Under the Social Security program current benefits are supposed to be paid by current workers. Contributions to the program are not intended to be set aside to be paid in the future. However, there is a Social Security trust fund that contained several hundred billion dollars in 1990. This money had accumulated and could help pay for the large number of people who will retire in the years after 2000. Do you remember learning about the "baby boom" of the 1940s and 1950s? These people will reach retirement age and begin to receive benefits sometime after the year 2000. Their needs will put a major strain on the ability of the Social Security system to provide adequate benefits to everyone who is entitled to them.

Summing Up   *Taxpayers have no control over the amount of money deducted from their earnings for Social Security. Earned income was taxed at a rate of 7.65 percent to a maximum amount of slightly more than $53,000 in 1991.* ◆

Vocabulary Builder

Earned income   Income that results from payment for one's labor.

FICA   Federal Insurance Contribution Act; payments support Social Security benefits.

Gross income   The total amount of an employee's earnings before any deductions are taken.

Medicare   An insurance program established by the federal government that provides basic medical coverage for Americans who are sixty-five years of age or older.

Net income   The remainder of an employee's earnings after withholdings for taxes, Social Security, and other deductions are taken.

Unearned income   Income that is not the result of payment for one's labor.

SECTION 2

WITHHOLDING FOR FEDERAL INCOME TAXES

While you read, ask yourself . . .
- ◆ *Why doesn't the government simply rely on taxpayers to send in the money they owe instead of using withholding?*
- ◆ *Would you ever consider using overwithholding as a means of saving?*

If you compare your FICA withholding with the amount taken from other people's paychecks, you will find that the percent taken is the same. This is not true of withholding for income taxes. The percent of your income that is withheld for income taxes will vary widely.

Why You Need to Complete a W-4

Unlike Social Security taxes, income taxes are progressive on the parts of income that are taxable. There are ways to reduce taxable income that you will learn about in Chapter 24. The greater your taxable income, the larger the percent you will pay for federal income taxes. Therefore, a larger part of your income is withheld as your income grows. Taxpayers, however, may reduce their taxable income by claiming **exemptions** for people they support or claiming **deductions** for some types of expenses they pay. This means that two people with the exact same earnings might need to have different amounts withheld for income taxes if they have different family sizes or types of expenses.

When you accept a job offer, you are asked to complete a federal form **W-4**. This form provides your employer with the information he or she needs to determine how much income to withhold from your earnings.

Consumer News

One Way to Reduce the Debt

In 1991 the federal debt grew by about $1,000 for every person in this country. It would have grown even more if the government had not used "creative" accounting methods.

Increases in Social Security and Medicare taxes in the late 1980s enabled the Social Security Administration to collect billions of dollars more than it needed to pay benefits. The purpose of this extra money was to save for benefits that will be paid to the millions of "baby boomers" who will retire after the year 2000. In 1986, however, the government decided to use the surplus in the Social Security fund to reduce the debt run up by other parts of the government. If this had not been done in 1991, the federal debt would have been about $150 larger for each American.

Using the Social Security surplus in this way does not change the fact that people will retire in the future and expect to receive benefits. Those benefits, as well as the rest of the government's debt, will have to be paid for by taxpayers. Remember, you are tomorrow's taxpayer.

How does this make you feel?

What a W-4 Asks For

In addition to your name, address, and Social Security number, the W-4 form asks you to provide information that will affect the amount of taxes you owe the government. This information includes your marital status, whether you make other tax payments to the **Internal Revenue Service (IRS)**, an estimate of other income you will earn, whether your spouse works, and the number of dependents you support. A worksheet is provided that shows you how to use this information to determine the number of **allowances** you should claim on your W-4. The more allowances you claim, the less money will be withheld from your earnings. It is against the law to claim an unreasonable number of allowances to reduce your withholding. If you do not have enough money withheld from your earnings, you will be charged interest on unpaid taxes and may be required to pay a penalty as well.

Your employer has received a table from the IRS that states how much should be withheld, depending on each employee's income and the number of allowances claimed. Employers are not responsible for checking W-4 forms for accuracy and honesty. If you make a mistake or provide inaccurate information, you will have to deal with the IRS.

Should You Claim Extra or Fewer Allowances?

There are special situations when a W-4 may not provide an appropriate amount of withholding. This may be the result of unequal income earned at different times of the year. If your pay is based on commissions, there may be some weeks when your income is very high and other times when it is almost nothing. As a result, too much money might be withheld in those times when your income is high. The same would be true if you have seasonal work. Employees who work in construction often earn large amounts in the summer and almost nothing in the winter. When your income varies, you may want to claim an extra allowance.

Some people have other sources of income that do not last the entire year. If you have a cottage that you rent only in the summer, you will earn extra income in June through August. You might not consider this income when you complete your W-4 because you won't know how many weeks the cottage will be rented. Therefore, you might need to reduce the number of allowances you claim.

Overwithholding as a Way to Save

Many taxpayers **overwithhold** both federal and state income taxes on purpose as a method of "forced" saving. They claim fewer allowances than they are entitled to so that they will receive a **refund** on their taxes from the government. This is usually a poor decision.

Vocabulary Builder

Allowance   A term used in completing federal tax form W–4; the more allowances a taxpayer claims, the less will be withheld from his or her earnings.

Deduction   Money subtracted from an employee's earnings for taxes, Social Security, and health insurance; withholding.

Exemption   An amount that may be subtracted from a person's income for each person supported to reduce his or her taxable income.

Internal Revenue Service (IRS)   The federal agency responsible for collecting income taxes.

Overwithholding   Withholding more money from a worker's earnings than are owed in taxes by that worker.

Refund   A return of excess taxes paid by the government to a taxpayer.

W-4 form   A federal tax form completed by employees that allows employers to determine how much of the worker's earnings should be withheld for income tax.

◆ When workers accept employment they must complete a W-4 form that helps their employer determine how much to withhold from their earnings for income tax. An inaccurate W-4 may cause too little money to be withheld and result in a taxpayer being charged interest and fined.

When taxpayers choose to have too much money withheld, they are really making an interest-free loan to the government. The government uses their money and pays them no interest. If you want to save, it is better to put an amount aside from each paycheck and place it in a savings account that pays you interest. Try to avoid getting a refund unless you find that it is the *only* way you can make yourself save.

The best situation is to end up each year having paid the government in withholding almost exactly what is owed. The W-4 form can help you do this, but it is only an estimate. Don't ex-pect it to always result in the exact amount of your tax being withheld. At the end of each year, the amount of your total tax bill will not change regardless of the amount of income that was withheld. If too much was taken, you will receive a refund. If too little was taken, you will owe money to the IRS. If the amount you owe is large, the government has the right to charge you interest and a penalty.

Summing Up *The amount of money that is withheld from employee earnings depends on the amount of their earnings and the number of allowances they claim on their W-4 forms. The best possible result is to have almost the same amount of money withheld that is owed in taxes.* ◆

SECTION 3

OTHER TYPES OF WITHHOLDING

While you read, *ask yourself . . .*
- ◆ *Why do unions often negotiate for the right to have dues withheld from workers' pay?*
- ◆ *Why do many people prefer to save using payroll deductions instead of depositing the money themselves?*

The largest amounts of money withheld from your pay are likely to be for FICA and federal income taxes. However, there are many other reasons for money to be withheld from your earnings.

State and Local Income Taxes

In 1988, forty-three states and the District of Columbia had income taxes. The rate of taxation ranged between a **flat tax** on all taxable income of 2.5 percent in Illinois to a maximum of 11 percent for people with over $57,580 in taxable income in California. Many cities also charged an income tax to support public services. For example, New York City charged 2 percent on taxable income in 1990. Employers use information from federal W-4 forms to determine how much income to withhold for state and local taxes.

The amount you pay for state and local income taxes may be deducted from your income when you figure your federal income tax. If you live in a state with high taxes, you will have a large deduction for your federal tax. You may find that you should claim more allowances on your W-4 to avoid having too much income withheld for federal taxes.

If you discover that too much or too little is being withheld from your income, you have the right to change your W-4 at any time. You may also elect to have an additional amount withheld by filling in the amount on line 5 on your W-4 form. Taxpayers do this when they find that too little is withheld from their pay, even when they claim no allowances. This is usually the result of having large amounts of untaxed income from other sources, such as rent or interest.

Nontax Withholding

There are reasons to have money withheld from your earnings that have nothing to do with taxes. Many people participate in **payroll savings** plans. With a payroll savings plan, an amount is taken out of each paycheck and deposited in a bank or credit union or used to buy government savings bonds. This method of saving is much better than overwithholding because the employee is paid interest on his or her savings.

Some businesses offer savings or stock purchase plans to their employees. In this case, money is set aside from the employee's pay that may be partially or totally matched by the employer. Often the employer's contribution increases when workers stay with the firm for longer periods of time. Businesses provide this type of incentive to encourage valued workers to stay with their jobs.

Employees often have money withheld from their pay to make contributions to retirement plans, insurance policies, or credit unions. Many **credit unions** have agreements with employers that allow workers to make loan payments directly from their wages. Workers may also have money taken from their wages to pay union dues. Another common reason to have money withheld is to make contributions to charities. Most employers allow workers to contribute to the United Givers Fund (UGF) or similar organizations in this way.

There are many reasons for your take-home pay to be smaller than your gross income. You have no control over some of these reasons. In other cases you may determine how much money should be withheld. Still, the amount of money you end up owing for federal taxes will not be affected by the amount of your withholding.

Summing Up *Employees may have money withheld from their earnings to pay for state and local taxes, to save, to pay union dues, and to make contributions.* ◆

Vocabulary Builder

Credit union A depository institution owned and operated by its members to provide savings accounts and low-interest loans to its members.

Flat tax A tax that remains at a constant rate of taxable income.

Payroll savings Money deducted from a worker's earnings to buy government savings bonds or to deposit in an account.

Consumers in Action

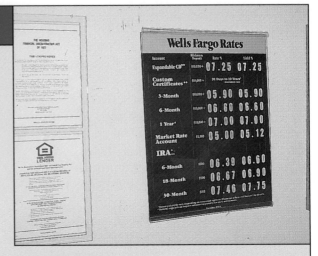

Reducing Taxes by Saving for Retirement

Do you believe that your retirement is so far in the future that there is no point in thinking about it now? Although your retirement is probably more than forty years in the future, your long-term goals should include plans for a secure retirement. If you rely on the government to provide for your retirement needs, you are likely to be disappointed. However, the government has taken steps to make it easier for people to save for their retirement years.

In 1981 a law was passed that allowed American taxpayers to set aside part of their income in an Individual Retirement Account (IRA) and not pay taxes on that part of their earnings until they withdrew the money sometime after they turned 59½ years old. This law was intended to encourage people to save for their old age by reducing their current tax bill and postponing taxes until they retired, when they would probably pay taxes at a lower rate. In 1986 this law was adjusted so that many people with larger incomes could no longer take advantage of it. However, if you do qualify, it provides a way to achieve a significant tax savings and set money aside for retirement.

Just how large is this tax advantage? Let's consider two taxpayers, Paula and Chad. Suppose that Paula began setting aside $2,000 a year in an IRA that paid 8 percent interest in 1981. If she paid taxes at a rate of 28 percent, the $2,000 saving would only reduce her current after-tax income by $1,440 because part of the money that she saved would have been paid to the government in taxes: $0.28 \times \$2,000 = \$560$ in taxes; $\$2,000 - \$560 = \$1,440$. After ten years, her $2,000 yearly contributions to the IRA would be

worth $28,973: $20,000 from Paula's deposits, the other $8,973 from interest earned on the account.

Now suppose that Chad was in the same tax bracket as Paula but paid taxes on his income before he saved. If he set aside $1,440 of his after-tax income in an ordinary account, it would only be worth $19,421 after ten years. Of this amount, $14,400 would be from his deposits, and $5,201 from interest. By putting the money in an IRA, Paula, in effect, earned interest on money that belonged to the government. She received $3,952 more interest than Chad. When Paula withdraws money from her IRA, she will have to pay taxes on it, but she will have more money to withdraw because of her extra interest. Paula may also benefit from paying taxes at a lower rate when she has retired.

People who still qualify for IRAs and can afford to set money aside until they are 59½ years old will gain a significant benefit by using this method to increase their retirement savings. If you are self-employed or earn less than $35,000 a year as a single person or less than $50,000 a year as a married couple, you qualify for an IRA as the law was written in 1991.

Review and Enrichment Activities

VOCABULARY REVIEW

1. Column A contains key consumer terms from this chapter. Column B contains a scrambled list of phrases that describe what these terms mean. Match the correct meaning with each term. Write your answers on a separate sheet of paper.

Column A	Column B
1. Flat tax	a. Money earned from a worker's labor
2. Taxable income	b. Earnings that have been reduced by deductions and exemptions
3. Allowance	c. Amounts of income withheld in excess of the amount needed to pay taxes
4. FICA	
5. Over-withholding	d. Money received from sources that did not involve a worker's labor
6. W-4 form	e. An indicator that helps employers determine how much to withhold from an employee's income
7. Payroll savings	
8. Earned income	f. A tax that takes the same percent of all taxpayers' income
9. Refund	g. The return of excess taxes paid or withheld by the government to a taxpayer
10. Unearned income	h. A document that employees complete to provide information to employers so they may know how much to withhold for federal income taxes
	i. The law that requires withholding to support Social Security
	j. Having money withheld from a worker's income and deposited in a bank or other similar institution

2. Explain the difference between gross income and net income.

Review and Enrichment Activities Continued

CHECKING WHAT YOU'VE LEARNED

Write your answers for the following exercises on a separate sheet of paper.

1. Identify five different types of withholding that could make your net income smaller than your gross income.
2. Explain why two people with the same earned income would have the same amount of FICA withholding but could have different amounts of federal income tax withholding.
3. Explain the purpose of a federal W-4 form.
4. If a taxpayer makes a mistake and fills out form W-4 incorrectly, who is responsible for the mistake?
5. Describe two situations when a taxpayer might want to claim an extra allowance on the W-4.
6. Describe two situations when a taxpayer might want to claim fewer allowances on the W-4.
7. Explain the difference between an exemption and a deduction.
8. Explain why it is not wise for most people to overwithhold as a method of saving.
9. Why might people choose to save by using payroll deductions instead of depositing money themselves into their bank accounts?

PRACTICING YOUR CONSUMER SKILLS

Write your answers for the following exercise on a separate sheet of paper.

1. Identify which of the following types of income would be taxed for Social Security.
   a. Income that a student earns from a part-time job at a grocery store
   b. Income earned by a sixty-six-year-old retired person who works at a polling place on election day
   c. Income earned from dividends paid to a retired person
   d. Income earned from a Christmas bonus by an executive who has a salary of $190,000
   e. Income earned from rent on an apartment building that you own
2. You have been given a blank federal W-4 form. Complete this form for Carol, using the following information.

   Carol S. Reese
   214 Loughton Drive
   Lake Success, NY 11042

Carol has just accepted a job that will pay her $21,000 a year. She is single and only has the one job. But she does earn an extra $500 a year delivering telephone books. Carol supports her elderly aunt, who lives with her in her house.

3. State whether the following people should probably claim more or fewer allowances on their W-4 forms. Explain your choice.

   a. Ted works at a winter resort as a ski instructor. His income is based on the number of customers he works with. In the winter he often earns $800 or more a week. In the rest of the year he does odd jobs and earns no more than $200 a week. Should he claim more or fewer allowances on his W-4 for the ski resort?

   b. Sally didn't work for the first half of this year. She started a job in September. Should she claim extra or fewer allowances for the rest of this year?

   c. Chad doesn't have any self-control. If he tries to save in a bank, he always takes the money out and spends it. Chad doesn't have much income. If he ever had to pay the government extra taxes on April 15, he would have no idea where to get the money. Should Chad claim extra or fewer allowances on his W-4 form?

   d. Polly is part owner of a copy business. She does no work there, but she did invest $20,000 in the firm. In exchange she is paid 20 percent of the firm's profits. This payment has ranged from nothing in some years to as much as $5,000. Polly never has any idea how much her share of the profits will be before the end of the year. Should Polly claim extra or fewer allowances on her W-4 form?

USING NUMBERS

Solve the following problem to help make the best possible choice. Write your solution on a separate sheet of paper. Be sure to show all your work.

Ted has always claimed too few exemptions on his W-4 form so that he would receive a large refund from the government. Last year his refund was $1,040. He filed early and received his refund April 1. If he had put $20 a week in a bank account that paid 6 percent interest last year, how much could he have earned by April 1 of this year? To make this problem easier, assume that he would have earned 6 percent on half the $1,040 for an entire year plus 6 percent on the full $1,040 for the first three months of this year.

PUTTING IDEAS IN YOUR OWN WORDS

The following quotations are from this chapter. Explain these quotations in your own words to make sure you understand what they mean. Write your answers on a separate sheet of paper.

Review and Enrichment Activities Continued

1. "He said that there were ways Beverly might increase her current take-home pay, but she would end up paying the government the same amount of tax regardless of how much was withheld from her earnings at the present."
2. "The Social Security program is not a retirement program."
3. "When taxpayers choose to have too much money withheld, they are really making an interest-free loan to the government."

BUILDING CONSUMER KNOWLEDGE

Write your answers for the following exercises on a separate sheet of paper.

1. Take a survey of adults to find out how many think it is better to receive a refund from the government, pay extra taxes, or break even? Ask them to explain the reasons for their answers.
2. Ask a member of a union why it is important to have union dues withheld from members' paychecks. Be prepared to explain what you learn to your class.
3. Complete a federal W-4 form for yourself.

Chapter 24

Paying Taxes

Chapter Objectives

After completing this chapter, you will be able to do the following:

● Describe the types of information provided by employers in form W-2, by banks in form 1099-INT, and by corporations in form 1099-DIV.

● Describe the types of information that taxpayers should record and maintain for themselves.

● Explain why taxpayers would use form 1040 EZ, 1040 A, or 1040.

● Explain the relationship between being organized and paying the minimum amount of tax necessary.

● Identify sources of help that taxpayers may use in completing their income tax returns.

Key Consumer Terms

In this chapter you will learn the meanings of the following important consumer terms:

● Voluntary compliance
● Audit
● Tax evasion
● Taxable income
● Tax credit
● Taxpayer number
● W-2 form
● Itemized deduction
● Standard deduction
● Dividend

● Filing status
● Adjusted gross income
● Volunteer Income Tax Assistance (VITA)
● Tax Counseling for the Elderly (TCE)
● Certified public accountant (CPA)

I t is safe to say that most people don't enjoy paying income taxes. Still, well over 150 million Americans filed individual income tax returns in 1990. Whether we like it or not, federal income taxes are here to stay. As taxpayers and citizens, we are ethically bound to pay our fair share of the cost of our government. However, we should not be paying more than our fair share of the tax burden.

PREPARING TO FILE YOUR INCOME TAX RETURN

While you read, ask yourself . . .
- *Why should you file a tax return even if you owe no taxes?*
- *Do you keep the records you would need to complete a tax return?*

Federal and state income taxes in the United States are based on **voluntary compliance**. This means that each taxpayer is responsible for determining the amount of tax he or she owes the government and making the appropriate payment. The biggest advantage of this system for the government is that smaller amounts of time and resources are used in collecting taxes. The greatest danger is that people may accidentally or on purpose pay less than their fair share of the tax burden. The Internal Revenue Service **audits** about 2 out of every 100 tax returns to check for mistakes. Any person found to be intentionally committing **tax evasion** may be fined or charged with a crime, convicted, and possibly sent to jail. Although our government relies on voluntary compliance, there is always the threat of legal action for those who do not comply with the law.

There are three basic individual income tax forms. These are forms 1040 EZ, 1040 A, and 1040. This choice of forms is intended to make filing income tax returns easier for people who have few complicating factors to report. As the number of factors that need to be reported

grows, the complexity of the form that must be used also increases. Most high school students and other people with relatively small incomes will be able to use either the 1040 EZ or 1040 A forms, which are less complicated than form 1040.

A little over half of the high school seniors in the United States have a job. They may only work a few hours each week, but they are gainfully employed and usually have federal and state withholding taken from their income. Most of these people need to file a tax return and qualify to use form 1040 EZ.

Who Must File? Who Should File?

People who have **taxable incomes** must file a tax return. Also people who have specific types of income, such as earnings from self-employment, must file. There are detailed instructions provided with each of the three 1040 forms that explain who must file.

Any person who has had income withheld should file a tax return, even if the earnings were so small that the person isn't required to file by law. There are at least two important reasons for this. First, if too much money was withheld from a worker's pay, he or she must file a return to receive a refund.

A second reason to file for many low-income workers and parents is the possibility of qualifying for **tax credits**. The government wants to encourage people to work even if they don't earn large incomes. As a result, laws have been passed that result in the government paying

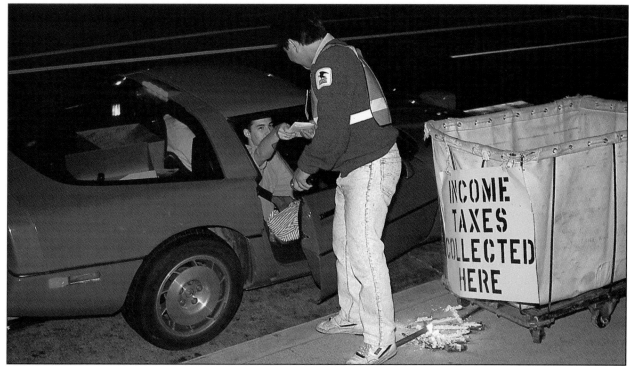

◆ Most taxpayers receive refunds on their income taxes. Why do you imagine millions of taxpayers put off filing their returns until the last possible minute each year?

some workers money instead of taxing them. These credits cannot be claimed by a taxpayer who does not file a return.

Information You Need to File Your Tax Return

Federal law was changed in 1990 to require all American citizens over one year old to register and receive a Social Security number. You have a Social Security number and will use it for many reasons throughout your life. Your Social Security number is also your **taxpayer number**. It identifies you in the records of the Internal Revenue Service. When you file your income tax, you are required to include this number.

If you work for an employer, you will receive three copies of a W-2 form in January of

Vocabulary Builder

Audit   A review of a financial statement or tax return to check for accuracy and completeness.

Taxable income   The amount of income on which taxes are levied (charged).

Tax credit   An amount that may be subtracted from the tax that people owe to encourage them to hold a job; may result in the government paying people more than they pay the government.

Tax evasion   A deliberate choice not to pay taxes owed by providing inaccurate or incomplete information on one's tax return.

Taxpayer number   A number that identifies an individual taxpayer; the same as the Social Security number in most cases.

Voluntary compliance   Refers to the fact that taxpayers are responsible for figuring and paying their own individual income tax.

Consumer News

Your Computer Can Help You

Where do you keep your financial records? Could you produce a receipt for any important purchases you made in the last year? Do you have any idea which of your expenses could be deducted from your income to reduce your taxes? You may not have enough income or expenses to worry about these questions now, but in a few years they will be very important to you.

In recent years many computer programs have been developed to help taxpayer gather and organize the information they need to complete their income tax returns. In 1991 two of the more popular programs were Turbo Tax, by Chip Soft, and Tax Shop 1040, from TenKey Publishing. These and other programs will keep track of expenses and total them in appropriate categories for use in tax forms. This is particularly useful when you think your calculations are complete only to find one more $72 deduction that could reduce your tax about $20. In the past, you had to ask yourself if it was worth doing all your calculations over for the $20. With these programs, you simply type in the extra deduction, and the computer does the work for you in a matter of seconds. Many programs include pictures of the actual tax forms with the amounts entered in the appropriate spaces. All you need to do is copy the numbers from your computer screen onto your own forms.

There are certain dangers in using these programs. If you type in the wrong values, they will not give you correct answers. Also, as soon as Congress changes the tax laws, you need to buy a new version of the program that considers the new laws.

each year. This form states your gross income for the previous year and the amount of withholding that was taken for FICA and federal, state, and local income taxes. You are required to include one copy of your W-2 with your federal income tax return and one copy with your state income tax return. The third copy is for your own records. A fourth copy of this information is sent by your employer to the Internal Revenue Service. This tells the IRS if a taxpayer isn't reporting all of his or her earned income.

Banks also send you a form that you need in order to complete your tax return. Form 1099-INT reports the amount of interest you earned from any bank accounts you own. You are not required to include this form with your tax return, but you will report the amount of interest income on the return. Your bank will send a copy of this information to the IRS. You must be sure to include all interest income on your return. If your numbers don't match those reported by the bank, you will almost certainly be audited. If you are paid **dividends** for corporate stock, you will receive a form 1099-DIV from the corporation that reports your dividend income. Like interest income, the information on this form is reported to the IRS.

Information You Must Save

Most people who are young and have relatively small incomes will not need to use information that they gather themselves to complete their income tax returns. However, as you grow older and take on more financial responsibilities, you will need to keep a careful record of your spending. Even if you don't need this information now, it is important to start learning how to keep track of how you spend your income. Getting in the habit of

◆   Although few people enjoy completing their returns and paying taxes this is much easier to do when you are organized and keep good records. What can you see that tells you this taxpayer is well prepared to complete his return?

keeping careful records now will make it easier for you to do in the future.

All taxpayers must choose which individual income tax form to use. To do this they need to know if they had enough deductible expenses to warrant using the **itemized deduction** that is part of form 1040. Using itemized deductions can reduce taxable income and the amount of taxes owed. A taxpayer who does not keep good records will not know if he or she would benefit from choosing form 1040. People who do not keep careful records may use the wrong form and pay more tax than they need to. A large part of keeping tax payments as low as is legally possible is a matter of good record keeping.

Summing Up   *All people who have federal taxes withheld from their earnings should file a tax return. To be able to choose the correct form and assure yourself of paying no more than your fair share of taxes, you need to keep accurate and complete records of your financial transactions.* ◆

Vocabulary Builder

Dividend   Money paid by a corporation to its stockholders; usually a share of its profits.

Itemized deduction   A listing of deductible expenses that may be subtracted from income to reduce taxable income; an alternative to a standard deduction.

CHOOSING THE PROPER FORM

While you read, ask yourself . . .
- ◆ *If you are employed, which form should you use? Which form do you believe your parents should use?*
- ◆ *What deductions could your family claim on a form 1040, schedule A?*

It is necessary for all taxpayers to choose one the three basic 1040 forms to file. Making the proper choice can save you time and money.

Choosing Form 1040 EZ

Federal tax form 1040 EZ got its name because it is relatively easy to complete. To find out whether you qualify to use this form, ask yourself the following questions:

Am I single?
Am I under sixty-five and not blind?
Can I only claim myself as an exemption?
Did I have less than $50,000 in taxable income last year? (This was the income limit in 1990.)
Did I only earn income from wages, salaries, tips, taxable scholarships, or interest that was $400 or less?
Did I have no adjustments to my income, are there no other taxes I owe, and did I have no tax credits?

If you can answer yes to each of these questions, you qualify to file your income tax return using form 1040 EZ. This does not mean you should necessarily use this form. If you had large medical bills, state income taxes, property taxes, interest payments on a mortgage, contributions to a charitable cause, or any

combination of these expenses, you may pay less tax by using form 1040.

The government allows taxpayers to reduce their income by an amount called the **standard deduction**. This amount is based on the assumption that all taxpayers have some deductible expenses. Rather than requiring all taxpayers to figure out their deductible expenses, the government allows them to claim a minimum amount established by law. In 1991 this amount was $3,400 for most single taxpayers. All people who use form 1040 EZ must take the standard deduction. If a taxpayer has deductible expenses that total more than the standard deduction, he or she should use form 1040 and itemize deductions. You will learn more about this form shortly.

Choosing Form 1040 A or Form 1040

Many taxpayers who do not qualify to use form 1040 EZ may still file their income tax return using the relatively simple form 1040 A. Deciding which form to use for most taxpayers is a matter of determining whether they have more itemized deductions than the amount of the standard deduction the government allows all taxpayers to take.

Either form 1040 A or 1040 may be used by people who have any **filing status**. They may be single, married but filing by themselves, filing jointly with their spouse, or filing as a widow or widower. Some taxpayers must use form 1040. For example, the maximum taxable income that could be reported on form 1040 A in 1991 was $50,000. People who had more income or special types of income, including self-employment income, rents, profit from the sale of stock, and alimony, were required to use form 1040.

◆ Many expenses people pay may be subtracted from their income on Schedule A before their taxes are figured. These include property taxes that are used to support public schools or local governments, part of losses people suffer to their property, or the interest people pay on mortgages they take out when they purchase a home.

Vocabulary Builder

Filing Status   A condition based on family situation that helps indicate which tax form to use when filing a tax return; single, married filing joint, and so on.

Standard deduction   An amount that the federal government allows taxpayers to subtract from their income, regardless of their actual deductible expenses, to reduce their taxable income.

Consumer News

Who Should Claim You as a Dependent?

Would you like to save your family money? If you work, you may be able to reduce your parents' tax bill.

Almost every person in the country may be claimed as a dependent on someone's tax return, but no one may be claimed twice. If your parents supported you in 1991, they could claim you to reduce their taxable income by $2,150. But if you were employed and they claimed you, you could not claim yourself again to reduce your own taxable income by another $2,150. However, you were allowed to subtract $550 from your income if your parents claimed you. If you claimed yourself as a dependent, your parents could not claim you at all.

How could your family decide who should claim you? A reasonable decision can be made by looking at the savings offered by each possible choice:

- If you claimed yourself, you would save 15 percent of $2,150, or $322.50, if you paid income taxes at a 15 percent rate.
- If your parents claimed you, they would save $322.50 if they paid at a 15 percent rate, $602 if they paid at a 28 percent rate, or $666.50 if they paid at a 31 percent rate. **Plus** you would save 15 percent of $550, or $82.50, for the $550 you could reduce your income by.

Unless you paid income taxes at a higher rate than your parents in 1991, it made sense for them to claim you.

Deductible Expenses

The most common reason for choosing to file using form 1040 is to be able to itemize deductions. Schedule A of form 1040 is for itemized deductions. On all three 1040 tax forms, you will determine your **adjusted gross income**. This is the income you earned before any amounts were subtracted for exemptions or deductions. On Schedule A, there are eight general classifications of expenses that may be deducted from your adjusted gross income:

- *Medical and Dental Expenses*. Taxpayers may deduct medical and dental expenses above 7.5 percent of their adjusted gross income.
- *Taxes You Paid*. Taxpayers may deduct many state and local taxes they paid, but not sales tax.
- *Interest You Paid*. Taxpayers may deduct interest payments and certain other payments on home mortgages and some other types of interest. They may not deduct interest paid on most consumer loans after 1990.
- *Gifts to Charity*. Taxpayers may deduct charitable contributions of either cash or property. When large donations of property are made, additional forms must be completed.
- *Casualty and Theft Losses*. Taxpayers may deduct losses resulting from accidents or theft that are over 10 percent of adjusted gross income and have a value over $100.
- *Moving Expenses*. Taxpayers may deduct the cost of moving when the move was necessary to accept new employment more than 35 miles from a former place of employment. To take this deduction, additional forms must be completed.
- *Job Expenses and Most Other Miscellaneous Deductions*. Many job-related expenses and costs associated with completing tax returns may be deducted in amounts that are over 2 percent of adjusted gross income.

Consumers in Action

How to Hire a Tax Consultant

Do you feel competent to complete your own tax forms? Most people your age should be able to file their tax returns with no more than an hour of work. However, as you grow older and your life becomes more complicated, you may need help with your tax returns. Almost half of all American taxpayers use professional tax preparers each year. If you ever decide you need professional help, how should you choose a consultant?

There are essentially three choices you can make if you want the services of a paid tax preparer. You can have your return completed by one of several nationwide firms like H & R Block that churn out millions of returns each year. For standard forms with few complications, these organizations provide fairly reliable services and charge relatively low fees. Although they can process routine forms, they may be less qualified to deal with more complicated returns that require specialized information.

A second choice you can make is to take your return to an accounting firm that hires specialists to prepare customers' taxes. These firms charge much more for their services than the nationwide organizations, but are often better qualified to deal with complicated returns. They may offer services that include estate and tax planning, which can reduce your tax liabilities in future years. If you do not have a complicated return or a large income, these firms probably cost more than they are worth.

You may also use the services of an independent tax preparer. These individuals are often well qualified and offer quality service for reasonable prices. However, some may be unqualified and possibly dishonest. The IRS designates some tax preparers as "enrolled agents." This means that they have either been employed as an IRS auditor for five or more years or passed a test given by the Treasury Department to evaluate their understanding of tax laws. You may find an enrolled agent in the yellow pages of your telephone book. Look for advertisements for accountants that include the words "Enrolled to Practice Before the IRS."

Consumers need to shop just as carefully when they buy the services of a tax consultant as when they buy any other product. Remember, it is *you* who is responsible for the accuracy of the return. If a preparer says that he or she can reduce your taxes to an "unbelievably low" amount—don't believe it.

- *Other Miscellaneous Deductions.* A few other special deductions may be taken. For example, if a taxpayer contributed to a pension that failed, he or she could deduct the loss here. Most taxpayers will have nothing to enter here.

When the total of itemized deductions exceeds the standard deduction, the taxpayer

Vocabulary Builder

Adjusted gross income A taxpayer's income after adjustments for factors such as business income, capital gains, or alimony paid, but before subtractions are made for exemptions or deductions.

should use form 1040. The standard deductions in 1991 were as follows:

Filing Status	Standard Deduction
Single (if you could be claimed as a dependent by someone else, this amount was $550 in 1991)	$3,400
Married filing joint return or qualifying widow(er) with dependent child	$5,700
Married filing separate return	$2,850
Head of household	$5,000

There are many other reasons why a taxpayer might need to use form 1040, but it is impossible to explain all these reasons here. Just remember that taxpayers may claim the standard deduction even if they do use form 1040. If you have any doubt about the form you should use, there are ways to get advice. Many of these sources are free and are identified in the next section.

Regardless of the specific 1040 form you use, you will determine your taxable income. This is the amount of income you must pay tax on after you have reduced your adjusted gross income by subtracting money for exemptions and deductions. There is a table in the back of the tax instruction booklet that you may use to determine the tax you owe according to your filing status and the amount of taxable income you earned. See Figure 24-1 for an example of part of this table.

Summing Up   *Some taxpayers must file their income taxes using form 1040 because of the amount or type of income they earn. Others choose to use this form so that they can itemize deductible expenses that total more than the standard deduction.* ◆

SECTION 3

GETTING HELP

While you read, *ask yourself . . .*
- ◆ *Do you know whether your parents prepare their own tax return?*
- ◆ *Would you rather receive tax assistance from an employee of the IRS, from a volunteer, or from a paid accountant?*

Although instructions are provided with all federal income tax forms, many taxpayers need help in filling out the forms or advice on which forms to use. This type of help is available from the government, from volunteer organizations, and from private businesses that will complete tax returns for a fee. Every taxpayer needs to realize that he or she is responsible for the forms and the tax that is due to the government regardless of who fills out the forms. If you hire an accountant who makes a mistake, *you* are responsible for any payments of taxes, interest, or penalties that must be paid to the government as a result of that mistake.

Help from the Government

The IRS employs representatives who will help you with your tax questions when you call their toll-free number. (That number varies from one location to another.) There are also special services for the hearing impaired and the blind. You may send written questions about your tax return to your IRS district director. The addresses and telephone numbers for these services may be found in the back of the tax instruction booklet you receive with your tax forms.

There are IRS offices in most large cities across the nation. Taxpayers may "walk in" to these offices for personal help with their returns. To find the office nearest you, look in the telephone book under "United States Government, Internal Revenue Service."

The IRS will complete your tax returns for you if you use forms 1040 EZ or 1040 A. You must determine your taxable income by completing form 1040 EZ through line 7, or form 1040 A through line 22 (in 1990). The IRS will complete the remainder of the form and either send you a refund or send you a bill for taxes you owe. If you owe taxes, you will be given thirty days to make your payment from the time your bill is sent.

Help from Volunteer Organizations

The **Volunteer Income Tax Assistance (VITA)** and **Tax Counseling for the Elderly (TCE)** are programs that provide volunteer help to many groups of taxpayers, particularly those who are older or who do not speak English. You may find the location of the nearest program by calling the same IRS taxpayer assistance numbers mentioned above.

Many libraries have entire sections devoted to taxpayer information. They may have videotapes in both English and Spanish to explain how to fill out the tax forms. Libraries also have most tax forms available or masters that may be copied. However, librarians are not qualified tax consultants. Don't expect them to help you fill out your return.

Many colleges, school districts, and education extension services provide tax preparation courses at no or little cost. If you would like to take a course in tax preparation, call your local educational institutions.

Help from Tax Preparation Businesses

There is a wide selection of firms and private entrepreneurs who will provide taxpayer assistance for a fee. Probably the best-known firm is H & R Block, with hundreds of offices across the nation. Many private accounting firms, banks, and **certified public accountants (CPAs)** offer their services for sale. Remember, all such firms are in business to earn a profit. They may or may not save taxpayers money, but they all charge a fee.

Many taxpayers prefer to use a professional tax preparation service because they believe that these firms can find more legal deductions and reduce tax payments. In some cases this may be true. However, the majority of taxpayers who have relatively simple returns should be able to complete their own returns or use government help. If you do use a paid preparer, remember that *you* are responsible for mistakes or fraudulent entries on the forms. If anyone gets into trouble, it is likely to be you.

Summing Up *Taxpayers may receive assistance in completing their returns from many sources. The IRS provides help directly and also organizes volunteer groups. Many libraries, schools, and community organizations also provide various forms of assistance. Taxpayers may also choose to pay for the services of a private tax preparer.* ◆

Vocabulary Builder

Certified public accountant (CPA) A person who has met state requirements and passed an examination to be approved by the state as a qualified accountant.

Tax Counseling for the Elderly (TCE) A volunteer program that helps older people complete their tax returns.

Volunteer Income Tax Assistance (VITA) A volunteer organization that helps taxpayers prepare their tax returns.

Review and Enrichment Activities

VOCABULARY REVIEW

1. Column A contains key consumer terms from this chapter. Column B contains a scrambled list of phrases that describe what these terms mean. Match the correct meaning with each term. Write your answers on a separate sheet of paper.

Column A

1. Voluntary compliance
2. Audit
3. Adjusted gross income
4. Tax evasion
5. Filing status
6. W-2 form
7. Tax credit
8. Schedule A
9. Taxpayer number
10. Volunteer Income Tax Assistance

Column B

a. A reduction in tax owed allowed to some low-income workers, especially those who have children

b. An organization of unpaid people who provide free assistance to tax payers in filing income tax returns

c. A deliberate attempt to not pay an appropriate amount of tax by providing incorrect information on a tax return

d. The system through which tax payers are responsible for figuring and paying their own taxes

e. A method of identifying individual tax payers; most often a Social Security number

f. The federal income tax form used to itemize deductions

g. A review of a tax return to check it for accuracy and completeness

h. A document provided by employers that states an employee's yearly earning and withholding

i. A taxpayer's income after it has been increased or decreased for factors such as business income, but before

any deductions or exemp-
tions are claimed
   j. The condition under which
       taxpayers file their income
       tax: married, single, etc.

2. Explain the difference between a standard deduction and an itemized
    deduction.

CHECKING WHAT YOU'VE LEARNED

Write your answers for the following exercises on a separate sheet of
paper.

1. Explain what we mean when we say that income taxes rely on voluntary
    compliance.
2. Is our income tax really entirely "voluntary?" Explain.
3. Why should citizens file a tax return even whey they don't owe a tax?
4. Identify the information that is included on a W-2 form.
5. Why must taxpayers be sure to include all interest and dividend income
    on their returns if they want to avoid an audit?
6. What is the reasoning behind the government's decision to allow tax-
    payers to take a standard deduction?
7. What are itemized deductions?
8. Describe three different ways that the IRS provides assistance to taxpay-
    ers who need help completing their tax returns.
9. If a paid tax preparer makes a mistake in preparing a tax return, who is
    responsible?

PRACTICING YOUR CONSUMER SKILLS

Write your answers for the following exercises on a separate sheet of
paper.

1. For each of the following situations, state how the taxpayer should ob-
    tain the needed information. (It is possible that some of these taxpayers
    should have recorded the information themselves.)
    a. Jerry has a savings account. He needs to know how much interest he
        earned.
    b. Fran spent three weeks in the hospital last year. She wants to know
        if her medical bills were large enough to make it worth her while to
        itemize her deductions.
    c. Karl wants to know how much state income tax was withheld from
        his pay last year so that he can put this value on schedule A of form
        1040.

Review and Enrichment Activities Continued

     d. Norine owns stock in many different corporations that pay her dividends. She needs to know how much she earned in dividends last year.

     e. Phyllis made many different charitable contributions last year. She needs to know the total amount that she gave.

2. Indicate which tax form each of the following individuals should probably use, and explain why.

     a. Alice is married. She and her husband earned a total of $39,432 in wages and $370 in interest income last year. They had no other income. They have two children. Their deductions, if they itemized, would total $4,390.

     b. Ned is single and earned $5,390 working part-time. He had interest income of $238. He had no other income and no special expenses.

     c. Fred is married. He and his wife each earned over $30,000 in wages at a factory. They had no other income, and the expenses they could itemize total $3,990.

     d. Patty is single. She earned $15,500 working in a florist shop. She also earned $390 in interest and $3,258 by doing typing at home. Her deductions, if she chose to itemize, would total $2,973.

     e. Elmer is single, but he supports his elderly mother in his home. His salary from working as a cook in a restaurant is $26,750. He earned $589 in interest and $1,000 in dividends. His deductions, if he chose to itemize, would total $7,927 because he paid for his mother's hospitalization for seven days.

3. Indicate which of the following expenses should be recorded and saved for possible use in itemizing deductions on schedule A. (Review the list of deductible expenses on page 394 to help you complete this exercise.)

     a. Contributions you made to charitable organizations

     b. Money you spent sending your son to Boy Scout camp

     c. Money you spent on new eyeglasses for your daughter

     d. The cost of uniforms you were required to buy by your employer

     e. The cost of moving to a new home in a better neighborhood when you did not change jobs

     f. The cost of the vacation you took to "get away from it all"

     g. The value of your bicycle, which was stolen and was not insured

     h. The cost of your homeowner's insurance policy

     i. Your union dues

     j. Your YMCA membership fee

     k. The amount of sales tax you paid when you bought a car

     l. The interest you paid on your credit card account

USING NUMBERS

Solve the following problem to help make the best possible choice. Write your solution on a separate sheet of paper. Be sure to show all your work.

In 1990 Gene and Norma were married with two young children. They wanted to know how much money they earned, how much of their earnings they could deduct, and whether they should use form 1040 EZ, 1040 A, or 1040 to file their tax return. Use the following information and the knowledge you gained from this chapter to answer their questions. Explain your choice of the proper form to use.

Together, Gene and Norma earned $43,897 in wages. They also earned $353 in interest from their bank account and $300 in dividends. They had no other income. Here are the expenses that they could report on schedule A. (Check the rules on page 394 for which expenses are deductible.)

$1,970 in medical expenses that were not paid by insurance
$1,132 in property taxes
$1,451 in state income taxes
$2,074 in interest paid on their home mortgage
$200 in charitable contributions
$250 uninsured loss when their car was dented in an accident
$371 in other miscellaneous deductible expenses

PUTTING IDEAS IN YOUR OWN WORDS

The following quotations are from this chapter. Explain these quotations in your own words to make sure you understand what they mean. Write your answers on a separate sheet of paper.

1. "Any person who has had income withheld should file a tax return, even if the earnings were so small that the person isn't required to file by law."
2. "A large part of keeping tax payments as low as is legally possible is a matter of good record keeping."
3. "If a taxpayer has deductible expenses that total more than the standard deduction, he or she should use form 1040 and itemize deductions."

BUILDING CONSUMER KNOWLEDGE

Write your answers for the following exercises on a separate sheet of paper.

1. Complete a form 1040 EZ for yourself. Assume that you earned $6,790 in wages from your job and $214 in interest from your savings account. Assume that $487 was withheld from your earnings for federal income tax.

Review and Enrichment Activities Continued

Your teacher will provide you with a copy of the tax table you may use. Use actual information about yourself to complete the remainder of the form.

2.   Complete a form 1040 A for yourself and your spouse, assuming that you have one child named Gordon. You earned $19,837 in wages, and your spouse earned $15,940. You had interest income of $381 and dividends of $300. You had no other income and no other adjustments to income. Gordon attends the school where your spouse works as a teacher's aide. You have no child care expenses. There was $2,120 withheld from your wages for federal income tax and $1,589 withheld from your spouse's income.

3.   Survey five different adults about the forms they use to complete their income tax. Try to choose people of various ages, filing statuses, and financial situations. *Do not ask them how much they earn or pay*! Ask each adult the following questions. Be prepared to report their answers to your class.

   a.   Do you complete your own tax return, or do you have someone else do it for you?

   b.   In how many of the past five years have you received a refund from the government?

   c.   Do you use form 1040 EZ, 1040 A or 1040?

   d.   Do you file as soon as possible, or do you tend to put off filing until April 15?

   e.   What is your opinion of a person who tries to cheat on their tax and pay less than they really should?

Chapter 25

Budgeting

Chapter Objectives

After completing this chapter, you will be able to do the following:

- Explain how creating and using short-term and long-term personal budgets can help you achieve your financial goals.
- Explain why trade-offs are often necessary between income, spending, and achieving your goals.
- Identify sources you may call on for help in developing and using a personal budget.

Key Consumer Terms

In this chapter you will learn the meanings of the following important consumer terms:

- Budget
- Short-term goal
- Long-term goal
- Fixed expenses
- Flexible expenses
- Luxury
- Receipt
- Equity
- National Foundation for Consumer Credit, Inc.

I magine what your life would be like if you were rich. If you were a famous movie star, businesses might pay you millions of dollars just to use your name. Or you might be a professional athlete. Some basketball and baseball players earn as much as $5 million in a single season. Boxing champions have been paid up to $20 million just for one fight. Executives of large corporations receive salaries and other benefits that total in the millions of dollars. However, even if you earned a large income, you would still need a **budget** to meet your financial goals. There is a limit to what even rich people can buy.

Unfortunately, most people never become wealthy. Typical American consumers need to make and follow financial plans to gain the greatest possible satisfaction from the money they receive. To be successful in managing your money, you must accept responsibility for yourself. You may receive advice from your parents, relatives, friends, or teachers, but in the end it is your money, your responsibility, and your life.

A budget is a projection of income and expenditures for a specific period of time. Personal budgets should be based on a financial plan that reflects an individual's goals and values. In Chapter 20 you completed a personal inventory that included a list of your goals and values. You should use your inventory to help you establish a financial plan for yourself.

SECTION 1

CHOOSING FINANCIAL GOALS

While you read, ask yourself . . .
- ◆ *How many goals do you have that you will be able to achieve without spending money?*
- ◆ *What changes in your priorities will probably take place over the next ten years?*

Review the goals you listed in your personal inventory in Chapter 20. To achieve most of these goals, you will probably need to spend money. Clearly, goals like owning a home or car require money. To achieve long-term goals like getting married, having a family, and saving for a secure retirement, you need to make and follow a financial plan. You will not be able to reach many of your personal goals if you can't afford to buy the goods and services you need or want.

Setting Your Priorities

To prepare your financial plan, start by listing your goals in two ways. First divide your goals into those that are **short-term** (ones you want to achieve within the next few years) and those that are **long-term** (those that will take longer than two or three years to achieve). When you have these two lists, arrange the goals on each list in order of your priorities. To do this, list the most important goal first, the second most important goal next, and so on.

You will probably discover that a number of your short-term goals are related to your long-term goals. Suppose that you want to attend a

◆   Many people have a goal of raising a family. Why does a personal goal like this require people to also set and achieve financial goals?

business school after you graduate from high school. This is a short-term goal. Although the two or three years you would need to achieve this goal may seem like a long time to you now, it is not long compared to the rest of your life. If you achieve this goal, your future income should increase and help you reach long-term goals like owning a home or raising a family.

The Need for a Logical Progression

Making a financial plan involves a logical progression. You should design your plan so that many of your short-term goals contribute to achieving your long-term goals. You should also be sure that your short-term goals don't interfere with your ability to achieve more important long-term goals. Suppose that you decided to use your money to go on a vacation to Florida instead of paying your college tuition. If you did this, you would probably be making a mistake. Satisfying your current desire for a vacation could prevent you from achieving your long-term goals of having a good job and financial security.

Vocabulary Builder

Budget   A plan for spending and saving income; a projection of income and spending over a period of time.

Long-term goal   A goal that one hopes to achieve over a period of time that is greater than several years: life goal.

Short-term goal   A goal that one hopes to achieve over several years or less.

Consumer News

How Much Is Enough?

Do you think you could "scrape" by on just $450,000 a month? It might be a struggle, but that's exactly what Donald Trump had to agree to do to gain roughly $60 million in credit he needed in June 1990. At that time Donald Trump's financial empire included an airline, hotels, a railroad yard, casinos, and a $3.8 billion debt. Although Trump had been very successful through most of the 1980s, his profits began to fall in 1989. He was unable to make payments on many of his loans on time. Trump's creditors told him he would have to cut back on his personal spending from the $583,000 he spent in May 1990 to just $450,000 a month to avoid losing control of his businesses. Even wealthy people need to make and follow budgets to help them live within their means.

studies teacher. As your goals change, you will need to adjust your priorities and your financial plans.

Summing Up   *In choosing your financial goals, it is important to set both short- and long-term goals. There should be a logical progression from the short-term to the long-term goals.* ◆

SECTION 2

DETERMINING YOUR INCOME AND EXPENSES

While you read, ask yourself . . .
- ◆ *What fixed expenses must you pay now?*
- ◆ *As you grow older and have more responsibilities, what is likely to happen to the number of fixed expenses you will need to pay?*

To make a current budget, you need to estimate your income and determine your expenses. You may know exactly what these amounts are for the present. Predicting what they will be in the future is more difficult but no less important.

It is not necessary for every short-term goal to contribute to long-term goals. If you want to own a good-quality bicycle, buying this product now may have no impact on your ability to achieve your long-term goal of having financial security.

Don't think of your priorities as "cast in stone." Your goals will almost certainly change as you grow older. At the present, your most important goal in life may be to become a computer programmer. Ten years from now, you might think that computer programming is boring and decide that you want to be a social

How Much Income Will You Receive?

No one can say for sure how much income he or she will receive in the future, but most people can make a reasonable estimate. You probably have a good idea of the income you will receive in the next two weeks, or even over the next year. The amount of your income five or ten years from now is more difficult to estimate, but will be an important factor in your ability to achieve your long-term goals. You should recognize that many of the decisions you make now will affect your future income.

There are a number of steps you can take now that will probably increase your future income. If you save part of your income every week, you will accumulate money that will earn interest. Saving now may allow you to avoid borrowing and paying interest in the future. Completing courses that provide training, education, or experience may help increase your future earnings. Choosing a job that will help prepare you for a career will also increase your earning power. While you may not be able to predict your exact future income, you can make choices that will help increase its size.

Fixed and Flexible Expenses

There are some expenses you must pay regardless of your income. If you drive, your automobile insurance payment must be made on time. If you rent an apartment, you must pay rent each month. If you take a bus to work, you must pay bus fare. People have little control over their **fixed expenses** in the short run. When a longer period of time is considered, most fixed expenses can be changed into **flexible expenses**. For example, you could stop driving a car and use public transportation to eliminate your need to pay automobile insurance. You could reduce your rent by finding a smaller apartment or by getting a roommate to share its expense. Still, there is a limit to how much most people are able to cut their fixed expenses. There is little advantage to living in poverty now to have more income and wealth than you need in the future.

Some expenses are almost always flexible. Money spent to buy **luxury** items, entertainment, and many consumer goods falls into this category. Suppose that you bought a $100 electronic watch that keeps track of phone numbers and addresses and performs mathematical

◆   Going to a movie is an example of a flexible expense. Although everyone needs some fun and relaxation it is possible to go to a park instead of a movie and to save the price of the ticket.

calculations as well as telling the time. While you may enjoy your purchase, a $15 watch would tell you the time just as well. Most of the price of an expensive watch is a flexible expense because you could have bought a less costly product that would still keep time. Although you may like going to the movies every weekend, they aren't necessary. The same is true of buying new clothes you don't really need or the latest recording by your favorite musical group. Most flexible expenses may be

Vocabulary Builder

Fixed expense A cost that must be paid at specific times, regardless of other events.
Flexible expense A cost that varies, depending on other events.
Luxury A product that is not necessary to maintain one's basic standard of living; demand for these products tends to be sensitive to changes in price.

reduced or eliminated without causing an important change in one's life.

Keeping Good Records

To determine your fixed and flexible expenses, you need to keep accurate records of how you spend your money. Many people say, "I don't know where my money goes, but I never have any left at the end of the week." They are often surprised when they record their expenditures. They find that they are spending money for products that really aren't very important to them. For example, spending an extra 50 cents on a bottle of soda each day at school totals over $90 for the school year. The cost of playing video games at a mall arcade can add up in a hurry. Even buying cosmetics can become very expensive over time.

You can keep track of your spending without having to take a record book with you when you go shopping. Almost all stores provide **receipts** for the purchases you make. Just be sure to save your receipts in one place and record them every so often. For the few cases where you don't receive a receipt for money you spend (like in some school cafeterias), keep a piece of paper in your pocket or purse to record these transactions.

If you use checks or credit cards to make purchases, your bank will provide you with a record of your spending. However, the statements you receive will only include the amount spent—not what you spent it on. People need to keep their own record of what each check or credit purchase was used for. You will learn more about how to use a checking account and make credit card purchases in Chapters 26 and 31.

Summing Up *To develop a personal budget, you need to predict your income and expenses by keeping accurate records. Expenses should be divided into two groups: those that are fixed and those that are flexible.* ◆

CREATING YOUR BUDGET

While you read, ask yourself . . .
◆ *How much time do you spend keeping track of your income and spending?*
◆ *Have you ever been surprised to find how little money you have left from your income?*
◆ *Do you try to save? If you do, how successful are you? If you don't, why not?*

Once you complete your record of current spending, you need to identify each type of expense as fixed or flexible and evaluate it in terms of its importance to your current lifestyle and to your ability to achieve future financial goals. Remember, reaching your financial goals involves a logical progression. What you do today affects what you are able to do tomorrow. Keep your priorities in mind as you prepare your budget.

Constructing a One-Month Budget Worksheet

Your first task in preparing a long-term budget is to construct a short-term budget worksheet as a way to test your ideas and understanding of your income and expenditures. Construct a form similar to the one shown in Figure 25-1 to help you predict your income and expenses. Adjust your worksheet to include your sources of income and expenses. When you are satisfied with your worksheet, fill it in, estimating your income and expenditures.

The income side should be easy to complete. You may receive income from wages, an allowance from interest you earn on a savings account, or from many other sources.

ONE MONTH BUDGET WORKSHEET

Estimated Income	Estimated Fixed and Flexible Expenses	

			Fixed or Flexible
Wages _____	Food	_____	_____
Allowances _____	Transportation	_____	_____
Other _____	Clothing	_____	_____
	Personal	_____	_____
Total Income _____	Recreation	_____	_____
	Other	_____	_____
	Total Expenses	_____	
	Difference	_____	

◆ **Figure 25-1** Completing one month budget worksheets may help you gain an understanding of your spending habits. This is an important step in creating a long-term budget that will help you achieve your financial goals.

Your next step is to prepare a list of the expenses you must pay and other types of spending you expect to carry out. Use a record of spending like the one described earlier to help you do this. Total the spending you intend to carry out, and compare this amount with your expected income. If your estimated income is greater than your expected spending, you will have money left over to save at the end of the month. If you don't expect to have money left over to save, you need to evaluate each type of spending you are considering. You should reduce or eliminate some flexible expenses so that you can save for the future. You can also try to find additional sources of income.

After completing your trial budget, try to follow it as closely as possible for a month. This will require you to keep an ongoing record of money you spend and may force you to give up some spending you might like to carry out. Being aware of your budget will

Vocabulary Builder

Receipt   A document that is given to a customer at the time a product is sold and which acts as proof of purchase.

Consumer News

Taking the Train Saves More Than Money

Would you consider taking a bus, train or public transportation instead of owning a car to save time and money? Americans paid an average of between $5,000 and $6,000 for each car they owned in 1990. By not owning a car, consumers would save the costs of insurance, gasoline, maintenance, and buying a new car every few years.

There are other reasons to take public transportation. If you lived in Los Angeles in 1990, the average speed you could drive on the freeways was 35 miles per hour. Remember, at 2 A.M. cars were able to drive the speed limit. To have an average of 35 mph, cars had to go much slower at other times. In addition, the number of cars on the road is growing every day. There will be an estimated 40 percent increase in traffic on the highways by the year 2010. How much do you like sitting in traffic?

To make it easier for commuters to use mass transit, a new electric train system is being built in Los Angeles. The first 17 miles were completed in 1991. The project will total over 150 miles when it is completed sometime in the next century.

help you limit your spending to the goods and services you need the most.

At the end of the month, compare your actual income and spending with your budget. You may find that you allocated too much money for some types of spending and too little for others. Make adjustments in your budget and try it again for another month. Eventually you will develop an understanding of your income and spending habits.

Developing a Long-Term Budget

Preparing a long-term budget is a more complex task because it includes a wider range of expenses and requires more estimates of future income and needs. However, long-term budgets offer great benefits to people who carry them out. A long-term budget is an important part of your lifetime plan. It can help you organize your income and spending to allow saving and investing for your future. When you become satisfied that you know what your current income and expenses are likely to be, you should use this understanding and your knowledge of your financial goals to create a long-term budget.

Remember that achieving long-term goals involves a logical progression. The financial decisions you make today will affect the income you earn in the future. In preparing your long-term budget, be careful that your short-term decisions do not prevent you from achieving your long-term goals.

Suppose that you want to own a car but can't afford to buy and maintain one with your current income. To pay for the car, you would need to find a new job and work longer hours. This could interfere with your ability to study and earn good grades in school. If you have good grades, you might win a scholarship that would increase your future income. Therefore, by deciding not to work long hours to pay for a car, but to study more instead, you will be taking steps to achieve your long-term goals and budget. In a way, you are paying for the time you need to study.

Consumer Close-Up

Can You Afford to Have Kids?

Try to picture yourself ten years from now. Do you see yourself as a parent with several "little ones" to take care of? If you are like most Americans, you expect to have children someday. We all know that children are expensive to raise, but many would-be parents don't understand just how expensive their family will be.

If we start with the basic needs, in 1990 the U.S. Department of Agriculture estimated that it would cost an average of $265,000 to feed and clothe a child to the age of twenty-two. Parents often pay an average of $6,000 a year for day care for each of their children until they reach school age. Then the average yearly expense drops to $2,500. Parents must add to these basic costs many other expenses, such as the cost of toys, health care, extra cars and insurance payments, and vacations. Estimates of the total cost of raising a child to the age of twenty-two ran between a low of about $350,000 to as much as $750,000 in 1990. The most important reason for the different amounts was the cost of private education.

The high cost of raising children has made dramatic changes in how Americans budget their income. In 1960 the average American family had 3.7 children and spent 28 percent of their income to provide for children's needs. By 1990 this average had increased to 35 percent, even though the average family had only two children. For families that were sending children to private colleges, the percentage of income devoted to their support was as high as 57 percent. Economists believe that the smaller size of American families is at least partially the result of the high cost of raising children.

If you want to have a family, you need to plan a budget that will allow you to support your children and give them the kind of life you want them to have. Remember, being a good parent means more than buying your children lots of "things." Raising children requires your time. You need to "budget" time for trips to the zoo or for teaching the baby to walk. These are often the most rewarding hours for a parent. However, every hour spent with your children is an hour that you will not be able to spend earning an income. Children affect family budgets in two ways. They cause families to change their spending habits, and they often bring about reduced family income.

It appears that this rapid growth in the cost of raising children will continue into the future. Government projections show that more children will require day care and that an increasing number of children will be sent to private schools. The cost of buying a house that is large enough for children will continue to grow. The number of "high-tech" and expensive toys children demand will increase. College and trade school costs are expected to continue to grow at a rapid rate. Many companies are requiring employees to make contributions to the cost of health insurance. Therefore, the cost of medical care is likely to increase.

This information is not intended to keep you from having children. It is intended to convince you to plan a budget that will help you pay for your children's needs. Having enough money won't guarantee your family a life of love and happiness. But it does help.

A long-term budget can help you get an overview of your spending habits and their relationship to your ability to achieve your goals. You should develop a worksheet for your long-term budget that is similar to the one you used for your monthly budget. Make sure that the worksheet you use is suited to your income, expenditures, and goals. Expect to adjust this form as you grow older and your needs change.

Budgets Change Over Time

Every successful budget requires periodic review. When you consider your income and spending, you should realize that many of these amounts will vary from month to month. If your car's transmission breaks down and costs $750 to be repaired, this cost will only appear in one month. If you work many hours of overtime in the Christmas shopping season, your higher level of income will not last past December. You can avoid making mistakes in your budget if you realize that some changes in income and expenditures are permanent, while others are temporary.

It is important to rethink your budget process as your needs change. For example, when you are a student, your clothing budget might be quite small. If you take a job in a bank after you graduate, you will probably need to spend much more on clothing to dress appropriately for your job. If you take a job in another community, you may need to use money to buy a car and pay for gasoline. A budget is part of your financial plan for your life. It should be adjusted as your plans and life change.

Summing Up   *To develop a long-term budget, start with a one-month budget worksheet for projecting income and expenses. Knowledge gained from this short-term budget may be used to construct a long-term budget. As your needs change over time, expect to adjust your budget.* ◆

SECTION 4

FITTING YOUR BUDGET INTO YOUR FUTURE

***While you read**, ask yourself . . .*
- ◆ *What items have you bought that you think will still be valuable to you five years from now?*
- ◆ *What items have you decided not to buy so that you can have more money to use in the future?*
- ◆ *Would you take a job that required you to work 24 hours a week during school and that paid $10 an hour?*

Your long-term budget is part of your overall plan for your future. Many of the long-term goals you want to achieve will affect the way you should prepare your current budget.

Trade-Offs Between Income, Expenditures, and Goals

Consider several of your most important long-term goals from the personal inventory you completed in Chapter 20. Many of these goals can only be achieved by careful planning. For example, if you want to own a large home in a better section of town, you might consider buying a small home in a less desirable location first. This will allow you to build value, or **equity**, in a home that can be used to help you buy a better home in the future. If you do this, there will be a trade-off between present and future goals. Buying a small home now may prevent you from renting a nice apartment, but could help purchase the home you want in the future.

If your goal is to manage a restaurant in a fine hotel someday, you could start by working at a hamburger stand in a shopping mall. You might say, "But I can earn more money by taking a different type of job." And you might be right. However, the experience you gain from working at a hamburger stand might be more valuable in terms of reaching your goal than the extra income you could earn from a different job. Still, taking the job with lower income will have an impact on your current budget and ability to spend. You would trade current income for a better chance of reaching your long-term goal.

If you want to have children, you should realize that they are very expensive. The cost of having a family goes beyond buying diapers and formula. It includes the cost of extra doctor bills, buying food in restaurants when you go on vacation, and saving for your children's future needs. Having children requires parents to look after them or pay for someone else to watch them. A two-income couple will experience a dramatic change in their ability to earn money and make expenditures when they have their first child. Most people want to have children. When they do, they are trading the rewards of parenthood for income and expenditures that they otherwise could have made. People who are parents have a particular need to make careful budgets for their family.

The National Foundation for
    Consumer Credit, Inc.
8701 Georgia Avenue, Suite 507
Silver Spring, MD 20910

Many communities have local budget assistance programs. You may find these organizations by inquiring at a bank or by calling educational institutions.

In recent years many computer software packages have been developed that can help you create a budget. Although there are excellent programs available, be sure that any program you buy fits your current needs and the needs you are likely to have in the next few years. Many colleges and school systems offer noncredit courses in personal budget computing that could be a wise investment of your time and money. More will be said of computer programs for consumer use in Chapter 39.

Summing Up   *A long-term budget should help you achieve your personal goals. This may require you to make trade-offs between current income and gaining knowledge or experience that can help you reach your goals. There are a number of sources you may use to receive help in creating a useful budget.* ◆

Getting Help

If you have difficulty with budgeting or debt management, there are many places you can go for assistance. Probably the best-known source for individual budget help is the **National Foundation for Consumer Credit, Inc.**, which coordinates roughly 400 Consumer Credit Services offices in the United States. You may find the nearest office by looking in the white pages of your telephone book or by writing to:

Vocabulary Builder

Equity   The value of an owner's investment in a business or house.
National Foundation for Consumer Credit, Inc.   An organization that helps consumers develop personal budgets through consumer credit service offices in many cities.

Review and Enrichment Activities

VOCABULARY REVIEW

1. Column A contains key consumer terms from this chapter. Column B contains a scrambled list of phrases that describe what these terms mean. Match the correct meaning with each term. Write your answers on a separate sheet of paper.

Column A	Column B
1. Short-term goal	a. A projection of income and expenditures for a specific period of time
2. Equity	b. A good that is considered to be the best and most costly
3. Long-term goal	c. Value of ownership that is built up in a good: often a house
4. Receipt	d. A record of a purchase that is given by a seller to a buyer
5. Luxury	e. Something one seeks to achieve over an extended period of time
6. Budget	f. An organization that helps consumers develop individual budgets
7. National Foundation for Consumer Credit	g. Something one seeks to achieve over a short period of time

2. Explain the difference between a fixed and a flexible expense.

CHECKING WHAT YOU'VE LEARNED

Write your answers for the following exercises on a separate sheet of paper.

1. Why should you expect different people with the same income to have different budgets?

2. Explain why short-term goals often contribute to achieving long-term goals.
3. Why do people need to set priorities for their goals?
4. Why is there often a logical progression of goals?
5. Why shouldn't a person think of his or her priorities and goals as being "cast in stone"?
6. Describe three fixed and three flexible expenses that your family pays.
7. Explain why keeping good records is important to having a budget.
8. Why should you construct a one-month budget worksheet before you attempt to complete a long-term budget?
9. Why do all budgets require a periodic review?
10. Describe a situation that demonstrates how giving up current income could help a person achieve a long-term financial goal.
11. Explain why people who have families have a particular need to complete and follow budgets.
12. What is the most widely known organization that offers assistance to people in preparing their budgets?

PRACTICING YOUR CONSUMER SKILLS

Write your answers for the following exercises on a separate sheet of paper.

1. Explain how the following people would benefit from making and using a budget.
    a. Carolyn has a job that pays well, and she has few fixed expenses. She plans to get married next year. At the end of each week she has almost no money left and doesn't know where it's gone.
    b. Nick has lived with his parents all his life. He has worked for several years and earns a respectable income. He used his savings to put a down payment on a house he will move into next month.
    c. Scott and Christine have been married for seven years. They have both had jobs most of this time and have been able to buy most things they wanted quickly. They are expecting their first child in five months.
    d. Shawn has worked all his life and made good money most of the time. He has managed to save about $50,000 and will receive both Social Security and a small pension when he retires next year. He expects his retirement income to be about 75 percent of what he earns this year.
    e. Helen has decided to quit her job as a secretary and go back to school to study elementary education. She wants to be a teacher but believes that she will need three years of college to complete her degree. Her husband Bill will keep his job as assistant manager of a grocery store.

Review and Enrichment Activities Continued

2. Charles works as a mechanic in a garage. He has held this job for eight years and has become convinced that the only way he will ever advance his career is to return to school and complete a business degree. He wants to save an extra $250 a month for the next year to help pay tuition at a local community college.

Identify each of the underscored expenses as either fixed or flexible. In your opinion, which of these expenses should he leave alone, and which should he reduce or eliminate? Explain your choices.

   a. Charles <u>rents</u> an apartment for $490 a month.
   b. Charles pays $800 in <u>dues</u> each year to a golf club. He tries to play at least 18 holes every week. Each time he plays, he must pay a $10 fee and rent a cart for $15.
   c. Charles runs his air conditioner almost all the time because he hates coming home to a stuffy house. His <u>electric bill</u> is usually about $320 every two months.
   d. Charles pays $1,100 each year for <u>car insurance</u>. He could reduce the coverage and save $400 a year, but if he had an accident, he would have to pay to have his car repaired.
   e. Charles doesn't like to cook, so he eats out most of the time. He spends an average of $75 a week on <u>meals</u> in restaurants.

3. Explain why you believe that the following choices will help or hurt the person's chance of achieving his or her long-term goal.

   a. Stan is a high school senior who wants to own his own photography shop someday. He was offered an after-school job in a shoe store that would have paid him $7 an hour. He turned down the job so that he could be a student photographer for the school yearbook.
   b. Lisa lives with her parents, but someday she wants to have a farm in the country and a big family. Six months ago she took a job in a boot factory that pays her well. She spends most of her money buying clothes and making payments on a new car.
   c. José would like to have a job that allows him to travel. He speaks both English and Spanish. He decided to sign up to take French in night school. The class will cost him $600 a semester that he could have spent on other products he would have enjoyed.
   d. Rita used to dream of owning a marina and renting slips where people could dock their boats. She completed two years of college by working in a small restaurant. In her junior year she married her employer and now has two children.
   e. Linda would like to learn how to repair airplane engines. She joined the air force, although she was offered a full scholarship at a local community college.

USING NUMBERS

Solve the following problem to help make the best possible choice. Write your solution on a separate sheet of paper. Be sure to show all your work.

Alex is 21 years old and is an assistant manager of a fastfood restaurant in St. Paul, Minnesota. He receives a paycheck every two weeks for $527.14, but always runs out of money before he is paid. He has decided to make and follow a budget because he wants to be able to save at least $100 a month so that he can put a down payment on a new car next year. To accomplish this, he has started keeping a record of all his expenses. His record for September is given here. Identify each expense as fixed or flexible (some expenses may be a little of each). What was his total for each type of expense in September? How much larger was his spending than his income? Which of these expenses are likely to change in the next few months? Identify three expenses you believe Alex could cut back on. Explain your choices.

Alex's Expenses for September

Groceries	$182.79
Gasoline	$ 72.60
Auto Insurance	
($\frac{1}{12}$ of year's total)	$121.98
Rent	$350.00
Utilities	$ 89.63
Entertainment	$122.42
Renter's insurance	
($\frac{1}{12}$ of year's total)	$ 12.34
Eating out	$ 72.19
Other	$ 35.68

PUTTING IDEAS IN YOUR OWN WORDS

The following quotations are from this chapter. Explain these quotations in your own words to make sure you understand what they mean. Write your answers on a separate sheet of paper.

1. "To be successful in managing your money, you must accept responsibility for yourself."
2. "A long-term budget is an important part of your lifetime plan."
3. "People who are parents have a particular need to make careful budgets for their family."

Review and Enrichment Activities Continued

BUILDING CONSUMER KNOWLEDGE

Write your answers for the following exercises on a separate sheet of paper.

1. Survey five adults. Ask them whether or not they keep a personal budget. Ask them to explain why they chose to keep, or not keep, a budget.

2. Use the personal inventory you prepared in Chapter 20 to make lists of your short-term and long-term goals. Prioritize each list from most valuable goal to least important goal. Write a paragraph that explains the relationship between these goals and your need to construct and use a personal budget.

3. Identify local sources of assistance that people may use to prepare their personal budgets. Contact one of these sources to ask for information about the specific services offered. Write an essay that explains the information you find.

Chapter 26

How Consumers Use Checking Accounts

Chapter Objectives

After completing this chapter, you will be able to do the following:

- Explain how to use a checking account.
- Explain the benefits and costs associated with different types of checking accounts that consumers may open and use.
- Explain the importance of keeping an accurate record of all deposits and checks written.
- Explain how checking accounts can help consumers achieve their financial goals.

Key Consumer Terms

In this chapter you will learn the meanings of the following important consumer terms:

- Commercial bank
- Savings and loan association
- Savings bank
- Minimum balance
- Service charge
- Maintenance fee
- Check register
- Insufficient funds
- Statement
- Outstanding check
- Electronic fund transfer
- Stop payment
- Automated teller machine (ATM)

H ow would you feel about carrying $20,000 or more around with you in cash? Would you be a little nervous? The largest value of paper money in circulation is the $100 bill. If you could afford to pay $20,000 in cash for a new car, you would need 200 of these $100 bills. Your money would be rather bulky. Imagine what it would be like if large firms paid million-dollar debts with currency. They would need a truck to carry all the money. Completing large, or even small, transactions is often much easier with checks. You may want to remind yourself of the ways in which checks are important to our economic system by reviewing Chapter 6.

Banks are in business to earn a profit. It costs banks money to offer checking services. They must pay employees to keep track of deposits and the checks that customers write. Banks need a way to generate income from checking accounts to pay their costs and earn a profit. The method of generating income will vary from institution to institution, but it will always be there. Banks are eager to have your checking business because they expect to earn a profit from your deposits and the checks that you write. As a responsible consumer, you must carefully choose the type of checking account that best suits your needs.

S E C T I O N   1

CHOOSING WHERE TO OPEN YOUR CHECKING ACCOUNT

While you read, *ask yourself . . .*
- *Do you now use a particular bank? If so, why do you use this bank?*
- *How often would you use a checking account if you had one? How often are you likely to use a checking account five years from now?*

Many types of institutions offer checking accounts to the public. There was a time when people could open checking accounts only at **commercial banks.** However, negotiable order of withdrawal (NOW) accounts are now offered by **savings and loan associations** and **savings banks.** Consumers may also open share draft accounts at credit unions. (All of these institutions will be called banks in this chapter to avoid repetition.) All of these accounts work essentially the same way. Consumers deposit money in their accounts and have the right to write checks to demand the use of their money at any time.

Benefits and Costs of Checking Accounts

Consumers may benefit from opening checking accounts that pay interest. Until the early 1970s, money deposited in checking accounts earned no interest. After that time, changes in bank regulations allowed greater competition between banks and other financial institutions. One result of this competition has been the creation of checking accounts that pay interest. To earn interest from a checking account, consumers are usually required to maintain a **minimum balance** that can range from as little as several hundred dollars to more than $2,000. Some checking accounts pay a fixed rate of interest, while others pay rates that go up or down with other interest rates.

To be able to pay depositors interest, banks must have a way to generate income from checking accounts. The most obvious source of income for banks is from loans that they make with the money that is deposited by customers. In 1992 banks were required to keep 10 percent of money deposited in checking accounts on reserve (see Chapter 6). They could loan out the remaining 90 percent. The interest rate that banks charge borrowers is greater than the interest rate paid to depositors. Banks use the difference between the two rates to pay their expenses and earn a profit.

Banks have other ways of earning income from checking accounts. They often require depositors to pay a **service charge** for each check written that is typically from 10 to 20 cents. Some banks have a monthly **maintenance fee** that may be from $2 to $5. These amounts may seem relatively small. However, when you consider the fact that banks may have several hundred thousand checking accounts and may process millions of checks every month, you will realize how important these fees are to banks.

Choosing Your Bank

When you are trying to decide which bank to choose for your checking account, you need to comparison shop the same way you would if you were buying a car or refrigerator. You need to find out what each bank's service charge is, the monthly maintenance fee, the interest rate that each pays, and what the minimum balance is to earn interest. When you consider bank policies, you must also think about your own financial situation. A good interest rate is only a benefit if you can receive it by meeting the minimum balance requirement.

Suppose that you are considering opening a checking account at one of two banks. You believe that you would write an average of ten checks in a typical month. You don't earn much money and would find it difficult to have an average balance that is much larger than $250.

If you open an account at bank A, you will be charged 10 cents for each check you write and a $2 monthly maintenance fee. There is no minimum balance requirement, and the account pays no interest. The account would cost you about $3 each month.

Bank B has no service charge or monthly fee for customers who keep a $750 average balance. It also pays 5 percent annual interest. However, if a customer's average balance falls below $750, bank B charges 20 cents per check and a $3 monthly maintenance fee, and it would pay no interest. Opening an account at bank B would cost you about $5 each month

Vocabulary Builder

Commercial bank A bank that offers a wide range of banking services; its main functions are to accept deposits, lend money, and transfer funds.

Maintenance fee A fee charged to keep an account open; often associated with checking accounts.

Minimum balance The smallest amount that can be kept on deposit in a bank account to receive a service.

Savings and loan association A depository institution that accepts deposits and lends money. Until recently, S&Ls could only make loans for home buying or improvements.

Savings bank A depository institution that accepts deposits and lends money; similar to savings and loan associations.

Service charge A fee charged by banks or other organizations for providing a service; often associated with checking accounts.

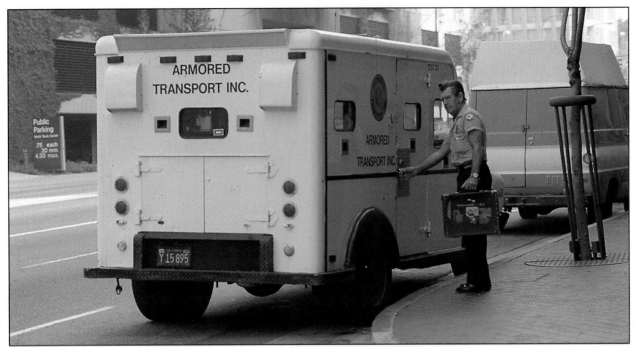

◆   Using checks to pay bills relieves consumers of the need to carry large amounts of money. Banks and other financial services are better equipped to transport and deal in cash than typical consumers.

because you probably would not be able to meet its minimum balance requirement.

Customers who are able to keep a $750 average balance should use bank B because they would not pay any fees and would earn interest on their deposits. People who are not able to maintain the minimum balance should choose bank A's account, even though it pays no interest.

When you choose a bank, also consider its location, its reputation for prompt, friendly service, and the attitude of its employees. It is sometimes better to accept a little less income to receive friendly, reliable service.

Summing Up   *There are many different ways consumers may open checking accounts that may result in service charges, maintenance fees, or free checking. The best arrangement for consumers depends on their needs and the amount of money they are able to keep in their account.* ◆

SECTION 2

USING YOUR CHECKING ACCOUNT

While you read, *ask yourself . . .*
- *What types of checks have you received?*
- *How would you benefit from having a checking account?*

Although you probably know how to endorse and cash a check, most high school students do not have checking accounts and have never written a check. This is something you will need to learn to do in the next few years.

Keeping a Check Register

When you first open your checking account, the bank will give you a small book of checks,

Consumer News

When Can I Have My Money?

Imagine wanting to write a check drawn on money you deposited in your checking account two weeks ago and being told you couldn't. In the past this often happened. Some banks made customers wait for weeks to use their money when they deposited a check drawn on a bank in another part of the country. This was changed when Congress passed the Expedited Funds Availability Act.

Starting on September 1, 1988, banks were required to allow customers the use of their money based on the following schedule. Some states require even shorter waiting periods.

Type of Deposit	When the Funds Must Be Available
Cash The first $100 of any deposit of checks	The next business day after the day of deposit

Type of Deposit	When the Funds Must Be Available
Government, cashier's, certified, and teller's checks Checks written on another account in the same institution Direct deposits and other electronic transfers	The next business day after the day of deposit
Checks written on local institutions	The third business day after the day of deposit (changed to second business day in 1990)
Checks written on nonlocal institutions Deposits made at an automated teller machine not belonging to the institution	The seventh business day after the day of deposit (changed to fifth business day in 1990)

deposit slips, and a **check register**. These are temporary documents that you may use until printed ones with your name and address can be prepared and sent to you.

It is very important for you to keep accurate and complete records of all your deposits and all the checks that you write in your check register. If you fail to do this and write a check that is returned for **insufficient funds**, you will be charged from $10 to $30 for each "bounced check." If this happens too often,

Vocabulary Builder

Check register The portion of a checkbook where one keeps a record of the checks written and remaining balance.

Insufficient funds Not enough money in a checking account to cover a check written against that account.

you will damage your credit history, and businesses will refuse to accept your checks. If you deliberately write checks that exceed the balance in your account, you can be charged with a crime, brought to trial, convicted, and be fined or sent to jail. Using a checking account requires a mature attitude and a sense of responsibility.

Every time you write a check, enter the check number, date, description of transaction, amount of the check, and any fee in your register first. Then subtract the amount of the check and fee from your balance to determine your new balance. Do this *before* you write the check so that you won't forget to do it later. After you have completed your register entry, you should then write your check.

When you make a deposit, follow the same procedure, except add the deposit to your previous balance. The bank teller will give you a receipt for your deposit. *Always* check to see that the receipt is for the correct amount, and then save the receipt. If there is ever any question about the amount of a deposit, you will need your receipt to prove when a deposit was made and its amount. If you don't check your deposit slips for accuracy and keep them in a safe place, you are asking for trouble.

Writing a Check

When you write a check, be sure to write clearly in ink so that your check cannot be easily changed. Your checks should contain the following six items:

1. *Check number.* Check numbers are usually printed in sequence in the upper right-hand corner of the checks. If your checks are not printed with numbers, you should write the numbers in this location and record them in your register.
2. *Date.* The current date should include the day, month, and year and should appear below the check number in the upper right-hand corner.
3. *Payee.* The person, business, or organization to whom the payment is being made is called the payee. The name should be written on the line following the words "pay to the order of."
4. *Amount.* The amount is written twice, once in figures and once in words. Write the amount to the far left on your check so that extra numbers cannot be added later. Draw a line to the right between the amount and the word "dollars" to prevent your check from being altered.
5. *Purpose.* Most checks have a line in the lower left-hand corner for recording the purpose of the payment. It usually follows the word "memo" or "for." When paying bills, it's a good idea to put your account number here. Put your Social Security number here when you are making tax payments.
6. *Signature.* You must sign your checks the same way you signed your application and signature card when you opened your checking account. If you opened your account as Charles A. Johnson, don't sign your checks "Chuck Johnson."

At least two other numbers appear on every check. In the upper right-hand corner there is a number that looks like a fraction. This is the number of the bank that the check is drawn on. In the lower left-hand corner is your account number. These numbers are important to banks because they allow them to transfer funds from the appropriate account in the correct bank.

Balancing Your Checkbook

It is important to keep an accurate record of the checks you write and deposits you make so that you know the balance in your account. It

Consumers in Action

You Don't Have to Use Checks to Send Money

Imagine your car breaking down in Winnemucca, Nevada, while you are on a coast-to-coast trip. You have used your credit card up to its limit and you're running short on cash. You need $200 to have your car repaired and another $100 or so to get to California. You call your parents for help. They agree to help, but how can they send you the money you need in a hurry? Actually it's not a problem. There are a number of ways to move money quickly if you are willing to pay.

Probably the least expensive way to send cash, if it isn't needed immediately, is to buy and send a postal money order. In 1991 postal money orders cost 75 cents to $1 each for amounts up to $700. They could be sent by Express Mail for $10 to arrive the next day. When delivered, these documents could be taken to any post office to be cashed. You simply endorse them much as you would a check. Some banks, drug stores, and supermarkets also sell money orders for fees that range between $1 and $2.

If you need to send money faster, you may have your bank wire money to another bank and receive it the same day if the request is made before noon. Both sending and receiving banks charge a fee for this service that is usually between $10 and $20. You may also charge a funds transfer to a credit card. Western Union provides this type of service over the telephone 24 hours a day, seven days a week. For this service, you will pay a fee to Western Union of between $25 and $40 and at least one month's interest on your credit card. American Express offers a similar service for about the same cost to its credit card holders. Both Western Union and American Express are able to transfer funds as quickly as in 15 minutes.

It is possible to send money quickly when necessary, but it is expensive. It is better to take enough cash or traveler's checks on a trip to avoid the need for such transfers. But it's nice to know you can have money sent quickly if you need to.

---

is equally important to compare your records with those of your bank. When you have a checking account, you will receive a **statement** of your account every month. Your statement will include most of the following information:

- Your balance at the beginning of the month

Vocabulary Builder

Statement   A document that reports transactions in an account over a period of time.

- A record of deposits made during the month
- A record of checks paid during the month
- A record of funds transferred to other accounts
- A record of payments made at your request (for example, to pay for a safety deposit box or insurance)
- Service charges and/or interest earned
- Your balance at the end of the month

When you receive your statement, you should check it against your own records to see that all deposits that you made are credited correctly to your account and that all checks that your bank paid were for the appropriate amounts. It is possible that some checks you wrote were not cashed during the month. They are still **outstanding** and will be paid in a future month. Therefore, it is possible for the bank to provide you with a correct balance that is different from your own. You should also adjust your records for any interest you have earned or special payments that were made.

If you discover that your records do not agree with those of your bank, you know that either you or your bank has made a mistake. Checking your records usually reveals that you have made the error. However, this is not always the case. Bank employees also make mistakes from time to time. A deposit you made could have been improperly entered in the bank's electronic data system. The amount could be wrong, or it could have been credited

◆   Consumers who use checking accounts need to balance their accounts and compare their records with those supplied in their bank statement. Why is it important for consumers to check and keep all of their deposit receipts?

Consumer News

Electronic Funds Transfer

Suppose that it is Sunday afternoon and all the banks in your community are closed. You have been looking for a used car for months and find just the right one. But the current owner demands a $500 down payment to hold the car for you or he may sell it to someone else. You would be happy to write him a check, but you only have $132.17 in your checking account. What can you do? Twenty years ago you might have had a problem. Today the solution is simple.

All you need to do is go to the nearest **automated teller machine (ATM)** and complete an **electronic funds transfer (EFT)** from your savings account to your checking account. Electronic funds transfer is the technical name for the movement of money from one account to another by computer. To complete an EFT, you need a special card that has your account number and other information on a strip of magnetic tape that the ATM reads, as well as a personal identification number (PIN) that you type into the machine to verify who you are. No cash changes hands, but by completing the EFT, you will be able to write your check without fear of it bouncing. In effect, we now have 24-hour, seven-day-a-week banking.

to the wrong account. Your account might have been charged for more than the check you wrote. Banks do not make mistakes intentionally, but mistakes do happen. Being able to find mistakes is one advantage of keeping accurate records of all your checking transactions.

If You Find a Mistake

If you discover a difference between your records and the bank's, examine your own records and computations first. Calling your bank when the mistake is yours can be embarrassing and a waste of the bank employee's time. When you are sure that a mistake was made by your bank, either call or visit your branch office. Many banks employ workers who are specially trained to help depositors with checking problems. Politely explain the situation as you understand it.

Disputes between banks and their depositors are almost always resolved quickly and easily when customers keep complete records. This is one reason it is so important to examine and keep all receipts for the deposits you make. Suppose that you deposited $243.20 but were credited with $24.32. If you have your receipt from that deposit, you can resolve the problem quickly. If you have lost or thrown the receipt away, you may never receive credit for the missing $218.88.

If you are not able to resolve a dispute with your bank, you should contact the appropriate regulatory agency. Study Figure 26-1 to find the agency that regulates your type of bank.

Summing Up *Consumers need to maintain complete and accurate records of their checking transactions. They should be sure to compare bank statements with their account registers and find and correct any differences.* ◆

Vocabulary Builder

Automated teller machine (ATM) A machine placed in convenient locations and used by consumers to complete many banking transactions.

Electronic Funds Transfer (EFT) Financial transactions completed through the use of a computer.

Outstanding check A check that has not been presented for payment at a bank.

WHERE TO FILE UNRESOLVED COMPLAINTS AGAINST YOUR BANK

Type of Bank	Identification Marks	Where to Complain
National bank	The word "national" appears in the bank's name, or the initials N.A. appear after the bank's name.	Consumer Activities Division Comptroller of the Currency 190 L'Enfant Plaza East, S.W. Washington, DC 20219 (202) 287-4265
State bank, member Federal Reserve, FDIC insured	Look for two signs at the bank: "Member, Federal Reserve System" and Deposits Insured by Federal Deposit, Insurance Corporation."	Consumer Affairs Board of Governors Federal Reserve System 20th St. and Constitution Ave., N.W. Washington, DC 20551 (202) 452-3946
State nonmember bank or state-chartered mutual savings bank	FDIC sign will be displayed; Federal Reserve sign will not.	Office of Consumer Programs Federal Deposit Insurance Corporation 550 17th St., N.W. Washington, DC 20429 (800) 424-5488 or (202) 898-3536
Federal savings and loan association	A sign on the door or in the lobby featuring an eagle surrounded by the words, "Backed by the full faith and credit of the United States Government."	Office of Thrift Supervision Office of Community and Consumer Division 17th and G Sts., N.W. Washington, DC 20552 (202) 377-6000
Federal credit union	Sign will be displayed reading "Member, National Credit Union Administration."	National Credit Union Administration Office of Public and Congressional Affairs 1776 G St., N.W. Washington, DC 20456 (202) 357-1050

◆ **Figure 26-1**   Where to File Unresolved Complaints Against Your Bank

SECTION 3

BENEFITS AND COSTS OF USING CHECKING ACCOUNTS

While you read, *ask yourself . . .*
◆ *What types of payments do members of your family make with checks?*
◆ *How much more difficult would it be to complete these transactions using cash?*

As in most economic decisions, the choice to open and use a checking account involves benefits and costs. It is clear that the benefits of using a checking account are greater than the costs because most of the money spent in our economy is spent by means of checks.

The Benefits of Using Checks

Probably the greatest advantage of having a checking account is that it reduces the amount

◆ Although paying bills with checks is convenient and safe having and using a checking account costs money. Why wouldn't it make sense to buy a single loaf of bread with a check?

of currency you need to keep on hand to carry out transactions. Holding large amounts of currency can be dangerous and inconvenient. Using checks also provides you with a positive record of the payments that you make.

Suppose that you pay your electric bill in cash and lose your receipt. If the electric company fails to record the transaction, you have no proof of your payment. However, if you pay with a check, your bank will keep a record of your payments. You will be able to show your canceled check as proof that you made your payment.

Spending money with a check is safer because only the person or organization that the check is made out to can legally cash it. If you write a check that is lost or stolen and someone

cashes it, the bank or business that paid the money is responsible for the loss. It is often possible to trace a person who illegally cashes a check because they are usually required to provide some form of identification. This is particularly valuable when sending payments through the mail. You should never mail cash. If you do, you will have no proof that your payment ever arrived. If you send a check, your payment will be recorded on your monthly statement.

There may be an occasion when you want to **stop payment** on a check. Suppose that you buy a bicycle and find that several parts are broken when you get it home. If you paid for the product with a check, you can call your bank and ask them not to pay the check when it is presented to them. There is a fee for this service that ranges between $10 and $20. Also, this must be done immediately, because once a payment has been made, it can no longer be stopped. However, if you paid in cash, you would have no opportunity to stop the payment at all.

Another benefit of using checks is the interest that many checking accounts pay. If you have an average balance of $500 in a checking account that pays 5 percent interest, you will earn an extra $25 a year. This is not an enormous amount of money, but it is money you would not have if you held the money in cash.

Keeping a checking account also becomes part of your financial history. If you ask to borrow $10,000 to buy a car, a bank may be more willing to make the loan if you have been a reliable checking customer for a number of years.

The Costs of Using Checks

Probably the greatest problem of using checks is the inconvenience of writing them out and keeping records. If you are only buying a quart of milk and a loaf of bread, it is easier to pay in cash. Also, some stores either don't accept checks or take a long time to have a check approved.

Some people might be better off not using checks if they have little self-control. It is difficult to spend cash that you don't have, but you can write a check when your balance is too small to cover your payment. If a consumer does not keep good records, having a checking account may cause considerable trouble and expense.

Having a checking account costs money. If you can't afford to keep a minimum balance, you will be required to pay a service charge, a maintenance fee, or possibly both. Even if your checking account pays interest, the money would earn more interest in other types of accounts. People who have little money may be better off financially if they don't have a checking account.

Although there are some costs of keeping a checking account, most adults choose to have them. As you grow older and your financial responsibilities increase, you will probably open a checking account of your own. When you do, it is important to choose the type of account that best suits your needs. Regardless of where you open your account, you must be certain to keep accurate records of all your transactions. This will help you be a responsible consumer.

Summing Up *Consumers benefit from the convenience and safety offered by checking accounts. Although some consumers don't really need a checking account or don't have the self-control to use a checking account properly, most adults choose to open and use checking accounts.* ◆

Vocabulary Builder

Stop payment   An order to one's bank not to honor a particular check when it is presented for payment.

Review and Enrichment Activities

VOCABULARY REVIEW

1. Column A contains key consumer terms from this chapter. Column B contains a scrambled list of phrases that describe what these terms mean. Match the correct meaning with each term. Write your answers on a separate sheet of paper.

Column A

1. Commercial bank
2. Statement
3. Check register
4. Maintenance fee
5. Minimum balance
6. Savings bank
7. Automatic teller machine
8. Service charge
9. Electronic funds transfer
10. Savings and loan association

Column B

a. A monthly payment made by a depositor to a bank to keep an account open
b. The smallest deposit possible to avoid paying fees and charges to banks
c. A payment made by a customer to a bank for each check written
d. A document that includes a record of deposits and checks paid sent by a bank to its depositors
e. A document depositors keep to record deposits, checks, and their current balance
f. A financial institution that offers a wide range of services; the only type that could offer checking accounts until the 1970s
g. Moving funds from one account to another using a computer
h. A financial institution that could only make loans for housing related purposes until the 1970s
i. A machine that consumers may use to complete many financial transactions without having to deal with a person

Review and Enrichment Activities Continued

   j. A financial institution that is
          similar to savings and loan
          associations but has slightly
          greater choice in the loans it
          can make; most commonly
          found in the north-eastern
          part of the United States

   2. Explain the difference between a check that is not paid due to insufficient funds and a check that is outstanding.

CHECKING WHAT YOU'VE LEARNED

   Write your answers for the following exercises on a separate sheet of paper.

   1. Explain why it is difficult to make large transactions with cash.
   2. What was the only type of financial institution where consumers could open checking accounts prior to the 1970s?
   3. Identify three different ways that banks may generate income from checking deposits.
   4. Explain why many people are not able to take advantage of checking accounts that pay interest.
   5. Explain why it is important to keep an accurate check register.
   6. Explain why it is important to save all deposit receipts.
   7. Give at least two reasons why people should avoid writing checks for which they have insufficient funds.
   8. Explain what you should do when you receive your monthly checking statement from the bank.
   9. Describe the steps you should take if you find your check register doesn't agree with your bank statement.
   10. Explain why you would use a stop payment order on a check.
   11. Describe two advantages of making payments with checks.
   12. Describe two situations where paying with a check would not be the best possible choice.

PRACTICING YOUR CONSUMER SKILLS

Write your answers for the following exercises on a separate sheet of paper.

1. Three financial institutions in a small town offer checking accounts. Each has different charges and rules for depositors:

    The Farmer's National Bank offers free checking and 5 percent interest to customers who maintain a minimum average balance of $1,500. If a customer's account falls below the minimum balance, the bank pays no interest and requires payment of a $5 monthly maintenance fee and a 10-cent service charge for each check written.

    The MidWest Savings and Loan offers free checking and 5 percent interest to customers who maintain a minimum average balance of $1,000. If a customer's account falls below the minimum balance, the savings and loan requires a $3 monthly maintenance fee and a 20-cent service charge for each check written. All accounts earn interest, regardless of their balance.

    The Employee's National Credit Union offers checking accounts that have no service charge for each check written, but there is a $5 monthly maintenance fee. The credit union pays 5 percent interest on all accounts, regardless of their balance.

    State which institution each of the following people should choose. Explain your choice.

    a. Melissa works in a food cannery. She believes that she could keep a minimum balance of $1,000 about half the time. She expects to write about ten checks a month.

    b. Roger works for a construction company. He will write at least 25 checks a month. He can keep a large minimum balance except in the middle of winter, when he usually is unemployed.

    c. Yvonne is retired. She is quite wealthy and wants to write many checks to various charitable organizations each month.

    d. Theresa just took her first job working in a grocery store. Right now she has about $300 to her name. She lives with her parents and expects to write no more than three or four checks a month. She hopes to earn more money after she graduates from a community college next year.

    e. Sean drives a soft-drink delivery truck for a living. He earns $250 a week plus a 1 percent commission on his sales. In the summer, when it's hot, he can earn as much as $400 in commissions in a week. In the winter there are weeks when his commission is less than $100. Sean believes that he would write about 20 checks a month.

2. Your teacher has given you a blank check register. Fill it in accurately and completely for each of the following transactions. Assume that there is a 10-cent service charge for each check if your average balance falls below $1,000.

Review and Enrichment Activities Continued

Date	Description of Transaction
11/2	Deposit #241 of $531.25
11/5	Check #1233 for $550 to James O'Brian for rent
11/7	Check #1234 for $34.57 to Oak Products Inc. for having a chair repaired
11/9	Check #1235 for $20 to the American Red Cross for a contribution
11/10	Deposit #242 of $431.25
11/15	Check #1236 for $97.21 to the National Gas Co. for gas to heat your home
11/22	Check #1237 for $34.65 to New York Telephone Co. for your telephone service
11/27	Check #1238 for $589.32 to the Bank of New York to pay your credit card balance
11/29	Deposit #243 of $381.25

Was your average balance more or less than $1,000? Were you charged 10 cents for each check you wrote? What is your ending balance?

3. Lydia has received a statement from her bank that does not agree with her register. She has checked all her deposit receipts and is sure that the amount for each deposit entered in her register is correct. If she maintains an average balance of $1,000, she receives free checking and 5 percent interest. She is concerned because her beginning and ending balances are different from those reported by her bank. Identify five mistakes or misunderstandings that were made by either the bank or by Lydia.

Lydia's Check Register					
Number	Date	Description	Payment	Deposit	Balance
Beginning Balance					$1672.31
2904	7/3	Joe's Hobby Shop	$ 24.33		$1647.98
2905	7/5	Electricity	$102.14		$1545.84
381	7/9	Deposit		$560.32	$2206.16
2906	7/11	Rent	$450.00		$1756.16
2907	7/13	Beauty shop	$ 54.00		$1810.16
382	7/16	Deposit		$260.32	$2070.48
2908	7/21	Telephone	$ 41.33		$2029.15
2909	7/22	Credit card	$123.42		$1896.73
383	7/23	Deposit		$260.32	$2157.05
2910	7/26	Airline tickets	$456.00		$1701.05
2911	7/28	Car payment	$283.17		$1417.88
2912	7/30	UGF contribution	$ 32.00		$1392.88

	Item			
Date	Number	Debit	Credit	Balance

Lydia's Bank Statement

Date	Item Number	Debit	Credit	Balance
7/1			Beginning Balance	$1928.45
7/4	2904	$24.33		$1904.12
7/5	2903	$256.14		$1647.98
7/7	2905	$102.14		$1545.84
7/9	381		$560.32	$2106.16
7/12	2906	$450.00		$1656.16
7/14	2907	$ 54.00		$1602.16
7/16	382		$ 26.32	$1628.48
7/22	2909	$123.42		$1505.06
7/23	2908	$ 41.33		$1463.73
7/23	383		$260.32	$1724.05
7/27	2910	$456.00		$1268.05
7/30	2911	$283.17		$ 984.88
7/31	Interest		$ 5.92	$ 990.80
			Ending Balance	$ 990.80

USING NUMBERS

Solve the following problem to help make the best possible choice. Write your solution on a separate sheet of paper. Be sure to show all your work.

Amy intends to open a checking account at her bank. If she maintains a minimum balance of $1,000, the account will be free and will pay her 5 percent interest. If her balance falls below $1,000, there is a 10-cent charge per check and a $2 monthly maintenance fee, although she will still earn 5 percent interest on her deposits. Amy expects to write about ten checks a month. Amy has $1,000 she had intended to put into a time deposit (you will learn more about these in Chapter 28) that would pay her 8 percent interest. She now wonders if she shouldn't simply take that money and put it in her checking account so that she will be sure to have the minimum deposit. Otherwise, she is sure she will fall below the $1,000 limit and will have to pay the fees for her checking account.

How much would Amy lose by not putting her $1,000 into the time deposit? How much would she save by putting her $1,000 into her checking account so that she would have no fees to pay? Which choice do you believe she should make? Explain the reasons for your recommendation.

PUTTING IDEAS IN YOUR OWN WORDS

The following quotations are from this chapter. Explain these quotations in your own words to make sure you understand what they mean. Write your answers on a separate sheet of paper.

Review and Enrichment Activities Continued

1. "When you are trying to decide which bank to choose for your checking account, you need to comparison shop the same way you would if you were buying a car or refrigerator."

2. "If you don't check your deposit slips for accuracy and keep them in a safe place, you are asking for trouble."

3. "It is possible for the bank to provide you with a correct balance that is different from your own."

BUILDING CONSUMER KNOWLEDGE

Write your answers for the following exercises on a separate sheet of paper.

1. Look through your telephone book to find a number of different banks and other financial institutions that offer checking services. Make a list of questions that you should ask a bank officer to help you decide which institution you should choose to open a checking account.

2. Ask your parents if they have a checking account. Ask them to identify the types of payments that they make with checks. Do not ask for the amounts. Be prepared to discuss the information you find with your class.

3. Assume that you made a deposit of $328.90 in your checking account two weeks ago. You received and kept your deposit receipt. The next week you wrote a check for $289.47 to pay for a new television set. The check was returned for "insufficient funds" on the same day you received your checking account statement. You noted that your bank had credited your account for a deposit of $32.89 instead of the correct amount. Your check should not have "bounced." You are angry and concerned about what this event will do to your credit rating. You also refuse to pay the $15 re-turned-check fee because it was not your mistake.

    Write a letter that will achieve the results you want. It must be clear and factual. State what you expect the bank to do about the situation. Remember, it might make you feel good to tell the bank employee what a terrible bank he or she works for, but this may not solve your problem.

Chapter 27

Saving and Investing Your Money

Key Consumer Terms

After completing this chapter, you will be able to do the following:

- Describe the relationship between saving and investing wisely and achieving financial security.
- Describe how a person should decide how much he or she can afford to save.
- Explain the difference between simple and compound interest.
- Explain the trade-offs people make between the risk and return they may expect from different uses of their money.
- Explain why different people need to make different plans for achieving financial security.

Chapter Objectives

In this chapter you will learn the meanings of the following important consumer terms:

- Save
- Invest
- Passbook account
- Simple interest
- Compound interest
- Yield
- Federal Deposit Insurance Corporation (FDIC)
- Joint account
- Savings bond
- Face value
- Diversification
- Risk-averse

437

S uppose that your average weekly income from your job is $60. After withholding is taken out for FICA and federal and state income taxes, you take home about $40 a week. Unless you give some of the money to your parents or someone else, there are really only two things you can do with your money. You can spend it or **save** it.

There are many ways to think about saving. One way is to regard it as delayed spending. By saving now, you should have a greater ability to spend in the future. You might also think of saving as a way to buy financial security. If you accumulate money, you won't need to worry about losing your job or many other problems as much as a person who has no savings. Saving is also a way to increase your future income. Money that is set aside can almost always earn a return. Most people should save for their future. Often the hardest part of saving is getting started. The answer to that problem is to make a plan and begin to save now.

SECTION 1

DIFFERENCES BETWEEN SAVING AND INVESTING

While you read, ask yourself . . .
- ◆ How much of your current income do you save?
- ◆ How much of your current income do you believe you could reasonably save?
- ◆ What reasons are there for any difference between these amounts?

If you spend money, you have sources of income. If you have a job, one source of your income is clear. Other sources may include an allowance or payment for jobs that you do at home. Regardless of your source of income, it is a good idea to get into the habit of saving. If you establish this habit when you are young, you should find it easier to save when you are older.

How Much Can You Afford to Save?

There are a number of ways to approach saving. It is often useful to make a rule for yourself to follow. You might decide to always save a certain amount, like $5, out of every paycheck. If your income varies from week to week, you might choose to save 10 percent of everything you earn. With this rule you would save $2 when you earned $20 and $10 when you earned $100.

A sensible way to save is to pay all fixed expenses first (see Chapter 25). Then you might choose to save some percent, possibly 25 percent, of any money that is left over. The other 75 percent would be used for flexible expenses. The advantage to this method is that it helps you pay the bills you must pay when your income isn't large, yet lets you save when you are able to. If you find that you can't save with

Consumer News

Interest Isn't the Only Thing You May Lose If You Don't Put Your Savings in a Bank

It seems that every few weeks you read a newspaper headline like this: "Elderly Woman's Life Savings Stolen from Shoe Box." Many Americans, particularly older people who remember the bank failures during the Great Depression of the 1930s, don't trust banks. They put their money in a jar and bury it, or they store it in their mattress, or they keep it someplace else—in cash. When people do this, they give up the interest they could be earning by putting their money in a bank account or in some other type of investment. However, they also give up safety.

In the summer of 1991 an eighty-four-year-old woman in Buffalo, New York, reported that over $120,000 in cash had been stolen from a closet in her home. Her savings were made up of more than 6,000 $20 bills she had been putting away over forty years. She had no insurance, and the police held out little hope of recovering her money.

Even if her money had not been stolen, she was losing interest. If she had deposited her money in an account that paid an average rate of 5 percent over the forty years, she would have earned more than $200,000 in interest. Keeping large amounts of money on hand in cash is not a responsible consumer decision.

How much cash do you keep on hand?

this method, you may have too many fixed expenses. You should consider steps that would reduce these costs, or you might take steps to increase your income.

At this time, the amount you save is probably less important than the fact that you do save what you can. There is no reason to live in poverty now so that you can live in luxury when you are old. Like so many other cases in economics, there is a trade-off between the value you receive from current consumption and what you gain from saving for the future. You must decide how much saving you can afford.

Saving and Investing

If you take $5 every week and put it in your cookie jar, you are saving. Your choice of how to save is not very wise, but you are saving. When your money is in your cookie jar, it isn't earning any interest. You also run the risk of having someone steal it from you. What's more, it loses purchasing power if there is inflation. It is a better choice to **invest** your savings in a way that earns you a return. Consumers who decide not to invest savings may be better off than other people who do not save at all, but they are not making the best possible use of their money.

If you deposit your savings into a bank account, you are making an investment because you will earn interest. **Passbook accounts**, also

Vocabulary Builder

Invest To place savings in a situation that will result in an increase in their value.

Passbook account A savings account for which a depositor receives a booklet in which transactions are recorded.

Save To not spend income at the present so that it may be spent in the future.

called day-in, day-out accounts, usually pay between 4 and 6 percent annual interest. Other types of deposits pay higher rates of interest. You will learn more about these accounts in Chapter 28.

Saving in bank accounts is not the only way to invest your money. You could buy corporate stocks or bonds or government savings bonds. You might purchase land, apartment buildings, or other types of real estate. Some people buy gold or silver or collect rare coins, stamps, or baseball cards. Investing directly by loaning money to homeowners or businesses is another possibility. There seems to be an endless list of possible investments you could make with the money you save. All people who make investments hope to earn a return on their money. However, not all investments are equally appropriate for all people.

Simple and Compound Interest

Have you ever gone into a bank and noticed a sign that said something like "Interest Compounded Daily" or "Annual rate 6.5%, Compounded to Yield 6.83%"? Did you wonder what these signs meant, or did you just ignore them? For people who are interested in earning the largest possible return from investing their

◆ The fact that this bank advertises both a rate and a yield for deposits shows it compounds the interest it pays. Which value should depositors be more concerned with?

savings, it is very important to understand the difference between **simple interest** and **compound interest**.

Suppose that Rita borrows $1,000 from Tim and agrees to pay him back $1,100 at the end of one year. If this happens, Rita and Tim have agreed that she will pay him a simple rate of interest equal to 10 percent per year. The extra $100 that Rita will pay Tim at the end of the year is 10 percent of the $1,000 loan. Simple interest is only figured once. It is not added to the amount that future interest is paid on. Compound interest, on the other hand, is added to the amount that interest is paid on. It has the effect of increasing the rate of interest or percentage **yield** of the loan.

Suppose that Rita agreed to compound the interest once after six months. This means that at the end of half a year, Rita would add $50 to the amount she owes Tim and pays interest on. For the second half of the year, Rita would pay an annual interest rate of 10 percent on $1,050. The amount of interest she would owe for the second half of the year would be $52.50. At the end of the year, Rita would pay Tim $1,102.50. The extra $2.50 would be the result of compounding. This compound interest results in a yield of 10.25 percent on the loan. You might think that $2.50 isn't very much to worry about, but if the loan is for $1 million, the difference is $2,500, a sizable amount indeed.

Compounding may happen once, twice, four times, 365 times, or any other number of times a year. The more often interest is compounded, the higher the resulting yield. When you deposit your money in a bank account or invest it in other ways, you need to be sure you understand whether the deposit pays simple or compound interest, and how often it is compounded.

Summing Up *It is important to have a plan to save and invest wisely. Starting to save when you are young should make it easier to save when you are older. Consumers need to understand the benefits offered by compound interest.* ◆

RISK VERSUS RETURN: WHAT INVESTMENT SHOULD YOU CHOOSE?

While you read, ask yourself . . .
◆ *Could you afford to lose any of your savings?*
◆ *If someone offers you an investment that is a "sure thing" and will pay you a 20 percent return each year, what should you think?*

Some people will tell you that every time you get up in the morning, you are taking a chance. Almost everything you do involves some risk. Events beyond your control could take place and harm you. However, when it comes to saving and investing your money, you may often choose the amount of risk you want to take.

Deposits Insured by the Government

Since 1933, money that is deposited in most banks has been insured up to a maximum amount by an agency of the federal government called the **Federal Deposit Insurance Corporation (FDIC)**. In 1991 the maximum that was insured for an individual account was $100,000. This means that if a bank is unable to repay a depositor for any reason, the FDIC will make the payment up to the maximum insured amount. Deposits over this amount will be paid to the extent that the bank's assets are great enough to cover the deposits.

Most people do not have over $100,000 deposited in their bank accounts. Therefore, the FDIC insures the entire deposits of most Americans. If a husband and wife, or other people, open **joint accounts**, in addition to accounts in their own names, it is possible for the total of their insured accounts to be several hundred thousand dollars. By making deposits in different banks, they can insure even greater amounts. When you deposit your money in an account insured by the FDIC, there is almost no chance that you will lose any of it unless you deposit more than the maximum amount.

Advantages of Buying Savings Bonds

Another way to save that has virtually no risk is to buy government **savings bonds**. When you buy a savings bond, you are helping to finance the national debt by making a loan to the federal government. Federal law allows each individual to buy up to $15,000 worth of series EE savings bonds a year in denominations of $50 to $10,000. Savings bonds may be purchased at commercial banks or through payroll deductions.

Vocabulary Builder

Compound interest Interest figured not only on the original funds deposited, but also on the interest those funds have earned.
Federal Deposit Insurance Corporation (FDIC) A corporation created by the federal government in 1935 that insures deposits in banks. In 1991 the limit on this insurance was $100,000.
Joint account An account owned by two people, often husband and wife.
Savings bond A bond sold by the U.S. Treasury for less than its face value, but which is worth purchase price plus interest when redeemed.
Simple interest Interest figured on the original amount deposited.
Yield The percentage return on an amount of money deposited or invested.

Consumer News

Should There Be a Limit on FDIC Insurance?

How much insurance do you believe the government should provide for people's deposits when their banks fail? Do you believe that the government should expect taxpayers to help pay for this protection?

In 1991, representatives of the Bush administration suggested limiting FDIC insurance to reduce the government's risk of being forced to pay many hundreds of thousands of dollars to individual depositors in failed banks. As the law was written, wealthy people could have millions of dollars insured by the FDIC by putting many $100,000 deposits in different accounts in different banks. They didn't need to be careful which bank they chose, because all their deposits were insured by the government. President Bush felt that this encouraged people to deposit money in poorly run banks that made risky loans because they took no personal risk. He suggested several possible changes. One suggestion was to limit the payment that any individual could receive from the FDIC to $100,000, regardless of how much was lost in how many accounts. Another was to limit the interest that banks could pay on insured deposits. To earn higher rates, people would need to take a risk of loss and would be more careful in where they put their money.

Series EE bonds are sold at a price equal to half their **face value**. This means that you would pay $25 for a bond that had a $50 face value. After you held the bond for ten to twelve years, the interest you earned would increase the bond's value to its face value. If you held the bond longer, it would continue to earn interest and become worth more than its face value.

Savings bonds paid a minimum 6 percent interest in 1991 and could pay more if other interest rates were high. If you do not hold a savings bond for at least five years, it will not pay the full rate of interest. The interest earned from a savings bond is taxed by the federal government when the bond is redeemed, but may not be taxed by state and local governments. This is an important consideration in states that have high taxes.

People who want to put off reporting income into the future often buy savings bonds. For example, if you intend to retire in ten years and expect to pay a lower tax rate at that time, you could benefit from owning savings bonds. You would not be required to declare the interest you earned until you redeemed your bonds after you retired.

Investments That Involve Greater Risks

There are many other ways to save and invest your money that involve varying amounts of risk. Corporations often sell bonds as a means of borrowing money to pay for new factories or equipment. If the corporation continues in business, it must pay interest at regular intervals and return the purchase price of the bond when it matures.

Bonds issued by large, successful corporations involve almost no risk. If you own a bond sold by IBM or General Motors, there is little chance you could lose either your interest or your original investment. However, if you buy a bond issued by a firm that is not financially sound, there is a substantial chance that you will not be repaid. People who owned bonds issued

◆ Investments in government securities like savings bonds involve less risk and lower return than investments in stocks or bonds sold by corporations. Why should different consumers make different investment decisions?

by Eastern Airlines and Federal Department Stores stood to lose large parts of their investments when these firms went into bankruptcy.

In Chapter 17 you learned that corporations are able to raise money by selling shares of stock. From the point of view of an individual, buying corporate stock is an investment. If the firm does well, it may pay dividends, and the value of its stock is likely to increase. Of course, not all corporations do well. There is no law that forces a corporation to pay dividends, and if the firm does poorly, you might have a difficult time finding someone who wanted to buy your stock. The amount of risk associated with buying either corporate bonds or stocks depends on the success of the issuing firm.

Vocabulary Builder

Face value   The value printed on a bond. It may or may not be the price the bond was first sold for.

Consumers in Action

Investing in the Environment

According to a recent survey, almost 80 percent of all Americans think of themselves as "environmentalists." The survey did not define what this word means, so it was up to each individual to use his or her own definition. However, many people who responded to the survey probably try to live their lives in a way that is helpful rather than harmful to the environment. Whatever being an environmentalist means, it is clear that consumers may invest their savings in stocks or bonds issued by firms that are producing goods or services that help the environment.

For example, about 80 percent of all U.S. garbage went into landfills in 1990. One way to reduce this volume of trash is to burn it to create energy. Wheelabrator Technologies ran ten trash-to-energy facilities in 1990, with plans to build four more. Wheelabrator executives expect their profits to grow 25 percent each year as more plants come into use. People who invest in Wheelabrator are able to help the environment while earning a good return.

Other possible investments include buying stock in Wellman Inc., which recycles plastic soda bottles into polyester fibers for carpets. Allwaste and Envirosafe Services are two companies specializing in removing or stabilizing asbestos in buildings. Some analysts predicted that these firm's earnings would grow rapidly in the 1990's.

The Environmental Protection Agency has determined that more than 17,000 bodies of water in the United States are polluted. Many of these lakes, rivers, and streams will be cleaned with filters made of activated charcoal. The nation's leading producer of this product is Calgon Carbon Inc. By investing in this firm, consumers can benefit from efforts to clean our water supply.

For investors who are willing to take a larger risk, there is the firm of Church & Dwight, which is trying to find a way to spray baking soda into industrial smokestacks to neutralize acid and prevent acid rain. This process was unproven in 1990, but if successful, it could generate enormous profits for the firm and its stockholders.

The list of firms that are helpful to the environment and offer a good return on investments goes on and on. However, don't lose sight of the fact that you need to be careful whenever you invest your savings. Environmental stocks and bonds are not magic. They can lose value just as easily as any other business you could invest in.

Risks That Involve Time

Some types of risk are not based on the possibility of nonpayment. Time is often an important factor that investors should consider.

Suppose that you buy a $1,000 bond that pays 8 percent interest and has a term of ten years. You will receive an interest payment of $80 each year, and you will get your $1,000 back when the bond matures. If prevailing interest rates go up to 10 percent the year after you buy your bond, you will miss out on earning 2 percent in interest for each of the next nine years. When you invest your money in any way that pays a fixed return over a long period of time, you take the risk that you could have earned more by waiting. Of course, there is the possibility that prevailing interest rates could go down, in which case you will do better by "tying in" the fixed rate of return.

The value of an investment also depends on the rate of inflation. If you invest money in a savings account and earn 5 percent interest, you probably won't have 5 percent more purchasing power when you take the money out one year later. If prices go up 4 percent, your purchasing power will have increased by only 1 percent. You should also consider the fact that most interest is taxable. If you pay federal income taxes at a rate of 15 percent and state income taxes at a rate of 5 percent, your purchasing power won't change at all. You will lose 4 percent to inflation and 1 percent to taxes (20 percent of 5 percent is 1 percent). Keep in mind that breaking even is better than losing 4 percent of your purchasing power. This is what would happen if you put your money in your cookie jar. When you make an investment, you should consider the effect of inflation on the value of your savings.

The Trade-Off Between Risk and Return

People who are able to afford greater risks can expect to be rewarded with greater returns. Other people who choose to avoid risk will not receive as great a return for their investments. Small savings accounts have virtually no risk of nonpayment, and depositors can withdraw their money at any time. These are some of the

reasons these accounts pay a relatively low interest rate of 4 to 6 percent.

Different types of accounts that require depositors to leave their money with a bank for a period of time pay higher rates of interest. However, the depositors must accept risks associated with time.

Investors who choose to buy corporate stocks or bonds may purchase ones that have high or low risks. The greater the risk, the greater the return the investor should receive. There is a direct relationship between risk and return. As the risk of an investment goes up or down, the return offered should move in the same direction.

Summing Up *There are many ways consumers may invest their savings that involve different amounts of risk and return. In general, the greater the return an investment offers, the greater the risk.* ◆

SECTION 3

DIFFERENT PEOPLE, DIFFERENT INVESTMENTS

While you read, ask yourself . . .
- ◆ *Should you consider making investments that involve significant risks at the present?*
- ◆ *Are there businesses you would not invest your money in as a matter of principle, even if they offered a high return?*

Different people have different incomes, needs, and financial goals. Therefore, different people need to make different investments with their savings. The personal inventory you made in Chapter 20 will once more be useful in determining the types of investments you should make.

The Value of Diversification

You have certainly heard the phrase, "Don't put all your eggs in one basket." When it comes to investing your savings, this means that you should not put all your money in one place. Rather, you should make a variety of investments. That way, even if one investment does poorly, you will have others that may do better. This idea is called **diversification**. Diversification means spreading out your savings among many different alternatives to avoid being too dependent on any one investment.

People who have very little income and savings cannot afford to lose any of their money. They have few choices in how they diversify their investments. They should put their savings in insured accounts or in government bonds. As people have greater incomes and savings, they may be able to choose investments that offer greater returns and involve accepting a degree of risk.

Income isn't the only factor that should be considered when people decide how to invest their savings. Personal responsibilities are as important as income in choosing what type of investments to make. People who have large, fixed expenses, who have family responsibilities, who hold insecure jobs, or who are chronically ill should not make risky investments where they could lose their savings. Other people with smaller incomes but few responsibilities may be better able to make investments that involve more risk.

Your Values and Your Investment Choices

When you choose how to invest your savings, you should also consider your personal values. Some people are very **risk-averse**. This means that they don't like to take risks. Putting their money in a risky investment may make

them nervous and irritable. They may spend so much of their time worrying about their investments that they have little time to enjoy the fruits of their labor. These people should avoid risky investments even if they can afford them. Never accept more risk than you can comfortably live with.

Values may also affect your investment decisions if you care how the money you invest is used. If you believe that development in your community should be encouraged, you might ask different banks how they use the money they receive as deposits. If a bank has a policy of returning a percentage of deposits to the community in loans, you could feel better about investing your savings with that bank rather than with a bank that does not have this policy.

If you are considering buying stock in a corporation, you might choose to invest in businesses that are environmentally responsible or that have strong equal opportunity programs. In some cases you might have to give up some return to avoid conflicts with your personal values. This is an individual choice that each saver and investor must make. For example, if you are in favor of protecting wildlife, you probably shouldn't invest in a firm that produces fur coats.

Summing Up   *Consumers should diversify their investments to avoid unnecessary risk. The amount of risk that an individual should accept depends on his or her income and responsibilities. Consumers should also consider their personal values when they choose which investments to make.* ◆

Vocabulary Builder

Diversification   Branching out into other types of investments.

Risk-averse   Wanting to avoid risk when possible.

Review and Enrichment Activities

VOCABULARY REVIEW

1. Column A contains key consumer terms from this chapter. Column B contains a scrambled list of phrases that describe what these terms mean. Match the correct meaning with each term. Write your answers on a separate sheet of paper.

Column A

1. Save
2. Invest
3. Passbook account
4. Yield
5. Face value
6. Savings bond
7. Joint account
8. Risk-averse
9. Federal Deposit Insurance Corporation
10. Diversification

Column B

a. Not willing to take a chance on losing money or something of value
b. To not spend after tax income
c. The percentage return a person receives from an investment
d. Investing in a selection of ways to reduce risk
e. To use money in a way that could earn a return
f. The value printed on a bond that may or may not be the price the bond was sold for
g. A bond sold by the U.S. Treasury to help finance the federal debt
h. A savings account for which a depositor receives a booklet in which transactions are recorded
i. An account that is owned and may be used by more than one person
j. A corporation created by the federal government that insures deposits in banks and other financial institutions

2. Explain the difference between **simple** and **compound** rates of interest.

Review and Enrichment Activities Continued

CHECKING WHAT YOU'VE LEARNED

Write your answers for the following exercises on a separate sheet of paper.

1. What are the three ways to think about saving that were mentioned at the beginning of this chapter?
2. Explain why making a rule for saving is helpful to most people who want to save.
3. Explain why two accounts paying 6 percent interest will have different yields if one pays simple interest and the other has interest that is compounded at the end of every three months.
4. What is the function of the FDIC?
5. Explain why a person who lives in a state with high tax rates might choose to buy federal savings bonds.
6. Explain why a person who currently pays a high rate of income tax might choose to buy federal savings bonds if he or she expects to pay at a lower tax rate in the future.
7. Describe two different types of risk that are associated with time.
8. What should an investor expect to happen to risk as the return on investments increases?
9. Why should people diversify their investments?
10. Why should different people choose investments that offer different combinations of risk and return?

PRACTICING YOUR CONSUMER SKILLS

Write your answers for the following exercises on a separate sheet of paper.

1. Consider the following three savings plans: to save $20 out of each paycheck; to save 10 percent of each paycheck; or to save 25 percent of income left over after paying fixed expenses. Choose the savings plan that you feel would be most appropriate for each of the following people. Explain your choice.
   a. Dan is single and lives by himself. He has a job selling used cars. Some weeks he earns over $1,000. In other weeks he earns nothing.
   b. Alice is a single parent with three children. She receives child support payments of $300 each month from her former husband and earns $350 a week working in a library. From this she must pay her rent and try to save for her children's future.

    c. Doris is a high school senior who lives at home with her parents. She works 14 hours every week in her uncle's drugstore. She earns $6 an hour.

    d. Gary is a construction worker. His wife is expecting their first child in four months. When Gary works, he has a good income. But he is often laid off for as many as 20 weeks a year.

2. Organize each of the following investments in order of their expected return and probable risk. Place the one with the least risk and return first. Explain your choices.

    a. Buying a $1,000 bond issued by a large corporation that sells natural gas

    b. Depositing $1,000 in a passbook savings account

    c. Buying stock for $1,000 in a corporation that is trying to find a way to recycle plastic waste into oil

    d. Depositing $200,000 in a small bank and agreeing to leave the money there for three years

    e. Buying a $500 federal government savings bond

3. Decide whether each of the following investment choices was appropriate for the person who made the investment. Explain your decision.

    a. Russel wants to save for a college education. He is single and lives alone. He works as a cook in a restaurant. He can only save about $20 a week. He decided to buy stock in a new firm he read about that manufactures computer games. He thinks that the firm will be successful and expects to earn a large profit from his stock when he sells it.

    b. Maria plans to be married next year. She and her future husband work in an office of an insurance company. They both earn about $400 a week and spend roughly 75 percent of their income. They use the rest of their income to buy federal savings bonds.

    c. Harold is a corporate vice president who earns over $100,000 a year. He saves all of his extra income in a passbook savings account that pays 6 percent interest. He has $189,742.29 on deposit now.

    d. Ester is a widow who received a $100,000 insurance payment when her husband died last year. She is sixty-three years old. She used her money to buy corporate bonds issued by three different large and successful businesses. Her average yield from these investments is 7.89 percent.

USING NUMBERS

Solve the following problem to help make the best possible choice. Write your solution on a separate sheet of paper. Be sure to show all your work.

Karen has $10,000 that she wants to invest. Although she would like to earn a good return, she does not wish to take any risk that could cause her to lose her money. She has narrowed her choices down to three investments.

Review and Enrichment Activities Continued

Determine how much each will earn for her over the next *two* years. She thinks that she may need the money after that. Which do you think she should choose? Explain the reasons for your choice.

Investment 1. To buy government savings bonds that pay a simple interest rate of 6 percent each year if they are held for five years

Investment 2. To buy a corporate bond issued by General Motors that will come due in ten years and that pays 9 percent each year to the owner

Investment 3. To deposit the money in an FDIC-insured bank account that pays 7.7 percent interest compounded to yield 8 percent a year

PUTTING IDEAS IN YOUR OWN WORDS

The following quotations are from this chapter. Explain these quotations in your own words to make sure you understand what they mean. Write your answers on a separate sheet of paper.

1. "At this time, the amount you save is probably less important than the fact that you do save what you can."
2. "For anyone who is interested in earning the largest possible return from investing their savings, it is very important to understand the difference between simple interest and compound interest."
3. "Different people have different incomes, needs, and financial goals. Therefore, different people need to make different investments with their savings."

BUILDING CONSUMER KNOWLEDGE

Write your answers for the following exercises on a separate sheet of paper.

1. Make a savings plan that you feel would help you achieve your financial goals. Write a paragraph that explains your plan and why it is appropriate for your income and needs.
2. Go to a bank or library to find the following types of information. Ask your librarian to help you. Describe the sort of people who you believe should make each type of investment.
   a. The interest rate paid by banks on passbook savings accounts. You may find this information by calling or visiting a local bank.

b. The current yield on a General Motors Acceptance (GMA) bond that will come due about five years in the future. This may be found in the last section of a *Wall Street Journal*, listed under "New York Exchange Bonds." The current yield is found in the second column of each quotation.

c. The current yield on a Sears Roebuck bond that will come due in about five years. This is found in the same location as the GMA bond.

d. The current yield on American Electric Power (AmElecPwr) stock dividends. This may be found in the last section of a *Wall Street Journal*, listed under "New York Stock Exchange Composite Transactions." The current yield is the sixth item listed in the quotation.

e. The current yield on Honda Motor Corporation (HondaMotor) stock dividends. This may be found in the same location as American Electric Power, but probably on the next page.

3. Survey five adults and ask them the following questions. Ask them to explain their answers to the extent that they feel comfortable giving you personal information. Be prepared to discuss the information you gather with your class.

a. Do you believe it is important to save for the future?

b. Do you try to save regularly?

c. Do you save to buy specific items or just to have money when you need it?

d. Are you as successful in saving as you would like to be?

e. If you could make a recommendation to young people about saving, what would it be?

Chapter 28

Different Ways to Invest

Chapter Objectives

After completing this chapter, you will be able to do the following:

- Identify the different types of investments that consumers can make, including bank deposits, corporate stocks and bonds, mutual funds, and government securities.
- Explain the benefits and costs associated with each type of investment.
- Identify investments that are currently appropriate for yourself and those which may become appropriate in the future.

Key Consumer Terms

In this chapter you will learn the meanings of the following important consumer terms:

- Certificate of deposit (CD)
- Money market account
- Common stock
- Capital gain
- Capital loss
- Preferred stock
- Discount
- Premium
- Corporate bond
- Principal
- Convertible bond
- Mutual fund
- Money market mutual fund
- Security
- Term
- Municipal bond
- Tax preference
- Default

S uppose that you made a decision last year to save $20 every week. You have carried out your plan and now have over $1,000 deposited in your savings account. You earn 5 percent interest on your savings, but you think you could do better. You don't intend to use the money soon and are willing to invest it where you wouldn't be able to withdraw it for several years. You need to study your alternatives before you decide what to do.

BANKING OPPORTUNITIES

While you read, ask yourself . . .
- *Do you have money that you could afford to set aside and not use for a number of years to achieve a higher return?*
- *How important is having government insurance for your savings?*

You learned about checking accounts in Chapter 26 and passbook savings accounts in Chapter 27. Banks offer many other types of deposits and investment opportunities.

Certificates of Deposit

Consumers who invest in **certificates of deposit (CDs)** agree to leave their money on deposit at a bank or savings institution for a specific period of time to earn higher rates of interest. This period may be as short as several days or as long as ten years. Banks and other financial institutions are often willing to pay higher rates of interest on certificates of deposit because they know that they will have the use of the money for an extended period of time. Therefore, they can make longer-term loans that will pay them higher returns. Banks earn more from certificates of deposit, so they generally to pay more to get them.

Certificates of deposit issued by banks offer customers safety because the FDIC guarantees the deposit up to a maximum of $100,000. In addition, the value of the deposit cannot fall. Once a depositor commits his or her funds to a CD, the interest rate it pays will remain the same regardless of what happens to other interest rates. This can help people make plans for their financial future. If a depositor needs money that has been placed in a CD, he or she can withdraw the money at any time, although there will be an interest penalty that must be paid.

There are important advantages of certificates of deposit, but there are also some disadvantages associated with them. CDs do not offer the highest possible returns on a saver's investment. CDs do pay higher rates of interest than passbook savings accounts, but there are other investments that pay more. Although money in CDs may be withdrawn at any time, the penalty that must be paid is usually equal to ninety days of interest. CDs usually have a minimum deposit that may be as low as $500 or as large as several thousand dollars. Not all savers have enough money to be able to take advantage of CDs.

Vocabulary Builder

Certificate of deposit (CD)   A document stating an amount of money deposited in an account, and the interest rate to be paid over the term of the account.

Money Market Accounts

Since the early 1980s, banks and other savings institutions have offered **money market accounts** to depositors. These accounts pay interest rates that change with prevailing interest rates. They have the advantage of being insured up to $100,000 by the FDIC. Money deposited in a money market account is immediately available to the depositor. In many cases customers can transfer funds to their checking account simply by making a phone call or by using an automated teller machine (ATM). Money market accounts are often used when customers have money that they will need to use in a short period of time. They pay higher rates of interest than passbook savings accounts and do not tie money up like CDs.

The greatest disadvantage of money market accounts is their relatively low rate of interest. Although they pay more than passbook savings, there are many other investments, including CDs, that offer greater returns. Still, in 1991 over $600 billion was deposited in this type of account.

Banks offer many other types of accounts that are intended to fill special purposes. If you feel that you have an investment need that cannot be met by an ordinary account, bank employees can provide you with advice. Their business depends on satisfied customers and a favorable public image. They will do what they can to meet your needs.

Summing Up ► *Banks offer consumers a variety of deposits that pay higher interest rates than checking or passbook savings accounts. In general, the longer a depositor agrees to leave money in an account, the greater the return will be.* ◆

SECTION 2

INVESTING IN CORPORATE STOCKS AND BONDS

While you read, ask yourself . . .
◆ *Do you or any members of your family own stock or corporate bonds?*
◆ *Are there any local corporations that you would consider investing in?*

Corporations sell stocks and bonds to raise money to buy buildings, tools, and resources they need to produce goods and services. People buy stocks and corporate bonds because they expect to share in the financial success of the firms they invest in. There are a number of ways to invest in corporations that offer various combinations of risk and expected return.

Buying Common Stock

Most corporate stock is **common stock**. A person who buys common stock is a part owner of the corporation and is said to own equity in the business. Common stock is voting stock. Stockholders are entitled to one vote for each common share they own when elections are held for the firm's board of directors or when other questions are put before the stockholders.

Common stockholders may receive dividends after other financial responsibilities of the firm have been satisfied. Corporations must pay their debts to the government, bondholders, and owners of preferred stock before they pay dividends to the common stockholders. Therefore, if the firm does poorly, it may have no money left to pay common stockholders dividends. On the other hand, if the business does well, there may be a large amount of money left over after other financial obligations have been met. In this situation, common

◆ A stock exchange helps people who want to buy and sell stock complete their transactions. When more people want to buy a type of stock than want to sell its price increases providing sellers with capital gains.

stockholders may receive much more from the firm than any other group of investors. Of the people who invest in corporations, common stockholders take the greatest risk but may receive the greatest return.

Owners of corporate stock may also earn income as the result of a **capital gain**. This occurs when they sell their stock for more than they paid for it. In Chapter 17 you learned that stocks and bonds may be bought or sold on stock exchanges. The price of any type of stock or bond is determined by what other people are willing to pay for it. If a firm is doing very well, many people will want to buy its stock,

Vocabulary Builder

Capital gain An increase in the value of a security or other asset between the time it was purchased and when it is sold.

Common stock A share of ownership in a corporation that entitles the owner to a portion of the firm's profits and a vote in choosing the board of directors and making certain other business decisions.

Money market account A bank account that pays a variable rate of interest that is tied to prevailing interest rates and which may be withdrawn at any time.

Consumer News

How's the Market Doing?

You have probably heard a reporter say something like, "The market rose 3.67 points today." Do you have any idea what the reporter was referring to?

The Dow-Jones Corporation is one of the oldest financial news-reporting services in the world. It publishes *The Wall Street Journal* and collects and distributes many types of financial information. In 1884 Charles Dow started to calculate a measure of the stock market's activities by taking an average of eleven important stock prices. This beginning developed into the current industrial average, which takes the values of stock issued by thirty industrial firms representing a cross section of American business and averages them together.

Although the value of individual stocks included in the Dow-Jones industrial average were generally less than $100 in 1991, the average exceeded 3,000 points or dollars. This was possible because over the years, many of the stocks had split, or been divided into more shares. The average is figured as if none of the stocks had ever been divided into more shares.

If the reporter said the market rose 3.67 points, he or she meant that the average price of the thirty stocks had gone up just over 0.1 percent (3.67 ÷ 3,000 = 0.0012 = 0.12 percent). This is a small change. On some days the market has changed by several hundred points. (This happened on October 19, 1987, when there was a crash.) By following the Dow-Jones industrial average, an investor can get a general idea of how the market is doing—but no specific information about particular stocks.

but few current owners will want to sell. As a result, there will be a shortage of the stock, and its price will go up. Those people who do sell will probably earn a capital gain. Of course, if the firm does poorly, few people will want to buy the stock while many will want to sell, causing a surplus. As a result the price will go down, and those owners who do sell will suffer a **capital loss**.

Buying Preferred Stock

Another way to buy ownership in a corporation is to purchase **preferred stock**. People who own preferred stock are not given the right to vote for the firm's board of directors or to help make other business decisions. Their "preference" is their right to be paid a set dividend before any dividends are paid to common stockholders. For example, suppose that you own 100 shares of Niagara Mohawk Power 9.95 percent preferred stock that has a face value of $100. You will be paid $9.95 each year for each share you own. This amount will never increase or decrease as long as the firm earns a profit, or even if it suffers only a small loss. If the firm suffers a loss, it is not required to pay preferred stockholders dividends. However, corporations must normally make up unpaid preferred dividends before they may pay any dividends to common stockholders.

If a corporation fails, its preferred stockholders will have claim on the assets of the firm before common stockholders are paid anything. The risk associated with owning preferred stock is much lower than that of owning common stock. On the other hand, if the firm does very well, preferred stockholders will not receive a share of the extra profit. They will continue to be paid their fixed dividend.

Preferred stock may be bought and sold on stock exchanges. The price of shares of preferred stock usually doesn't change as much as the price of common stock. The price of preferred stock fluctuates mostly with changes in interest rates. Suppose that you own preferred stock that pays a dividend of 8 percent. If most interest rates go up to 10 percent, people will want to put their money in other places where it can earn a higher return. To find someone who is willing to buy your stock, you might have to lower (**discount**) its price. However, if other interest rates go down to 6 percent, your stock will be attractive to other investors. They will be willing to pay you more (a **premium**) to own your stock. The price of preferred stock and interest rates are inversely (oppositely) related. When one goes up, the other goes down.

Buying Corporate Bonds

If you buy a **corporate bond,** you do not own any part of the business that issued the bond. Whoever bought the bond first, in effect, made a loan to the corporation. Bonds may be resold. If you own a corporate bond, you probably bought it from another person, not from the corporation itself.

Corporations must pay the interest on their bonds on time and repay the original **principal** on a designated date. They must do this even if they are losing money. If a corporation fails to make its payments, it may be forced into bankruptcy. If the business does fail, owners of corporate bonds receive payment from the firm's assets before the preferred or common stockholders. Owners of corporate bonds take the least risk of the three groups discussed in this section.

The price of bonds that are resold depends largely on prevailing interest rates. It works exactly the same way as the price of preferred stock. If a bond pays 8 percent when most interest rates are 10 percent, it must be sold at a discount. But if other interest rates are at 6 percent, it can be sold for a premium. Unless there is a chance that the firm may fail, interest rates

are almost the only factor that affects the price of a corporate bond.

Some firms issue special types of corporate bonds called **convertible bonds.** People who own these bonds receive interest and have the right to trade in their bonds for common stock at a specific price if they choose to do so. Suppose that you own a convertible bond that allows you to trade your bond for stock at a price of $25 a share. If the firm does well and its stock's price goes up to $30, you may convert your bond to stock to hold or sell at a profit. This is an advantage to the owners of convertible bonds because it allows them to share in the success of the firm.

Buying either stocks or corporate bonds involves some risk. There is always a chance that a firm could fail and not pay its bond- or stockholders. Before you invest your money in either stocks or bonds, you should be sure that

Vocabulary Builder

Capital loss   A decrease in the value of a security or other asset between the time it was purchased and when it is sold.

Convertible bond   A bond that may be exchanged for stock in the corporation that issued the bond.

Corporate Bond   A certificate issued by a corporation or government in exchange for borrowed money. A bond promises to pay a stated rate of interest over a stated period of time and to repay the original amount paid for the bond at the end of that time.

Discount   To offer to sell something, possibly a bond, for less than its original purchase price.

Preferred stock   A type of stock that guarantees the holder a certain amount of dividend but does not carry voting rights in the company's affairs.

Premium   When a person pays more for a bond than its original price. A fee paid for insurance coverage.

Principal   The original amount of a loan or investment.

you can afford to take a risk. Ask for information from brokers or other qualified advisors. You can also get information about investing from books in the library. And there are courses on investing offered in most communities. Investing in stocks and corporate bonds often offers higher returns than depositing money in banks. However, stocks and corporate bonds are not insured by the government. To get a higher return, you must accept a greater risk.

Investing in Mutual Funds

Many people want to invest in stocks and bonds but lack the time, ability, or interest to keep track of their investments. These people often invest in **mutual funds**. A mutual fund is an organization that accepts investments from many individuals and uses their money to buy stocks or bonds or to make other types of investments. The managers of the funds take a percentage of the value of each investment to pay their expenses and earn a profit. The remainder of the income generated by the investments is paid to the investors.

There are hundreds of mutual funds in the United States. Each has a specialty intended to attract investors. Some only buy stock in large, secure corporations. Others look for new businesses that are just getting started to invest in. There are mutual funds that buy oil company

◆   Mutual funds allow consumers to place their savings in almost any type of investment. This fund had an average gain of 18.67% per year in the past five years. Can you be sure it will do as well in the next five?

stocks, transportation stocks, or stock in electric utilities. Investors can find almost any type of mutual fund they want. In recent years some mutual funds have specialized in buying stock in firms that try to protect the environment or that try to work for equal rights.

One special type of mutual fund is called a **money market mutual fund**. This type of fund buys short-term securities (usually ones that will come due in thirty to sixty days) and works exactly like the money market deposits described earlier in this chapter. These funds generally pay somewhat higher interest rates than the money market deposits offered by banks.

Summing Up *Consumers may invest in corporations in a number of ways. They may become part owners by purchasing either common or preferred stock. They may buy corporate bonds or invest in mutual funds. Although investing in corporations offers higher returns, consumers take greater risks than with government-insured bank accounts.* ◆

SECTION 3

INVESTING IN GOVERNMENT SECURITIES

While you read, ask yourself . . .
- ◆ *Would buying Treasury securities or municipal bonds be a wise choice for your investments now?*
- ◆ *Do you believe that it is fair for people who earn interest from municipal bonds to not pay tax on this income?*

The federal, state, and local governments borrow money by selling bonds or other types of **securities**. The federal savings bonds you have already learned about are only one of many types of investments that consumers can make in government securities.

Buying Treasury Securities

The Treasury of the United States sells securities other than savings bonds to raise money for our government. These other securities are called treasury bills, notes, and bonds. The difference between these securities is in their **term**, or how long it takes them to mature. This period of time may be as little as three months or as long as thirty years. Unlike savings bonds, these securities will not be paid off by the Treasury until their term expires. However, they may be sold to other people. These securities have face values that range from $1,000 for some bonds to over $10,000 for some treasury bills. Anyone can buy this type of security by submitting a bid at a Federal Reserve Bank or by paying a commercial bank or stockbroker to buy the security for them.

There is no risk of nonpayment for a federal security. However, there is the risk of changing

Vocabulary Builder

Money market mutual fund   A mutual fund that pays a variable rate of interest that is tied to prevailing interest rates and may have checks written against the individual's investments.

Mutual fund   An investment company that pools the money of many individuals to buy stocks, bonds, or other investments.

Security   A stock or bond representing an obligation of the issuer to provide the purchaser with a specific or expected return on the purchaser's investment.

Term   The period of time required for a bond or account to mature; its life.

The  Consumer

Foreign Sales of U.S. Government Securities

Do you think it's a good idea to send American dollars to people who live in other countries? In 1991 more than $300 per American was paid in interest to foreigners by the federal government. The reason for this is easy to understand. Our government's debt grew by almost $2 trillion in the 1980s to an amount that exceeded $3.2 trillion at the start of 1991. During the 1980s almost 40 percent of all new federal borrowing was financed by selling government securities to foreign people or businesses. By 1991, foreigners owned about one-fourth of the national debt and therefore received about one-fourth of the interest paid by the Treasury.

Americans have received benefits and paid costs as a result of foreigners buying our government's securities. We have benefited because the willingness of foreigners to buy our securities has kept interest rates lower than they otherwise would have been. Foreign money has allowed our government to provide public goods and services without increasing current taxes.

Unfortunately, there are some disadvantages of our foreign debt that some economists believe are greater than any advantages. When the U.S. government pays interest to Americans, the money stays in our economic system and provides jobs. When interest payments leave the country, they provide jobs in other countries. In 1991 the federal government paid roughly $65 billion in interest to foreigners.

Some economists believe that the enormous amount of U.S. securities owned by foreigners gives them the ability to influence our economy. They say that foreigners could control interest rates and the value of government securities if they buy or sell large quantities of securities in the market. On the other hand, there is a concern that foreigners might refuse to buy more of our securities. If this happened, it would be more difficult for the government to finance its debt and to continue providing services to our citizens. The government could be forced to raise taxes, which would affect our ability to consume.

Clearly, the American economy and American consumers are only one part of a larger global economic system.

interest rates over time for owners who want to sell their securities. If a federal bond promises to pay 8 percent over ten years and interest rates increase, the current value of the bond will fall. If interest rates go down, the current value of government securities will increase. Of course, if the security is held until it comes due, the original face value of the security will be paid to its owner by the Treasury.

One important advantage to owning any federal government security is the fact that interest paid by the federal government may not be taxed by either state or local governments. This is a particularly important fact to consider in states with high tax rates.

Buying Municipal Bonds

Securities sold by state and local governments are called **municipal bonds**. The most important advantage to investing in a municipal bond is the fact that except in special circumstances, the interest paid on a municipal bond may not be taxed by federal, state, or local governments. The law was written to provide this **tax preference** so that state and local governments could borrow money at relatively low interest rates.

Investors are willing to buy municipal bonds that pay lower interest rates because they are able to keep all of their interest income. Suppose that you pay state and federal income taxes at a combined total rate of 33 percent. In this case, a municipal bond that pays 6 percent will allow you to keep as much income as a taxable corporate bond that pays 9 percent. Many wealthy taxpayers avoid paying taxes by buying municipal bonds and accepting a lower interest rate for their investment.

Municipal bonds may be bought and sold just like federal or corporate bonds. Most often, the price of municipal bonds depends on changes in interest rates. In a few cases the value of some municipal bonds have changed for other reasons. Some cities and states have experienced difficulty in paying interest on the bonds they have issued. Some local governments have even **defaulted**, that is, not paid the interest or principal when they were supposed to.

In the late 1970s New York City almost defaulted on its debts. The city was saved by the creation of a special agency, the Municipal Assistance Corporation (MAC), which was funded by the state of New York and helped by the federal government. Bonds issued by cities and states that experience financial difficulty will also lose value. People should not buy municipal bonds unless they are well informed and understand what they are buying.

Summing Up *Consumers can invest their savings in federal government securities or in municipal bonds issued by state or local governments. These securities usually involve little risk and provide different types of tax preferences.* ◆

Consumer News

Bridgeport Goes "Belly Up"

Did you know that cities can go bankrupt? This doesn't happen often, but it can take place. In June 1991, Bridgeport, Connecticut, filed for bankruptcy because it didn't have enough money to pay all its bills. The value of the municipal bonds issued by Bridgeport plummeted, losing as much as 20 percent of their value in less than a week. The mayor of Bridgeport stated that the city did have enough money to pay interest on its bonds and would fulfill its obligations to bondholders. It was believed by many people that the city filed for bankruptcy to try to break contracts with city workers and cut expenses. Regardless of the actual reason for the filing, the result was a significant loss for people who had invested in Bridgeport Bonds. But the problem was not limited to Bridgeport's bondholders. The city's difficulties worried investors and caused the value of bonds issued by other cities and states that were not financially strong to fall. This event shows that there is some risk associated with almost any investment you can make.

Vocabulary Builder

Default Failure to pay a debt on time.
Municipal bond A bond issued by a state or local government.
Tax preference Having the tax rate on a specific type of income less than on most other types of income.

Review and Enrichment Activities

VOCABULARY REVIEW

1. Column A contains key consumer terms from this chapter. Column B contains a scrambled list of phrases that describe what these terms mean. Match the correct meaning with each term. Write your answers on a separate sheet of paper.

Column A	Column B
1. Discount	a. Failure to pay a debt on time
2. Default	b. Paying more for a bond than its face value
3. Principal	c. The original amount of a loan
4. Mutual fund	d. The length of time until a bond or loan is paid off
5. Premium	e. When the tax on a particular type of income is less than on other types of income
6. Municipal bond	f. A bond issued by a state or local government
7. Tax preference	g. A security issued by a corporation
8. Term	h. To sell a bond for less than its face value
9. Corporate bond	i. An organization that pools money of many people to buy stocks, bonds, or other investments
10. Money market mutual fund	j. An organization that pools money of many people to buy short term securities and that often allows investors to write checks against the value of their investments

2. Explain two differences between common stock and preferred stock.

CHECKING WHAT YOU'VE LEARNED

Write your answers for the following exercises on a separate sheet of paper.

1. Describe two advantages and two disadvantages of certificates of deposits as an investment.
2. Explain why banks are willing to pay higher rates of interest for certificates of deposit than they pay for passbook savings.
3. Why are money market accounts more "liquid" (easier to turn into cash) than certificates of deposit?
4. Explain why buying common stock in a firm is a more risky investment than buying either preferred stock or a bond issued by the same firm.
5. How would a person earn a capital gain by owning and then selling shares of stock?
6. Explain why the value of preferred stocks and bonds usually goes up when most interest rates go down.
7. Explain why a firm's corporate bonds usually offer a lower return than the return from that firm's preferred stock.
8. Explain what would cause the value of a federal government security to go down.
9. What is the tax preference enjoyed by people who own municipal bonds?
10. Why do people with large incomes usually benefit more from owning municipal bonds than people with smaller incomes?
11. How may the owner of a government security receive money for his or her bond before its term is completed?
12. Why shouldn't a person invest in a municipal bond without first doing research about the government that issued the bond?

PRACTICING YOUR CONSUMER SKILLS

Write your answers for the following exercises on a separate sheet of paper.

1. Here are six possible investments:
   1. A one-year bank CD that pays 7.5 percent interest
   2. A three-year bank CD that pays 8 percent interest
   3. A type of common stock that currently pays a dividend equal to 6 percent of its purchase price per year and has increased in value at an average rate of 5 percent a year over the past ten years
   4. A type of preferred stock that currently pays a dividend equal to 10 percent of the purchase price per year
   5. A corporate bond that returns 9 percent a year on its current price
   6. A municipal bond that pays 6.54 percent and will come due in seven years

   Identify the type of investment that you feel is most appropriate for each of the following people. Explain each of your choices.

Review and Enrichment Activities Continued

a. Rose Ann has $5,000 in her bank account. She is a working mother with two children. She is dissatisfied with the return she has been earning. On the other hand, she really doesn't like to take risks and can't afford to lose her money.

b. Vivian has saved $10,000 that she intends to use to go back to college. She knows that she will have to pay her first tuition bill in just over one year. She can't afford to lose any of her money.

c. Phillip is a high school senior. He has just signed up for a three-year enlistment in the navy. He inherited $4,000 from his grandfather's estate and would like to put it somewhere that is absolutely safe while he is gone.

d. Harold is twenty-four years old. He was disabled in an accident several years ago. He has a job but often misses work and has many doctor bills. After the accident, Harold received a settlement of $50,000 from an insurance company. Harold wants a large return on his money, but doesn't want to take much of a risk.

e. Robin is a successful real estate salesperson. She has earned at least $45,000 in each of the last five years. She has saved $50,000 and wants to put at least $20,000 of it in an investment that will yield her a high return. She would rather not lose the money, but she would not live in poverty if she did.

f. Derrick is the owner of a chain of fast-food restaurants. He earns several hundred thousand dollars each year. He has accumulated nearly $500,000 in savings. He is distressed by the high rate of tax he must pay on his income.

2. Read the following two paragraphs. Then copy over paragraph 2, substituting the correct term from this chapter for each *underscored* word or phrase. Possible answers are: equity, money market deposit, corporate bond, FDIC, certificate of deposit, common stock.

(1) Greg recently inherited $10,000 from his aunt's estate. When he received his check in the mail, he deposited it in a savings account that paid him 5½ percent interest. Greg knew that he wanted to put the money somewhere else, but at least it was earning some return while he made up his mind. Greg asked many of his relatives and friends what they thought he should do with his money.

(2) Greg's mother told him that he should put his money in a *bank and leave it there* so that it can earn a higher interest rate and be insured by *an agency of the government*. Greg's father told him he ought to buy *into a corporation* so that he can earn a return from his *ownership* and participate in choosing the leadership of the firm. Greg's sister advised him to take less risk and buy *some of a corporation's debt*. In the end, Greg couldn't make up his mind, so he put the money in a *special account* at his bank that pays interest rates that change with other interest rates.

3. Each of the following people could have made a better investment choice. Identify the problem for each of the choices that were made.
   a. Earl has kept $5,000 deposited in a passbook savings account that has paid him 5 percent interest for the past five years.
   b. Carol put $14,000 in a three-year CD because it paid 8 percent interest. Seven months later she took the money out to buy a car she had planned to purchase for over a year.
   c. Paul only earns $6,000 a year. He won $5,000 in a contest and used the money to buy a municipal bond that pays 6 percent interest that is not taxed.
   d. Wendy bought a twenty-year corporate bond that paid 8 percent interest, although a newspaper article said that most interest rates were about to go up.
   e. Terry bought 100 shares of stock in a firm that sells military equipment to the government. The firm made large profits last year, but it just lost a big contract to produce machine guns.

USING NUMBERS

Solve the following problem to help make the best possible choice. Write your solution on a separate sheet of paper. Be sure to show all your work.

Jayson is a successful businessman who earns well over $100,000 a year. As a result he pays federal income taxes at a 31 percent rate and state taxes at a 5 percent rate. He is considering buying a municipal bond that would pay him 6 percent interest. Another alternative would be to buy a federal government security that pays 8 percent interest and is taxable for federal income taxes but not for state taxes. He could also put his money in a CD that would pay him 9 percent interest. Calculate which investment will allow Jayson to keep the largest amount of after-tax income.

PUTTING IDEAS IN YOUR OWN WORDS

The following quotations are from this chapter. Explain these quotations in your own words to make sure you understand what they mean. Write your answers on a separate sheet of paper.

1. "Banks and other financial institutions are willing to pay higher rates of interest on certificates of deposit because they know that they will have the use of the money for an extended period of time."
2. "Of the people who invest in corporations, common stockholders take the greatest risk but may receive the greatest return."
3. "There is no risk of nonpayment for a federal security. However, there is the risk of changing interest rates over time."

Review and Enrichment Activities Continued

BUILDING CONSUMER KNOWLEDGE

Write your answers for the following exercises on a separate sheet of paper.

1. Visit three different local banks or savings and loan associations to find the following information for each institution.
   a. The interest rate paid on passbook savings
   b. The interest rate paid on one-year CDs
   c. The interest rate paid on three-year CDs
   d. The interest rate paid on money market deposits
   How much difference is there between different institutions in interest rates offered for similar investments?

2. Identify three large corporations that do business in your community. These could be automobile firms, producers of foods or medicine, or oil companies. Go to a library and ask the librarian for help in looking up the price of these firms' common stock one year ago and today. Find the dividend paid by each firm in the last year. Figure out the return you would have earned on each stock if you had bought the stock one year ago. (Add the change in price to the dividend.) What does this show you about the risk associated with owning stock?

3. Identify a public project that was recently completed in your community. This could be a new school, bridge, sewage treatment plant, or any other government building. Call or visit the appropriate local government and ask how the project was financed. Find out what rate of interest the government had to pay to borrow money. Compare this interest rate with rates being paid by corporations or with the prime interest rate that you learned about in Chapter 6. Why would people be willing to loan your local government money at an interest rate that is lower than they could earn by loaning their money to a business?

UNIT 8

Understanding Credit

Unit 8 explains what credit is and why you should use credit wisely. You will learn why it so important to develop a good credit history, as well as learning about your credit rights and responsibilities. The advantages and disadvantages of various sources of credit are also discussed. Unit 8 emphasizes the importance of shopping for credit when you determine that borrowing is a wise choice.

Chapter 29

What Is Credit?

Chapter Objectives

After completing this chapter, you will be able to do the following:

- Describe several situations in which consumers need to borrow money to meet their personal goals.
- Explain the rights that borrowers are entitled to under the law and explain the responsibilities that they are expected to fulfill.
- Explain steps that consumers may take to establish a credit history and a favorable credit rating.
- Explain why consumers should use credit in moderation.
- Explain why consumers should shop for credit to be sure that they borrow funds at the lowest possible cost and in a way that is best able to meet their individual needs and financial situation.

Key Consumer Terms

In this chapter you will learn the meanings of the following important consumer terms:

- Credit
- Mortgage
- Self-liquidating loan
- Austerity
- Truth-in-Lending Act
- Disclose
- Finance charge
- Annual percentage rate
- Right of recession
- Equal Credit Opportunity Act
- Cosign
- Credit bureau
- Fair Credit Reporting Act
- Collection agency
- Write off
- Foreclose
- Insolvent
- Character
- Collateral
- Capacity
- Capital

I t has been said that part of the "American dream" is to own your own home. How many Americans do you know who could afford to buy a house if they couldn't borrow money? Most Americans could never save enough money to buy expensive products without the use of **credit**. Here's how credit works: A person or business supplies a good, service, or resource (such as money) in exchange for the promise of future payment. Most American consumers depend on credit to maintain their standard of living.

SECTION 1

WHEN USING CREDIT MAKES GOOD SENSE

While you read, *ask yourself . . .*
◆ *What sorts of purchases does your family make using credit?*
◆ *Can you think of a time when borrowing money to buy a product would have been a wise choice for you?*

Consumers complete many types of financial transactions in their lives. Some of these transactions are only possible through the use of credit. Although there are times when the use of credit is wise or even necessary, there are other times when credit really should not be used. One of the most important skills a consumer can acquire is the ability to know when to use credit—and when not to.

When Credit Is Necessary

Suppose that Maria and her husband Raymond rent an apartment for $680 a month. At the end of each year they have nothing to show for the money they have paid in rent. Although they both work, they only take home about $2,000 a month. After Maria and Raymond pay for their rent, heat, electricity, phone, food, clothing, car, and insurance each month, they have very little money left over. The most they

have ever been able to save is about $2,500 a year. In many years they have saved less. Maria and Raymond have been married for seven years and have accumulated almost $12,000 in savings. They have picked out a modest house in a rural area that they would like to buy for about $65,000.

The price of housing in the area where Maria and Raymond want to buy has been going up about 7 percent a year. When they first looked at these houses five years ago, they cost about $45,000. Raymond thinks that if they don't buy a house soon, they will never be able to own a home. Like Maria and Raymond, very few people can afford to buy a house without taking out a **mortgage**. If they are able to qualify for a mortgage, Maria and Raymond can become homeowners. If they cannot borrow the money they need, they probably will never own a home.

Another situation where credit is almost a necessity is borrowing to pay the cost of college tuition. Private colleges can cost well over

Vocabulary Builder

Credit   Allowing a person, business, or government to use money, goods, or services at the present in return for a promise of future payment.

Mortgage   A long-term debt owed on real property, such as a house.

◆   Almost all people who buy homes finance their purchase with a mortgage. What other types of purchases do consumers most often make with borrowed money?

$20,000 a year. Even state-supported colleges and universities can cost $5,000 to $8,000 or more when the cost of books and housing is included. Most students could not earn this amount of money and attend college at the same time. Unless your parents can afford to help, you may have to borrow to attend college.

Borrowing may also be necessary to meet expenses that result from family emergencies. If you break your leg and can't work, you may be forced to borrow to pay for your living 'expenses. If your son or daughter needs braces, you can't wait five years until you have saved the $3,000 they will cost. If you own a home and discover that the wall of your basement is caving in, you might have to borrow to have it fixed before more damage is done. There are many situations where using credit is simply necessary.

When Using Credit Is a Wise Choice

There are times when using credit is not absolutely necessary but is a wise choice. Assume that you have been saving to buy a motorcycle. The model you want costs $1,799. You have saved $1,200. While reading the newspaper one evening, you see an advertisement for the exact motorcycle you want on sale for just $1,599. If you are willing to borrow $400, you can save $200 off the regular price. In this situation it is wise to use credit.

Suppose that after you graduate from high school you are offered a job working for a business in a community 10 miles from your home. You don't want to move, and there is no public transportation you can use to get to your new job. You have saved $2,000, but you don't want to spend all your savings on a car. Besides, you know that you could not buy a dependable used car for much less than $5,000. If you borrow money to buy a car, you can accept the new job.

Borrowing to increase your income is called a **self-liquidating loan**. This means that the loan is used to pay for something that increases your income, which in turn makes you better able to pay your debt. This term is most often used when businesses borrow to build factories or buy machines. But consumers also use credit in this way. Using credit to buy a car makes sense if it will allow you to accept a new job and earn the money to pay your debt.

Only Borrow When You Need To

Unfortunately, many Americans do not use credit wisely. In recent years as many as twenty-three out of every thousand adults in this country have been forced to file for bankruptcy. Other people have lived through years of **austerity** to make up for having borrowed too much money. Before you borrow money to buy a product, there is a series of questions you should ask yourself:

1. Do I really need to buy the product now?

2. Do I need to borrow money to buy the product?
3. Can I afford to make the payments on the loan I would take out?
4. Will I be able to buy other things I need more if I buy the product?

If you can answer yes to each of these questions, you should be willing to borrow the funds you need to buy the product.

There are many times when using credit is a reasonable decision because it can help you achieve your personal goals.

Summing Up   *Consumers need to learn to recognize when using credit is necessary and when it is a wise choice. They should be able to distinguish these situations from those when credit should not be used.* ◆

SECTION 2

YOUR RIGHTS AND RESPONSIBILITIES AS A BORROWER

***While you read**, ask yourself . . .*
- ◆ *What characteristics do you have that you would want a potential lender to know about?*
- ◆ *When you borrow money from your friends or relatives, do you always pay it back on time?*

If you decide to borrow money, it is important for you to understand your rights and responsibilities as a borrower. Many people who

Vocabulary Builder

Austerity   Spending the least amount possible to achieve an objective.
Self-liquidating loan   A loan used to buy something that generates income to pay for the loan.

Consumers in Action

Bad Times for Some Are Good Times for Others

Is it better to borrow money to buy a home or car when the economy is booming and most people have a secure income—or during a recession when most people are worried about the future? You might think the better time is in an expansion, but you could be wrong.

In the mid-1980s the American economy was recovering from a recession. Unemployment was down and production was up. Interest rates for automobile loans were as high as 16 percent, and consumers had to pay 13 percent or more to borrow money to buy a house. With the recovery, more people wanted to borrow money, which helped to keep interest rates high. Many consumers were willing to pay these high interest rates because they had confidence in the future.

By the end of the 1980s the situation had changed. The economy was going into a recession. In many parts of the country too many new homes had been built by contractors who couldn't find buyers. With unemployment growing, some people were forced to sell their homes to find less expensive places to live. The failure of many savings and loan associations caused the government to seize and sell homes that these financial institutions owned. The result was a surplus in housing, causing a decline in prices for new and used homes in many parts of the country. For example, the price of typical housing units fell as much as 17 percent in New York City and 15 percent in Chicago and Los Angeles. Similar problems plagued the American automobile industry. New car sales were about 15 percent less in 1990 than in 1989. There was a surplus of cars offered for sale on the market. Automobile manufacturers reacted by offering rebates and special low-cost financing to try to attract customers.

When people buy fewer products, they also borrow less money. The Federal Reserve System took steps to lower interest rates in 1990 and 1991 to try to encourage borrowing and spending. As a result, by the summer of 1991, interest rates for new car loans were about 12 percent, and interest rates for mortgages were less than 10 percent. Still, many consumers were too worried to borrow and buy.

When you consider all these events together, you will see that borrowing to buy expensive products in a recession can be a wise choice for people who can afford to do this. Interest rates are likely to be lower, and sellers are usually more willing to compromise on price. People who are able to buy should be able to find good deals.

These events also point out the importance of planning for your future. A consumer who could afford to buy in 1991 may have been able to find a good house at a low price. However, a seller in 1990 was likely to be forced to take a loss when he or she sold. Many Americans "bit off" too much in the expansion of the mid-1980s. When economic times turned down, they couldn't pay their bills. Some of these people could have avoided financial hardships if they had been more careful when times were good.

use credit don't understand interest rates or many of the other charges they may be required to pay when they borrow money. It is hard to make a wise choice about something you don't understand. For this reason, the government has passed a number of laws that are intended to protect consumers who choose to use credit.

Truth in Lending

Probably all Americans know that using credit to buy goods and services costs money. However, for many years the contracts that consumers signed when they borrowed money were often so complicated that it was difficult to tell what the actual cost would be. This situation was changed with the passage of the **Truth-in-Lending Act** in 1968. This law requires lenders to **disclose**, or make known, to the borrower all credit terms so that the consumer will be able to compare different sources of credit and make an informed decision. Lenders are required by this law to explain the actual cost of credit to the borrower, including the interest and other fees under one label called the **finance charge**. This prevents lenders from having "hidden" fees that borrowers are charged but not informed of.

The same type of procedure is used to compute a single rate known as the **annual percentage rate**. This rate includes the interest and all other fees the lender charges as a percent of the money borrowed. Knowing the finance charge and annual percentage rate for each possible source of credit allows consumers to make informed choices when they borrow money.

The Truth-in-Lending Act also gives consumers the **right of recession** for certain credit agreements. This means that consumers have three business days to change their mind if they have borrowed money against the value of their home. For example, if you owned a

home and signed an agreement to have new siding put on it, you would have three days to change your mind and receive a full refund of any money you had put down on the agreement.

The Truth-in-Lending Act controls or limits many other phases of credit agreements. It regulates advertising for consumer credit. A 1970 amendment provides regulation on the use of credit cards and establishes a maximum limit of $50 that consumers may be charged for the unauthorized use of a credit card. This means that when the loss or theft of a card is promptly reported, the most the cardholder may be charged is $50.

The Truth-in-Lending Act does not assure consumers that they cannot be taken advantage of. It only guarantees consumers access to information. Whether or not consumers choose to use this information is their decision.

Equal Credit Opportunity

Since the **Equal Credit Opportunity Act** was passed in 1975, it has been illegal to dis-

---

Vocabulary Builder

Annual percentage rate   The cost of credit expressed as a yearly percentage. The Truth-in-Lending law requires lenders to provide this figure.

Disclose   To provide relevant information.

Equal Credit Opportunity Act   A law that makes discrimination in credit based on sex or marital status illegal.

Finance charge   The cost of credit expressed in dollars and cents that must be paid over the life of a loan.

Right of recession   The right to cancel a contract or a signed agreement.

Truth-in-Lending Act   A law passed in 1968 that requires lending institutions to tell borrowers the annual percentage rate and finance charge for loans.

Consumer News

What if Your Credit History Contains Mistakes

Three companies control most of the credit bureau business in this country. They are TRW, Equifax Inc., and Trans Union Corporation. These firms believe that their procedures for gathering and reporting consumer credit information are reliable and fair. However, in 1991 Cathy Saypol ordered a copy of her confidential credit report for $20 and discovered that there were three accounts on her record that she had never opened. Two were marked "closed at lender's request." Saypol wondered if her incorrect report had anything to do with her being granted a smaller loan than she had requested in 1990. She was eventually able to correct the mistakes after many telephone calls to TRW, but worries that other incorrect information could be placed in her record in the future.

Critics of the credit-reporting industry point out that of the 9 million consumers who received copies of their files in 1989, 3 million disputed information and requested changes. The industry admits that there may be a problem and has even found a way to earn money by offering consumers a way to protect themselves from incorrect credit reports. In 1990, all three firms offered services for $20 to $40 a year that regularly report changes in credit files to consumers.

What is your opinion of this practice?

- Asking for information about a credit applicant's intention to have a family
- Requiring some individuals to have other people **cosign** loan applications when other applicants with similar qualifications are not asked for a cosigner
- Discouraging an applicant from asking for credit because of his or her sex or marital status
- Terminating or changing the conditions of credit because of an applicant's sex or change in marital status
- Ignoring alimony or child-support payments as a source of income in deciding whether to grant credit to an applicant

Basically, the Equal Credit Opportunity Act was intended to guarantee women the right to get or keep credit in their own name rather than in their husband's. Today women have the legal right to have a credit history and rating equal to that of their husband or former husband.

Access to Your Credit Rating

Credit histories may include records of consumers' transactions, incomes, bad debts, and court actions. There are a number of businesses called **credit bureaus** that provide lenders with consumers' credit histories. There is no guarantee that all the information included in the files of such credit-investigating agencies is complete or accurate. Inaccurate information about consumers has often been sent to lenders and prevented deserving people from receiving credit.

There was a time when it was nearly impossible to find out what was included in your credit history. However, in 1971 the **Fair Credit Reporting Act** went into effect. This law requires businesses or banks that turn anyone down for credit to provide the applicant with the name and address of the credit-investigat-

criminate on the basis of sex and marital status when granting credit. Under this act, the following actions are against the law:

ing agency that was used. This allows the individual to contact the agency and demand access to his or her credit record. A consumer whose credit application has been refused has thirty days to request a free copy of his or her file. After the thirty days, a fee may be charged that is often between $20 and $40.

The Fair Credit Reporting Act requires credit bureaus to disclose the "nature and substance of all information" that is included under a consumer's name in its records. If a consumer discovers that his or her record includes misleading or false information, the law requires the credit agency to investigate any disputed information within a "reasonable period of time." This does not mean that the credit agency will investigate every dispute as quickly as it should, but it does mean that consumers have the law on their side and may take the credit agency to court if necessary. Even if the credit bureau eventually refuses to remove information from your record, you have the right to file a personal version concerning disputed entries.

Your Responsibilities as a Borrower

People who borrow money have rights, but they also have responsibilities. These responsibilities are to the businesses they receive credit from, to other consumers, and to themselves.

Businesses that extend credit to consumers expect to earn a profit. However, in doing so, they help consumers satisfy their needs by allowing them to buy goods and services on credit. When customers fail to pay their debts on time, businesses have higher costs. At the least, there will be extra mailing costs to send past-due notices. The firm may hire a **collection agency**, pay the cost of taking the customer to court, or eventually **write off** the debt and take a loss. When firms pay higher costs, they usual-

ly pass these increased costs on to consumers in higher prices. Therefore, consumers who fail to pay their debts on time cause other consumers to pay more for the goods and services they buy. Ethical consumers pay their debts on time if they possibly can.

It is possible for firms to be forced out of business by customers who do not pay their debts on time. In the late 1980s and early 1990s the prices of homes in many parts of the United States fell. People who were laid off or had other financial problems often found that they could not sell their homes for as much money as they owed. As a result, some people chose to simply stop making payments and allow banks to **foreclose** on their property. In many such cases banks lost large amounts of money because they could not sell the homes for as much as they had loaned their customers. Some of these banks became **insolvent** and were taken over by the FDIC. The bank owners lost their investment, and it is likely that American taxpayers will need to support the FDIC.

Consumers who do not pay their debts on time create a credit history that may prevent

Vocabulary Builder

Collection agency   A business that attempts to secure payment of overdue debts for a fee.

Cosign   To sign a loan contract along with a borrower and promise to repay the loan if the borrower does not.

Credit bureau   An agency that collects and distributes information about people's credit histories.

Fair Credit Reporting Act   A law passed in 1971 that gives individuals access to files that concern them held by credit bureaus.

Foreclosure   To take title to a property because of nonpayment of a debt.

Insolvent   Describing a person or business that has current debts that exceed their ability to pay, resulting in a non payment of debts.

Write off   To decide that a debt will not be paid and no longer count it as an asset.

them from obtaining credit in the future. Consumers who do not have access to credit often find it difficult to achieve their personal goals. If you decide not to make a payment of several hundred dollars to a bank on time because you are a little short of cash, you may hurt your chance to own a home in the future. Banks and other lending institutions are not likely to loan many thousands of dollars to someone who has failed to pay a few hundred dollars on time. Consumers have a responsibility to themselves and to their families to establish a positive credit history.

Summing Up   *Consumers have many rights guaranteed to them by the law. Although consumers should be aware of these rights, they also need to be aware of their responsibilities.* ◆

ESTABLISHING YOUR CREDIT HISTORY

While you read, ask yourself . . .
◆ *Would you want to loan money to someone who did not demonstrate a willingness and ability to pay on time?*
◆ *What steps could you take now that would help you develop a positive credit history?*

People are not born with a credit history. They must develop one by being responsible consumers and borrowers. Having a good credit history means more than earning a good income. It also depends on a demonstrated

◆   Paying bills on time is one important step you may take to establish a positive credit history. When you send your payment through the mail be sure to allow enough time for delivery.

willingness to pay bills on time. If you earn $100,000 a year but don't pay your bills on time, businesses won't want to loan you money. They would rather extend credit to a person who earns only $20,000 a year and takes his or her credit responsibilities seriously.

When businesses decide whether or not to grant you credit, they consider four factors, commonly called the four Cs of credit: **character, collateral, capacity,** and **capital**.

Demonstrating Your Character

Many young people have difficulty getting their first loan. They may be asked to have a parent or some other adult cosign their application. This means that if the applicant fails to pay, the bank can force the cosigner to pay instead. The bank is asking the cosigner to accept most of the risk of extending credit to a person who does not have many assets or an established credit history. Many young borrowers think that this is unfair. They can't get a loan without a credit history, and they can't have a credit history without getting a loan.

Although you may not be able to borrow money on your own at this time, there are steps you can take that will make it easier to borrow in the future. One positive step would be to establish a pattern of saving regularly. A bank is more likely to make a loan to a person who saves $5 every week for several years than to someone who has never demonstrated a willingness to save regularly. You could also open and use a checking account to pay your bills. Again, showing the bank that you are able to pay bills on time will help create a positive credit history. Some businesses allow young people to buy a limited value of products on credit. This may only be $100 to $200 worth, but it is enough for you to show your ability and willingness to pay your debts on time.

If you do borrow money, be sure that your debt never exceeds your ability to pay. Getting in over your head just once can ruin your credit history for many years. Federal laws allow a bankruptcy to be kept on your credit record for ten years. Few banks or businesses will want to extend credit to a person who has filed for bankruptcy. If you have filed for bankruptcy and are granted a loan, it may be by an institution that will require you to pay high interest rates.

Collateral

Assets such as homes, land, cars, boats, and other property that could be easily sold may be used as backing, or collateral, for a loan. Financial assets like stocks or bonds may also be used. Collateral is an asset that is pledged to back a loan. If the borrower fails to pay his or her debt on time, the lender can take and sell the property to satisfy the debt. When a bank or other lending institution knows that it may take the property of a borrower, the risk is much lower. The greater a borrower's collateral, the more likely he or she is going to be

---

Vocabulary Builder

Capacity   The difference between a person's or firm's current income and the fixed costs that must be paid; one of the "four Cs of credit."

Capital   All property—machines, buildings, and tools—used to produce goods and services; in some situations, the money necessary to undertake a business venture. Value of a person's or business's assets; one of the "four Cs of credit."

Character   A person's demonstrated willingness to make payments on a debt on time; one of the "four Cs of credit."

Collateral   Assets used as security or backing for a loan; one of the "four Cs of credit."

granted a loan and the lower the interest rate that may be charged.

Unfortunately, most young people do not have much property to pledge as collateral against a loan. Possessions that have personal value to you may have little market value. For example, you may have spent hundreds of dollars to buy every CD ever produced by your favorite musical group. However, if you tried to pledge the CDs as collateral on a loan, the bank wouldn't be interested.

The best way to develop collateral is to start small. Save as much money as you can. If you can put down half the cash you need to buy an automobile, banks are more likely to loan you the rest of the money you need. A bank can always take the car and sell it to satisfy your debt if you don't make your payments. If the bank loaned you the full price of the car, it could not sell the car for what you owe.

Capacity and Capital

When you ask to borrow money, the potential lender will look at your income and the amount of current payments you must make to determine your capacity to pay your debts on time. Capacity is not determined by income alone. A person who earns $900 a month and has no current debts would probably be a better risk than a person with $1,500 a month in income but who already must pay $1,100 of that income to other creditors. The lender will also be interested in how steady your income is and how long you have held your current job. If you are a salesperson who earns $1,000 some weeks and nothing in others, a bank would be concerned about your capacity to pay on a loan.

Capital is similar to collateral. They are both assets that have market value, but collateral has been pledged to back a specific loan, while

capital has not. If you own a home, a bank will feel better about making you a loan to go on a vacation to Europe, even if the house is not pledged as collateral. The fact that you own the home means that you are likely to return to live in your home and not stay in Europe. In general, the more capital people own, the more they can be counted on to make their payments on time.

There are millions of Americans who have good credit histories and an ability to borrow money when they need to. These people had to develop their credit histories over time. They accomplished this by being responsible consumers.

Summing Up *Consumers need to establish a positive credit history to be able to borrow money when necessary. In doing this, they need to consider how they rank with the four Cs of credit: character, collateral, capacity, and capital.* ◆

SECTION 4

SHOPPING AROUND FOR CREDIT

While you read, ask yourself . . .
  ◆ *What sources of credit are available for consumers in your community?*
  ◆ *What types of purchases do you expect to make in the next five years that will probably require the use of credit?*

Many consumers think that the kinds of credit offered by most lending institutions are much the same. If you believe this, you are wrong and your mistake could cost you a great deal of money. Annual percentage rates charged by different lending institutions vary widely. When consumers need to borrow, they should carefully compare alternative sources of credit that are available to them.

◆ If you need to borrow money don't automatically accept the first loan offer you receive. Paying half a percent more in interest can make a big difference in the cost of a loan over several years.

Different types of institutions offer credit in various ways that have different costs. You will learn more about different financial institutions that loan money in Chapters 30 and 31.

You should never borrow money until you are sure you have found the best possible deal. There was a time when it was very difficult for consumers to know what rate they were being charged when they borrowed money. But with the Truth-in-Lending Act, it is now relatively easy to compare credit costs. Lending institutions are required to tell you the annual percentage rate they will charge, including all interest and other fees. By asking each poten-

tial source of credit for this rate, a consumer can find the best offer.

There are other factors that borrowers should consider. For example, what will the lender do if the borrower wants to pay off a loan early to avoid paying extra interest? Most institutions have no penalty for early payments, but a few do. If you think you might want to pay off your loan early, this is important information for you to have.

It is also important to know what the institution will do if a borrower is late making a payment. Are there penalties—and if so, how large are they? Borrowers also need to find out if the

Consumer News

Special Accounts Build Credit Histories

Some banks have introduced special credit accounts for students to help them develop a credit history. To qualify for the account, a student is required to keep $1,000 or more deposited in the bank. In exchange, the bank issues the student a credit card with a $1,000 limit on the amount that can be charged. The interest rate on any unpaid balance is often set as low as 7.5 percent, a rate that probably doesn't cover the bank's cost of servicing the account.

The advantage of this type of account to the students is that they can establish a credit history without having a cosigner. They also enjoy the convenience and safety of using credit cards instead of carrying cash. The banks benefit by gaining future credit customers while taking no risk of nonpayment. If a student fails to pay his or her bills, the bank has the right to take the money from student's deposit.

lending institution can sell the debt to another organization. There have been cases where consumers have borrowed money from one organization and found later that they were required to make payments to a different organization.

Borrowers should also consider the character of the people that represent the institutions they borrow from. Some banks or other lending institutions are more pleasant to work with than others. It may be worth paying a little more to borrow money at a location that is convenient and that employs workers who are friendly and helpful.

When you borrow, try to put yourself in the place of the institution you want to borrow from. It wants to loan you money because that is how it earns a profit. Your job is to assure the institution that you will pay your debts on time. You can't expect anyone to take a high risk loaning you money that often is not even theirs. Remember, the money that you borrow from a bank was deposited by savers who expect their money back and a return on their investment. If you have not demonstrated responsible financial habits, you should not expect others to trust you with their money.

Summing Up   *When consumers need to borrow money, they should shop for the best possible offer.* ◆

Review and Enrichment Activities

VOCABULARY REVIEW

1. Column A contains key consumer terms from this chapter. Column B contains a scrambled list of phrases that describe what these terms mean. Match the correct meaning with each term. Write your answers on a separate sheet of paper.

Column A	Column B
1. Character	a. A borrower's right to change his or her mind and not buy a product for which the borrower's home has been pledged
2. Cosign	b. A borrower's ability to make payments on a loan; current income minus current payments
3. Annual percentage rate	c. The total amount a borrower must pay in interest and fees
4. Right of recession	d. To take property pledged to back a loan as the result of nonpayment
5. Capacity	e. The total amount a borrower must pay in interest and fees each year as a part of the amount borrowed
6. Write off	f. A loan used to finance the purchase of a house
7. Foreclose	g. To decide that a debt will not be paid and no longer count as an asset
8. Mortgage	h. A borrower's demonstrated willingness to pay debts on time
9. Finance charge	i. A loan that is used to buy something that will increase the income of the borrower to pay for the loan
10. Self-liquidating loan	j. To sign a loan agreement with a borrow and promise to repay the loan if the borrower does not

Review and Enrichment Activities Continued

2. Explain the difference between collateral and capital as these terms are used in deciding whether or not to grant a person a loan.

CHECKING WHAT YOU'VE LEARNED

Write your answers for the following exercises on a separate sheet of paper.

1. Describe two situations when borrowing money would be a necessity.
2. Describe two situations when borrowing money would be a wise choice.
3. Name two amounts or rates that the Truth-in-Lending Act requires lenders to tell potential borrowers.
4. Describe the purpose of the Equal Credit Opportunity Act.
5. Describe a situation in which rights guaranteed by the Fair Credit Reporting Act should be used.
6. Explain how consumers who do not pay their debts on time can harm other consumers.
7. Explain what character means when it is used as one of the four Cs of credit.
8. Describe several steps that young people may take to begin to develop a positive credit history.
9. Explain how a person with a small income could have a better capacity to pay for a new loan than a different person with a larger income.
10. What are the four questions you should ask yourself when you are considering borrowing money?
11. Explain why consumers should never borrow from the first institution that offers them credit.

PRACTICING YOUR CONSUMER SKILLS

Write your answers for the following exercises on a separate sheet of paper.

1. Explain whether you believe that each of the following decisions was a wise choice, and explain your opinion.
   a. Stacie has always wanted to be an actress on the stage or in the movies. She has acted in community theaters but has never had a lead role. She works as a clerk in a drugstore. She borrowed $2,000 to take a trip to Hollywood to see the movie studios. She has a secret dream that she will be "discovered" while she is there.

    b. Harold delivers advertising circulars to earn an extra $50 every weekend. His old car had more than 100,000 miles on it, so he borrowed $5,000 to buy a "new" used car.

    c. Gail is a single parent who often gets home from work late. She has little time to cook for herself or her two children. She decided to borrow $300 to buy a microwave oven, so that she can prepare food more rapidly.

    d. Chet likes to work out. He has won several weight-lifting competitions and has been interviewed by local newspaper and television reporters about his bodybuilding methods. His job is directing an athletic program at the YMCA. He borrowed $2,500 to buy exercise equipment of his own to keep in his basement.

    e. Peggy and her husband Thad have a son named William. William is disabled and needs a wheelchair to get around. Their insurance would only pay for an ordinary wheelchair that made William tired. Therefore, Peggy and Thad borrowed $2,000 to buy William an electric wheelchair.

2. Describe the probable effect that each of the following situations will have on the person's credit history and ability to obtain credit in the future.

    a. Roger went on vacation for three months and forgot to arrange to have his utility bills paid. When he returned home, his electricity had been turned off.

    b. Beverly decided long ago to never use credit unless it was absolutely necessary. Although she is twenty-seven years old and is looking for a house to buy, she has never owed anyone a penny.

    c. Margo doesn't believe in paying her bills until the last possible moment. She sees no reason to give anyone the use of her money "for free." Although she is never intentionally late with her payments, she often pays bills several days after they are due.

    d. Robert is an impulse buyer. He never intentionally buys things he can't afford. It just seems to happen. Last week he bought a $1,200 kayak and agreed to pay $56.88 for each of the next twenty-four months. He now realizes that he won't be able to make the payments.

    e. Sandra works in a restaurant and lives at home with her parents. She is going to be married next year. Last week she signed a contract to buy an entire set of kitchen pots, pans, and cooking utensils for $799. She will pay $72.19 each month for twelve months and make her last payment six weeks before she gets married.

3. At least one of four Cs of credit—character, collateral, capacity, and capital—are demonstrated in each of the following situations. In each case identify the C that is demonstrated. Explain your choice.

    a. Jacob owns a small farm and farm equipment that he pledged against a loan he needed to buy seed and fertilizer.

    b. Lucy has saved over $1,500 this year by depositing 10 percent of every paycheck she received in her savings account.

Review and Enrichment Activities Continued

    c. Lois earns $997.32 every two weeks. Of this amount she takes home $803.34. She currently has bills she must pay each month that total about $800.

    d. Ryan earns about $1,000 every two weeks selling appliances. He also owns an apartment building worth about $130,000 that he inherited from his uncle two years ago. He borrowed $2,000 to take a trip to California but did not pledge the apartment building against his loan.

USING NUMBERS

Solve the following problem to help make the best possible choice. Write your solution on a separate sheet of paper. Be sure to show all your work.

Shelly had an accident with her car and needs to borrow $1,200 to have it repaired. She did not have collision insurance, so she must pay for the work herself. Shelly has found three sources of credit. Figure out how much she would pay in each case and recommend a choice to Shelly. Explain your recommendation.

Source 1. Shelly's brother has offered to loan her the money if she agrees to pay him $100 plus 1 percent of the unpaid balance each month for twelve months. At the end of the first month she would pay $112, since $100 + ($1,200 \times 0.01) = 112, leaving an unpaid balance of $1,100. At the end of the second month she would pay $111, since $100 + (1,100 \times 0.01) = 111, leaving an unpaid balance of $1,000. And so on, until she paid off her loan at the end of a year.

Source 2. Shelly can borrow the money from a bank and pay the bank $107 at the end of each month for a year.

Source 3. Shelly can pay for the repair by charging it on her credit card and paying an annual rate of 18 percent (1.5 percent per month) on the unpaid balance at the end of each month. Shelly believes that she could pay $100 plus the interest charge each month if she uses this method. The advantage of this method is that she won't be charged any interest in her first billing period. If she pays $100 of her debt in the first month, her first interest payment will be 1.5 percent of the remaining balance of $1,100 in the second month. She will only pay interest in eleven of the twelve months it takes her to pay off the debt. Using this method, she would pay $100 the first month and $116.50 in the second month, since $100 + (0.015 \times $1,100) = 116.50. In the third month she would pay $115, since $100 + (0.015 \times $1,000) = 115. And so on, until the debt was paid off after twelve months.

PUTTING IDEAS IN YOUR OWN WORDS

The following quotations are from this chapter. Explain these quotations in your own words to make sure you understand what they mean. Write your answers on a separate sheet of paper.

1. "Most American consumers depend on credit to maintain their standard of living."
2. "The Truth-in-Lending Act does not assure consumers that they cannot be taken advantage of. It only guarantees consumers access to information."
3. "Consumers who fail to pay their debts on time cause other consumers to pay more for the goods and services they buy."

BUILDING CONSUMER KNOWLEDGE

Write your answers for the following exercises on a separate sheet of paper.

1. Describe one specific use of credit by a member of your family. What did this person need to do before being granted credit?
2. Use the four Cs of credit to evaluate yourself as a credit risk.
3. Suppose that a relative or friend about the same age as you asks to borrow $200. He or she wants the money to buy a new bicycle. Assume that you have the money to loan if you want to. This person promises to pay you back $10 a week for the next twenty-two weeks, so that you will receive $20 extra if you are paid on time. Write this person a letter explaining why you will or will not grant the loan. You don't want to offend the person, but you don't want to lose $200 either.

Chapter 30

Consumer Loans

Chapter Objectives

After completing this chapter, you will be able to do the following:

- Discuss types of consumer credit offered by banks and other financial institutions.
- Explain the differences between fixed- and variable-rate mortgages.
- Identify alternative sources of home financing.
- Explain how a home equity loan works and the tax advantages offered by such loans.

Key Consumer Terms

In this chapter you will learn the meanings of the following important consumer terms:

- Consumer credit
- Repossess
- Delinquent
- Restructuring the debt
- Bill consolidation loan
- Point
- Conventional mortgage
- Fixed interest rate
- Closing costs
- Adjustable-rate mortgage (ARM)
- Graduated-payment mortgage
- Federal Housing Administration (FHA)
- Veterans Administration (VA)
- First mortgage
- Second mortgage
- Home equity loan

How do you feel about banks? Would it make you nervous to ask a bank for a loan? It shouldn't. Regardless of all the polished desks and thick carpets, a bank is only a business that has the purpose of earning a profit by loaning money. If you are a qualified borrower, the bank's employees want to talk to you.

Banks loan roughly $1 out of every $5 borrowed to buy consumer goods in this country. The other $4 are loaned by savings and loan associations, credit unions, finance companies, and private businesses. Most people who borrow large sums began by borrowing a few hundred or a few thousand dollars to buy a consumer product they needed. Although there are differences between these financial institutions, they all intend to earn a return by loaning money and providing other services.

SECTION 1

WHAT IS CONSUMER CREDIT?

While you read, ask yourself . . .
- ◆ *What are several products that your family owns that were purchased through consumer credit?*
- ◆ *How would your life be different if your family could not borrow to buy consumer goods?*

Consumer credit is money that is borrowed to purchase consumer goods or services. Consumer credit differs from other types of borrowing in at least two ways.

One feature of consumer credit is that it usually does not increase a borrower's future income. In general, people who use consumer credit are trading future consumption for current consumption. Suppose you moved into a new apartment and did not have enough cash to buy furniture. You would probably be willing to borrow money and make payments over several years to have a bed to sleep in and chairs to sit on now. A loan to pay for a big wedding, a vacation, or an appliance is also a form of consumer credit. None of these uses of borrowed money increases the borrower's future income.

Consumer credit is used to buy products that will either decrease in value as they grow older or retain no value at all. If you borrow money to buy a new boat, it will lose 10 to 15 percent of its value the second you take it out of the dealer's showroom. Even slightly used boats have less value than new ones. The same is true of furniture, appliances, or clothing you could buy on credit. If you borrow money to take a trip or receive personal counseling, you will have nothing you could resell to others after you have spent the money.

Summing Up   *People use consumer credit to buy goods and services that will not increase in value over time or increase their future income.* ◆

Vocabulary Builder

Consumer credit   Money borrowed to finance the purchase of consumer goods and services.

Consumer News

Increase in Delinquent Loans

According to the American Bankers Association (ABA), in the spring of 1991 there was a significant increase in the number of consumers who were unable to make payments on their loans. Every three months this trade association asks it members how many of their consumer loans are **delinquent**, or overdue, by more than thirty days. In April 1991 this rate stood at 2.67 percent or 0.31 percent higher than it had been a year earlier. This may not seem like much of an increase, but the amount of money involved was several billion dollars. The ABA blamed the increase on higher unemployment, lower personal income, and the difficulty that consumers were having in "catching up" with Christmas bills.

When consumers can't pay their bills on time, what does it show about the health of the economy?

SECTION 2

GETTING A CONSUMER LOAN

While you read, *ask yourself . . .*
- ◆ *Would a bank want to loan me money?*
- ◆ *What could I do to convince a bank I would pay back a loan?*

When you ask for a consumer loan at a bank or other financial institution, think of the loan from the bank's point of view. The good or service you intend to buy will have limited or no resale value. If you don't make your payments and the bank **repossesses** the product, the bank will not be able to sell it for nearly as much money as it cost. What's more, the product you buy is not likely to increase your future income and ability to pay. For these reasons, a bank will not be willing to loan you the full price of a consumer purchase unless you have assets you are willing to pledge as collateral against the loan.

Banks and other financial institutions want to make loans that they believe will be paid back on time. It is your job to convince the loan officer that you are willing and able to make your payments on time. To do this you will be asked to provide financial information. The institution will check with a credit agency to be sure that the information you provide is accurate. The worst thing you can do when you ask for a loan is to lie. The institution will almost certainly discover the truth and refuse to make the loan.

Applying for a Consumer Loan

When you apply for a loan, you may expect to be asked to provide the following information:

- Your place of residence, how long you have lived there, and whether you own or rent your dwelling. You may also be asked to identify your previous place of residence.
- Your place of employment, how long you have worked for this organization, who your supervisor is, and how much you earn. You may also be asked to provide your previous place of employment.
- A list of other sources of income you have and assets you own.
- A list of your savings, checking, and any other accounts you have.
- A list of your current debts and the monthly payments you must make. You may also be asked if you have filed for bankruptcy

in the last ten years or had court judgments filed against you.

Banks and other lending institutions are allowed to ask you for almost any information that is directly related to your ability and willingness to pay your debts on time. However, there are many questions that banks may not legally ask. For example, a bank may not ask if you are getting along with your spouse or if you intend to have children anytime soon. Banks also may not inquire about your religion or ethnic background or about the financial condition of your relatives. If a bank loan officer asks questions that are not directly related to your ability and willingness to make your payments on time, he or she is probably breaking the law.

Making Payments on a Consumer Loan

Whether you borrow a few hundred dollars or several thousand dollars, it is important to make your payments on time. Your credit history and future ability to borrow depends on your ability and willingness to fulfill your financial obligations. Not making a small payment now might prevent you from being able to borrow at some future time when you want to buy a house or finance your education. A decision not to pay a debt that you are really able to pay is not a wise choice.

If you owe money and discover that you will not be able to make your payment on time, the worst thing you can do is ignore the problem. Banks do not want customers to default on their loans. The extra costs that the bank would need to pay are only one reason for this. Banks want to keep their customers. If you need extra time to satisfy a debt, most banks are willing to negotiate **restructuring the debt** to help you. If you find you cannot make a

payment on time, the best thing you can do is talk to a loan officer at a bank. Banks need to see that borrowers care about their debts and that they plan to eventually make their payments. When banks see customers doing their best to meet financial obligations, they are likely to be sympathetic and do their best to help.

Some consumers may benefit from taking out a **bill consolidation loan**. In this case a single loan for an extended period of time is made to allow a borrower to pay off many smaller debts. Because of the longer term, the monthly payment is often smaller on the new loan. This allows the borrower to meet his or her financial responsibilities more easily. The mistake that many people make when they take out a bill consolidation loan is to borrow even more money from other sources. Before a bill consolidation loan is made, the bank or other financial institution will want to be sure that the customer seriously wants to address his or her financial problems. The borrower may be asked to seek counseling and make a financial plan for the future.

Summing Up   *Lending institutions want to make consumer loans but must be assured that customers will pay their debts on time. To receive such a loan, consumers must provide financial information about themselves and should expect the institution to check this information for accuracy.*

Vocabulary Builder

Bill consolidation loan   A new long-term loan that is used to pay off many shorter-term loans and to reduce the total amount of monthly payments a creditor must make.

Delinquent   Describing a debt that is more than thirty days overdue.

Repossess   To take a product as the result of non-payment of a debt; often associated with consumer credit.

Restructuring the debt   Extending payment on a debt over a longer period of time to reduce the amount of monthly payments.

BORROWING TO BUY A HOME OR CAR

While you read, *ask yourself . . .*
- ◆ *Do you ever expect to own a home of your own?*
- ◆ *What steps can you take now that will improve your chances of being able to own a home in the future?*
- ◆ *Do you (did you) expect to pay cash for your first car?*

The two biggest purchases that most consumers make is buying a home and buying a car. Almost all Americans must borrow to buy a house, and most people use credit to purchase an automobile. When consumers borrow the large amounts of money necessary to make these purchases, they should be particularly careful to find the best offer possible.

Obtaining a Mortgage

Mortgage loans are made by banks and other types of financial institutions. These institutions often feel that there is less risk in granting a loan to buy a home than in loaning money for cars or vacations. For one thing, unlike most consumer products, homes usually increase in value over time. In many parts of the country a house that was worth $60,000 in 1981 might have increased in value to over $100,000 by 1991. If a bank had to foreclose on a home, it would normally have little trouble selling the property for more than the amount of money owed. Although housing values have not always increased in every neighborhood, more often than not they do. The other advantage from the point of view of the bank is the fact that houses are not very portable. If you own a home at 246 Elm Street that is pledged to back a loan, that home is likely to stay at 246 Elm Street while the loan is paid off.

Before you go house hunting, you should sit down and talk with your loan officer to see how large a mortgage you qualify for. The four Cs of credit apply to borrowing money to buy a house as much as to any other type of loan. The down payment you put on the house you buy may serve as your collateral and capital, but it does not prove anything about your character or capacity. Financial institutions will look at your credit history, your sources and amount of income, and your current debts that must be paid when they decide how much money to loan you for a mortgage. If you have $20,000 to put down on a home and the most you can borrow is another $60,000, there is little point in looking at homes that cost $100,000 or more.

Never assume that the first bank or lending institution you talk to will always give you the best possible deal. Such institutions are competing for your business. You should probably start by shopping for your loan at a bank where you already have a savings or checking account. But don't stop there. You may find that other organizations are willing to loan you more or charge you a slightly lower interest rate or lower fees.

When you are approved for a loan and complete the transaction, there are expenses that must be paid in addition to interest. You will probably be required to pay a number of **points**. A point is a fee charged by banks and other lending institutions when a mortgage is first granted. It is a way for these firms to increase their income without *apparently* charging higher interest rates. A point is equal to 1 percent of the amount loaned and is subtracted from the loan before it is given to the borrower. Suppose that you agreed to pay four points when you borrowed $60,000 to buy a home. The bank would keep 4 percent of the $60,000, or $2,400. You would only receive $57,600 but be expected to repay the full $60,000.

◆ Finding a house you want to buy may be easier than choosing the best mortgage. Before you sign any mortgage agreement be sure to have a qualified professional examine the document so you know what you are signing.

Points were originally created as a way to get around state laws that limited the interest rates that could be charged on mortgages. In theory they cover the costs of processing your loan application. There are many other fees that home buyers must pay. You will learn more about these other fees in Chapter 36. All fees become part of the total finance charge that lending institutions are required to inform borrowers of when they take out loans. It is important to compare this amount between lending institutions to find the best offer.

Fixed, Variable, and Other Types of Mortgages

Twenty-five years ago almost all mortgages were **conventional mortgages** that had **fixed interest rates**. When banks or savings and loan associations made conventional mortgage loans, they required the customer to put down from 5 to 25 percent of the price of the house in cash and to pay **closing costs**. The remainder

Vocabulary Builder

Closing costs   Fees charged by a lender for various costs involved with completing the sale of housing; may include fees for legal costs, taxes, and so on.

Conventional mortgage   A mortgage with a fixed interest rate.

Fixed interest rate   An interest rate that remains the same over the full term of a loan.

Point   A fee paid to a lender that is computed as a percentage point of a mortgage. A mark placed on one's driver's license when convicted of a moving violation.

Consumer News

Impact of Lower Housing Values

How would you feel if you bought a $200,000 vacation home on Nantucket Island in 1988 and found that by 1989 the most you could sell it for was $130,000? Then think how you would feel if the price was down to $115,000 in 1990.

In the 1980s many families bought vacation homes as an investment. They thought that they could enjoy their property for a few years and then sell it for a profit. By 1990 5.5 million American families owned second homes. One major problem was that many people who thought they could afford to support two homes in the 1980s discovered that they couldn't in the 1990s. This meant that they were forced to sell their vacation homes at reduced prices and take large losses. But some of these borrowers weren't able to sell their property. Their banks foreclosed on their property and sold it at auction. These sales tended to force the price of vacation homes down even more.

If you were a bank officer who had made many loans so that people could buy vacation homes, how would you have felt in 1991? Remember, many of these loans were made with down payments that were as small as 10 to 20 percent of the purchase price.

Is a mortgage always a "safe" loan?

went up after the mid-1970s, many lending institutions lost large amounts of money. They received 6 to 8 percent from the loans they had made but paid depositors 10 to 12 percent or even more. As a result, **adjustable-rate mortgages (ARMs)** became common in the 1980s.

There are different kinds of adjustable-rate mortgages. However, they all share certain characteristics. The most obvious is the fact that their interest rates can change over time. The rate charged is tied to some other type of interest rate that changes over time. This may be the prime interest rate or the interest rate paid by the federal government on its securities. Whatever the rate is, it must not be controlled by the lender.

Most ARMs have cap or a maximum interest rate that may be charged. There may also be a limit on the amount the rate may be increased in a year or the number of times it may go up. It is very important for a borrower who takes out an ARM to understand exactly what he or she is agreeing to. ARMs are always something of a gamble. Banks are willing to offer lower rates for ARMs than for conventional mortgages because they know that they can adjust the interest rate if necessary. On the other hand, customers may end up having to pay much more for an ARM if interest rates increase during the life of the mortgage.

There are many other types of mortgages that borrowers may be offered. One that has been popular among young, first-time home buyers is the **graduated-payment mortgage**. In this type of agreement the borrower makes small payments at the beginning of a loan's term. As time goes by, the payments increase. This type of loan can be helpful to borrowers who expect to have growing incomes. However, they can cause hardships and financial losses for people whose incomes fail to increase when the size of their payments goes up.

The federal government and many states have special agencies that can help people borrow money to buy homes. The **Federal Hous-**

of the necessary money was loaned at an interest rate that *did not change*. In the 1960s and early 1970s this interest rate was commonly in the range of 6 to 8 percent. When interest rates

ing Administration (FHA) and **Veterans Administration (VA)** both provide special help to specific groups of home buyers. Information can be obtained at banks and savings and loan associations. The same is true of state-sponsored programs. Your best source of information about borrowing money to buy a house is a selection of loan officers at several different banks.

Obtaining a Car Loan

There are a number of sources of credit that consumers may use when they borrow to purchase an automobile. Virtually all new or used car dealer in the country will have some sort of arrangement with a bank or finance company that will allow them to provide "on-the-spot" financing. Dealers are likely to encourage consumers to use this type of credit because it is so "convenient" for the customer. Another reason they will recommend it is that they will receive a share of the income that the loan generates. If you accept this type of financing, only do so after you have checked to see that there are no other sources that are less expensive.

Banks, savings and loan associations, and credit unions offer automobile loans. Although the interest rates charged by these institutions will often be about the same, credit unions are likely to offer somewhat lower rates because they have lower costs.

When you borrow money to buy a car, you may be offered an insurance policy at the same time. This policy would make your car payments for you if you were disabled and unable to make them yourself. Generally, there are other types of disability insurance you could buy that would provide similar coverage for less cost. Again, call around to find the best deal before you agree to any important transaction.

Consumer News

Benefits of Reverse Mortgages

Elderly homeowners who are cash-poor are being given a way to avoid being forced out of their homes by rising taxes and expenses for upkeep. The Federal Housing Administration announced on May 21, 1991, that it will allow some homeowners who are at least sixty-two years old to convert the equity in their homes into a monthly income. With these "reverse mortgages," banks will pay these homeowners an income that can last as long as they are able to live in their homes. When the homeowner moves or dies, the amount borrowed comes due. The home can be sold to satisfy the debt, or relatives can pay off the loan to take possession of the house. This program will allow many older Americans to live in their homes for a longer period of time.

Vocabulary Builder

Adjustable rate mortgage (ARM) A mortgage with an interest rate that may change over the term of the loan.

Federal Housing Administration (FHA) A federal agency that helps people who would not qualify for a conventional mortgage to borrow money to buy a house.

Graduated-payment mortgage A mortgage for which the amount of monthly payments grows over the term of the loan.

Veterans Administration (VA) An agency of the government that serves the needs of former members of the armed forces, including assistance in obtaining mortgages.

Many automobile firms offer rebates (a refund of part of the purchase price paid by the manufacturer to the customer) or low-interest-rate financing as a method of encouraging customers to buy. Consumers are usually better off to take the rebate but obtain financing from some other organization. Don't be talked into any decision until you have checked around for the best offer. A good way to determine what you should do is to compare the total finance charge of the dealer with the total finance charge of other institutions less the rebate. The method that results in the least cost is probably the best deal.

Summing Up *The two most important uses of credit for most people are mortgages and car loans. Mortgages may have fixed or variable interest rates and will have closing costs that must be paid. Car loans are offered by many financial institutions. Consumers should compare the total finance charges of different loans to choose the best one for their needs.* ◆

SECTION 4

HOME EQUITY LOANS

While you read, *ask yourself . . .*
  ◆ *Have you heard adults discuss home equity loans? If you have, what did they say about them?*
  ◆ *Do you think it's fair for people who own homes to be able to take advantage of home equity loans while people who rent cannot?*

Before the Tax Reform Act of 1986 went into effect, interest paid on personal loans was deductible on people's federal and state income taxes. This meant that people who paid taxes at a 25 percent rate spent only $75 of after-tax income for each $100 they paid in interest. The other $25 was in effect paid by the government through reduced tax collection. However, after 1986 the amount of personal interest that was deductible for most loans was gradually reduced until it was totally eliminated in 1991.

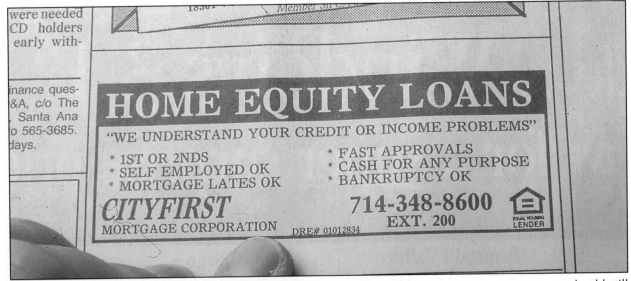

◆ Although home equity loans offer low interest rates that are deductible on income tax, consumers should still shop for the best deal. Would you immediately trust the firm that placed this ad?

Consumer Close-Up

Our Declining Home Equity

In the past many Americans used their homes as a way to save for their old age. They paid mortgages for many years, and their home's resale value usually grew, building up equity in homes that people could borrow against or sell in later years. The widespread use of home equity loans is rapidly reducing this type of saving for many Americans and may make their retirements more difficult. Some may even need to ask their children for help.

The amount of borrowing that consumers made against the equity in their homes reached $100 billion in 1990. As a result, the total equity that consumers had built up in their homes fell in that year instead of increasing. This trend was at least partially the result of the tax law of 1986 that allowed homeowners to deduct interest paid on home equity loans from their income. Another factor that contributed to reduced equity in homes was the falling value of real estate. Home values decreased by as much as 40 percent in some parts of the country between 1989 and the end of 1990. These two factors put sort of a "double squeeze" on homeowners' equity. Homeowners were borrowing more while their homes were decreasing in value. Both trends reduced homeowners' equity. The average amount that Americans owed on their homes was 57.5 percent of the structure's value in 1990.

Most of the money borrowed through home equity loans is used to finance consumer purchases like cars, boats, vacations, and college educations for children. With the exception of higher education, these goods and services lose most or all of their value very quickly but leave payments to be made in the future. The ease of borrowing against home equity has encouraged many people to buy expensive products or send their children to expensive schools that they might not otherwise have considered.

As a result of reduced home equity, many people will be leaving smaller estates for their children when they die. In the past, many people have been able to buy homes or pay for their children's education with inherited money. This source of financing is declining as home equity falls. Some people believe that the trend toward reduced home equity will reverse itself in the future. If it doesn't, many older Americans and their children could experience economic hardships.

Would you be willing to help support your parents in their old age?

Mortgage Interest Still Tax Deductible

Although interest paid on most consumer loans is no longer deductible, one exception is interest paid on **first** and **second mortgages**. A first mortgage is the loan that a person originally takes out to buy his or her home. A second mortgage is a different loan that is taken out sometime later and that uses the homeowner's equity in the home as collateral.

Suppose you put $20,000 down on an $80,000 house five years ago. In that time the

Vocabulary Builder

First mortgage The original mortgage used to buy a home or piece of property.
Second mortgage A loan taken out against an owner's equity in a home.

market value of the home has grown to $100,000, and you have paid off $5,000 of your original mortgage. You would have accumulated $45,000 in equity in your home. (Its $100,000 value minus the $55,000 you still owe the bank equals your equity of $45,000.) You could pledge your equity against a second mortgage loan. Most lending institutions will allow customers to borrow up to 80 percent of the equity they have in their homes. In your case the amount would be $36,000, since $45,000 × 0.80 = $36,000. A popular name for a second mortgage is a **home equity loan**.

At one time home equity loans were used almost exclusively to finance home improvements like remodeling, room additions, swimming pools, or new siding. Since 1986 they have been used for almost any purpose you can think of, including college educations, cars, and trips. The reason for this change is the tax advantage offered by home equity loans. People who have equity built up in their home may borrow money against that value and deduct their interest expenses from their taxes. The interest rates they pay are also likely to be lower because they are pledging the value of their home against the loan, which reduces the lending institution's risk. However, these interest rates vary according to some measure of prevailing interest rates. Therefore, the rate that is in effect when a home equity loan is taken out is not necessarily the same rate the borrower will be charged a year later.

Unfortunately, only homeowners are able to qualify for this type of loan. One reason to buy a home is to be able to take advantage of home equity loans.

Extra Costs of Home Equity Loans

Consumers obtaining a home equity loan are required to pay a number of costs. There will be a fee of several hundred dollars to have their property appraised by a professional to determine its value and therefore the amount of credit that may be extended. There will probably be an application fee of roughly $100 to cover the bank's or other lending institution's cost of processing the application. It is common for consumers to be charged 1 or 2 percent of the amount that may be extended when a home equity loan is approved. There may be attorney's fees, the cost of a title search, or taxes that must be paid, depending on the laws of each state. There may also be a fee charged each time money is drawn from the amount that may be loaned.

Home equity loans cost hundreds of dollars to establish. Consumers should not complete such agreements unless they are sure they will save enough in taxes and interest to make up for the cost of taking out the loan. If you know that you need to borrow $40,000 for ten years to send your children to school, a home equity loan makes sense and can save you thousands of dollars. If you think you may borrow a few hundred dollars to buy a new television, you are probably making a mistake to take out a home equity loan.

Summing Up *Homeowners may deduct the cost of interest they pay for mortgages and home equity loans from their earnings to reduce their taxable income. There are costs as well as benefits of opening a home equity loan that homeowners should evaluate.* ◆

Vocabulary Builder

Home equity loan A loan secured by a person's equity in a home; second mortgage. The interest paid on this type of loan was generally tax deductible in 1991.

Review and Enrichment Activities

VOCABULARY REVIEW

1. Column A contains key consumer terms from this chapter. Column B contains a scrambled list of phrases that describe what these terms mean. Match the correct meaning with each term. Write your answers on a separate sheet of paper.

Column A		Column B	
1.	Closing costs	a.	Money borrowed to pay off many smaller debts and reduce a person's total monthly payment
2.	Adjustable rate mortgage		
3.	Delinquent	b.	1 percent of the amount of a mortgage deducted from the loan at closing
4.	Fixed interest rate	c.	An interest rate that does not change over the life of a loan
5.	Bill consolidation loan		
6.	Repossess	d.	A loan that uses the value an owner has built up in his or her home as collateral
7.	Restructuring the debt	e.	An agreement that allows a borrower to trade short term debt for long term debt that will be paid over more time
8.	Point		
9.	Home equity loan	f.	Fees paid by a borrower to take out a loan to buy a home
10.	Graduated payment mortgage	g.	A mortgage for which the amount of monthly payments grows over the term of the loan
		h.	A mortgage with an interest rate that may change over the term of the loan
		i.	When a debt is not paid on time
		j.	When a lender takes property that was pledged for a loan as the result of nonpayment

2. Explain the difference between a first and second mortgage.

Review and Enrichment Activities Continued

CHECKING WHAT YOU'VE LEARNED

Write your answers for the following exercises on a separate sheet of paper.

1. Describe two characteristics of consumer credit that distinguish it from many other types of credit.
2. Explain why it is unlikely that a bank would be willing to lend the full price of a product purchased through a consumer loan unless other assets are pledged as collateral.
3. Identify five general types of information that a bank or other lending institution is likely to ask for when you apply for a consumer loan.
4. Describe the type of information that banks are not legally allowed to ask for when you apply for credit.
5. What type of events could cause a borrower to want to restructure his or her debt?
6. Why do banks usually take less risk when they make a loan to finance the purchase of a home?
7. Why did many lending institutions begin to offer more adjustable-rate mortgages than conventional mortgages in the 1980s?
8. Explain why borrowing money through an adjustable-rate mortgage is almost like gambling.
9. Explain how a graduated-payment mortgage works.
10. What important tax preference may homeowners take advantage of that people who do not own homes are not able to use?
11. Explain the extra costs that must be paid to take out a home equity loan.

PRACTICING YOUR CONSUMER SKILLS

Write your answers for the following exercises on a separate sheet of paper.

1. Which of the following types of information are you likely to be asked to provide when you apply for a loan at a bank? Which can you not legally be asked about?
   a. Your yearly income
   b. How long you have lived at your present address
   c. Where you graduated from school
   d. How many children you have
   e. If you were ever fired from a job
   f. What debts you currently own

     g. Whether you ever received welfare payments

     h. If you expect to change jobs in the next five years

     i. If you have filed for bankruptcy in the past five years

     j. If you have ever been convicted of a crime more serious than a traffic violation

2. Choose the type of mortgage that you feel would be most appropriate for each of the people described. Explain your choice.

Possible Choices

1. A conventional thirty-year mortgage that requires a 20 percent down payment and charges a 10 percent annual rate

2. An adjustable-rate mortgage that requires a 10 percent down payment and starts with an interest rate of 8½ percent that can be adjusted by as much as ½ percent twice a year, with a 13 percent maximum cap

3. A twenty-five-year graduated-payment mortgage that requires a 10 percent down payment and starts with a 6 percent interest rate for three years that increases by 1 percent a year until it reaches 11 percent in eight years

     a. William and Thelma both have good jobs, but medical expenses have prevented them from saving very much money. They need to buy a one-story home because Thelma uses a wheelchair. They have found a house that they would like to buy for $100,000. They have $13,000 saved. Their current combined income is almost $60,000 a year. They both believe that their jobs are secure, although they doubt that they will receive any large raises.

     b. Patrick is a plumbing contractor. In some years he has earned as much as $80,000, but in others his total income has been as low as $25,000. His wife Jenny earns about $6,000 working as a clerk in a store. They have found a larger home that they would like to buy for their growing family. This new home costs $120,000. Pat and Jenny have almost $40,000 saved for a down payment.

     c. Evelyn is working to put her husband Bill through veterinary school. He is doing well and will graduate in two years. After that he will need to set up an office and develop a business. Evelyn inherited $10,000 from her grandmother. She would like to use her money to put a down payment on a small home that costs $65,000.

3. Each of the following people (1) would benefit from using a home equity loan to finance going to school, (2) would not benefit from using a home equity loan to finance going to school, or (3) would not even qualify for a home equity loan. Identify which category each person falls in. Explain your answer.

     a. Deborah owns a small cabin in the woods that is worth perhaps $20,000. She only earns about $5,000 a year as a fishing guide and pays no income tax. She would like to go back to school to improve her financial situation.

     b. Terry earns about $35,000 a year as a marketing specialist for a building contractor. He rents an apartment for $560 a month. He needs to take several specialized courses at a local college to qualify for a promotion.

Review and Enrichment Activities Continued

c. Holly and her husband Arthur bought a new home for $80,000 last year. They put $15,000 down and have paid off about $1,000 of their loan. Housing prices in their neighborhood have stayed about the same or fallen just a little in the past year. Holly wants to go to school to become a laboratory technician.

d. Gordon and Brenda have been paying for their home for almost twenty years. When they bought it, it cost $30,000. Since then, they have had an addition put on. Brenda thinks that they could sell the house for at least $150,000. They only have $7,800 left to pay off. Gordon intends to start his own business next year and wants to take a few courses in accounting at a local college.

USING NUMBERS

Solve the following problem to help make the best possible choice. Write your solution on a separate sheet of paper. Be sure to show all your work.

Joyce wants to borrow $10,000 so that she can go back to college next year. She owns a house that is worth $100,000. If she borrows the money she needs from a bank, she will pay a 12 percent fixed rate of interest that is not tax deductible. She pays federal, state, and local income taxes at a combined rate of 25 percent. She could also take out a home equity loan that currently charges 12 percent interest that is tax deductible. To do this, Joyce would have to pay various fees to the bank that would total $700 to open her account. In either case, Joyce has made an agreement with the bank that she will pay only interest for the four years while she completes her degree. After that she will pay both interest and amounts toward the original loan. How much will Joyce save in taxes in each of the first four years if she takes out the home equity loan and interest rates don't change? Which method of borrowing do you recommend that she use? Explain your recommendation.

PUTTING IDEAS IN YOUR OWN WORDS

The following quotations are from this chapter. Explain these quotations in your own words to make sure you understand what they mean. Write your answers on a separate sheet of paper.

1. "The worst thing you can do when you ask for a loan is to lie."
2. "It is very important for a borrower who takes out an ARM to understand exactly what he or she is agreeing to."
3. "People who have equity built up in their home may borrow money against that value and deduct their interest expenses from their taxes."

BUILDING CONSUMER KNOWLEDGE

Write your answers for the following exercises on a separate sheet of paper.

1. Identify a consumer purchase that a member of your family, or someone you know made by borrowing money from a bank. Ask the person who borrowed the money about the process that he or she had to go through to qualify for the loan. Be prepared to report the information you gather to your class.

2. Contact several local banks to find the current rate on conventional mortgages. Imagine that you have $20,000 to put down and want to borrow $80,000 to buy a $100,000 home. Use the following table to determine how much your monthly payment would be for a thirty-year mortgage. Round off the current rate to the nearest rate on the table. How would this information affect your willingness to agree to an adjustable-rate loan? Write a paragraph explaining the importance of interest rates to borrowers.

Monthly Payments at Different Interest Rates for a 30-Year Mortgage

Amount Financed	8%	9%	10%	11%	12%	13%	14%	15%
$80,000	$587	$644	$702	$762	$823	$885	$948	$1,012

3. Think of a relative or friend who owns a home. Suppose that this person has decided to buy a $20,000 car and intends to finance $15,000 of its price through an ordinary new car loan for which he or she will be charged 12 percent interest a year. Assume that this person pays federal taxes at a 28 percent rate and state taxes at a 7 percent rate. Also assume that home equity loans are being offered by banks in your community at a rate of 11 percent. Write a letter to this person explaining the benefits and costs of borrowing through a home equity loan instead of through a normal car loan. Try to convince this person that this is what he or she should do.

Chapter 31

Credit Cards

Chapter Objectives

After completing this chapter, you will be able to do the following:

- Explain the benefits and costs to consumers of using credit cards.
- Identify different interest rates and fees that may be charged by institutions that offer credit cards to consumers.
- Explain consumer rights and responsibilities of having and using credit cards.
- Explain why it is important to comparison shop when choosing a credit card.
- Describe methods of minimizing the cost of having and using credit cards.

Key Consumer Terms

In this chapter you will learn the meanings of the following important consumer terms:

- Charge account
- Credit card
- Debit
- Billing period
- Credit limit
- Annual fee
- Preapproved credit cards
- Fair Credit Billing Act
- Credit terminal
- Home equity line of credit
- Debit card

Years ago your parents or even grandparents may have had a **charge account** at a local store. Under this type of agreement the store would allow them to charge items they wanted to buy. At the end of the month the store would send them a bill that they could pay or make payment on. The trouble with opening a charge account is that it can only be used at the one store that has approved your credit. If you go to any other store, you can't use your charge account and have to pay with cash or a check. As consumers began to travel and shop at many different businesses, charge accounts became impractical. Although charge accounts still exist, they have been largely replaced by **credit cards** in our economic system.

HOW CREDIT CARDS WORK

***While you read**, ask yourself . . .*
- *Do members of your family have credit cards? What sort of purchases do they make with their cards?*
- *What uses could you make of a credit card at the present? How will your need for a credit card change in the next five years?*

Three-quarters of all American families have at least one credit card. In 1990 there were almost 1 billion credit cards in use. That works out to be about four credit cards for every person in the country. The two types of credit cards that are most frequently issued are VISA and MasterCard. These are both national organizations that have banks and other organizations as customers. In return for a fee, banks receive permission to issue the VISA or MasterCard to their customers. Banks bill their own cardholders, but transfers of funds between banks to pay for credit card purchases flows through the credit card organization. Although these are the most common types of credit cards, there are many others that consumers may choose.

What Is a Credit Card?

A credit card is essentially a form of financial identification. By presenting your credit card at a store, you are telling the store who you are and allowing the store to **debit** (charge) your account at your bank or other financial institution for your purchases. To be allowed to accept credit cards, businesses agree to pay the organization that issued the card a percentage of the credit sale (most often 4 to 5 percent). When a business makes a credit card sale, it has its own bank account credited for the portion of the sale it is allowed to keep.

The responsibility for collecting credit card debts from customers belongs to the bank or

---

Vocabulary Builder

Charge account An agreement that allows a customer to buy goods or services from a particular company and pay for them later.
Credit card A credit device that allows a person to make purchases without paying cash. The person is billed at the end of a billing period by the firm that issued the credit card.
Debit To charge an amount to an account.

organization that issued the card. This is an important advantage for retail businesses, since they do not need to maintain a credit or billing department of their own. Accepting credit cards also increases the number of consumers who are likely to buy from their firm using credit.

At the end of each **billing period** the issuing institution sends a statement to each cardholder. This statement identifies each time the card was used, the amount charged, any payments made, interest charged, and the current balance. The customer may pay the account balance entirely or pay a lesser amount. There is always some minimum amount that must be paid. Interest will be charged in the next billing period on any unpaid balance. If the customer does not pay off his or her account balance, the resulting interest is earned by the bank or issuing organization. None of it goes to stores where purchases were made.

Obtaining a Credit Card

To obtain a credit card, a consumer must fill out an application that asks for the same types of information as other consumer loans (see Chapter 30). Most people who are approved for credit cards have a **credit limit**, a maximum value that they may charge to their account at any one time. This limit may be as low as several hundred dollars for young people who are just beginning to develop a credit history. People who have demonstrated their ability to pay may have limits as high as $10,000 or more. Some special types of credit cards have no limit.

When a consumer receives a credit card, the first thing the person should do is sign the back of the card. The back of most cards also has a strip of magnetic tape that identifies the cardholder and his or her account number. This allows stores to report transactions and ask for approvals electronically when a card is presented as payment for a sale. This information is gathered by the issuer of the card to keep customer accounts up-to-date in a computer. Stores usually call in charges for approval to be sure that customers have not exceeded their credit limit.

Many institutions issue credit cards. The most obvious sources are banks and other savings institutions. However, many other organizations now offer credit cards. Labor unions, charities, and even social clubs may have credit cards issued to their members. In reality this is a way for these organizations to earn money. They do not actually loan money or service the card. They are in effect acting as a marketing organization for the real card issuers. The issuing businesses (VISA or MasterCard, for example) pay the organizations a fee for encouraging members to use their cards. These cards do raise money for the organization, but such organizations usually are not the least expensive source of credit cards available to consumers.

Benefits of Using Credit Cards

Consumers benefit in many ways from using credit cards. People with credit cards don't need to carry large amounts of cash with them or keep large amounts of money on deposit in checking accounts. Another advantage is being able to buy products when "good deals" are available. Have you ever walked into a store and seen something you want on sale, only you didn't have the cash to buy it? With a credit card, you can just charge it and pay for it later.

Credit cards have many other advantages. They may be used to borrow cash at ATMs or in bank offices. Statements are sent to cardholders at the end of each billing period that help them keep track of how they are spending their money. A few credit cards even provide

◆   Although spending money with credit cards is quick and easy consumers still need to pay for their purchases. Using a credit card wisely requires the use of self-control.

cardholders with discounts on purchases, insurance for rented cars and travel, and even small cash rebates on purchases made with the card.

Wise use of a credit card is a good way for a young person to develop a positive credit history. If you demonstrate your sense of responsibility by making your payments on time and never exceeding your credit limit, you may be granted higher limits in the future. This should also help you qualify for mortgages or other types of loans. If you apply for a credit card but are only approved for a credit limit of a few hundred dollars, don't be disappointed.

If you use your card wisely, you will soon have a higher credit limit.

Vocabulary Builder

Billing period   The time between one regularly scheduled billing for an account and the next.
Credit limit   A maximum amount of credit that will be extended to a specific individual or business under an agreement with a bank or other financial institution; often associated with credit cards.

Costs of Using Credit Cards

Consumers are offered credit cards because they are an excellent source of income for banks and other financial institutions. Unpaid balances on credit card accounts may result in consumers paying interest rates as high as 24 percent a year, although a 15 to 18 percent rate is more common. The interest rates charged on unpaid credit card balances are higher than most other interest rates that consumers pay. Banks and other financial institutions justify these high rates by saying that their costs of keeping records on the accounts are high. They also argue that there are more defaults on credit card accounts than on other types of consumer credit. In any case, carrying a balance on a credit card results in relatively high interest rates for consumers.

Most credit cards also have an **annual fee**. While this fee may be as high as $100 or more, an annual fee of $20 to $30 is more common. A few cards charge no fee, although there is usually some other method the issuing organization uses to increase its income. Such cards may have higher interest rates or may start charging interest at the time of purchase instead of at the end of a billing period, as with most credit cards. Banks sometimes provide free credit cards to customers who maintain large deposits with the bank.

Shopping at stores that accept credit cards may result in consumers paying higher prices. The fee that the store pays to the credit card company increases its cost of doing business. The owners of the business are likely to pass this increased cost on in higher prices to all customers, including those who pay cash. A few businesses provide discounts for people who pay cash. This may be seen at gasoline stations, where there is often a cash price and a higher credit card price.

The greatest danger of credit cards may be the ease with which consumers can accumulate a large debt in a very short period of time. Many organizations issue **preapproved credit cards** through the mail. It is not uncommon for an adult to receive five to ten credit card solicitations (invitations to take out a credit card) in a month. Many of the issuing organizations do not check with each other about the people they issue credit cards to. It is entirely possible for a person who does not have a large income to have twenty or thirty credit cards. Although the credit limit on each card may be no more than $500 to $1,000, together these cards give the consumer the ability to borrow and spend many thousands of dollars in very little time. By failing to use credit cards wisely, consumers who lack good money sense or self-control can pile up debts that they can never hope to pay off. The unwise use of credit cards has forced many people into bankruptcy.

Summing Up *Most American families use at least one credit card. Credit cards offer consumers the advantages of convenience and safety but may result in large costs for people who do not use them wisely.* ◆

SECTION 2

CREDIT CARD RIGHTS AND RESPONSIBILITIES

While you read, ask yourself . . .
◆ *How would you feel if you were billed for something on your credit card statement that you did not buy?*
◆ *Do you feel that you have the self-control to use a credit card wisely?*

When credit cards were first coming into widespread use about thirty years ago, they were treated like other types of credit by the law. Over the years it became apparent that credit cards are different for a number of reasons. Therefore, laws have been written or adjusted to take care of the needs of credit card users.

Credit Card Rights

How would you feel if you received a credit card in the mail, preapproved and ready to use? All you had to do was sign it and go out and charge a purchase. What if you received ten or twenty such cards in a single month?

In the late 1960s many Americans received cards that they had never asked for. Banks and other financial institutions wanted to capture a larger part of the credit card market, so they simply sent credit cards to people who might be willing to use them. A document was sent with the cards explaining the charges that users would have to pay. However, these contracts were often written in language that ordinary people could not understand. When consumers signed the card and charged something, they were agreeing to the contract and its charges. Many people ran up large debts very quickly without understanding what they were doing.

To prevent the mass distribution of preapproved credit cards, the Truth-in-Lending Act was amended in 1970. This amendment made it illegal to send people credit cards that they hadn't asked for. Firms could still send applications and advertising, but they could no longer send cards unless a consumer requested one in writing. The amendment also placed a $50 limit on the consumer's liability for unauthorized use of a credit card that was lost or stolen. In 1982 another amendment was added that required all credit contracts to be written in English that most consumers could understand.

When credit cards are used, there may occasionally be disputes over billing, the quality of products, or undelivered goods. The **Fair Credit Billing Act** guarantees consumers the

right not to be required to pay for a charged transaction until a dispute is resolved. It is the responsibility of the firm that issued the credit card to try to bring about a settlement to any dispute. When a consumer believes that a product purchased with a credit card is defective, that person may refuse to make payment—but only if the consumer also makes a "good faith" effort to gain satisfaction from the seller. This means that the consumer must actively try to get the seller to correct the problem. The consumer is not required to tell the credit card company what is occurring, although doing so can avoid confusion and misunderstandings.

As a result of the Fair Credit Billing Act, consumers are not required to pay portions of credit card bills that they believe are incorrect. Suppose that you are on vacation and you want to buy a shirt as a souvenir. You choose one with long sleeves that costs $19. You give the clerk your card, and she starts to enter the sale in her **credit terminal**. About halfway through the sale, you change your mind. You decide that you want a short-sleeved shirt instead that costs $15. The clerk says, "No problem" and changes the transaction. But when you receive your bill the next month, you find that you

Vocabulary Builder

Annual fee   A charge made by a bank once a year for the service of keeping an account open; often associated with credit card accounts.

Credit terminal   An electronic device that allows stores to report a credit card purchase to the organization that issued the credit card and to receive approval for the purchase.

Fair Credit Billing Act   A law passed by the federal government that protects consumers' billing rights.

Preapproved credit card   A credit card that a consumer is promised if he or she completes an application form.

Consumers in Action

How to Avoid Credit Card Fraud

A "credit card crook" doesn't have to steal your card to use your account. All he or she needs is your card number. Using your number, the thief can order merchandise from thousands of mail-order firms over the telephone. These goods may be sent to addresses where the thief knows no one will be home and picked up by the thief after delivery. It can be more than a month before you discover that someone is using your number. Although you are only liable for the first unauthorized $50 spent on your account, you must report the use of your card to your bank.

There are many ways credit card crooks can get your number. When you pay your account, perhaps you write your account number on the check. This check will pass through many hands before being returned to you. A dishonest bank employee could copy the number down and use it. Other crooks sort through trash at businesses or apartment buildings looking for charge receipts. For this reason, always be sure to destroy carbons, old statements, and old charge slips. And never write your charge account number down or give it to someone else to use.

A crook who has both your account number and your address can send for replacement cards. To try to prevent this, never write your address on your charge slips. In some states, like New

York, it is against the law for stores to require such information. In other states credit card issuers recommend that you "manufacture" a false address rather than provide your correct one.

Never give your account number to someone who has called you on the phone. One common scam is to tell people that they have won a prize but must verify their identity by giving their charge card number. Of course, they never receive a prize, but they may get a surprise when they see their next statement.

Consumers who are careful with their account numbers will have less chance of being hurt by credit card fraud. However, it is still necessary to check your charge record against your statement every month to be sure that no one else is using your account.

---

have been charged $19 for the $15 shirt. What can you do? What are your consumer rights?

When billing errors take place, consumers have the right to refuse to make payment. They have sixty days to write to the credit card company briefly explaining the situation. The issuing firm must write and tell them it received their letter within thirty days and settle the

problem within ninety days. If it fails to do these things, the consumer is not responsible for the debt. Consumers may not be charged interest or have their accounts closed while the dispute is being resolved. However, if it is later found that they made the mistake, consumers may be charged interest on the amount that they should have paid.

If you ever want to give up a credit card you have received, you should cut the card up and send it along with an explanation of your choice to the firm that issued the card. You will still owe any debts that you have already charged on the card as well as the annual fee. However, if you never used the card, you may be entitled to a refund of the annual fee.

Credit Card Responsibilities

Many credit card responsibilities that consumers have are to themselves. Anyone who uses a credit card should keep a record of all charges made, including the amount, the location, and what the purchase was for. This practice allows consumers to know how much they owe on their account, when they are approaching their credit limit, and when they should reduce their charges because the account balance is getting too large for them to comfortably carry.

Probably the single most important thing that credit card users should do is to keep the receipts they are given when a charge transaction is completed. If there is ever a dispute over billing, this receipt will be very important in settling the problem. If you are charged $19 for a $15 shirt and you can produce your $15 charge receipt, you should have little problem in resolving the dispute in your favor. If you have lost or thrown away the receipt, you could have a problem proving that you are right. Choose a place to keep all of your receipts, and make a habit of always putting your receipts in this place.

Credit card users are required to notify card issuers of lost or stolen cards as soon as they realize the cards are missing. If they fail to do this, they may be held responsible for unauthorized use of their cards in excess of the $50 limit set by the Truth-in-Lending Act. Card

Consumer News

Never "Loan" a Credit Card

What does "unauthorized" mean? Support that a friend of yours asks to borrow your credit card to buy "just this one pair of shorts" one day when you are shopping at a mall. You lend your friend your card and believe him when he says that he will only charge $25 and give the money to you next week. Your friend doesn't return for almost 3 hours, but you're not worried. Eventually, he does give you back your card and says, "Thanks, I'll pay you next week."

When you receive your next statement from the bank, you find that your friend had charged $786.43 in that 3 hours. You call his number and hear a recorded message that his phone has been disconnected. What should you do? Are you responsible for paying for the things he charged? In many court cases the answer has been yes, you are responsible. If you give someone your card to use, then it isn't considered "unauthorized use." Even if this individual charges more than you had given permission to charge, you are still responsible. If you have a credit card, you must be very careful about letting other people use it. You could end up owing more money than you ever bargained for.

holders should treat their credit cards like cash. You wouldn't leave a $50 bill sitting on a counter in a store unattended. Don't be careless with your credit card either.

Summing Up   *Consumers who have credit cards have rights and responsibilities that are established by law. However, their greatest responsibility is to themselves.* ◆

Consumer News

What's a Debit Card?

If you are unable to qualify for a credit card, or if you are worried that you may charge too much or pay too much interest, you might benefit from having a **debit card**. These cards look exactly like ordinary VISAs or MasterCards. When they are used in a store, they work the same way. But instead of a bank loaning you money to purchase products, the cost is debited (billed) directly to an account that you hold in a bank. Therefore, no interest is charged for the purchase. Many banks offer debit cards as an alternative to credit cards.

You might wonder if there is any advantage of using a debit card instead of just writing a check or paying cash. The answer is yes. When you travel, it is often difficult to use an out-of-town check, but a debit card may be used as easily as a credit card. Debit cards eliminate the need to carry checks or to maintain two sets of records for checks and credit card purchases. Many stores that do not accept credit cards will take debit cards.

There are some disadvantages of using debit cards. Probably the greatest is that they do not provide consumers with a few days of "free credit," as credit cards do. When you use most credit cards, you may pay your bill up to thirty days after you make the purchase and pay no interest. When you use a debit card, you pay the bill the same day you make the purchase. People who have self-control and who qualify for credit cards are probably better off using a credit card instead of a debit card.

MANAGING CREDIT CARD COSTS

While you read, ask yourself . . .
- ◆ *Would you choose to pay off credit card balances at the end of each billing period if you could?*
- ◆ *Would you benefit more from using a credit card that offers lower interest rates or a lower annual fee?*

Credit cards offer many advantages to consumers who use them wisely, and they don't have to cost a lot of money. Consumers who make and follow plans for using their credit cards may even be able to borrow money almost for "free."

The Cost of Unpaid Balances

When consumers leave an unpaid balance on their credit card accounts at the end of a billing period, they are choosing to pay a higher rate of interest than they probably need to pay. About two-thirds of the states had a legal limit on the interest rate or annual fee that could be charged cardholders in 1991. These limits ranged from a low of 12 percent in the state of Washington to rates as high as 30 percent in New Jersey. The other third of the states had no interest rate limit at all. In most states the rate that credit card accounts could be charged exceeded other rates available to consumers. In addition, the interest paid on credit card accounts is no longer deductible from taxes. With a little financial planning, consumers who use credit cards can reduce the rate of interest they pay on their unpaid balances.

Suppose that you have charged a $500 television set on your credit card and find that you simply cannot pay off the account at the end of the month. You can leave the charge on your account and end up paying an annual rate of about 18 percent. Or you can take out a conventional consumer loan to pay off the balance. Conventional consumer loans, particularly those offered by credit unions, should charge 2 to 4 percent less than most credit cards. It is better to pay 14 percent than to pay 18 percent.

An even better choice for people who qualify is to draw on a **home equity line of credit**. This is a form of home equity loan that allows consumers to borrow against their home whenever they want to and in amounts they need. These loans charge much lower interest rates, and the interest paid is tax deductible. If you can qualify for such a loan, paying interest on a credit card makes very little sense.

The Trade-Off Between Interest Rates and Fees

Many different organizations offer credit cards. The exact interest rate and annual fee charged for a credit card can vary widely between the different cards you could choose. If you are able to put a relatively large deposit (most often $15,000 or more) in a bank, you may be able to avoid paying a fee at all. To choose the best credit card for your needs and abilities, you need to consider your own financial situation. If you expect to pay off your account at the end of each billing period, the interest rate charged on most cards makes no difference to you. You should find the card with the lowest annual fee. On the other hand, if you do expect to leave unpaid balances on your card, you should look for the lowest interest rate.

Some credit cards have no fee and may provide special benefits. For example, in 1991 the Sears Discover Card offered cash rebates to customers who used this card. However, there was a trade-off. It wasn't accepted at all stores. VISA and MasterCard are accepted at more businesses than most other cards both in the United States and in other countries. The Discover Card was growing in acceptance in 1991, but was still not taken in as many stores.

In addition to the more common types of credit cards, there are a number of special cards offered by some organizations. The American Express Card offers consumers a card with no credit limit. If you are in business or if you travel extensively, this can be an important advantage. On the other hand, this card has a larger annual fee than most cards and expects balances to be paid in shorter periods of time.

Many oil companies issue credit cards that are good at their filling stations and for other travel expenses, such as hotels and airline tickets. There is a selection of "gold" or even "platinum" cards available for higher annual fees that offer special services like travel insurance and discounts on car rentals.

Before you pay for the use of any credit card, weigh the benefits you believe you will receive against the cost you will be required to pay. Using a credit card is just like any other consumer choice. If you make your decisions carefully, you will increase the satisfaction you receive when you spend your income.

Summing Up   *Most consumers must pay an annual fee or have money on deposit to obtain a credit card. However, interest costs can be controlled by paying off balances from other sources. Using a home equity loan to pay a balance also offers tax advantages.* ◆

Vocabulary Builder

Debit card   A coded plastic card used to transfer money from a customer's account to a store's account.

Home equity line of credit   An agreement between a consumer and a bank that guarantees the consumer a home equity loan up to some maximum amount on demand.

Review and Enrichment Activities

VOCABULARY REVIEW

1. Column A contains key consumer terms from this chapter. Column B contains a scrambled list of phrases that describe what these terms mean. Match the correct meaning with each term. Write your answers on a separate sheet of paper.

Column A	**Column B**
1. Debit Card	a. A device used by stores to receive approval for a credit card purchase
2. Annual fee	b. A payment made each year for the right to have and use a credit card
3. Credit limit	c. The time between when a payment for a credit card account is due and the next time a payment must be made
4. Billing period	
5. Debit	
6. Fair Credit Billing Act	d. A maximum amount that a consumer may charge on his or her credit card
7. Credit terminal	e. To charge a credit card account
8. Preapproved credit card	f. Assurance that a credit card will be granted to a person who completes an application
9. Home equity line of credit	g. A card that results in money being taken from a user's account when the card is used to make a purchase
	h. A law that establishes consumer credit card rights and responsibilities
	i. An agreement that allows people to borrow against the value of the equity in their homes when, and in amounts they choose

2. Explain the difference between the way a **charge account** at a particular store and a **credit card** may be used.

CHECKING WHAT YOU'VE LEARNED

Write your answers for the following exercises on a separate sheet of paper.

1. Why have charge accounts become less useful than they were thirty years ago?
2. Explain what a credit card is and how it works.
3. Describe two different advantages that businesses receive from accepting credit cards.
4. Describe the greatest cost to businesses of accepting credit cards.
5. Describe three different benefits that consumers may receive from using credit cards.
6. Explain the two basic types of costs that consumers commonly pay to have and use credit cards.
7. Explain how it is possible for a person with a relatively low income to have many credit cards and the ability to borrow many thousands of dollars immediately.
8. Why might stores that accept credit cards tend to charge higher prices than stores that don't accept them?
9. Describe the content of the 1970 amendment to the Truth-in-Lending Act.
10. Describe the rights of a credit card user who believes that his or her statement is incorrect.
11. What is a cardholder required to do when he or she loses a credit card?
12. Why is leaving an unpaid balance on a credit card often a mistake for consumers?
13. What type of credit arrangement should a homeowner make for paying any balance on his or her credit card account?

PRACTICING YOUR CONSUMER SKILLS

Write your answers for the following exercises on a separate sheet of paper.

1. Explain how the use of a credit card could help the consumer achieve his or her goals in each of the following situations.
   a. Evelyn is a buyer for a department store. She travels to many trade shows. Her employer pays her expenses, but she must save her receipts to be paid back. Although she tries to do this, she often thinks that she may have forgotten to keep some of her receipts and therefore may receive less money than she deserves.
   b. Jack is paid only once a month. He often finds himself running short on cash toward the end of each pay period.

Review and Enrichment Activities Continued

    c. Annette doesn't like to carry much cash with her when she goes shopping. She is always afraid that she will lose it or that someone will steal it.

    d. Dan can pay cash for the things he buys now, but wants to develop a good credit history so that he will be able to get a mortgage when he starts looking for a home in a few years.

2. Describe the legal right and/or responsibility of the cardholder in each of the following situations.

    a. Richard lost his wallet and all his credit cards while he was on vacation. Someone found it and charged $350 on his VISA card.

    b. Donna paid for a new skirt with her credit card. When she got it home, she found a tear in it and intends to refuse to pay for it.

    c. Beth received her monthly credit card statement yesterday and discovered that she had been charged for a purchase of $123.21 from a mail-order firm that she has never called in her life.

    d. Chris applied for a credit card that was advertised in a letter he received in the mail. When his card arrived, he decided that he didn't want it after all.

3. Decide whether or not each of the following people is making a wise use of his or her credit cards. Explain your answer.

    a. Kim has five different MasterCards, each issued by a different bank. The credit limit on each card is between $500 and $800. Kim is a responsible consumer and never charges more than she can afford to pay.

    b. Bruce doesn't like to pay bills before he has to. He tries to pay off his credit card balance on the last possible day of each billing period. Sometimes he forgets and doesn't pay until several days later.

    c. Ikuko isn't able to pay off his credit card balance every month because he wants to be sure to make other payments, such as his mortgage payment on the home he bought ten years ago.

    d. Gwen puts $20 in her savings account every week no matter what. Sometimes she chooses not to pay off her credit card bill so that she can afford to save the $20.

USING NUMBERS

Solve the following problem to help make the best possible choice. Write your solution on a separate sheet of paper. Be sure to show all your work.

Barney wants to have a credit card. There are three local banks that will issue him a card, but each charges a different fee and a different interest rate on unpaid balances. Barney believes that he will have an average unpaid balance of about $500 a month. He works in construction and does not expect to be able to pay off his debts when his income is low in the winter. He belongs to a credit union that will loan him money at 13 percent but does not issue credit cards. He wants a card for its convenience. Use the information about the three banks to figure out how much Barney is likely to pay for each card. Then recommend a choice and explain the reasons for your recommendation.

- Bank A has an annual fee of $35 and charges 15 percent on unpaid balances.
- Bank B has an annual fee of $15 and charges 20 percent on unpaid balances.
- Bank C has no annual fee for people who maintain at least $5,000 on deposit and charges 18 percent interest. If their deposit ever falls below $5,000, there is a $30 fee.

PUTTING IDEAS IN YOUR OWN WORDS

The following quotations are from this chapter. Explain these quotations in your own words to make sure you understand what they mean. Write your answers on a separate sheet of paper.

1. "A credit card is essentially a form of financial identification."
2. "Probably the single most important thing that credit card users should do is to keep the receipts they are given when a charge transaction is completed."
3. "When consumers leave an unpaid balance on their credit card accounts at the end of a billing period, they are choosing to pay a higher rate of interest than they probably need to pay."

BUILDING CONSUMER KNOWLEDGE

Write your answers for the following exercises on a separate sheet of paper.

1. Survey five adults. Ask each person the following questions:
   - How many credit cards do you own?
   - Roughly how many times a week do you use a credit card?
   - How do you benefit from having and using credit cards?
   - What costs must you pay to have and use credit cards?
2. Watch your family's mail for a week. Find the number of credit card applications received. Bring these applications to school to discuss.
3. Survey the businesses in your community to identify those that accept credit cards and those that don't. List each group of businesses. Do the businesses in each group share any other characteristics? Why do you believe each group has chosen to accept or not accept credit cards?

UNIT 9

Insurance

onsumers need to protect themselves from losses that are greater than they can bear. Unit 9 describes the types of insurance that you can buy to protect your home, automobile, wealth, and future income from loss. It explains your insurance rights and responsibilities. You will also learn a number of methods for controlling your insurance costs. Finally, you will see how some types of insurance may be used to help prepare for your retirement.

Chapter 32

How Insurance Works

Chapter Objectives

After completing this chapter, you will be able to do the following:

- Explain why some risk is unavoidable in life and how buying insurance can help consumers manage risk by sharing it with other people.
- Describe the benefits that consumers receive when they buy insurance.
- Identify services offered by insurance companies.
- Explain the importance of comparison shopping and checking the financial stability of insurance companies before buying insurance.

Key Consumer Terms

In this chapter you will learn the meanings of the following important consumer terms:

- Law of probability
- Insurance
- Risk management
- Premium
- Shared risk
- Insurable interest
- Appraise
- Insurable risk
- Property insurance
- Liability insurance
- Personal insurance
- Whole life
- Rider
- Deductible

A t one time or another, everyone suffers a loss. Some losses are very small and will have little effect on the rest of your life. If you drove your car over a board full of nails, you might have to spend $70 to buy a new tire. Such an event surely wouldn't please you, but over the course of your life, the $70 wouldn't be very important. On the other hand, if your house and everything in it were blown away in a tornado, it could be years before you recovered financially. People need to protect themselves from losses that are greater than they can afford.

SECTION 1

LIMITING RISK THROUGH INSURANCE

While you read, *ask yourself . . .*
- *What important loss have you, a member of your family, or a friend suffered?*
- *Was the loss insured? How would this person's life have been different if his or her loss had (or had not) been insured?*

Although everyone suffers losses, there is no sure way to know when a loss will happen to a particular person or how important it will be. However, when large numbers of people are considered, the **law of probability** can provide helpful information. The law of probability takes events that have happened in the past and uses them as the basis for making predictions about the future. For example, by keeping a record of the characteristics of people who have been involved in accidents in the past ten years, we could predict that 5 out of every 100 eighteen-year-old male drivers in Detroit will have an automobile accident before they reach the age of twenty-one. We could also predict that the average loss per accident will be $3,783.17. This process allows insurance companies to set insurance rates and to help people avoid devastating financial losses.

Risk Management

There is no way for consumers to prevent all losses. They should only be concerned with protecting themselves against losses that are greater than they can financially handle. The most common way to reduce the risk of unmanageable loss is to buy **insurance**. When you buy insurance, you pay an organization (insurance company) to take the risk of a particular type of loss. Businesses, governments, and people buy different types of insurance. By doing this they are trying to limit their risks. This is called **risk management**.

The payment that consumers make when they buy insurance is called a **premium**. The size of a premium depends on the value of the item that is being insured and the predicted risk of something happening to destroy or damage that item. Insurance companies use some of the money they receive from premiums to pay claims filed by policyholders. The rest they use to invest in stocks and bonds, make loans to businesses, or buy real estate. These investments create a store of value that insurance companies may call on if customers have many large losses in any one year. This may happen in the event of a hurricane or earthquake. Much of the income that insurance companies earn comes from the investments they make.

When consumers buy insurance, they receive no economic benefit if they have no loss. Suppose that you buy homeowner's insurance for $347 a year. Your house does not burn down, no one sues you, and nothing is stolen from you. When you have no losses, you file no claims and receive nothing for your premium other than peace of mind. Suppose that the people next door also pay $347 for homeowner's insurance, but their house is destroyed in a fire. As a result, they received $84,900 from the insurance company to rebuild their home. At the end of the year, they are no better or worse off than you. Insurance does not result in a gain. It is designed to prevent a large loss through **shared risk**.

The premium that consumers pay when they purchase insurance is a cost that will never be recovered. You might think of it as a small financial loss that consumers take to avoid the possibility of a greater loss in the future. Because many people are willing to accept the small loss of paying a premium, the insurance company has the money to pay for larger losses suffered by its policyholders. The company makes sure it has enough money by determining the probability of different types of losses and the amount of value that the losses are likely to involve. This helps the firm set premiums that will allow it to pay claims made by its customers.

How Insurance Companies Decide What to Insure

People who buy insurance must have an **insurable interest**. This means that the person must own something of value that needs to be insured. This may sound simple, but it is important. If you own an old house that is worth $20,000, you can't insure it for more and receive $50,000 if it burns down.

Sometimes an object is **appraised**. That is, its value is determined by a professional appraiser who has specialized knowledge and knows the value of particular types of items. This may be the case when paintings or rare coins are insured. In other cases the amount of the insurance is determined by market value or replacement cost. This method of setting value is used when homes or automobiles are insured. In some situations the amount of insurance is determined by prior agreement and is reflected in the amount of the premium that must be paid. This is the case when people buy life insurance. If you insure your life for $200,000, you will pay roughly ten times the premium of insuring your life for $20,000. The value of the insurable interest is one of the factors that insurance companies consider when they set premiums.

The second factor that insurance companies look at when they set premiums is the **insurable risk**. This is the insurer's understanding of and willingness to accept the risk that is

Vocabulary Builder

Appraise   To determine the value of something that is to be insured.

Insurable interest   Ownership of something of value that is to be insured.

Insurable risk   Insurer's understanding of the risk of insuring property or a condition.

Insurance   An agreement in which people pay for protection against specific losses they might suffer.

Law of probability   A measurement of the likelihood of an event based on mathematical relationships or past experience.

Premium   When a person pays more for a bond than its original price. A fee paid for insurance coverage.

Risk management   Taking steps intended to reduce the risk of a major loss.

Shared risk   Spreading the risk of a major loss among many people or businesses by agreeing to accept the certainty of a smaller cost.

Consumer News

The Policyholders' Revolt

Do you think that automobile insurance premiums are too high? If you do, is there anything you can do about it? The people of California tried in 1988 when they passed Proposition 103. This law was intended to impose government regulation on insurance companies and force automobile insurance premiums down by at least 20 percent for all drivers and 40 percent for those with good driving records. California insurers immediately appealed to the courts to have the law overturned. Finally, on May 4, 1989, the California Supreme Court upheld the law with one major change: Instead of an automatic 20 to 40 percent cut, there would be controlled rates that must afford the companies a "fair and reasonable" profit. As a result, it was unclear what effect, if any, the law would have on premiums. One representative of the insurance industry said that the law's biggest impact would be to force the companies to communicate better with policyholders and to explain why their premiums were so high.

building down on purpose, you cannot expect payment for its value.

3. The loss must be financially measurable. The insurance company must know the value of what it is insuring to determine the premium it will charge. If you own a vase that is a family heirloom, you can't expect an insurance company to pay $100,000 for it if another vase that is just the same can be purchased for $50.

4. The insurance company must be able to determine how much risk it will accept and when it will refuse to take a risk. If you have an incurable disease and have six weeks left to live, you can't expect an insurance company to offer you life insurance at the same rate it would charge other people.

Summing Up   *Buying insurance is a way of sharing the risk of a major loss among many people. For insurance companies to set appropriate premiums, there must be an insurable interest and a measure of the insurable risk.* ◆

SECTION 2

THE BENEFITS OF HAVING INSURANCE

While you read, ask yourself . . .
- ◆ *Do you know of any insurance claims that members of your family have recently made?*
- ◆ *Does your family have health insurance? What could happen to families that do not have health insurance?*

taken when a particular item or condition is insured. The insurer's decision to issue a policy is based on four conditions:

1. The likelihood of a loss taking place must be predictable based on previous losses or other reliable information.
2. An understanding that losses must be the result of chance, not due to an action of the insured party. If you burn your own

The ability to buy insurance allows consumers to do more than simply share risks. Insurance allows consumers to make choices they could not afford to make without sharing their risk with other policyholders. Insurance contributes to our nation's economic stability. Without insurance many businesses could not

Consumer Close-Up

Protecting Your Right to a Fair Settlement

Suppose that you suffered a loss. Perhaps you had an accident with your car or your home was damaged in a windstorm. Not to worry—you're insured, right? Well, maybe not. Every year thousands of Americans suffer losses, only to have their insurance company say, "It wasn't covered." It pays to know what your insurance rights are and to fight to protect them. Here are a number of suggestions for consumers who file claims:

- Demand a written explantion if a claim is refused.
- It is better to file quickly, but you don't give up your legal

rights if you don't. Check to see that filing claims after a number of months, or even years, is not considered a reason for refusing payment in most states.
- Any exclusions (property that is not covered) in a policy are stated clearly and put in a location where policyholders are likely to notice them. When they are not, many courts have ruled in favor of the policyholder. Read your policy to see if it is easy to understand.
- If statements in a policy are not clear, courts generally give the benefit of any doubt to the policyholder.
- Don't be frightened because

the insurance company is large and you aren't. If you feel you have a legitimate claim, talk to a reputable lawyer to receive professional advice.
- If you have suffered an important loss, sign nothing until you have spoken to a qualified lawyer. If you sign something while you're upset that relieves an insurance company of its responsibilities, the agreement may be overturned in court. But to save yourself trouble, sign nothing from an insurance company until you are confident that you understand what it says and means.

---

operate and our economic system would not function as well as it does. Americans would have a lower standard of living.

Benefits Made Possible by Insurance

In Chapter 30 you learned about mortgages that are offered to consumers by banks and other financial institutions. Mortgage holders are required to have insurance for their homes. If you want to borrow $60,000 to buy a house, you have to take out a homeowner's insurance policy before you will be given a mortgage. No bank will risk its investment in a structure

that is uninsured. If your home is destroyed, your insurance company will pay off your loan. Without insurance there would be no asset to satisfy your debt if you failed to pay. Thus, insurance makes it possible for consumers to borrow money to buy homes.

Most Americans depend on their cars to get around. We use our automobiles to commute to work and go shopping. We drive them when we take vacations or visit relatives. To register and drive an automobile in most states, you must have insurance. Therefore, insurance allows Americans to use their automobiles.

Insurance also allows people to continue to spend when they suffer losses. If your house burned down when you were uninsured, your

◆   Consumers may protect themselves from destruction caused by natural disasters like hurricanes by buying insurance. What would the future of communities like this be if people couldn't buy insurance?

ability to buy other consumer goods would be reduced. If there were a general disaster, like a hurricane, flood, or earthquake, uninsured people would be forced to cut back on their spending. This reduced spending would force people out of work and could cause businesses to fail. However, when losses are paid for by insurance companies, people are able to continue spending and support the economy. Insurance contributes to our nation's economic stability.

What May Be Insured?

There are three basic types of loss that may be insured against:

1. **Property insurance** is placed on homes, automobiles, or other property to protect consumers from loss to their possessions. If someone broke into your apartment and took your furniture, your renter's insurance would pay for your loss.

2. **Liability insurance** protects consumers from the cost of damage they may do to another person's property ˎof from injuries they cause to others. If you accidentally back into a pedestrian and break the person's leg, the liability insurance you carry on your automobile will pay for doctor bills and other related costs.

3. **Personal insurance** protects you or your relatives from loss related to your health or

physical condition. If you die or are injured so that you are unable to work, your life insurance or health insurance will pay benefits to you or your survivors.

How Consumers Benefit When Businesses Buy Insurance

Businesses, like people, sometimes have accidents or suffer losses. And so businesses, like individuals, need to protect themselves from unmanageable loss by sharing risk through buying insurance. This ability is important to business owners and to the consumers they serve. For example, we all rely on trucks to deliver the goods we consume. Trucks are sometimes involved in accidents. If trucking firms could not buy insurance, their owners might choose not to stay in business. As a result, stores would have trouble maintaining an inventory of products to offer consumers.

Businesses insure themselves against losses suffered by their customers as the result of defective products or services. When a person deposits money in a bank, that account is insured up to $100,000 by the FDIC. The bank pays a premium to the FDIC for this insurance. If a child is injured by a toy that is improperly designed, the manufacturer may be sued. Businesses buy insurance to protect themselves against such suits. If firms could not buy insurance, they might be forced out of business when mistakes were made. Consumers generally do not benefit when businesses fail. They end up having a smaller number of products to choose from and could suffer from reduced competition among manufacturers.

Summing Up *Consumers and businesses need insurance to carry out their normal activities. Without insurance we might not be able to buy homes, drive cars, or purchase many of the consumer goods we need.* ◆

SECTION 3

HOW TO CHOOSE AN INSURANCE POLICY

While you read, ask yourself . . .
◆ *What types of insurance do members of your family have now?*
◆ *What types of insurance do you expect to need ten years from now?*

One cost of obtaining insurance is the time you spend choosing the best policy for your financial ability and personal needs. On the other hand, if you don't spend the time making a careful choice, you could regret your decision for many years.

Checking the Reputation of the Insurance Company

There is little point in asking an insurance agent if the firm he or she represents is reliable and sound. No salesperson is going to tell you, "I really don't think you should buy insurance from me because the firm I represent is about to fail." It makes more sense to do the research yourself. You can start by asking an agent for the name of a customer who has filed a claim recently. If you find such a person, ask

Vocabulary Builder

Liability insurance   Insurance that pays for bodily injury and property damage suffered by others as a result of actions of the insured party.
Personal insurance   Insurance that protects people from losses due to illness or injury.
Property insurance   Insurance that protects people from losses to their property.

◆ Choosing an insurance agent you trust is important but consumers need to be sure the protection they buy is the right kind and amount for their needs. Why should consumers always shop around for the best insurance buy?

about the kind of service that the individual received from the firm. Another possibility is to go to the public library and look up the firm in *Best's Annual Insurance Guide*. Find out how long the firm has been in business and its financial condition. Many small insurers may offer lower premiums but might experience financial difficulty if too many claims were filed at one time.

Choosing an Agent

It is always pleasant to work with friendly, considerate, and polite salespeople, whether they are selling insurance or any other product. However, you are buying a product and not a friendly smile. Don't stop thinking after you decide you like an agent's personality. Listen to and evaluate the information that he or she provides.

Any agent you do business with should understand his or her product thoroughly. If you can't get an understandable answer from an agent who is trying to sell you a policy, you should not expect this person to know much more when you need to file a claim. Insurance agents should be honest. An agent who never says anything bad about a policy or who refuses to point out any limitations is probably not giving you the whole story. As in any other purchase, consumers should be skeptical of a deal that seems too good to be true. All insurance companies have similar costs. A policy that is offered at a much lower price probably has much less to offer.

Many consumers choose to use an independent agent who sells policies from many firms instead of policies offered by a single company. Independent agents may be better able to meet the specific needs of different customers because they have a wider choice of policies to sell. Even so, policyholders must be sure that the policy they buy is the one they need.

Buying the Right Amount of Insurance

Buying insurance involves making a trade-off between the value of reducing your risk of loss and the value you could currently receive from spending your money for something else you want. Trying to reduce your risk to zero is impossible and a waste of your money. If your house is worth $80,000, there is no point insuring it for $150,000. If the house was destroyed, you would only receive its fair market value. Almost half of your insurance would be wasted. If you are looking for life insurance and your income is only $14,000 a year, it would be a mistake to insure your life for $200,000 and pay an annual $1,200 premium. You would end up living in poverty so that your survivors could have a large settlement if you died.

When people buy insurance, they should comparison shop. Although the cost of insurance may not differ very much between firms, there is clearly some difference. A common problem is that many firms do not offer the exact same benefits in their policies. One way to approach this problem is to ask each firm how much a specific quantity of insurance would cost. For example, if you are buying life insurance, ask how much you would need to pay each year for $50,000 of conventional **whole life insurance**. If a firm charges less for this amount of insurance, it probably charges less for other types and amounts of insurance as well.

Make sure you understand what is insured by your policy and how much you will be required to pay. Many insurance policies require special **riders** or additions to insure jewelry, boats, or valuable paintings against losses. Special insurance usually must be purchased for protection from floods or earthquakes. These riders may be quite expensive but can be equally important. If your home is in a river valley that sometimes is flooded, it makes little sense to have a policy that does not include flood insurance. The best way to know what a policy insures is to read it carefully. If you don't understand what a part of the policy means, ask your agent to explain it. Don't take no for an answer. If an agent can't explain a part of his or her policy so that you can understand it, the chances are that he or she would rather you didn't understand it. Don't buy something you don't understand.

One way to lower the cost of many types of insurance is to increase your **deductible**. This is the amount that the insured party must pay before the insurance company pays anything.

Vocabulary Builder

Deductible   The initial amount of money that an insured party must pay before the insurance company pays the remainder of a claim.

Rider   A written attachment to an insurance policy that alters the policy to meet certain conditions or special needs.

Whole life insurance   Insurance that has both death benefits and living benefits.

Consumer Close-Up

Why The Rates Went Up

During the 1980s premiums for automobile and home insurance increased at a rate that was roughly twice the rate of inflation. Many drivers and homeowners with limited income were squeezed between paying for their insurance and paying for their basic needs of food, shelter, and clothing. Why did insurance premiums increase so rapidly? Insurance companies have given at least four basic reasons.

Insurance companies believe that 10 percent of the increase is the result of more people filing fraudulent claims. For example, one woman in New York recently had her car buried in her backyard and then reported it stolen. Another cause that is often mentioned is the increase in the number of unreasonable lawsuits. One insurer tells of a woman who poured gasoline on a pile of coal to start a fire. When she lit it, the gasoline exploded and burned her. She sued a neighbor who had helped her with the coal for not stopping her from using the gasoline. Although many suits fail, they still force insurance companies to pay legal fees.

The rapid increase in medical costs have forced personal injury premiums up. Insurers attribute almost 25 percent of the increase in these premiums to improved and more costly medical technology. Keeping injured people alive is something we would all like to do, but it is also costly.

According to insurance companies, the greatest cause for increased premiums has been the large awards that juries have given injured parties in liability suits. Multimillion-dollar settlements are not uncommon when people are seriously injured. Whether or not you agree with such settlements, they have certainly forced premiums up. The insurance companies don't really pay these amounts themselves. They collect larger premiums from insured parties to pay them.

Do you know anyone who has cheated on an insurance claim?

How would you feel about someone who did this?

What would an ethical consumer do?

For example, suppose that your homeowner's policy has a $250 deductible on property loss. If a tree falls on your roof and does $1,400 in damage, you pay the first $250 and the insurance company pays the remaining $1,150. You could reduce your insurance premium by agreeing to a deductible of $500. This would mean that you would pay more if you had a loss, but you would still be protected from large losses. Remember, the purpose of insurance is to protect yourself from losses that are too large for you to deal with, not to protect yourself from all losses.

There are many different types of insurance that consumers may need to buy. But they all involve buying protection from losses that are larger than individuals are able to deal with by sharing risk among many people.

Summing Up *When consumers buy insurance, they must be sure that the firm that they choose is financially sound and provides good service. They should also choose an agent who is pleasant to work with and who understands their needs. Consumers should only buy enough insurance to protect themselves from losses that are too large to deal with.* ◆

Review and Enrichment Activities

VOCABULARY REVIEW

1. Column A contains key consumer terms from this chapter. Column B contains a scrambled list of phrases that describe what these terms mean. Match the correct meaning with each term. Write your answers on a separate sheet of paper.

Column A	**Column B**
1. Appraise	a. A payment made to purchase insurance
2. Insurable risk	b. A portion of a loss that must be paid by the insured party before any part is paid by an insurance company
3. Shared risk	
4. Rider	c. An agreement that insures something in addition to a basic policy
5. Deductible	d. Something of value that is to be insured
6. Personal insurance	e. An understanding of the probability of a loss being suffered
7. Insurable interest	f. To determine the value of something that is to be insured
8. Insurance	g. Taking steps to reduce the possibility of a major loss
9. Risk management	h. Spreading the risk of a major loss among many people or businesses
10. Premium	i. An agreement in which people pay for protection against specific losses they might suffer
	j. Insuring the health or life of an individual

2. Explain the difference between property and liability insurance.

Review and Enrichment Activities Continued

CHECKING WHAT YOU'VE LEARNED

Write your answers for the following exercises on a separate sheet of paper.

1. Describe how insurance companies use the law of probability to help them set insurance premiums for consumers.
2. What are two uses of the premiums that insurance companies receive?
3. Describe an insurable interest that your family owns that demonstrates your understanding of this term.
4. Explain the meaning of insurable risk.
5. Describe something that consumers would have difficulty doing if they could not buy insurance.
6. Describe three types of risks that may be insured.
7. Give an example of how consumers benefit from businesses' ability to purchase insurance.
8. Explain why consumers should investigate the financial stability of an insurance company before purchasing a policy.
9. Although it is nice to work with a friendly agent, what factors should consumers be more interested in when they choose an agent?
10. Describe two steps that consumers may take to reduce the amount of their premiums.

PRACTICING YOUR CONSUMER SKILLS

Write your answers for the following exercises on a separate sheet of paper.

1. Explain why each of the people described in the following situations should consider purchasing the type of insurance indicated.
   a. Becky has recently graduated from high school. She has rented an apartment and used almost all of her savings to buy furniture. She also borrowed $3,000 from her parents to buy a used car. She would have a hard time raising another $100 at the present. She wonders if she should spend $12.43 a month to buy renter's insurance to protect her new furniture.
   b. Robert has recently joined the merchant marine. He earns a very good salary but is gone from home for long periods of time. He works on oil ships that visit places like the Persian Gulf. He wonders if he should buy $100,000 of life insurance to provide for his wife and children if anything happened to him. It would cost $450 a year.

    c. Kerry owns a speedboat and takes his friends waterskiing on weekends. They often ask him to drive fast. Kerry wonders if he should buy liability insurance for $239 to pay up to $100,000 for doctor bills if anyone is injured by his boat.

    d. Beth inherited a diamond ring from her grandmother that has been appraised for $8,500. Her present homeowner's policy does not insure it. She wonders if she should pay an extra $35 a year to buy a special rider that would cover the ring.

2. Identify each of the following as an example of (1) property insurance, (2) liability insurance, or (3) personal insurance. Then explain how you know that your answer is correct.

    a. Harold bought insurance that will pay him money if he is injured and unable to work.

    b. Margerie bought insurance that will pay for anyone who is injured while they are riding one of the horses that she keeps on her farm.

    c. Wayne bought insurance that will pay off his mortgage if either he or his wife is injured and can't work or is killed.

    d. June bought insurance that will pay her if her stamp collection is damaged or stolen.

3. Each of the following individuals has purchased insurance. Some may have bought too much, others too little. Evaluate each decision and explain your answer.

    a. Fred works as a cook's helper in a restaurant where he earns $280 before taxes a week. He spends most of his spare time working on his 1965 Ford Mustang convertible. Fred insured his car for $25,000 and pays $180 every month for his premium.

    b. Diane receives basic health insurance from her employer. She has decided not to spend $13 of her own each month to have dental insurance added to her policy. Diane has had two root canals in the past year and may soon need another.

    c. Todd has a job that requires him to work with high-voltage electricity. Although he is a single parent, he decided not to buy life insurance.

    d. Jody works as a cleaning person in a restaurant. She worries about being sued. She bought an insurance policy that will protect her up to $10 million if any guests are injured in her home. She pays $128 every month for this insurance.

USING NUMBERS

Solve the following problem to help make the best possible choice. Write your solution on a separate sheet of paper. Be sure to show all your work.

Peter bought a homeowner's insurance policy for his new house. He has a $100 deductible, and his premium is $445 a year. The premium is so high that it makes it difficult to pay his other bills. He is considering lowering the premium by accepting a larger deductible. With a $500 deductible, the premium would be $320 a year. With a $250 deductible, the premium would be

Review and Enrichment Activities Continued

$380 a year. How many claims could Peter file in ten years and still save money by taking the $500 deductible? Answer the same question for a $250 deductible. Which deductible would you recommend to Peter? Explain the reasons for your recommendation.

PUTTING IDEAS IN YOUR OWN WORDS

Explain the following quotations from this chapter in your own words on a separate sheet of paper so it is clear you understand their meanings.

1. "People need to protect themselves from losses that are greater than they can afford to bear."
2. "Insurance does not result in a gain, it is designed to prevent a large loss by **sharing risk**."
3. "The ability to buy insurance allows consumers to do more than simply share risks."

CONSUMER ECONOMICS IN ACTION

Write your response to each exercise on a separate sheet of paper.

1. Ask adults in your family to identify and generally describe the types of insurance they have. Which policies do they pay for and which are paid for by their employers or someone else?
2. At your age insurance is less important than it will be in ten years. Write several paragraphs that identify changes in your life that may take place and cause you to need more insurance. Show how these policies will be important to achieving your personal goals.
3. Look up three different advertisements for insurance sales people in your telephone book or newspaper. Explain what factors in the advertisement impress you favorably and which do not. What other facts would you want to know about these insurance representatives before you chose one to be your agent?

Chapter 33

Automobile and Property Insurance

Chapter Objectives

After completing this chapter, you will be able to do the following:

- Explain the basic types of insurance that consumers may purchase to protect themselves from losses while they operate a car.
- Explain the basic types of insurance that homeowners and renters may purchase to protect themselves from losses that occur at their place of residence.
- Explain the trade-offs that consumers can make to reduce the premiums they pay for insurance.

Key Consumer Terms

In this chapter you will learn the meanings of the following important consumer terms:

- Medical payments insurance
- Collision insurance
- Deductible
- Comprehensive insurance
- Uninsured motorist insurance
- No-fault Insurance

- Book value
- Gender-based insurance rates
- Risk pool
- Assigned risk
- Standard fire insurance
- Homeowner's insurance
- Replacement value
- Residence contents broad form policy

O ne of the first major expenses that most Americans pay is the cost of buying automobile insurance. In many parts of the United States the annual cost of insurance for an automobile is greater than the cost of buying an older used car. Although automobile insurance is expensive, it is necessary to protect yourself from loss due to theft, fire, liability, medical expenses, and other types of damage. Choosing to drive without insurance is never a wise consumer choice and is against the law.

SECTION 1

CHOOSING THE RIGHT AUTOMOBILE INSURANCE

While you read, *ask yourself . . .*
- *What types of coverage should your family members have on any cars they own?*
- *Have any members of your family ever had a loss that resulted from an automobile accident? What was their experience with insurance companies?*

It is possible for people to lose almost all of their life savings and much of their future earnings as the result of one automobile accident. All drivers should have at least a basic liability insurance policy. In addition, there are other types of coverage that consumers may purchase to protect themselves from loss. The type and amount of additional coverage that are right for an individual consumer depends on the person's income and wealth and on the type of car the person drives.

Types of Automotive Coverage

There are five basic types of automobile insurance that drivers may buy.

1. Liability insurance covers injuries to other people or damage to their property when it is the fault of the insured driver. The amount of liability that will be covered by a policy is described by a series of three numbers. For example, 100/300/50 means that a policy will cover up to $100,000 in liability for a person who is injured in an accident, up to $300,000 in total liability for all people injured in an accident, and up to $50,000 in property damage resulting from an accident. Many states set minimums on the amount of liability insurance that drivers must have. (See Figure 33-1).

2. **Medical payments insurance** covers medical expenses for the driver and passengers who are in an accident while riding in a car driven by the insured party. Consumers may have other health insurance that covers them in case of injury and may choose not to buy this type of coverage. Some insurance policies allow consumers to buy this type of coverage only for passengers.

3. **Collision insurance** covers the cost of repairing a car when it is damaged in an accident. It usually has a **deductible** of $100, $200, or $500. Suppose that you had an accident that resulted in $1,893 worth of damage to your automobile when you had a $200 deductible policy. You would pay $200 and the insurance company would pay the remaining $1,693. The larger the deductible, the smaller the premium will be for collision insurance.

4. **Comprehensive insurance** covers losses to a person's automobile if it is damaged or destroyed by fire, storms, or vandalism or if it is stolen. Again, there is a deductible

included with comprehensive. This type of insurance is quite expensive and may not be a wise purchase if your car is old and not worth very much.

5. **Uninsured motorist insurance** covers losses that result from being in an accident with a driver who has no insurance or in cases of hit-and-run drivers. May states require this type of coverage to be sold with all automobile insurance policies. It is not very expensive and is important to have for the times when it is needed.

No-Fault Insurance

No-fault insurance became popular in the United States in the 1960s. Fourteen states have this type of insurance and ten others have modified versions of no-fault insurance. Under this type of insurance, each driver's own insurance company is responsible for covering injuries resulting from an accident, regardless of who is at fault. Therefore, there are many fewer court cases with no-fault insurance.

People who support this type of insurance believe that it has two important advantages. It speeds up payments to injured people because there is no need to determine fault in a court of law. No-fault insurance was also expected to reduce legal costs and therefore premiums. In states that have no-fault insurance, a larger part of each premium dollar does go to benefits. However, there is not much evidence that premiums have gone down. Premiums continue to remain high because many more people receive compensation now, even though the amount of each settlement tends to be smaller.

The biggest problem with no-fault insurance is that it limits the rights of people to sue for pain and suffering. In most cases there is a limit on when people may sue and for how much. This may prevent people from receiving just compensation for their injuries. Since the mid 1970s, no additional states have adopted no-fault insurance.

Which Type of Insurance Is Right for You?

All drivers need at least a certain amount of liability insurance. Some states may require you to carry uninsured motorist insurance. The choice of carrying collision or comprehensive insurance, as well as the amount of liability insurance you carry, depends on the type of car you drive and on your income and wealth.

People who are wealthy have more to lose than people who are not. They also can afford to pay more for insurance. If you had $500,000 in the bank and an annual income of $75,000, you would probably be making a mistake to buy only 20/40/10 liability insurance. Many accidents result in damages and injuries that

---

Vocabulary Builder

Collision insurance   Insurance that pays for car damage that is the result of an accident.

Comprehensive insurance   Insurance that pays for car damage that is not the result of an accident.

Deductible   The initial amount of money that an insured party must pay before the insurance company pays the remainder of a claim.

Medical payments insurance   Insurance that pays medical expenses of a driver and passengers in a car involved in an accident.

No-fault insurance   A type of coverage stating that in case of an accident, each driver's insurance company pays for damages and medical bills for that driver without trying to determine who was at fault.

Uninsured motorist insurance   Insurance that pays for medical treatment for people injured in an accident caused by a driver who had no insurance.

AUTOMOBILE FINANCIAL RESPONSIBILITY/COMPULSORY LIMITS

State	Liablity Limit[1]	State	Liablity Limit[1]
Alabama	20/40/10	North Dakota	25/50/25
Alaska	50/100/25	Ohio	12.5/25/7.5
Arizona	15/30/10	Oklahoma	10/20/10
Arkansas	25/50/15	Oregon	25/50/10
California	15/30/5	Pennsylvania	15/30/5
Colorado	25/50/15	Rhode Island	25/50/10
Connecticut	20/40/10	South Carolina	15/30/5
Delaware	15/30/10	South Dakota	25/50/25
District of Columbia	25/50/10	Tennessee	25/50/10
Florida	10/20/5	Texas	20/40/15
Georgia	15/30/10	Utah	20/40/10
Hawaii	35/unlimited/10	Vermont	20/40/10
Idaho	25/50/15	Virginia	25/50/10
Illinois	20/40/15	Washington	25/50/10
Indiana	25/50/10	West Virginia	20/40/10
Iowa	20/40/15	Wisconsin	25/50/10
Kansas	25/50/10	Wyoming	25/50/20
Kentucky	10/20/5		
Louisiana	10/20/10	**Canada**	
Maine	20/40/10		
Maryland	20/40/10	Alberta	$200,000 inclusive[3]
Massachusetts	10/20/5	British Columbia	200,000 inclusive
Michigan	20/40/10	Manitoba	200,000 inclusive
Minnesota	30/60/10	New Brunswick	200,000 inclusive
Mississippi	10/20/5	Newfoundland	200,000 inclusive
Missouri	25/50/10	Northwest Territories	200,000 inclusive
Montana	25/50/5	Nova Scotia	200,000 inclusive
Nebraska	25/50/25	Ontario	200,000 inclusive
Nevada	15/30/10	Prince Edward Island	200,000 inclusive
New Hampshire	25/50/25	Quebec	50,000 prop. damage[4]
New Jersey	15/30/5	Saskatchewan	200,000 inclusive
New Mexico	25/50/10	Yukon	200,000 inclusive
New York	10/20/5[2]		
North Carolina	25/50/10		

1. The first two figures refer to bodily injury liability limits and the third figure to property damage liability. For example, 10/20/5 means coverage up to $20,000 for all persons injured in an accident, subject to a limit of $10,000 for one individual, and $5,000 coverage for property damage.
2. 50/100 in cases of wrongful death.
3. "Inclusive" means that the amount of liability insurance shown is available to settle either bodily insurance or property damage claims—or both.
4. Quebec has a complete no-fault system for bodily injury claims, scaled down for non-residents in proportion to their degree of fault. The $50,000 limit relates to liability for damage to property in Quebec and to liability for bodily injury and property damage outside Quebec.
   SOURCE: *Insurance Facts*, 1988–89 edition, Insurance Information Institute, 110 William Street, New York, NY.

◆ **FIGURE 33-1**   Automobile Financial Responsibility/Compulsory Limits

exceed these limits. A wealthy person should buy a policy that has higher limits. Consumers with less wealth and income often cannot afford to buy policies that have high limits, although they still need to be adequately covered. The cost of increasing your liability limits is usually not very great.

Buying collision or comprehensive coverage for an older car may be a waste of money. The insurance company will only pay up to the **book value** for the car if it is damaged. This may be as little as $1,000 or less for an older car. If you have a $200 or $500 deductible on such an automobile, the policy becomes almost useless. It is usually better to save the premium and pay for damages to the car yourself.

Summing Up   *All drivers need to have basic liability insurance. Most states require some minimum coverage that may include no-fault insurance. Additional types and amounts of insurance may be purchased, depending on individuals' needs and ability to pay premiums.* ◆

SECTION 2

SHOPPING FOR AUTOMOBILE INSURANCE

While you read, ask yourself . . .
- ◆ *How did members of your family who have automobile insurance choose their insurance company?*
- ◆ *Do you know people who have been unhappy with their automobile insurance company? Why were they dissatisfied?*

Shopping for automobile insurance is usually easier than buying a car. Most insurance companies offer policies that provide almost identical coverage. When you decide on the type and amount of insurance you want, ask several different firms what they would charge for this coverage. You should be able to find the least expensive company in only a few days. Even if you eventually decide to have slightly different coverage, the firm that made the best first offer is likely to be the one with the lowest price.

When you are young, it may be much less expensive to buy insurance through your parents' policy. Insurance premiums are also smaller when young people are only occasional drivers of cars that belong to their parents, rather than primary drivers of cars that they own in their own name. Before you buy a car, be sure to find out how much your insurance will cost.

Cost Isn't the Only Factor to Consider

Although there is no reason to spend unnecessary money on premiums, the least expensive policy is not always the best policy. It may be worth paying a little more to have an insurance company that provides quick and friendly service. One way to find out about insurance companies is to ask your friends and relatives what their experience has been when they filed claims with their insurance companies or agents. If they received superior service and quick settlements, their company may be a good choice for you.

Some insurance companies do not have local agents and expect customers to transact their business over the phone using toll-free 800 telephone numbers. These firms are often able

Vocabulary Builder

Book value   The average value of a used car according to the *Official Used Car Guide*.

Consumers in Action

How Not to Get Taken When You Rent a Car

Although you may never have rented a car, the chances are very good that you will in the next few years. There are many reasons why you may need to rent a car. You may need a replacement when your own car is being repaired. You may want to rent a car when you go on vacation. You may need a larger or additional car when you have guests or large objects to move. Whatever the reason, when you rent a car, you will need to make decisions about your insurance coverage.

The rental firm will almost certainly try to convince you to buy a collision damage waver (CDW). This is insurance that "guarantees" that the rental firm will not charge you for damage to their car while it is in your possession as long as you don't "abuse" the car or drive it "recklessly." For this insurance you will be asked to pay from $9 to $15 a day. For many of the less expensive cars, this in effect doubles the price of renting. Most people don't need to buy this insurance because they already have adequate coverage from their own policies.

Before you rent a car, call your insurance agent and ask what coverage your automobile policy (or in some states homeowner's or renter's policy) gives you on a rented car. Many states require insurance companies to extend coverage to rented cars. You will probably find that you are covered. If you have no car insurance of your own, you may purchase this type of protection for around $60 a year from a number of insurance companies. If you only rent a car for a few days, this is not a wise choice, but if you frequently rent cars,

it can save you money. You might also consider choosing a credit card that automatically provides this insurance. Gold VISA, MasterCard, and cards issued by American Express and by the American Automobile Association give cardholders this type of coverage.

If you are asked to leave your credit card number with the rental agency, demand that they give you the customer copy of the charge slip so that you can prove that there was no amount on it when you signed the slip. Also, inspect the car before you drive it away. If it is damaged, demand that this be noted on your contract so that you will not be charged for damages done by someone else.

CDWs may be a thing of the past in a few years. There have been a number of state laws proposed to eliminate them. However, smaller car rental companies say that they can't pay the cost of insurance themselves and need CDWs to stay in business. If you are asked to pay for a CDW, be prepared to say no.

to offer lower premiums because they have fewer employees to pay. However, this also means that there is no one to go to locally when you need help or special documents. For

example, most states require proof of insurance to register automobiles. It may take several days to receive these documents through the mail when there is no local office or agent.

What Determines the Price of Automobile Insurance?

The premiums charged by automobile insurance companies are the result of past experience. Insurance companies collect and evaluate data about people who file claims. They have found that policyholders may be grouped according to age, sex, marital status, and the number of miles driven each year to predict the likelihood of individuals filing a claim. For example, statistically, single males who are sixteen to twenty-five years old have the highest probability of being involved in an accident. In addition, this group is likely to have larger claims than other groups. For this reason, young single males pay higher premiums than older married couples.

◆   The cost of receiving a ticket is likely to be felt in higher insurance premiums more than in the amount of the fine. What other reasons are there for obeying traffic laws?

Until recently, most insurance companies charged women less than men who were alike in all other ways. This is because women statistically have fewer accidents. However, a number of states have passed laws making these **gender-based insurance rates** illegal because they ignore such factors as driving records and social habits.

The highest premiums are charged to people who have been placed in a **risk pool**. Most drivers in this group have been refused insurance under normal conditions because of their driving record. When they are unable to obtain insurance, they become an **assigned risk**. The state assigns these drivers to insurance companies who must insure them for a minimum amount of liability. To receive this insurance, these drivers must pay premiums that are much higher than normal insurance rates. Not being placed in a risk pool is one of the most important advantages of having a good driving record.

How to Lower Your Insurance Premiums

There are a number of steps that consumers can take to lower their insurance rates. The

Vocabulary Builder

Assigned risk   A driver who is unable to obtain insurance often because of a poor driving record and who is assigned by state authorities to be insured by an insurance company that does business in that state.

Gender-based insurance rates   Insurance premiums set according to the sex of the insured party.

Risk pool   A group of drivers who have been unable to obtain insurance often because of poor driving records and who have been assigned to insurance companies by their state government.

Consumer News

If Cars and Highways Are Safer, Why Do We Pay More for Insurance?

Federal laws now require cars to have many types of safety equipment that reduce the danger of injuries in traffic accidents. Speed limits have been lowered and highways improved. The national fatality rate (death rate) per 100 million miles driven fell from 4.88 in 1970 to 2.55 in 1987. All these factors should keep insurance rates down, but instead they have increased rapidly. What other factors have caused insurance rates to go up?

One important factor has been an increase in the use of small cars. Nationally, the market share of small cars increased from 20 percent in 1975 to 32 percent in 1986. In California and many urban areas, up to 44 percent of the cars on the roads weigh less than 3,000 pounds.

Small cars have many social and economic benefits. They are less expensive to buy and run. They use less fuel and create less pollution. They put less wear on our roads. However, they are also more dangerous. People involved in an accident are almost twice as likely to sustain serious injuries if they are driving a small car rather than a large car. Big, heavy cars are safer to drive.

When you buy an automobile of your own, do you expect to buy a large car or a small one?

What trade-offs will you make?

best way to keep premiums down is to have a good driving record. Insurance companies often reward good drivers with lower premiums. Another choice that consumers may make is to not carry collision or comprehensive insurance or to increase the amount of their deductibles. They can also join car pools or use public transportation to receive special discounts.

Many people want to buy high-performance cars. Such cars may be fun, but they almost always result in higher insurance premiums. Less powerful cars may not be as exciting, but they are less expensive. You should regularly review your coverage and the prices offered by competitive insurance companies. Although a particular firm may offer the lowest rates one year, it may not the following year. On the other hand, it is not a good idea to change insurance companies to save only a few dollars. There is value in developing a good working relationship with an insurance company and an agent.

Summing Up   *Consumers should shop carefully for automobile insurance. The amount of premiums and quality of service are factors that they should consider. There are a number of steps that consumers may take to reduce their premiums.* ◆

SECTION 3

INSURING YOUR PLACE OF RESIDENCE

While you read, *ask yourself . . .*
- ◆ *What type of insurance does your family carry on your place of residence?*
- ◆ *Has anyone in your family ever filed a claim for theft or other property loss in your home?*

One of the basic costs of having a home is buying insurance to protect yourself from personal suits and to protect your property from theft or damage. The amounts and types of insurance will vary from person to person. However, all homeowners and renters need some sort of insurance coverage.

Homeowner's Insurance

There are two basic types of insurance policies that homeowners may buy. A **standard fire insurance** policy protects a home from loss that results from fire, weather damage, and explosions (a natural gas explosion, for example). Protection offered by a homeowner's insurance policy typically is more extensive and includes two types of coverage: property and liability.

Homeowner's policies protect consumers from losses to their house, garage, furniture, and other personal property whether they are at home, at work, or traveling. These policies cover losses due to fire, weather damage, theft, or vandalism. They usually pay for the cost of living somewhere else while your home is being rebuilt or repaired as the result of covered damage. For an additional premium, homeowners may buy protection against floods, earthquakes, or other types of damage.

There are three basic types of liability coverage that homeowner's policies provide:

1. Personal liability, in case someone is injured on your property or you damage someone else's property
2. Medical payment for injury to others who are on your property
3. Coverage for the property of others that you damage

Consumers may choose to buy a basic form policy that covers a limited number of risks or a comprehensive form policy that covers almost all risks of loss except flood, war, or nuclear attack. Homeowners who own specific pieces of valuable property like jewelry or paintings may need to buy additional insur-

ance for these items. To obtain this type of insurance, consumers must provide a list of the items to be insured with a statement from an appraiser of their current value.

Most homeowner's insurance policies cover the personal items for their fair market value, not for their replacement cost. Suppose that you bought a living room set five years ago for $2,800. To replace it today you might have to pay $4,000. However, if was stolen or destroyed, the insurance company would only pay you the current value of your used set, perhaps $1,300. You would have to pay the other $2,700 to buy a new set. Insurance that will pay the **replacement value** may be purchased for a little more than a normal policy.

How Much Insurance Should You Buy?

Homeowners should always insure their dwellings for at least 80 percent of the value. If the structure was destroyed in a fire or storm, the foundation, driveway, and land would still be there. Therefore, the cost of rebuilding would be less than the original value of the property. If a house is insured for 80 percent or more of its value, the insurance company must pay the total cost of repairing any damage up to the maximum covered amount. Suppose that a tree fell on your house and did $4,000 worth of damage. If your house was only insured for 60 percent of its value, the insurance

---

Vocabulary Builder

Replacement value The current cost of replacing an insured piece of property.

Standard fire insurance An insurance policy that protects a homeowner from property losses due to fire, weather, or explosions.

Consumer News

Buying a Little
Peace of Mind

In 1990 only one out of every four renters in the United States had renter's insurance. Barbara Foley was one of them, and for good reason. In 1983 Foley's apartment was broken into and destroyed by vandals. They tore up her clothing, broke her furniture, and kicked in her television. At that time she had no insurance to pay for her loss. For the next six months she slept in a sleeping bag on the floor and sat on an aluminum lawn chair because she could not afford to buy new furniture. She said that it took her years to put her life back together. By paying a little over $100 a year in 1990, Foley bought renter's insurance to give herself a degree of security and peace of mind.

company would not be required to pay the entire cost of the repair. You would pay $1,000 while the insurance company would pay $3,000 because you had only three-quarters of the 80 percent insurance you should have had.

It is important to review your insurance coverage regularly. Housing values and rebuilding costs increase most of the time. You may need more insurance even in areas where housing prices are going down. If land values were falling when construction costs were going up, it could cost more to rebuild a house on a piece of property that was worth less. Some insurance policies are automatically adjusted by the insurance company to reflect increased hous-

ing values. If other cases the homeowner must request an adjustment in the coverage.

Renter's Insurance

Most renters make the mistake of failing to insure themselves against loss. There is no reason to believe that no one will be injured in your home simply because you rent. If you accidentally pour a pot of boiling water on someone in your apartment, you may be sued just as easily as if you owned your own home. What's more, being a renter won't prevent your furniture from being stolen or destroyed in a fire. Clearly, renters need insurance.

Renter's insurance is typically called a **residence contents broad form policy**. Such a policy roughly parallels the same coverage as a homeowner's policy except that it does not provide protection for the structure itself. Typical renter's policies may be purchased for between $200 and $300 a year. Renters who have particularly valuable possessions will need to buy extra protection for these items.

Controlling Premiums

There are several ways to reduce homeowner's and renter's insurance premiums. The most obvious is to increase deductibles. Changing a deductible on property coverage from $100 to $500 should reduce a policy's premium by about 30 percent. Smaller decreases may be achieved by installing smoke detectors or dead bolt locks. It is also important to make sure that you don't buy more insurance than you need. There is little point in protecting a home that is worth $80,000 for $100,000.

Some insurance companies allow consumers to prepay insurance policies for an extended period of time at a reduced rate. This allows

◆   Renters may enjoy features most homeowners could not afford. However, like homeowners, they should protect themselves against loss. What types of insurance should people who live in these apartments purchase?

consumers to know how much their insurance will cost over a period of time and protects them from rate increases. Unfortunately, people who cannot afford to pay a year or more in advance are not able to take advantage of this choice.

The cost of buying insurance is significant, but it is money well spent. Insurance prevents consumers from suffering losses that are so great that their quality of life would be destroyed. For most people it is better to pay a limited cost than to suffer a large loss. The exact type and amount of insurance that a consumer should buy depends on the person's individual needs and ability to pay premiums.

Summing Up   *Consumers need to protect themselves from losses that occur in their place of residence by buying homeowner's or renter's insurance. The type and amount of coverage that each individual should buy depends on the person's individual needs and ability to pay premiums.* ◆

Vocabulary Builder

Residence contents broad form policy   A type of insurance that protects renters from losses to their property and from liability losses; renter's insurance.

Review and Enrichment Activities

VOCABULARY REVIEW

1. Column A contains key consumer terms from this chapter. Column B contains a scrambled list of phrases that describe what these terms mean. Match the correct meaning with each term. Write your answers on a separate sheet of paper.

Column A	Column B
1. Replacement value	**a.** Pays for the car damage that is not the result of a traffic accident
2. Gender-based insurance	**b.** Pays for injuries suffered by a driver or passenger in a traffic accident
3. Assigned risk	**c.** Pays for car damage that is the result of a traffic accident
4. Comprehensive insurance	**d.** Insuring a product for the amount it would cost to buy a new one
5. Medical payments insurance	**e.** Premiums based on the sex of the insured party
6. Collision insurance	**f.** When states require insurance companies to provide automobile insurance to people with poor driving records
7. Standard fire insurance	**g.** The average market value of a used car according to the *Official Used Car Guide*
8. Homeowner's insurance	**h.** Insurance that protects a home and its owner against a wide range of possible losses
9. Book value	**i.** A group of drivers who have been assigned to insurance companies because of their driving records
10. Risk pool	**j.** Insurance that only protects against damage from fire, weather, or explosions

2. Explain the difference between no-fault and uninsured motorist insurance.

CHECKING WHAT YOU'VE LEARNED

Write your answers for the following exercises on a separate sheet of paper.

1. Identify the five basic forms of automobile insurance.
2. Explain how no-fault insurance works.
3. Explain why many people thought that no-fault insurance would result in lower costs and premiums.
4. Explain why consumers might be better off by not buying collision or comprehensive insurance for older cars.
5. How could an insured party benefit from accepting a larger deductible for collision and comprehensive insurance?
6. What factors should consumers consider in addition to cost when they choose an insurance policy?
7. Describe how insurance companies set premiums for different customers.
8. Explain the difference between a standard fire insurance policy and a homeowner's policy.
9. Identify the three types of liability protection provided in homeowner's policies.
10. Why would a consumer choose to have insurance for the replacement cost of his or her property?
11. Explain why people who rent should purchase a residence contents broad form policy.

PRACTICING YOUR CONSUMER SKILLS

Write your answers for the following exercises on a separate sheet of paper.

1. Each of the following people has purchased automobile insurance. Evaluate each choice and explain the reason for your opinion.
   a. Heather is a college student who drives a 1983 Plymouth. She bought 100/300/50 liability, collision, and comprehensive insurance with a $100 deductible.
   b. Edgar is a corporate vice president who earns more than $100,000 a year. He thinks that he is a good driver, so he only bought 20/40/10 liability insurance for his new $80,000 Porsche.
   c. William and Evalynn both work and have two children. They bought 100/300/50 liability, collision, and comprehensive insurance with a $500 deductible for their new minivan.
   d. Harriet drives a new luxury car that costs $50,000. She carries 20/40/10 liability insurance, collision, and comprehensive with a $100 deductible.

Review and Enrichment Activities Continued

2. Identify the type of insurance that would protect a consumer in each of the following situations.

   a. Martin was stopped at a red light when a person with no insurance ran into his car and broke Martin's leg.

   b. Kathy left her car in her driveway one night when there was a hail storm. When she came out the next morning, she found little dents all over her car.

   c. Greg fell asleep while he was driving home late one night. He ran his car through the window of a store. No one was hurt, but there was $8,971.34 in damage done to the building and its contents.

   d. Rachel was driving home in a storm when her car slid into a ditch. Although the car was not seriously damaged, Dave, a passenger in her car, suffered a broken arm.

   e. One day Mark hit a telephone pole when he was turning into his driveway. There was $943.80 in damage done to his car.

3. Explain how each of the following people could have avoided their problems by purchasing insurance.

   a. Terry invited many people to his house for a pool party. One guest broke her leg by falling down a flight of stairs. She sued Terry for $10,000.

   b. Austin rented an apartment near Dayton, Ohio, that was destroyed by a tornado. He lost over $6,000 worth of furniture and clothing.

   c. Gretta had a gold and ruby necklace that she inherited from her grandmother. It was worth $5,000 but was stolen when her home was broken into last year.

   d. When there was a small fire in Tom's home, he was forced to rent a hotel room and eat out for five days while his home was cleaned and repainted.

USING NUMBERS

Solve the following problem to help make the best possible choice. Write your solution on a separate sheet of paper. Be sure to show all your work.

Shelly and Ted have been looking for a house to buy. They have found two that they could afford that are almost identical in every way. However, one is on the side of a hill far above where any flood could come. The other is only 200 feet from a river that has a history of flooding at least once in every twenty years. They can buy the house near the river for $68,000. The house on the hill would cost $80,000. If they buy the house near the river, they would need to buy flood insurance that would cost about $500 a year. How long would they be able to pay for the flood insurance from the savings they would receive by purchasing the house near the river? Which house do you think they should buy? Explain the reasons for your opinion.

PUTTING IDEAS IN YOUR OWN WORDS

The following quotations are from this chapter. Explain these quotations in your own words to make sure you understand what they mean. Write your answers on a separate sheet of paper.

1. "Choosing to drive without insurance is never a wise consumer choice."
2. "The biggest problem with no-fault insurance is that it limits the rights of people to sue for pain and suffering."
3. "Most homeowner's insurance policies cover the personal items for their fair market value, not for their replacement cost."

BUILDING CONSUMER KNOWLEDGE

The following quotations are from this chapter. Explain these quotations in your own words to make sure you understand what they mean. Write your answers on a separate sheet of paper.

1. Ask your parents or other family members to tell you the amount of automobile insurance coverage they have purchased. Evaluate their choice in relation to the type of car they drive and their apparent financial situation. Be prepared to explain your opinion to the class. It is not necessary to identify the person whose insurance you evaluate.
2. Investigate how much it would cost you to obtain automobile insurance on your own. Would you be willing and able to pay this amount to be able to drive? What steps could you take to reduce the amount you would have to pay?
3. Talk to three different people who rent their places of residence. Ask them to explain why they have or don't have renter's insurance. Be prepared to report your findings to the class.

Chapter 34

Health and Life Insurance

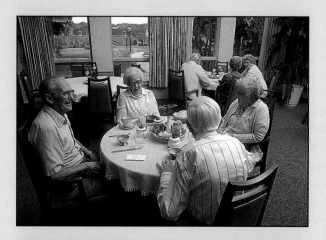

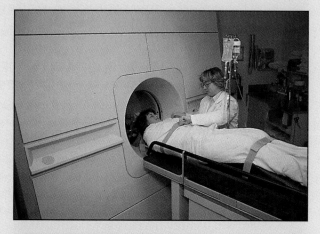

Chapter Objectives

After completing this chapter, you will be able to do the following:
- Identify different types of health insurance that may be used to protect consumers against injury or illness.
- Discuss issues involved in providing adequate health insurance for all citizens.
- Explain how consumers may choose the type of insurance that best meets their needs.
- Identify different types of life insurance that consumers may buy to protect their families in case of their death and to plan for their own retirement.

Key Consumer Terms

In this chapter you will learn the meanings of the following important consumer terms:
- Life expectancy
- Malpractice
- Medicare
- Medicaid
- Major medical insurance
- Health maintenace organization (HMO)
- Preferred provider organization (PPO)
- Cost-management system
- Whole life insurance
- Death benefit
- Beneficiary
- Living benefit
- Annuity
- Uniform decreasing term life insurance
- Standard term life insurance

I f you had an extra $2,800 to spend, what would you do with the money? You could buy a used car, pay for a vacation, or save for a college education. The fact is, in 1990, enough money was spent on health care in the United States to give every man, woman, and child in the country $2,800. This amount was about 12 percent of all the income people earned in that year. Even after spending this amount of money, there were many Americans who had inadequate health care. These were often people who had no health insurance. When it is possible, consumers should provide themselves and their families with health insurance to protect themselves from the possibly devastating costs of injury or illness.

People who have health insurance are likely to feel a sense of security. They know that if a member of their family becomes ill, many of their medical expenses will be paid by their insurance company. Psychologists believe that people want to feel secure more than just about anything else in life. Just worrying about the possibility of having to pay hospital bills could make you sick enough to need medical treatment.

SECTION 1

WHO PAYS FOR HEALTH INSURANCE?

While you read, ask yourself . . .
- *Do the members of your family have health insurance?*
- *How have members of your family benefited from health insurance? If you do not have health insurance, how has your family suffered?*

There was a time when many Americans believed that being employed automatically meant having employer-provided health insurance. Although many people do have this type of insurance today, there are many others who do not have basic health insurance provided by their employer. Some of these people may be part-time workers, some may be self-employed, and some may work for a firm that does not provide this benefit to its employees. An even larger number of employees find that they are now required to contribute to the cost of their health insurance.

The Skyrocketing Cost of Health Insurance

Between 1980 and 1988 the cost of health insurance in the United States increased at an average rate of about 12 percent a year in a time when most prices were going up about 4 to 5 percent a year. Not only are health insurance rates growing, but their rate of growth is accelerating. A typical increase in 1988 was 18 percent compared to increases of 20 to 30 percent in 1990. A family policy that could be purchased for $800 in 1980 cost roughly $3,600 by 1990. If this rate of growth continues through the year 2000, a basic family policy could cost around $12,000. With costs increasing at such a rapid rate, it is not surprising that employers would want to reduce the insurance coverage that they provide for employees.

Consumer News

Costs of Various Hospital Stays

In 1989 Joseph Califano, the former secretary for Health, Education and Welfare, said, "By the year 2000 the only person in the United States who can afford to get sick will be Donald Trump." Although this may be an exaggeration, it does point out the problem. According to the government, the average cost of a stay in the hospital more than doubled between 1980 and 1988. A typical chest X-ray that cost $27.50 in 1979 was up to $59 by 1989. A coronary bypass operation increased from $18,000 to $37,300 in the same time. Even dentures increased from $350 to $600.

If you or a member of your family became seriously ill, how would the medical bills be paid?

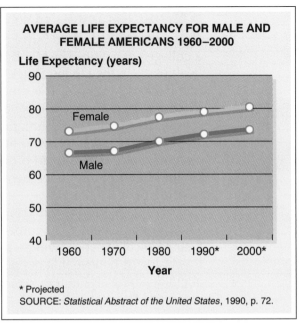

Figure 34-1   Life Expectancy

There are several reasons for the rapid increase in the cost of health insurance. One important reason is that Americans now have longer **life expectancies** than they used to. Medical advances have allowed doctors and other health care providers to give better treatment to people who are ill or have been injured, keeping alive many people who would have quickly died only a few years ago. A newborn American male could expect to live to be 72.1 years in 1988, while a newborn girl had a life expectancy of 79 years. When people live longer, they must be cared for. This adds to our medical costs and increases the price of health insurance. Average American male and female life expectancies are shown in Figure 34-1.

Many of the technological advances that allow us to live longer are very expensive. For example, a new method of looking inside a person's body to diagnose diseases and monitor changes is called magnetic resonance imaging (MRI). This procedure has saved or extended thousands of lives in recent years. However, each time MRI is used, it may cost between $1,000 and $2,000. People who have cancer may have this procedure done several times a year. When people are involved in accidents that cause brain damage, they may have MRIs done several times in one week. Although technological advancements have helped people live longer, they have come at high costs and have added to the expense of our medical care.

Many people believe that one of the most important causes for the increase in the cost of medical care has been increased doctors' earnings. However, available data do not give much support to this belief. In 1970 the average American doctor earned $41,800 per year.

By 1987 this amount had grown to $116,000, for a 177 percent increase. This may appear to be a rapid increase, but inflation in the same time totaled 193 percent. The purchasing power of the income that doctors earned actually fell. There were, of course, individual doctors who charged and earned much more, just as there were other doctors who earned less. Even if an increase in doctors' earnings contributed to the increased cost of medical care, it clearly was not one of the most important causes.

To some extent, the increase in doctor fees has been the result of the increase in the cost of **malpractice** insurance that doctors must pay to protect themselves from lawsuits. Some doctors have been sued and forced to pay settlements of over $1 million for mistakes in treatment. All doctors pay for these settlements in the form of higher premiums, regardless of whether they themselves have made mistakes that caused them to be sued. The cost of these higher premiums are passed on to consumers and their insurance companies in the form of higher doctor bills.

Government-Supported Health Care

Approximately 67 million of the almost 250 million Americans in 1989 benefited from at least one type of government-sponsored health care. Roughly half of these individuals were older people who participated in the **Medicare** program that is part of Social Security. Medicare was established in the 1960s to assure older Americans of at least a minimum amount of health coverage. Participants in the program must be sixty-five years of age. They pay a relatively small premium each month to qualify for limited coverage that is less expensive than coverage they could buy from private firms. Many older Americans buy supplemental policies to extend their Medicare coverage. These policies often cost them more than the

amount they must pay for the insurance provided by Medicare.

One reason the cost of Medicare has grown very rapidly is because it provides coverage and care at much lower costs than had previously been available to many Americans. Therefore, many more people use its services than would have purchased other types of insurance programs if Medicare was not available.

Steps were taken in the 1980s to slow the growth in the cost of this program. Beginning in 1983, hospitals and doctors were paid fixed fees for specific types of treatments. This meant that doctors and hospitals would receive a certain amount of money for a Medicare patient who broke a leg regardless of what the hospital spent to treat the patient. This did slow the growth of Medicare spending and save the government money. The amount saved in 1983 alone was estimated to be as great as $25 billion. On the other hand, the new fee system may have resulted in Medicare patients being given less care than they needed by hospitals and doctors who wanted to save money.

Many other Americans receive medical benefits paid for by the government through **Medicaid**. This program is not an insurance policy because the participants do not pay premiums

---

Vocabulary Builder

Life expectancy The average number of years that people of a particular age, sex, or other characteristic can expect to live.

Malpractice Inappropriate treatment given to a patient, resulting in injury or death.

Medicaid A government program that provides health care for people with low income and the disabled.

Medicare An insurance program established by the federal government that provides basic medical coverage for Americans who are sixty-five years of age or older.

Consumer News

Buying "Medigap Insurance"

Older Americans often buy "Medigap insurance" to supplement the insurance provided by Medicare. In 1990 more than 20 million senior citizens spent over $15 billion on Medigap insurance policies. Many of them were wasting their money buying coverage that was of little value or in some cases nonexistent. Congressman Ron Wyden of Oregon stated, "Many [seniors] have been ripped off, and many are being cheated out of their limited fixed incomes." The problem was that too many different types of policies were available and written in language that most people could not understand. Older Americans who were afraid of being wiped out by medical bills or of becoming a burden on their families would buy almost anything. Some paid more than half their income in premiums.

In December 1990 Congress passed a law that "invited" the National Association of Insurance Commissioners (NAIC) to reduce the types of Medigap policies that could be offered and to make the policies more understandable. If they failed to do so in nine months, more decisive action was threatened by the Congress. Do you have older friends or relatives who buy Medigap insurance? Ask them about their experiences with this type of insurance.

into the program. It is a part of the welfare program that is found in all states. Medical benefits and the quality of care provided by this program vary widely from state to state. In 1989 almost 34 million Americans received medical care through this program.

Private Sources of Health Insurance

About half of all Americans who have health insurance receive this protection from programs paid in part or totally by their employers. The number of Americans with this type of health insurance was slightly over 100 million in 1990. At that time a growing number of firms were requiring employees to contribute to the cost of their health coverage.

Other people paid for their own health insurance because they were self-employed, received no insurance from their employer, or were unemployed. Although most Americans had some type of coverage in 1990, there were approximately 35 million Americans who had no health insurance at all. For these people, illness or injury could mean financial disaster.

Summing Up *Most Americans enjoy the benefits of some health insurance. About one-third of these people participate in either Medicare or Medicaid. A little more than half receive health insurance that is partially or totally paid by their employers. The remaining people either pay for their own insurance or have no health insurance.* ◆

SECTION 2

TYPES OF HEALTH INSURANCE

While you read, ask yourself . . .
- ◆ *Do members of your family have to pay for routine visits to the doctor, or do they have insurance that pays for routine checkups?*
- ◆ *Do you know someone who was seriously injured or ill? How did the cost of medical bills affect that person's family?*

Over recent years many health insurance policies have been extended to cover medical expenses beyond those associated with treating injuries and illnesses. Regular checkups and diagnostic testing are paid for by some policies. The costs of such policies have turned out to be smaller than some experts had expected. People who have regular checkups tend to have illnesses that are discovered earlier and are therefore less serious and not as costly to treat. More money spent on regular checkups has resulted in less money being spent for treatment.

Group Health Insurance

Until quite recently, most consumers who had health insurance were members of specific groups, usually employees of a single firm or industry. Insurance companies usually have lower bookkeeping costs for group policies and therefore offer coverage at lower rates to members of the group. Under group policies people are covered to a certain maximum amount if they are injured or become ill. These policies sometimes have deductibles or pay a percentage of a patient's medical costs but not the entire bill.

A distinction is often made in group policies between outpatient and inpatient treatment. Outpatient treatment occurs when a person is treated in a hospital but does not stay overnight. Coverage of this type of treatment is often limited or in some cases not covered at all. Inpatient treatment is provided to patients who spend at least one night in a hospital. Generally, a larger portion of the cost of this type of treatment is covered by group medical insurance policies.

Many group policies have **major medical insurance** associated with them. Major medical policies cover a portion of the cost of medical care after a maximum amount has been paid by an ordinary group medical insurance policy. There is frequently a deductible of $50 or $100 that must be paid by the insured party before his or her major medical insurance will go into effect. Let's see how this works. Suppose that you are hospitalized for a serious illness. Your total bill amounts to $150,000, but your ordinary group medical insurance policy has a $100,000 maximum amount that it will pay. So your group policy pays the first $100,000. Then you pay the next $100 (your major medical deductible). Then 80 percent of the remaining $49,900 will be paid by your major medical insurance ($39,920), and you are expected to pay the remaining 20 percent ($9,980). Although this is a large amount, it is much less than the $50,000 you would have been required to pay without your major medical coverage.

Most major medical policies also have limits that are commonly between $1 million and $10 million. In recent years some policies have offered unlimited coverage.

Health Maintenance Organizations

Although **health maintenance organizations (HMOs)** have existed for over fifty years, they have become more popular in recent years. An HMO is an insurance plan that makes agreements with specific health providers to treat members of a group for a preset fee. Doctors and hospitals are often willing to charge these organizations less because they are assured that the members of the

Vocabulary Builder

Health maintenance organization (HMO) A type of insurance plan in which members receive medical services from participating doctors and medical facilities for a flat fee paid by them or their employer.

Major medical insurance Insurance that covers a percentage of medical costs after the benefits provided by a basic health insurance policy have been exhausted.

Consumer News

Being Paid to Lead a Healthy Life

With the rapid growth in the cost of health insurance, some employers have started programs that reward workers for leading healthy lives. For example, Ventura County, California, offers its employees a $300 bonus each year if they don't smoke, if they exercise regularly, and if their weight falls within designated ranges, depending on their age, sex, and height.

Would you be willing to live a more healthy life if you were paid more?
Do you feel that such plans are fair?

group will use their services. As a result, the costs of HMOs tend to be lower than other types of insurance.

HMOs pay all or most of the cost of regular physical examinations for members. Thus, many illnesses are caught in their early stages because HMO members are not afraid of the cost of seeing a doctor. This is probably the most important reason why HMO members are sent to hospitals 40 percent less often than other insured people. The greatest disadvantage of HMOs from the patient's point of view is the limitation on the choice of health care providers. Members of HMOs must receive treatment from doctors who belong to the organization. Patients do not have the freedom to use other doctors who they might prefer but who have not reached agreements with the HMO. If they do use these nonmember doctors, they must pay for the treatment themselves.

◆ People insured through preferred provider organizations may receive health care from doctors who accept its payments in full. They may also seek care from non-member doctors and pay any extra costs themselves.

Preferred Provider Organizations

Another type of organization that reduces medical costs and is similar to HMOs is the **preferred provider organization (PPO)**. PPOs give members a list of doctors and hospitals that have agreed to accept a preset fee as total payment for services provided. However, patients may choose to use nonparticipating health providers. They pay the doctor themselves and file claims with their PPO for the preset fee. The PPO sends the patient a check for the amount it covers, and the patient ends up paying the difference between the fee and the amount of the doctor's bill.

The lower costs of HMOs and PPOs have made them the most common type of health insurance in the United States. In 1984, 85 percent of all people who had health insurance were insured by traditional group policies. By 1990, 75 percent were covered by HMOs or PPOs. This means that most health care consumers have less choice in the medical care they receive. But the use of HMOs and PPOs has prevented costs from going up even more rapidly than they have. Both HMOs and PPOs may have major medical plans associated with them.

Cost-Management Systems

Many health insurance companies have tried to control medical costs by implementing **cost-management systems**. Under this type of system, patients must receive prior approval by the insurance company for hospitalization and treatment except in emergency situations. For example, if your doctor recommends that you have heart surgery, then your doctor must contact your insurance company and receive authorization before you enter the hospital. Frequently, the doctor will be asked a series of computer-generated questions about your physical condition. This information is fed into a computer that determines whether or not the treatment is justified by comparing your condition with other people who have had this type of surgery. If the computer rejects the proposed medical treatment, your doctor must discuss your condition with a physician who works for the insurance company before your treatment is approved.

Many doctors have expressed resentment about being "second-guessed" by a computer. They also argue that this procedure uses up large amounts of their time that could be better spent with their patients. However, this method of eliminating unnecessary treatment to cut costs is likely to become more common. Even the American Medical Association has begun to collect its own data in computerized form to check on the need for treatment.

Summing Up *People may receive health insurance from traditional group insurance policies or from HMOs and PPOs. These policies are often supplemented with major medical policies to help pay for large costs of serious illness or injury. All these forms of insurance have tried to find ways to limit the cost of medical treatment.* ◆

Vocabulary Builder

Cost-management system A system in which insurers require prior approval for a medical treatment to be insured, except in emergency situations.

Preferred provider organization (PPO) A type of health insurance that gives an insured party the choice of using a member health care provider, who will accept the plan's fee as total payment, or using another provider who is not a member. The insured party is then responsible for any difference between the insurance company's fee and the amount of a bill.

Consumer News

Your Doctor, Your Nurse, and Your Insurance Representative

Suppose that you just received the bad news from your doctor. You're sick and you must spend the next six months in the hospital receiving constant treatment. The total cost of your hospital stay will run into the hundreds of thousands of dollars.

If this happened, you would expect your doctors and nurses to keep track of your progress and to hold regular conferences to determine the best type of care for you. However, more and more you could also expect a representative of your insurance company to demand the right to be present at these meetings. "Case managers" are assigned by many insurance companies to work with doctors to find the best and most cost-effective treatments for patients they insure. For example, Cost Care Inc., a subsidiary of John Hancock Insurance, works to control the costs associated with premature births. Pregnant women in the program are required to consult with a Cost Care nurse about their progress to receive benefits. If they consult and receive advice and treatment fewer will have expensive premature births.

Some people believe that programs like this are an invasion of the doctor-patient relationship. Others say that it is a practical way to hold down the cost of medical insurance.

What do you think?

SECTION 3

SHOULD THERE BE UNIVERSAL HEALTH INSURANCE?

While you read, ask yourself . . .
- *What would your life be like if you had no health insurance?*
- *How much would your family be willing to pay to be sure that all Americans had at least a minimum amount of health coverage?*

The United States is the wealthiest nation in the world. We have more doctors and hospitals than any other nation. And yet there were roughly 35 million Americans who had no health insurance in 1990—and the number of uninsured people was growing.

The Costs of Not Having Health Insurance

It is clear that people who have no health insurance pay costs. But society and our economic system also pay significant costs when there are so many uninsured Americans. Most people who lack health insurance are the working poor. These people are employed and therefore do not qualify for Medicaid. On the other hand, they do not have employer-provided health coverage and cannot afford to purchase their own. Buying basic family coverage for people who were not members of a group in 1990 cost between $3,000 and $5,000, depending on where the family lived and the amount of insurance purchased. A person who earned $8,000 to $12,000 could not afford to pay 30 to 50 percent of his or her income to buy health insurance.

People who do not have health insurance are likely to put off seeing a doctor until they absolutely have to. By this time their illness may have progressed so far that it is life threatening; and their treatment will in any case be much more expensive. These people often cannot pay large hospital or doctor bills. When they become ill, their bills often end up being paid by Medicaid after their limited resources are exhausted. These government payments are often larger than they needed to be because of the time wasted while people put off seeing a doctor.

When people who are uninsured become ill, they tend to be sick for a longer period of time than other people. This means that they are unable to work and earn a living, often forcing them and their families onto welfare. While they are sick, they are not able to contribute to production or pay taxes. They also do not earn money to spend and support businesses. In one way or another, all Americans pay a cost when people do not have health insurance.

Should We Have a National Health Care Plan?

Most countries that are economically developed have some form of national health care paid for by the government. In Canada, for example, there is no private medical insurance. There is one comprehensive health care plan that insures all citizens. When someone becomes ill or simply doesn't feel well, he or she may see a doctor and pay no bill. As a result, the incidence of illness and death is lower in Canada than in the United States. Of course, the taxes that Canadians pay are higher than those in the United States to support this medical care. Canadian employers also pay taxes to support this system, but they do not have to worry about finding a health care program for their employees.

Many people are opposed to national health care in the United States. One reason they give

is the high cost of the system. Some people believe that if patients paid nothing when they went to see a doctor, they would make an appointment for every little pain and end up wasting much of our doctors' time and our health care resources. Another problem is that until recently, most doctors have opposed the plan. The American Medical Association (AMA) has lobbied against universal health care for most of the twentieth century. They have argued that fixed payments to doctors and hospitals would result in inferior care and discourage people from becoming doctors.

Some people have suggested that one reason some doctors may be opposed to national health care is that they might not be able to earn as much income. For national health care to function successfully, we would need the support of our health care providers. In the early 1990s the AMA appeared to be slowly changing its position to favor some form of national health care.

Although it is not necessary for the United States to have the exact same health care plan that Canada or other nations have, it is clear that uninsured people are made to suffer unreasonably under the mixed type of insurance available in 1990. Many Americans believe that we need to provide some form of health insurance for all citizens of the United States. Public opinion surveys taken in 1990 showed that about two-thirds of all Americans favor some form of universal health insurance. Some people have even suggested amending the constitution to guarantee all Americans the right to basic health care paid for by the government.

Summing Up *Uninsured people tend to have more serious illnesses and to remain ill longer than other people. When uninsured people become ill, they often must be helped by Medicaid. Many people support plans for a national health care program.* ◆

INSURING YOUR LIFE AND RETIREMENT

While you read, ask yourself . . .
- ◆ *How much do you expect to earn over your lifetime?*
- ◆ *Who would be hurt if you were not alive to earn an income?*

Almost everyone would like to live a long and healthy life. Unfortunately, not everyone is lucky enough to do this. When a person suffers an early death in an accident or from illness, he or she often leaves financial burdens for the family left behind. Although medical expenses may be covered by health insurance, there are often other expenses that will not be covered. This is particularly true when a parent dies. The responsibility and cost of raising children can be overwhelming for a single parent. It is important for consumers to consider the needs of their family and to buy an adequate amount of life insurance if they can possibly afford to. Parents should also recognize that both husband and wife should be insured. If there are two wage earners in a family, or even when one parent stays home with the children, the death of one adult may put financial strain on the other.

Whole Life Insurance

What most people think of when they consider life insurance is **whole life insurance**. This type of insurance usually provides two types of benefits. If a person suffers an early death, the policy will pay a **death benefit** in the form of a lump sum or an alternative type of payment to a designated **beneficiary**. If policyholders live into retirement years, they usually receive some sort of payment to help with their living expenses.

Generally, the annual premium of a whole life policy remains the same. The benefit that will paid if the insured party dies also remains the same. This means that as time goes by, inflation will tend to make the premium and the benefit smaller in terms of their purchasing power. If you buy $50,000 worth of whole life insurance at the present, it may seem like quite a lot. Twenty years from now the value of a $50,000 policy may be rather small.

Whole life insurance policies build up cash value over time. In the first year the majority of the premium covers the insurance company's risk and costs associated with the policy. However, as time goes by a larger portion of the premium is accumulated as a value that belongs to the policyholder. This value may be borrowed against at low-interest rates if the policyholder needs cash. A whole life policy may also be terminated and "cashed in" for its value. This is usually not a good choice because buying similar coverage in the future will be much more expensive.

When insured parties reach retirement age, they may choose among a variety of alternatives. They may continue to pay their premiums and receive protection for the remainder of their lives, but at a reduced level. They may continue to receive full protection, but only for a specified number of years. They may also elect to take a financial settlement that is based on the value of their policy. Most whole life insurance policies provide **living benefits** for people who live to retirement age. The policyholders are allowed to convert the value in their policy into some form of retirement income. They may take the value of their policy as a lump sum, or they may choose to receive an **annuity** for the remainder of their lives. An annuity is a monthly payment that is based on the value a policyholder has built up in a policy and the period of time he or she may be expected to live. The exact form that these payments may take varies from one company to another. Consumers should check into this

◆   The early death of a parent often creates financial burdens that life insurance benefits can eliminate. What trade-offs do consumers make when they buy life insurance?

type of benefit when they are choosing a policy. On an average, 60 percent of the payments made by life insurance companies are of this type.

The amount that an individual must pay for a premium and the amount that the person will receive as an annuity depends in part on the person's life expectancy. This is the length of time a person of that age and sex can expect to live on an average. Although some people will live much longer than their life expectancy, others will live less. Insurance companies keep a small portion of funds on hand to pay annuities to beneficiaries.

Consumers should start buying life insurance as soon as possible. In this way they will

Vocabulary Builder

Annuity   A form of payment made by an insurance company that provides a monthly income for the remainder of a beneficiary's life.

Beneficiary   The designated person or persons who will receive payment for any insurance policy.

Death benefit   The amount an insurance company pays if an insured person dies while a policy is in effect.

Living benefit   A benefit paid on a whole life insurance policy while the owner is living.

Whole life insurance   Insurance that has both death benefits and living benefits.

Consumers in Action

Checking Up on Your Life Insurance Company

How would you feel if you had paid thousands of dollars into an insurance policy to have a financially secure retirement only to have the company fail just before you were ready to retire? This is exactly what happens to many consumers every year. They certainly are angry, but unfortunately, there isn't much they can do about it. The best step you can take to avoid this problem is to check out the financial condition of the insurance company before you purchase a policy.

Money "saved" in life insurance policies is *not* insured by a federal government agency like the FDIC. Most states have "guaranty funds" that pay off customers of failed insurance companies for amounts up to but not over $100,000. When firms fail in states with guaranty funds, customers eventually receive their money, but they may have to wait years while the courts review the situation and make decisions. In 1990, Alaska, California, Colorado, Louisiana, New Jersey, Wyoming, and Washington, D.C., had no guaranty funds. When insurance companies fail in these states, settlements might never come.

Although most life insurance companies are financially strong, it is worth your time to be sure you don't chose one that isn't. The A.M. Best Company of Oldwick, New Jersey, rates insurance companies. Even this rating service is not foolproof, and it is possible for a firm's rating to change. For example, Baldwin-United was rated A+ in 1981 but failed in 1983 after making a series of unwise investments.

An insurer's investment choices are a clue to its financial health. You should ask your agent for a list of the firm's investments. This list should include 15 to 20 percent in government securities and a significant share of investments in large, reputable firms. There is no reason to be put off by a few investments in smaller ventures, but they should not be the largest part of the insurance company's assets. You should also ask what the firm's surplus is as a percent of its assets. The surplus is money or assets set aside to pay for unexpected losses. A healthy firm should hold 10 percent or more of its assets as a surplus.

Size is not a guarantee of security, but it doesn't hurt. Small insurance companies have a history of experiencing financial difficulties more often than larger ones. Whatever firm you consider, ask your agent many questions. If your agent is unable or unwilling to answer your questions, look elsewhere for insurance.

have the necessary insurance should they become injured or ill. Also, premiums are smaller when people start paying them early in their lives. A man who buys life insurance at the age of twenty-five will pay roughly half the annual premium of another man who begins his policy at forty-two.

Term Life Insurance

Premiums for whole life insurance tend to be quite high and are therefore more expensive than many consumers can afford. A less expensive alternative is **uniform decreasing term life insurance**. This insurance pays a death benefit that becomes smaller as time goes by. It has a relatively low premium, so people who are young or are just starting families can afford to buy it without being forced to lower their standard of living. There is no accumulated cash value in this type of policy. What it does is provide a substantial death benefit to help a family cope with the unexpected loss of a wage earner—something that could otherwise be financially devastating.

Suppose that a husband and wife each buys a $50,000 thirty-year decreasing term policy at the age of twenty-six. He will pay about $65 a year, while she will pay roughly $60. The difference in their premiums reflects the fact that women have longer life expectancies than men. As they pay into the policies, the amount of their premiums will decline, and the amount of the benefits will also go down. This type of insurance allows maximum coverage with minimum premiums. When these people become older, they may be able to afford whole life insurance coverage.

Some term policies only last for a short period of time, perhaps as little as five years. **Standard term life insurance** is renewable at the end of these short periods of time at a higher premium. This system lasts until the person retires or reaches some specific age like sixty-five or seventy, at which time all coverage stops. The advantage of renewable term insurance is that its benefit does not go down over time.

Often term insurance can be converted into whole life insurance without the necessity of a medical examination. This means that people who buy such policies when they are young know that they will be able to buy whole life insurance when they are older regardless of their health. Term policies that are convertible will cost somewhat more than term policies that cannot be converted.

Consumers should take steps to protect themselves and their families from the financial consequences of injury, illness, or premature death. The amount and type of coverage that each individual should purchase will vary, depending on income and family situation. It is important to start young so that you may protect your future. Many insurance companies offer slightly different types of policies than those described in this chapter. Be sure to investigate many different firms before you choose the policy that you believe best suits your needs and financial situation.

> *Summing Up* *Consumers should consider purchasing life insurance to protect their families from financial loss due to death at a young age. Although whole life policies usually offer living as well as death benefits, they are more expensive. Many young people can start building their protection through term policies.* ◆

Vocabulary Builder

Standard term life insurance A form of life insurance that provides a fixed amount of protection for a short period of time, but which may be renewed for more time at a higher premium.

Uniform decreasing term life insurance Insurance that provides progressively less protection over a certain period of time.

Review and Enrichment Activities

1. Column A contains key consumer terms from this chapter. Column B contains a scrambled list of phrases that describes what these terms mean. Match the correct meaning with each term. Write your answers on a separate sheet of paper.

Column A	Column B
1. Life expectancy	a. An insurance policy that pays a death benefit that grows smaller over time
2. Cost-management systems	b. A payment made by a life insurance firm when an insured party retires
3. Beneficiary	c. The person who receives a payment from an insurance company
4. Uniform decreasing term life insurance	d. An insurance policy that must be renewed at a higher premium after a specific period of time
5. Standard term life insurance	e. Insurance that pays a share of medical costs after a basic insurance policy's benefits have been used up
6. Living benefit	f. The average length of time a person of a particular age, sex, and condition may be expected to live
7. Death benefit	g. Insurance purchased by health care providers to protect themselves from suits by patients
8. Major medical insurance	h. A plan that requires prior approval for many treatments to be paid for by an insurance company
9. Malpractice insurance	i. Insurance that usually provides benefits when an insured parties die or retirement benefits when they live
10. Whole life insurance	

j. A payment made by a life insurance company when an insured party dies

2. Explain the difference between a health maintenance organization and a preferred provider organization.

CHECKING WHAT YOU'VE LEARNED

Write your answers for the following exercises on a separate sheet of paper.

1. Describe four possible reasons for the rapid increase in medical costs in this country during the 1980s.
2. Explain the difference between Medicare and Medicaid.
3. Why are group insurance premiums usually lower than individual health insurance premiums?
4. Describe how major medical policies provide extra coverage for consumers.
5. What type of benefit is provided by HMOs and PPOs that is not normally provided by group health insurance policies?
6. What is the most likely reason that members of HMOs and PPOs spend less time in hospitals than other people?
7. What type of person was most likely to have no health coverage in 1990?
8. Describe how people who have health insurance may be affected by people who do not.
9. Explain two reasons why many people are opposed to providing some form of national health care.
10. What two types of benefits are offered by most whole life insurance policies?
11. Why is uniform decreasing term life insurance less expensive to buy than other forms of life insurance?
12. What benefit does convertible term insurance offer consumers?
13. Why is it usually a wise choice for consumers to buy life insurance when they are young?

PRACTICING YOUR CONSUMER SKILLS

Write your answers for the following exercises on a separate sheet of paper.

1. Each of the following consumers has some form of health insurance: (1) group health insurance, (2) individual health insurance,(3) HMO insurance, (4) PPO insurance, or (5) Medicare. Identify the type that each person has. Explain how you know your answer is correct.

Review and Enrichment Activities Continued

    a. When Paul started feeling ill each morning he went to his doctor. He paid the bill and was reimbursed for part of this amount by his insurance company. His doctor has not agreed to belong to his insurance company's group of member care providers.

    b. When Mary broke her hip falling down the stairs at the retirement home where she lives, her insurance only paid for part of her medical costs. She ended up paying about 30 percent of the bills herself.

    c. When Bill was laid off from his job, he couldn't afford to buy much health insurance. When his son became ill, he had to pay almost half the bill himself.

    d. When Wanda had a baby, she chose a pediatrician from a list provided by her insurance company so that she would not end up paying the cost of doctor visits for her child.

    e. When Lou has his annual checkup, he pays the bill himself. However, the insurance provided by his employer paid for his hospital stay when he had surgery on his hand last year.

2. Identify each of the following points of view as being (1) in favor of or (2) opposed to national health insurance. Give your opinion of each argument.

    a. If we had national health care, fewer people would become seriously ill. As a result, we would need to spend less money building hospitals. We would have more healthy Americans working and contributing to production and taxes.

    b. If we had national health care, our taxes would go right through the roof. People would go to the doctor every time they had a sore toe. Doctors would charge the taxpayers a fortune and wouldn't have enough time to treat people who are really sick.

    c. If we had national health care, fewer people would become doctors, and hospitals wouldn't provide quality treatment. They would only be interested in keeping their expenses down because of the fixed fees they would receive from the government.

    d. If we had national health care, our country would be a better place to live. People would feel more secure and happier because they would know that they could not suffer devastating costs if they became seriously ill.

3. Recommend a type and amount of insurance for each of the following people using the following table. Explain each of your recommendations.

Annual Insurance Premium for a 25-Year-Old Woman			
Amount	Whole Life	Decreasing Term	Standard Term
$ 10,000	$ 85.40	$ 40.80	$ 36.40
$ 50,000	$303.00	$ 57.00	$ 53.00
$100,000	$508.00	$102.00	$ 98.00
$150,000	$705.00	$146.00	$138.00
$200,000	$902.00	$190.00	$178.00

a. Molly owns a flower shop and is a single mother of three children. She wants to put most of her income back into her business, which has been growing rapidly. She also wants to protect her children if anything happened to her.

b. Ronda is single and has no intention of getting married. She works as a receptionist in a doctor's office. She would like to put money away for her old age. She also wants to be sure that if anything happened to her, her relatives would not be forced to pay any of the bills for her funeral.

c. Alice is married to Richard. They both work and can afford to buy many things. They expect to have children someday. Richard has been promoted twice in recent years and expects to be vice president of the firm he works for within ten years.

d. Brenda just graduated from college with a teaching degree. She has a job, but as a new teacher her pay is low. She thinks that she may get married in a year or two but really can't be sure.

USING NUMBERS

Solve the following problem to help make the best possible choice. Write your solution on a separate sheet of paper. Be sure to show all your work.

James fell from a ladder while he was painting his house last year. He broke both his legs, his collar bone, and an arm. He spent almost three months in the hospital and had to return for therapy every week for almost a year. He is now feeling well again but has his medical bills to deal with. His group insurance policy will pay all of the first $100,000 of his expenses. He also has $1 million in major medical coverage, but he must pay the first $100 before this policy begins to pay 80 percent of the remaining cost. Jim's total medical bill for his treatment was $212,600. Of this amount, how much will be covered by his group policy, how much will be covered by his major medical policy, and how much will Jim have to pay?

Review and Enrichment Activities Continued

PUTTING IDEAS IN YOUR OWN WORDS

The following quotations are from this chapter. Explain these quotations in your own words to make sure you understand what they mean. Write your answers on a separate sheet of paper.

1. "The cost of Medicare has grown very rapidly because it provides coverage and care at much lower costs than had previously been available to many Americans."

2. "The greatest disadvantage of HMOs from the patient's point of view is the limitation on the choice of health care providers."

3. "The amount that an individual must pay for a premium and the amount that the person will receive as an annuity depends in part on the person's life expectancy."

BUILDING CONSUMER KNOWLEDGE

Write your answers for the following exercises on a separate sheet of paper.

1. Ask five different adults how much they are required to pay when they visit a doctor for a regular checkup. Also ask them how often they get checkups. Does it seem like there's a relationship between the amount that people must pay and the number of doctor visits they make? Be prepared to report your findings to the class.

2. Interview friends or relatives who receive medical coverage either through Medicare or Medicaid. Ask them to describe the quality of the treatment they receive and the amount of paperwork they must complete to receive care. Be prepared to report your findings to the class.

3. Write an essay describing what you believe would happen to your family if the primary wage earner died. Be as specific as possible. What does this essay show you about the importance of buying life insurance?

UNIT 10

Making Your Dollars Count

All consumers have a limited amount of income to spend to satisfy their needs and wants. Unit 10 describes various methods you can use to help get the greatest satisfaction possible from the money you spend. You will learn about the factors to consider when you choose where to live, how to travel, and which food products to buy. You will also learn how to get information that will help you make better choices. You will discover how changes in technology have made your life different from that of your parents, and you will learn about the changes that may take place in the future. The message in this unit is that consumers need to keep learning so that they can make rational and responsible choices.

565

Chapter 35

How to Be a Smart Shopper

Chapter Objectives

After completing this chapter, you will be able to do the following:

- Identify four questions that consumers should ask before they purchase goods or services.
- Explain why consumers should read labels on packaged food products to make better choices.
- Describe the trade-offs between quality, convenience, and price that consumers make when they buy food products.
- Identify the important characteristics of appliances, and explain how these characteristics may be taken into account when purchasing an appliance.
- Explain why consumers buy different types of clothing, and explain how they may receive the best value for the clothing dollars that they spend.

Key Consumer Terms

In this chapter you will learn the meanings of the following important consumer terms:

- Recommended daily allowance (RDA)
- Unit pricing
- Quantity buying
- Name-brand product
- Store-brand product
- Generic product
- Bulk product
- Convenience food
- Buying service
- Custom
- Fabric content
- Care instructions

H ave you ever seen something in a store that you wanted very much? It may have been expensive. Or perhaps it was something you could only use one time. But you knew you had to have it. If you bought the product, were you satisfied with it after several weeks? Did you later find that you could have bought a similar product somewhere else for less? Maybe other people bought the exact same product, and you decided you didn't want it so much. When you used it, you might have found that it broke or tore easily. After a few weeks you may have decided that it wasn't what you really wanted after all.

This sort of experience happens to just about everyone. To keep it from happening often is an important reason to shop carefully.

SECTION 1

DECIDING WHAT TO BUY

While you read, ask yourself . . .
- What products have you bought that you later wished you hadn't?
- What knowledge and skills have you gained from your experiences that make you a better shopper?

If you don't live on a desert island or in the wilderness, you have a wide range of choices you can make when you decide where to shop. You should take the time to find the best deal for the products you need or want to buy.

Before you buy any product, ask yourself the following four questions:

1. *Do I really need this product?* Consumers are often attracted to products that are promoted in clever or original ways. Being attracted to something is not the same as needing that product. Learn to distinguish between products that are merely attractive and those that you really need and should spend your money on.

2. *How will I feel about this product in the future?* Consumers frequently change their minds about products in a relatively short period of time. Think carefully about a product that you feel you need now. You may realize that in a few weeks you won't want it so much. Learn to distinguish between products that have lasting value and those that are only a "passing fancy."

3. *Is this the best deal available?* Most products may be purchased at more than one location. Take the time to find the best offer for the products you decide to buy.

4. *If I buy this product, will I have enough money left over to buy other products that are more important to me?* Not all products that consumers want have equal importance. Be sure to buy the products that will give you the greatest satisfaction for your money. Avoid buying a product that will prevent you from buying more important products in the future.

Answering these questions is really a form of decision making similar to the process you learned about in Chapters 1 and 15. Of course, when you make simple decisions like which brand of soft drink to buy, you won't take the time to work through all seven steps of this process. However, to make good consumer choices, people need to consider their goals, values, and alternatives.

Summing Up *Before consumers buy a product, they should be sure that they really need the good or service, that they will want it in the future, that they have found the best deal, and that buying the product won't prevent them from buying something else of greater value in the future.* ◆

MAKING THE MOST OF YOUR FOOD DOLLAR

While you read, ask yourself . . .
- ◆ *How much money do you personally spend on food?*
- ◆ *How will your need to shop for food carefully change when you have your own family?*

Americans spent about $550 billion on food in 1990. This worked out to about $2,200 per person in the country. When people earn more income, they don't necessarily eat a greater quantity of food, but the type of food (prepared versus raw) and the service that comes with it (having someone else cook it for you) does change. Unfortunately, there may be little relationship between the amount of money that people spend on food and its nutritional value. Many inexpensive foods are good for you, while those that are more expensive may have little food value. It is important to know the difference between food that just tastes good and food that is good for you.

Read the Label!

Government regulations require packaged food products to be labeled with the following information:
- Name of the product
- Name and address of the manufacturer, packer, or distributor
- Net contents in terms of weight, measure, or count
- Details of dietary characteristics, if applicable

◆ Consider the food products this shopper has chosen. What might she learn about the nutritional value of these items if she read their labels? Do you think she is making a rational choice for her health?

- Mention of whether the product contains artificial coloring, flavoring, or chemical preservatives
- Serving size
- Servings per container
- Calories per serving
- Grams of protein, carbohydrate, and fat per serving
- Percentage of U.S. **recommended daily allowance (RDA)** of protein and selected minerals and vitamins

These are the minimum label requirements. Many manufacturers put additional information on their packages. Consumers need to be careful when they read this additional information. For example, if your breakfast cereal lists nutritional information *when* it is served with 3 ounces of milk, it is possible that much of the nutritional value is from the milk and not the cereal. Businesses put this added information on their packages for a reason. This reason may not always be to provide useful information to consumers.

Ingredients in foods must be listed in order of their content share. The ingredient that makes up the largest share must be listed first. The second largest ingredient will be listed next and so on. If a product's list of ingredients starts off with "sugar, corn syrup, milk solids, wheat flour, salt ...," then it probably isn't very good for you. Sugar and corn syrup make up the largest parts of the product. Another product whose ingredients read, "wheat flour, eggs, milk solids, corn oil, sugar, salt, ..." is likely to be a healthier choice.

Meat, poultry, eggs, milk, and many other food products are graded for quality by the U.S. Department of Agriculture (USDA). These grades are intended to provide information that will help consumers make better choices.

All fresh meats sold by retailers, with the exception of pork, are "voluntarily" labeled as prime, choice, or select. Prime meats have the highest fat content, select meats the least. Although this system may appear useful, you should realize that 92 percent of the meat sold in 1990 was labeled "choice." When consumers buy meat in a grocery store, they usually have little or no choice in the grade they buy.

Poultry has been inspected and graded since 1968. This grading is solely based on observable characteristics (those that can be seen), such as freezer burn or broken parts. The grade that poultry receives has no relation to the flavor of the meat or its quality. In recent years poultry inspection has been criticized for its lack of thoroughness. Consumers should not put all their faith in government inspections.

The Trade-Off Between Quality, Quantity, and Price

By reading labels, you can compare products according to their price, quantity, and quality. Many states require stores to provide **unit pricing** for food and other products. This allows consumers to easily compare the price of different products for a standard amount. Cooking oil, for example, might have a unit price that is expressed in cents per ounce. If two brands of oil come in different-size bottles, a unit price of 5.6 cents per ounce for one and 6.3 cents for the other tells the consumer immediately which is least expensive.

Products are often less expensive when consumers take advantage of **quantity buying**, but this is not always the case. You might be surprised to find that larger packages of some

Vocabulary Builder

Quantity buying Purchasing products in large amounts to reduce the cost per unit.
Recommended daily allowance (RDA) An amount of various nutrients recommended for daily consumption by the U.S. government.
Unit pricing Expressing prices in an amount per standard unit of measure.

Consumer News

Can One Person Make a Difference?

How often have you seen something that really bothered you, but you thought, "I'm just one person. What difference can I make?" You may have felt this way, but not Phil Sokolof.

In 1988 Phil Sokolof got fed up with misleading advertisements and labeling used by producers of processed foods. He took $1 million of his own money and placed full-page advertisements in newspapers across the nation that identified specific misleading claims and the firms that made them. One claim that offended Sokolof was for Swiss Miss Light Cocoa Mix, which achieved most of its claimed 36 percent drop in calories by reducing the serving size by 25 percent. Another claim that bothered Sokolof was the statement that a product contained only "pure vegetable oil." Unfortunately, palm oil, one of the worst oils that people can consumer, is a vegetable oil. Some claims made by food processors were simply untrue. Kraft Foods claimed that one slice of its Kraft Singles cheese had as much calcium as 5 ounces of milk, when in fact it had only 67 percent as much calcium. The list went on and on.

As a result of Sokolof's ads, twelve firms announced that they would change the ingredients in their food products. These firms included Borden's, General Foods, Heinz, and Kellogg's. We do not all have $1 million to invest in honesty, but this shows that one person can make a difference.

products are more expensive per unit than smaller ones. Although this makes little sense in terms of the cost of producing and packaging products, it does happen. Unit pricing allows consumers to discover this type of pricing easily.

How Much Could You Save?

Have you ever wondered how much you could save by shopping carefully for your groceries? To answer this question, the editors of *Consumer Reports* conducted an experiment in 1988. Two people were given an identical shopping list and asked to purchase all the items on the list from the same large grocery store. One shopper was asked to buy impulsively, without thinking of price. The other shopper was instructed to choose carefully, comparing nutritional value and prices. The result was that the impulsive shopper selected mainly **name-brand products** for a total cost of $110.05. The careful shopper, on the other hand, purchased mostly **store-brand products** and paid a total of $59.35. By shopping carefully, this person saved more than 45 percent of the expense of buying the groceries.

In other studies *Consumer Reports* asked consumers to judge products for quality and ease of use. In these studies name-brand products were consistently rated superior to most store-brand products. What this shows is that in many cases there is a trade-off between price and quality. Brand-name products tend to have both higher quality and higher prices. Consumers must decide for themselves when to choose price over quality and when to choose quality over price.

In addition to name-brand and store-brand products, consumers may buy **generic products** and **bulk products**. Generic products have no advertised brand name and may be recognized by the yellow or white and black containers they are usually packaged in. Their quality is generally adequate but not superior.

◆   Bulk foods are often convenient and inexpensive when compared to name brand products. Do members of your family buy bulk foods? What reasons do they have for their choice?

Because firms that manufacture these goods spend little or nothing on advertising they are able to price generic goods significantly lower than other similar products. Bulk products are usually found in large containers. Consumers simply take whatever amount they want. These products are usually less expensive than prepackaged goods.

Consumers Buy Convenience Too

The packaging of many food products costs the manufacturer as much or more than the food itself. Plastic-coated packages with bright colors add much to the cost of the product and little to its quality. Since most of these packages aren't biodegradable, they also add to our landfill problems. The quality of food in ordinary cardboard packages or reusable containers is often as good as other products, and the price is usually lower.

Vocabulary Builder

Bulk products   Products sold by weight, often unbranded.

Generic products   The general name for a product that is not advertised or marketed under brand names by manufacturers.

Name-brand product   A product with a well-known, often advertised name, trademark, or logo.

Store-brand product   A product that bears the name or brand of the store that offers it for sale.

Buying **convenience food** requires consumers to make another type of trade-off. Microwave meals are much quicker and easier to prepare. However, they are almost always more expensive, and many consumers believe that they are less pleasing and wholesome than other types of food. Not all convenience food is bad for you. Some is quite nutritious. But it is always more expensive. Again, each consumer must decide when the extra convenience of easy-to-prepare foods is worth the extra cost or possibly inferior taste.

When consumers buy food products, the best type of protection they have is their own good judgment. Meals that are prepared in your own home from unprocessed food products are more likely to be wholesome and inexpensive. However, not all consumers have time to cook each meal "from scratch." They must make the best possible choice between price, convenience, and quality.

Summing Up   *When consumers buy food products, they should read the labels to be sure they know what they are buying. Often they can use unit prices to compare the values of different products. Consumers should also consider packaging when they choose between price, convenience, and quality.* ◆

SECTION 3

BUYING PRODUCTS FOR YOUR HOME

While you read, ask yourself . . .
- ◆ *How do members of your family decide where and when to buy appliances or other household goods?*
- ◆ *What appliances does your family own that you believe are necessities? Which appliances are not necessities?*

When people buy furniture, appliances, linens, and other products for their home, they are able to save money and receive quality goods if they are careful shoppers. As in other decisions, consumers who are patient and take the time to find the best offer are most likely to receive the greatest satisfaction from the money they spend.

Steps to Wise Shopping

There is no way to be sure you will always get the best deal possible, but you can take certain steps to avoid being taken advantage of. Consumers should make a practice of following these five steps whenever they purchase goods:

1. *Always check the quality of any product you consider buying.* Look up the product in the *Consumer Reports Buyer's Guide* to find their recommendation for brands that have good quality. This publication is available in most libraries and ranks many products for quality and price. Although it does not include all makes and models, it is a good place to start. It also suggests features to consider when buying various products.

2. *Always check the price at three or more stores.* There are often significant price differences between businesses. It may be a better choice to pay slightly more to shop at a convenient or more reputable store, but take the time to find out how much you need to pay for this added value.

3. *Always find out what type of service and warranty is offered with a product you buy.* Many stores do not service the products they sell. If the good is defective or breaks, it may need to be sent to some other location for service. This can take weeks or months. Find out who is expected to pay for shipping, parts, and labor. It makes little sense to save $5 to buy a microwave that will cost you $100 or more to have serviced. If you buy products that were manufactured in

other countries, check into the availability and cost of parts.

4. *Always try to buy products when they are on sale.* Many goods go on sale regularly. For example, linens are sold at reduced prices in most stores every January. Buying sheets or towels in December is not a wise choice if it is possible to wait a few weeks for prices to go down. Many organizations, such as unions, have **buying services** that offer reduced prices to members. If you belong to any organizations, check to see if they offer this type of service.

5. *If you are dissatisfied with a product, take it back.* Most businesses want satisfied customers who will be repeat shoppers and who will recommend the store to their friends and relatives. A customer who isn't satisfied should complain to the store, thereby giving the firm an opportunity to correct the problem. Otherwise, the customer is as responsible for the problem as the business.

By following these steps, consumers can make better choices when they buy most products. The final responsibility for making good consumer choices belongs to each consumer.

How to Choose an Appliance

Most Americans make large investments in their furniture, appliances, and other household goods. When consumers buy furniture, they usually have plenty of time to consider their purchase. This is not always the case when they buy appliances. If your furnace breaks in February and you live in North Dakota, you will need to buy a new one quickly. Consumers are often faced with the need to buy appliances on short notice and therefore have less time to consider their purchases.

Today, consumers have an easier time choosing an appliance that suits their needs than they did twenty years ago. Government regu-

lations require manufacturers to label appliances according to the amount of energy they consume and their estimated cost to operate each year. These labels make it much easier for consumers to make wise choices.

All appliances have some of the following characteristics:

- They provide service over an extended period of time. Although they do wear out, they may last twenty years or more.
- They tend to be relatively expensive and are often purchased on credit.
- They require regular maintenance and repair.
- They are often insured by homeowner's or renter's insurance policies.
- They often must be replaced quickly after they wear out.
- They are sometimes purchased as a status symbol rather than out of need.

When you are ready to choose which make and model of an appliance to buy, be sure to identify your needs *before* you go shopping. Salespeople earn their wages largely from commissions. It is to their advantage to encourage you to buy the most expensive product available. When you ask for a simple refrigerator-freezer, you should not be surprised if a clerk tells you how important and valuable it is to have a model that dispenses ice cubes through the door of the freezer for only $400 more. If you have made up your mind about the features you want, it will be easier to resist spending more than necessary.

Vocabulary Builder

Buying service   An organization that provides information to consumers that helps them complete transactions at lower prices.
Convenience food   Food products that are totally or partially prepared so that they are relatively easy and quick to serve.

Consumer News

Beware of "Rent-to-Own" Agreements

People who are short on cash or are denied consumer credit are sometimes offered "rent-to-own" plans at stores where they shop. Under these plans a buyer "rents" an appliance by paying a weekly or monthly charge. At the end of a specified time they are given ownership of the product by the store. Does this sound fair to you? In general, consumers should avoid such plans.

The *Journal of Consumer Affairs* completed a survey that compared the cost of buying a 19-inch color television by paying cash and by using a "rent-to-own" plan. It discovered that the cash price ranged between $325 and $399 for the TV, but under different rent-to-own plans the consumer paid anywhere from $720 to $1,213 for the same television. These agreements allow stores to avoid legal limits on the interest rates they charge because they "rent" the appliances instead of selling them.

If you really need a product you can't afford to buy new, it is usually better to consider purchasing a used product than to agree to a rent-to-own contract. The best choice of all may be to put off the purchase entirely until you save enough money to pay cash for a new product.

Price is only part of the cost of owning an appliance. Consumers must also pay for operating and maintaining the products they own. Appliances have labels that indicate the amount of energy they use. If you have trouble understanding this type of measurement, ask a salesperson to explain it. Be suspicious of those who are unable to explain this information clearly. It may mean that they don't want to tell you what it means or that they don't understand it themselves. Either situation does not speak well of the firm you are considering buying an appliance from.

Borrowing to Buy an Appliance

When consumers borrow to buy appliances, they must pay interest as well as the price of the product. Consumers should always use good judgment when they borrow. If an appliance is truly necessary, consumers may make a responsible decision by deciding to borrow money. However, they should resist buying a more expensive appliance than they need. If your stove breaks and must be replaced, you may need to borrow $500 to buy a good-quality electric range. However, taking out a loan for $1,000 or more to purchase a stove with its own vented indoor grill probably is not a responsible consumer decision.

The choice of where to borrow money is also important. Many appliance stores offer credit to their customers but tend to charge high interest rates. Generally, credit unions or banks offer lower rates. When possible, the best choice in terms of interest rates and tax deductibility is a home equity loan. Unfortunately, people who do not own homes cannot use this alternative. Remember, when you borrow to buy an appliance or any other consumer good, you are trading future consumption for current consumption. Be sure that you don't go so far into debt that you cannot afford to buy products you will need in the future.

Summing Up   *When consumers buy household goods, they should decide what features they need before they talk to a salesperson, and they should resist buying more than they need. If they use credit to pay for their purchase, they should make sure they have found the best rate offered.* ◆

HOW TO CHOOSE CLOTHING PRODUCTS

While you read, ask yourself . . .
◆ *How much of your budget do you spend on clothing?*
◆ *Do you care more about the quality or the style of clothing you buy? How many garments do you own that you don't wear, even though they're not worn out?*

Consumers spent over $200 billion on shoes, pants, hats, underwear, socks, suits, ties, shirts, skirts, and other types of clothing in 1990. Most Americans spend about 10 percent of their income buying products to wear. The fact that clothes are necessary to stay warm and dry often has little to do with consumer choices in what they wear. In many cases clothing styles cause people to dress in ways that make them too hot or too cold to be comfortable.

What Styles of Clothing Do You Buy?

Think of a man whom you respect. Picture him wearing a skirt. Would your feelings toward this person change? Many of the clothes we buy are the result of **customs**. In the United States men usually wear pants, while women frequently wear dresses or skirts. There are, and have been, other societies where men wore skirts and women wore garments that were much like pants. Another example of our clothing customs is the fact that men's buttons are on the right side of their shirts and jackets, while women's buttons are on the left. There is no logical reason for this difference—it is simply the custom.

You probably own a wide selection of clothes because you realize that different types of clothing are appropriate in different situa-

◆ Bright colored garments with distinctive styles may be popular and make consumers feel good when they wear them. Does this guarantee they are well made or easy to care for?

tions. You wouldn't wear a formal dress or suit to a beach party, and you wouldn't go to a graduation dance wearing a tennis outfit. You simply would not be appropriately dressed. You own other types of clothes to be comfortable in different types of weather.

Clothing styles change over time. Bell-bottom pants were fashionable in the early 1970s. Few people would have chosen to buy and wear such products in 1990. Some changes in style are the result of fashion designers' new "creations." Others just seem to happen. In the mid-1980s many women in this country wore small pillbox hats because President Reagan's wife Nancy frequently wore them. Athletes and movie stars can also set fashion trends.

Many consumers buy clothing as a means of expressing their feelings or values. People who are native to other parts of the world or who wish to identify with their ancestors' values or

Vocabulary Builder

Custom   Buying products out of habit or because members of a consumer's social group purchase this type or brand of product.

Consumers in Action

Should You Buy Mail-Order Clothes?

Would you buy a product you had never seen? Many American consumers do. In 1987 more than $20 billion worth of goods were ordered from mail-order firms in the United States. The annual rate of growth in mail-order shopping was roughly 20 percent between 1982 and 1987, and every indication is that it will continue to grow in the future. The probability is very high that you either already have or someday will order clothing from a mail-order catalog. When you do, what should you look for?

Mail-order shopping has many advantages. It is easy to do in the comfort of your own home, so you don't have to drive or fight crowds of other shoppers. Mail-order firms usually have a toll-free 800 number that you may call. They are more likely to have your size, and if they don't, they can back-order the product. In many cases they offer a wider selection and have better prices than local stores because they have fewer employees and less overhead to pay.

When you consider buying a mail-order garment, the first thing you should look for is the firm's return policy. A garment that looks attractive in a picture taken by a professional photographer may not look so good on you. The actual garment may be a different color or made of inferior fabric or poorly constructed—or it simply may not fit. Be sure you can return your purchase for a full refund. You should also find out who must pay for shipping. Will you be refunded the cost of shipping the product to you and the cost of your return postage? It is possible that a product you don't keep could end up costing you $10 or more in transportation.

You should check the firm's shipping costs and whether you will be charged state sales tax. Some mail-order firms have quite reasonable shipping charges. Others are very expensive. A $15 shirt may not seem like such a good deal if you must pay a $7 shipping charge to get it. If the firm is located in your state, it will charge you any sales tax that is applicable.

If a mail-order firm is large and reputable, you can be reasonably sure that it will stand behind its products. This is not always the case with smaller firms. The failure rate for mail-order firms is almost 20 percent per year. Although there are many large firms that have been in business offering quality products for decades, smaller firms come and go. In general, it is better to make payment for mail-order goods with a credit card. Then if you are dissatisfied with the product, or if it fails to arrive, you may refuse payment when you receive your credit card billing (see Chapter 31). When used carefully, mail-order shopping can be a responsible consumer choice.

customs often wear clothes that demonstrate their heritage. Regardless of your individual motivation for buying a particular type of clothing, you should be careful to make the best consumer choice possible.

Buying Quality Garments

There is often a direct relationship between quality and price. Clothing products that are well made out of durable fabrics tend to cost more than inferior goods. However, this is not always the case. Frequently, clothes that are considered "new" or fashionable are not well made. Choosing well-made clothes is a responsibility of all consumers. No one else will do it for them.

When you buy a clothing product, you should always look at its label to find the **fabric content** and the **care instructions**. A beautiful linen blouse may look wonderful in the store but will certainly be difficult to care for. Pure cotton garments frequently shrink when they are washed. Bright colors may run and stain other clothes. Most silk and rayon products must be dry-cleaned. If you want clothes that are easy to care for, you should be careful to buy products that are "wash and wear."

Quality construction is as important as fabric content when you choose a garment to buy. When you consider a piece of clothing, check the fabric for flaws or runs. Be sure that the seams line up and are straight. Check to see that the buttons or other fasteners are firmly attached. Examine any lining to see that it is well made and lies smoothly when the garment is worn. When you put the garment on, does it fit well? Are there strings that hang out? Are the sleeves or legs the same length? Choosing a well-made product is each consumer's responsibility.

How Much Is a Name Brand Worth?

There was a time when fashion designers ignored ordinary consumers and marketed their creations to the wealthy. Those days are a thing of the past. In the 1970s there was a designer craze that saw labels stitched on the back pockets of jeans and on almost every other consumer product imaginable. It is now possible to buy chocolates or automobiles designed by Bill Blass.

There is no guarantee that a designer product will be superior to any other similar product. Famous people may have designed the products, but they did not control their production. When there are millions of products produced with a designer label, it is hard to be sure that they are all well made. There is also the problem of "counterfeit" garments that imitate designer goods and are sold by many outlets at lower prices.

When you buy designer clothing, you should realize that part of the price you are paying covers the cost of advertising. The manufacturer also had to pay the designer a royalty to use his or her name. These costs increase the product's price but add little if anything to the quality of the good. The choice becomes a matter of how much extra you are willing to pay to wear designer clothes.

There are far too many consumer goods to cover them all in one chapter. However, if you ask yourself the four questions identified in Section 1 and follow the five steps for making good consumer choices from Section 3, you will be able to make better decisions when you buy almost any consumer product. Making good consumer choices is largely a matter of using common sense and being patient enough to find the best buy available.

Summing Up *Consumers should read fabric content and care labels on garments they are considering buying. They should also examine garments for quality construction. Each consumer must decide what the best trade-off is between price, quality, and style.* ◆

Vocabulary Builder

Care instructions Instructions found on a label attached to clothing that explains how the garment should be cared for.

Fabric content The type of fiber that an article of clothing is made from, indicated on an attached label.

Review and Enrichment Activities

VOCABULARY REVIEW

1. Column A contains key consumer terms from this chapter. Column B contains a scrambled list of phrases that describe what these terms mean. Match the correct meaning with each term. Write your answers on a separate sheet of paper.

Column A

1. Fabric content

2. Quantity buying

3. Generic product

4. Customs

5. Convenience food

6. Buying Service

7. Care instructions

8. Bulk product

9. Unit pricing

10. Recommended daily allowance

Column B

a. Packaged product that has no trade name and generally is less expensive than a brand product

b. A product that is packed by customers from large containers in the quantity they want

c. Food that is prepared and that requires minimum effort by the consumer

d. Purchasing large amounts of a product to reduce the price paid per amount

e. Prices that are expressed in terms of a standard amount of a product

f. The type of fiber that an article of clothing is made from, indicated on an attached label

g. An amount of various nutrients recommended for daily consumption by the U.S. government

h. Buying products out of habit because members of a consumer's social group purchase this type of product

i. An organization that provides information to consumers that helps them complete transactions at lower prices

    j. Directions found on a label attached to clothing that explains how the garment should be cared for

2. Explain the difference between a store-brand product and a name-brand product.

CHECKING WHAT YOU'VE LEARNED

Write your answers for the following exercises on a separate sheet of paper.

1. Name the four questions that consumers should ask themselves before they make a purchase.
2. Describe the types of information that must be included on packaged food labels.
3. Why do many people believe that the current system of grading meat and poultry products by the government has limited value?
4. Explain how unit pricing can help you choose the least expensive size of container of a soap product.
5. Describe the results of the 1988 *Consumer Reports* study of careful shopping that was described in Section 2.
6. Describe the trade-offs that consumers make when they buy convenience foods.
7. Identify five steps that people should take when they buy consumer goods.
8. Why should consumers try to decide what features they want in a product before they go shopping?
9. Name several appliances that consumers may have to purchase quickly.
10. Give several reasons why people might have to buy different types of clothing.
11. Describe several factors that consumers should consider when they decide which clothing products to buy.
12. What trade-offs do consumers make when they buy designer fashions?

PRACTICING YOUR CONSUMER SKILLS

Write your answers for the following exercises on a separate sheet of paper.

1. Explain how each of the following consumers can find the information that he or she needs to help make a good decision.
    a. Peggy wants to buy the type of salad dressing that is lowest in calories and fat. When she finds the salad dressing shelf in her store, she discovers twelve different brands that all claim to be "light" or "reduced calorie" products. How can she choose the best product for her needs?

Review and Enrichment Activities Continued

    b. Dan had expected to spend about $300 for a 19-inch color TV set. When he went to an appliance store last week, the salesperson tried to sell him a brand of television he had never heard of that had a remote control and that cost $350. Dan likes the convenience of the remote control but is concerned about never having heard of the manufacturer.

    c. Rachel has a limited budget for clothing. She saw a really pretty suit in a store last week, but it cost more than she wants to spend. On the other hand, she would be willing to pay a little more if she is sure that it will last a long time.

    d. Fred's hot-water heater sprung a leak yesterday. He feels that he must replace it immediately. When Fred visited a store, he was shown several different models at various prices. Fred wants to buy the product that will end up costing him the least to buy and operate over the next ten years.

2. Read each of the following advertisements, and explain why they provide little information that would be useful to consumers.

    a. Mark's Butcher Shop—The Store That Sells Only USDA Choice Meat

    b. Buy ZAPPY FLAKES—a nutritionally balanced breakfast when served with fruit and milk.

    c. Mr. Big Floor Shampoo comes in a convenient, long-lasting, 24-pound box.

    d. The ACME electric space heater is the least expensive brand on the market. It costs only $59.99 to buy and can keep a 6-by-6 foot room warm in temperatures down to 20° below zero.

3. Evaluate each of the following consumer choices, and explain your reasoning.

    a. Susan buys only designer clothing products because she feels that they are more likely to have good quality.

    b. Harold decided he wanted a new air conditioner for his bedroom one day and simply went out and bought one at his neighborhood appliance store.

    c. Gary buys mostly generic and bulk foods because he thinks that they are almost as good as name-brand products and cost much less.

    d. Greta likes the feel of cotton clothing. She refuses to buy products that are made of anything else.

USING NUMBERS

Solve the following problems to help make the best possible choice. Write your solution on a separate sheet of paper. Be sure to show all your work.

Suppose that you are building a new home. You need to decide what type of heating system to install. You have collected the following information about electric, gas, and oil heat. Use this information to determine how much each type of heat is likely to cost on an average each year. Choose the type of heat that you believe would be best, and explain your answer. Why can't you be sure that your choice will really turn out to be the best one in the future?

1. *Electric baseboard heat* would cost $3,800 to install. These units have an expected life of sixteen years and would cost an average of $960 to operate at current electric rates. They have an average maintenance cost of $10 a year.
2. An *oil furnace with forced air* would cost $5,500 to install because of the ductwork that would be needed. These units have an expected life of twenty years and would cost an average of $540 to operate at current oil prices. They have an average maintenance cost of $50 a year.
3. A *gas furnace with forced air* would cost $6,500 to install because a gas line would need to be run to the house. It would also require ductwork. These units have an expected life of nineteen years and would cost an average of $380 to operate at current gas prices. They have an average maintenance cost of $40 a year.

PUTTING IDEAS IN YOUR OWN WORDS

The following quotations are from this chapter. Explain these quotations in your own words to make sure you understand what they mean. Write your answers on a separate sheet of paper.

1. "There may be little relationship between the amount of money that people spend on food and its nutritional value."
2. "The grade that poultry receives has no relation to the flavor of the meat or its quality."
3. "The final responsibility for making good consumer choices belongs to each consumer."

BUILDING CONSUMER KNOWLEDGE

Write your answers for the following exercises on a separate sheet of paper.

1. Name three examples of convenience foods that your family buys. List the benefits received and costs that are paid when each type of item is purchased.

Review and Enrichment Activities Continued

2. Name an appliance that was purchased by a member of your family in the past year. List the factors that were considered when this particular purchase was made. Did the product live up to your family's expectations? Explain how it did or did not. If this choice could be made over, would it be made in the same way? Explain.

3. Survey the clothing in your closet. Roughly what portion of the clothes that you own do you still wear on a regular basis? Roughly what portion of the clothes that you own have provided you with good value? Roughly what portion of the clothes that you own are designer or "fashionable" garments? Write an essay describing how you choose the clothing you buy based on the answers you have just given.

Chapter 36

Paying for Housing

Chapter Objectives

After completing this chapter, you will be able to do the following:

- Identify factors that consumers should consider when they choose the general location where they would like to live.
- Explain how consumers can determine how much they are able to spend on housing.
- Explain the benefits and costs associated with buying or renting a home.
- Describe the services offered by real estate agents and the costs of obtaining these services.
- Explain the financial considerations related to home ownership.

Key Consumer Terms

In this chapter you will learn the meanings of the following important consumer terms:

- Security deposit
- Landlord
- Tenant
- Lease
- Real estate agent
- Multiple real estate listing
- Contingency offer
- Earnest money
- Escrow account
- Title
- Title insurance
- Condominium

here would you like to live? Perhaps you have had dreams of owning a beautiful house in a wonderful location. Would you choose to live in a secluded forest setting, in an exclusive penthouse in the clouds, or on your own island in the South Pacific? You may have dreamed of living in these or other special places, but reality will probably force you to make a different choice in your life. Although you may not be able to afford the home you would like the most, you should be careful to choose one that best fits in with your values and personal goals and that you can afford.

SECTION 1

DECIDING WHERE TO LIVE

While you read, ask yourself . . .
◆ *How did your family choose where to live?*
◆ *What benefits and costs do members of your family pay to live where they do?*

There are towns in the United States where you could buy a well-kept three-bedroom house on a good-sized lot for little more than $40,000. Unfortunately, most communities that have such low housing prices are economically depressed and are often in rural areas. Other locations have housing prices that are very high. Trying to buy a three-bedroom house near the ocean in San Diego would cost hundreds of thousands of dollars. When consumers choose where they live, they must make a trade-off between location and the kind of home they are able to buy.

Factors You Should Consider

Choosing where to live involves more than looking for a good price or a location that has the climate or recreational facilities that you enjoy. Consumers must also consider how a location will affect their ability to earn a living or the sort of family life they may have. Before making a housing decision, consumers should think about their personal characteristics, values, and goals, like those included in the personal inventory you prepared in Chapter 20.

Suppose that you made a career choice to be an electronics technician. You would need to live near businesses that offer that type of employment. Buying a nice inexpensive home in a farming community would be a mistake for you, regardless of its low price.

If you intend to raise a family, you should investigate the schools and other public facilities in an area where you might live. Consumers who want to obtain a higher education need to live near the college or university that they want to attend. If you need regular medical care, you should be sure to live where doctors or hospitals are easily available.

Consumers who consider buying homes should investigate the trends in housing values in different areas where they might live. Although most homes increase in value over time, this is not always the case. In some locations housing values have gone down or failed to increase at the same rate as other prices. Choosing to buy a home in an area that is rapidly growing may increase the value of your investment. Buying a home in an area that is economically depressed may result in a loss of value over time.

Local property tax rates are another important factor in deciding where to live. Property taxes affect people who rent as well as those who own their own homes. Areas with high property taxes are also likely to have higher

Consumer Close-Up

Living with a Friend

Many young people are able to afford their first home by sharing the cost of an apartment with one or more friends. If you and several of your friends ever decide to do this, you will learn many things about each other quickly, and they may not all be good. *Before* you move in together, you should agree on how responsibilities will be shared. People who live together need a clear understanding of what is expected of each person, both financially and in terms of maintaining their home. Putting this type of agreement in writing is a good idea.

If you rent, your landlord will probably want the lease to be signed by only one person. When this happens, one person is financially responsible for the apartment. You and your friends must determine who is best qualified to take this responsibility and how the other renters will contribute to the cost of the apartment. A good idea is to have each

renter put an amount of money into a bank account in the name of the person who has signed the lease. This money can be used to pay rent for people who don't contribute their share on time or who move out of the apartment. The same money can be used for unpaid telephone bills or an individual's share of the heating or electricity expense. You may want to make a written agreement that states how this money can be used. If you don't make this type of agreement, someone may be left "holding the bag" when other renters leave or fail to pay their bills.

The renters should agree on how to pay household expenses before they move in together. Cleaning supplies, dishes, linens, light bulbs, and other basic needs must be purchased. You need to decide whether food will be purchased individually or as a group. Ownership of furniture that individuals buy for the apartment should be determined. If you don't agree on these things

at the beginning, they will surely result in disagreements later.

Another question that should be settled early is who is responsible for cleaning and doing laundry. Almost certainly there will be arguments when a messy person and a "clean freak" are living together. Few people want to wade through someone else's wet towels and underwear when they use the bathroom. This is almost as disagreeable as trying to cook in a kitchen that is full of someone else's dirty dishes. Household duties should be shared fairly and completed in a reasonable period of time.

Finally, renters should have regular weekly meetings to discuss any problems. If you want to take advantage of the financial benefits of sharing an apartment, you must recognize the need to divide responsibilities fairly and to be considerate of one another. You will soon discover that being someone's friend and living with that person are two different experiences.

---

rents. It is wise to consider what is likely to happen to taxes in the future. For example, if a town has few schools and a rapid growth in families who have children, it will soon need to tax property to pay for the construction of new schools. The same is true of sewage treatment facilities, water systems, and other public services. Low tax rates in areas that are rapidly growing may soon be much higher tax rates.

Should You Live Near Friends and Relatives?

An important consideration for many people who are choosing a place to live is the location of their friends and family. If you want to be able to see certain people often, you should choose to live somewhere that is convenient to their homes. This is particularly important for young parents if they expect their friends or family to watch their children. Roughly one-third of working parents leave their children with relatives on a regular basis while they go to work.

In other cases it may be necessary to provide help to elderly or disabled relatives. As people grow older, they often rely on their adult children for help in maintaining their homes or providing limited health care. If you believe that you will need to help your parents in the future, you might want to live closer to them rather than farther away.

Summing Up *There are many factors that consumers should consider when they choose a place to live. These include housing prices, the availability of employment and education, trends in housing values, taxes, and where friends and relatives live.* ◆

SECTION 2

DECIDING WHETHER TO BUY OR TO RENT

While you read, ask yourself . . .
- ◆ *Why did your family choose to buy or rent the place where you live?*
- ◆ *When you establish your first residence, do you expect to buy or rent? Why would you probably make this choice?*

It's easy to be carried away when you buy or rent a home and commit yourself to spending more money than you can afford. Suppose that you found an especially nice place where you could live if you were willing to pay $50 or $100 more each month than the amount you had hoped to pay. Having a nice place to live may give you a sense of pride or make you appear to be more wealthy than you actually are. You might enjoy the comfort or convenience offered by this location. However, if you truly cannot afford this greater cost, you may have

to give up buying other products that you need. You could even be forced into bankruptcy. Consumers need to be sure that they do not commit themselves to paying more for housing than they can afford.

Paying the Cost of Housing

Finding a place to live involves more costs than just a monthly rent or mortgage payment. If you buy a house, you must pay the closing costs that you learned about in Chapter 30. Whether you rent or buy a home, you need to spend money for furnishings, appliances, linens, and many other basic necessities. You

◆ There are costs and benefits of owning or renting a home. Why are most young people likely to choose renting even if they have a goal of owning a home in the future?

will probably be required to make a **security deposit** to receive electricity or natural gas. There will be charges for installing your telephone or for cable television. You will also need to protect yourself by buying homeowner's or renter's insurance. Consumers need to keep all these expenses in mind when they choose a place to live.

In addition to the costs necessary to set up a new dwelling, there are also a number of ongoing costs that must be paid. Whether you rent or buy, you must regularly pay for heat, electricity, water, and telephone. There may be other monthly payments you must make as well, depending on where you live. Many housing developments require members to pay monthly fees to maintain community facilities. There may also be fees for garbage collection or sewage treatment.

Before you decide how much you can afford to pay for rent or for a mortgage, you should consider the other expenses that you will have to pay. A good way to accomplish this task is to set up a checklist of expenses similar to the one shown here. By completing this type of form in Figure 36-1 and comparing the total with your after tax income, you will be able to judge how much you can afford to pay for housing each month.

Checklist for Average Monthly Expenses	
Food	_____
Transportation	_____
Clothing	_____
Furniture, appliances, etc.	_____
Insurance	_____
Heating, electricity, telephone, water, waste disposal, etc.	_____
Maintenance	_____
Health care	_____
Other	_____
Total Expenses	_____

Figure 36-1   Average Monthly Expenses

Benefits and Costs of Renting

Two important advantages associated with renting are lower costs and greater independence. People who rent are not responsible for maintaining the property. Their **landlords** pay these costs from the rents they collect from their **tenants.** Renters are often better able to budget because they usually know what their rent will be for an extended period of time. Although rents reflect tax increases, they are less likely to change as rapidly or as much because higher taxes may be distributed among a large number of renters. People who rent are often able to use common facilities like swimming pools or tennis courts that they could never afford to build for themselves. Although renters usually must make a security deposit equal to several months rent, they do not need to worry about putting a large down payment on a home. And while renters should purchase renter's insurance, this is less expensive than homeowner's insurance because renters do not need to protect the structure they live in.

Renters generally must sign a **lease** committing themselves to pay rent for a period of time (most often one year), but they are not tied into one location to the same extent as a homeowner. If they need to move, they do not need to worry about selling their home. If their family grows or becomes smaller when children move out, it is much easier for renters to move to a different location or size of home.

Vocabulary Builder

Landlord   A person who rents property.
Lease   A long-term agreement describing the terms under which property is being rented.
Security deposit   Money paid by a renter to a landlord to pay for any damage done to rented property; it is normally refunded at the end of the rental period.
Tenant   Someone who lives in rented property.

Consumer News

A Place to Live

In 1988 there were 840,000 families, or almost 5 million people, who were on the government's waiting list for public housing. It is estimated that by the year 2003 there will be 7.8 million people who will need low-income housing. Although the government is helping to pay for the construction of some new units, its efforts will fall far short of the need. To accomplish the task, private organizations and businesses will need to contribute to the effort.

Probably the most successful private low-income housing program is the Enterprise Foundation, started by James W. Rouse in Washington, D.C., in 1973. By 1990 his organization had rebuilt 6,000 housing units and had another 5,700 in various stages of completion. Rouse, a real estate developer in the Baltimore area, became wealthy running his own business for nearly twenty years. When he was persuaded to get into the low-income housing business, he used his experience to rebuild existing buildings rather than construct new ones. He was able to accomplish his task at roughly two-thirds the cost that the government spent on similar units. He even wrote a book explaining how to rebuild structures at low cost. Although he did not intend to earn a profit at this business, he nevertheless has. The equity that the Enterprise Foundation has in its buildings was estimated to be roughly $200 million in 1990.

Probably the greatest disadvantage of renting is that renters do not have anything to show for their money after they pay their rent. A person who buys a home and pays a mort-gage of $700 a month will build up equity in his or her property. A person who pays $700 in rent may have a nicer place to live, but will own nothing when he or she is ready to move. Renters also do not benefit from increases in real estate value.

Renters have less choice in how they live. Many apartments will not allow pets. People who rent have less freedom to decorate their homes as they see fit. They may not remodel, change the location of walls, or add windows. There may be restrictions on the number of guests that renters may have or on the space they may use for parking.

Most people start out by renting because they lack the money needed to buy a house and because they do not know where they eventually want to live. As people grow older, they are more often able to pay the costs of home ownership and are more likely to know where they want to settle down and live.

Benefits and Costs of Buying

Possibly the most important advantage of home ownership is the investment opportunity it offers people. Houses usually increase in value over time. Therefore, most homeowners benefit from appreciation in the value of their homes. Housing is not the only investment that people should have because homes are not easy to convert into cash on short notice. However, it does offer a distinct advantage when compared to paying rent for a place to live. Home ownership is generally a good way to protect your savings from the effects of inflation.

There are also tax benefits to home ownership. Property taxes and interest paid on home mortgages are deductible from income for both federal and state income taxes. People who have built up value in their homes may borrow through home equity loans that charge interest that is tax deductible. When people rent, they indirectly pay property taxes, but receive no tax advantage from their payments and cannot benefit from home equity loans.

There are many other advantages that people who own homes enjoy. Homeowners are able to remodel their homes as they see fit. They can landscape or build additions. Generally, they are able to have pets and more freedom to invite guests to outdoor parties. Homeowners have greater freedom to choose how to live in their homes.

There are important costs of home ownership that consumers should be aware of. Homeowners may lose part of their investment if housing values go down when they sell their homes. Even worse, sometimes homeowners need to move but are unable to sell their homes. People who own houses have less freedom to travel because they must either maintain their property themselves or pay someone else to do it. If you lose your job, it may be difficult to keep up mortgage and property tax payments on a home. In general, people who buy houses need to be more financially secure than people who rent.

Summing Up *Whether consumers choose to buy or rent, they will enjoy benefits and pay costs. Both renters and buyers need to evaluate their ability to pay for housing. Generally, renters have more freedom and less responsibility than homeowners but do not benefit from growth in the home value or tax advantages.* ◆

SECTION 3

HOW TO BUY A HOUSE

While you read, *ask yourself . . .*

- ◆ *Would you enjoy the responsibility of home ownership?*
- ◆ *What steps can you take now to be able to buy a home in the future?*

Once a consumer has decided to buy a house, it is necessary to find one that suits his or her needs and that is affordable. This can be both an enjoyable and a difficult task. To find the right home and complete the transaction, consumers need to be organized and patient.

Getting Help from a Real Estate Agent

Real estate agents are in the business of selling information. For a fee, they provide both buyers and sellers with information about people who might be opposite participants in a transaction. They relieve buyers of much of the time and effort that they would need to spend looking for a home that fits their needs and budget. They relieve sellers of much of the time and effort that they would need to spend looking for qualified buyers. Real estate agents reduce the transaction cost of buying and selling homes.

When people offer their home for sale through a real estate agent, their property is placed in a **multiple real estate listing**. This is a catalog of homes and other properties that are for sale in an area. It includes property offered for sale through many real estate firms. Information about the size of the home, its location, type of heat, property taxes, whether it has air conditioning, and many other facts are provided in multiple listings. By studying the homes in this publication, potential buyers can

---

Vocabulary Builder

Multiple real estate   A publication that identifies and describes all property offered for sale through real estate firms in an area.

Real estate agent   A person who earns a living by helping people who want to buy and sell property to complete their transactions.

◆   Real estate agents earn their income by providing information. What types of help can they offer home buyers and sellers? Why would they try to make people feel buying a home is the right decision?

decide whether it is worth their time to visit any of the listed homes.

When consumers select a real estate firm to work with, they may be shown any home offered through the multiple listing service, regardless of which real estate firm originally listed the property. This allows customers to visit many homes without dealing with more than one agent. When a home is sold, the commission is divided between the firm that listed the property and the firm that made the sale. This system also benefits sellers because they know that people who are qualified buyers will be able to consider their property, regardless of which real estate firm they use.

Real estate agents offer other services to consumers. They have learned about neighbor-

hoods, public services, types of financing that are available, laws that must be considered when homes are purchased, and closing costs that must be paid by buyers and sellers. This type of information can help consumers avoid many problems that could slow or prevent them from buying a home.

Consumers should shop for real estate agents just as they shop for any other good or service. The 6 to 7 percent fee that is charged by most real estate firms will be approximately the same. It is important to find an agent who understands your needs and who is friendly and helpful. However, keep in mind that the agent will only earn a commission if you buy a home. Some agents may try to convince you to buy a home that does not meet your needs just to earn a commission. Remember, although real estate agents provide helpful information, the final decision to buy must be yours.

Before you sign any document, be sure that the home you are buying is the one that you want and that it is structurally sound. Spending several hundred dollars to have an expert examine a home you want is money well spent. If faults are found, you should demand that the selling price be reduced by the amount it would cost to have the defect repaired. Be sure that any agreement to have a problem fixed is included in a written contract. Verbal agreements are almost never legally binding. Also be sure to have your lawyer review the purchase contract *before* you sign it.

Making the Deal

Houses are most frequently bought through a process of negotiation. When sellers list their property, they set an asking price. Most sellers ask for more than they expect to receive for their property so that they will have room to negotiate. On the other hand, most buyers offer less than they are willing to pay. When an offer is made, the seller may accept the offer,

Consumer Close-Up

Buying a Condominium

Millions of Americans own a home that is not a house. They have chosen to buy **condominiums**, which offer many of the advantages of both renting an apartment and home ownership. The owner of a condominium essentially owns part of a building. Like the owner of a house, the owner of a condominium is responsible for obtaining a mortgage, paying utilities and property taxes, and maintaining appliances within the condominium. However, there is an association of condominium owners that maintains the building, its grounds, and community facilities such as swimming pools or tennis courts. Each owner in the group pays a fee to the association to support this maintenance.

Condominium owners enjoy the independence of being able to leave their property for extended periods of time without worrying about who will cut the grass or trim the bushes. They also have the advantage of a possible increase in the value of their property. They may deduct their interest payments and property taxes from their federal and state income taxes.

Owners of condominiums do risk not being able to sell their property quickly or for a price they would have hoped to receive. In a number of places, more condominiums have been built than there are people who want to buy them. The result has been a decline in the price of the units and significant losses for people who already owned condominiums and were forced to sell at these reduced prices.

Condominiums are quite common as vacation homes. There are even organizations that allow people to exchange the use of condominiums in different parts of the country. Someone who owns a unit in Florida can trade with someone who owns a unit in Colorado for part of the year.

make a counteroffer, or demand the full asking price. In return, the buyer may make another offer. This process of offer and counteroffer can go back and forth many times before a price is agreed on. Remember, it is important to be patient. Unless you are positive that this is the house you want and you are afraid that someone else may buy it first, you should be willing to take the time to go through the negotiation process. You may save thousands of dollars by taking a few extra days.

Contingency offers are often made when a consumer already owns a home. With this type of offer, potential buyers are given time to sell a home that they currently own so that they are able to afford to buy a new home. Their offer is contingent on (depends on) their ability to sell their current home. This type of offer is usually good for some specified period of time, such as three or six months. If the buyer does not sell his or her home in that time, the offer ends.

When an offer is accepted, a payment of **earnest money** is made by the buyer to the seller to bind the agreement. This earnest

Vocabulary Builder

Condominium   A single unit of a larger building that is owned separately by the resident of that unit.
Contingency offer   An offer to buy property that depends on some other event, usually selling a house currently owned.
Earnest money   Money put up to show that you are serious about an offer you make to buy a house.

Consumer News

Why Home Buyers Need Title Insurance

How would you feel if you purchased a home, made mortgage payments for two years, and then had a stranger show up who said that half of your house belonged to her? This may sound impossible, but it has happened.

In the early 1980s a young couple bought a home in Florida from a man and a woman who he introduced as his "wife." A title search was completed that showed that these people did have clear ownership of the house, so the transaction was completed. Two years later the man's *real* wife showed up. She said that she had been separated from her husband for five years and that she owned half the home. Her lawyer argued that her husband couldn't sell her half of the house and that she was entitled to a payment from the young couple equal to half what the husband had received. A state court upheld her claim. If the young couple had not purchased title insurance, they would have been required to pay the wife the thousands of dollars that their insurance carrier had to pay.

Remember, a deed is not legal proof of clear ownership to property. It is a document that is used to transfer ownership. It tells a buyer nothing about any claims on the property by other parties. For example, if a house or land has been pledged as collateral for a loan, a seller does not have a clear title to transfer to a buyer. A buyer who does not discover such an obligation can be held responsible for the debt if the seller cannot be found. Consumers who buy property should always purchase title insurance to protect themselves from unpleasant surprises.

money is forfeited in most cases if the buyer backs out of the deal before it is completed. Generally, earnest money is not forfeited if the buyer is not able to obtain a mortgage.

Banks and other institutions that lend money for home mortgages often require borrowers to deposit money into **escrow accounts** until a transaction is completed. This amount is usually about 10 percent of the price of the home. Such accounts guarantee the buyer's ability to make the required down payment. After an agreement is reached, the **title** to the property must be examined to be sure that there are no debts owed on the land and house by the current or any previous owner and that the current owner has a clear title to the property to sell. **Title insurance** should be purchased to protect the new owner from any future claims against the property that are not discovered. This insurance is relatively inexpensive and can protect the new owner from a significant expense. The new owner must also obtain insurance on the property before a mortgage will be provided by a bank.

Summing Up   *Consumers often benefit from hiring real estate agents to help them buy and sell homes for a fee. Home buyers should remember the features they want in a home and not be talked into buying a house that they don't want. Before buying a house, they should have it inspected and the sales contract reviewed by their lawyer.* ◆

Vocabulary Builder

Escrow account   An account opened by a buyer before the completion of a home purchase to assure the institution that will provide the mortgage of his or her ability to make the necessary down payment.

Title   The physical representation of your legal ownership of a house or piece of property.

Title insurance   The insurance that a prospective homeowner buys to be assured that the title, or legal ownership, to the house is free and clear.

Review and Enrichment Activities

VOCABULARY REVIEW

1. Column A contains key consumer terms from this chapter. Column B contains a scrambled list of phrases that describe what these terms mean. Match the correct meaning with each term. Write your answers on a separate sheet of paper.

Column A	Column B
1. Lease	a. An agreement made between a property owner and a renter that sets the terms of their rental agreement
2. Contingency offer	b. Money deposited in a bank by someone who has agreed to take out a mortgage and which guarantees the down payment
3. Title	c. A legal document that serves as proof of ownership of property
4. Condominium	
5. Real estate agent	d. A person who rents property from another person
6. Escrow account	e. A person who rents property to another person
7. Tenant	f. A publication that identifies property offered for sale through real estate firms in an area
8. Title insurance	
9. Landlord	g. A single unit of a larger building that is owned separately by an individual
10. Multiple real estate listing	h. An offer to buy property that depends on the person making the offer being able to sell other property already owned
	i. Protection that is purchased by a home owner to prevent losses if ownership to property is not free and clear
	j. A person who earns a living by helping buyers and sellers of property complete transactions.

2. Explain the difference between a security deposit, which is made by a person who rents an apartment, and earnest money, which is paid by someone who intends to buy a house.

CHECKING WHAT YOU'VE LEARNED

Write your answers for the following exercises on a separate sheet of paper.

1. Describe four different factors that consumers should consider when they choose a location for their home.
2. Identify two benefits and two costs that homeowners have.
3. Identify two benefits and two costs that renters have.
4. Describe how a multiple real estate listing works.
5. What do real estate agents have to sell?
6. Why should consumers be suspicious of real estate agents who recommend houses that don't really fit their needs?
7. Describe the negotiation process through which most homes are bought and sold.
8. Explain how a contingency offer works.
9. Explain what title insurance is and why it is important.

PRACTICING YOUR CONSUMER SKILLS

Write your answers for the following exercises on a separate sheet of paper.

1. Write a brief description of the personal, family, and financial situation of consumers who should consider responding to each of the following real estate advertisements. What do you suppose these places really look like?
   a. For Rent - Fifth-floor studio apartment, 600 square feet, electric heat, new appliances, $400 a month plus utilities.
   b. For Sale - Exclusive executive retreat on Lake Mitchell. Features five bedrooms with six baths, central air, five acres of landscaped grounds, 300 feet of sandy beach, boat house, and too many other features to mention. Just $1,750,000.
   c. For Rent - Three-bedroom ranch home in friendly suburban setting. Features a family room with fireplace and a full basement. One-car garage. $800 a month plus utilities.

    d. For Sale - Handyman's dream, older home in up-and-coming neighborhood. Four bedrooms, one bath, oil heat. Needs a little tender loving care. $32,000 or best offer.

    e. For Sale - Two-bedroom condominium on the third floor of Warmwater Estates #63. Features include a view of the Atlantic ocean from your own balcony, total electric climate control, use of a community swimming pool and shuffleboard courts. Only 10 minutes from downtown Miami. The price has just been reduced from $98,000 to only $84,000. Hurry, this one won't last!

2. Suppose that you are a real estate agent and the following consumers ask you to help them find a home. Explain why you think each person should buy or rent, and describe the type of home you believe each individual should choose.

    a. Barbara and Tim have been married for two years. They have a one-year-old daughter. Their monthly income is now $2,100 from Tim's job as a truck driver. It should grow to about $3,900 when Barbara returns to work next month. Barbara and Tim do not expect to move or change their basic life-style in the next few years.

    b. Peter is single. He graduated from technical school six months ago. He recently accepted a job with an engineering firm that has factories in twelve states. He is currently in a training program where he earns $1,800 a month. He has a student loan to pay off that costs him $235 a month, as well as car payments that cost him $467 each month.

    c. Sonny is a well-known fashion designer. His income varies widely from one year to another. To be successful in his business, he must give many large parties for fashion buyers. He wants to give these parties in a lavish and memorable setting.

    d. Clara owns her own bakery. Although her firm is successful, she wants to put as much of her profit into her business as possible. She is separated from her husband, who is not always dependable with his child-support payments. Her two sons are now in high school and want to attend college soon.

    e. Mike is a successful computer programmer and is disabled. He uses a wheelchair to get around. Wherever he lives he will need ramps and other special features to help him.

3. Explain what you would do if you found yourself in the following situations.

    a. You bought a new house three years ago for $80,000. Unfortunately, housing values in your community have recently fallen. You believe that the most you could get for your home would be about $65,000 today. Yesterday you received a job offer from a firm in another city that would increase your annual salary by almost $8,000 a year.

    b. You own a two-bedroom bungalow on a large lot in a pleasant neighborhood. Your doctor told you a month ago that you and your spouse are about to become the parents of twins. You need a larger home but cannot find one you can afford.

Review and Enrichment Activities Continued

    c. You are sixty years old. You and your spouse have raised three children who have now moved into homes of their own. You are tired of taking care of your four-bedroom home in the hills above San Francisco.

    d. You are twenty-two years old and are the assistant manager of a clothing store. You are single and earn a good salary. You do not expect to be married at any time in the near future. You have saved over $12,000 and no longer want to live at home with your parents.

USING NUMBERS

Solve the following problem to help make the best possible choice. Write your solution on a separate sheet of paper. Be sure to show all your work.

Otis and Diane have been looking for a new place to live. Otis is a foreman in a factory. He earns $3,000 a month. Diane has a part-time job that pays her $6,000 a year. Otis and Diane have saved $18,000 in cash. They have two young children. They now have fixed expenses of $1,880 a month. Of this amount, $750 is the rent they pay on their current apartment, which is too small. Otis and Diane want a larger and nicer place to live. They would also like to live in a more pleasant neighborhood, which would be better for their children.

Otis and Diane have narrowed the choice down to three possible locations. Use the following information to determine how much each location would cost them to move into and how much they would have to pay per month. Use this information to make a recommendation to Otis and Diane. You don't have to recommend the least expensive location. Explain the reasoning behind your recommendation.

Location #1. An older home in a middle-class neighborhood. It has three bedrooms and has been well cared for. It is on a fenced lot that is 70 by 120 feet. The kitchen was recently remodeled, and there is new carpeting. This house would cost $69,000 to buy. If Otis and Diane put $10,000 down on it, there would be closing costs of $2,100. They would have to pay about $800 for moving expenses. Security deposits and other costs would add about $400 to the initial cost of this home. Their mortgage payment would be $620 a month, and they would have property taxes of $1,320 a year. They believe that their fixed monthly costs would increase by about $300 except for their rent, which they would no longer pay.

Location #2.   A brand-new home in a suburban subdivision. It has three bedrooms and was built by a reputable contractor. It is on an unlandscaped lot that is 100 by 150 feet. This house would cost $79,000 to buy. If Otis and Diane put $10,000 down on it, there would be closing costs of $2,300. They would have to pay about $1,200 for moving expenses. Security deposits and other costs would add about $700 to the initial cost of this home. Their mortgage payment would be $750 a month, and they would have property taxes of $1,760 a year. They believe that their fixed monthly costs would increase by about $450 except for their rent, which they would no longer pay.

Location #3. A farm home in a rural community 15 miles from town. It has five bedrooms and is in need of a new roof. It is on 3 acres of land with many large trees and a small stream. This house would cost $75,000 to buy, but it would need another $8,000 in work almost immediately. If Otis and Diane put $10,000 down on it, there would be closing costs of $2,175. They would have to pay about $1,500 in moving expenses. Security deposits and other costs would add about $500 to the initial cost of this home. Their mortgage payment and the cost of borrowing another $8,000 for the roof would total $800 a month. They would have property taxes of $1,440 a year. They believe that their fixed monthly cost would increase by about $500 except for their rent, which they would no longer pay.

PUTTING IDEAS IN YOUR OWN WORDS

The following quotations are from this chapter. Explain these quotations in your own words to make sure you understand what they mean. Write your answers on a separate sheet of paper.

1. "Low tax rates in areas that are rapidly growing may soon be much higher tax rates."
2. "Finding a place to live involves more costs than just a monthly rent or mortgage payment."
3. "Verbal agreements are almost never legally binding."

BUILDING CONSUMER KNOWLEDGE

Write your answers for the following exercises on a separate sheet of paper.

1. Make a list of the types of expenses your family must pay for your home. (Do not list the amounts paid.) Which of these costs are fixed, and which are flexible?
2. If you were trying to convince someone else to live where you do, what features of your home would you tell them about? What would you avoid pointing out? How does this demonstrate the need for home shoppers to be careful?
3. Study a real estate advertising section from a local newspaper. Identify a home that is for sale and an apartment that is for rent that you believe would be suitable for your family. Write an essay explaining your choices.

Chapter 37

Getting from Place to Place

Chapter Objectives

After completing this chapter, you will be able to do the following:

- Explain the benefits and costs of owning a car.
- Explain how consumers should choose a car that best fits their needs and financial situation.
- Describe the negotiation process that consumers go through to buy a car.
- Describe the costs of operating a car.
- Identify different forms of public transportation and explain the benefits and costs associated with these alternatives.

Key Consumer Terms

In this chapter you will learn the meanings of the following important consumer terms:

- Depreciation
- Extended protection plan (EPP)
- Option
- Add-on
- Blue book
- Lemon law
- Arbitration
- Moving violation
- Point
- Driving while intoxicated (DWI)
- Passive restraint

In the United States the automobile is more than a means of transportation. It is almost a way of life. Automobiles are the first major goods that most people purchase. They take us to work, school, and play. We drive to go shopping, to visit friends and relatives, or just to go "cruising" on Saturday night. To many Americans, an automobile is almost like an extension of their personality. It is a way to show others who they are and what they believe in. Cars may be many things to different people, but most of all, they are expensive. Consumers need to choose what kind of car to buy carefully.

SECTION 1

THE COSTS OF OWNING A CAR

While you read, *ask yourself . . .*
- *How much could you afford to pay for a car?*
- *What benefits would you receive from owning a car?*
- *If you bought a car, what other products would you need to give up?*

Most Americans know that buying an automobile is expensive. They are also aware that there is a cost of maintaining and insuring an automobile. Some consumers may not be aware of some of the other costs of owning a car. Whether they think about all these costs or not, Americans paid an average of from $5,000 to $6,000 a year for each car they owned in 1990.

The Growing Cost of New Cars

Most car models have changed significantly in recent years. Therefore, it is difficult to compare prices between older models and newer models. One exception is the Chevrolet Caprice Classic sedan. This model was introduced by General Motors in the late 1970s and remained essentially unchanged for more than ten years. It is possible to make a reasonable comparison between a 1977 Caprice Classic with a list base price of $4,878 and a 1989 Caprice Classic with a list base price of $14,445. These two cars were not exactly the same, but they were very similar.

In 1978 the average American had a yearly income of $7,567. At that time a new Caprice Classic cost not quite 65 percent of an average person's annual income. In 1988 (when 1989 models were introduced) the average American's income had grown to $16,489, but the Caprice Classic's price had grown even more rapidly. Its price was almost 88 percent of the average American's income in that year. In recent years car prices have been going up more rapidly than our income. This has reduced the number of Americans who can afford to buy a new car.

One important reason for increasing car prices is the legal requirement that automobile manufacturers meet federal pollution, mileage, and safety standards. Although our environment has clearly benefited from reduced automobile emissions, these benefits are costly. In 1990 it was estimated that the pollution control and safety devices on the average new car sold in this country added almost $1,000 to its price.

Increasing mileage has meant developing lighter materials. However, lighter automobiles tend to be less safe. To build cars that are both light and strong, manufacturers have invested billions of dollars in research and development and in new production methods. These increased costs have been passed on to consumers in higher prices. Most new cars today are very different from the automobiles of the 1960s and 1970s. They are better products and they cost more.

Safety equipment adds to the cost of a new car. The following safety devices are required on all cars sold in the United States today:

- Dual braking systems
- Nonprotruding interior appliances
- Over-the-shoulder safety belts in the front seat
- Head restraints on all front seats
- Seat-belt warning systems and ignition interlocks
- Collapsible, impact-absorbing arm rests
- Impact-absorbing instrument panels
- Passive-restraint systems

Another reason for high automobile prices may be the relatively high wage rates that workers and managers receive in the automobile industry. In the 1960s and 1970s numerous studies showed that employees in the U.S. automotive industry were paid as much as 15 percent more for their labor than similarly skilled workers in other industries. There are many possible reasons for this wage difference. Auto workers may have had more powerful unions than other workers. Their wages may be the result of monopoly-like powers that U.S. auto manufacturers once had. Auto workers may have been more productive than workers in other industries. Regardless of the reason, some experts believe that these higher wages are part of the reason why automobile manufacturers have had to charge higher prices. In recent years the wage difference between auto workers and other employees has fallen to be a little less than 10 percent.

The Cost of Operating a Car

In Chapter 33 you learned about the high cost of insuring a car. There are, of course, many other costs of keeping a car on the road.

Gasoline in 1991 cost an average of about $1.27 a gallon for unleaded regular. This means that a driver who put 15,000 miles on the average car would have paid $1,058 for fuel in 1991. Buying new tires, having car repairs, paying for licenses and registration fees, and other expenses add to the costs of owning a car.

Another expense that most car owners pay is the cost of interest for money that they borrow to buy cars. In 1990 over 80 percent of the people who bought new cars financed at least part of their purchase. The average interest rate for car loans in that year was roughly 13 percent. This added about $2,130 to the price of a car when $10,000 was borrowed and paid off over three years. Even people who pay cash for their cars give up the interest they could have earned if they had left their money in the bank.

Depreciation

With the possible exception of insurance, **depreciation** is the greatest cost of owning an automobile. A good rule of thumb is that a car will depreciate or lose about one-fifth of its value each year you own it. Suppose that you spend $20,000 on a new car. When it is one year old, it will probably be worth about $16,000, or one-fifth less than its purchase price. This value will fall by roughly another fifth, or $3,200, to $12,800 in the second year you own the car. By the end of the third year, its value will be about $2,560 less, or $10,240. See Table 37-1 comparing resale values of several makes of cars.

The longer you own a car, the less it will depreciate in each year. However, there is another factor to consider. As automobiles become older, they also require greater maintenance. A five-year-old car may not depreciate much over a year, but you will probably need to spend more money on repairs than on a newer car. There are few things more distasteful to consumers than paying to fix a car that is only worth a few thousand dollars in the first place.

Resale Values of Different Models of Automobiles			
	1988 Price	**1990 Value**	**Percent of Purchase Price Retained**
Honda Accord DX Sedan	$10,535	$ 8,925	84.7%
Toyota Corolla Deluxe	$ 8,898	$ 7,275	81.8%
Oldsmobile Cutlass Ciera	$10,656	$ 8,275	77.7%
Mercedes-Benz 300E	$42,680	$30,250	70.9%
Chevrolet Blazer	$16,500	$11,550	70.0%
Cadillac Sedan DeVille	$23,049	$15,975	69.3%
Plymouth Voyager LE	$18,500	$11,950	64.6%
Hyundai Excel GLS	$ 7,750	$ 4,600	59.4%

Source: *Business Week*, September 17, 1990, p. 153.

◆ **Table 37-1**   Resale Values

Not all cars depreciate at the same rate. By checking *Consumer Reports* or other sources, you can find out which cars are most likely to hold their value and which will depreciate most rapidly. There are two ways to use this information. If you are interested in buying a new car, it may be a better choice to purchase one that holds more of its value. However, if you are interested in buying a used car, you may be better off buying one that has depreciated rapidly. You may find that you can buy a car that has been driven relatively few miles and that is in good condition for a low price. Most of the depreciation will have been suffered by the original owner of the car.

Should You Buy a Used Car?

More consumers buy used cars each year than new ones. There are many good reasons for this. Probably the greatest advantage to buying a used car is that someone else has already suffered most of the cost of depreciation. Used cars do not require as much of an investment and therefore will cost less in terms of interest. Used cars cost less to insure than new cars, and they are less likely to be stolen. Many consumers buy used cars because they cannot afford new ones. Although there are many advantages to buying a used car, there are many dangers as well.

When you buy a used car, you may be buying someone else's problem. If a car is relatively new, the original owner must have had a reason for selling it. The car may have been defective. It might have been a demonstrator, rental, or leased car. Although dealers are supposed to tell consumers when cars have been used in these ways, they don't always do this. Many used cars carry the leftover warranty from the original owner. However, warranties offered on some used cars may be less extensive than on new cars and may require the payment of a deductible. If you buy a used car, be sure you understand what, if anything, is covered by a warranty.

Vocabulary Builder

Depreciation   A loss in value that occurs as a result of wear and age. A fall in the value of a nation's currency due to the forces of demand and supply.

◆ There are costs consumers should expect to pay and benefits they should receive when they buy used cars. What steps should you take to make sure you don't buy someone else's problem if you purchase a used car?

If you plan to buy a used car, be certain to have it checked over by a mechanic who you know and trust and who is not employed by the dealership that is offering the car for sale. This will not guarantee that the car will be perfect, but it will improve your chances of buying a good used car. The $20 to $50 that this will cost is money well spent.

Consumer Reports and other publications regularly collect and report data on new and used cars. You should consult these publications to check the reliability record of whatever type of car you are considering. But remember, such data are only an average and are not reliable for specific cars. Even when a certain model has the best average reliability record, a specific car may still be defective.

Many consumers buy used cars from private individuals. By doing this, they often pay a lower price than a dealer would charge. They also have an opportunity to talk to the previous owner about the car. However, when you buy from a private party, there is no warranty to protect you if the car is defective. You may take a private party to court for deliberately misrepresenting the car, but it will be expensive, and you may not win.

Warranties and Repair Costs

New cars and some used cars purchased from dealers come with warranties to protect the new owner from the cost of repairs for a

Consumers in Action

Should You Lease a Car?

Could you afford to drive a $40,000 car in a few years? If you couldn't afford to buy one, you could lease an expensive car instead. In recent years dealers have turned more and more to leasing luxury or sports cars that are too expensive for many people to buy.

On the surface, lease agreements appear to be a good deal. They allow consumers to drive expensive cars while making only a small beginning payment and lower monthly payments than if they bought the car. In 1990 consumers could lease a $22,000 Mazda RX-7 for $350 a month. After four years the car would be returned to the dealer, and the consumer could lease another new car. Buying the car outright with a 13 percent loan would have resulted in monthly payments of about $500. What these consumers might not realize is that they paid $16,800 for the use of a car that they don't even own. At the end of four years, consumers could buy their car from the leasing firm for about $8,500, but they would be buying a four-year-old car. In addition, most leases required consumers to pay extra if they drive more than 15,000 miles a year.

Consumers who want to lease a car should try to negotiate for a better price. Few consumers

pay the sticker price on a new car. In the same way, most dealers would probably be willing to negotiate the monthly fee to lease a car. There are a number of points to remember when you negotiate. The price that the dealer is likely to mention is the car's sticker price. Remind the dealer that the sticker price is probably not what the car would sell for. Dealers may also state that the car will have little value at the end of a lease to make their costs appear larger than they really are.

Be sure that you understand any lease agreement *before* you sign it. If there are any terms that are not clear to you, ask the dealer to explain them. If you do not receive a satisfactory explanation, don't sign. Once you have signed a contract, there is little you can do to change the agreement.

---

specific period of time or number of miles, whichever comes first. In 1991 most manufacturers offered a warranty on new cars that ranged from a minimum of 36,000 miles or three years to a maximum of 70,000 miles or seven years. Used car dealers commonly offered warranties ranging from 3,000 miles or ninety days to 12,000 miles or one year. Most dealers offer consumers **extended protection plans (EPPs)** that provide more protection

over greater lengths of time. In general, these plans cost more than they are worth. It is com-

Vocabulary Builder

Extended protection plan (EPP) An agreement through which the buyer of a product pays a fee to have the product's warranty extended for a longer period of time.

mon for more than half the price of such plans to be dealer profit.

Consumers need to learn to read warranties carefully and to find out what the warranties actually protect the consumers from. Many warranties have deductibles after a certain number of miles have been driven. There are parts of automobiles that may not be covered in the same way as other parts. For example, tires are usually covered by their original manufacturer, not by the automobile firm. A car's drive train may be covered for more miles than radios or windshield washers. The bodies of many automobiles were covered against rust-through for up to 100,000 miles in 1991. The difference between warranties offered by different manufacturers may be important enough to cause you to buy one car instead of another.

When a repair becomes necessary and it's not covered by a car's warranty, the consumer may take it to the dealer that sold the car or to an independent garage. Wherever the car is taken, it is important to choose a reputable business that will provide a written estimate before work is begun.

Sometimes it is impossible to know how much a repair will cost when it is started. For example, when an automatic transmission fails, there is often no way to tell how much a repair will cost until the transmission is taken apart. In this situation, you should state that you want to be consulted before work that will cost more than $200 is begun. It is possible that the bill for fixing your car may end up being more than the car is worth.

Summing Up   *There are many costs that consumers pay to own cars. Of these costs, depreciation is often the largest. When consumers buy new or used cars, they should be sure to know what warranties are offered. Consumers who buy used cars should have them inspected by a professional before they complete the transaction.* ◆

SECTION 2

STEPS TO BUYING A CAR

While you read, *ask yourself . . .*
- *How did a member of your family choose the car he or she owns?*
- *Was this person satisfied with the car one year later?*

For most people, buying a car is the second most expensive purchase they will ever make. (Buying a house is the most expensive.) Such an important decision should not be made lightly or rushed into. Taking a few extra days to be a wise shopper can save years of aggravation. Consumers should never buy a car until they are sure that they have made the best choice for their needs and financial situation.

Gathering Information

Many people who buy cars never carefully think about the features that they need. They may be attracted to a particular model that they saw advertised, or they may simply like a certain style. Unfortunately, many attractive cars are not very practical. For example, if there are three teenagers in your family, buying a sports car with almost no back seat would probably be a mistake. If you need a car to commute 40 miles to work every day, you shouldn't buy a car with a powerful engine that gets poor gas mileage. If your garage was built in the 1920s and is quite small, you should not consider buying a full-sized van. Consumers should make a list of what they require in their car before they even begin to shop around. This will prevent them from wasting their time investigating cars that can't fill their needs.

Car buyers should read through publications that report on the quality and features of cars. *Car and Driver, Road and Track*, and the

April issues of *Consumer Reports* contain the results of tests on new cars. You will also be better prepared to negotiate with a car dealer if you have some idea of the cost that the dealership had to pay to purchase its cars. This type of information can be found in the December issues of *Changing Times* and *Edmund's New Car Prices* or can be obtained from many buying services offered through labor unions, the American Automobile Association (AAA), or other organizations. You cannot expect a dealer to accept no profit when a car is sold. On the other hand, knowing how much the dealer paid for a car can prevent you from helping the dealer make an unreasonable profit.

It is important for consumers to know what they can afford to pay for a car before they begin to negotiate with a dealer. If the most you can possibly pay is $400 a month, you should not consider a car that would require a monthly payment of $550. Don't allow yourself to be talked into buying more of a car than you can afford.

Whey you buy a car, you are also buying the service of the dealer. Good service is almost as important as the quality of the car you buy. You should take the time to investigate specific car dealers you might buy from. By asking friends and relatives about their experiences with various car dealers, you can choose one that is reliable and fair. You should also choose a dealer that is in a convenient location. You will need to take your car in for regular service. If the dealer is far from where you live or work, this can be a significant problem. You should also ask if you will be given a "loaner" while your car is being worked on.

Deciding What Options to Buy

Very few consumers buy "basic" or "stripped" models of automobiles. There are several reasons for this. Some consumers buy

Consumer News

How Much Do "Add-Ons" Cost?

In 1991, researchers for *Consumers' Research Magazine* completed a survey of the cost of various consumer "add-ons." The following table shows only a few of their findings. For the "add-ons" surveyed, the dealer price averaged 185 percent more than the price of similar products offered by other businesses.

Add-On	Dealer Price	Price at Other Stores
Honda floor mats	$ 99	$10 to $45
Rear step bumper for a Toyota Truck	$895	$100 to $160
Aluminum wheels for a Toyota Camry	$995	$500 to $620
Volkswagen Passat radio	$579	$40 to $300

options because they want the convenience or luxury they offer. For example, most cars sold in the United States have automatic transmission, power steering, and power brakes for making driving easier. Air conditioning is becoming almost a standard feature on all but the least expensive cars.

Vocabulary Builder

Option An extra feature installed at a factory and which may be added to a base product; for example, air conditioning on a car.

Unfortunately, consumers often buy options that they don't really need or want because they buy cars "off the lot." Most dealers order large quantities of automobiles to hold in inventory. They can't predict exactly what features customers will want so they tend to order cars that are equipped with many options. These options add to the price of the cars and to the dealer's profit. Unless you are willing to wait many weeks to receive a special-order car, you must accept one of the cars already in stock with its options.

In addition to factory options, dealers often try to sell consumers special "**add-ons**" that most often add to the dealer's profit more than to the value of the car. Almost all new cars sold in the United States have been built and treated to resist rust. Many have "rust-through" warranties that last for 100,000 miles. Still, dealers often try to convince consumers to spend an extra $300 to $500 to have their cars rustproofed. Dealers are also likely to offer special waxes or leather treatments. They often encourage consumers to buy extended protection plans. In general, dealers benefit much more from these "add-ons" than consumers.

Making the Deal

Consumers who are in the market for a new or used car should always remember that dealers need them more than they need the dealer. Regardless of any statements made by salespeople, there will be other sales, and today is not your "last chance" to get a good price. If you are not satisfied with what you are offered, or if you feel that someone is trying to "railroad" you into buying a car you don't want, all you have to do is leave.

Before you talk about trading in your used car, try to find out what you would have to pay if you bought a new car for cash. Most dealers won't want to give you a price until they think

you are ready to buy. Salespeople often say that they must have deals "approved" by their superiors after they have negotiated with you. The chances are very good that this supervisor will decide that you should pay a few hundred dollars more. The best policy is to say that you want a price on a specific car. Give the salesperson a reasonable amount of time to provide you with an answer. If you are refused, simply walk out the door. The world is full of car dealers who would like your business.

Once you have a clear idea of what the dealer would be willing to accept for a car in cash, you can start talking about trading in your old car. The National Automobile Dealers Association publishes its *Official Used Car Guide*, or "**blue book**," which lists average used car values. Banks usually have copies of these books that you can look at. You should expect to receive the blue book value for your car. To find out how much you are being offered for your car, you should look at the difference between the cash price and the trade-in price. The car's sticker or list price usually has little importance.

Suppose that you decide to buy a car with a sticker price of $18,200. After negotiations you are able to get the dealer to agree to sell it to you for $17,400 in cash. If the dealer then agrees to sell you the car for $15,000 when you trade in your used car, you are being given $2,400 for your car ($17,400 − $15,000 = $2,400). The salesperson is likely to tell you that the trade-in value is $3,200 ($18,200 − $15,000 = $3,200). This is not the case because you would not have needed to pay the list price of $18,200 in the first place.

If you don't feel that you are being offered enough for your used car, you have the option of trying to sell it yourself. This can save you money, but it is also likely to be time-consuming and aggravating. The value of this type of trade-off depends on the time you can afford to take selling your old car and your financial situation.

◆ Consumers should be prepared to negotiate for a car they want to buy. They can't expect to pay less than a fair price for an automobile, but they should not agree to a deal that provides a dealer with an unreasonable profit.

Many automobile salespeople will try to get you to give them money toward the price of a car to show them you are "serious" about the deal. Don't give anyone money until you are sure of the car you want to buy. After you give a dealer money, it is often difficult to get it back if you decide not to buy the car. Many consumers also consider it insulting to have to pay a dealer just to prove that they are serious customers. Remember, you came into a dealership through a door. You can just as easily leave the same way.

When you find a dealer who treats you well, it is worth protecting this relationship by giving this firm your business. A dealer who feels that you will be a repeat customer is more likely to be cooperative and helpful in providing service and charging fair prices in the future.

Summing Up *Before consumers buy a car, they should investigate the types of cars that are offered for sale. They should also decide what features they want in a car. When consumers negotiate for a car, they should remember that they have the right to say no and leave at any time. They should not allow a salesperson to talk them into buying a car that they don't really want.* ◆

Vocabulary Builder

Add-on An extra feature sold and added to a product by a dealer.

Blue book The *Official Used Car Guide*, which lists the average market value of different types and years of used cars.

SECTION 3

USING YOUR CAR

While you read, ask yourself . . .
♦ *When you buy a new product, do you always read the instructions? If you don't read the instructions that come with your new car, what might happen?*
♦ *Do you know someone who owns a "lemon"? What has this person done to resolve the problem?*

It has been said that when you buy a car, your fun has just begun. Although this may be true, buying a car is also just the beginning of your responsibilities. Consumers need to spend the time and money necessary to maintain their cars. If they don't, they are likely to experience many unexpected problems at inconvenient times.

Reading the Owner's Manual

All new cars come with an owner's manual that explains how the car functions and how to make simple repairs. It also includes a schedule of maintenance procedures that must be performed at various times—usually after a certain number of miles have been driven. Following this maintenance schedule is important for two reasons. First, the manufacturer provided the schedule because your car will run better and last longer if it is properly maintained. Second, following the schedule protects your car's warranty. If a major component breaks, you may have to pay the cost of repairs if you have not maintained the car properly.

Owner's manuals also include information about where to look for help if you are dissatisfied with the service provided by a dealer or if your car breaks down while you are far from home. There is almost always a toll-free 800 number to call to either seek assistance or to lodge a complaint. You might not think about this when you buy a car, but it may become important later.

What to Do When Your Car Breaks Down

At one time or another, almost every car will break down. It may only be a dead battery or a clogged fuel line, but if you are stuck at night on the shoulder of a deserted highway 30 miles from the nearest town, you still have a big problem. Some expensive cars come with roadside service. By calling a toll-free 800 number, you can have a service truck sent to you. Or you may join road service clubs like the Ameri-

♦ If your car breaks down you should be sure a mechanic doesn't take you for a ride. Demand a written estimate before work is begun and be sure the work is guaranteed for a reasonable period of time after it is completed.

can Automobile Association. Again, a call to the appropriate number will bring you help in a reasonable period of time. Many insurance policies will reimburse you for road service, but you must first pay the bill and then file for payment from the company.

Drivers should prepare for the worst by carrying emergency supplies in their car. You should always have a basic first-aid kit with you. Tools, flares, and a flashlight are also a good idea. If you are traveling in the winter, you should carry a blanket in case you are stranded in the cold. Regularly check the air pressure in your spare tire. There are few things worse than having a flat tire and finding that your spare is also flat. A little planning can prevent small problems from becoming big problems.

What You Should Know About Lemon Laws

In 1990 all but five states had some form of **lemon law**. Under these laws owners of new cars are protected from defects that can't be fixed in a reasonable period of time. Most lemon laws state that if your new car has a major problem and your dealer is unable to repair it in four attempts, you have the right to demand your money back or a different new car. This protection usually lasts for one year or 12,000 miles, although limits vary from state to state. For lemon laws to be used, the defects must be covered by the car's warranty and substantially reduce the usefulness, value, or safety of the car.

When there is a dispute over whether a car qualifies for free repairs under its warranty or is subject to a lemon law, consumers may seek **arbitration**. When this is done a third party listens to both sides of a disagreement and is given the power to make a final decision. Most states have laws that require dissatisfied car owners to notify the dealer or manufacturer of a problem with their car. This gives the firm a chance to solve the problem. If the problem is not resolved, the owner may submit complaints to an arbitration program specified in the car's owner's manual. These programs are free to the consumer and are generally binding on the manufacturer but not on the owner. If the arbitration panel rules in favor of the consumer, the business must repair, replace, or refund the price of the car. If the panel rules in favor of the company, the consumer still has the right to take the dispute to court.

If you are a new car owner and you believe that your car is defective, you may contact your state's attorney general's office or the Center for Auto Safety (2001 S Street, NW, Suite 410, Washington, DC 20009) to ask for information about your rights under the lemon law in your state.

The Costs of Breaking the Law

Every year millions of tickets are issued by police agencies across the United States. The cost of paying tickets is only part of the expense that consumers must pay when they are caught breaking the law. In most cases receiving a ticket for a **moving violation** will result in **points** being placed on the violator's dri-

---

Vocabulary Builder

Arbitration   When a third party is given the power to determine the resolution to a dispute.

Lemon law   A law that protects consumers from defective new cars.

Moving violation   Violation of a traffic law while driving a car.

Point   A fee paid to a lender that is computed as a percentage point of a mortgage. A mark placed on one's driver's license when convicted of a moving violation.

Consumer News

ATVs Are Fun and Deadly

Many consumers buy motorcycles, snowmobiles, jet skis, and all terrain vehicles (ATVs), not so much to travel on as to have a good time. Unfortunately, many consumers seem to forget basic safety rules when they drive for fun. Between 1982 and 1989 there were 1,037 reported deaths and 365,000 injuries as a result of ATV accidents.

In 1987 the Consumer Product Safety Commission filed suit against ATV manufacturers to try to force them to take the vehicles off the market and to recall units that had already been sold. On April 28, 1988, a settlement was reached between the U.S. Department of Justice and the ATV manufacturers. The agreement stopped the sale of all three-wheel ATVs and began removing existing three-wheel vehicles by offering to buy them back. The manufacturers agreed to spend $1 million on advertising to inform consumers of the dangers of ATVs. More complete instructions and safety warnings were included with four-wheel models that could still be sold, and extensive training programs were begun.

Some people believe that this agreement was an invasion of individual freedom of consumers to decide what products they want to buy for themselves.

What do you think?

ver's license and an increase in the insurance premium that the driver must pay. When drivers receive too many points, their license may be suspended. This can prevent them from driving to work and earning an income.

People who break traffic laws and are involved in accidents may also be subject to the cost of legal fees and to liability judgments placed against their property or future income. Many lawsuits have resulted in settlements in the millions of dollars. Most people do not carry insurance that would cover such a large judgment.

Probably the most serious traffic offense is driving under the influence of alcohol or drugs. In 1990 roughly half of the accidents in this country involved people who had been drinking. Most people who are convicted of **driving while intoxicated (DWI)** have their license suspended. They may be sent to jail if they caused a fatal accident. It is important to remember that part of being a responsible consumer is to not drink and drive.

People pay a cost for poor driving when they injure themselves or other people in accidents. One mishap can have results that last a lifetime. To reduce the possibility of being seriously injured in an accident, you should drive responsibly and use the safety devices that your car is equipped with. Since 1990 all automobiles have been required to have **passive restraints** that prevent people from being thrown forward in a head-on collision. Many states require child seats to reduce the possibility of injury to children in an accident. Responsible consumers use safety equipment to protect themselves and their passengers.

Summing Up *Consumers who own cars should take responsibility for properly maintaining them. They should also keep emergency equipment in their cars. If they are dissatisfied with their new cars, they have rights under lemon laws in most states. Consumers also are responsible for following traffic laws to protect themselves and others.* ◆

USING PUBLIC TRANSPORTATION

While you read, ask yourself . . .
◆ *How often could you take public transportation instead of a private car?*
◆ *Would you save money if you used public transportation more frequently?*

There are times when driving an automobile is not the only or even the best way to travel. Many consumers can save both time and money by using public transportation.

Local Transportation

There are many people in the United States who could save hundreds or even thousands of dollars a year if they were willing to use public transportation. In urban areas most forms of public transportation cost between $1 and $2 a trip. Over the course of a year this cost may add up to several hundred dollars for each person in a family. At first this may seem like a large cost. But when compared to the cost of owning an automobile, public transportation in urban areas is almost always the less expensive choice.

One of the greatest savings offered by public transportation is not having to pay for parking. In many major cities the cost of parking a car can be as much as $100 a month or more. Insurance, maintenance, gasoline, and depreciation add thousands more to the cost of keeping a car. All of these costs can be avoided by using public transportation.

Public transportation is frequently more convenient than using a car. If you take a bus or a subway to work, you do not need to worry about finding a place to park. There are other ways public transportation may be more convenient—not having to fight traffic jams dur-

◆ Most people who live in cities could save time and money by using public transportation. Why do many people own cars that are expensive and often not very useful?

ing rush hour; leaving the driving to someone else, especially in bad weather; talking to other passengers or reading.

There are times, of course, when a car is necessary. You can't move large pieces of furniture on a bus. What's more, there may not be any public transportation to certain places you want to go. In these cases one of the best alternatives is to rent a car. This may cost $50 to $100 a day, but is much less expensive than owning a car that is not needed most of the time.

Vocabulary Builder

Driving while intoxicated (DWI)   Driving a vehicle while under the influence of alcohol or drugs.
Passive restraint   A device that automatically prevents people from being thrown forward during an automobile accident.

Consumer News

Taking the Train South

Would you like to be in Florida tomorrow? If you lived in New York City in 1990, you could spend $269 for a round-trip "slumbercoach" ticket to Fort Lauderdale and arrive in the sun in just over 24 hours. For your money you would receive a "cozy" private room with a fold-out bed, a sink, and a toilet. Advantages of taking the slumbercoach included not having to get to and from airports, being able to take extra baggage without paying extra money, being able to watch the scenery, and getting to know other travelers. Slumbercoach services were also available from Chicago to California, and there was talk of extending them to other routes.

Traveling Over Greater Distances

When you need to travel between cities, there are often several alternative forms of public transportation to choose from. Interstate bus lines, such as Greyhound, offer transportation between most major cities. Travelers can take trains that are relatively quick and inexpensive. Since airlines were deregulated in the late 1970s, the cost of flying has fallen to levels that are affordable to many consumers.

Taking public transportation not only saves money, but allows travelers to use their time to look at scenery, read, or complete other types of work on their way. There is also less of a chance of becoming lost when you take public transportation.

Although it may not always be restful, consumers may travel at night when they use public transportation. By taking a train, it is possible to get from San Francisco to Los Angeles overnight or from Washington, D.C., to Florida in just over 24 hours. You can even travel from New York City to Seattle in just over two days if you are willing to travel at night. Flying between cities saves even more time, although you may suffer from "jet lag."

The price of air travel varies widely, depending on where and when you choose to travel. Airlines continually adjust prices to try to fill flights and get as much revenue as possible. If you call up today to take a 9 A.M. flight tomorrow and return the next day, expect to pay a high price. On the other hand, if you make your reservation several weeks ahead of time and are willing to fly on a Thursday afternoon and return the following Tuesday at 6 A.M., you will be charged a much lower price.

Consumers should realize that many less expensive tickets are not refundable. If you want to be sure that you can fly on a particular day, you might purchase a full-price, refundable ticket for the flight you want. Then you should call different travel agents at different times to see if you can find a better price. When you believe that you have the lowest-priced ticket possible, buy another ticket and cancel your original reservation. This causes more paperwork for the airline, but it also improves your chances of paying the lowest price possible.

Airline prices and billing procedures change frequently. By the time you read this text, there may be newer ways to get the best price. You should check with several travel agents to find the current method that is best for your needs.

Summing Up *American consumers spent over $275 billion on trips that took them more than 100 miles from their homes in 1987. They took 455 million pleasure trips and another 155 million business trips. To be sure that you receive fair value for the travel dollars you spend, you need to shop carefully, just as you would for any other product you buy.*

Review and Enrichment Activities

VOCABULARY REVIEW

1. Column A contains key consumer terms from this chapter. Column B contains a scrambled list of phrases that describe what these terms mean. Match the correct meaning with each term. Write your answers on a separate sheet of paper.

Column A	Column B
1. Moving violation	a. Legislation that protects new car buyers from defective cars
2. Points	b. Device that automatically protects passengers from being thrown forward in a head-on collision
3. Passive restraint	
4. Depreciation	c. A decline in the value of a car, a result of the car becoming older over time
5. Blue book	d. A listing of the average value of various cars according to their model, options, and age
6. Arbitration	
7. Lemon Law	e. A mark that is placed on a person's driving record when he or she is convicted of a moving violation
8. Driving while intoxicated	
9. Extended protection plan	f. To be caught breaking a traffic law while driving a motor vehicle
	g. An agreement through which a buyer pays for a longer warranty on a product
	h. When a third party has the power to settle a dispute
	i. To be caught driving a car while under the influence of drugs or alcohol

2. Explain the difference between factory options and dealer "add-ons."

Review and Enrichment Activities Continued

CHECKING WHAT YOU'VE LEARNED

Write your answers for the following exercises on a separate sheet of paper.

1. How much did it cost to own the average car in 1990?
2. Describe three possible causes for the relatively high price of new cars.
3. Explain what depreciation is and why it is often the greatest cost of owning a car.
4. Describe three advantages of buying a used car rather than a new automobile.
5. Why should people who buy used cars have them inspected by an independent mechanic before they complete the transaction?
6. What types of useful information can car buyers find in *Consumer Reports*?
7. Why do many car buyers end up buying options that they don't need or want?
8. Explain how a car buyer should determine how much he or she is actually being offered for a trade-in.
9. Explain what a "lemon law" does for consumers.
10. Explain why people who are able to use public transportation usually save money.
11. Describe several advantages of using public transportation in addition to saving money.

PRACTICING YOUR CONSUMER SKILLS

Write your answers for the following exercises on a separate sheet of paper.

1. Consider the following types of cars: (1) a new subcompact economy car for $8,999; (2) a used full-size station wagon with 22,000 miles for $12,899; (3) a new sports car with a powerful engine for $58,999; (4) a new van that will hold nine people for $19,600; (5) a used four-door compact with 48,000 miles for $3,500. Identify the type of car that you believe would be most appropriate for each of the following people. Explain your choices.
   a. Norman has three children of his own and is the scoutmaster of a Boy Scout troop. He often takes his troop on weekend camping trips. Norman has a good job and can afford most any car he wants to buy.

   b. Barbara is a successful model with an important New York City agency. She has been on the cover of several fashion magazines. It is important for her to project an image of being "up with the times."

   c. Lora has a job that requires her to deliver and install draperies in customers' homes. She must provide her own transportation. Lora's income is respectable, but she has many expenses to pay.

   d. Joe is a college student. He commutes 30 miles a day to classes as part of a car pool with three other students. He has a part-time job but can't afford to pay very much for a car.

   e. June lives by herself in an old farmhouse about 50 miles from Billings, Montana. She writes romance novels for a living. She is able to support herself, but her books have not sold all that well. She drives to town once a week to buy her groceries and to collect her mail.

2. Each of the following consumers made at least one important mistake when they bought a car. Identify each mistake, and explain how it could have been avoided.

   a. Maria found a car that she wanted to buy with a sticker price of $16,459. When she bought the new car, she traded in her old car. The dealer told her he was giving her $4,459 for her old car because he only charged $12,000 for the new one.

   b. Gary needed a car to get to work. He thought that he could afford to pay about $300 a month. He expected to buy a basic model that was around two years old for about $8,000 and to pay it off over three years. The dealer convinced him to take out a four-year loan to buy a five-year-old luxury model that cost $10,000. The dealer pointed out that Gary would still pay about $300 a month but would pay one year longer.

   c. Karen lives in Reno, Nevada, where it doesn't rain or snow very much. She bought a small pickup truck that she expects to keep about three years. The dealer convinced her to pay an extra $359 to have her truck rustproofed.

   d. Vern has a wife and four children. He doesn't earn much money. Vern wanted to buy a small station wagon with a standard transmission and a radio with no other options. He expected to pay about $11,000. Vern went shopping in June but found that it was too late to order the car he wanted before the next year's models came out. The dealer said that there was going to be a 5 percent increase for the new models but that he would sell Vern one of last year's full-size station wagons for just $17,899. Vern decided to buy the full-size car.

3. Explain how each of the following people could benefit from using public transportation.

   a. Terry is a financial analyst for a bank in New York City. He lives on Long Island and spends about 3 hours every day driving to and from work. He never seems to have enough time to keep up with the reading he needs to do for his job.

b. Ricky owns a car in Los Angeles. He has been involved in three accidents in the past two years. He is in the risk pool and must pay $3,600 each year for insurance.

c. Sara works in Boston. She drives about 5 miles to work each day and parks in an underground garage six blocks from her job. She pays $120 a month to rent her parking space.

d. Mark is a retired bus driver who lives in the suburbs of Chicago. He doesn't have much income and finds his car to be a financial burden. Although he does use the car from time to time, weeks go by when he does not drive it at all.

USING NUMBERS

Solve the following problem to help make the best possible choice. Write your solution on a separate sheet of paper. Be sure to show all your work.

Richard has budgeted $6,500 for each of the next three years to pay for transportation. He has decided to buy either a new car for $13,000 or the same type of car that is three years old for $7,000. Richard will pay insurance of $1,110 if he buys the new car or $890 if he buys the used model. He estimates that he will spend about $500 a year for gas regardless of which car he buys. Registration and other costs would add another $100 a year for either car. Richard expects almost no maintenance costs if he buys the new car because it will be under warranty. He figures that he should set aside $300 a year for repairs on the used car. Richard will need to take out a loan to buy either car. If he buys the new car, he must borrow $10,000. For the used car he would borrow $4,000. Current interest rates for new cars are 12 percent. For used cars they are 14 percent. Use the following table to help determine how much Richard would have to pay each year for each of the two cars. Which car would you recommend he buy? Explain the reasons for your answer.

Cost of a Three -Year-Loan per $1,000 Borrowed at Different Interest Rates		
Interest Rate	Monthly Payment	Total Finance Charge Over 3 Years
10%	$32	$161
12%	$33	$196
14%	$34	$231

PUTTING IDEAS IN YOUR OWN WORDS

The following quotations are from this chapter. Explain these quotations in your own words to make sure you understand what they mean. Write your answers on a separate sheet of paper.

1. "With the possible exception of insurance, depreciation is the greatest cost of owning an automobile."
2. "When you buy a car, you are also buying the service of the dealer."
3. "Consumers who are in the market for a new or used car should always remember that dealers need them more than they need the dealer."

BUILDING CONSUMER KNOWLEDGE

Write your answers for the following exercises on a separate sheet of paper.

1. If your family owns a car, describe this vehicle and explain why this particular car was purchased. If your family does not own a car, describe alternative means of transportation that the members of your family use.
2. Suppose that you have two close friends who are married and have two young children. This couple does not have a large income. One evening they tell you that they are thinking of buying a used sports car with a powerful engine because they think that their life is too dull. They ask for your opinion. Write an essay describing what you would recommend to your friends. Be sure to explain the reasons for your recommendation.
3. Suppose that your Great-uncle Harry left you his six-year-old Cadillac with 74,000 miles on it in his will. Make a list of the costs that you would have to pay to put this car on the road. Which do you believe would be a better idea: to sell the car or keep it? Explain your answer.

Chapter 38

Health and Recreation

Chapter Objectives

After completing this chapter, you will be able to do the following:

- Describe the benefits and costs of weight control programs.
- Describe the benefits and costs of eating a nutritious diet.
- Describe the benefits and cost of regular exercise.
- Explain how consumers can achieve the benefits of weight control, nutritious diet, and regular exercise at reduced costs.

Key Consumer Terms

In this chapter you will learn the meanings of the following important consumer terms:

- Metabolism
- Diet supplement
- Nutrition
- Cholesterol
- Weight loss program
- Saturated fat
- Unsaturated fat
- Fiber
- Basic food groups
- Anabolic steroid

W hen you look in a mirror, are you pleased with what you see? Do you think you are too heavy, too thin, or just about right? Are you pretty, handsome, plain, or something else? A 1990 poll revealed that 39 percent of adult American men and about half of our nation's women believe that they are overweight. According to government standards, the real figures of overweight Americans are 24 percent for men and 27 percent for women. At any given time, over one-third (about 37 percent) of American adults are on some type of diet to lose weight. Of those who succeed, more than half will gain the weight back within a year.

Why do many Americans think that they are fat? Have our self-images or values been changed by advertising? Do we all want to look like movie stars? Do we care more about our appearance than how we feel or act? Being thin is not necessarily the same as being healthy.

Medical research has made it clear that diet, exercise, and lifestyle affect a person's health and life expectancy. To an extent, the quality of your life is determined by the health habits that you follow. Other people may tell you how to live a more healthy life, but only you can take the steps to do it. Being a responsible consumer includes taking care of your body.

SECTION 1

CHOOSING A HEALTHY WEIGHT

While you read, ask yourself . . .
- ◆ *Do you feel that you weigh too much, too little, or just about right? How important do you believe your weight is to your health and appearance?*
- ◆ *Have you or other members of your family tried to lose weight in the past year? Was the diet successful?*

Many tables and guides have been created that are intended to tell Americans how much they should weigh. The National Academy of Sciences proposed the following table in 1990 as illustrated in Table 38-1. It indicates a range of weights for both men and women according to age and height. The proper weight for someone within a range depends on the person's sex (most men can be a little heavier than most women), the size of the person's bones, and the physical condition that the person is in (an extra 5 pounds of muscle is different from an extra 5 pounds of fat). How does your weight fit on this chart?

The people who prepared this table emphasized that being in the range of weight indicated for your age and height does not prove that you are healthy. Nor does it mean that there is something wrong with you if your weight is not within the appropriate range. This and similar tables are merely one indicator of physical condition that consumers should consider when they evaluate their health.

Good and Bad Ways to Diet

If you decide that you want to lose weight, ask your doctor for advice before you do anything *drastic*. There is probably no danger to your health if you decide to lose a few pounds by cutting out snacks between balanced meals. However, if you plan to change your total diet to lose large amounts of weight in a short period

Healthy Weight Ranges for Men and Women				
	Age			
Height	**19–24**	**25–44**	**45–65**	**Over 65**
5-0	97-123	102-133	112-143	123-148
5-1	100-127	106-137	116-148	127-153
5-2	104-131	109-141	119-152	130-157
5-3	107-135	113-146	124-156	135-163
5-4	110-139	116-150	127-162	139-168
5-5	114-143	120-156	132-167	144-178
5-6	117-147	123-159	135-167	147-178
5-7	121-152	127-165	140-178	152-185
5-8	124-157	131-170	144-183	157-189
5-9	128-161	133-172	148-188	161-196
5-10	131-166	135-175	152-193	166-202
5-11	135-171	142-185	157-198	171-207
6-0	139-175	146-190	161-204	175-213
6-1	143-181	151-196	166-211	181-219
6-2	147-187	154-201	170-216	185-226
Source: St. Cloud Star Tribune, May 2, 1990, p. 13.				

◆ **Table 38-1** Healthy Weight Ranges

of time, you need professional help. People who lose weight rapidly by eating an unbalanced diet are likely to do more harm than good. Dieters who try to lose weight rapidly on their own have been classified into several groups.

Starvers try to lose weight by eating almost nothing for long periods of time. There are several important drawbacks to such a diet. People who starve themselves don't consume proper vitamins and minerals and may become ill. When people don't eat normally, their body's **metabolism** automatically slows down to conserve food energy. When they finally do eat, the food is used more efficiently. The result is that these people may not lose weight at all and in fact may end up gaining.

Stuffers overeat one day and then eat very little for the next two or three days. They believe that their metabolism will increase by overeating, helping them to lose weight rapidly on the days when they consume fewer calories. One problem with this plan is the cheating. The increased metabolism is likely to make these dieters feel very hungry on days that they are not supposed to eat. As a result, they are likely to have a "little something" just to tide them over.

Skippers try to lose weight by giving up eating lunch or breakfast. As a result, they often eat far too much in the evening. Calories eaten later in the day are not burned by exercise when people are asleep. They tend to be stored as fat. Many people who skip meals lose little weight, and some end up weighing more.

Fad dieters try to lose weight by giving up certain types of foods or eating combinations of foods that are supposed to suppress the appetite or not metabolize well together. Some buy **diet supplements** or special diet foods that supposedly will allow them to lose weight rapidly. The greatest danger from this type of diet is poor **nutrition**. Eating too much or too little of any type of food tends to be bad for your health.

Any diet that allows a person to lose weight rapidly probably is unhealthy unless it is supervised by a qualified doctor. Rapid weight loss tends to cause **cholesterol** to collect in the gallbladder, increasing a person's risk of forming gallstones. People who have lost weight rapidly are more likely to suffer a heart attack than people who have lost weight more slowly. Rapid weight loss is often the result of water loss that will be regained quickly when a dieter returns to eating a more normal diet. Furthermore, water loss is not healthy. It can cause people to be dizzy and to have all sorts of chemical imbalances.

People who want to lose more than just a few pounds should seek the advice of a qualified medical specialist. They will probably be advised to eat a balanced diet with a reduced total number of calories. They may be advised to eat smaller amounts of food more often and have a regular exercise routine. If they stick to their diet and exercise plan, they will lose

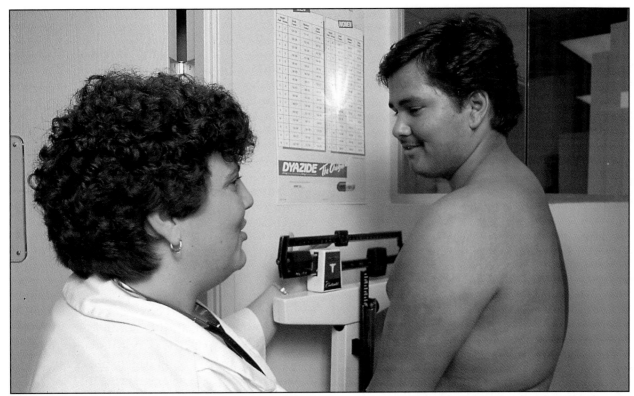

◆   What problem do these people appear to have in common? How could they benefit from a plan that includes eating a controlled but balanced diet and regular exercise?

weight slowly and have a much better chance of keeping the weight off in the future. One fact that medical researchers agree on is that repeatedly losing weight and gaining it back is bad for a person's health.

How Useful Are Weight Loss Programs?

There are many programs that consumers may join that are designed to help them lose weight. Some provide counseling and medical advice, others include exercise programs, and a few sell prepared foods that have premeasured calorie contents. Some organizations that only provide counseling or personal support are relatively inexpensive. Those that offer packaged food products are quite expensive.

Vocabulary Builder

Cholesterol A fatty acid found in many food products. Some forms of this compound are thought to contribute to circulatory diseases.

Diet supplement A manufactured compound that may be added to a person's diet to provide more balanced nourishment; for example, vitamin pills.

Metabolism The process through which an organism converts food into energy and body tissue.

Nutrition Consuming a combination of foods that will help the body build tissue and remain healthy.

Consumer News

Weight Watchers Lasagna at Burger King?

Many Americans may find it hard to picture fast food that's good for you, but that's exactly what started to happen in the early 1990's. McDonald's was first with its McLean Deluxe hamburger, advertised as 91 percent fat free. Hardee's followed with its own version of a reduced-fat burger. Burger King, however, took a different step. Rather than trying to "de-fat" its traditional menu items, it made a deal with Weight Watchers, a unit of H. J. Heinz Co., to market low-fat, reduced-calorie food items in its outlets. These Weight Watchers products included such eatables as low-calorie syrup and cinnamon rolls for breakfast and lasagna and fettuccine with broccoli for dinner. A representative of Burger King commented, "You want to have something for everyone."

Many people who join **weight loss programs** benefit from the companionship and support they receive from other members of the program. It has been said that "misery loves company." Few people would tell you that dieting is fun. Working on a weight problem with other people who share the problem may make dieting easier. There is also the possibility of peer pressure. When your group gets together for its "weekly weigh in," you don't want to be the only member who failed to lose weight.

There are financial dangers that may be associated with some weight loss organizations. One common problem is that there is a high rate of business failure in this industry. Consumers have often paid hundreds of dollars for a membership in a weight loss program only to lose their money when the program went bankrupt. If you are considering buying a membership in a weight loss organization, be sure that it is financially secure before you pay any money.

Americans spent over $10 billion on weight loss programs in 1989. Among the larger organizations was *Physicians' Weight Loss Centers*, which had over 400 centers and charged its customers an average of $35 a week for its services. *Nutri-System* operated in 1,500 locations. Its fee was based on the amount of weight a customer wanted to lose, ranging from a low of about $300 to as much as $600. Customers were also expected to buy packaged food from this organization, adding another $50 to $65 to this weekly cost. It was not uncommon for a Nutri-System customer to pay the organization over $3,000 for a year's services. *Diet Center Inc.* had the most locations in 1990, with 2,100 centers across the nation. Its customers paid from $35 to $50 a week for an average total of about $700.

Although American consumers have paid weight loss programs billions of dollars, it is not clear that they benefited as much as they paid. Many lawsuits have been filed against these organizations for damage to consumers' health or for misleading advertising. Congressional hearings were held in 1990 to investigate weight loss advertising that made unrealistic claims. Soon after, many organizations dropped specific claims and substituted statements like "Lose as much weight as you can." Even such vague advertisements may be misleading to people who want to lose weight in a hurry.

Clearly, some people are more successful when they try to lose weight as a member of a group. This does not mean that they must pay a high price for this benefit. Community organizations often have weight loss clubs at little or no cost. If you are interested in such a program, start by asking for information at your local YMCA or YWCA. Even some employers offer their workers weight loss programs.

Summing Up *When consumers decide to lose weight, it is important for them to obtain professional advice. They should see their doctor or other qualified person. Consumers should not try to lose a lot of weight in a short period of time.* ◆

THE IMPORTANCE OF WHAT YOU EAT

While you read, ask yourself . . .
- ◆ *How carefully do you keep track of your own nutrition?*
- ◆ *Do you think that you might feel healthier if you were more careful about your diet?*
- ◆ *What factors may prevent you from eating a better diet?*

Unless you cracked the eggs yourself and used homemade bread for your toast, you probably don't know what you ate for breakfast this morning. Suppose that you had a cheese omelet, bran muffin, and glass of breakfast drink. Does this sound healthy to you? Let's investigate a little further.

To make your omelet healthy, you could have used Egg Beaters, a product made largely from egg whites to satisfy people who are trying to avoid high-cholesterol foods. Most of the food value of a whole egg is in its yolk. Therefore, the manufacturer of Egg Beaters adds protein, vitamins, minerals, and other ingredients to its product to approximate those found in a whole egg. This meets the requirements of the FDA, but there is no way to be sure that this type of egg product has the same nutritional value as a whole egg.

To avoid unnecessary **saturated fats**, you may have used a cheese substitute in your omelet. The wrapping on this "cheese food" stated that the milk fat had been replaced with vegetable oil, an **unsaturated fat**. Frankly, you didn't think it tasted too much like cheese when you ate it.

Perhaps you chose an oat bran muffin to be sure that you were getting enough natural **fiber** in your diet. The muffin did have oat bran as an ingredient, but it also had sugar, corn syrup, dates, and honey. It also contained more flour than bran. It is not even clear how much benefit there is to bran fiber by itself. Bran is only one source of fiber, and studies have shown that a combination of different types of fiber is needed to help people stay healthy.

Your glass of "orange-flavored drink with added vitamin C" tasted fine, but it had almost no fruit in it. Federal standards do not require fruit-flavored drinks to contain even 10 percent fruit juice. These drinks are basically sugar, water, and some sort of flavoring.

You may have thought that your breakfast was healthy for you. Compared to some other foods you might have chosen, it was. However, the more prepared foods we buy and eat, the more difficult it becomes to know if we are eating a nutritious diet.

Vocabulary Builder

Fiber   Threadlike filaments found in many foods; thought to help the digestion of food and to reduce the risk of some diseases.

Saturated fat   A fatty acid that contains as many hydrogen atoms as possible. Consumption of saturated fats has been associated with an increased risk of circulatory diseases.

Unsaturated fat   A fatty acid that does not contain as many hydrogen atoms as possible. Consumption of unsaturated fats has been associated with a reduced risk of circulatory disease.

Weight loss program   A program in which consumers pay for assistance in losing weight.

Consumer News

What Is Saturated Fat?

Almost all the fat in our diet is in the form of compounds that contain different types of fatty acids. These compounds may be saturated or unsaturated, depending on the number of hydrogen atoms in the fat. A compound that can accept more hydrogen atoms is unsaturated. A compound that can't accept any more hydrogen atoms is saturated. Generally, fats that are liquid at room temperature contain more unsaturated fat than those that are solid. An ideal diet will have a balance of saturated and unsaturated fats. However, because our diet tends to have more meat, eggs, and other sources of saturated fats, many Americans take steps to reduce their consumption of this type of fat. Eating too much saturated fat has been associated with high cholesterol levels in the blood and increased risk of heart disease.

Eating from the Basic Food Groups

Repeated surveys have shown that many Americans do not understand what good nutrition is or how to achieve it. The government's recommended daily allowances (RDAs) of various nutrients may be useful to professionals, but many consumers do not understand what they mean. For example, many consumers who try to follow these allowances don't realize that the various nutrients must be consumed regularly in a balanced diet. Eating foods with lots of iron one day and other foods with little or no iron for the next week will not supply enough iron to a person's body. RDAs may also result in misleading advertising claims by some food manufacturers. Some Americans think that if they eat one bowl of a particular breakfast cereal that has 100 percent of many of the RDAs, then they can eat whatever they want the rest of the day and still be healthy.

Nutritionists suggest that the best place for consumers to begin building a balanced diet is with the **basic food groups**. In 1943 a list of seven basic food groups was introduced. This list was largely replaced by a simplified and reduced list of four food groups after 1955:

1. Enriched or whole grain bread, flour, cereal, and potatoes
2. Meat, poultry, fish, eggs, and legumes
3. Fruits and vegetables
4. Milk, cheese, and ice cream

By eating a selection of foods from each of the four groups every day, consumers can be reasonably sure that they are eating a balanced, nutritious diet. Even this reduced list may be confusing to some people, particularly those who are young. In 1984 a study of elementary school children showed that most of them could not classify many ordinary food products into the basic food groups. This problem was partly the result of the kind of prepared foods we eat. For example, a can of spaghetti and meat sauce contained elements of groups 1, 2, and 4. As a result, many children classified the product incorrectly, placing it in just one group—or they gave up and did not classify it at all.

When you think about how many prepared foods we eat, it is not surprising that so many adults have similar problems. Where would you classify a microwave burrito? It has a little bit of many foods and does not fit neatly into any group. Because of these difficulties, there has been a movement to teach consumers to think about foods in terms of their original ingredients. Thus, a burrito becomes wheat flour, cheese, legumes, and meat. Unfortunately, it is

◆   When you eat convenience foods how often do you bother to read the label? Why should you care about the nutritional value of the meals you eat?

not always easy to break foods down into their basic groups, and many people simply don't bother to try. Try classifying a bacon double cheeseburger with lettuce and tomato. It has foods from all four groups and a great deal of fat. It is also not clear just how much of the original food value remained once these foods had been processed.

Eating a Balanced Diet of Unprocessed Foods

As a general rule, you will receive more nutritional value from food that has not been processed than from food that has. This does

not mean that all packaged, prepared foods are bad for you. Fish that was "flash frozen" when it was caught may be fresher than fish that was flown to your grocery store and is three days old. However, unprocessed foods are often more nutritious and easier to evaluate. If you

Vocabulary Builder

Basic food groups   Four categories of foods established by the federal government. When eaten together in appropriate amounts, these foods result in a balanced diet.

Consumer News

How Much Should You Rely on Vitamin Supplements?

Do you take vitamin pills on a regular basis? More than half of all Americans do. Between 1980 and 1990 the consumption of vitamin supplements in this country roughly doubled. Manufacturers and marketers made claims for their products that included preventing the common cold, reducing stress, and even preventing some types of cancer. Many doctors warn that people who consume large quantities of vitamins risk taking too much of a good thing.

Research has shown that taking large doses of vitamin D can cause calcium deposits to form in soft muscle tissues. Too much vitamin A can cause damage to the liver. Other supplements when taken in excessive amounts have caused blood disorders. The National Research Council cautions consumers against large doses of any vitamin supplement. Instead, they recommend that consumers eat a balanced diet and take one multivitamin tablet to provide any of the RDAs they may have missed.

cook a meal of fish and vegetables with brown rice and a slice of melon, you know what you are eating. If you eat a package of Aunt Sally's Frozen Seafood Entrée, you probably won't know what you are really having for supper. The more often you are able to eat a well-balanced meal, the better your chances of having a good diet.

Another important step that you can take to protect your health is to limit your intake of foods that clearly add little nutritional value to your diet. Sweets, soft drinks, snack foods, and most chips or "crunchies" have little or no nutritional value. They taste good, and you may enjoy eating them, but they don't make an adequate diet. They should be eaten in limited quantities as an addition to a balanced diet of other foods. They should not form anyone's basic diet.

Use your common sense. No food product is good for you in large quantities. Your body can only absorb so much vitamin C in a short period of time. If you drink gallons of orange juice in a single day, you will end up using the sugar in the juice and wasting most of its vitamin C. Again, the key is eating a balanced diet from all four food groups.

There is something else that you should keep in mind. Eating a balanced diet of foods that you have prepared yourself is likely to be less expensive than eating prepackaged foods that are of questionable nutritional value. Eating a healthy diet can save consumers money.

When to Ask for Help

If you do not feel well, or if you gain or lose weight for no apparent reason, or if you are tired or have pain for no apparent reason, then you should seek professional help. When you experience any unexplained symptoms, visit your doctor. Your doctors may find a physical problem or recommend that you join an organization to help you plan an appropriate diet. If you don't know as much as you should about meeting your nutritional needs, ask for help.

It is particularly important for pregnant women or people with young children to seek help. They are responsible for providing their children with a diet that will allow them to grow and develop into healthy adults. Damage done by poor nourishment in childhood cannot be cured by a better diet in later life.

Consumers can also learn about preparing and eating a balanced diet by reading books on nutrition that are available in the public library. Also, there are often community education courses on nutrition offered by school districts and colleges. These classes are frequently free or charge a small fee. Most Americans can afford to eat a balanced, nutritious diet if only they know how to do it.

Summing Up *Consumers should eat a balanced diet from the four basic food groups every day. They should avoid consuming unnecessary fats and sugar. Consumers who lack an understanding of how to eat a balanced diet should seek professional help.* ◆

SECTION 3

THE BENEFITS OF REGULAR EXERCISE

While you read, ask yourself . . .
- ◆ *How often do you exercise? Do you feel weak and out of breath when you climb a flight of stairs?*
- ◆ *How could you rearrange your schedule to include time for regular exercise?*

Many Americans believe that if they aren't too fat or too thin, then they must be in pretty good physical condition. Unfortunately, this is not necessarily true. You do not need to be overweight to be out of shape. Regular exercise is an important part of maintaining your health. Consumers spend many billions of dollars every year buying goods and services that are intended to help them exercise and stay fit.

The Economics of Health Clubs

By 1990 there were over 20,000 private health clubs in the United States with annual sales in excess of $12 billion. In addition, there were many other types of athletic organizations that provided exercise opportunities. If you wanted to join a tennis, swimming, or racquetball club, you could in most cities. There were also rowing, riding, and even hang-gliding groups to belong to. The total bill that Americans paid for membership in athletic organizations of one kind or another came to over $100 billion in 1990. Exercise is big business.

Have you ever wondered why people join health clubs and other types of organizations that provide facilities for exercise? Why don't they just get out and jog or go for a walk? Many types of exercise are free to those who make the effort.

Market researchers have found that consumers join health clubs for reasons other than a desire to stay fit. Many people join for the companionship and professional help. Others seek specialized programs that offer personalized types of support. For example, the Association of Quality Clubs reports that more than one-quarter of its 1,550 clubs offer their members courses in nutrition, stress management, and how to quit smoking. About 200 of the clubs teach classes on self-esteem. People who apply to join Club Corporation of America have their personalities assessed. Many fitness centers hire doctors to be on call to advise their clients on what the best type of exercise would be for their individual needs. Certainly, exercise is one reason why consumers pay to join health clubs. But there are other reasons as well—including their self-image.

Exercise and Health

Exercise is more than a personal goal. It is also an objective set by the Public Health Service of the United States. According to this government agency, at least 90 percent of all youths from ten to seventeen should participate regularly in physical activities. In addition, the service states that 60 percent of adults should exercise vigorously at least three times a week, and at least half of all elderly Americans should participate in appropriate physical activity on a regular basis. Why does the government feel so strongly about exercise and physical fitness?

Various studies have shown that there are many benefits of regular exercise. One study showed that *on an average*, people in their mid-sixties will have the strength and metabolism of a typical fifty-year-old if they have followed a program of regular exercise for most of their lives. There is also clear evidence that regular exercise can reduce the risk of heart disease. Even moderate exercise on a regular basis has been shown to significantly reduce high blood pressure. Other diseases that may be prevented or treated through exercise include diabetes, arthritis, osteoporosis, some forms of cancer, and some infections. People who have had surgery recover more quickly when they exercise as directed by their physicians.

The evidence is clear. People who participate in regular exercise are healthier on an av-

◆ Although regular exercise is important for good health people should avoid strenuous exercise at irregular times. Do you exercise on a regular basis?

erage than people who don't. It also appears that they have more energy and probably more self-esteem. Other studies show that people who exercise call in sick to work roughly 20 percent less than those who don't exercise. Clearly, people who exercise are more successful employees and business owners. Exercise may not solve all problems for all people, but it can help many people lead fuller, more rewarding lives.

Going Too Far

There is such a thing as too much exercise. There is extensive evidence that people, particularly men, who exercise irregularly but vigorously have an increased chance of suffering a heart attack. This is evident when men who have "desk jobs" try to shovel heavy snow in winter storms and suffer heart attacks. People who have suffered one heart attack should only exercise under the supervision of a physician.

It is possible to tear or break body tissues from the strain of exercise. Again, this is most likely to happen when people don't exercise on a regular basis. Children should be protected from impacts or the strain of excessive exercise because their bones are not hard and can be easily broken or damaged. Pregnant women usually need regular exercise, but should consult their doctor about the sort of physical activity that is most appropriate for them. Studies have shown that regular exercise often makes childbirth easier, but premature birth may be brought on by excessive exercise.

There is a difference between exercise and bodybuilding. In recent years the number of men and women in bodybuilding programs has grown to an estimated 500,000 to 1 million people. People who exercise are trying to protect their health. Those involved in bodybuilding commonly set goals for themselves in terms of being able to lift some amount of weight or exert an amount of pressure. For some people, increasing the physical size of their muscles is also an important goal. No one should undertake a program of bodybuilding without the professional advice of a qualified trainer. People who try to lift too much weight can do permanent damage to their bodies.

Anabolic Steroids

Another danger that has been in the news in recent years is the widespread use of **anabolic steroids** by athletes. Through the use of this type of drug, athletes can experience incredible increases in their strength, weight, and speed in very little time. High school athletes have gained as much as 40 pounds in one summer and have been able to increase the weight they could bench press by more than 100 pounds in the same time. Generally, the immediate side effects of taking steroids appear to be increased cases of acne and a bloated appearance for some people. The long-term effects are much more serious and may be life threatening.

The use of steroids may cause damage to a person's liver, kidneys, and reproductive system. Steroids tend to increase the body's retention of calcium in the bones. There is an increased probability of both heart attacks and strokes among steroid users. People who use steroids tend to be moody and irritable. They are more often involved in physical violence and have been convicted of violent crimes at a higher rate than other members of the general

Vocabulary Builder

Anabolic steroids   A drug that causes people to gain body weight and muscle tissue rapidly.

The *Global* Consumer

Steroids at the Olympics

We all know that the world is not a perfect place. But there are a few places where honesty and virtue prevail, like the Olympics. Or are there? Canadian sprinter Ben Johnson and seven other athletes were disqualified from the 1988 Seoul Olympics when they tested positive for anabolic steroids. Johnson later admitted the use of steroids. He and his coach were barred from competition for two years.

Although Johnson's case may have been the most widely publicized example of steroid use by Olympic athletes in recent years, it certainly was not the only one. Bulgaria's Mitko Grablev lost his weight-lifting gold medal, and Angel Myers never even went to Seoul as a result of steroid use. In 1987 an East German athlete, Birgit Dressel, died of a massive allergic reaction to the combination of over twenty drugs she was taking. Similar tragedies have occurred among football, basketball, and soccer players throughout the world.

In 1976 the International Olympic Committee (IOC) ruled that steroids could not be used by athletes in the games. There were more than 3,000 drugs on the IOC's restricted list in 1988. Urine tests were given to all participating athletes. However, people with knowledge of the games believe that in track-and-field events and in weight lifting, as many as half the participants may have used steroids. New methods of testing are making it more difficult to escape detection, but many athletes have apparently been able to use the drugs and then stop in time to avoid being disqualified. The IOC has set a goal of having a totally drug-free Olympics in 1992.

The danger of steroids is even greater for athletes who do not participate in the Olympics or other national and international events. Olympic athletes at least have the supervision of trainers who have some knowledge of what these drugs can do. People who simply take steroids to add strength and body weight usually have no knowledge of what they may be doing to their bodies. Steroids are one product all consumers should avoid.

population. When people stop taking steroids, they tend to lose most of their extra strength and body weight, but other types of physical changes or damage often remain.

One of the greatest dangers of using steroids has to do with the fact that they are prescription drugs. Doctors cannot ethically prescribe them for the purpose of increasing strength and weight. As a result, most steroid users obtain these drugs illegally and do not have the benefit of professional advice on how to use them. They may buy impure drugs or misuse the drugs that they buy. Using steroids is a very dangerous business.

Consumers should regard exercise as a way to help themselves stay healthy. In choosing the type of exercise that is most appropriate for their own needs, they should consider their values and life-style. Many people who enjoy nature may simply choose to walk several miles a day. Others may prefer to join a swim club or play basketball. It is more important to do some sort of regular exercise than to spend lots of money on club memberships and fancy equipment. The biggest commitment you need to make is to take the time to protect your health through a program of regular physical activity.

Summing Up   *Consumers almost always benefit from a program of regular exercise. They should avoid irregular exercise or putting excessive strain on their bodies. Consumers should never use steroids as a method of increasing their strength or weight.* ◆

Review and Enrichment Activities

VOCABULARY REVIEW

1. Column A contains key consumer terms from this chapter. Column B contains a scrambled list of phrases that describe what these terms mean. Match the correct meaning with each term. Write your answers on a separate sheet of paper.

Column A	Column B
1. Cholesterol	**a.** Taking in and using foods to replace and repair body tissues
2. Weight loss program	**b.** The chemical reaction through which food is broken down to create energy in the body
3. Nutrition	
4. Basic food group	**c.** A drug that promotes growth of muscle tissue but that has many harmful side effects
5. Diet supplement	**d.** A threadlike substance found in many foods that is generally thought to be beneficial to health
6. Anabolic steroid	
7. Metabolism	**e.** General classifications of foods that are necessary for a balanced diet
8. Fiber	**f.** A fatty acid thought to contribute to circulatory diseases
	g. A manufactured compound that may be added to a diet to provide more balanced nutrition
	h. An organization that consumers pay for help in losing weight

2. Explain the difference between saturated and unsaturated fats.

Review and Enrichment Activities Continued

CHECKING WHAT YOU'VE LEARNED

Write your answers for the following exercises on a separate sheet of paper.

1. Explain why being in the recommended weight range for your height and age does not guarantee that you are healthy.
2. Describe each of the four types of dieters identified in this chapter.
3. Describe several possible dangers of rapid weight loss.
4. What are several possible benefits of belonging to a weight loss program?
5. Explain one reason for the difficulty many consumers experience in placing foods in their appropriate food groups.
6. Why are meals prepared at home from basic foods often more nutritious than meals made from packaged food products?
7. Why are balanced diets often less expensive than diets that provide only poor nutrition?
8. Identify several benefits that are commonly associated with regular exercise.
9. How much did American consumers spend joining various athletic clubs in 1990?
10. What is the difference between a program of regular exercise and bodybuilding?
11. Identify several dangers of using anabolic steroids.

PRACTICING YOUR CONSUMER SKILLS

Write your answers for the following exercises on a separate sheet of paper.

1. Each of the following people has attempted to lose weight with varying degrees of success. Evaluate each person's plan, and explain why the person was or was not successful.
   a. Last year Phyllis thought that she was a few pounds overweight. She decided to stop drinking a can of soda with her lunch and when she got home from school each day. Over ten weeks she lost 8 pounds and has managed to keep this weight off for more than eight months.
   b. Ward decided that his social life would be better if he weighed about 50 pounds less. His solution was to simply give up eating lunch. He ate his normal breakfast of coffee with toaster waffles and syrup and nothing else until he got home from work. By then he was so hungry that he often ate an entire pizza by himself. After a month of this diet, Ward had gained 8 pounds.

c. Melody read about a swordfish diet in a magazine that she picked up at the checkout stand at her grocery store. The article said that by eating swordfish instead of red meat every other day, she would be able to lose up to 3 pounds in a week. Melody ate her fish on schedule. She fixed it with cream sauce, in butter and mushrooms, with garlic and oil, and in many other ways, but she never lost an ounce.

d. Louise thought that she was fat. To lose weight, she ate whatever she wanted one day and then nothing but lettuce and dry toast for the next three days. In her first week she lost 8 pounds. She was so pleased with her results that she let herself cheat a little in the second week. She rewarded herself with a "little ice cream" on days when she wasn't supposed to eat much. She kept up her diet for six months but only ended up weighing 10 pounds less than when she started. She eventually gave up and decided that she just "couldn't lose weight."

e. Pedro, an overweight banker, asked his doctor how he could lose weight. She told him to eat fewer foods that were high in fat and to exercise regularly. By changing the foods he ate, he reduced the number of calories he consumed each day by about 400. He also began to walk 2 miles to work each morning instead of taking the bus. He lost a few pounds each week and eventually weighed 30 pounds less than when he began his diet.

2. Study the following ingredients for different food products, and identify which food groups they belong in. Can you identify what the food products are? What other factors should you consider in choosing each product to be a part of your diet?

Food Groups

1. Enriched or whole grain bread, flour, cereal, and potatoes
2. Meat, poultry, fish, eggs, and legumes
3. Fruits and vegetables
4. Milk, cheese, and ice cream

a. Dried potatoes, vegetable oil, white corn flour, potato starch, salt, sugar, potassium chloride, citric acid, spices

b. Tomato paste, distilled vinegar, corn syrup, salt, onion powder, spice, natural flavoring

c. Beef stock, enriched egg noodles, cooked beef, tomatoes, vegetable oil, water, salt, potato starch, monosodium glutamate, dehydrated onions, caramel color, natural flavorings

d. Wheat bran, raisins, sugar, corn syrup, malt flavoring, salt

3. Evaluate each exercise program in terms of its probable harm or benefit to the consumer described.

a. Paul is a forty-six-year-old teacher. He believes that yard work is a good form of exercise. He plants flowers in the spring, cuts the grass in the summer, rakes leaves in the fall, and shovels snow in the winter.

b. Nancy walks for exercise. When the weather is nice, she walks in a park near her home. If it is too hot or if it is raining, she walks in an indoor mall. In either location she walks about 2 miles five days a week.

Review and Enrichment Activities Continued

c. Jerry play center for his high school football team. He weighs about 210 pounds and would like to work his way up to around 250. During the football season he works out every day. For the rest of the year he doesn't do too much, but he keeps on eating.

d. Sharon swims for exercise. She is on her school's swim team and has joined the YWCA so that she can swim in the off-season. She does 150 laps or more at least three days a week.

e. Randy is into "pumping iron." He works out in his garage 2 to 3 hours almost every day on weights that he bought from a friend. He has a 48-inch chest and is working up to a goal of being able to lift 400 pounds.

USING NUMBERS

Solve the following problem to help make the best possible choice. Write your solution on a separate sheet of paper. Be sure to show all your work.

Brad would like to lose about 10 pounds. He has decided to reduce his consumption of calories by changing the type of food he eats. In the past he always had the same breakfast every morning. He had an 8-ounce glass of whole milk, two eggs fried in half a tablespoon of butter, two strips of bacon, two pieces of toast with a tablespoon of butter and two tablespoons of jelly, and a 4-ounce glass of orange juice.

With his new diet his breakfast is a 2-ounce bowl of cornflakes with a teaspoon of sugar, half a cup of fresh strawberries, and 4 ounces of skim milk and a cup of black coffee. (*Note*: 3 teaspoons = 1 tablespoon.) Use the information in the following table to determine roughly how many calories his old breakfast and new breakfast contain. Do you believe that Brad is making a wise choice? Explain the reasons for your answer.

Type of Food	Quantity	Number of Calories
Whole milk	1 8-ounce cup	160
Skim milk	1 8-ounce cup	90
Butter	1 tablespoon	100
Eggs	1 large	80
Bacon	2 strips fried crisp	100
Orange juice	4 ounces	55
Strawberries	1 cup	55
White bread	1 slice	60
Cornflakes	1 ounce	110
Sugar	1 tablespoon	45
Jelly	1 tablespoon	55
Coffee	1 cup	0

PUTTING IDEAS IN YOUR OWN WORDS

The following quotations are from this chapter. Explain these quotations in your own words to make sure you understand what they mean. Write your answers on a separate sheet of paper.

1. "The proper weight for someone within a range depends on the person's sex, the size of the person's bones, and the physical condition that the person is in."
2. "One fact that medical researchers agree on is that repeatedly losing weight and gaining it back is bad for a person's health."
3. "There is such a thing as too much exercise."

BUILDING CONSUMER KNOWLEDGE

Write your answers for the following exercises on a separate sheet of paper.

1. Ask two adults whether they feel that they should lose weight. Then ask them to determine if they fit within the recommended weight ranges in the table prepared by the National Academy of Sciences. Does the table provide the same answer, or do some people think that they should lose weight when they are already in the recommended ranges? Ask these people how much weight they would like to lose and how they would expect to benefit from the weight loss. Is their goal one of health or appearance? Be prepared to report your findings to the class.
2. Make a list of the foods you eat on a typical day. Evaluate these foods in terms of how well they represent each of the four food groups and in relation to their fat content. Do you believe that you eat a healthy diet?
3. Make a list of ten people you know. Your list should include both men and women and people of different ages. State whether each person on your list exercises regularly and seems to be healthy. Try to determine whether there is any apparent relationship between exercise and health among these people. Be prepared to discuss your findings with the class.

Chapter 39

Computers, Technology, and Today's Consumers

Chapter Objectives

After completing this chapter, you will be able to do the following:

- Describe technological changes that have recently affected the lives of American consumers.
- Describe the capabilities of personal computers that can help consumers keep track of information and make better decisions.
- Describe various components of computer systems.
- Identify organizations that collect, use, or distribute information about consumers.
- Explain the rights that consumers have to protect their privacy.
- Explain why consumers need to stay aware of technological advancements that may change their lives in future years.

Key Consumer Terms

In this chapter you will learn the meanings of the following important consumer terms:

- Facsimile
- Personal computer (PC)
- Software
- User-friendly
- Computer file
- Word processing program
- Spreadsheet
- Data base
- Graphics program
- Random access memory (RAM)
- Byte
- Megabyte
- Monitor
- Dot matrix printer
- Laser printer
- Mouse
- Modem
- Mainframe computer
- Computer terminal
- Interactive computer program

I magine how your grandparents must have lived when they were your age. They would have known about electric lights and radios, and they might have had a refrigerator. But most of the appliances and electronic devices that you take for granted would have been a mystery to them. Perhaps computers and all the tasks that they can do would have been most amazing of all.

SECTION 1

HOW COMPUTERS HELP YOU

While you read, ask yourself . . .
- *How have you and your friends made use of personal computers?*
- *What advantages do people who understand personal computers have over other people?*

Computers and electronic devices that use computers are invading our everyday lives. Businesses use computers to keep track of their inventory, to maintain accounts, to send bills, and to pay the wages of their employees. Banks, businesses, and the government transfer funds electronically across thousands of miles in mere seconds. When you use a credit card, your purchase is often reported, approved, and recorded electronically. You can now cash checks, pay bills, and make deposits at thousands of grocery stores by using automated teller machines that are electronically connected to your bank's computer system. Computers help organizations keep files on people from the day they are born until they die. Your name and all sorts of information about you probably appear in the records of hundreds of businesses and organizations.

You are able to "go shopping" by simply turning on your television and phoning in your order to several home-shopping television services. When you're in your car, a cellular phone may be as near as your dashboard.

If you have documents that must be in Arizona, you can use a **facsimile** and "fax" them there in just minutes. When you answer your phone, you may find yourself listening to a computer trying to sell you something. We have compact disk players that fit in our hands and satellite dishes that allow us to receive hundreds of television channels. Our phones are answered automatically while machines clean our swimming pools.

The age of technology is here. There is little we can do to change progress. Consumers need to learn how to live with machines and make use of the opportunities they offer. They also need to learn how to protect themselves from machines when they need to.

Personal Computers

When **personal computers (PCs)** were first introduced in the 1970s, a machine with limited ability and small memory typically cost several thousand dollars. At that time personal computers were quite rare, however they have become very common. (See Table 39-1.) Many

Vocabulary Builder

Facsimile   A reproduction of a document; often sent to another location by a device that uses the telephone lines.
Personal computer   A computer originally designed for individual use in a home or small business.

Personal Computers in the United States, 1981–1988	
Year	Number Used (in millions)
1981	2.1
1982	5.5
1983	12.2
1984	19.2
1985	25.3
1986	31.2
1987	37.8
1988	45.1

Source: Statistical Abstract of the United States, 1990, p. 756.

◆ **Table 39-1** Personal Computers, 1981–1988

of the computer programs, or **software** packages, consumers could buy were not **user-friendly**. If you didn't follow directions exactly, the computer would refuse to operate or flash a message like "Fatal Error" and crash the program you were working on. Those days are gone. PCs are now much less expensive, able to carry out complicated functions quickly, and easy for people to learn to use. Many consumers use computers on a regular basis.

An important advantage of computers is their ability to help people complete tasks in minutes that would otherwise take hours or days to finish by hand. For example, you can buy computer programs that will keep your tax records and complete your tax returns. If you discover one additional charitable contribution to deduct at the last minute, the computer will completely refigure your tax return in seconds. Doing the same task by hand on paper could take hours.

Because of computers, consumers can organize information more efficiently and even perform jobs that they otherwise would not have been able to do. For example, people who

never would have dreamed of writing a book twenty years ago have become successful authors because of computers. They are able to move sentences, change ideas, and check their spelling without having to lift a pencil. Greater speed and accuracy in writing is only one of the advantages offered to consumers in the computer age.

Automated Checkbooks

Many consumers used to find keeping a record of their checking transactions bothersome and time-consuming. There are now hand-held computerized devices that look like calculators and that keep track of checking transactions. Also, many computer programs will maintain a record of checking transactions in a **computer file.** Some even allow consumers to designate which checks are tax deductible. Other programs will sort checks according to whom they were written to or when they were written. All of this information is helpful for people who are keeping budgets or preparing tax returns.

Although a computer can make the job of keeping a checkbook easier, it cannot do all the work for a consumer. The correct amount of each check and deposit must be entered in the computer file. The program will complete computations correctly only if the correct amounts are provided by the user. If you write a check for $51.32 and enter $15.32 in your computer, you will end up with a balance that is wrong.

Basic Computer Applications

Although computers may be used in many ways, there are four types of applications that are most frequently used by consumers. These are word processing programs, spreadsheets, data base files, and graphics.

◆   Computers are an every-day fact of life in almost every office. Do you believe you could qualify for most secretarial, accounting, or management positions without having a basic knowledge of computers and how to use them?

A **word processing program** allows users to edit and rearrange the order of sentences and paragraphs without having to copy words over. Margins, spacing, underlining, and different typefaces may be specified in written documents simply by typing commands into the computer file. When you are finished with your work, hundreds of pages of written material may be sent through the mail on one 3½-inch disk. Word processing programs are used by many students to prepare reports for school. Some teachers even require it.

A **spreadsheet** is similar to a computerized checkbook, except that it keeps track of many different accounts and allows users to interrelate these accounts. When you change one amount in one account, the program automatically changes all other related accounts and totals in the program. Suppose that you have

Vocabulary Builder

Computer file   A quantity of information stored together under a specific heading on a computer disk that may be accessed with a particular software program.

Software   Programs that tell computers what tasks to carry out.

Spreadsheet   A type of software that interrelates accounts and allows a user to make adjustments in all accounts by changing an entry in one account.

User-friendly   Describing software that is easy to learn and that often provides extensive help and instructions to the user.

Word processing program   A software program that allows a user to move words, sentences, or paragraphs without retyping what has been written.

Consumer News

Buying a Computerized Encyclopedia

You may now carry a complete encyclopedia in your shirt pocket. A twenty-one volume *Grolier's Academic American Encyclopedia* has been offered for sale on a single compact disk. This is no ordinary computer disk. It is a special CD-ROM (compact disk read only memory). Ordinary disk drives cannot read them. If you want to use CD-ROM disks, you must buy a special player that cost roughly $1,000 in 1990. Some new PC systems now come with these players as standard equipment, but they cost over $3,000. This price will probably come down over the next few years. One of these disks can hold high-resolution copies of over 3,000 famous paintings or the entire works of William Shakespeare. Someday your library may fit in a space the size of a shoe box.

placed your family's budget in a spreadsheet. You have created an account for housing repair expenses and related it to another account for total housing expenses. If you entered a payment of $149 for a new storm door in your repair account, your total housing expense account would automatically increase by the same $149. Spreadsheets allow consumers to make changes in their accounts without having to copy and adjust other related accounts by hand.

A **data base** file contains information that will be used in some other application. Sup-

pose that you want to send a holiday greeting to fifty of your friends and relatives. If their names and addresses have been placed on your data base, you can write the letter one time in a word processing program and command the computer to print an individualized, addressed copy for each person you want to send the letter to. A data base may also contain numerical information that can be used in a spreadsheet application.

Graphics programs allow computer users to print illustrations or pictures already provided in the program or to create new graphs and diagrams of their own. Many spreadsheet applications have graphics programs included in them. With such a program, users may generate graphs of numerical relationships in the spreadsheet. For example, you could create a bar graph that shows how you spent your income last year from data you gathered in your spreadsheets. Graphs that once took hours to draw can now be completed in minutes through the use of graphics programs.

In recent years many software packages that include all of these capabilities have been placed on the market. One popular package in 1990 was called Windows and was produced by Microsoft Corp. Alternative packages with similar capabilities were available for Apples and other types of computers.

When consumers use computer programs, it is important to have a backup file and to regularly print out a hard copy. Computer disks can be lost or damaged. There are few things that are more discouraging or time-consuming to replace than a lost computer file.

Choosing the Right Computer

There are many types of computers you may buy. To choose the right computer, you need to ask yourself how much you can afford to spend and what you will use the computer for.

It is also important to consider your future needs. If you spend a little more now to buy a computer that has more capacity than you currently need, you may avoid having to buy a new computer in the future.

There are many features that consumers should look for when they buy a computer. The amount of memory (**random access memory**, or **RAM**) is one of the most important considerations. A computer uses its RAM when it completes computations or manipulates words and letters. The more RAM a computer has, the more complex operations it will be able to carry out. When home computers were first introduced, many had as little as 16,000 **bytes** of RAM. By 1990 most PCs offered 512,000 bytes or more. Many popular programs require several hundred thousand bytes of memory just to run.

There are many ways to store data entered in computer files. There are 5¼-inch floppy disks, 3½-inch disks, and hard disks that can hold 100 **megabytes** or more of data. By the time you read this text, there are likely to be new types of memory devices that can hold even more information. You should investigate the products that are available by consulting recent issues of *Consumer Reports* or computer magazines.

You will need to purchase a **monitor** for your computer. There are monochrome (one-color) or color monitors available. They may be large or small and have high or low resolution (clear or fuzzy). The better the monitor you buy, the more it will cost. Consumers must decide which trade-off between expense and quality of picture is best for their needs and financial situation.

You will need a printer for most computer applications. Printers can be quite cheap or quite expensive. You could pay as little as $200 for a simple **dot matrix printer** or more than several thousand dollars for a **laser printer**. The quality and speed of the copies you want and the amount of money you can afford to

spend will help you determine which printer is best for your needs.

Another device that you may need for your computer is a **mouse**—a device that lets you move an indicator around the screen to give commands without typing. You could also buy a **modem** which allows computers to exchange information over telephone lines. There are various other devices that can transfer pictures or drawings into computer memory or generate music.

By the time you read this text, there will be many new uses for computers that can make your life easier and more interesting—for a price. How you use computers in your home

Vocabulary Builder

Byte   A unit of memory in a computer system.

Data base   A file of information that can be integrated with work done in another computer application.

Dot matrix printer   A relatively inexpensive type of printer that makes impressions on paper by hitting a ribbon with multiple pins.

Graphics program   A software program that allows users to generate graphs, pictures, and other images on their computer.

Laser printer   A type of printer that forms letters by projecting a laser beam on paper that is sensitive to light; tends to be relatively expensive but produces a high-quality product.

Megabyte   One million bytes of memory in a computer system.

Modem   A device that allows two computers to communicate information over telephone lines.

Monitor   The device upon which images are displayed in a computer system.

Mouse   A device that allows a user to give commands to a computer without typing them on a keyboard.

Random access memory (RAM)   The part of a computer that performs basic computations and other functions as directed by a software program.

Consumer News

Filing Your Taxes with a Computer

Filing your tax return to receive a refund used to be a 'slow process. You could wait for as long as eight weeks from the time you sent in your forms until you received your refund. However, for those who file electronically, the time is cut to as little as two weeks. In 1990 there were roughly 18,000 tax preparers whose computers were electronically tied into the IRS's **mainframe computer**. By paying a fee of between $25 and $75, taxpayers could have their taxes filed in seconds instead of the weeks it takes paper forms to be entered into the system by IRS employees.

This system could even save some taxpayers money if their refund was substantial. Suppose that your refund was $10,000 and you invested the money at 6 percent. The interest you would earn for the extra six weeks would be about $70. This is not a great deal of money, but most people would rather have it in their own pocket than in the government's.

is your decision. In the workplace and in other parts of your life, you may be required to use computers whether you want to or not.

Summing Up *Consumers are now able to purchase personal computers that can help them write, keep their budgets, store information, and create graphs and tables. In choosing the best personal computer, consumers should weigh the cost of features against their current and future needs.* ◆

SECTION 2

ARE WE WITNESSING THE END OF PRIVACY?

While you read, ask yourself . . .
- ◆ *Have you or a friend ever been accused of doing something you did not do because you were mistaken for someone else? If so, how did you feel?*
- ◆ *Why is it a good idea to try to develop a good academic and attendance record while you are in school?*

When you walk into your local grocery store, do you notice the television cameras that peer at you from brackets mounted on the ceiling? Does it concern you that your picture is taken every time you go to your bank? Are you offended by the flood of "junk mail" you receive offering you everything from birdseed to silk pajamas? How do you feel about marketing organizations keeping track of the number of children you have or if you watch football on Sunday afternoons in the fall? Almost everything we do has become a matter of public knowledge. This loss of privacy has been made possible by technological advancements.

Who's Keeping a File on You?

Many organizations gather data and maintain computer files on Americans. We clearly benefit from some of these efforts. In other cases it appears that we suffer from an invasion of privacy. We may have even greater problems when incorrect information about us is circulated. The following list describes some of the ways that your life has become a matter of public knowledge:

- The Census Bureau keeps confidential files on individuals. Employees of the bureau must take an oath every year that they will not give out any information that they find

◆   How have computers helped to stuff your mailbox with junk mail that you may never look at? Do you think junk mail is an invasion of your privacy or a form of free speech guaranteed by the Constitution?

about any individual. Although the Census Bureau maintains files on many individuals, it shares this information with no other organizations. The data are maintained for the sole purpose of determining population trends in this country.

• The Social Security Administration gathers information about Americans so that it can provide benefits that citizens are entitled to. This information is shared with other federal organizations and with some private ones as well. The greatest danger to consumers from this practice is the possibility of incorrect earnings data being circulated. Individual Americans have the right to see their Social Security records

and may obtain this information by completing form SSA 7004 at any Social Security office.

• The Internal Revenue Service maintains files on more than 100 million individual taxpayers in the United States. By law these records must be kept confidential with sev-

Vocabulary Builder

Mainframe computer A central computer, or processing unit, that may be accessed and used at the same time from many different computer terminals.

eral exceptions. The Federal Bureau of Investigation and other law enforcement organizations may receive access to this information to investigate the possibility of criminal activity.

- State agencies keep information about citizens that is often open to the public. State agencies even sell the names and information about people to marketing organizations. Auto insurance companies have direct access to individual driving records. If your insurance company refuses you insurance or raises your rates, you have the right to demand to see the file it keeps on you. This will tell you whether the firm received incorrect information from a state agency about your driving record. Your right to correct such information will vary from state to state. If you believe that incorrect information about you is included in state agency files, you may contact your state's public information or assistance office for advice.

- Marketing mailing lists are kept by many firms that sell your name and information about you and your family to businesses and charities. These lists are notorious for including inaccurate information. Information that is gathered is passed back and forth so often that it seems amazing to many people that they include any correct data at all. As a result, you may be a twenty-three-year-old female and receive advertisements for hair coloring for men who are turning gray. If "junk" mail or phone calls offend you, you may send your name and address to the Direct Marketing Association, Mail Preference Service, P. O. Box 3861, Grand Central Station, New York, NY 10163, or to the Telephone Preference Service, Six E. 43rd Street, New York, NY 10017, and ask that you no longer be contacted by their members. This may reduce the number of letters and calls you receive, but it won't stop them entirely.

- Health care providers, such as doctors and hospitals, keep and share records on individuals' medical histories. They are also likely to keep records of insurance coverage and payments for treatment. In the past, health care providers have resisted sharing this information with patients for fear that they might misunderstand the information in these files. However, in recent years a number of states have passed laws that require medical files to be opened to individuals. The federal Privacy Act guarantees the right of patients to be given access to their records at Public Health Service facilities such as veterans hospitals.

- Employers keep personnel files on employees that contain information gathered from their experience with the worker and from other sources, such as credit bureaus. This information is sometimes passed from one employer to another when people move from job to job. Although some states and the federal government require that their employees be given access to these files, many workers in the United States have no idea what is in their employee files. If workers believe that incorrect or unfair information is included in their files and has been passed on to other parties, they may sue but their chances of winning are slim. Courts have generally upheld the right of employers to gather and pass on such information.

- Credit bureaus keep the most extensive and potentially damaging records about consumers. These files include information about a consumer's employment, marital status, bankruptcies, tax judgments, arrests, and convictions. Although consumers are supposed to have free access to their files if they are denied credit, it is not clear that this always happens. What's more, because credit bureaus continually share information, incorrect information may be removed by one bureau only to reappear several months later when it is sent out from a different source. In the early 1990s many states began to require greater control over credit bureaus.

Protecting Your Right to Privacy

The Supreme Court has recognized a constitutional right to privacy. The federal government and thirteen states have passed laws that protect people's privacy and guarantee them access to information concerning them that appear in government files. For example, in many states adult students or parents must be shown school records. Access to federal tax records is restricted and there are limits on the types of information banks may gather. States also have a wide variety of laws that guarantee citizens access to their files. Unfortunately, there are some states and businesses that do not allow people access to their files. As a result, incorrect or misleading information about people may be repeatedly circulated. Thus, our rights to privacy under the law are not entirely clear.

The Privacy Act permits lawsuits by anyone who believes that they have been "adversely affected" by inaccurate records. If you think that you have been libeled or slandered, wrongfully fired from a job, bothered without a reason or in other ways harmed by false information, you have the right to sue for damages. This, of course, does not guarantee that you will win.

Summing Up   *There are many organizations that maintain computerized files of personal and financial information about consumers. Although consumers often benefit from the availability of such information, they suffer a loss of privacy and may be harmed by the circulation of incorrect information. Consumers should try to be aware of information that concerns them that is kept in these files.* ◆

Consumer News

TRW Sued Over Credit-Reporting Practices

In July 1991, Texas, California, Alabama, Idaho, Michigan, and New York filed suit against TRW, one of the three largest credit-reporting services in the United States, charging "fraudulent and illegal practices." A Texas assistant attorney general, Stephen Gardner, described one of over 700 complaints filed against TRW in his state in the preceding two years. He said that TRW repeatedly provided incorrect information about a surgeon, making it impossible for him to obtain a mortgage. According to Gardner, TRW told the doctor that it was his responsibility to get each firm that had filed incorrect information about him to correct their report.

TRW and other credit-reporting services contend that for the number of reports they provide, they have relatively few complaints. They also state that the mistakes are most often not theirs, but the result of businesses providing them with incorrect information. Attorneys for the states suing TRW claimed that TRW simply accepts whatever information it receives as the truth and does not ask for any supporting evidence. The states also believe that TRW has inadequate methods of preventing incorrect information from being refiled in consumer records.

Regardless of the result of this and other suits against credit-reporting services, it is probably worth your money to pay to see your credit record every few years. It is better to try to correct a problem early than to let it get out of hand.

HOW TECHNOLOGY IS CHANGING YOUR LIFE

While you read, ask yourself . . .
- ◆ *How would your life be different if you were growing up in the 1950s?*
- ◆ *What new type of technology has resulted in a product that you would like to own?*

In 1990 the chances were 4 to 1 that your family owned a VCR. There was more than a 50 percent probability that you had a microwave oven in your kitchen. About one-quarter of American families had a video camera, and there was at least one PC in more than 20 percent of our homes. People who study trends believe that the 1990s may be the decade of the facsimile machine, when most American families will buy a machine for their home that can send letters and documents across the country the way they made telephone calls in the 1980s. This may or may not be true, but one thing is for sure: Technological advancements will continue to change our lives and the types of decisions we will need to make.

Technology Thirty Years Ago and Today

Thirty years ago, when your parents may have been in high school, their lives were very different from yours. Although they probably had a television in their home, it did not have a remote control, and they certainly did not have a VCR. There was no cable television, and most sets could only receive four or five commercial channels. Microwave ovens had been invented but were far too expensive for most families to own. Home computers and video games were unheard of. If your parents were lucky, their family had a mechanical adding machine to help them keep their budget. The family car probably weighed about 2 tons and often got no more than 15 miles to the gallon. Of course, the speed limits were much higher, and many cars could easily hit 120 miles per hour or more.

In school, your parents never asked whether they could use calculators to solve math problems because there were no calculators to use. They learned how to type on manual machines. Students who wanted to study computers took classes where they learned how to punch holes in paper cards. Electronics classes were likely to teach students how to fix a toaster. Technology in education meant wearing a headphone to listen to recordings in a foreign language class. The most sophisticated audio-visual equipment was probably a movie or film-strip projector. Think how life has changed in just a few years.

To be successful in school today, it is almost necessary to learn how to use a computer. In English classes you may be required to write reports using a word processing program. In business classes you learn how to use spreadsheets. Many art classes require you to use computer graphics. The chances are good that you will be required to learn basic concepts of computer programming. Many science labs have computers that both teach and test students. Some libraries have already eliminated their card catalogs and replaced them with **computer terminals**. These terminals provide access to a mainframe computer that contains in its memory a listing of all the books in the library. Students often see videotaped lessons in class and may even watch televised lectures or demonstrations that are broadcast from other locations.

At home your life has changed too. More parents work today than in the past. Therefore, the chances are good that you are expected to do more tasks for yourself. You may have to

Consumers in Action

What to Look for in a Fax

Throughout history there have been many ways for people to communicate over distances. Native Americans used smoke signals, Africans used drums, sailors used flags or lights, and spies in the eighteenth century used carrier pigeons. None of these methods offer the speed and ease of today's facsimile machines.

Some people have said that watching a fax curl out of a machine is sort of like tasting ice cream for the first time. Until you've experienced it, you really can't know what it's like. Most new technologies take many years to be accepted. The ballpoint pen was patented in 1888 but was not widely used until after World War II. On the other hand, the facsimile machine became a standard feature in most offices in less than five years. It is now rapidly moving into our homes as well.

Facsimile machines offer many possibilities to consumers. The fax can almost replace the mails. In England there are eight times as many fax machines per 1,000 people than in the United States. In 1988 the postal workers in England went on strike and most people hardly noticed. Some universities are accepting records that are faxed from other schools as "official." A few colleges allow students to fax their homework or reports to their instructor's office. Courts in some states have begun to accept faxed documents as evidence. The list of possible uses seems endless.

If you decide to buy a facsimile machine, there are a number of features you should consider:

- An automatic document feed and paper cutter so that you don't have to be present while the machine works
- A copier that will make multiple copies of faxes as they are received
- Delayed transmission that sends faxes at night when telephone rates are lower
- A memory to store incoming faxes and a password so that unauthorized people cannot see them
- An activity feature that prints the time and date of any transmission
- A voice request that tells a person when a fax transmission is completed and allows a voice conversation on the phone line

Special features like these add to the cost of facsimile machines but also increase their usefulness. If you ever buy a fax machine, there will probably be other new features to choose from. As in most consumer decisions, you will need to make a trade-off between the value of the features you want and the cost you will have to pay.

operate a dishwasher that must be programmed. Your microwave oven may look a little like the control panel of a spaceship. You may have a television with a remote control that also runs a VCR. Your coffee maker and

Vocabulary Builder

Computer terminal A keyboard and monitor that are attached to and provide access to a mainframe computer.

even your alarm clock may need to be set electronically. There isn't one thing mentioned here that your parents knew how to operate when they were your age. Yet you probably use these devices without even thinking about them.

When you look for a job, you will probably find that there are few openings for untrained workers. To advance beyond the position of clerk or dishwasher, you will need at least a high school diploma and probably some form of specialized training. You can't even repair a car anymore without knowing how to use computer equipment. Having a strong back and willing hands assures you of almost nothing. But if you know how to repair computers or VCRs, you should earn a good living.

What Will the Next Thirty Years Bring?

If your life is different from that of your parents, you can be sure that your children's lives will be just as different from yours. In July 1991, IBM announced that it had succeeded in manipulating single atoms of silicon. This may eventually lead to super computers no larger than a typewriter. The time when cash purchases are made may be rapidly coming to an end. We now use credit cards for major purchases. It is possible that the stores of the future will be "wired" into the banking system so that our accounts will be immediately charged when we buy something.

Every sign points to more automation and technology in our schools. **Interactive computer programs** already allow students to almost "discuss" problems with computers. With television satellite linkups, students will watch courts make decisions, Congress debate issues, and markets function. Entire libraries will be put on a small number of memory disks, reducing the vast size of our libraries and allowing different people to use the same resource at the same time.

Our automobiles will become more fuel efficient and probably more electronically controlled. There are already "on-board" computers in our cars that monitor many functions. It is possible that driving on major highways will become automated and controlled by computers. The list of technological innovations that will change our lives seems endless.

For the average consumer, technological advancements will require a constant learning process. To make responsible decisions, consumers need to understand the products that they purchase and use. Thirty years ago your parents would not have had a clue how to choose the best VCR. Thirty years from now you may need to choose the best pocket super computer. If you have not studied these products, you could end up purchasing the wrong product for your needs. Being a responsible consumer means committing yourself to a life of learning. If you don't understand the products you buy, you should not expect to make the best use of the money you spend.

Summing Up *Technological advancements have changed consumers' lives, forcing people to gain new types of knowledge. In the future, people will need to continually learn new skills so that they can make informed consumer decisions.* ◆

Vocabulary Builder

Interactive computer program A type of software that allows the user to ask the computer questions that it will answer.

Review and Enrichment Activities

VOCABULARY REVIEW

1. Column A contains key consumer terms from this chapter. Column B contains a scrambled list of phrases that describe what these terms mean. Match the correct meaning with each term. Write your answers on a separate sheet of paper.

Column A	Column B
1. Monitor	a. Any program that directs a computer to perform specific tasks
2. Modem	b. A device that allows computers to share information over telephone lines
3. Software	c. A program that keeps track of and interrelates various accounts
4. Data base	d. A unit of memory in a computer
5. Computer terminal	e. A record of information that may be used with other programs
6. Facsimile	f. The device upon which images are displayed in a computer system
7. Mouse	g. A quantity of information stored together under a specific heading in a computer's memory or on a disk
8. Byte	h. A device that allows a user to give commands to a computer without typing them on a keyboard
9. Computer file	i. A keyboard and monitor that are attached to and provides access to a mainframe computer
10. Spreadsheet	j. A reproduction of a document; often sent to another location by a device that uses telephone lines

Review and Enrichment Activities Continued

2. Explain the difference between a personal computer and a mainframe computer.

CHECKING WHAT YOU'VE LEARNED

Write your answers for the following exercises on a separate sheet of paper.

1. Describe three different electronic devices that have made your life different from the lives your parents led thirty years ago.
2. Identify each of the four basic computer applications listed in this chapter, and explain how you might be able to use each of these applications.
3. Explain what random access memory is.
4. Why is it often a good idea to buy a computer with more memory than you currently need?
5. Why don't computers always provide correct answers?
6. Identify several organizations that probably maintain files on you or other members of your family.
7. How have computers made it easier for organizations to keep files on consumers and invade their privacy?
8. What are your legal rights if you believe that your credit file includes incorrect information?
9. Explain why consumers will need to continue to learn about new types of technology in the coming years.

PRACTICING YOUR CONSUMER SKILLS

Write your answers for the following exercises on a separate sheet of paper.

1. Describe how new technology would allow consumers to accomplish each of the following tasks more easily than the methods described here, which were used in the 1960s.
    a. Around the first of every April, Harold would take out all his receipts and the other records he had saved from a shoe box and spend hours sorting them to prepare his income tax return.
    b. When Karen got home late, she would look in her refrigerator to find something to eat. She often ended up eating her food cold because she was too hungry to wait for it to warm in her oven.
    c. Although Rita always took movies of her children's birthday parties, she almost never looked at them because setting up her projector and screen was so much trouble.

    d. When Peter went to the bank to ask for a car loan, it took more than a week to have it approved because the bank had to send for information about his credit history.

    e. Carol often stayed up half the night typing copies of letters that she sent regularly to all of her relatives.

2. Describe new technology that has made each of the following events possible.

    a. About two months ago Janine placed a $23 order for a few flower bulbs from a mail-order catalog she borrowed from a friend. In the past three weeks she has received thirty-one catalogs from different gardening firms that want her to buy everything from "beneficial nematodes" to dwarf bonsai pine trees.

    b. Al wanted to borrow $2,000 to buy a new engine for his fishing boat. He applied for the loan last Monday morning. The loan was approved at about 2 P.M. the same afternoon.

    c. Kathy wrote a report for her English class that was eleven pages long. When she was almost done, she discovered that she had left out a paragraph that she wanted to include on page 2. She simply inserted the paragraph in the appropriate location and printed out her report.

    d. Linda went to a new doctor and received a prescription for a drug to help her arthritis. When she took the prescription to her druggist to have it filled, he told her that the drug would have a bad reaction if she took it with one prescribed for her by a different doctor about a year ago.

    e. After Todd left work, he remembered that his wife had asked him to buy something on his way home, but he couldn't remember what it was. Although he was driving on the freeway, he gave her a call to find out what he was supposed to buy.

3. How do you imagine each of the following problems may be solved through new forms of technology thirty years from now?

    a. When William was taken to the hospital after an accident, the doctors didn't know who he was and couldn't find his medical records.

    b. Jerry used to write mystery novels for a living, but has given this up since he became blind several years ago.

    c. Mr. Kramer would like to have all the students in his social studies classes witness a criminal trial, but there aren't enough seats in the courtroom for more than ten students to attend at any one time.

    d. The college's alumni organization tried to raise $5 million to enlarge the school's library, but only collected $1,700,000.

USING NUMBERS

Solve the following problem to help make the best possible choice. Write your solution on a separate sheet of paper. Be sure to show all your work.

Ted writes a newsletter about financial events that he sells for $100 each to firms who invest millions of dollars in the stock market. Ted's reports are

Review and Enrichment Activities Continued

usually six pages long. At the present he has 239 customers. It is very important to his customers that they receive Ted's information quickly. Ted is trying to decide the best way to send his information. Determine how much each of the following methods would cost. Then recommend the one that you believe would be best for Ted to use. Explain the reasons for your choice.

1. Send them first-class mail so that they would arrive in three days or less most of the time (29 cents per stamp in 1991).
2. Send them Express Mail to arrive the next day ($10 each in 1991).
3. Fax them to arrive the same day. It takes 20 seconds per page, and each phone call costs an average of $1.20 per minute. How long would it take him to fax his report to all his customers? What problem could this time create for him?

PUTTING IDEAS IN YOUR OWN WORDS

The following quotations are from this chapter. Explain these quotations in your own words to make sure you understand what they mean. Write your answers on a separate sheet of paper.

1. "When consumers use computer programs, it is important to have a backup file and to regularly print out a hard copy."
2. "Our rights to privacy under the law are not entirely clear."
3. "To advance beyond the position of clerk or dishwasher, you will need at least a high school diploma and probably some form of specialized training."

BUILDING CONSUMER KNOWLEDGE

Write your answers for the following exercises on a separate sheet of paper.

1. Make a list of the technical skills that you have that your parents probably did not have thirty years ago. Identify the one that you believe has made the biggest difference in your life, and explain your choice in a brief essay.
2. Choose a task that you are responsible for that you could use a computer to complete. Write a brief essay explaining how a computer could make your work easier and quicker than doing the task by hand. If you have access to a word processing program, use it to complete this task, and explain how it helped you finish your essay.
3. Write an essay or draw a picture of what you think your child's room could look like twenty years from now. Explain what the specific devices in the room are able to do. Use your imagination, but try to be reasonable at the same time.

Glossary

Ability to pay principle   A system of taxation in which people with larger incomes pay a higher rate of tax than those with lower incomes.

Absolute advantage   The ability of one country, using the same amount of resources, to produce a particular product at a lesser cost than another country.

Accounting   Measuring, interpreting, and communicating financial information for internal and external decision making.

Accounting process   Steps that firms take to maintain records that are used to prepare financial statements for evaluating the firm's performance and for planning for the future.

Acid rain   Acid compounds in the air that are formed from sulfur and nitrogen oxides and that fall to earth in rain; thought to be the result of burning fossil fuels like coal.

Add-on   An extra feature sold and added to a product by a dealer.

Adjustable rate mortgage (ARM)   A mortgage with an interest rate that may change over the term of the loan.

Adjusted gross income   A taxpayer's income after adjustments for factors such as business income, capital gains, or alimony paid, but before subtractions are made for exemptions or deductions.

Aid to Families with Dependent Children (AFDC)   Public assistance program that provides money to needy families with children.

Allocation of resources   The way that resources are distributed and used.

Allowance   A term used in completing federal tax form W–4; the more allowances a taxpayer claims, the less will be withheld from his or her earnings.

Anabolic steroids   A drug that causes people to gain body weight and muscle tissue rapidly.

Annual fee   A charge made by a bank once a year for the service of keeping an account open; often associated with credit card accounts.

Annual percentage rate   The cost of credit expressed as a yearly percentage. The Truth-in-Lending law requires lenders to provide this figure.

Annuity   A form of payment made by an insurance company that provides a monthly income for the remainder of a beneficiary's life.

Antitrust law   Legislation that prohibits attempts to monopolize or dominate a particular market.

Appraise   To determine the value of something that is to be insured.

Appreciation   An increase in the value of a currency under a flexible exchange rate.

Apprenticeship   A form of on-the-job training in which new employees must complete a period of instruction to become certified as having a skill.

Aptitude   A potential or natural ability that may be developed into a skill.

Aquifer   A geological structure that is a source of water.

Arbitration   When a third party is given the power to determine the resolution to a dispute.

Asset   Anything of monetary value that is owned by a consumer, business, or government.

Assigned risk   A driver who is unable to obtain insurance often because of a poor driving record and who is assigned by state authorities to be insured by an insurance company that does business in that state.

Attitude   One's basic outlook on life.

Audit   A review of a financial statement or tax return to check for accuracy and completeness.

Austerity   Spending the least amount possible to achieve an objective.

Automated teller machine (ATM)   A machine placed in convenient locations and used by consumers to complete many banking transactions.

Bait and switch   Advertising a product at a bargain price but then informing customers brought in by the offer that only a more expensive product is available; normally an illegal sales practice.

Balance   The amount of money presently in an account; to determine how much money is in an account.

Balance sheet   A financial statement that shows a firm's assets, liabilities, and net worth at a point in time.

Bankruptcy   An inability to pay debts based on an individual's or firm's wealth and income.

Barrier to trade   Obstacle to free trade, such as a tariff or quota.

Barter   Exchanges that take place without the benefit of money.

Basic food groups   Four categories of foods established by the federal government. When eaten together in appropriate amounts, these foods result in a balanced diet.

Beneficiary   The designated person or persons who will receive payment for any insurance policy.

Benefits-received principle   A system of taxation in which those who use a particular government service support it with taxes in proportion to the benefit they receive.

Better Business Bureau   A private agency supported by businesses and intended to improve customer relations and resolve disputes.

Bill consolidation loan   A new long-term loan that is used to pay off many shorter-term loans and to reduce the total amount of monthly payments a creditor must make.

Billing period   The time between one regularly scheduled billing for an account and the next.

Biodegradable   A quality of a product that allows it to break down into basic components over prolonged contact with the environment.

Blue book   The *Official Used Car Guide*, which lists the average market value of different types and years of used cars.

Bonus   A form of compensation usually given in a lump sum at a particular time of the year to reward workers for their effort.

Book value   The average value of a used car according to the *Official Used Car Guide*.

Boom   That portion of the business cycle in which economic activity is at its highest point.

Boycott   An activity in which the public is urged not to purchase a particular product to exert economic pressure on the producer of that product.

Brand-name advertising   Advertising that features a firm's name, picture, or logo to help consumers distinguish that firm's products from other similar products; intended to create consumer loyalty to the brand.

Budget   A plan for spending and saving income; a projection of income and spending over a period of time.

Bulk products   Products sold by weight, often unbranded.

Bureau of Land Management (BLM)   The federal agency that oversees and controls the cutting of trees in national forests.

Business cycle   The periodic ups and downs in the nation's economic activity.

Buying service   An organization that provides information to consumers that helps them complete transactions at lower prices.

Byte   A unit of memory in a computer system.

Capacity   The difference between a person's or firm's current income and the fixed costs that must be paid; one of the "four Cs of credit."

Capacity planning   The decisions made concerning the right amount of products or services to manufacture or offer for sale.

Capital   All property—machines, buildings, and tools—used to produce goods and services; in some situations, the money necessary to undertake a business venture. Value of a person's or business's assets; one of the "four Cs of credit."

Capital gain   An increase in the value of a security or other asset between the time it was purchased and when it is sold.

Capitalism   Another name for a free market economy.

Capital loss   A decrease in the value of a security or other asset between the time it was purchased and when it is sold.

Career   A sequence of work-related experiences over a person's lifetime.

Career consultation   A meeting with someone to obtain information about that person's career.

Care instructions   Instructions found on a lable attached to clothing that explains how the garment should be cared for.

Cash flow   The flow of money into and out of a person's, business's, or government's accounts.

Caveat emptor   Latin for "Let the buyer beware."

Caveat venditor   Latin for "Let the seller beware."

Cease-and-desist order   An administrative or judicial order commanding a business to stop conducting "unfair or deceptive acts or practices."

Certificate of deposit (CD)   A document stating an amount of money deposited in an account, and the interest rate to be paid over the term of the account.

Certified public accountant (CPA)   A person who has met state requirements and passed an examination to be approved by the state as a qualified accountant.

Chamber of Commerce   An organization whose purpose is to improve business conditions within a community.

Character   A person's demonstrated willingness to make payments on a debt on time; one of the "four Cs of credit."

Charge account An agreement that allows a customer to buy goods or services from a particular company and pay for them later.

Charter A state's written agreement giving a corporation the right to operate a business.

Check register The portion of a checkbook where one keeps a record of the checks written and remaining balance.

Chlorofluorocarbon Any of a group of chemicals used in many products that contribute to the depletion of the earth's ozone layer.

Cholesterol A fatty acid found in many food products. Some forms of this compound are thought to contribute to circulatory diseases.

Claimant The person who sues someone else in a court of law.

Classified want ads Advertisements in newspapers that seek qualified applicants for current job openings.

Clean air act The basic federal law that sets standards and limits for emissions of pollutants into the air.

Clear-cut To cut all trees in an area of forest, regardless of their size.

Closely held corporation A corporation in which most of the stock and control is held by a single family or small group of people.

Closing costs Fees charged by a lender for various costs involved with completing the sale of housing; may include fees for legal costs, taxes, and so on.

Collateral Assets used as security or backing for a loan; one of the "four Cs of credit."

Collection agency A business that attempts to secure payment of overdue debts for a fee.

Collision insurance Insurance that pays for car damage that is the result of an accident.

Command economy An economic system in which the government owns the factors of production and makes decisions about their use.

Commercial bank A bank that offers a wide range of banking services; its main functions are to accept deposits, lend money, and transfer funds.

Commission A payment based on a percentage of the total amount or value of a good or service sold by a salesperson.

Commodity money Money that has value as a commodity or a good, aside from its value as money.

Common stock A share of ownership in a corporation that entitles the owner to a portion of the firm's profits and a vote in choosing the board of directors and making certain other business decisions.

Comparative advertising A form of advertising that compares a firm's product to specific competing products.

Compensation The direct and indirect payments that employees receive for their labor or job performance.

Competition The rivalry among producers or sellers of similar goods to win more business by offering the lowest prices and best quality.

Competitive market A market characterized by firms that are in competition.

Compound interest Interest figured not only on the original funds deposited, but also on the interest those funds have earned.

Comprehensive insurance Insurance that pays for car damage that is not the result of an accident.

Computer file A quantity of information stored together under a specific heading on a computer disk that may be accessed with a particular software program.

Computer terminal A keyboard and monitor that are attached to and provide access to a mainframe computer.

Condominium A single unit of a larger building that is owned separately by the resident of that unit.

Conservation Taking steps to reduce the use of scarce resources.

Constant dollars Dollar amounts that have not been adjusted for inflation.

Consumer Any person or group that buys or uses goods or services to satisfy personal needs and wants.

Consumer Affairs Council (CAC) A group of representatives from cabinet-level department that guides federal agencies in responding to consumer issues.

Consumer Bill of Rights Seven consumer rights identified by the federal government in the 1960s and 1970s.

Consumer credit Money borrowed to finance the purchase of consumer goods and services.

Consumer Credit Protection Act A truth-in-lending law that requires lenders to inform borrowers of the annual rate of interest and the finance charge they will pay for their loan.

Consumer decision A choice made by a person concerning how to use resources or products.

Consumer economics The study of how people consume goods and services that are produced.

Consumer price index (CPI) A measure of changes in average prices over a period of time for specific group of goods and services used by the average household.

Consumer Product Safety Commission A federal agency that regulates all potentially hazardous consumer products.

Consumer recognition A feeling of knowing and trust amount consumers for a particular brand of product.

Consumer Reports A magazine published by Consumers Union that provides information to help consumers make rational decisions about products they buy.

Consumer sovereignty A situation in which consumers decide which products and styles will survive in the marketplace through their buying decisions.

Consumers' Research, Inc. An organization that publishes *Consumers' Research Magazine.*

Consumers Union A not-for-profit organization that publishes *Consumer Reports.*

Contingency offer An offer to buy property that depends on some other event, usually selling a house currently owned.

Contraction A portion of the business cycle in which economic activity is slowing down.

Controlling Evaluating and adjusting an organization's activities and performance to help it accomplish its objectives.

Convenience food Food products that are totally or partially prepared so that they are relatively easy and quick to serve.

Conventional mortgage A mortgage with a fixed interest rate.

Convertible bond A bond that may be exchanged for stock in the corporation that issued the bond.

Cooperative education program School program that allows students to earn school credits for learning that takes place while they work.

Corporate Bond A certificate issued by a corporation or government in exchange for borrowed money. A bond promises to pay a stated rate of interest over a stated period of time and to repay the original amount paid for the bond at the end of that time.

Corporation An organization owned by many people but treated by the law as though it were a person. It can own property, pay taxes, make contracts, sue or be sued, and so on.

Cosign To sign a loan contract along with a borrower and promise to repay the loan if the borrower does not.

Cost-management system A system in which insurers require prior approval for a medical treatment to be insured, except in emergency situations.

Cost of production Money spent producing or marketing a product.

Cost-push inflation An increase in prices that is the result of wage demands of labor, an increase in the costs of raw materials or tools, or the excessive desire for profits by owners.

Counteradvertising Advertising ordered by the Federal Trade Commission to correct earlier false claims made about a product.

Cover letter A brief letter written to a potential employer intended to convince the employer to read the enclosed resume.

Credit Allowing a person, business, or government to use money, goods, or services at the present in return for a promise of future payment.

Credit bureau An agency that collects and distributes information about people's credit histories.

Credit card A credit device that allows a person to make purchases without paying cash. The person is billed at the end of a billing period by the firm that issued the credit card.

Credit history A record of an individual's credit transactions and subsequent payments; often used as the basis for deciding a future extension of credit.

Credit limit A maximum amount of credit that will be extended to a specific individual or business under an agreement with a bank or other financial institution; often associated with credit cards.

Credit terminal An electronic device that allows stores to report a credit card purchase to the organization that issued the credit card and to receive approval for the purchase.

Credit union A depository institution owned and operated by its members to provide savings accounts and low-interest loans to its members.

Curie A measure of an amount of radioactivity.

Currency Cash, or paper money and coins, that may be used to buy goods and services.

Current dollars Dollar amounts that have not been adjusted for inflation.

Custom Buying products out of habit or because members of a consumer's social group purchase this type or brand of product.

Cyclical unemployment Unemployment that is the result of a downturn of the business cycle.

Data base A file of information that can be integrated with work done in another computer application.

DDT Dichlorodiphenyltrichloroithane, a powerful insecticide banned in the U.S. in 1972.

Death benefit   The amount an insurance company pays if an insured person dies while a policy is in effect.

Debit   To charge an amount to an account.

Debit card   A coded plastic card used to transfer money from a customer's account to a store's account.

Debt   Something of value that is owed to someone else.

Decentralized   Located or made in many places rather than in only one.

Deceptive advertising   Advertising that is intended to mislead consumers.

Deductible   The initial amount of money that an insured party must pay before the insurance company pays the remainder of a claim.

Deduction   Money subtracted from an employee's earnings for taxes, Social Security, and health insurance; withholding.

Default   Failure to pay a debt on time.

Defensive advertising   Advertising intended to rebut claims made by competing firms about a firm's product or business practices.

Deficit   The difference between income and spending in an accounting period (or in a specific period of time).

Delinquent   Describing a debt that is more than thirty days overdue.

Demand   The amount of goods and services that consumers are willing to pay for at various prices.

Demand deposit   Money deposited in a bank that can be withdrawn at any time; checking accounts are demand deposits.

Demand-pull inflation   An increase in prices that is the result of a total demand for goods and services that exceeds their supply.

Dependability   Ability to complete a task on time and in the appropriate manner.

Depreciation   A loss in value that occurs as a result of wear and age. A fall in the value of a nation's currency due to the forces of demand and supply.

Depression   A major slowdown of economic activity, during which millions are out of work, many businesses fail, and the economy operates far below its capacity.

Devaluation   Lowering the value of a nation's currency in relation to other currencies by government order.

Dictionary of Occupational Titles   Publication that provides a brief description of over 20,000 jobs.

Diet supplement   A manufactured compound that may be added to a person's diet to provide more balanced nourishment; for example, vitamin pills.

Differentiation   The process used by manufacturers to convince customers that their products are in some way superior to similar products offered by other firms.

Directing   Supervising and guiding workers to accomplish organizational goals.

Disclose   To provide relevant information.

Discount   To offer to sell something, possibly a bond, for less than its original purchase price.

Disposable personal income   The income that people have left to spend or save after all taxes have been paid.

Dissolved   Describing a business that is closed, its assets distributed to the owners.

Diversification   Branching out into other types of investments.

Dividend   Money paid by a corporation to its stockholders; usually a share of its profits.

Division   One of ten types of businesses that all firms are divided into in the government's Standard Industrial Classification; a subheading under the two sectors, goods and services producing firms.

Domestic   A good or service that is made within the country in which it is sold.

Dot matrix printer   A relatively inexpensive type of printer that makes impressions on paper by hitting a ribbon with multiple pins.

Double coincidence of wants   A situation in which two individuals each want exactly what the other has, allowing a direct exchange of goods or services without the use of money.

Double counting   Including the value of a product in national income accounting more than once.

Driving while intoxicated (DWI)   Driving a vehicle while under the influence of alcohol or drugs.

Earned income   Income that results from payment for one's labor.

Earnest money   Money put up to show that you are serious about an offer you make to buy a house.

Easy money   A policy designed to stimulate the economy by making credit inexpensive and easy to get.

Economic decision   Basic choices concerning what products should be produced, who should produce them, how they should be produced, and for whom they should be produced that must be made in all economic systems.

Economics   Study of how individual and nations make choices about ways to use their scarce resources to fill their needs and wants.

Economic system   A set of understandings that governs how resources are used to satisfy people's needs and wants.

Electronic Funds Transfer (EFT)   Financial transactions completed through the use of a computer.

Employment agency   An organization that matches people with jobs.

Endangered Species Act   A law that protects animals and plants designated as endangered species by the federal government.

Entrepreneur   A person who takes the risks necessary to operate a business.

Entrepreneurship   The ability and willingness to be resourceful and innovative and to take the risks associated with operating a business.

Environment   The sum of our surroundings that we live in.

Environmental Protection Agency (EPA)   The federal agency charged with monitoring and enforcing laws that concern the protection of our environment.

E-PERM Test   A test used to determine the amount of radon gas in the air.

Equal Credit Opportunity Act   A law that makes discrimination in credit based on sex or marital status illegal.

Equilibrium price   The price for a product at which the amount producers are willing to supply is equal to the amount consumers are willing to buy.

Equity   The value of an owner's investment in a business or house.

Escrow account   An account opened by a buyer before the completion of a home purchase to assure the institution that will provide the mortgage of his or her ability to make the necessary down payment.

Ethical behavior   Acting in accordance with one's moral convictions as to what is right and what is wrong.

Exchange rate   The value of a nation's currency in relation to that of any other nation or to a fixed standard, such as gold.

Exemption   An amount that may be subtracted from a person's income for each person supported to reduce his or her taxable income.

Expansion   A portion of the business cycle in which economic activity is increasing: also called recovery.

Expansion of money   Repeated cycles of deposits, loans, spending, and new deposits that provide a large part of the money used to buy goods and services in our economic system.

Export   A good or service sold to individuals or groups in another country.

Extended protection plan (EPP)   An agreement through which the buyer of a product pays a fee to have the product's warranty extended for a longer period of time.

External data   Information gathered from sources outside of an organization. Electronic funds transfer (EFT). The movement of money from one account to another through the use of an electronically transmitted signal; often carried out at an automatic teller machine (ATM).

External recruitment   Recruiting applicants for a job opening from among people who are not current employees of a firm.

Fabric content   The type of fiber that an article of clothing it is made from, indicated on an attached label.

Face value   The value printed on a bond. It may or may not be the price the bond was first sold for.

Facility location   Choosing the location for a business that is most likely to contribute to its profitability.

Facsimile   A reproduction of a document; often sent to another location by a device that uses the telephone lines.

Factors of production   Economic resources such as land, labor, capital, and entrepreneurship used to produce goods and services.

Fair Credit Billing Act   A law passed by the federal government that protects consumers' billing rights.

Fair Credit Reporting Act   A law passed in 1971 that gives individuals access to files that concern them held by credit bureaus.

Federal Deposit Insurance Corporation (FDIC)   A corporation created by the federal government in 1935 that insures deposits in banks. In 1991 the limit on this insurance was $100,000.

Federal Housing Administration (FHA)   A federal agency that helps people who would not qualify for a conventional mortgage to borrow money to buy a house.

Federal Reserve System   An agency created by the federal government to regulate banking in the United States and implement monetary policy.

Federal Trade Commission (FTC)   Most important federal consumer protection agency, created in 1914.

Feedback   A method of collecting and retaining information about an event or process. To help managers judge whether changes need to be made.

Fiat money   Money that has value because a government has established it as an acceptable means for the payment of debts.

Fiber Threadlike filaments found in many foods; thought to help the digestion of food and to reduce the risk of some diseases.

FICA Federal Insurance Contribution Act; payments support Social Security benefits.

Filing Status A condition based on family situation that helps indicate which tax form to use when filing a tax return; single, married filing joint, and so on.

Finance charge The cost of credit expressed in dollars and cents that must be paid over the life of a loan.

First mortgage The original mortgage used to buy a home or piece of property.

Fiscal policy The federal government's policies concerning spending and taxing that are intended to stabilize economic conditions.

Fixed exchange rate A system in which a government sets the value of its currency in relation to other types of currency so there is an official exchange rate between currencies that does not change for extended periods of time.

Fixed expense A cost that must be paid at specific times, regardless of other events.

Fixed interest rate An interest rate that remains the same over the full term of a loan.

Flat tax A tax that remains at a constant rate of taxable income.

Flexible exchange rate System of setting the values of currencies in terms of each other according to the demand and supply for each type of money.

Flexible expense A cost that varies, depending on other events.

Food and Drug Administration (FDA) Federal agency responsible for administering federal laws that regulate the quality of foods and drugs offered for sale.

Foreclosure To take title to a property because of nonpayment of a debt.

Formaldehyde A chemical found in many consumer products that has been associated with an increased incidence of cancer.

Fractional reserve system A method of banking in which banks must keep a fraction of money deposited on reserve; the remainder may be lent out or otherwise invested.

Franchise A business that buys the right to operate using an established name and method of production.

Fraud Providing incorrect information for the purpose of obtaining payments one does not deserve.

Free market A market in which individuals own the factors of production and decide the answers to the basic economic questions; also referred to as capitalism.

Free market economy An economic system characterized by individuals who own the factors of production and decide the answers to the basic economic questions.

Frictional unemployment A situation in which people are unemployed for a short time; people between jobs.

Fringe benefits Compensation other than salary or wages provided by employers to employees or their families.

Full-bodied money Money backed by a commodity that people believe has value, like gold.

Full warranty A promise by a supplier to provide for the repair or replacement of faulty merchandise within a reasonable period of time; meets minimum federal standards.

Gain sharing A form of compensation where employees are paid a share of a firm's increase in profit or reductions in cost.

Gender-based insurance rates Insurance premiums set according to the sex of the insured party.

Generic products The general name for a product that is not advertised or marketed under brand names by manufacturers.

Global Related to the world as a whole.

Global warming A gradual increase in the average temperature of the earth's atmosphere.

Goal Something to be accomplished in a certain period of time.

Goods Items of value that can be physically touched or measured.

Graduated-payment mortgage A mortgage for which the amount of monthly payments grows over the term of the loan.

Graphics program A software program that allows users to generate graphs, pictures, and other images on their computer.

Gross domestic product (GDP) The total dollar value of all final goods and services produced by a nation regardless of ownership during a given period, usually one year.

Gross income The total amount of an employee's earnings before any deductions are taken.

Ground water Water held in a geographical area's aquifer.

Group A sub-heading for one of the ten divisions in the government's Standard Industrial Classification.

Guide for Occupational Exploration A publication that organizes jobs into twelve interest groups that are further divided into sixty-four worker trait groups.

Headhunter A firm that specializes in locating employees for firms to hire, particularly managers.

Health maintenance organization (HMO) A type of insurance plan in which members receive medical services from participating doctors and medical facilities for a flat fee paid by them or their employer.

Hiring decision Decision as to who is the best-qualified applicant for a job opening.

Home equity line of credit An agreement between a consumer and a bank that guarantees the consumer a home equity loan up to some maximum amount on demand.

Home equity loan A loan secured by a person's equity in a home; second mortgage. The interest paid on this type of loan was generally tax deductible in 1991.

Homeowner's insurance Insurance that protects a dwelling and its owners against a wide range of possible losses, including property and liability losses.

Human resource management The process of acquiring, training, developing, motivating and using people properly to achieve an organization's objectives.

Imperfect competition A market situation in which firm's sell or customers buy products and are able to affect prices on their own.

Implied warranty of fitness An implied promise that a product is appropriate for the buyer's stated purpose.

Implied warranty of merchantability An implied promise by the seller that an item is in good condition and can be used for the purpose for which it was sold.

Import A good or service bought from another country.

Incentive A reason for doing something.

Income redistribution Taking income from some groups of people or businesses and paying it to members of other groups.

Income statement A financial statement that shows a firm's revenues, costs, and net income over a period of time.

Industry A group of businesses that operate in a similar fashion to provide the same type of goods or services.

Inflation A sustained increase in the prices of goods and services.

Informative advertising Advertising that provides information about a product.

Insolvent Describing a person or business that has current debts that exceed their ability to pay, resulting in a non payment of debts.

Insufficient funds Not enough money in a checking account to cover a check written against that account.

Insurable interest Ownership of something of value that is to be insured.

Insurable risk Insurer's understanding of the risk of insuring property or a condition.

Insurance An agreement in which people pay for protection against specific losses they might suffer.

Interactive computer program A type of software that allows the user to ask the computer questions that it will answer.

Interest Payment for the use of borrowed funds.

Interests The activities, objects, causes, or people that an individual finds personally rewarding or gratifying over extended periods of time.

Intermediary A go-between between the producer of a product and its consumer.

Internal data Information gathered from sources within an organization.

Internal recruitment Recruiting for a job opening from a firm's current employees.

Internal Revenue Service (IRS) The federal agency responsible for collecting income taxes.

Inventory control The process of keeping adequate supplies for production and sale while keeping down the cost of carrying inventory.

Invest To place savings in a situation that will result in an increase in their value.

Investigative reporting Actions taken by news media to investigate and report on various situations, including consumer issues.

Invisible hand Symbol of Adam Smith's theory of economic competition that states that individuals will serve the interest of society in general when they are allowed to work for their own self-interest.

Itemized deduction A listing of deductible expenses that may be subtracted from income to reduce taxable income; an alternative to a standard deduction.

Job   A group of tasks to be accomplished while at work.

Job evaluation   A method of determining job worth, often used to set levels of compensation.

Job referral   Giving a person's name to an employer as a possible candidate for a job opening.

Joint account   An account owned by two people, often husband and wife.

Labor   Work or effort performed by people to produce goods and services.

Labor force   All people who are sixteen or older who are able to work and who either hold a job or are looking for a job.

Laissez-faire   French term meaning "do not touch"; applies to Adam Smith's theory of economic competition.

Land   In economic terms, natural resources; all things found in nature.

Landlord   A person who rents property.

Laser printer   A type of printer that forms letters by projecting a laser beam on paper that is sensitive to light; tends to be relatively expensive but produces a high-quality product.

Law of demand   An economic rule stating that as the price of a good or service falls, a larger quantity of it will be bought; as the price of a good or service rises, a smaller quantity will be bought.

Law of probability   A measurement of the likelihood of an event based on mathematical relationships or past experience.

Law of supply   An economic rule stating that as the price of a good or service falls, a smaller quantity of it will be offered for sale; as the price of a good or service rises, a larger quantity will be offered for sale.

Leading indicator   A statistic that points to what will happen in the economy in the near future.

Lease   A long-term agreement describing the terms under which property is being rented.

Legal entity   An organization, such as a corporation, that is recognized by the law and given many of the rights of a person under the law.

Lemon law   A law that protects consumers from defective new cars.

Liability   The claim of a firm's creditors on its assets.

Liability insurance   Insurance that pays for bodily injury and property damage suffered by others as a result of actions of the insured party.

Life expectancy   The average number of years that people of a particular age, sex, or other characteristic can expect to live.

Life values   Values that determine how a person chooses to live.

Limited liability   The risk taken by a shareholder in a corporation that is limited to the value of money invested in the firm.

Limited warranty   A warranty that does not meet minimum federal standards and must state how it fails to meet these standards.

Litigation   Law suit.

Living benefit   A benefit paid on a whole life insurance policy while the owner is living.

Lobby   Special-interest group that pressures members of Congress to vote for or against legislation that would support the group's point of view or benefit the group.

Logical progression   A series of steps that when taken in sequence will help a person or organization reach a goal.

Long-term goal   A goal that one hopes to achieve over a period of time that is greater than several years: life goal.

Luxury   A product that is not necessary to maintain one's basic standard of living; demand for these products tends to be sensitive to changes in price.

Magnuson-Moss Warranty Act   A law passed in 1975 that sets federal standards for warranties.

Mainframe computer   A central computer, or processing unit, that may be accessed and used at the same time from many different computer terminals.

Maintenance fee   A fee charged to keep an account open; often associated with checking accounts.

Major medical insurance   Insurance that covers a percentage of medical costs after the benefits provided by a basic health insurance policy have been exhausted.

Malpractice   Inappropriate treatment given to a patient, resulting in injury or death.

Management   The achievement of organizational objectives through organizing, directing, and controlling employees and their use of resources.

Market   The actions through which an exchange of goods, services, money, and other things of value takes place.

Marketing   The actions associated with supplying products consumers want when, where and in the form that they want them, and making consumers aware of these products' availability.

Marketing concept   A business's decision to be sales oriented in its functions, to produce goods and services that consumers want, and to produce them when, where, and in the form they want them.

Market research   Gathering, recording, and analyzing information about the types of goods and services that people want.

Mediation   Procedure by which a neutral person steps into a negotiation to try to get both sides to reach an agreement.

Medicaid   A government program that provides health care for people with low income and the disabled.

Medical payments insurance   Insurance that pays medical expenses of a driver and passengers in a car involved in an accident.

Medicare   An insurance program established by the federal government that provides basic medical coverage for Americans who are sixty-five years of age or older.

Megabyte   One million bytes of memory in a computer system.

Metabolism   The process through which an organism converts food into energy and body tissue.

Minimum balance   The smallest amount that can be kept on deposit in a bank account to receive a service.

Mixed market economy   An economic system that has elements of both free market and command economies.

Modem   A device that allows two computers to communicate information over telephone lines.

Monetary policy   The decisions of the Federal Reserve System concerning the money supply, intended to influence interest rates and help our economic system meet objectives.

Money   Anything used as a medium of exchange, a unit of account, and a store of value.

Money market account   A bank account that pays a variable rate of interest that is tied to prevailing interest rates and which may be withdrawn at any time.

Money market mutual fund   A mutual fund that pays a variable rate of interest that is tied to prevailing interest rates and may have checks written against the individual's investments.

Monitor   The device upon which images are displayed in a computer system.

Monopolistic competition   A market situation in which there are numerous sellers, each with some control over price as the result of having successfully differentiated their products.

Monopoly   A market situation in which only one firm offers a product for sale with no competition.

Mortgage   A long-term debt owed on real property, such as a house.

Mouse   A device that allows a user to give commands to a computer without typing them on a keyboard.

Moving violation   Violation of a traffic law while driving a car.

Multiple real estate   A publication that identifies and describes all property offered for sale through real estate firms in an area.

Municipal bond   A bond issued by a state or local government.

Mutual fund   An investment company that pools the money of many individuals to buy stocks, bonds, or other investments.

Name-brand product   A product with a well-known, often advertised name, trademark, or logo.

National debt   Total amount of debt owed by the federal government.

National Foundation for Consumer Credit, Inc.   An organization that helps consumers develop personal budgets through consumer credit service offices in many cities.

National income   Total income earned by everyone in the country.

National income accounting   Measuring the economy's income and output and the interaction of its major parts—consumers, businesses, and government.

Negative balance of trade   When the value of a country's imports is greater than the value of its exports.

Net income   The remainder of an employee's earnings after withholdings for taxes, Social Security, and other deductions are taken.

Net national product   The value of GDP less wear-out or depreciation.

Net worth   The difference between the value of a business's assets and its liabilities.

No-fault insurance   A type of coverage stating that in case of an accident, each driver's insurance company pays for damages and medical bills for that driver without trying to determine who was at fault.

Nominal value   A value that has not been adjusted for inflation.

Notice   The advance warning that employees give their employer when they intend to leave their job.

Nuisance suit   A suit filed for the purpose of bothering a person or organization rather than for redress of a grievance.

Nutrition   Consuming a combination of foods that will help the body build tissue and remain healthy.

Objective   A specific condition that an individual or organization wishes to achieve.

Occupational Outlook Handbook   A publication that provides general information about 250 occupations, covering about 80 percent of all jobs in the United States.

Off-the-job training   Training that takes place away from the workplace.

On-the-job training   Training that takes place in the workplace.

Old-growth forest   Forest made up of trees that are in the climax stage of the forest's growth.

Opportunity Cost   The value of a second choice that is given up when a first choice is taken.

Option   An extra feature installed at a factory and which may be added to a base product; for example, air conditioning on a car.

Organizing   Coordinating the efforts of employees to help meet a business's goals.

Outstanding check   A check that has not been presented for payment at a bank.

Over withholding   Withholding more money from a worker's earnings than are owed in taxes by that worker.

Ozone layer   A layer in the atmosphere that contains high levels of ozone that block most ultraviolet rays from reaching the earth's surface.

Partnership   A form of business organization owned and operated by two or more people under a contractual agreement.

Passbook account   A savings account for which a depositor receives a booklet in which transactions are recorded.

Passive restraint   A device that automatically prevents people from being thrown forward during an automobile accident.

Payroll savings   Money deducted from a worker's earnings to buy government savings bonds or to deposit in an account.

Peak   A portion of the business cycle in which economic activity is at its highest point.

Personal computer   A computer originally designed for individual use in a home or small business.

Personal income   Total income received by individuals before personal taxes are paid.

Personal insurance   Insurance that protects people from losses due to illness or injury.

Personal inventory   An exploration of personal assets, needs, values, and personality.

Personality   Sum of the outward signs and characteristics that show the inner values that a person holds.

Persuasive advertising   Advertising intended to persuade consumers to buy a product by appealing to their need to be happy or socially accepted.

Pesticide   A chemical intended to kill insects, and other pests.

Point   A fee paid to a lender that is computed as a percentage point of a mortgage. A mark placed on one's driver's license when convicted of a moving violation.

Positive balance of trade   When the value of a country's imports is less than the value of its exports.

Preapproved credit card   A credit card that a consumer is promised if he or she completes an application form.

Preferred provider organization (PPO)   A type of health insurance that gives an insured party the choice of using a member health care provider, who will accept the plan's fee as total payment, or using another provider who is not a member. The insured party is then responsible for any difference between the insurance company's fee and the amount of a bill.

Preferred stock   A type of stock that guarantees the holder a certain amount of dividend but does not carry voting rights in the company's affairs.

Premium   When a person pays more for a bond than its original price. A fee paid for insurance coverage.

Price   The exchange value of a good or service.

Price discrimination   Selling the same product at different prices to different customers.

Price taker   A firm in perfect competition.

Principal   The original amount of a loan or investment.

Priority   A ranking of goals or objectives in the order of their value or importance.

Private property   Goods or assets owned by individuals or groups of individuals rather than by the government.

Product   Any good or service that satisfies a human need or want.

Production Combining factors of production to create goods and services that satisfy human needs and wants.

Productive resources Any of the factors of production; land, labor, capital, or entrepreneurship.

Productivity The measure of the relationship between the value of resources used to make goods and services and the value of the products produced.

Profit The amount of money left over after all expenses of a business are paid.

Profit motive A desire to earn money from running a business that provides the basic incentive for producing goods and services in a free market economy.

Profit sharing A form of compensation in which employees are paid a part of a firm's profit, the amount often set by a contractual agreement.

Progressive tax Tax that takes a larger percentage of higher incomes than of lower incomes.

Property insurance Insurance that protects people from losses to their property.

Proportional tax A tax that takes the same percentage of all incomes.

Public assistance Government programs that make payments to people based on their need.

Public goods Goods or services supplied to everyone by the government; can be used by many individuals at the same time without reducing the benefit that each person receives.

Punctuality Arriving at work and completing tasks on time.

Quantity buying Purchasing products in large amounts to reduce the cost per unit.

Quota A fixed limit on the importing or exporting of a product.

Radon gas A colorless, odorless, radioactive gas that occurs naturally in the soil.

Random access memory (RAM) The part of a computer that performs basic computations and other functions as directed by a software program.

Range The geographical area in which a particular plant or animal may be found.

Rational choice The decision that maximizes the benefits at the lowest possible cost.

Real estate agent A person who earns a living by helping people who want to buy and sell property to complete their transactions.

Real value A value corrected for inflation.

Rebate A return of part of the purchase price of a product.

Receipt A document that is given to a customer at the time a product is sold and which acts as proof of purchase.

Recession A portion of the business cycle in which a nation's output does not grow for at least six months.

Recommended daily allowance (RDA) an amount of various nutrients recommended for daily consumption by the U.S. government.

Recovery A portion of the business cycle in which economic activity is increasing.

Recruitment The process of attracting the best-qualified candidates for a job opening.

Recyclable A product which leaves remains that may be used as the raw material to make a new product.

Redress The right to seek and obtain satisfaction for damages through legal action.

Reference A written recommendation supporting a person who is being considered for a job opening.

Refund A return of excess taxes paid by the government to a taxpayer.

Regressive tax A tax that takes a larger percentage of lower incomes than of higher incomes.

Replacement value The current cost of replacing an insured piece of property.

Repossess To take a product as the result of notpayment of a debt; often associated with consumer credit.

Representative money Money that is not valuable in itself for nonmoney uses, but which can be exchanged for valuable items.

Reserve requirement The percentage of deposits that a bank must keep as cash or deposited with a Federal Reserve bank.

Residence contents broad form policy A type of insurance that protects renters from losses to their property and from liability losses; renter's insurance.

Resource Anything people can use to make or obtain the goods or services they need or want.

Responsible consumer A person who is aware of how his or her decisions impact other members of society and takes other people's interests into consideration when decisions are made.

Restructuring the debt Extending payment on a debt over a longer period of time to reduce the amount of monthly payments.

Résumé   A one- or two-page summary of a person's job qualifications.

Retail   When a firm sells to consumers.

Reusable   A quality of a product that allows it to be used repeatedly.

Rider   A written attachment to an insurance policy that alters the policy to meet certain conditions or special needs.

Right of recession   The right to cancel a contract or a signed agreement.

Risk-averse   Wanting to avoid risk when possible.

Risk management   Taking steps intended to reduce the risk of a major loss.

Risk pool   A group of drivers who have been unable to obtain insurance often because of poor driving records and who have been assigned to insurance companies by their state government.

Salary   Employee compensation provided in exchange for labor over a specific period of time.

Saturated fat   A fatty acid that contains as many hydrogen atoms as possible. Consumption of saturated fats has been associated with an increased risk of circulatory diseases.

Save   To not spend income at the present so that it may be spent in the future.

Savings and loan association   A depository institution that accepts deposits and lends money. Until recently, S&Ls could only make loans for home buying or improvements.

Savings bank   A depository institution that accepts deposits and lends money; similar to savings and loan associations.

Saving bond   A bond sold by the U.S. Treasury for less than its face value, but which is worth purchase price plus interest when redeemed.

Scarcity   A condition that results from people being unable to obtain enough goods and services to satisfy all their needs and wants.

Schedule A   The federal income tax form used to itemize deductions.

Scheduling   Making sure that workers, raw materials, and tools are where they are needed at the appropriate time so that production can be efficient.

Seasonal unemployment   A situation in which people are unemployed during a specific time of the year.

Second mortgage   A loan taken out against an owner's equity in a home.

Sector   One of the two basic classifications in the government's Standard Industrial Classification; either goods or services producing.

Security   A stock or bond representing an obligation of the issuer to provide the purchaser with a specific or expected return on the purchaser's investment.

Security deposit   Money paid by a renter to a landlord to pay for any damage done to rented property; it is normally refunded at the end of the rental period.

Self-concept   The way one sees oneself and one's feeling of self-worth.

Self-liquidating loan   A loan used to buy something that generates income to pay for the loan.

Service charge   A fee charged by banks or other organizations for providing a service; often associated with checking accounts.

Services   Tasks completed by people or machines to satisfy human wants and needs and which cannot be touched or measured.

Shared risk   Spreading the risk of a major loss among many people or businesses by agreeing to accept the certainty of a smaller cost.

Shortage   A situation in which there is a larger quantity of a product demanded than supplied at a particular price.

Short-term goal   A goal that one hopes to achieve over several years or less.

Simple interest   Interest figured on the original amount deposited.

Skill   The ability to accomplish a specific task.

Small claims court   A state court that allows people to sue other parties for limited amounts of money without the services of a lawyer.

Social insurance   Programs designed to provide insurance against the problems of old age, illness, and unemployment.

Social security   A federal program that provides monthly payments to millions of people who are retired or unable to work.

Software   Programs that tell computers what tasks to carry out.

Sole proprietorship   A form of business organization owned by only one person, who is totally responsible for the business.

Specialization   Producing a good or service for which a person, business, or nation is particularly well suited.

Spreadsheet   A type of software that interrelates accounts and allows a user to make adjustments in all accounts by changing an entry in one account.

Standard deduction   An amount that the federal government allows taxpayers to subtract from their income, regardless of their actual deductible expenses, to reduce their taxable income.

Standard fire insurance An insurance policy that protects a homeowner from property losses due to fire, weather, or explosions.

Standard industrial classification (SIC) A government listing of businesses and industries divided into ten basic classifications that are further divided into groups and industries.

Standard term life insurance A form of life insurance that provides a fixed amount of protection for a short period of time, but which may be renewed for more time at a higher premium.

Statement A document that reports transactions in an account over a period of time.

Stock A share of ownership in a corporation that entitles the owner to a share of profits distributed to owners.

Stock Exchange An organization that helps people who want to buy and sell stock in corporations complete transactions.

Stop payment An order to one's bank not to honor a particular check when it is presented for payment.

Store-brand product A product that bears the name or brand of the store that offers it for sale.

Structural unemployment A situation in which people are unemployed because they lack the skills that employers demand.

Substitute Goods Two or more goods that may be used to fill the same purpose.

Supply The amount of products businesses are willing to offer for sale at a particular price.

Surplus A situation in which there is a greater quantity of a product supplied than is demanded at a particular price.

Tangible Something that can be touched.

Target market A group of consumers toward which a firm directs its marketing efforts.

Tariff Tax levied on imported products.

Taxable income The amount of income on which taxes are levied (charged).

Tax Counseling for the Elderly (TCE) A volunteer program that helps older people complete their tax returns.

Tax credit An amount that may be subtracted from the tax that people owe to encourage them to hold a job; may result in the government paying people more than they pay the government.

Tax evasion A deliberate choice not to pay taxes owed by providing inaccurate or incomplete information on one's tax return.

Taxpayer number A number that identifies an individual taxpayer; the same as the Social Security number in most cases.

Tax preference Having the tax rate on a specific type of income less than on most other types of income.

Technology The use of knowledge and tools in an effort to find better ways to satisfy human needs and wants.

Temporary agency An agency that hires individuals for employers who need help for limited periods of time.

Tenant Someone who lives in rented property.

Term The period of time required for a bond or account to mature; its life.

Tight money Policy designed to slow the economy by making credit expensive and in short supply.

Title The physical representation of your legal ownership of a house or piece of property.

Title insurance The insurance that a prospective homeowner buys to be assured that the title, or legal ownership, to the house is free and clear.

Trade-off A term that implies an opportunity cost in which one alternative is accepted at the cost of a second alternative that is given up.

Training Instructing, or helping people acquire new skills or knowledge.

Transfer payment Financial assistance by the state or federal government that is not in exchange for any current productive activity by an individual.

Trough A portion of the business cycle in which economic activity is at its lowest point.

Truth-in-Lending Act A law passed in 1968 that requires lending institutions to tell borrowers the annual percentage rate and finance charge for loans.

Underground economy The production of goods and services resulting in income that is not reported to the government.

Unearned income Income that is not the result of payment for one's labor.

Unemployment The situation in which people are unable to find a job.

Unemployment compensation Money paid by the government to people who have recently become unemployed.

Uniform decreasing term life insurance Insurance that provides progressively less protection over a certain period of time.

Uninsured motorist insurance   Insurance that pays for medical treatment for people injured in an accident caused by a driver who had no insurance.

Unit pricing   Expressing prices in an amount per standard unit of measure.

Unlimited liability   The risk that sole proprietors and partners take that all their assets may be taken to satisfy the debts of their firm.

Unlimited life   A characteristic of corporations that allows them to function through a majority of voted stock, even when an individual stockholder dies.

Unsaturated fat   A fatty acid that does not contain as many hydrogen atoms as possible. Consumption of unsaturated fats has been associated with a reduced risk of circulatory disease.

U. S. Department of Justice   The department of the federal government that is most responsible for enforcing federal laws.

User-friendly   Describing software that is easy to learn and that often provides extensive help and instructions to the user.

Utility   An economic term that means value, or added value.

Values   The personal standards that a person feels are important and worthwhile.

Verifiable claim   Claim made in comparative advertising that has been proved true.

Veterans Administration (VA)   An agency of the government that serves the needs of former members of the armed forces, including assistance in obtaining mortgages.

Voluntary compliance   Refers to the fact that taxpayers are responsible for figuring and paying their own individual income tax.

Voluntary exchange   Transactions in which buyers and sellers work out their own terms of exchange without outside interference.

Volunteer Income Tax Assistance (VITA)   A volunteer organization that helps taxpayers prepare their tax returns.

W-2 form   A document provided to employees and to the federal and state governments that reports the employee's yearly earnings and withholding.

W-4 form   A federal tax form completed by employees that allows employers to determine how much of the worker's earnings should be withheld for income tax.

Wage   Employee compensation calculated on an hourly basis.

Warranty   A guarantee made by the seller of a product that it will meet specific standards over a period of time, or it will be repaired, replaced, or its price will be refunded.

Weighted average   An average that counts some components (parts) more often than others.

Weight loss program   A program in which consumers pay for assistance in losing weight.

Whole life insurance   Insurance that has both death benefits and living benefits.

Wholesale   When a firm buys products from a manufacturer for resale to another business.

Withholding   Money subtracted by employers from employee earnings to pay for income taxes or social security; deduction.

Word processing program   A software program that allows a user to move words, sentences, or paragraphs without retyping what has been written.

Work environment   The general conditions in which people work in a particular type of job.

Workers compensation   A state-run program to extend payment for medical care to workers injured on the job.

Work-study program   A school program that arranges jobs that allow students to work around their class schedule.

Work value   Values that help a person choose a job and career.

Write off   To decide that a debt will not be paid and no longer count it as an asset.

Yield   The percentage return on an amount of money deposited or invested.

Index

Photo Credits

it; **187 (right)** Alan Oddie / PhotoEdit; **193** Phil Borden / PhotoEdit; **197** Charles Gupton / Stock, Boston, Inc.; **204 (left)** Nancy L. Fix / Stock, Boston, Inc.; **204 (right)** Laima Druskis / Stock, Boston, Inc.; **207** Tony Freeman / PhotoEdit; **211** Tony Freeman / PhotoEdit; **219 (left)** Tony Freeman / PhotoEdit; **219 (right)** George E. Jones, III / Photo Researchers, Inc.; **221** Rick Browne / Stock, Boston, Inc.; **223** Lawrence Migdale / Photo Researchers, Inc.; **229** David Young-Wolff / PhotoEdit; **230** David Young-Wolff / PhotoEdit; **235 (left)** Tony Freeman / PhotoEdit; **235 (right)** Tony Freeman / PhotoEdit; **237** Francois Delaprte / Photo Resarchers, Inc.; **239 (left)** Charles Kennard / Stock, Boston, Inc.; **239 (right)** Linc Cornell / Stock, Boston, Inc.; **243** Stacy Pick / Stock, Boston, Inc.; **249** Richard Hutchings / InfoEdit; **250 (left)** Stacy Pick / Stock, Boston, Inc.; **253** Tony Freeman / PhotoEdit; **255** PhotoEdit; **256** Richard Hutchings/ Photo Researchers, Inc.; **258** Bill Gillette / Stock, Boston, Inc.; **259** Bryce Flynn / Stock, Boston, Inc.; **261** Michael Grecco / Stock, Boston, Inc.; **266 (left)** Jon Feingersh / Stock, Boston, Inc.; **266 (right)** Ellis Herwig / Stock, Boston, Inc.; **268** Herb Snitzer / Stock, Boston, Inc.; **272** C. Vergara/ Photo Researchers, Inc.; **276** David R. Frazier / Photo Researchers, Inc.; **279** PhotoEdit; **285 (left)** Michael Grecco / Stock, Boston, Inc.; **285 (right)** Charles Gupton / Stock, Boston, Inc.; **287** Mike Mazzaschi / Stock, Boston, Inc.; **291 (left)** Charles Gupton / Stock, Boston, Inc; **291 (right)** Tony Freeman / PhotoEdit; **293** PhotoEdit; **303 (left)** Tony Freeman / PhotoEdit; **303 (right)** Edward Miller / Stock, Boston, Inc.; **308** Bob Daemmrich / Stock, Boston, Inc.; **312** Jerry Wachte / Photo Researchers, Inc.; **317** John Neubauer; **318** Amy Etra / PhotoEdit; **319 (left)** Tony Freeman / PhotoEdit; **319 (right)** Tony Freeman / PhotoEdit; **322** Stephen Frisch / Stock, Boston, Inc.; **325** Richard Hutchings / InfoEdit; **328 (left)** David Young-Wolff / PhotoEdit; **328 (right)** Richard Hutchings / InfoEdit; **335 (left)** John Neubauer; **335 (right)** Bob Daemmrich / Stock, Boston, Inc.; **340** Michael Newman / PhotoEdit; **343** Ann McQueen / Stock, Boston, Inc.; **346 (left)** Tony Freeman / PhotoEdit; **346 (right)** Tony Freeman / PhotoEdit; **353 (left)** Bob Daemmrich / Stock, Boston, Inc.; **353 (right)** Will/ Deni McIntyre / Photo Researchers, Inc.; **355** Elena Rooraid / PhotoEdit; **358** Tony Freeman / PhotoEdit; **362** Tony Freeman / PhotoEdit; **364** Tony Freeman / PhotoEdit; **374** David Young-Wolff / PhotoEdit; **375 (left)** Tony Freeman / PhotoEdit; **375 (right)** Alan Oddie / PhotoEdit; **377** David Young-Wolff / PhotoEdit; **380** Tony Freeman / PhotoEdit; **382** Tony Freeman / PhotoEdit; **387 (left)** Michael Newman / PhotoEdit; **387 (right)** Phil McCarten / PhotoEdit; **389** Michael Newman / PhotoEdit; **391** Tony Freeman / PhotoEdit; **393 (top)** Susan Van Etten / PhotoEdit; **393 (bottom left)** PhotoEdit; **393 (bottom right)** PhotoEdit; **395** Rhoda Sidney / PhotoEdit; **403 (left)** Blair Seitz / Photo Researchers, Inc.; **403 (right)** Felicia Martinez / PhotoEdit; **405** Myrleen Ferguson / PhotoEdit; **407** Elizabeth Zuckerman / PhotoEdit; **419 (left)** David Young-Wolff / PhotoEdit; **419 (right)** Tony Freeman / PhotoEdit; **422** Alan Oddie / PhotoEdit; **425** Tony Freeman, PhotoEdit; **426** David Schaefer / PhotoEdit; **429** Rhoda Sidney / PhotoEdit; **437 (left)** Tony Freeman / PhotoEdit; **437 (right)** David Young-Wolff / PhotoEdit; **440** Robert Brenner / PhotoEdit; **443 (top)** Susan Van Etten / PhotoEdit; **443 (bottom)** Myrleen Ferguson / PhotoEdit; **444** Daniel Brody / Stock, Boston, Inc.; **452 (left)** Elena Rooraid / PhotoEdit; **452 (right)** Tony Freeman / PhotoEdit; **455** Bachmann / PhotoEdit; **458** Tony Freeman / PhotoEdit; **467** Robert Brenner / PhotoEdit; **468 (left)** Leslye Borden / PhotoEdit; **468 (right)** Tony Freeman / PhotoEdit; **470** Tony Freeman / PhotoEdit; **472** Michael Newman / PhotoEdit; **476** David Young-Wolff / PhotoEdit; **479** Tony Freeman / PhotoEdit; **486** Tony Freeman / PhotoEdit; **491** David Young-Wolff / PhotoEdit; **494** Tony Freeman / PhotoEdit; **502** Tony Freeman / PhotoEdit; **505** Mary Kate Denny / PhotoEdit; **508** Michael Newman / PhotoEdit; **516** Calvin Larsen / Photo Researchers, Inc.; **517** David Young-Wolff / PhotoEdit; **522** James Lester / Photo Researchers, Inc.; **524** Art Stein / Photo Researchers, Inc.; **531 (left)** Robert Brenner / PhotoEdit; **531 (right)** Tom Hollyman / Photo Researchers, Inc.; **536** David Young-Wolff / PhotoEdit; **537** Mark Burnett / Photo Researchers, Inc.; **541** PhotoEdit; **546 (left)**